The **Rough G**

Montréal

written and researched by

Arabella Bowen and John Shandy Watson

NEW YORK • LONDON • DELHI

www.roughguides.com

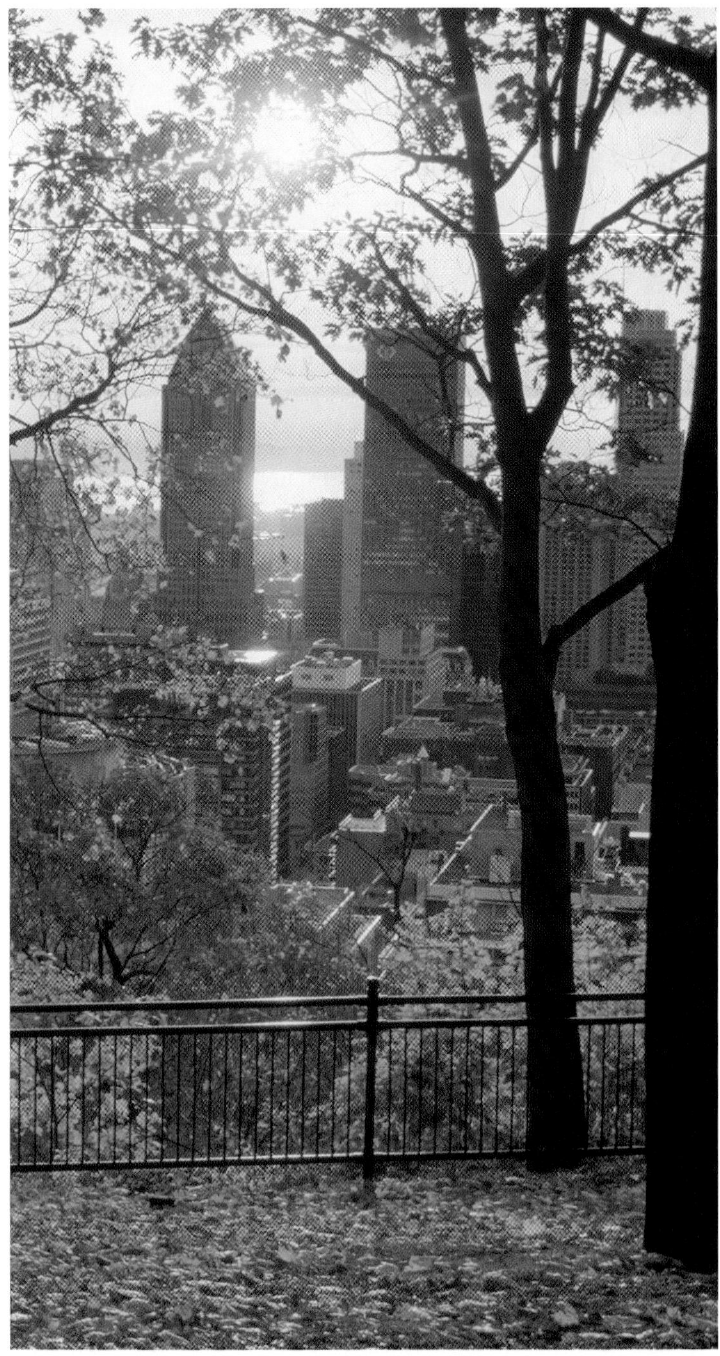

Introduction to

Montréal

Montréal is by far Canada's most cosmopolitan city. Toronto may have the country's economic power and Vancouver its most majestic scenery, but the centuries-old marriage of Protestant English and Catholic French cultures that defines Montréal has given the city a dynamic allure that is unique in North America. Its captivating atmosphere combines the best of both traditions, tempered with the Scottish merchants and Irish workers who built much of the city and also the diverse mix of Italians, Greeks, Eastern Europeans, Jews, Chinese and Portuguese who have put down roots in various neighbourhoods over the last century. And yet Montréal's free-spirited ambience – at once laid-back and highly style-conscious – is a product of the city itself rather than merely a sum of its multi-ethnic parts.

Ever since the French first flew the flag here in the 1600s, the struggle for the city's soul has centred on – and largely set apart – its English and French factions. As such, Montréal has always been a pivotal player in the tense politics of Québec separatism, which reached its lowest point in the late 1960s, when the Front de Libération du Québec waged a terrorist campaign on the city. This occurred in the wake of legislation that enshrined French-language dominance in Québec, causing English-Quebecers to flee in droves, tipping the nation's economic supremacy from Montréal to Toronto. After decades of linguistic dispute, though, a truce appears to have at last settled in, and nowadays it's hard to believe that hardly a decade ago a narrowly failed 1995 referendum on separation transformed the city into a pitched battlefield over linguistic and territorial rights. It seems virtually everyone can speak French, while the younger generation of Francophones also speak *l'anglais* – certainly a blessing for English-speaking visitors, who should have no problem finding someone who speaks the language.

The duality of Montréal's social mix is also reflected in its urban make-up. Sandwiched between the banks of the St Lawrence River and the forested, trail-covered rise of Mont Royal (233m high, but a "mountain" in the minds of Montrealers) the heart of the city is an engaging melange of Old and New World aesthetics. Busy Downtown, with its wide boulevards lined by sleek office towers and rambling shopping malls, is emblematic of a typical North American metropolis, while just to the south, Vieux-Montréal preserves the city's unmistakable French heritage in its layout of narrow, cobblestone streets and town squares. Closer investigation belies both these cliches, however, for there are charming nineteenth-century churches dotted about Downtown, while the bulk of Vieux-Montréal's buildings are actually the fruits of the Anglophone merchant class that made its fortunes off the country's plentiful natural resources and later during the Industrial Revolution, when the nearby Lachine Canal was "Canada's Pittsburgh". Ironically, the impetus for the canal – the Lachine Rapids in the St Lawrence River – was the reason for the city's early success in the first place: Montréal was as far as ships could travel into the interior, and so became a major port and trading centre.

It's the street-level vibe that makes Montréal such a great place to visit. Like the homegrown Cirque du Soleil, Montréal has a ceaseless and contagious energy that infuses its café

Fact file

- Montréal, founded in 1642, is the third-largest French-speaking city in the world (after Paris and Kinshasa).
- What Montrealers consider "north" is actually northwest – this is because the street grid was set up parallel to the St Lawrence, which flows northeast where it passes Vieux-Montréal. The further "north" from there you go, the greater the house number in addresses. Boulevard St-Laurent divides the city into east and west.
- On average, it snows nearly every second day during December, January and February. The heaviest snowfall on record was on March 4, 1971 – the 102cm that dropped that day is nearly half the average snowfall for the whole year.
- The population of the new city of Montréal is 1.8 million, of which 54 percent have French as a mother tongue, 17 percent English and 29 percent another language (a fifth of these are Italian). The population of greater Montréal, including the off-island cities and suburbs, is just under 3.5 million.
- The roughly triangular Île de Montréal covers nearly 500 square kilometres and is dominated by 233m-high Mont Royal – known by everyone as "the mountain". The island has 267km of shoreline, surrounded by the St Lawrence River to the south and east and the Rivière des Prairies to the northwest. Montréal's top three most attended events are the Juste pour Rire (Just for Laughs), Festival de Jazz and Divers/Cité.

culture, the thrilling, into-the-wee-hours nightlife, and the boisterous summer festivals – celebrating jazz, comedy, music and film. Nowhere captures the city's free-spirited ethos better than Plateau Mont-Royal, the trendiest neighbourhood in town and effective meeting point of Montréal's founding and immigrant cultures. Here, the best restaurants, bars and clubs hum and groove along boulevard St-Laurent, the symbolic divide between the city's French and English communities, all under the watchful gaze of the city's most prominent landmark: the cross atop Mont Royal that recalls Montréal's initial founding as a Catholic colony.

What to see

Invariably, most first-time visitors head straight for **Vieux-Montréal**, the oldest part of the city, where the continent's finest collection of seventeenth- to nineteenth-century buildings line the atmospheric streets between rue St-Antoine and rue de la Commune. Sights are clustered around a number of public spaces, and **Place d'Armes**, dominated by the radiant **Basilique Notre-Dame**, is the best place to start from. The neighbouring streets are home to historic museums as well as the delicately steepled **Chapelle Notre-Dame-de-Bon-Secours** and the silver-domed **Marché Bonsecours**, one of the city's best-known landmarks. In the district's southwest corner, the excellent **Musée d'Archéologie** provides a good introduction to Montréal's three and a half centuries of history, while the reclaimed land of the **Vieux-Port**, running the length of Vieux-Montréal along the St

Lawrence River, is lined with promenades, parks and a number of harbourfront attractions.

Between Vieux-Montréal and the mountain, you'll find Montréal's modern **Downtown**, centred on the east–west artery **rue Ste-Catherine**, and filled with a collection of department stores, hotels, restaurants and cinemas. Nearby, the scaled-down (but still massive) rendition of St Peter's – the **Basilique-Cathédrale Marie-Reine-du-Monde** – as well as the warm-hued interior of **St Patrick's Basilica** contrast with the soberer Protestant churches dotted about. Although no longer the tallest of Montréal's skyscrapers, the cross-shaped **Place Ville Marie** seems to tower over the city; it sits atop the shopping mall that began the **Underground City**'s network of pedestrian tunnels linking the Métro system to shopping centres, offices and cultural institutions. The foremost example of the latter is the complex of theatres that, along with the **Musée d'Art Contemporain de Montréal**, comprises **Place des Arts**, half a dozen blocks east of Place Ville Marie.

The west end of Downtown overlaps the **Golden Square Mile**, the historic enclave of Montréal's wealthy Anglophone elite, which clings to the southern slopes of the mountain. This neighbourhood's contributions to the city include a number of sumptuous mansions and such public institutions as **McGill University** and the **Musée des Beaux-Arts** facing onto rue Sherbrooke, the premier address for upscale galleries and boutiques. By contrast, the eastern edges of Downtown are marked by the small yet bustling **Chinatown** and the bars and cafés of the **Quartier Latin**, stomping ground of students from the Université du Québec à Montréal. A similarly vibrant energy infuses the **Village**, the openly gay and lesbian district further east along rue Ste-Catherine.

The **Plateau Mont-Royal** district on the mountain's eastern flank mixes Montréal's typically down-to-earth quality

A taste of Montréal

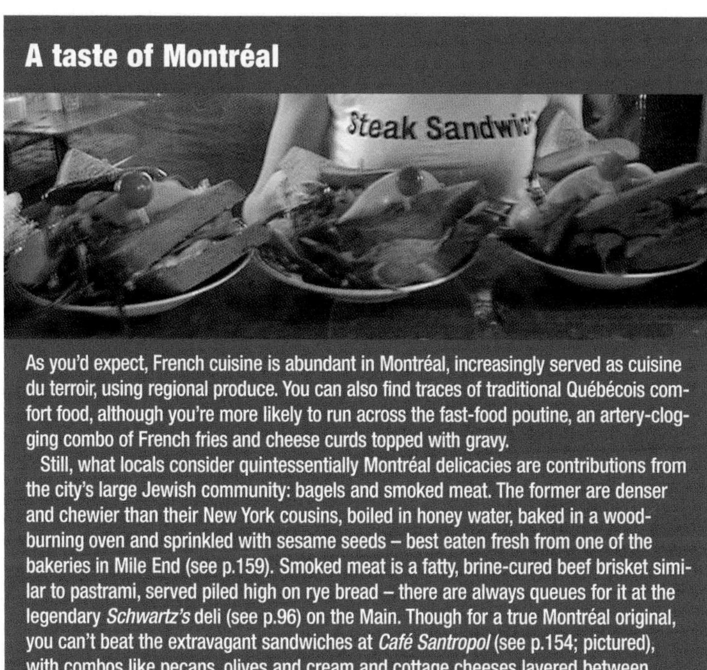

As you'd expect, French cuisine is abundant in Montréal, increasingly served as cuisine du terroir, using regional produce. You can also find traces of traditional Québécois comfort food, although you're more likely to run across the fast-food poutine, an artery-clogging combo of French fries and cheese curds topped with gravy.

Still, what locals consider quintessentially Montréal delicacies are contributions from the city's large Jewish community: bagels and smoked meat. The former are denser and chewier than their New York cousins, boiled in honey water, baked in a wood-burning oven and sprinkled with sesame seeds – best eaten fresh from one of the bakeries in Mile End (see p.159). Smoked meat is a fatty, brine-cured beef brisket similar to pastrami, served piled high on rye bread – there are always queues for it at the legendary *Schwartz's* deli (see p.96) on the Main. Though for a true Montréal original, you can't beat the extravagant sandwiches at *Café Santropol* (see p.154; pictured), with combos like pecans, olives and cream and cottage cheeses layered between slices of the best bread in the city.

with hip style and ethnic charm. The largely Francophone neighbourhoods of the Plateau lie to the east of the chic boutiques and cafés of **rue St-Denis** – ideal for people-watching – while a panoply of ethnic businesses and trendy restaurants are clustered on and around **boulevard St-Laurent**, more commonly known as "The Main". Rising above Downtown but best accessed from the Plateau, **Parc du Mont-Royal** is the city's largest park, wound about with trails and terrific views over the city. The **Oratoire St-Joseph** and its massive dome rise above the western flank of the mountain, while to the north, a pair of vast cemeteries give way to tony, Francophone **Outremont** and the Greek and Jewish communities of **Mile End**. Further north still, **Little Italy** is a major foodie destination, as much for its espresso and Italian dishes as for the enticing produce stalls and gourmet shops surrounding the **Marché Jean-Talon**.

Some of Montréal's chief tourist attractions are a bit far from the centre, but remain easily accessed via the Métro. In the city's east end, the **Stade Olympique**, with its unique inclined tower, lies between the **Biodôme**, featuring four ecosystems under one roof, and the enormous **Jardin Botanique**, notable for its replica Chinese and Japanese gardens and creepy-crawly **Insectarium**. To the south, in the middle of the St Lawrence oppo-

Franglais

Despite Québec's linguistic battles, there's often a great deal of crossover between English and French and it's not uncommon to hear Montrealers switching from one to the other in the course of a single conversation. Francophones and Anglophones have also each picked up words and phrases from the other's language – a combination of French and anglais dubbed "franglais". So while you might hear a Montréalais say something like, "Je suis allé à un party ce weekend – c'était full fun", it's no less natural for a Montrealer to throw in French expressions while making plans for the evening: "Let's try to grab a seat on the terrasse for the cinq à sept before heading to that new resto on the Plateau – we'll need to grab a bottle of wine at the dep along the way, though."

site the Vieux-Port, visitors and locals alike head to **Parc Jean-Drapeau**, consisting of **Île Ste-Hélène** and man-made **Île Notre-Dame**, for its green spaces, amusement park, casino and racing track (built for the Grand Prix). West of Downtown is the staid Anglophone enclave of **Westmount**, while strung along the **Lachine Canal** to the south are a few workaday communities, notably **Pointe St-Charles** and **St-Henri**, which grew up during the area's Industrial Revolution heyday. An excellent bicycle path runs through these neighbourhoods, from the Vieux-Port to the canal's end at the former fur-trading post of **Lachine**.

Beyond Montréal, two enchanting regions – the **Eastern Townships** (Les Cantons-de-l'Est) and the **Laurentian mountains** (Les Laurentides) – provide excellent year-round escapes with plenty of activities (especially top-notch skiing), away from the teeming city centre. In contrast to Montréal, **Québec City**, around 250km northeast, seems immune to outside forces, its walled old town steadfastly embodying the province's French roots. Perched atop a promontory with a commanding view of the St Lawrence and

laced with winding, cobblestone streets flanked by seventeenth- and eighteenth-century stone houses, it ranks as the country's most romantic and beautifully situated city.

When to go

Montréal's climate is one of extremes – bone-chilling **winter** temperatures morph into sweaty summer highs with barely an iota of spring to ease the transition. Though tourist authorities are fond of minimizing the true extent of the city's winters, the season is in fact bitterly cold; temperatures often fall well below the zero mark and snowfalls don't dust the city – they bury it. Though a boon for avid skiers and snowboarders, the period between November and April can be positively grim for everyone else. That said, if you're here during a cold snap, the labyrinthine Underground City provides an escape from the elements and spending the afternoon tucked inside a cozy café is a wonderful antidote.

The transition from winter to **summer** passes almost unnoticed, and locals quickly replace their complaints about the cold to gripes about the humidity. The population seems to double come summer as the city's residents come out of hibernation; still, despite the heat and the crowds, late June through August is one of the best times to visit, thanks in part to a rotating menu of wild festivals. Likewise, Montréal can be simply glorious during the **autumn** months. Though it's cooler in the evenings, the days remain quite warm and, best of all, the changing leaves set the city ablaze with bursts of yellows, oranges and reds. Indeed, the season is perfect for hikers as the provincial parks resonate with colour, though traipsing up Mont Royal can be just as splendid.

Average monthly temperatures and rainfall

	Temp °C		Temp °F		Rainfall	
	max	min	max	min	mm	inches
Jan	-6	-15	22	5	63.3	2.5
Feb	-4	-14	24	8	56.4	2.2
March	2	-7	36	20	67.6	2.7
April	11	1	51	33	74.8	2.9
May	19	7	65	45	68.3	2.7
June	23	13	74	54	82.5	3.3
July	26	15	79	60	85.6	3.4
August	29	19	84	67	104	4.1
September	20	9	68	49	86.5	3.4
October	13	4	55	38	75.4	3.0
November	5	-2	41	28	93.4	3.7
December	-3	-11	27	12	85.6	3.4

21

things not to miss

It's not possible to see everything that Montréal has to offer in one trip – and we don't suggest you try. What follows is a selective and subjective taste of the city's highlights: memorable restaurants, lively festivals, engaging museums and exciting outdoor activities. They're arranged in five colour-coded categories to help you find the very best things to see, do and experience. All entries have a page reference to take you straight into the Guide, where you can find out more.

01 Biosphère Page **119** • Built by Buckminster Fuller as the US pavilion for Expo '67, this space-age geodesic dome now holds a fun, family-friendly collection of ecosystem displays, focusing on water.

02 Basilique Notre-Dame

Page **70** • Looking more like Westminster Abbey than its Parisian namesake, Montréal's basilica has a stern exterior that belies the impossibly lush nature of its interior decor.

03 Strolling the Plateau

Page **91** • Checking out the distinctive architecture of the Plateau's staircase-lined streets and back-lane courtyards, called "Balconville" by locals, is as good an excuse as any to explore this hip neighbourhood.

04 The Village

Page **89** • The heart of Montréal's gay and lesbian community, this vibrant neighbourhood offers an abundance of restaurants, cafés, bars and shops.

05 Festival International de Jazz de Montréal Page **214** • Montréal's storied jazz scene is celebrated at this massive annual concert series, which draws big names and hundreds of thousands of visitors from all over the world.

06 Schwartz's Deli Page **96** • No matter how long the queue at this local institution on the Main, it's worth it for their smoked-meat sandwiches, a Montréal speciality.

07 Mont Royal Page **101** • At 233 metres, the "mountain" is hardly deserving of the name, yet its many trails, stunning views and central location make it a more than worthwhile destination.

08 Mont Tremblant Page **231** • This sprawling resort complex in the Laurentians north of Montréal offers luxurious lodgings and almost 100 ski runs.

09 Vieux-Montréal

Page **77** • The impressive, silver-domed Marché Bonsecours (pictured) is but one of the architectural highlights in Old Montreal's jumble of narrow, lamp-lit streets lined with eighteenth-century houses and elaborate nineteenth-century commercial buildings.

10 Biking the Lachine canal

Page **128** • Once the centre of Montréal industry, this waterway has been rehabilitated with a lengthy, picturesque walking and biking trail.

11 Marché Jean-Talon

Page **100 & 198** • Drawing foodies, tourists and locals alike, this market at the heart of Little Italy overflows with fantastic fresh produce, bread, cheeses and meats seven days a week.

12 Café society on Rue St-Denis Page **185 &157** • Located in the heart of the Plateau, this bustling avenue is thick with fantastic French restaurants and terrace-fronted cafés perfect for lunching and people-watching.

13 Insectarium Page **114** • Not only is this bug-shaped building a fascinating repository of all kinds of creepy-crawly creatures, but once a year at the winter insect tastings invited chefs prepare many of those same bugs as courage-testing delicacies.

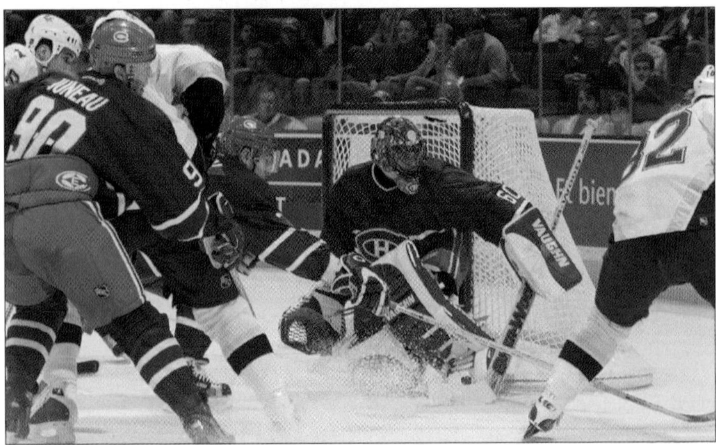

14 Montréal Canadiens Page **201** • Though the Canadiens are a long way from their glory days, seeing them play at the Molson Centre is still an action-packed, invigorating way to spend an evening.

15 Molson Indy Page **203** • Even if the Grand Prix leaves Montréal, there's always this championship CART race to keep speed-lovers happy.

16 Centre Canadien d'Architecture Page **65** • Incongruously located on the outskirts of Downtown, the CCA is more like a severely designed temple to architecture than just another museum.

17 Dancing at the Tam Tam Page **102** • Every summer Sunday afternoon, the area around the Sir George-Étienne Cartier monument on Mont Royal is flooded by drummers and dancers taking part in this freewheeling jam session and celebration.

18 Oratoire St-Joseph Page **104** • This copper-domed edifice, an awe-inspiring tribute to religious devotion, towers over the western slopes of Mont Royal.

19 Quebéc City Page **242** • Much of New France's religious and military history is bound up within the fortification walls encircling this beautiful and atmospheric city.

20 Summertime fireworks Page **212** • For ten nights in June and July, the sky over Parc Jean-Drapeau plays host to awesome displays of colourful pyrotechnics.

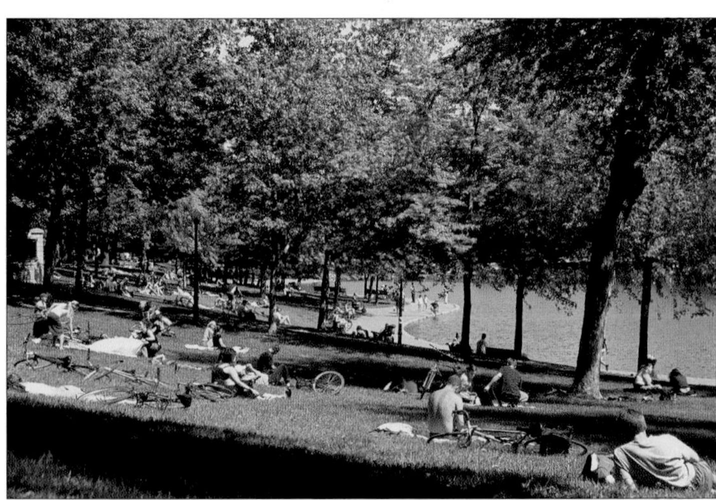

21 Relaxing in Parc La Fontaine Page **95** • Take a break from sightseeing at this urban oasis, where you can lie in the sun, take a boat out on the ponds, or even catch a free play at the outdoor Théâtre de Verdure.

Contents

Using this Rough Guide

We've tried to make this Rough Guide a good read and easy to use. The book is divided into nine main sections, and you should be able to find whatever you want in one of them.

Colour section

The colour section offers a quick tour of Montréal. The **introduction** aims to give you a feel for the city, with suggestions on where to go. We also tell you what the weather is like and include a basic fact file. Next, our authors round up their favorite aspects of Montréal in the **things not to miss** section – whether it's great food, amazing sights or a special activity. Right after this comes the Rough Guide's full contents list.

Basics

The Basics section covers all the **pre-departure** nitty-gritty to help you plan your trip and the practicalities you'll want to know once there. This is where to find out about money and costs, Internet access, transportation, car rental, local media – in fact just about every piece of **general practical information** you might need.

The City

This is the heart of the Rough Guide, divided into user-friendly chapters, each of which covers a different Montréal neighbourhood. Every chapter begins with an **introduction** that helps you to decide where to go, followed by an extensive tour of the **sights**, all plotted on a neighbourhood map.

Listings

Listings contain all the consumer information needed to make the most of your stay, with chapters on **accommodation**, places to **eat** and **drink**, live music and performing arts venues, **shopping**, sports and festivals.

Out of the City

Here we detail the sights and attractions of the city's surrounding areas, from the skiing resorts of **Les Laurentides** to the old world atmosphere of **Québec City**.

Contexts

Read Contexts to get a deeper understanding of what makes Montréal tick. We include a brief **history**, along with a detailed section that reviews numerous **books** and **films** relating to the city.

Language

The Language section gives useful guidance for speaking **French**, Montréal-style, pulling together all the **words and phrases** you might need on your trip, including a comprehensive menu reader. Here you'll also find a **glossary** of words and terms peculiar to the city.

Index + small print

Apart from a **full index**, which includes maps as well as places, this section covers **publishing information**, credits and acknowledgements, and also has our contact details in case you want to send in updates and corrections to the book – or suggestions as to how we might improve it.

Colour maps

The back colour section contains seven detailed **maps** to help you explore the city up close and locate every place mentioned in the guide.

Map and chapter list

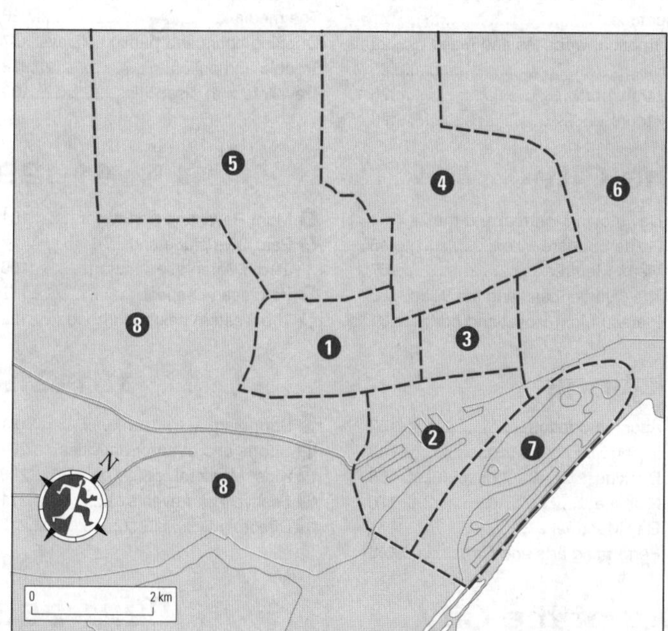

Contents

Contexts 265–278

Language 279–285

Rough Guides advertising 287–292

Index + small print 293–303

Colour maps at back of book

Map symbols

Maps are listed in the full index using coloured text

International boundary
Chapter boundary
Autoroute
US interstate highway
Provincial highway
Major road
Minor road
Pedestrianized street
Steps
Bridge
Underground tunnel
Path
Bike path
Railway
Gondola
Coastline/river
Ferry
Wall
Point of interest
International airport
Cliff

Information office
Hospital
Accommodation
Restaurant
Monument
Statue
Viewpoint
Fort
Monastery
Ski resort
Métro station
Parking
Bus stop
Gate
Building
Church (town maps)
Stadium
Cemetery
Park
Beach

Basics

Basics

Getting there

From most places in North America – and from anywhere overseas – the fastest and easiest way to get to Montréal is to fly to Aéroport de Montréal-Dorval (YUL). If you are coming from anywhere within 500–600 kilometres of the city, however, a train, bus or car journey may be cheaper and, after factoring in airport formalities, just as quick.

Airfares always depend on the **season**, with the **highest** being around June to early September, when the weather is nicest; you'll get the best prices during the **low season**, November to February (excluding mid-December through the New Year when prices are hiked up and seats are at a premium); during the **shoulder seasons** the smaller crowds and moderate prices are balanced out by the uncertainty of good weather. Note also that flying on weekends ordinarily adds a bit to the round-trip fare; price ranges quoted throughout this section assume midweek travel and a Saturday night stay. When comparing prices, always check whether they include taxes – many companies don't include taxes and other charges in their initial advertised price, while others do.

You can often cut costs and avoid having to call all the airlines by going through a **specialist flight agent** – either a **consolidator**, who buys up blocks of tickets from the airlines and sells them at a discount, or a **discount agent**, who in addition to dealing with discounted flights may also offer special student and youth fares and a range of other travel-related services such as travel insurance, rail passes, car rentals, tours and the like. Some agents specialize in **charter flights**, which may be cheaper than scheduled flights, but often have fixed departure dates and high cancellation penalties. In between, there are a number of **low-fare and no-frills airlines** keeping things competitive. For Montréal, you may even find it cheaper to pick up a bargain **package deal** from one of the tour operators described below (or from the extensive list of local travel agents available on the Canadian Tourism Commission website www.travelcanada.ca) and then find your own accommodation when you get there.

If you have already arrived from overseas, or live in Québec, Ontario or the northeast US, there are a number of alternatives to the hassles of flying. The most comfortable route is to take a **train** – VIA Rail operates frequent services in the Windsor–Québec City corridor and Amtrak provides a direct train from New York and a train–bus combo from Washington. If you're on a budget, a **long-distance bus** trip is the cheapest way to get to Montréal, with Greyhound services from the US and a number of Canadian carriers also available.

Online booking agents and general travel sites

Many discount travel websites offer you the opportunity to book flight tickets and holiday packages **online**, cutting out the costs of agents and middlemen; these are worth going for, as long as you don't mind the inflexibility of non-refundable, non-changeable deals. There are some bargains to be had on auction sites too, if you're prepared to bid keenly.

Ⓦ**www.cheapflights.ca** Bookings from Canada only (for US, Ⓦwww.cheapflights.com; for UK & Ireland, Ⓦwww.cheapflights.co.uk; for Australia and New Zealand, Ⓦwww.cheapflights.com.au). Flight deals, travel agents, plus links to other travel sites.

Ⓦ**www.cheaptickets.com** US-only discount flight specialists.

Ⓦ**www.destina.ca** Bookings from Canada only. Air Canada's online travel website, with flights and holiday web deals. Allows you to double-up on Aeroplan points.

Ⓦ**www.ebookers.com** Efficient, easy-to-use flight finder, with competitive fares.

Ⓦ**www.etn.nl/discount.htm** A hub of consolidator and discount agent links, maintained by the nonprofit European Travel Network.

Ⓦ**www.expedia.ca** Bookings from Canada only

(for US, Ⓦ www.expedia.com; for UK, Ⓦ www.expedia.co.uk). Discount airfares, all-airline search engine and daily deals.
Ⓦ **www.flyaow.com** "Airlines of the Web" – online air travel info and reservations.
Ⓦ **www.gaytravel.com** US-only gay travel agent, offering accommodation, cruises, tours and more.
Ⓦ **www.geocities.com/thavery2000** An extensive list of airline websites and US toll-free numbers.
Ⓦ **www.hotwire.com** Bookings from the US only. Last-minute savings of up to 40 percent off regular published fares. Airline and flight time is not available until after paying, though, and there are no refunds, transfers or changes allowed.
Ⓦ **www.lastminute.com** Bookings from UK only (for Australia, Ⓦ www.lastminute.com.au; for New Zealand, Ⓦ www.lastminute.co.nz). Good last-minute holiday package and flight-only deals.
Ⓦ **www.opodo.co.uk** Popular and reliable source of low UK airfares. Owned by, and run in conjunction with, nine major European airlines.
Ⓦ **www.orbitz.com** Bookings from the US only. Cut-rate flights comparing major airlines at a glance (including the five US majors who started the site).
Ⓦ **www.priceline.com** US bookings only (for UK, Ⓦ www.priceline.co.uk). Name-your-own-price website that has deals at around 40 percent off standard fares.
Ⓦ **www.skyauction.com** Bookings from the US only. Auctions tickets and travel packages to destinations worldwide.
Ⓦ **www.travelocity.ca** Bookings from Canada only (for US, Ⓦ www.travelocity.com; for UK, Ⓦ www.travelocity.co.uk; for Australia, Ⓦ www.zuji.com.au). Destination guides, hot fares and great deals for car rental, accommodation and lodging.
Ⓦ **www.travelshop.com.au** Australian site offering discounted flights, packages, insurance, and online bookings.
Ⓦ **www.travel.yahoo.com** Incorporates some Rough Guides material in its coverage of destination countries and cities across the world, with information about places to eat and sleep.

Flights and other approaches from Canada and the US

From most of the US and Canada, the easiest and often cheapest way to get to Montréal is to **fly**; there are direct flights from larger Canadian cities and from most major US hubs. Via Rail's corridor **train** services are a viable alternative to flying from Ontario and Québec (it takes about the same amount of time once getting to the airport and check-in are tacked on). Amtrak trains from New York and Washington, DC require most of the day but are worth it mainly for the scenery. If money is more important than comfort and speed, **buses** will eventually get you to Montréal from anywhere on the continent. Finally, there's the old standby, the **car** – flexible, just as fast for shorter journeys and cheaper if there's a group of you.

By plane

Aéroport de Montréal-Dorval (see p.25), renamed **Aéroport International Pierre-Elliott-Trudeau de Montréal** in January 2004, handles all but a few of the flights to Montréal. There are dozens of flights daily from Toronto, and at least five a day from the **Canadian cities** of Ottawa, Québec City and Halifax. Air Canada provides by far the most comprehensive service, reaching all parts of the country through its flagship brand and regional Air Canada Jazz. It launched an independent low-fare airline, Zip, as well as no-frills Tango, to fend off increasing **competition** from WestJet in western Canada, CanJet to the east and Jetsgo, which cherry-picks the busiest routes across the country. For the time being, Air Canada's higher published fares are somewhat irrelevant in the face of their almost weekly seat sales, web specials and last-minute offers. Keep an eye out in the travel section of your local newspaper and re-visit the airlines' websites regularly (or sign up for e-mail alerts) to be sure of getting a good deal. One bonus of all the competition is that it is now possible to get one-way fares for half the price of a return.

Rates tend to vary widely – play around with dates and times to get the best fares. In general, for economy fares you should multiply the one-way price by three for a rough idea of the final cost of a return (including taxes and charges). You should be able to fly from Toronto for as low as $300 including taxes; Maritime cities start at around $400. Out west, Calgary to Montréal runs to $450–700 and Vancouver ranges from $500 during a sale or a no-frills flight on Tango to around $700 economy on Air Canada.

Service **from the US** is also competitive – New York's three airports bring in almost as many planes as Toronto's does, and there's a good range of flights daily from the eastern hubs of Atlanta, Boston, Chicago, Cincinnati, Philadelphia and Washington, DC on the main carriers and their regional affiliates. There are fewer direct flights from the south and west – you might have to change planes to get a time and price to suit. Expect to pay US$200–300 from New York, Boston or Washington, DC, US$275–350 from Chicago, US$350–450 from Miami and US$400–550 from LA. If you are coming from the West Coast on a budget (and time isn't a factor), you can save around US$100 flying to New York and travelling overland from there.

Airlines in Canada and the US

Air Canada ⓣ1-888/247-2262, ⓦwww.aircanada.com. Also operates under regional Air Canada Jazz and no-frills Tango (ⓣ1-800/315-1390, ⓦwww.flytango.com) brands.
Air Transat Canada ⓣ1-800/587-2672, ⓦwww.airtransat.com. Charter airline.
American Airlines ⓣ1-800/433-7300, ⓦwww.aa.com.
Canjet Airlines ⓣ1-800/809-7777, ⓦwww.canjet.com.
Continental Airlines ⓣ1-800/231-0856, ⓦwww.continental.com.
Delta Canada ⓣ1-800/221-1212, US ⓣ1-800/241-4141, ⓦwww.delta.com.
Jetsgo ⓣ1-866/440-0441, ⓦwww.jetsgo.net.
Northwest/KLM ⓣ1-800/225-2525, ⓦwww.nwa.com.
United Airlines Canada ⓣ1-800/241-6522, ⓦwww.united.ca, US ⓣ1-800/538-2929, ⓦwww.united.com.
US Airways ⓣ1-800/428-4322, ⓦwww.usair.com.
WestJet ⓣ1-888/WEST-JET or 403/250-5839, ⓦwww.westjet.com.
Zip ⓣ1-866/4321-ZIP, ⓦwww.4321zip.com. Owned by Air Canada but independently run.

Flight and travel agents

Airtech ⓣ212/219-7000, ⓦwww.airtech.com. Standby seat broker; also deals in consolidator fares. No flights to Montréal, but may get you cheaply to New York.
Airtreks ⓣ1-877/AIRTREKS, ⓦwww.airtreks.com. Round-the-world and Circle Pacific tickets. The website features an interactive database that lets you build and price your own round-the-world itinerary.
Educational Travel Center ⓣ1-800/747-5551 or 608/256-5551, ⓦwww.edtrav.com. Low-cost fares worldwide, student/youth discount offers, and car rental and tours.
Flightcentre Canada ⓣ1-888/WORLD-55, ⓦwww.flightcentre.ca, US ⓣ1-866/WORLD-51, ⓦwww.flightcentre.us. Rock-bottom fares worldwide.
Long Haul Travel ⓣ1-866/548-4548, ⓦwww.longhaultravel.com. Canadian partner of Airtreks (see above).
STA Travel Canada ⓣ1-888/427-5639, US ⓣ1-800/329-9537, ⓦwww.statravel.com. Worldwide specialists in independent travel; also student IDs, travel insurance, car rental, rail passes, and more.
TFI Tours ⓣ1-800/745-8000 or 212/736-1140, ⓦwww.lowestairprice.com. Consolidator with global fares.
Travel Avenue ⓣ1-800/333-3335, ⓦwww.travelavenue.com. Full-service travel agent that offers discounts in the form of rebates.
Travel Cuts Canada ⓣ1-888/246-9762, US ⓣ1-800/592-CUTS, ⓦwww.travelcuts.com. Popular, long-established Canadian student-travel organization, with worldwide offers and cheap domestic flights for students and non-students. Also student IDs. Also known as Voyages Campus in Québec.
Travelers Advantage ⓣ1-877/259-2691, ⓦwww.travelersadvantage.com. Discount travel club, with cashback deals and discounted car rental. Membership required ($1 for 3 months' trial).

Package tours

A day or two in Montréal and Québec City often features in **package tours**, either as a base for camping, skiing or wilderness trips or as part of a 10-day-or-so bus tour of Québec and Ontario. Some operators offer rail and fly-drive alternatives, while for a completely different experience you can take a 10- to 14-day cruise from eastern seaboard ports like New York. Finally, there are city-breaks to Montréal – either a simple flight-and-hotel deal or one centred around a theme – many of which include a day's sightseeing in Québec City.

Tour operators in Canada and the US

Adventure Center ⓣ1-800/228-8747 or 510/654-1879, ⓦwww.adventurecenter.com. Hiking and "soft adventure" specialists worldwide.

They offer a 10-day trip to Québec City and its hinterland, including four days canoeing, from US$980.

Adventures Abroad ⓣ1-800/665-3998, ⓦwww.adventures-abroad.com. Adventure specialists with a 9-day tour of Montréal, Québec City and Charlevoix (whose only real adrenaline rush is a whale-watching trip). From US$1310.

Classic Journeys ⓣ1-800/200-3887 or 858/454-5004, ⓦwww.classicjourneys.com. Walking trips with an emphasis on culture. Itinerary includes Québec City, small towns and countryside in Charlevoix and the inevitable whale-watching cruise in the Saguenay. Six days for US$2095.

Contiki ⓣ1-888/CONTIKI, ⓦwww.contiki.com. 18- to 35-year-olds-only tour operator. Montréal and Québec City are included in a couple of multi-city bus tours for around $160 (US$100) a day.

Cosmos ⓣ1-800/276-1241, ⓦwww.cosmosvacations.com. Planned vacation packages with an independent focus. Nine-day bus tour of Ontario and Québec's major cities for US$750–850.

Delta Vacations ⓣ1-800/654-6559, ⓦwww.deltavacations.com. City-breaks (such as a foodie tour of Montréal) and some last-minute deals on air and hotel packages.

Far and Wide ⓣ1-866/FAR-WIDE, ⓦwww.farandwide.com. Very broad array of deals, from customized trips to group tours. Offerings include a 9-day bus tour of Ontario and Québec's major cities for US$1700 plus flights and a 3-day trip to Montréal that concludes with a 10-day cruise down the St Lawrence and along the Atlantic coast to Boston (from US$2650 including flights).

Globus ⓣ1-866/755-8581, ⓦwww.globusjourneys.com. Planned vacation packages such as a 9-day bus tour of Ontario and Québec's major cities for US$1200–1450 plus a longer option that takes in the northeast US.

Maupintour ⓣ1-800/255-4266, ⓦwww.maupintour.com. Luxury independent and escorted tours that take in Québec's big cities and scenic countryside.

Moose Travel Network ⓣ905/853-4762 or 1-888/816-6673, ⓦwww.moosenetwork.com. The same outfit (see p.14) that runs hop-on and -off backpacker mini-coach tours in summer also organizes $399 week-long winter circuits that take in Montréal, Québec City, Mont Tremblant and Ottawa (youth hostel accommodation and activities extra).

Suntrek Tours ⓣ1-800/SUNTREK, ⓦwww.suntrek.com. Soft adventure specialists who offer a 3-week camping tour of the northeast US and eastern Canada that'll give you a couple of days in Montréal and Québec City (US$1300).

Trek America ⓣ1-800/221-0596, ⓦwww.trekamerica.com. Walking and soft adventure tours all over the US, Canada and Mexico, year-round. Among their "Trek America" offerings – 1–9 week camping adventure trips for 18–38-year-olds – Montréal figures in their 3-week cross-country "Frontier Canada" trip, priced at US$1200–1400.

Trek Holidays ⓣ1-800/661-7265, ⓦwww.trekholidays.com. Canadian agent that handles a vast array of deals from adventure companies worldwide. Their 10-day trip to Québec City includes four days back-country canoeing and starts at $1500.

Train passes

VIA Rail pass (validity)	off-peak rates	peak rates
Corridorpass (10 days)	$235	$235
Canrailpass (12 days in 30)	$448	$719

Amtrak pass (validity)	off-peak rates	peak rates
North East Rail Pass (5/15/30 days)	US$149/185/225	US$149/205/240
Coastal Rail Pass (30 days)	US$235	US$285
East Rail Pass (15/30 days)	US$210/265	US$260/320
National Rail Pass (15/30 days)	US$295/385	US$440/550
North America Rail Pass (30 days)	$690 (US$495)	$975 (US$699)

VIA Rail passes and the North America Rail Pass can be purchased by anyone; the other Amtrak passes are only available to overseas visitors. Sales outlets include: **UK** 1st Rail ⓣ0845/644 3553, ⓦwww.1strail.com; Trailfinders ⓣ020/7937 5400, ⓦwww.trailfinders.com; **Ireland** USIT ⓣ0818/200 020, ⓦwww.usit.ie (Amtrak only); **Australia** Asia Pacific Travel Marketing ⓣ02/9319 6624, ⓦwww.aptms.com.au; **New Zealand** Holiday Shoppe (ⓣ0800/808 480, ⓦwww.holidayshoppe.co.nz) and United Travel (ⓣ0800/730 830, ⓦwww.unitedtravel.co.nz).

VIA Rail Ⓦwww.viarail.ca. Although they don't organize tours, VIA's website does provide a lengthy list of US and Canadian operators who offer rail and sightseeing trips that include Montréal.
Viator Ⓦwww.viator.com. Bookings for local tours and sightseeing trips in destinations around the world, including Montréal, Québec City and the surrounding regions.

By train

Montréal is one of the main hubs of Canada's skeletal rail network, operated by **VIA Rail** (Ⓣ514/989-2626 or 1-888/842-7245, Ⓦwww.viarail.ca) – all trains from eastern Canada terminate here, as do corridor services from Toronto, Ottawa and Québec City. The trains are comfortable, if a little antiseptic – more akin to air travel than the romantic rolling stock of old – but you'll probably be too busy gawking at the scenery to take much notice. In addition to economy service, the busier routes have VIA1 first-class cars – the extra price is reflected in the free booze and good-quality meals rather than any extra space to stretch out. Students with an ISIC card cop a 35 percent discount, while anyone can save 25–35 percent (depending on route) by booking at least five days in advance (there are only limited seats at this rate, though, so book well ahead).

The most heavily travelled route links Toronto and Montréal six times per day (plus one overnight train) in as little as four hours for $210 ($336 on VIA1 and from $363 sharing a double sleeper cabin). If coming from the Maritimes, you'll pay almost as much as flying – the twenty-hour Halifax to Montréal trip costs $272–362 return – unless you actually want to spend the night sleeping (from $486 in a berth, $592 per person in a triple cabin). From out west, the only conceivable reason to take the train (aside from fear of flying) is for the scenery – you'll see a lot of it on the three-day-plus, $700 minimum (one-way, seated; berths from $1224) journey.

In addition, **Amtrak** (Ⓣ1-800/USA-RAIL, Ⓦwww.amtrak.com) lines run to Montréal directly from New York – the 10-hour trip costs from US$125 return. The last leg of the 15-hour, US$180 return journey from Washington, DC, is usually by bus from St Albans, VT.

By bus

The scope of North America's **bus** services is as vast as the continent itself – something you may want to think about before considering travelling from, say, San Diego to Montréal, an epic, three-day-plus journey. But if you're on a tight budget, the US$238 fare (if purchased a week in advance) may be compelling – though be sure to factor in three days worth of food and drink – plus you get to see a whole lot of country in between. A similar Canadian odyssey from Vancouver takes just as long, but, if you purchase two weeks in advance, it'll cost just $230 – a third of the regular fare.

For most travellers, however, the bus is only bearable for a day at most. Common trips to Montréal are **from Toronto** on Coach

Bus passes

Bus pass (validity)	**year-round rates**
RoutPass (7/14/18 days)	$213/242/300
Canada Discovery Pass (7/15/30 days)	$275/415/515
Eastern CanAm Pass (10/21 days)	US$285/385
CanAm Pass (15/30 days)	US$419/529
Ameripass (7/15/30 days)	US$229/349/439

Although RoutPass is provided by a separate company (Ⓦwww.routpass.com), it is available, along with the Greyhound passes, to North American and international travellers at major bus terminals or directly from Greyhound (see main text) or Greyhound Canada (Ⓣ1-800/661-8747, Ⓦwww.greyhound.ca). Overseas Greyhound agents include STA Travel in the UK, Australia and New Zealand, and Galway Student Travel Centre (Ⓣ091/528 488) in Ireland.

Canada (ⓣ1-800/461-7661, ⓦwww.coachcanada.com); the express takes six and a half hours and costs $130–150. Voyageur (ⓣ1-800/668-4438, ⓦwww.voyageur.com) makes the two-hours-and-twenty-minute trip **from Ottawa** for $65 return ($54 booked a day in advance) and Orléans Express (ⓣ1-888/999-3977, ⓦwww.orleansexpress.com) handles most routes in Québec; the **Québec City** express takes two hours and twenty minutes and goes for $57 return. Student discounts can take up to a third off the regular fare.

From the US, Adirondack Trailways (ⓣ1-800/858-8555, ⓦwww.trailways.com) and **Greyhound** (ⓣ1-800/229-9424, ⓦwww.greyhound.com) compete on the New York to Montréal run, offering half a dozen trips per day. Fares for the eight-hour journey are US$109 return. Greyhound subsidiary Vermont Transit Lines (ⓣ1-800/552-8737, ⓦwww.vermonttransit.com) runs most trips from Boston; they cost US$111 (US$98 if bought a week in advance) and take around seven hours. Count on fourteen hours from Washington, DC (US$118–142), as you'll need to transfer in New York.

The **Moose Travel Network** (ⓣ905/853-4762 or 1-888/816-6673, ⓦwww.moosenetwork.com) provides a completely different experience – a mini-coach service aimed at backpackers, it hits the major destinations on the travellers' circuit between May and mid-October (for winter packages, see p.12). The jump-on, jump-off service stops three days a week at youth hostels in the major cities and interesting smaller towns. Their Loonie Pass covers Montréal, the Laurentians, Québec City and as far east as Tadoussac (for whale-watching) and costs $249 ($239 with ISIC or hostelling membership).

By car

A network of *autoroutes* (expressways or motorways) funnel into Montréal from all directions, and, apart from rush hour and bottlenecks on the bridges from the south shore, traffic generally flows quite smoothly. The two main freeways **from Ontario**, Hwy-401 from Toronto and Hwy-417 from Ottawa, converge just west of the island, from where Hwy-40 and Hwy-20 continue straight across Montréal and extend eastward to Québec City. **From the US**, a number of interstate highways provide access to Montréal from the south. I-87 travels straight up from New York City, becoming Hwy-15 as it crosses the border. If you're coming from Boston, following I-93 to I-89 (which becomes Hwy-133) provides the most direct route; alternatively, take I-91 (Hwy-55 in Québec), which leads to Hwy-10, the main route through the scenic Eastern Townships.

Roadside assistance is available from the CAA – the Canadian Automobile Association (ⓣ514/861-5111 or 1-800/CAA-HELP for emergency assistance, ⓦwww.caaquebec.com) – who have reciprocal agreements with the AAA and motoring groups from other countries. The Ministère des Transports (ⓣ514/284-2363, ⓦwww.mtq.gouv.qc.ca) has information on road conditions as well as a detailed on-line map; local radio stations broadcast up-to-date traffic reports.

Driving in Québec

Road signs in Québec are the same as elsewhere in North America but usually in French. Drivers can make a right turn at a red light except on the island of Montréal. Unless indicated otherwise, maximum speed limits are 100kph on *autoroutes*, 80kph or 90kph on other highways and 50kph in built-up areas. Slower speeds are advisable in adverse winter conditions; throughout the colder months, snow tires are a necessity.

An International Driving Permit is recommended, although it is not legally required for visits of less than six months. A minimum of $50,000 third-party liability insurance is required. Non-residents may be covered for compensation under the province's no-fault insurance if driving a vehicle registered in Québec or a province or US state with a reciprocal arrangement – see p.22 for further details.

Note that motorists are not only prohibited from using radar detectors, they may not even be carried in your car. Seatbelts are compulsory for all passengers. Finally, do not drive under the influence of alcohol – penalties are steep and often include jail time; the maximum legal alcohol-to-blood ratio for driving is 0.08 percent.

By boat

Aside from expensive cruises from US ports like Boston and New York, the only way to get to Montréal by water is aboard the **jetfoil** service from Québec City – a unique way to experience the St Lawrence with a bit of commentary thrown in. From late May to mid-October, Les Dauphins du St-Laurent (Ⓣ1-877/648-4499 or 514/288-4499, Ⓦwww.dauphins.ca) runs daily, four-and-a-half-hour trips to Quai Jacques-Cartier in Montréal, with a stop in Trois-Rivières en route, for $109 ($149 July and August, when there are two sailings a day).

Flights from the UK and Ireland

Prices from the UK vary widely, with flights out of **London** as cheap as £250 in low season (though £300–400 is more typical) and you'll be hard pressed to find much below £500 in the peak summer season. Shop around on a few of the online booking engines to get an idea of which airlines have seat sales; prices can also vary considerably depending on routing and time of day (you'll usually be less jet-lagged with a daytime return and higher prices reflect the demand for these flights).

Only Air Canada and British Airways offer direct scheduled flights for the seven-and-a-half-hour trip from London to Montréal, you can often get a cheaper fare by connecting through a major European or US hub, which adds a few hours to your journey. KLM/Northwest often have the best deals – it's worth paying a bit extra to fly via Amsterdam than Detroit's dreadful airport, though. Charters offer consistently cheaper fares (£260–420) but only fly direct from May to October – MyTravel's newer planes make it the better of the two carriers (Air Transat being the other).

You'll have to change planes regardless if you're travelling from one of the UK's **regional airports**, either via London, Toronto or a US or European hub; again, prices vary – expect to pay anywhere from the same rates as if flying directly from London to a couple of hundred pounds more. It may work out cheaper to travel to London by land or on a low-cost carrier; though you'll need to factor in the hassle of getting from one London airport to another if you choose the latter option. There are no direct flights **from Ireland**, and even though you'll be transiting through the same airports, you'll often pay less if starting from there – count on €400–500 in low season and upwards of €600–700 in summer, plus taxes of around €100.

Airlines in the UK and Ireland

Aer Lingus UK Ⓣ0845/084 4444, Republic of Ireland Ⓣ0818/365 000, Ⓦwww.aerlingus.com.
Air Canada UK Ⓣ0870/524 7226, Republic of Ireland Ⓣ01/679 3958, Ⓦwww.aircanada.com.
Air France UK Ⓣ0845/359 1000, Republic of Ireland Ⓣ01/605 0383, Ⓦwww.airfrance.com.
Air Transat Ⓦwww.airtransat.com. Bookings through Globespan – see below.
American Airlines UK Ⓣ0845/7789 789, Republic of Ireland Ⓣ01/602 0550, Ⓦwww.aa.com.
bmi UK Ⓣ0870/607 0555, Ⓦwww.flybmi.com.
British Airways UK Ⓣ0870/850 9850, Republic of Ireland Ⓣ1800/626 747, Ⓦwww.ba.com.
Continental Airlines UK Ⓣ0845/607 6760, Republic of Ireland Ⓣ1890/925 252, Ⓦwww.continental.com.
Delta UK Ⓣ0800/414 767, Republic of Ireland Ⓣ1800/768 080 or 01/407 3165, Ⓦwww.delta.com.
KLM/Northwest UK Ⓣ0870/507 4074, Ⓦwww.klm.com.
Lufthansa UK Ⓣ0845/773 7747, Republic of Ireland Ⓣ01/844 5544, Ⓦwww.lufthansa.com.
MyTravel Bookings through Canadian Affair – see p.16.
Swiss UK Ⓣ0845/601 0956, Republic of Ireland Ⓣ1890/200 515, Ⓦwww.swiss.com.
Thomas Cook Airlines UK Ⓣ0870/750 0316, Ⓦwww.thomascookpromotions.com/tca.
United Airlines UK Ⓣ0845/844 4777, Ⓦwww.unitedairlines.co.uk.
Virgin Atlantic UK Ⓣ01293/450 150, Ⓦwww.virgin-atlantic.com.

Flight and travel agents

Apex Travel Republic of Ireland Ⓣ01/241 8000, Ⓦwww.apextravel.ie. Specialists in flights to Australia, East Asia and North America. Consolidators for BA, American and SAS Scandinavian.
Aran Travel First Choice Republic of Ireland Ⓣ091/562 595, Ⓦwww.firstchoicetravel.ie. Good-

value flights worldwide, as well as package deals and tailor-made holidays.

Bridge the World UK ⓣ0870/443 2399, ⓦwww.bridgetheworld.com. Specialists in long-haul travel, with good-value flight deals, round-the-world tickets and tailor-made packages, all aimed at the backpacker market.

Canadian Affair UK ⓣ0870/075 3000, ⓦwww.canadian-affair.com. Good-quality and consistently cheap charter flights on MyTravel planes to Montréal (late May to October) and Toronto (year-round) as well as scheduled flights. Also accommodation packages, self-drive itineraries and car and motorhome hire.

ebookers UK ⓣ0870/010 7000, ⓦwww.ebookers.com, Republic of Ireland ⓣ01/241 5689, ⓦwww.ebookers.ie. Low fares on an extensive selection of scheduled flights and package deals.

Flightcentre UK ⓣ0870/890 8099, ⓦwww.flightcentre.co.uk. Rock-bottom fares worldwide.

Flynow UK ⓣ0870/444 0045, ⓦwww.flynow.com. Large range of discounted tickets.

Globespan UK ⓣ0870/556 1522, ⓦwww.globespan.com. Agent for Air Transat charter flights to Montréal (late May to October) and Toronto (year-round) as well as scheduled flights. Also car and motorhome hire.

Joe Walsh Tours Republic of Ireland ⓣ01/676 0991, ⓦwww.joewalshtours.ie. Long-established general budget fares and holidays agent.

Lee Travel Republic of Ireland ⓣ021/427 7111, ⓦwww.leetravel.ie. Flights and holidays worldwide.

McCarthys Travel Republic of Ireland ⓣ021/427 0127, ⓦwww.mccarthystravel.ie. General flight agent.

North South Travel UK ⓣ01245/608 291, ⓦwww.northsouthtravel.co.uk. Friendly, competitive travel agency, offering discounted fares worldwide. Profits are used to support projects in the developing world, especially the promotion of sustainable tourism.

Premier Travel UK ⓣ028/7126 3333, ⓦwww.premiertravel.uk.com. Discount flight specialists.

Rosetta Travel Northern Ireland ⓣ028/9064 4996, ⓦwww.rosettatravel.com. Flight and holiday agent, specializing in deals direct from Belfast.

STA Travel UK ⓣ0870/160 0599, ⓦwww.statravel.co.uk. Worldwide specialists in low-cost flights, overlands and holiday deals. Good discounts for students and under-26s.

Trailfinders UK ⓣ020/7938 5400, ⓦwww.trailfinders.com, Republic of Ireland ⓣ01/677 7888, ⓦwww.trailfinders.ie. One of the best-informed and most efficient agents for independent travellers.

Travel Bag UK ⓣ0870/890 1456, ⓦwww.travelbag.co.uk. Discount deals worldwide.

Travel Care UK ⓣ0870/112 0085, ⓦwww.travelcare.co.uk. Flights, holiday deals and city-breaks around the world.

Travel4Less UK ⓣ0871/222 3423, ⓦwww.travel4less.co.uk. Good discount airfares, bargain global city-breaks and discounted package deals, including cruises, fly-drives and ski holidays in the Laurentians. Part of Lastminute.com.

USIT Northern Ireland ⓣ028/9032 7111, ⓦwww.usitnow.com, Republic of Ireland ⓣ0818/200 020, ⓦwww.usit.ie. Specialists in student, youth and independent travel – flights, trains, study tours, TEFL, visas and more.

World Travel Centre Republic of Ireland ⓣ01/416 7007, ⓦwww.worldtravel.ie. Excellent fares to Europe and worldwide.

Package tours

Although **package tours** from the UK and Ireland tend to focus more on western Canada, Montréal and Québec City crop up as a base for camping, skiing or wilderness trips, which include canoeing or snowmobiling adventures and more sedate whale-watching excursions. You'll also get a couple of days in the cities as part of a ten-day-or-so bus tour of Québec and Ontario or longer trips that span the entire country. Some operators offer rail and fly-drive alternatives (which works out cheaper than hiring a car on the spot), and you can also cruise to Montréal from New York or Boston. Most operators can also tailor-make city-breaks to Montréal – a simple flight-and-hotel deal that might include a day's sightseeing in Québec City.

Tour operators in the UK and Ireland

1st Class Holidays UK ⓣ0845/644 3545, ⓦwww.1stclassholidays.com. Rail and coach tours of Ontario and Québec starting around £400 per week plus flight. Fly-drives include a number of off-the-beaten-track itineraries.

All Canada Travel and Holidays UK ⓣ01494/688 924, ⓦwww.all-canada.co.uk. Canada specialists offering Montréal and Québec City as a 4-night city-break or as part of a longer coach, rail or fly-drive package with wildlife and activity extras.

American Holidays Northern Ireland ⓣ028/9023 8762, Republic of Ireland ⓣ01/673 3840, ⓦwww.american-holidays.com. Full range of package deals from Ireland to all parts of the US and Canada. The two-week "Eastern Canada Discovery" and fly-drive packages feature Montréal; the agency also books hotel packages focusing solely on the city.

Arctic Experience UK ⓣ01737/214 214, ⓦwww.arctic-experience.co.uk. Well-established wildlife holiday specialist (part of the Discover the World group of companies), which takes groups led by naturalists on chilly (and pricey) adventures up north. For a blast of fun, you can spend three days zooming around the hinterland and warm up again with three days in Montréal and Québec City as part of the £1320 (including flights) "Snowmobile Adventure".

Bales Worldwide UK ⓣ0870/241 3208, ⓦwww.balesworldwide.com. Family-owned company offering high-quality escorted tours to Canada's wilder reaches, as well as tailor-made itineraries.

British Airways Holidays UK ⓣ0870/240 0747, ⓦwww.baholidays.co.uk. An exhaustive range of package and tailor-made holidays around the world, using British Airways and other quality international airlines.

CIE Tours International Republic of Ireland ⓣ01/703 1888, ⓦwww.cietours.ie. Wide range of escorted bus tours from €1330 for eight days in Ontario and Québec.

Contiki UK ⓣ020/8290 6777, ⓦwww.contiki.co.uk. Tours and trips for 18–35-year-old party animals.

Crystal Holidays UKⓣ0870/160 6040, ⓦwww.crystalski.co.uk. Ski holiday specialist that offers Mont Tremblant packages, with a couple of nights in Montréal as an option.

Explore Worldwide UK ⓣ01252/760 000, ⓦwww.explore.co.uk. Small-group tours such as a ten-day trip to Québec City and its hinterland including four days canoeing from £1100 (including flights).

Frontier Travel UK ⓣ020/8776 8709, ⓦwww.frontier-canada.co.uk. Tailor-made holidays as well as ski and St Lawrence cruise packages. Tours of Laurentians by snowmobile in winter or by hiking and canoeing while black-bear-spotting in summer.

Headwater UK ⓣ01606/720 099, ⓦwww.headwater.com. Walking and cross-country skiing holidays, including a week in the Laurentians near Mont Tremblant for £1050 (as high as £1650 Christmas week).

Inghams UK ⓣ020/8780 4433, ⓦwww.inghams.co.uk, Republic of Ireland ⓣ01/661 1377, ⓦwww.inghams.ie. Comprehensive ski holiday bookings, with Mont Tremblant and Québec City-area resorts on the books from around £800 low season including flights, accommodation, lift tickets and rentals. Also offer summer "Lakes and Mountains" coach tours.

Kuoni Travel UK ⓣ01306/747 002, ⓦwww.kuoni.co.uk. Award-winning major tour operator running flexible package holidays to long-haul destinations worldwide. Especially good deals for families. Offers a pair of twelve-day coach tours – one hits Ontario and Québec City, the other covers similar ground quicker then hops out west. Note – minimum age limit of 10 years. Also one- and two-week fly-drives.

Maxwells Travel Republic of Ireland ⓣ01/677 3662. Agent for a wide array of deals from adventure operators worldwide, with a number of outdoorsy Canadian options. Also offer flight-hotel and fly-drive packages for Montréal and tailor-made trips.

Thomas Cook UK ⓣ0870/750 0512, ⓦwww.thomascook.co.uk. Long-established one-stop travel agency for package holidays, city-breaks or flights, with bureau de change issuing Thomas Cook-branded travellers' cheques, plus travel insurance and car rental.

Wildlife Worldwide UK ⓣ020/8667 9158, ⓦwww.wildlifeworldwide.com. Tailor-made trips for wildlife and wilderness enthusiasts. Their 15-day Québec trip includes enough time in Tadoussac to see belugas and bigger whales and a long self-drive to the end of the Gaspé peninsula, with stops at reserves frequented by snow geese and gannets; the £1800–1900 price tag includes flight, car and rooms.

Flights from Australia and New Zealand

There are no direct **flights** for the 24-hour haul to Montréal from Australia or New Zealand – you'll need to change planes at least once and more likely twice depending on the airline and routing. Almost all flights are via the West Coast – principally Los Angeles, though some pass through San Francisco or Vancouver – and you may need to change planes again on the way to Montréal. There are often deals from the big Asian carriers via their home airports, which can allow for an interesting stopover, depending on the city, often at no extra charge. It's also worth considering a stopover in Honolulu or the South Pacific.

Air passes

If you're planning to visit a number of destinations in North America, one of the various **air passes** may save you a bundle on flights (but be sure to compare prices with what's available by booking direct). Typically these are unavailable to North Americans and must be booked overseas at the same time you book your flight to Canada or the US (some passes restrict your first flight to one country or the other). For most passes, like Continental's Visit USA (VUSA) pass, United's Skypass and Star Alliance's North America Airpass, you purchase a minimum of three and a maximum of eight to twelve coupons (depending on the airline), which are each valid for a single flight; costs average out around US$100–130 per flight segment, US$10–30 more in the June–August high season (if you can, ensure that your first flight is in May – fares are based on the first day of travel).

If you're planning to travel mainly in the northeast US and eastern Canada, Oneworld's Visit North America Pass may work out cheaper since you pay for each flight segment based on mileage, starting at US$80 for up to 430km and ranging up to US$300 for over 4020km (to or from Montréal, you're looking at US$110 for Toronto or New York, US$150 for Washington, DC and US$250 for Vancouver). Note that for any of these passes you may be required to fly to North America on whichever carrier (or partner of that carrier) is offering the programme; some airlines provide it to travellers on competitors' flights at extra cost.

There are also a number of train and bus passes, many of which are also available to Americans and Canadians (see boxes, pp.12–13).

Sydney offers the most choice for flights **from Australia** and, along with Melbourne, is the cheapest city to fly from – you'll pay around A$400 more from Perth, for instance. Fares for flights to Montréal vary seasonally and you can expect to pay A$2400–2700 (and up). It's well worth considering purchasing an air pass (see box, above) and connecting via Los Angeles, which costs around A$800–1000 less than a ticket straight through to Montréal – you'll pay under A$1500 if you hit upon a good fare.

From New Zealand, the best deals are out of Auckland – you'll need to factor on an extra NZ$200 from Wellington and NZ$300 from Christchurch. Fares through to Montréal start as low as NZ$2300 but you'll more likely pay in the NZ$2500–3200 range. As with Australia, you may be better off flying directly to Los Angeles and using an air pass from there (see box, above); flights to LA cost NZ$1800–2400 but drop as low as NZ$1600 during a seat sale.

Airlines in Australia and New Zealand

Air Canada Australia ⓣ1300/655 747 or 02/8248 5757, New Zealand ⓣ09/379 3371, ⓦwww.aircanada.com.
Air New Zealand Australia ⓣ13 24 76, ⓦwww.airnz.com.au, New Zealand ⓣ0800/737 000, ⓦwww.airnz.co.nz.
Air Pacific Australia ⓣ1800/230 150, New Zealand ⓣ0800/800 178, ⓦwww.airpacific.com.
Air Tahiti Nui Australia ⓣ02/9244 2899, New Zealand ⓣ09/308 3360, ⓦwww.airtahitinui-usa.com.
American Airlines Australia ⓣ1300/130 757, New Zealand ⓣ0800/887 997, ⓦwww.aa.com.
Cathay Pacific Australia ⓣ13 17 47, New Zealand ⓣ0508/800 454 or 09/379 0861, ⓦwww.cathaypacific.com.
China Airlines Australia ⓣ02/9244 2121, New Zealand ⓣ09/308 3371, ⓦwww.china-airlines.com.
Continental Airlines Australia ⓣ1300/361 400, New Zealand ⓣ09/308 3350, ⓦwww.continental.com.
Delta Australia ⓣ02/9251 3211, New Zealand ⓣ09/379 3370, ⓦwww.delta.com.
EVA Air Australia ⓣ02/8338 0419, New Zealand ⓣ09/358 8300, ⓦwww.evaair.com.
JAL Japan Airlines Australia ⓣ02/9272 1111, New Zealand ⓣ09/379 9906, ⓦwww.jal.com.
Korean Air Australia ⓣ02/9262 6000, New Zealand ⓣ09/914 2000, ⓦwww.koreanair.com.au.
Malaysia Airlines Australia ⓣ13 26 27, New Zealand ⓣ0800/777 747, ⓦwww.malaysiaairlines.com.my.
Qantas Australia ⓣ13 13 13, New Zealand ⓣ0800/808 767 or 09/357 8900, ⓦwww.qantas.com.

Singapore Airlines Australia ⓣ13 10 11, New Zealand ⓣ0800/808 909, ⓦwww.singaporeair.com.
Thai Airways Australia ⓣ1300/651 960, New Zealand ⓣ09/377 3886, ⓦwww.thaiair.com.
United Airlines Australia ⓣ13 17 77, ⓦwww.united.com.

Flight and travel agents

ecruising Australia ⓣ1300/369 848 or 02/9249 6060, ⓦwww.ecruising.com.au. Searchable fare database of cruises worldwide; many of the New England to Canada cruises stop in Québec City and Montréal.
Flight Centre Australia ⓣ13 31 33, ⓦwww.flightcentre.com.au, New Zealand ⓣ0800 243 544, ⓦwww.flightcentre.co.nz. Rock-bottom fares worldwide.
Holiday Shoppe New Zealand ⓣ0800/808 480, ⓦwww.holidayshoppe.co.nz. Great deals on flights, hotels and holidays.
OTC Australia ⓣ1300/855 118, ⓦwww.otctravel.com.au. Deals on flights, hotels and holidays, including 10-day cruises from New York to Montréal.
STA Travel Australia ⓣ1300/733 035, ⓦwww.statravel.com.au, New Zealand ⓣ0508/782 872, ⓦwww.statravel.co.nz. Worldwide specialists in low-cost flights, overlands and holiday deals. Good discounts for students and under-26s.
Student Uni Travel Australia ⓣ02/9232 8444, ⓦwww.sut.com.au, New Zealand ⓣ09/379 4224, ⓦwww.sut.co.nz. Great deals for students.
Trailfinders Australia ⓣ02/9247 7666, ⓦwww.trailfinders.com.au. One of the best-informed and most efficient agents for independent travellers.
travel.com.au and **travel.co.nz** Australia ⓣ1300/130 482 or 02/9249 5444, ⓦwww.travel.com.au, New Zealand ⓣ0800/468 332, ⓦwww.travel.co.nz. Comprehensive online travel company, with discounted fares.

Package tours

Many **package tours** include a couple of cosmopolitan days in Montréal and Québec City before exploring the countryside on a camping or wilderness trip or heading off to the ski hills. Montréal and Québec City also feature on itineraries of ten-day bus tours of Québec, Ontario and, for longer trips, New England or the Rockies. Many operators offer a more comfortable rail alternative, though for flexibility a fly-drive package can't be beat and is cheaper than renting on the spot. If you'd prefer to approach the city by water, as the earliest settlers did (but in greater comfort), there are 10- to 14-day cruises from eastern seaboard ports like New York. A short city-break just to Montréal is pretty much out of the question but may be worthwhile as an add-on to extend a tour or if you're planning a number of stops in North America and want to sort out your accommodation in advance. Many of these include a day's sightseeing trip to Québec City.

Tour operators in Australia and New Zealand

Adventure World Australia ⓣ02/8913 0755, ⓦwww.adventureworld.com.au, New Zealand ⓣ09/524 5118, ⓦwww.adventureworld.co.nz. Agents for a vast array of international adventure travel companies that operate trips to every continent. The 15-day "Highlights of Canada" coach trip in the Rockies and eastern Canada includes stops in Montréal and Québec City; from A$2400 plus flights. Also on offer are winter activity holidays, 3-week cross-country camping trips with Trek America (A$2150–2500; NZ$2500–2900) and a 9-day rail and coach tour of Ontario and Québec's major cities for A$1700–2400.
Australian Pacific Touring Australia ⓣ1800/675 222 or 03/9277 8555, New Zealand ⓣ09/279 6077, ⓦwww.aptours.com. Long-established, award-winning operator running package tours and independent travel. Montréal is a stop on the 10-day Niagara Falls to Québec City coach tour; longer trips include the Rockies or US destinations.
Canada & America Travel Specialists Australia ⓣ02/9922 4600, ⓦwww.canada-americatravel.com.au. North American specialists – accommodation, train travel, adventure sports, car and motorhome rentals, Greyhound and other long-distance bus passes, cruises, escorted tours, independent travel, and more.
Contiki Australia ⓣ02/9511 2200, New Zealand ⓣ09/309 8824, ⓦwww.contiki.com. Frenetic trips for 18-to-35-year-old party animals.
Explore Holidays Australia ⓣ02/9423 8080, ⓦwww.exploreholidays.com.au. Coach and rail tours of eastern Canada for A$1600–2000, with optional extended stays in Montréal and Québec City. If you want to make your own way, a week's self-drive and hotels works out to A$800–1100 per person.

Ski and Snowboard Travel Company Australia ⓣ1300/766 938, ⓦwww.skiandsnowboard.com.au. Customized skiing holidays.
Talpacific Australia ⓣ1300/137 727 or 02/9244 1850, New Zealand ⓣ0800/888 099, ⓦwww.talpacific.com. Deals include a 4-night Montréal and Québec City break.
USA Travel Australia ⓣ02/9250 9320, ⓦwww.usatravel.com.au. Good deals on flights, accommodation, city stays, car rental and trip packages. Packages include a cruise from New York to Montréal starting at A$4100.
Viator ⓦwww.viator.com. Bookings for local tours and sightseeing trips in destinations around the world, including Montréal, Québec City and the surrounding regions.

Red tape and visas

Entry to Canada is relatively straightforward. Citizens of the EU, Scandinavia and most Commonwealth countries do not need an entry visa – all that is required is a valid passport. United States citizens simply need some form of official identification.

Visitors **from the US** should ideally carry their passport, but can also cross the border with one piece of current photo ID and proof of citizenship (birth certificate, naturalization certificate or certificate of citizenship; non-US permanent residents should also bring their US Resident Alien Card, or green card). If you plan to travel to Canada regularly, investigate the joint Canada-US programmes designed to speed up border crossing for low-risk travellers (ⓣ1-866/639-8726, ⓦwww.ccra-adrc.gc.ca/nexus) – otherwise expect a wait at land border crossings and the possibility that your vehicle may be searched.

If you're coming from **anywhere else** in the world, you'll need a passport and possibly a visa; nationals of Australia, New Zealand, the UK and most western European countries are exempt from the latter requirement for tourist visits of up to a maximum of six months (the limit is more usually three – a Canadian immigration officer decides the length of stay permitted at the point of entry). You should also have a return ticket, proof of sufficient funds to support yourself, be in good health and not have a criminal conviction. Visitors with a criminal record – including drinking-and-driving convictions – may be refused entry to Canada; contact the embassy before planning your trip. Unaccompanied visitors under 18 years old require a letter of permission from their parent or guardian.

For longer stays or if you are planning to work or study in Canada, a **visa** is required: enquire at the Canadian embassy or consulate in your country (see below) well in advance of departure. The Government of Canada's "Canada International" website (ⓦwww.canadainternational.gc.ca) contains useful information and links for anyone planning to visit, study or work in Canada. If you plan to visit or transit through the **US,** check what the requirements are for nationals of your country as they may be different than for Canada, especially in the wake of the terrorist attacks in September 2001 – more information can be found at ⓦwww.travel.state.gov/visa_services.html.

Canadian embassies and consulates

A full list of Canadian overseas representatives is available on ⓦwww.dfait-maeci.gc.ca/world/embassies/menu-en.asp; offices that deal specifically with visas can also be found at ⓦwww.cic.gc.ca/english/offices/index.html. Details of foreign consulates in Montréal are given on p.217.

Australia Commonwealth Ave, Canberra, ACT 2600 ⓣ02/6270 4000; Level 6, Quay West Building, 111 Harrington St, Sydney, NSW 2000 ⓣ02/9364 3000 or 3050 (visas), ⓦwww.dfait-maeci.gc.ca/australia.

Ireland 65 St Stephen's Green, Dublin 2 ⓣ01/417 4100, ⓦwww.dfait-maeci.gc.ca/canadaeuropa/ireland. For visa services contact the Immigration Division in London.

New Zealand PO Box 12 049, 3rd Floor, 61 Molesworth St, Thorndon, Wellington ⓣ04/473 9577 or freephone ⓣ09/309 8516 from Auckland, ⓦwww.dfait-maeci.gc.ca/newzealand. For visa services contact the consulate in Sydney.

UK 1 Grosvenor Square, London W1K 4AB ⓣ020/7258 6600, ⓦwww.dfaitmaeci.gc.ca/canadaeuropa/united_kingdom; Canada House, Trafalgar Square, London SW1Y 5BJ; Immigration Division, 38 Grosvenor St, London W1K 4AA ⓣ020/7258 6699, ⓦwww.canada.org.uk; Unit 3, Ormeau Business Park, 8 Cromac Ave, Belfast BT7 2JA ⓣ028/9127 2060; Standard Life House, 30 Lothian Rd, Edinburgh EH1 2DH ⓣ0131/220 4333.

US 501 Pennsylvania Ave, NW, Washington, DC 20001 ⓣ202/682-1740, ⓦwww.canadianembassy.org; 550 South Hope St, 9th Floor, Los Angeles, CA 90071 ⓣ213/346-2700, ⓦwww.dfait-maeci.gc.ca/los_angeles; 1251 Ave of the Americas, Concourse Level, New York, NY10020 ⓣ212/596-1783, ⓦwww.dfait-maeci.gc.ca/new_york. Immigration services are also provided by Canadian consulates in Buffalo, Detroit and Seattle but not at the other Canadian consulates general in the US.

Insurance

The only thing worse than an accident or having something stolen on holiday is being out of pocket for it. You'd do well to take out an insurance policy before travelling to Canada to cover against theft, loss and illness or injury, especially as Canada's generally excellent health service costs non-residents anything from $50 to $1000–2000 a day for hospitalization. There is no free treatment to non-residents but if you do have an accident, medical services will get to you quickly and charge you later.

Before paying for a new policy, however, it's worth checking whether you are already covered: some all-risks home insurance policies may cover your possessions when overseas, and many private medical schemes include cover when abroad. For residents from elsewhere in Canada, provincial health plans usually provide full cover for hospitalization but for a visit to a physician you may need to pay up front and seek reimbursement later. Holders of official student/teacher/youth cards in Canada and the US are entitled to meagre accident coverage and hospital in-patient benefits. Students will often find that their student health coverage extends during the vacations and for one term beyond the date of last enrollment. Some credit card companies also offer coverage if your holiday is purchased using your card, however coverage is generally minimal.

After exhausting the possibilities above, you might want to contact a specialist travel insurance company, or consider the travel insurance deal offered by Rough Guides (see box, overleaf). A typical travel insurance policy usually provides cover for the loss of baggage, tickets and – up to a certain limit – cash or cheques, as well as cancellation or curtailment of your journey. Most of them exclude so-called dangerous sports unless an extra premium is paid: in Canada this can mean scuba-diving, whitewater rafting, windsurfing, snowmobiling, skiing and trekking, though probably not canoeing or cycling. Many policies can be chopped and changed to exclude coverage you don't

Rough Guides travel insurance

Rough Guides offers its own low-cost travel insurance, especially customized for our statistically low-risk readers by a leading British broker, provided by the American International Group (AIG) and registered with the British regulatory body, GISC (the General Insurance Standards Council). There are five main Rough Guides insurance plans: **No Frills**, for the bare minimum for secure travel; **Essential**, which provides decent all-round cover; **Premier** for comprehensive cover with a wide range of benefits; **Extended Stay** for cover lasting four months to a year; and **Annual multi-trip**, a cost-effective way of getting Premier cover if you travel more than once a year. Premier, Annual Multi-Trip and Extended Stay policies can be supplemented by a "Hazardous Pursuits Extension" if you plan to indulge in sports considered dangerous, such as scuba-diving or trekking. For a policy quote, call the Rough Guide Insurance Line on the UK freefone ⓣ0800/015 09 06 or ⓣ+44 1392/314 665 from elsewhere. Alternatively, get an online quote at ⓦwww.roughguides.com/insurance.

need – for example, sickness and accident benefits can often be excluded or included at will. If you do take medical coverage, ascertain whether benefits will be paid as treatment proceeds or only after return home, and whether there is a 24-hour medical emergency number. When securing baggage coverage, make sure that the per-article limit – typically under $500 – will cover your most valuable possessions. If you need to make a claim, you should keep receipts for medicines and medical treatment, and in the event you have anything stolen, you must obtain an official statement from the police.

If you are **driving** to Montréal, you must have at least $50,000 liability coverage. Under the Société de l'Assurance Automobile du Québec (SAAQ) insurance scheme, you are fully covered if injured in a Québec-registered automobile (including rental cars). If your car isn't registered in Québec (or a Canadian province that has a reciprocal agreement), or you are a pedestrian or cyclist, you can also claim compensation to the degree that the accident wasn't your fault. For more information, visit the SAAQ website (ⓦwww.saaq.gouv.qc.ca) or call ⓣ1-888/810-2525 within the province, ⓣ1-800/463-6898 from elsewhere.

Information, websites and maps

The best way to get information about the city is from one of the tourist boards – Tourisme Montréal naturally covers the city in the greatest detail, but Tourisme Québec also provides a wealth of brochures and maps on Montréal and should be your first resource for travel elsewhere in the province. From abroad, you can order brochures from Tourisme Québec or the Canadian Tourism Commission but the easiest way to find out about Montréal is on the Internet – we've provided a list of useful sites below to get you started.

Tourist information

The main tourist information office in Montréal is the Downtown **Centre Infotouriste** located in the Dominion Square Building facing Square Dorchester, just south of rue Ste-Catherine (daily: June to early Sept 7am–8pm; early Sept to May 9am–6pm; ⓣ514/873-2015 or 1-877/266-5687, ⓦwww.bonjourquebec.com). Run by Tourisme Québec, it has loads of brochures and information on Montréal sights (including free maps and the useful *Montréal Official Tourist Guide* booklet), and those of the rest of the province, making it an excellent stop if you're planning to do some travelling outside the city. In addition, there's an accommodation service and a counter where private companies offer currency exchange, car rental and city tours – most bus tours depart from directly in front of the office.

The city-run tourist office, the **Bureau d'Information Touristique de Vieux-Montréal**, is on the corner of Place Jacques-Cartier at 174 rue Notre-Dame E (early June to early Sept 9am–7pm; early Sept to early June 9am–5pm; ⓦwww.tourism-montreal.org). There are also a number of smaller information offices or kiosks dealing with specific districts – these are described in the relevant sections of the guide.

Tourist offices

You can contact the following organizations with postal and telephone enquiries only:

Canadian Tourism Commission 5th Level, Quay West, 111 Harrington St, Sydney NSW 2000, Australia. Canada Travel Information Line ⓣ1300/300-576 or 02/9954 3377, ⓦwww.travelcanada.ca.

Destination Québec PO Box 1939, Maidenhead, Berkshire SL6 1AJ. UK brochure requests only ⓣ0870/556 1705, ⓦwww.quebec4u.co.uk.

Tourisme Québec PO Box 979, Montréal, Québec H3C 2W3. US and Canada toll-free ⓣ1-877/266-5687; overseas callers dial ⓣ514/873-2015, ⓕ864-3838.

Travel Canada Inquiries 55 Metcalfe St, Suite 600, Ottawa, Ontario K1P 6L5. US only toll-free ⓣ1-877/822-6232, overseas callers dial ⓣ613/946-1000, ⓕ952-7475.

Websites

The **Internet** provides an excellent way of finding out everything from what's happening in Montréal's rapidly changing nightlife scene to the latest blockbuster exhibitions at the city's museums – if the homepage is in French, you can usually click through to an English version (usually with slimmed-down content). We've listed relevant websites throughout the guide, but below you'll find a few of the more helpful and interesting general sites on offer.

Commerce Design Montréal ⓦwww.commercedesignmontreal.com. Photos and virtual tours of some of the city's trendiest bars, shops and restaurants, which have won awards for their interior architecture.

Heavyweight Art Installation ⓦwww.hvw8.com. Site featuring the works of a popular Montréal urban art collective, Heavyweight, which hold frequent public-art happenings.

Jazz Montréal ⓦwww.jazzmontreal.com. Reviews, listings and news from the city's jazz scene.

Montréal CAM ⓦwww.montrealcam.com. If you can't wait to see Montréal, check out this site for live web-cam images taken from around the city.

Montrealplus ⓦwww.english.montrealplus.ca. This portal features thousands of reviews (which aren't always up to date) on everything from local shops and galleries to bars, restaurants and clubs, along with a handy mapping device that locates venues for you.

MoreMontreal.com ⓦwww.moremontreal.com. Directory-style site with hundreds of links organized by category, along with a quick menu of popular websites and an opinionated e-guide to the city.

Museums to Discover ⓦwww.musees.quebec.museum. The Société des Musées Québécois has a comprehensive guide to every museum and interpretation centre in the province, large and small. Search by area or discipline or plan a thematic itinerary.

Place des Arts ⓦwww.PdArts.com. Montréal's primo cultural venue has a calendar of events and online booking here.

Tourisme Montréal ⓦwww.tourism-montreal.org. The city tourist office's official site, with listings of sights, hotels, restaurants, entertainment and events.

Tourisme Québec ⓦwww.bonjourquebec.com. The official site of the province's tourist board has information on towns across the province and links to regional tourist-board sites.

Urbanphoto ⓦwww.urbanphoto.net. Photo and text essays about cities and their neighbourhoods, with an especially strong focus on Montréal.

Ville de Montréal ⓦwww.ville.montreal.qc.ca. The municipal government's main website covers all facets of city life, though the English-language coverage is patchy.

Virtual Museum of New France ⓦwww.civilization.ca/vmnf/vmnfe.asp. Online exhibition on the history and personalities of Québec's earliest days, up until the Conquest.

YULBlog ⓦwww.billegible.org/yulblog. Directory listing of weblogs run by Montrealers – one of the best for keeping up to date and focusing on local issues is Montreal City Weblog (ⓦwww.montreal.com/mtlweblog).

Maps

The tourist information offices (see p.22) provide a comprehensive **map** of Montréal's main sightseeing areas, which, along with the maps in this guide, should be sufficient for your needs. If you're planning to use city buses, the free map available from the STM (see p.26) covers the whole island but lacks the detail you'd need for driving. If you're a member of a motoring organization, it's worth checking if they provide maps free of charge; otherwise, there are a number of commercial options (below). You can also download maps: Transports Québec (Ⓦwww.mtq.gouv.qc.ca) has a road map of the province, the city website has plans of districts and tourist areas (Ⓦwww.ville.montreal.qc.ca – click on "Cartographie") and the STM has detailed (if dated) maps of the areas surrounding each Métro station (Ⓦwww.stm.info/English/metro/a-mapmet.htm) as well as various transit maps.

MapArt produces the best general map of the city, a fully indexed map of the island at 1:31,250 with an enlargement of the Downtown area at 1:15,625 (Rand McNally produces one at a similar scale). Larger scale maps at around 1:15,000 that cover the main tourist areas (essentially the same area as the enlargement on the map mentioned above), and highlight attractions, hotels and the like include MapArt's *Downtown Montréal Map* and *Montréal FastTrack Map*, as well as the laminated *Insight FlexiMap*, National Geographic's *Montreal Destination Map*, and the more conventional GeoCenter one. MapArt also publish a series of street atlases of Montréal and the surrounding area.

Map outlets

Large general bookstores and online retailers usually have some maps of Montréal but if you want to compare maps to find one that suits, you're better to try one of the following specialist map and/or travel bookshops or websites.

In Canada and the US

110 North Latitude US Ⓣ336/369-4171, Ⓦwww.110nlatitude.com.
Aux Quatre Points Cardinaux 551 rue Ontario E, Montréal, PQ H2L 1N8 Ⓣ1-888/843-8116, Ⓦwww.aqpc.com.
Book Passage 51 Tamal Vista Blvd, Corte Madera, CA 94925 Ⓣ1-800/999-7909, Ⓦwww.bookpassage.com.
Distant Lands 56 S Raymond Ave, Pasadena, CA 91105 Ⓣ1-800/310-3220, Ⓦwww.distantlands.com.
Globe Corner Bookstore 28 Church St, Cambridge, MA 02138 Ⓣ1-800/358-6013, Ⓦwww.globecorner.com.
Librairie du Voyage Ulysses 4176 rue St-Denis, Montréal, PQ, H2W 2M5 Ⓣ1-877/542-7247, Ⓦwww.ulyssesguides.com.
Longitude Books 115 W 30th St #1206, New York, NY 10001 Ⓣ1-800/342-2164, Ⓦwww.longitudebooks.com.
Map Town 400 5 Ave SW #100, Calgary, AB, T2P 0L6 Ⓣ1-877/921-6277, Ⓦwww.maptown.com.
Travel Bug Bookstore 3065 W Broadway, Vancouver, BC, V6K 2G9 Ⓣ604/737-1122, Ⓦwww.travelbugbooks.ca.
World of Maps 1235 Wellington St, Ottawa, ON, K1Y 3A3 Ⓣ1-800/214-8524, Ⓦwww.worldofmaps.com.

In the UK and Ireland

Stanfords 12–14 Long Acre, London WC2 Ⓣ020/7836 1321, Ⓦwww.stanfords.co.uk. Also at 39 Spring Gardens, Manchester Ⓣ0161/831 0250, and 29 Corn St, Bristol Ⓣ0117/929 9966.
Blackwell's Map Centre 50 Broad St, Oxford Ⓣ01865/793 550, Ⓦwww.maps.blackwell.co.uk. Branches in Bristol, Cambridge, Cardiff, Leeds, Liverpool, Newcastle, Reading & Sheffield.
The Map Shop 30a Belvoir St, Leicester Ⓣ0116/247 1400, Ⓦwww.mapshopleicester.co.uk.
National Map Centre 22–24 Caxton St, London SW1 Ⓣ020/7222 2466, Ⓦwww.mapsnmc.co.uk.
National Map Centre Ireland 34 Aungier St, Dublin Ⓣ01/476 0471, Ⓦwww.mapcentre.ie.
The Travel Bookshop 13–15 Blenheim Crescent, London W11 Ⓣ020/7229 5260, Ⓦwww.thetravelbookshop.co.uk.
Traveller 55 Grey St, Newcastle-upon-Tyne Ⓣ0191/261 5622, Ⓦwww.newtraveller.com.

In Australia and New Zealand

Map Centre Ⓦwww.mapcentre.co.nz.
Mapland 372 Little Bourke St, Melbourne Ⓣ03/9670 4383, Ⓦwww.mapland.com.au.
Map Shop 6–10 Peel St, Adelaide Ⓣ08/8231 2033, Ⓦwww.mapshop.net.au.
Map World 371 Pitt St, Sydney Ⓣ02/9261 3601, Ⓦwww.mapworld.net.au. Also at 900 Hay St, Perth Ⓣ08/9322 5733.
Map World 173 Gloucester St, Christchurch Ⓣ0800/627 967, Ⓦwww.mapworld.co.nz.

Arrival

With direct international flights from across Canada and the US, as well as many European cities, Montréal is an easy city to get to. A number of rail lines also converge on the city, bringing VIA Rail trains from the rest of Canada and Amtrak trains from the US. Orléans Express buses link the city with other Québec destinations, while a variety of companies handle transborder routes. The train station is right downtown with the bus station just to the east and both are well integrated into the city's efficient public-transport system. Numerous *autoroutes* provide a relatively quick way to reach Downtown, though access to the island, via the Tunnel Lafontaine and many bridges, suffers from traffic bottlenecks at rush hour.

By air

All flights on major airlines to the city touch down at **Aéroport de Montréal-Dorval** (ⓣ514/394-7377 or 1-800/465-1213, ⓦwww.admtl.com), 25km west of Downtown. Amid some controversy, the airport was renamed **Aéroport International Pierre-Elliott-Trudeau de Montréal**, though it may be some time before the name catches on. The airport's layout is simple, with the domestic and international wings connected by a large concourse on the upstairs Departures level and separated by a long corridor on the ground-floor Arrivals, where currency exchange and car-rental desks are available outside the baggage-claim areas. ATMs are dotted throughout. Ongoing construction through 2005, including a new transborder and international arrivals area, may mean that parts of the airport will be temporarily inaccessible.

The cheapest way to get Downtown is by **local bus**, a complicated, 60–90-minute journey you don't want to think about unless on an extremely tight budget. From outside the terminal catch #204 to the Dorval bus and train station due south of the airport. From there, switch to either one of the infrequent commuter trains downtown or bus #211 (or Métrobus #190 or #221 during rush hour) to Métro Lionel-Groulx, from where you can take the orange or green line downtown.

Instead, most visitors opt for the straightforward and luggage-friendly **Aérobus shuttle** (ⓣ514/931-9002; 2 hourly, daily 7am–1am; tickets from the booth just outside the terminal between domestic and international Arrivals), which drops passengers off at the Downtown Aérobus Station (adjacent to the main rail station) and main bus station in 35 to 45 minutes. Included in the $12 fare ($21.75 return) are free minibuses that connect the Aérobus Station with 40 hotels in Downtown, Vieux-Montréal and the Quartier Latin.

Taxis queue up outside Arrivals and will take you anywhere within the wider Downtown area (from Vieux-Montréal to around avenue des Pins, between Atwater and Papineau) for a flat rate of $28 (plus tip); other destinations are metered.

By train

VIA Rail and Amtrak **trains** loop south of Downtown before diving under Place Bonaventure to reach the main terminus, **Gare Centrale**. Located at 895 rue de la Gauchetière O in the heart of Downtown, the station is accessible from a number of spots in the surrounding blocks via the Underground City, which also links it to Métro Bonaventure and other Métro stations. Escalators from the platforms lead up to the grand main concourse, where facilities include a labyrinthine food court, ATMs, newsstands, Internet kiosks and left luggage facilities (for passengers only; $2.50/24hr, $5 oversized; Mon–Fri 6am–11pm, Sat & Sun 8am–11pm). If you have a lot of luggage, you might want to avoid the trek to the Métro and take a taxi instead – follow the signs to the covered taxi rank.

By bus

The main terminus for long-distance buses to the city, **Station Centrale d'Autobus Montréal**, lies on the eastern edge of the Quartier Latin at 505 boul de Maisonneuve E (☎514/842-2281), and connects directly with Métro Berri-UQAM. It's a pretty impersonal spot, though there are adequate facilities for visitors, including ATMs, newsstands, a café/restaurant, pay-Internet terminals, currency exchange, lockers and left luggage for larger items. The area outside the station can be a bit sketchy at night – if you are carrying luggage, head directly to the Métro or catch one of the taxis that queue up outside the station. Buses from Québec City also stop at the Longueuil terminus on the South Shore, at the end of the yellow Métro line.

By car

If you're coming to Montréal by **car**, you'll approach the city on one of the numerous *autoroutes* (motorways or expressways) that, outside of rush hours, provide speedy access into town. There are two main east–west routes: **Hwy-40** (stretches of which are known as the Route Transcanadienne and the Autoroute Métropolitaine) crosses the island through the city's northern suburbs and is often congested; the poorly marked exits that veer off suddenly to either side can make it daunting for new arrivals. **Hwy-20** more closely follows the southern shore, passing Dorval airport and continuing as **Hwy-720** (Autoroute Ville-Marie) as it approaches Downtown. From the east, Hwy 20 crosses to the island along Pont Champlain, coinciding for a stretch with two other *autoroutes*: **Hwy-10** (Autoroute Bonaventure) leads directly downtown from the south and **Hwy-15** splits off north of the junction of hwys 20 and 720 as the trench-like Autoroute Décarie. The city's bridges are notorious bottlenecks, and it's worth listening to the radio traffic reports (such as CJAD 800 AM) to see if Pont Victoria or Pont Jacques-Cartier may be less time-consuming options. In any event, care should be taken in planning out your route as signage is in French and often gives inadequate warning of an impending exit. Although drivers can now turn right at red lights elsewhere in Québec (unless signposted otherwise), it is forbidden on the island of Montréal.

City transport

If you're not planning to stray too far from the city centre, you can easily get around in Montréal without a car. Certainly in Vieux-Montréal with its narrow streets and nightmarish parking, walking is your best bet. The Métro and buses offer a frequent and fairly speedy way for seeing the rest of the city. Taxis are plentiful and relatively cheap. In the warmer months, cycling is an excellent way to get a flavour of the city.

The public transit system is run by the **STM** (Société de transport de Montréal; ☎514/288-6287, Ⓦwww.stm.info), whose website and phone line can provide you with detailed journey information. Free maps of the Métro and bus network are also available at most stations – if they've run out, drop by the system's main information desk at Métro Berri-UQAM, opposite the turnstiles nearest to the Station Centrale d'Autobus exit. There are also a number of commuter train lines, however these are of little use to visitors.

The Métro

The clean and quiet **Métro system** has four lines that are colour-coded and identified by the terminus in each direction – refer to the back of this guide for a colour plan of the system. The most heavily used lines both pass through Downtown – the **green line** snakes along from west to east, heading out past the Stade Olympique, while the **orange line** makes a large "U", with the arms heading north from Downtown on either side of the mountain. The east–west **blue line** runs north of the mountain, intersecting with the orange line at Snowdon and Jean-Talon stations. The **yellow line** only has three stops, but is the best way to get to Parc Jean-Drapeau – you can transfer from the orange or green lines at Berri-UQAM station. Service starts at 5.30am daily on all lines. The last trains on the blue line are at 12.15pm; the others stop running at 12.30am, 1am on Saturday.

Single tickets cost $2.50 but you can buy a strip of six tickets for $10 at retail outlets such as pharmacies and *dépanneurs* (cornershops) throughout the city as well as at the stations themselves. Just after passing through the turnstiles, be sure to take a transfer from one of the machines if you intend to continue your journey by bus. If you're planning to make more extensive use of the Métro and bus system, it's worth investing in a **Tourist Card** – the one-day pass is $7 from Downtown stations (but is only available at Berri-UQAM and Bonaventure stations from November–March). If you want any longer than that, the **CAM Hebdo** (a weekly commuter pass) is $16, giving you more days for a bit more money than the three-day tourist card at $14; the only drawback is that the pass is valid starting Monday and ends on Sunday.

Buses

The city's fleet of **buses** supplements the Métro system, filling in the gaps between the lines and fanning out into the suburbs. Prices are the same as for the Métro (exact fare required if paying cash rather than using a ticket) and if you want to transfer from one bus to another or on to the Métro, ask the driver for *une correspondance* when you pay your fare. Bus stops indicate which Métro station the bus is heading towards and many also have a unique telephone number you can call for the schedule for that particular stop. Night services run on a limited number of routes after midnight; these vary from the day-time routes and are marked on the back of the STM map mentioned above.

Taxis

Taxis are relatively cheap and easy to find Downtown and on the main roads everywhere, and can also be found at taxi ranks near the larger hotels and transport termini. The largest and most reliable of the city's taxi firms are Taxi Diamond (☎514/273-6331)

Useful bus routes

#11 (Montagne) From Métro Mont-Royal across the top of the mountain.
#24 (Sherbrooke) From Métro Sherbrooke through Downtown and Westmount to Métro Villa-Maria.
#36 (Monk) From Métro Square-Victoria along rue Notre-Dame past the Marché Atwater to Métro Angrignon.
#51 (Édouard-Montpetit) From Métro Laurier via Outremont and past the Oratoire to Métro Snowdon and beyond.
#55 (St-Laurent) From Place d'Armes in Vieux-Montréal to Little Italy via the Main.
#80 (Du Parc) From Métro Place-des-Arts alongside the mountain to Outremont and Mile-End; #129 (Côte-Ste-Catherine) follows the same route before veering off north of the mountain.
#144 (Av des Pins) From Métro Atwater to Métro Sherbrooke along the mountain's south flank and past Molson Stadium.
#165 (Côte-des-Neiges) and #166 (Queen Mary) From Métro Guy-Concordia along the mountain's west side for access to the main gate of Cimetière Notre-Dame-des-Neiges and the Oratoire.
#167 (Casino) Follows a circuit around the islands from Métro Jean-Drapeau.
#535 (R-Bus Du Parc / Côte-des-Neiges) Rush-hour service that combines the #80 and #165 routes via boulevard René-Lévesque.

and Taxi Co-op (☎514/725-9885). **Fares** start at $2.80 and the meter clocks another $1.13 for each kilometre travelled; a fifteen percent tip is standard. A short ride within Downtown will cost little more than $5, to the Plateau is about $10–12. Trips between Downtown and the airport are a fixed $28, not including tip.

Ferries

Although it's less convenient (and more expensive) than taking the Métro, the passenger **ferry** that runs from the Quai Jacques-Cartier in the Vieux-Port to Île Ste-Hélène affords striking views of Montréal's skyline. The ferry runs regularly from mid-May to early October (☎514/281-8000 for schedules) and the ten-minute ride will set you back $3.75 each way.

Driving

You don't really need a car when visiting Montréal unless you're planning a day out from the city. If you do insist on **driving**, avoid Vieux-Montréal where the narrow streets make life difficult and parking can be a pain – for advice on your best options, see box, p.68. Downtown traffic can be a bit slow and, while you might have difficulty finding a metered spot, there's plenty of parking otherwise. There are numerous open-air lots (which the city hopes to reduce) and more secure underground parking as well – the car park below Dominion Square is one of the most central.

In most of the city, traffic doesn't pose too many problems outside of rush hour, which is at its worst at *autoroute* junctions and the bridges off the island that form natural bottlenecks. If you're driving in the winter, make sure you have snow tires and antifreeze and know how to control a skid in icy conditions; in general, drive more cautiously than you would on dry roads.

Montréal is one of the only places in North America where you cannot turn right at a red light – and with good reason. Montréal drivers are renowned in Canada for their laissez-faire driving skills and for them it often seems that the word "arrêt" on the red, octagonal signs is not a literal translation of "stop". Otherwise, signage in the city conforms to North American norms, albeit in French – you'll have the most difficulty when it comes to parking. Even Francophone Montrealers get caught out occasionally by the bewildering array of restrictions limiting parking at certain hours, days of the week or months of the year. In residential areas, pay especially close attention to signs indicating if a resident's permit is required. Be aware that during and after a snowfall, extra no-parking signs are temporarily installed so that snow-removal crews can do their job.

If you need a **rental car**, you'll find plenty of competition at the airport and throughout Downtown (see box, below). You'll need to have a credit card and, if you have an overseas driver's licence, an International Driver's Permit is recommended. Some car rental firms won't accept drivers under 25; others will charge a premium for younger drivers (minimum 21 years old). It may be worth booking a fly-drive package if you plan to do a lot of

Car rental agencies

Alamo ☎1-800/462-5266, ⓦwww.alamo.com.
Avis Canada ☎1-800/272-5871, ⓦwww.avis.ca, US ☎1-800/230-4898, ⓦwww.avis.com.
Budget Canada ☎800/268-8900, ⓦwww.budgetcanada.com, US ☎1-800/527-0700, ⓦwww.budgetrentacar.com.
Discount ☎514/286-1554, ⓦwww.discountcar.com.
Dollar US ☎1-800/800-4000, ⓦwww.dollar.com.
Enterprise Rent-a-Car ☎1-800/736-8222, ⓦwww.enterprise.com.
Hertz Canada ☎1-800/263-0600, ⓦwww.hertz.ca, US ☎1-800/654-3001, ⓦwww.hertz.com.
Kangouroute ☎1-888/768-8388, ⓦwww.kangouroute.com.
National ☎1-800/227-7368, ⓦwww.nationalcar.com.
Thrifty ☎1-800/847-4389, ⓦwww.thrifty.ca or ⓦwww.thrifty.com.
Via Route ☎514/871-1166, ⓦwww.viaroute.com.

driving, but if you're only planning a day or two out of the city it will likely cost more and you'll have to worry about parking the beast.

Allô-Stop, 4317 rue St-Denis (Ⓣ514/985-3032, Ⓦwww.allo-stop.com), is a **ridesharing** service that matches drivers with passengers for destinations within Québec. Membership costs $6 per year, and you pay for your share of petrol – it's about $15 to Québec City, which also has a branch, located at 467 rue St-Jean (Ⓣ418/522-0056). They also post ads on their website for rideshares further afield; otherwise, try bulletin boards at university student centres and youth hostels for a driver going your way.

Cycling

Cycling is a great way to get a feel for the city's many neighbourhoods and get a bit of exercise while trekking out to more distant attractions. The main places to **rent** a bike are in Vieux-Montréal (see box, p.80) – handy for checking out the industrial landscapes along the Lachine Canal or exploring the islands – and the Plateau (see p.204), where there are a number of bike shops within a short distance of the rue Rachel bike path that runs from the mountain out to the Big O. Most of the city's **bike paths** have two lanes side-by-side, separated from the traffic by a curb or a series of waist-high posts; be careful at intersections, especially when you are travelling counter to the main flow of traffic. In addition to the rue Rachel path, the other main urban one you are likely to use is the north-south route on rue Berri from Vieux-Montréal, which detours through Parc Lafontaine north of rue Sherbrooke. You can bring your bike onto the front car of the Métro at any time outside of rush hour (Mon–Fri before 10am and 3–7pm); as there are no lifts, be prepared to hike it up stairs and/or escalators. For car-free cycling, the paths on the islands and the route along the Lachine Canal are both good options, though the latter gets congested with bladers and Sunday cyclists. For further details, see Chapter 16, "Sports and outdoor activities".

City tours

There's a wide range of options for organized sightseeing in Montréal. To decide on one of the bus tours or cruises on the St Lawrence we've listed below, it's easiest to compare what's on offer at the Centre Infotouriste (see p.22). More interesting, though, are the possibilities outlined under walking tours.

For general information on cycling tours and where to rent bicycles, see Chapter 18, "Sports and outdoor activities" and p.80 for the Vieux-Port area in particular. If you want to delve into the Lachine Canal's industrial heritage, check out the cruises and thematic walking tours detailed in the box on p.128. For more highbrow culture, you can take a stroll around the district surrounding the Musée des Beaux-Arts (see p.65). If your French is really up to scratch, there are a variety of thematic tours in addition to those listed here, (including a tour of the year's Commerce Design Montréal winners, see p.23) – ask at the tourist office for further options.

Walking tours

Guidatour Ⓣ514/844-4021 or 1-800/363-4021, Ⓦwww.guidatour.qc.ca. Tours of Vieux-Montréal depart at 11am and 1pm (July & Aug also at 4pm) from the front of Basilique Notre-Dame daily from late June to September and weekends from late May to mid-October. The 90-minute tours focus on the history and architecture of the area and cost $13.50. On Saturdays in July and August, a lamplighter leads visitors on a 75-minute tour of Vieux-Montréal's illuminated buildings (9pm, $10).

Heritage Montréal ⓣ514/286-2662, ⓦwww.heritagemontreal.qc.ca. This non-profit preservation group runs an excellent series of 2hr "Architectours" in the warmer months, with historians covering the architectural legacy and history of city neighbourhoods. Tickets are $10.

Mobile literary workshops ⓣ514/345-2627 ext 3017, ⓦwww.jewishpubliclibrary.org. On the occasional summer Sunday, local English teacher Stan Asher leads evocative literary rambles, full of anecdotes and quotations from the works of Montréal writers such as Mordecai Richler and A.M. Klein. A donation of a non-perishable kosher food item is all it costs.

Old Montréal Ghost Trail ⓣ514/868-0303, ⓦwww.phvm.qc.ca. Costumed actors pop up as ghosts of famous Montrealers on these summer tours (Wed–Sun 8.30pm; $15); tickets from the kiosk near the foot of Quai Jacques-Cartier 6–8.30pm.

Land and water tours

Amphi-Bus ⓣ514/849-5181, ⓦwww.amphitours.com. From May to October, you can see Vieux-Montréal by land and by water from a customized military landing craft. The 1hr tour costs $20.75 ($39.15 during the fireworks); hourly departures are from the corner of boulevard St-Laurent and rue de la Commune or the Centre Infotouriste (10am–midnight).

Autocar Impérial ⓣ514/871-4733, ⓦwww.autocarimperial.com. Similar offerings and prices to Gray Line (see below), though they also have a hop-on, hop-off ticket valid for two days on an open-top double-decker bus for $31.

Le Bateau Mouche ⓣ514/849-9952 or 1-800/361-9952, ⓦwww.bateau-mouche.com. Day-time cruises give fine views onto the Vieux-Port and the skyline before circling around Île Ste-Hélène (4 daily, one and a half hours, $21), while longer dinner cruises travel downriver to the Îles de Boucherville before returning to the lit-up city (three and a half hours, $68.50–123.00). Departures during the May to October season are from Quai Jacques-Cartier.

Calèches Horse-drawn carriages are a romantic (if expensive) way to see the sights of Vieux-Montréal, though the quality of such a tour depends on the driver's abilities as a raconteur. You can hire one at Place d'Armes, on rue Notre Dame est near the Hôtel de Ville and at the foot of Place Jacques-Cartier opposite the Vieux-Port for $35/30min or $60/hr.

Croisières AML ⓣ1-800/563-4643, ⓦwww.croisieresaml.com. A variety of cruises on *Le Cavalier Maxim* are available with or without meals, ranging from one and a half to 4 hours ($23.75–37.95) and departing from Quai King-Edward. The cheaper sunset cruise ($17.50) uses the passenger ferry boat and departs from Quai Jacques-Cartier.

Gray Line ⓣ514/934-1222, ext 3, ⓦwww.coachcanada-montreal.com. Standard bus tours on a regular coach or one dollied up as a tram take in the city's main sights, with various excursions and combo packages available. The 90-minute basic tour (May–Oct) visits Downtown, Vieux-Montréal and Mont Royal for $26. The year-round three-hour tram tour throws a wider net, also taking in the Parc Olympique, Parc Jean-Drapeau and other sights for $35.

Costs, money and banks

Montréal ranks among the cheaper of Canada's major cities, and the perennially low Canadian dollar makes it a bargain for visitors from the US and the UK. Accommodation will eat up the largest chunk of your budget – unless you take advantage of Montréal's pricier gastronomic restaurants or go full-tilt on the nightlife front.

Average costs

Unless you purchased a package deal, your biggest on-the-ground layout will be for **accommodation**. Aside from a no-frills youth hostel or student residence room, count on spending around $50–75 for a budget one- or two-star hotel. Many of these places can be fairly grim and it's worth spending closer to $100 for B&B accommodation (the large breakfasts go some way to making up the difference) or one of the city's charming small hotels. Downtown and even more so in Vieux-Montréal, you'll be hard-pressed to find a decent place below $150 and you're looking at over $300 for the most spectacular properties. Many hotels offer promotional deals in the off-season.

You can get by on as little as $20 a day for **food** if you stick to cheap fry-up breakfasts, a sandwich for lunch and a fast-food shawarma (kebab) pita, noodle dish or pizza by the slice for dinner. That would be a shame, though, as Montréal has a fantastic array of restaurants that are cheaper than ones of comparable quality in Europe or America's foodie capitals – figure on around $50 a day for moderately priced meals and a drink or two, though you can easily spend that on dinner alone (double it for a quality bottle of wine) at finer places. Another thing to remember is taxes and tips – these add almost a third onto restaurant bills.

Both the federal and provincial governments get their share of taxes: the 7 percent GST (TPS in French) goes to the former and the 7.5 percent QST (TVQ in French) the latter. As a visitor, you can claim some of it back – see box, p.32. In restaurants, it's customary to **tip** 15 percent of the total before taxes. Note that "TPS" or "GST" that appear on the bill are not abbreviations for "tips" or "Good Service Tip" – these are the taxes mentioned above. If there's a group of you, the restaurant may insist on adding the tip to your bill. Bar staff expect 15 percent (or about a buck a beer), even if you pick up your own drinks from the bar, as do taxi drivers and hairdressers. For porters, doormen and bellhops, tip $1 per bag.

Youth and student discounts

Once obtained, various **youth/student ID cards** soon pay for themselves in savings. Full-time students are eligible for the International Student ID Card (ISIC, Ⓦwww.isiccard.com), which entitles the bearer to special air, rail and bus fares and discounts at museums, theatres and other attractions. The card costs $16, US$22, £6, A$16.50 and NZ$21 in New Zealand. You only have to be 26 or younger to qualify for the **International Youth Travel Card**, which costs US$22/£7 and carries the same benefits. Teachers qualify for the **International Teacher Card**, offering similar discounts and costing $16, US$22, £7, A$16.50 and NZ$21. All these cards are available in Canada from Travel CUTS, in the US from Council Travel, STA and Travel CUTS, in the UK from STA, and in Australia and New Zealand from STA or Campus Travel.

Banks and ATMs

Banks are widespread and are generally open Monday to Friday 10am–4pm; it's very rare to find one open on Saturday. The major banks are Banque Royale, Banque de Montréal, CIBC, Banque TD, Banque Scotia, Banque Nationale and Banque Laurentienne. Almost all have *guichets* *automatiques* (**ATMs**), which accept Plus and/or Cirrus networked cards (all are on the Canadian Interac system). You'll also find ATMs at *caisses populaires* (credit unions) and independently owned machines in bars, restaurants, some Métro stations and elsewhere. Most machines charge a fee of $1 or $2 in addition to any banking fees your home institution may charge. Large Downtown branches offer **currency exchange**, as do private outfits at the airport and in tourist areas – see p.217 for a list. Many establishments will accept US dollars, though often at derisory rates.

Credit and debit cards

Credit cards are a very handy backup source of funds, and can be used either in ATMs or over the counter. MasterCard and Visa are good just about everywhere, and American Express and Diners Club are often accepted as well, but other cards may not be recognized. Remember that all cash advances are treated as loans, with interest accruing daily from the date of withdrawal; there may be a transaction fee on top of this. However, you may be able to make withdrawals from ATMs in Canada using your **debit card** if it's compatible with the Plus, Cirrus or Interac systems. Make sure you have a personal identification number (PIN) that's designed to work overseas.

A compromise between travellers' cheques and plastic is **Visa TravelMoney**, a disposable pre-paid debit card with a PIN which works in all ATMs that take Visa cards. You load up your account with funds before leaving home, and when they run out, you simply throw the card away. You can buy up to nine cards to access the same funds – useful for couples or families travelling together – and it's a good idea to buy at least one extra as a back-up in case of loss or theft. There is also a 24-hour toll-free customer assistance number (Ⓣ1-800/847-2911). The card is available in most countries from branches of Thomas Cook and Citicorp. For more information, check the Visa TravelMoney website at Ⓦwww.usa.visa.com/personal/cards/visa_travel_money.html.

Travellers' cheques

Travellers' cheques are no longer widely used in Canada – you'll have the most luck at banks and currency exchange offices (you can often save commission fees if you cash them at a branch of the issuing company), though you should also be able to cash them at major hotels, large stores and some restaurants. American Express is the most widely recognized brand, with Visa and Thomas Cook (MasterCard) vying for second place. Ask for cheques in Canadian dollars to avoid any surprises on exchange rates upon arrival.

The usual fee for travellers' cheque sales is one or two percent, though this fee may be waived if you buy the cheques through a bank where you have an account. It pays to get a selection of denominations. Make sure to keep the purchase agreement and a

Tax refunds

You can claim a rebate on the GST for items you take outside of Canada, as well as on short-term accommodation (including the accommodation portion of a package holiday): the total pre-tax value must exceed $200, with each individual receipt being at least $50. Apply directly to the Canada Customs and Revenue Agency (Ⓣ902/432-5608 or 1-800/668-4748, Ⓦwww.ccra-adrc.gc.ca/visitors). Keep an eye out for their plain-looking brochures (rather than the glossy ones for private companies), which include the forms you'll need, at the Centre Infotouriste, the airport, and duty-free shops on the US/Canada border. You must have proof of export to reclaim the tax on goods you take with you – allow extra time at the airport for customs to look at your receipts and purchases. You can get your cash refund straight away at duty-free shops at a number of land border crossings; otherwise you will need to post the forms after you have returned home. If you are below the $200 limit and are planning to visit Canada again within a year, get your receipts stamped anyway as you can claim them along with later purchases.

Passes

If you're planning to see a lot of museums while in Montréal, it's worth picking up a **Carte Musées Montréal** (Montréal Museums Pass), which gives you access to some 25 attractions, including the Musée des Beaux-Arts, the Centre Canadien d'Architecture and the Musée d'Archéologie, for only $20. It's valid for two out of three consecutive days and you can buy it at any of the participating museums or at either of the tourist information centres listed on p.22. However, the main attractions east of Downtown aren't included. Instead, you can see the Biodôme and Jardin Botanique with the **Nature Package** for $17, while the $25 **Get an Eyeful** pass adds on a trip up the Stade Olympique's tower.

record of cheque serial numbers safe and separate from the cheques themselves. In the event that cheques are lost or stolen, the issuing company will expect you to report the loss forthwith to their office in Montréal; most companies claim to replace lost or stolen cheques within 24 hours.

Wiring money

Having money wired from home using one of the companies listed below is never convenient or cheap, and should be considered a last resort. It's also possible to have money wired directly from a bank in your home country to a bank in Canada, although this is somewhat less reliable because it involves two separate institutions. If you go this route, your home bank will need the address of the bank branch where you want to pick up the money and the address and telex number of the head office, which will act as the clearing house; money wired this way normally takes two working days to arrive, and costs around US$40/£25 per transaction.

Financial services

American Express Canada and US ⓣ1-888/269-6669, ⓦwww.americanexpress.com, UK ⓣ0870/600 1060, ⓦwww.americanexpress.co.uk. In Montréal: 1141 boul de Maisonneuve 0 ⓣ514/284-3300.
Thomas Cook Canada ⓣ1-888/823-4732, ⓦwww.thomascook.ca, US ⓣ1-800/287-7362, Great Britain ⓣ01733/318 922, ⓦwww.thomascook.co.uk, Northern Ireland ⓣ028/9055 0030, Republic of Ireland ⓣ01/677 1721. In Montréal: Centre Eaton, 705 rue Ste-Catherine 0 ⓣ514/284 7388.
Travelers Express MoneyGram Canada ⓣ1-800/933-3278, US ⓣ1-800/955-7777, UK ⓣ0800/018 0104, Republic of Ireland ⓣ1850/205 800, Australia ⓣ1800/230 100, New Zealand ⓣ0800/262 263, ⓦwww.moneygram.com.
Western Union Canada and US ⓣ1-800/325-6000, UK ⓣ0800/833 833, Republic of Ireland ⓣ1800/395 395, Australia ⓣ1800/501 500, New Zealand ⓣ0800/270 000, ⓦwww.westernunion.com.

Communications

With healthy telecommunications and new media sectors, it's no surprise that Montréal is so well hooked-up with broadband Internet and mobile phone coverage, in addition to plenty of pay phones and a reasonable postal service for keeping in touch with family and friends back home.

Telephones

Local calls cost 25¢ at **public telephones**, which can be found along commercial streets and in shopping malls, hotels, restaurants and bars. Private subscribers pay nothing for local calls, so you'll find that shops often don't mind you using their phone to dial locally. Note that for local calls you must dial the full 10-digit number, including the 514 area code. If you'll be making a number of calls and don't feel like carrying around a stack of quarters, pick up a prepaid **phone card**, which are available from Bell-Canada outlets, newsagents and the Centre Infotouriste. The La Puce card comes in a variety of denominations and is inserted in phones with a yellow card-reader; it works like a debit card and local calls are charged at the same rate as cash. Bell's other cards are better for long-distance and international calls, but there are a variety of competing cards and access-numbers – see below. Many public telephones also accept credit cards though you'll be charged at a higher rate; collect calls to elsewhere in Canada and the US can likewise be costly. Commercial establishments often have toll-free (freephone) numbers, which begin with 1-800, 1-866, 1-877 or 1-888. Unless you don't mind throwing away money, avoid using hotel room phones – there's usually a service charge even for local and toll-free calls.

Calling home from Montréal

One of the most convenient ways of phoning home from abroad is via a **telephone charge card** from your local phone company. Using a PIN number, you can make calls

Useful telephone numbers

Emergencies ☎911 for fire, police and ambulance
Police ☎514/280-2222 for non-emergencies
Operator ☎0
Directory assistance (local) ☎411
Directory assistance (long-distance) ☎1 + area code + 555-1212
Directory assistance (toll-free numbers) ☎1-800/555-1212
Area codes ☎514 Montréal; ☎450 off-island suburbs, Lower Laurentians and western areas of the Eastern Townships; ☎819 Upper Laurentians and rest of Eastern Townships; ☎418 Québec City.

International and long-distance dialling
Montréal From the US and Canada, dial 1 + 514 + number; from overseas dial your international access code + 1 + 514 + number
US and Canada 1 + area code + number
UK 011 + 44 + city code + number
Republic of Ireland 011 + 353 + city code + number
Australia 011 + 61 + city code + number
New Zealand 011 + 64 + city code + number
Note that the initial zero is omitted from the area code when dialling the UK, Ireland, Australia and New Zealand from abroad.

from most hotel, public and private phones that will be charged to your account. Since most major charge cards are free to obtain, it's certainly worth getting one at least for emergencies; enquire first though whether calls from Canada are covered, and bear in mind that rates aren't necessarily cheaper than calling from a public phone. In addition to the services mentioned below, it's also worth checking out the calling cards offered along with ISIC and Hostelling International memberships. A number of companies sell prepaid phone cards in Montréal; you dial a local or toll-free number and enter the PIN number written on the card. Look closely at the terms on the card – a cheap per-minute rate may be offset by a high connection charge (which makes getting an answering machine all the more annoying).

In the **US**, AT&T, MCI, Sprint and other American long-distance companies all enable their customers to make credit-card calls from Canada, billed to your home number. Call your company's customer service line to find out what the toll-free access code is.

In **the UK and Ireland**, British Telecom (Ⓣ0800/345 144, Ⓦwww.chargecard.bt.com) will issue free to all BT customers the BT Charge Card, which can be used in 116 countries; AT&T has the Global Calling Card (dial Ⓣ0800/890 011, then 888/641-6123 when you hear the AT&T prompt to be transferred to the Florida Call Centre, free 24 hours); while NTL (Ⓣ0500/100 505) issues its own Global Calling Card, which can be used in more than sixty countries abroad, though the fees cannot be charged to a normal phone bill.

To call **Australia and New Zealand** from Canada, telephone charge cards such as Telstra Telecard or Optus Calling Card in Australia, and Telecom NZ's Calling Card can be used to make calls abroad, which are charged back to a domestic account or credit card. Apply to Telstra (Ⓣ1800/038 000), Optus (Ⓣ1300/300 937), or Telecom NZ (Ⓣ04/801 9000).

Mobile phones

Calling a Canadian (or American) **mobile phone** costs no more than making a call to a landline in that area code. If you want to use your own mobile in Canada, you'll need to check with your service provider whether it will work abroad; it's unlikely that a mobile bought for use outside Canada or the US will work in Montréal.

Visitors from other parts of Canada may be able to make local calls at the same rates as in their home area code. If that's the case, you're better off not answering an incoming call and instead phoning the caller right back; otherwise you, and possibly they as well, will pay long-distance charges. Some US phones will only work within the region designated by the area code in the phone number (ie 212, 415, etc) – check with your service provider whether this applies to your phone.

In the UK, you'll generally have to inform your phone provider before going abroad to get international access switched on. There are usually hefty charges even for local calls as well as extra charges for incoming calls when in Canada. If you want to retrieve messages while you're away, you'll need a new access code from your provider. Most UK mobiles – as well as those in Australia and New Zealand – use GSM, which gives access to most places worldwide, except Canada and the US. For further information about using your phone abroad, check out Ⓦwww.telecomsadvice.org.uk/features/using_your_mobile_abroad.htm.

Email

One of the best ways to keep in touch while travelling is to sign up for a free Internet **email** address that can be accessed from anywhere, for example Yahoo! Mail or Hotmail. Once you've set up an account, you can use these sites to pick up and send mail from any Internet café (see p.217 for a list), or photocopy shop or hotel with Internet access; many larger post offices now offer free Internet access. You'll also find Bell Internet kiosks in transport termini and shopping malls but access ($2/10min) costs about twice the going rate of Internet cafés. One useful website is Ⓦwww.kropla.com, which gives details of how to plug your laptop in when abroad, phone country codes around the world, and information about electrical systems in different countries.

Mail

The main Downtown **post office** is at 1250 rue University (Mon–Fri 8am–5.45pm). Most other post office opening hours are Monday to Friday 8.30am to 5.30pm, though a few places are open on Saturday between 9am and noon. Service counters are also found inside larger stores, pharmacies and the like, so look out for Postes Canada / Canada Post signs or look up the nearest outlet (Ⓣ1-800/267-1177, Ⓦwww.canadapost.ca). Newsstands, pharmacies, hotels and souvenir shops usually sell stamps either individually or in a pack of six or so. Within Canada, letters and postcards up to 30g cost 48¢, to the US 65¢ for under 30g, and international mail up to 20g is $1.25. If you're posting letters to Canadian addresses, always include the postcode or your mail may never get there.

Letters can be sent poste restante to any Canadian main post office by addressing them c/o Poste Restante. Make a pick-up date if known, or write "Hold for 15 days", the maximum period mail will usually be held. After that time the post is returned to sender, so it's a good idea to put a return address on any post. Take some ID when collecting.

The media

English-language print media in Montréal isn't too strong on quality news reporting but does provide good local coverage (in both mainstream and alternative varieties) and up-to-date listings on events around town. Television is broadly similar to that in the US but with some home-grown programming and international shows. Likewise, radio is pretty middle-of-the-road; tune into university radio or the CBC for the most interesting broadcasts.

Newspapers and magazines

The city's only English daily **newspaper**, *The Montreal Gazette* (75¢ weekdays, $1.90 Saturday; Ⓦwww.montrealgazette.com), has been keeping locals abreast of all the latest news for over two centuries and contains fairly comprehensive entertainment listings; watch out for special supplements tied to the starts of major festivals. Its national and international coverage is fairly patchy – for better quality news, pick up the Toronto-based *Globe and Mail* or *National Post*. The best place to find out what's happening entertainment-wise are the free **alternative weeklies** – the two tabloid-size English papers, *Hour* (Ⓦwww.afterhour.com) and the *Montreal Mirror* (Ⓦwww.montrealmirror.com) are virtually indistinguishable in content from one another and you can pick them up all over town. Their French counterparts are *Voir*, the most respected of the lot, and *ici*. Look in cafés and bookstores for other free magazines that cover various cultural and nightlife scenes, specific neighbourhoods, or gay and lesbian issues. There have also been sporadic attempts at city lifestyle magazines, however none of these seem to stick around for long. For publications in English, as well as to catch up on the news from back home, head to one of the many branches of Multimags or Maison de la Presse Internationale.

TV and radio

Despite the primacy of French in the city, there are three local English-language **TV stations**: CBC on channel 6, CFCF (CTV) on channel 12 and CKMI (Global) on channel 46. The main French channels are Radio-

Canada (2), TVA (10), Télé-Québec (17) and Télévision Quatre-Saisons (35). If you have a TV in your hotel room, it's most likely hooked-up to **cable** – the channels for the above stations will vary depending on which cable company the hotel deals with. You'll also have access to the whole range of US networks as well as sports and music video channels and international news broadcasters like the BBC and CNN.

On the **radio**, CBC One (88.5 FM) is the national broadcaster's flagship station, with programming focusing on news and commentary, while CBC Two (93.5) plays classical music. For rock, stick to the FM dial: CHOM (97.7 FM) and MIX 96 (95.9) are the best of a mediocre lot, though if you can pull in "The Buzz" (WBTZ at 99.9 FM) from across the border you'll get a more alternative bent. If you want some Francophone rock along with North American chart-toppers, try CKOI (96.9 FM) or RockDétente (107.3 FM). English talk-radio stations are on AM frequencies – try CJAD (800 AM) to hear what has the local "angryphones" up in arms this week; it's also a good source for news, sports, weather and traffic reports, as is the all-news station 940 News (940 AM). McGill University's student-run CKUT (90.3 FM) has a hit-or-miss schedule of music and spoken word covering all genres.

Opening hours and public holidays

The opening hours of specific visitor attractions, stores and offices are given in the relevant accounts throughout this guide. Telephone numbers are provided so that you can check current information with the places themselves.

Opening hours

As a general rule, most **museums** are open from 10am to 5.30pm, though many are closed one day of the week (usually Monday) and may be open late one day during the middle of the week (often free of charge). Government **offices**, including post offices, are open during regular business hours, typically 8.30 or 9am until 5 or 5.30pm, Monday to Friday. **Shops** are generally open Monday to Friday 10am–6pm (with many staying open as late as 9pm on Thursday and Friday), Saturday 11am–5pm and Sunday noon–5pm. Smaller specialty shops may be closed Sunday and/or Monday.

Montrealers tend to dine a bit later than the rest of North America, so **restaurants** are typically open until around 11pm; quite a few open for dinner at 6pm, especially on weekends. Many diner-type places, however, close earlier in the evening (or much later, if they cater to the nightlife crowd). Places that specialize in breakfasts open early, between 6am and 8am and shut mid-afternoon. **Bars** open anywhere between 11am and mid-evening and continue serving until 3am in most cases. Clubs don't open their doors until around 10pm and, except for after-hours clubs, shut at 3am.

Time of year makes a big difference to opening times of information centres, museums and other attractions, many of which have shorter winter hours or close altogether. Many attractions have extended opening hours for the **summer season**, which typically begins on the weekend nearest the Fête St-Jean and extends until Labour Day, though some may commence summer operations as early as the Fête des Patriotes and/or carry through to Thanksgiving in October. Note that Canada's Thanksgiving is a month earlier than the American one and coincides with Columbus Day in the US.

Public holidays and festivals

Banks, schools and government buildings close on **public holidays** although many shops, restaurants, museums and sights remain open (in fact, many museums that are normally closed on Mondays open on holidays).

Once Montréal shakes off winter, it positively explodes with **annual festivals and events**, see Chapter Eighteen, "Festivals and Events". Hotel rooms can be scarce (and many places ratchet up their prices) during the major festivals and big events like the Grand Prix and Molson Indy car races – book well in advance if you plan to visit Montréal at these times.

Official public holidays

January
1: New Year's Day
March/April
Good Friday
Easter Monday
May
Monday preceding May 25: Fête des Patriotes (Victoria Day)
June
24: Fête St-Jean-Baptiste
July
1: Canada Day
September
1st Monday: Labour Day
October
2nd Monday: Thanksgiving
November
11: Remembrance Day (partial holiday)
December
25: Christmas Day
26: Boxing Day

Trouble and police

In contrast to comparable-sized cities in the US, there's very little street crime in Montréal. You shouldn't have any problems in terms of personal safety if you stick to the main parts of town, though it's obviously advisable to be cautious late at night. During the day, the usual rules apply – don't flash money around or leave bags unattended or visible in your car.

The main exceptions are the drug-dealing areas around Parc Émilie-Gamelin and to the east of the bus station, and the red-light district along rue Ste-Catherine near boulevard St-Laurent (although this is relatively tame by American standards and much of the activity is being pushed away eastwards). As well, avoid the larger parks late at night. Public transit is generally safe at any time of the day – any problems tend to be well out in the suburbs.

Montréal is generally a safe place for **women**, though the usual common sense rules apply: avoid walking alone late at night outside of well-lit, populated areas. Don't take short-cuts through parks or vacant lots, and when walking along the sidewalk stay close to the curb away from dark nooks in buildings and alleyways. Women who are travelling on city buses at night can take advantage of the "Entre deux arrêts" service, whereby you can ask the bus driver to let you off between stops after 7.30pm (May–Aug after 9pm).

Theft is also uncommon, though it's obviously a good idea to be on your guard against petty thieves. Always keep an eye on your luggage at bus and train stations, secure your things in a locker when staying in hostel accommodation or in a safe at hotels, and if you need to leave valuables in your car, stow them in the trunk and park in a well-lit area. If you are unlucky enough to be attacked or have something stolen, phone the **police** on ⓣ911 or ⓣ514/280-2222 for non-emergencies. If you're going to make an insurance claim or travellers' cheque refund application, ensure the crime is recorded by the police and make a note of the report number.

Travellers with disabilities

Montréal is one of the best places in the world to travel if you have mobility problems or other physical disabilities. All public buildings are required to be wheelchair-accessible and provide suitable toilet facilities, almost all street corners have dropped curbs, and public telephones are specially equipped for hearing-aid users. The city's main failing in this regard is with public transport: the Métro is inaccessible to wheelchair users, although this is offset somewhat by a system of adapted-transport buses.

Planning your trip

Most **airlines**, both transatlantic and internal, will do whatever they can to ease your journey, and will usually allow attendants of more seriously disabled people to accompany them at no extra charge – Air Canada is the best-equipped carrier.

All VIA Rail **trains** can accommodate wheelchairs that are no larger than 81cm by 182cm and weigh no more than 114kg, though 24 hours notice is required for the Québec–Windsor corridor and 48 hours on other routes. They offer an excellent service, and will help with boarding and disembarking. Those who need an attendant can apply for a two-for-one fare with a "Disability Travel Card"; it's available from the Easter Seals / March of Dimes National Council (ⓣ514/866-1969, ⓦwww.esmodnc.org); you can download an application form, which must be signed by a health professional, from their website.

Although **buses** are obliged to carry disabled passengers if their wheelchairs fit in the luggage compartment, access is often difficult. However, you can arrange to have an elevator-platform-equipped bus on most inter-city routes in Québec. Nearly all bus companies accept the two-for-one "To Accompany Card", and drivers are usually extremely helpful. Contact the Québec Bus Owners Association for more information and forms, which must be submitted at least a month in advance (ⓣ418/522-7131, ⓦwww.apaq.qc.ca). The larger **car-rental companies** can provide cars with hand controls at no extra charge, though these are only available on their most expensive models; book one as far in advance as you can.

Disabled access

The major hotel chains are the best bet for accessible **accommodation** but wherever you choose to stay you should confirm that they are able to meet your needs before making a reservation. For **getting around**, the Métro is not an option as there are no lifts, but many city buses have low-floor access for wheelchair users. As well, Paratransit is a door-to-door transportation service for persons with disabilities that requires reservations. Unless you are using a wheelchair, you need to register for the service first, however – forms and further information are available from the STM (ⓣ514/280-8211,

Ⓦwww.stm.info – click on the "Paratransit" link).

Montréal is also blessed with an organization that works to make tourist facilities accessible: **Kéroul** (Ⓣ514/252-3104, Ⓦwww.keroul.qc.ca) provides information on, and publishes the *Accessible Québec* ($15) guide to, accommodation, attractions and other services in the city and around the province. Much of their documentation is in French, however, so it may also be worth contacting the Canadian Paraplegic Association (CPA), who can provide a wealth of information on travelling in Canada (see below). The provincial tourist office is also an excellent source of information on accessible hotels, motels and sights. As well, keep an eye out for the tourist and leisure companion sticker (TLCS, also known by its French acronym VATL), which allows free access for the companion of a person living with a disability or a mental health problem when they visit tourist and leisure activity sites. For a list of participating establishments, visit Ⓦwww.vatl.qc.ca.

Information for disabled travellers

Canada and the US

Access-Able Ⓦwww.access-able.com. Online resource for travellers with disabilities.

Access to Travel Ⓦwww.accesstotravel.gc.ca. A government website that provides information on accessible transportation and travel across Canada.

Canadian Paraplegic Association Ⓣ1-800/720-4933, Ⓦwww.canparaplegic.org. Their main office is at Suite 230, 1101 Prince of Wales Drive, Ottawa, Ontario K2C 3W7 T613/723-1033, F613/723-1060, however there are branches in most other provinces. Comprehensive resources for persons with spinal cord injuries and other disabilities; their website has hundreds of links to useful sites.

Directions Unlimited 123 Green Lane, Bedford Hills, NY 10507 Ⓣ1-800/533-5343 or 914/241-1700. Travel agency specializing in bookings for people with disabilities.

Kéroul Box 1000, Station M, 4545 avenue Pierre-de-Coubertin, Montréal, Québec H1V 3R2 Ⓣ514/252-3104, Ⓕ514/254-0766, Ⓦwww.keroul.qc.ca. Provides information on the accessibility of accommodation and attractions around the province; they also offer tour packages to various Québec destinations.

Mobility International USA 451 Broadway, Eugene, OR 97401 Ⓣ541/343-1284, Ⓦwww.miusa.org. Information and referral services, access guides, tours and exchange programmes. Annual membership $35 (includes quarterly newsletter).

Society for the Advancement of Travelers with Handicaps (SATH) 347 5th Ave, New York, NY 10016 Ⓣ212/447-7284, Ⓦwww.sath.org. Non-profit educational organization that has actively represented travellers with disabilities since 1976.

Wheels Up! Ⓣ1-888/38-WHEELS, Ⓦwww.wheelsup.com. Provides discounted airfare, tour and cruise prices for disabled travellers, also publishes a free monthly newsletter and has a comprehensive website.

UK and Ireland

Holiday Care 2nd floor, Imperial Building, Victoria Rd, Horley, Surrey RH6 7PZ Ⓣ0845/124 9971, minicom Ⓣ0845/124 9976, Ⓦwww.holidaycare.org.uk. Provides free lists of accessible accommodation abroad – European, American and long-haul destinations – plus a list of accessible attractions in the UK. Information on financial help for holidays available.

Irish Wheelchair Association Blackheath Drive, Clontarf, Dublin 3 Ⓣ01/818 6400, Ⓦwww.iwa.ie. Useful information provided about travelling abroad with a wheelchair.

RADAR (Royal Association for Disability and Rehabilitation) 12 City Forum, 250 City Rd, London EC1V 8AF Ⓣ020/7250 3222, minicom Ⓣ020/7250 4119, Ⓦwww.radar.org.uk. A good source of advice on holidays and travel in the UK; their website also has contacts and general information for travel abroad.

Tripscope Alexandra House, Albany Rd, Brentford, Middlesex TW8 0NE Ⓣ0845/7585 641, Ⓦwww.tripscope.org.uk. This registered charity provides a national telephone information service offering free advice on UK and international transport for those with a mobility problem.

Australia and New Zealand

ACROD (Australian Council for Rehabilitation of the Disabled) PO Box 60, Curtin ACT 2605; Suite 103, 1st floor, 1–5 Commercial Rd, Kings Grove 2208; Ⓣ02/6282 4333, TTY Ⓣ02/6282 4333, Ⓦwww.acrod.org.au. Provides lists of travel agencies and tour operators for people with disabilities.

Disabled Persons Assembly 4/173–175 Victoria St, Wellington, New Zealand Ⓣ04/801 9100 (also TTY), Ⓦwww.dpa.org.nz. Resource centre with lists of travel agencies and tour operators for people with disabilities.

The City

The City

1

Downtown Montréal and the Golden Square Mile

Although **Downtown Montréal** lacks the charm of Vieux-Montréal or the edginess of the Plateau, it's dotted with enough old churches and museums to more than fill a few days' exploration. Besides historical and cultural attractions, Downtown affords plentiful opportunities for both **shopping** and **nightlife**, especially along **rue Ste-Catherine**, where many of Montréal's best cinemas, music venues, bars and clubs are found.

The main thoroughfares Downtown run east–west, giving it a long, rectangular shape bounded by rue Sherbrooke to the north, rue St-Antoine to the south, and boulevard St-Laurent to the east, beyond which it merges with the Quartier Latin (see p.85). The western border is harder to define, as it overlaps with the remnants of the historic Anglophone enclave of the **Golden Square Mile**.

Downtown Montréal

A number of public spaces, such as **Square Dorchester** and **Place du Canada**, break up Downtown's long stretches of commercial establishments, which helps keep the area from feeling too claustrophobic. The centrally located cruciform skyscraper and attendant plaza of **Place Ville Marie** mark the southern end of the city's truncated "Champs d'Elysées", while to the east can be found **Christ Church Cathedral**, the **Musée d'Art Contemporain de Montréal** and the performance halls of **Place des Arts**. South of there are the bustling restaurants and shops of Montréal's small **Chinatown**.

Some history

For the first couple of centuries of Montréal's existence, most development was concentrated in Vieux-Montréal and the *faubourgs*, residential areas clustered outside the gates of the former city walls. At the start of the nineteenth century, when rue Ste-Catherine was laid out, the area that is now Downtown was little more than a spread of farms. But within a few decades, rue Ste-Catherine was lined with townhouses, schools and churches, and by the 1840s had become the city's main commercial thoroughfare. Houses continued to be built along the side streets, with middle-class neighbourhoods sprouting up and the wealthier nabbing prime estates on the mountain's slopes for their mansions.

In 1865, the first horse-drawn streetcars began running along rue Ste-Catherine year-round, leading to Downtown's expansion as the Anglophone population moved further north and west into villa and rowhouse subdivisions clutching at the skirts of the wealthy's estates, and financial institutions began to make their mark. It wasn't long before Downtown became increasingly urbanized, spurred by the opening of the Gare Windsor in the 1880s and the first of the big department stores around Square Phillips a decade later. In the 1890s, electric streetcars began running along rue Ste-Catherine, making it the largest commercial artery in Canada by the time Ogilvy opened its doors at its present location on the corner of rue de la Montagne in 1912. The following decades saw the advent of the big movie palaces, theatres and cabarets that would become a part of the fabled nightlife that drew Prohibition escapees from the US for riotous weekends. Hotels and restaurants cropped up on middle-class residential side streets such as rue Peel, while businesses as well as shops began choosing Downtown instead of Vieux-Montréal for their headquarters (notably Sun Life's giant wedding-cake of a headquarters, built between 1914 and 1933).

Montréal's answer to New York's Rockefeller Center, the signature Place Ville Marie skyscraper and the vast climate-controlled shopping centre at its base, opened in 1962 (the year construction on the Métro began), with Royal Bank as its principal tenant. This coup sealed Vieux-Montréal's fate: the other large, conservative banks followed the Royal Bank's lead in the ongoing exodus from the old city to Downtown. An explosion of other major works in the 1960s, including Place des Arts and a number of other office towers, completed Downtown's transformation as the city's cultural and business centre. The first phase of the Métro went into operation in 1966, linked to ten Downtown buildings (including the monstrous Place Bonaventure) that formed the nucleus of the now famous Underground City (see p.50), just in time for Expo '67 and Montréal's debut as an "international city".

Most of the rest of Downtown's present-day character was formed in a massive construction boom in the Eighties and early Nineties, when McGill College was widened and a number of skyscrapers shot up to rival Place Ville Marie in height and add to the Underground City with their lower floor shopping malls and passageways. Today, the process continues towards Downtown's fringes with the towers of the Cité du Commerce Électronique (E-Commerce Place) near the Centre Bell and the filling in of the gap between Downtown and Vieux-Montréal with the Quartier International development. But other than a recessionary blip in the mid-1990s that caused quite a few boarded-up shopfronts, rue Ste-Catherine continues to be Downtown's bustling commercial heart.

Square Dorchester and Place du Canada

Square Dorchester, on the east side of rue Peel between rue Ste-Catherine and boulevard René-Lévesque, is a good place to get your bearings as Montréal's main **Infotouriste** office (daily: June to early Sept 7am–8pm; early Sept to May 9am–6pm; Ⓣ514/873-2015 or 1-877/266-5687, Ⓦwww.bon-

△Édifice Sun Life

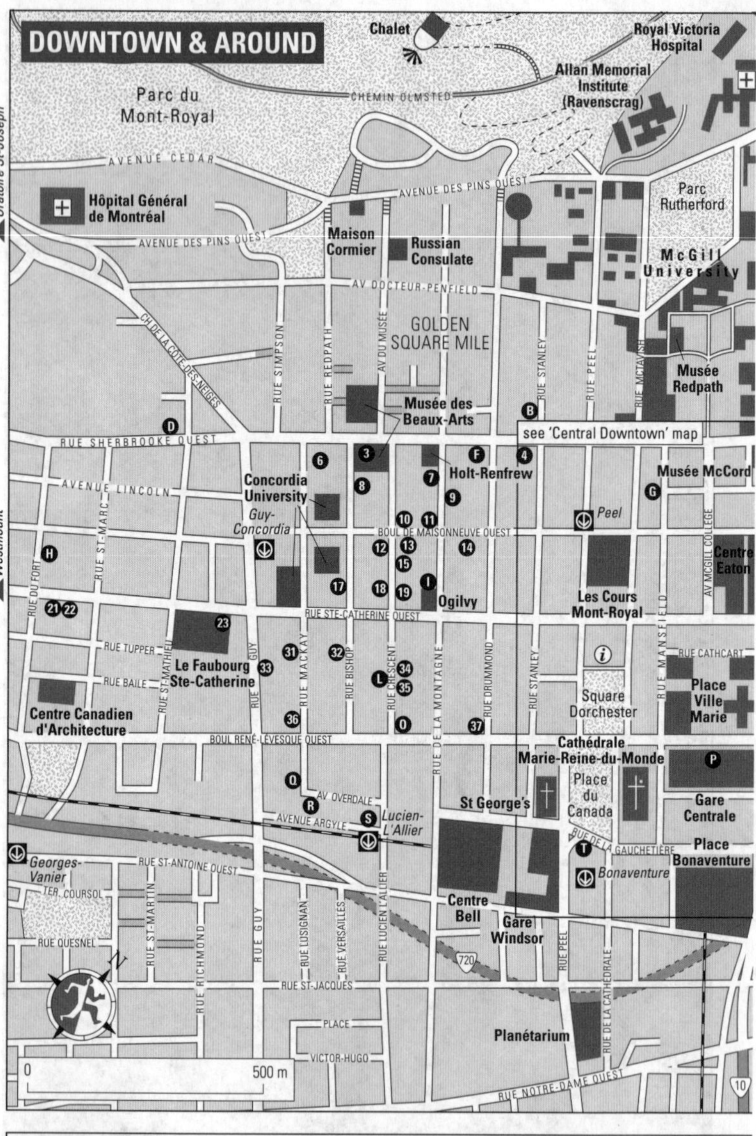

ACCOMMODATION

- L'Appartement Hôtel — C
- Auberge de Jeunesse Internationale de Montréal — R
- Aux Berges — Q
- Château Versailles — D
- Le Germain — G
- La Maison du Prêt d'Honneur — M
- Manoir Ambrose — B
- Marriott Château Champlain — T
- McGill University Residences — A
- Hôtel de la Montagne — I
- Petite Auberge les Bons Matins — S
- Quality Inn Downtown — L
- Queen Elizabeth — P
- Ritz-Carlton — F
- Royal Victoria College — E
- Le Square Phillips — K
- Le St-Malo — H
- Travelodge Montréal-Centre — N
- Wyndham — J
- Hôtel Y des Femmes (YWCA) — O

RESTAURANTS & CAFÉS

- Bar-B-Barn — 33
- Bâton Rouge — 25
- Le Café des Beaux-Arts — 3
- Ben and Jerry's — 13
- Brûlerie St-Denis — 4
- Les Chenêts — 8
- Ciné-Express — 22
- Eggspectation — 11
- Hong Kong — 41
- Idée Magique — 40
- Il Cortile — 6

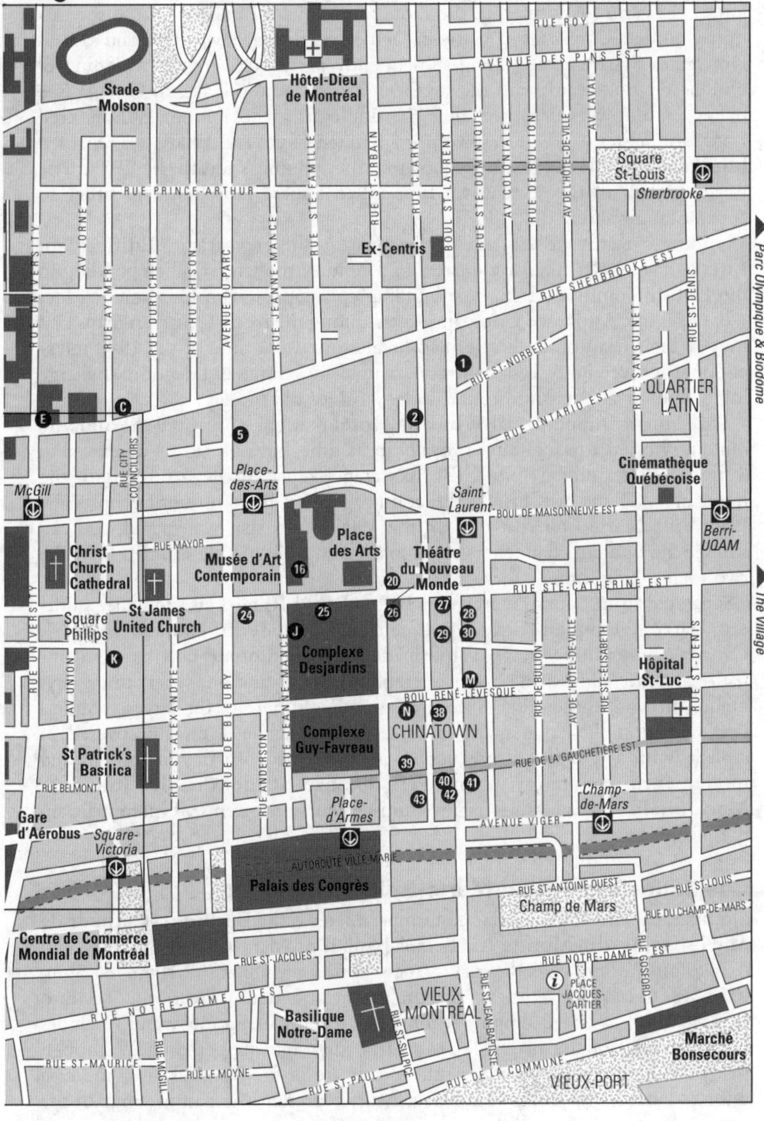

Jardin de Jade	39
Katsura	7
Lotté-Furama	38
Montréal Pool Room	29
Le Café du Nouveau-Monde	26
Pho Bac 97	42
Queue de Cheval	37
Café République	19 & 20
La Rotonde	16
Ruby Rouge	43
Café Tramezzini	9

BARS & CLUBS

Agora	36
Brutopia	35
Cabaret	1
Club Soda	28
Cock n' Bull Pub	21
Comedyworks	32
Dôme	27
Hurley's Irish Pub	34
Jimbo's Pub	32
Luba Lounge	5
Madhatter Café	14
Magnétic Terrasse	I
McKibbin's Irish Pub	17
Newtown	12
Café Sarajevo	2
SAT	30
Sharx	23
Sir Winston Churchill Pub (Winnie's)	15
Spectrum	24
Stogies	10
Upstairs	31
Club Vatican	18

jourquebec.com) is located in the Dominion Square Building on the square's north border. Originally a Catholic cemetery, the area was first laid out as Dominion Square in 1872 and subsequently partitioned by the widening of Dorchester Boulevard, with the southern half becoming Place du Canada (see below). Controversy erupted after the boulevard, whose moniker honoured Lord Dorchester, the British governor for much of the late 1700s, was renamed **boulevard René-Lévesque** following the premier's death in 1987. The northern half of the square was later called Square Dorchester in order to appease Anglophones.

Lording over the eastern side of the square is the grey-granite **Édifice Sun Life**, built in 1918 and for a quarter of a century the largest office building in the British Commonwealth. The building's principal tenant for many decades – the Sun Life Assurance Company – was among the many Canadian firms that moved their head offices out of Montréal around the time of the 1980 referendum on sovereignty. Today, the cool marble and minimalist decor in the large lobby behind the massive bronze doors speak of old money.

The similarly monumental **Windsor Hotel** that once mirrored the Sun Life building hosted a procession of royalty in its time, but was mostly destroyed in a fire. The streamlined Tour CIBC skyscraper replaced the main part of the hotel in 1962 and was briefly the country's tallest building until eclipsed by Place Ville Marie later that year. In the 1906 annex that was spared, you can still see the opulent chandelier-lit Peacock Alley, a gilt marble hall that links the two formal ballrooms.

Separated from Square Dorchester by boulevard René-Lévesque, the southern half of Dominion Square was renamed **Place du Canada** in 1967, Canada's centennial year. Its name made it an appropriate rallying point for national unity during the 1995 referendum on separation, when three days before the vote some 300,000 federalists gathered here in the largest political demonstration the country has ever seen. The square – mostly covered in asphalt, with a few bits of greenery – is dotted with various memorials and monuments, including an imposing bronze statue of **Sir John A. MacDonald**, Canada's first prime minister, but most items of interest lie on the periphery.

Basilique-Cathédrale Marie-Reine-du-Monde

Dominating Place du Canada's eastern perimeter is the **Basilique-Cathédrale Marie-Reine-du-Monde** (Cathedral-Basilica of Mary Queen of the World; daily 7am–7.30pm except during mass at 7.30am, 8am, 12.10pm & 5pm; ⓣ514/866-1661, ⓦwww.cathedralecatholiquedemontreal.org; Métro Bonaventure), a scaled-down version of St Peter's in Rome which includes faithful copies of the original's massive portico and copper dome. Although many think the statues crowning the facade are of the Apostles (as is the case with St Peter's), the thirteen figures actually represent the patron saints of the parishes that donated them.

Bishop Ignace Bourget commissioned the building to replace the previous cathedral, St-Jacques, which was located in the present-day Quartier Latin and burned in 1852. He chose St Peter's as the inspiration to emphasize the dominant role of Catholicism in what was then the largest city in the new Dominion of Canada. Construction was delayed until 1870 due to a number of factors, including the uproar over his chosen site – a predominantly Protestant Anglophone neighbourhood – and services did not finally begin until 1894.

Inside it's not as opulent as you might expect from the grand exterior (and million-dollar price tag – a record at the time for Montréal), with the exception of the high altar of marble, onyx and ivory that's surmounted by a reproduction of Bernini's baldachin over the altar in St Peter's. As in Rome, the gilded copper baldachin's spiralling columns support an altar canopy topped by statues of angels. Back towards the entrance along the eastern aisle is the Chapelle des Souvenirs, which contains various relics collected by the enthusiastic Bourget, including the wax-encased remains of the immensely obscure St Zoticus, an early Christian martyr. Paintings throughout the cathedral depict prominent members and events of the early colony.

West of Place du Canada

Opposite the southwestern corner of Place du Canada, at the intersection of rues Peel and de la Gauchetière, the Victorian **St George's Anglican Church** (Tues–Sun 8.30am–4pm, Sat from 9am; ⓣ514/866-7113, ⓦwww.st-georges.org) is the only one of the six Protestant churches constructed around Dominion Square between 1865 and 1875 that remains standing. Its solid Neo-Gothic exterior gives way to a lofty interior with vaulting double hammer-beam trusses that rise in a series of arches to support the gabled roof. A tapestry used at the Queen's coronation in Westminster Abbey in 1953 contrasts nicely with the darker wood fixtures, including the altar and choir hand-carved from English oak. Free guided tours are available in July and August (Tues–Sat).

Gare Windsor, the large Romanesque Revival structure facing the church's main entrance on rue de la Gauchetière, was Montréal's main rail terminus from 1887 until 1938, helping draw much business to Downtown away from Vieux-Montréal. Just inside the doors on rue de la Gauchetière is a plaque bearing an eloquent tribute to the employees of the railway who perished in World War I (the eulogy is repeated on the monument – a statue of an angel lifting a soldier to heaven – at the end of the otherwise bland concourse).

Although it continued to serve as a terminus for commuter trains until the mid-1990s (trains now stop a block to the west), the station's demise was finally sealed with the construction of the **Centre Bell** on the western side of the courtyard at 1200 rue de la Gauchetière O (ⓣ514/925-5656 or 1-800/363-3723, ⓦwww.centrebell.ca; Métro Lucien-L'Allier or Bonaventure). This 21,000-seat amphitheatre is home to ice hockey's **Montréal Canadiens** (or "Habs"), the most successful team in the history of the National Hockey League. When there isn't a hockey game, it's the place for rock concerts, classical music performances and family entertainment. Guided tours focusing on the legacy of the once great Habs take place in English daily at 11.15am and 2.45pm ($8) and can be purchased at the box office or the boutique, where fans can pick up a hockey jersey or other Canadiens paraphernalia.

Rue Ste-Catherine

Retrace your steps to Square Dorchester and head north on rue Peel (see below). You will quickly come to the corner of what has been the city's main commercial thoroughfare since the early 1900s, **rue Ste-Catherine**. The intersection of the two is the busiest in the city and along the stretch east of here are the main shopping centres and department stores overlying the core of the **Underground City** (see box, p.50). Exclusive boutiques and mid-priced chain stores interspersed with souvenir shops and fast-food outlets line the street westward as far as rue Guy, after which the area becomes a bit more

The Underground City

Montréal's **Underground City** was planned as a refuge from outrageously cold winters and humid summers. It began with the mall beneath Place Ville Marie in the 1960s. Montrealers flooded into the first climate-controlled shopping arcade, and, spurred by the opening of the **Métro** in 1966, the Underground City duly spread. With each newly constructed commercial development linking to the complex, it now has 31km of passages – the largest such subterranean network in the world – providing access to the Métro, major hotels, shopping malls, transport termini, thousands of offices, apartments and restaurants, and a good smattering of cinemas and theatres to boot. Around half a million people pass through it each day, mostly on their way to and from work – the sixty building complexes linked to the system contain 80 percent of Downtown's office space. Calling it a "city" is appropriate because of the way that it has developed gradually, with each addition bringing its own design style to the network, but is also misleading – because each component is privately owned, anything undesirably urban, like beggars or protest marches, are excluded.

In the largest section of the system, you can walk all the way from the Centre Bell to La Baie – over a kilometre in a straight line, several times that below ground with all the twists and turns that take you past a year-round skating rink, along the train station's grand concourse and through a shopping mall built below the foundations of Christ Church Cathedral. And from Cours Mont-Royal in the northwest, you can wend your way as far as the Centre de Commerce Mondial on the edge of Vieux-Montréal. A recent series of links now connects this to the other major axis, between the Palais des Congrès (the city's mammoth convention centre) and Place des Arts. The third main component is the area around Métro Berri-UQAM, which includes the bus station and the pavilions of the Université du Québec à Montréal (UQAM).

Although tourist-office hype makes the Underground City sound somewhat exotic, don't plan to make a day out of visiting: the reality is pretty banal and most Montrealers use it solely as a way to get from place to place. It does offer a variety of experiences, though, from bustling Métro concourses and brightly lit shopping malls to long stretches of depressing, empty, brown-brick corridors, all of it connected by a convoluted circuit of escalators and stairs that lead to sudden expanses of glass providing unexpected views outside. And if you want cheap and quick food, check out the **food courts** on the lowest floor of any of the malls en route – also handy for public toilets.

downmarket. There's a similar tailing off in quality east of Square Phillips (see p.53) before things perk up around the entertainment district anchored by Place des Arts (see p.54). But for all its consumerist gloss, rue Ste-Catherine still has seedy bits scattered throughout, with peepshows and strip clubs enlivening the streetscape.

Rue Peel

Largely residential until the 1920s, **rue Peel** has now become one of the main north–south Downtown routes, stretching from the Lachine Canal to the verge of the mountain, where a series of steps lead to the chalet and lookout (see p.103). Half a block north of rue Ste-Catherine at no. 1430 lies one of the city's architectural curiosities, replete with battlements and a fake portcullis, and apparently modelled on a sixteenth-century Scottish castle. Built in 1929 for Seagram – the Bronfman-owned company that cleaned up in the liquor trade after Prohibition was introduced in the United States – it was recently donated to the McGill Alumni Association (Ⓦwww.mcgill.ca/alumni), who have retained Samuel Bronfman's office in its original state but at press time had not decided if tours

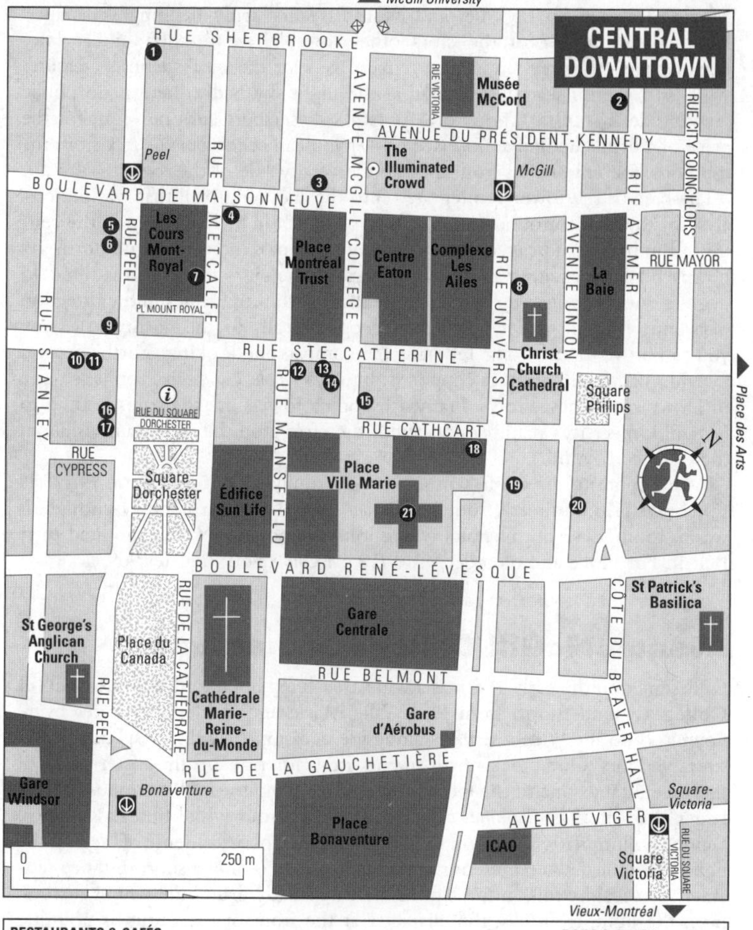

RESTAURANTS & CAFÉS

Altitude 737	21	Ferreira Café Trattoria	6	Café République	17
Basha	12	Le Grand Café	20	Reuben's	10 & 13
Ben's	4	Marché Mövenpick	18	Sushi Shop	3
Boccacinos	15	Le Parchemin	8	Takara	7
Le Commensal	14			Zen	1

BARS & CLUBS

Alexandre et Fils	5
Club 6/49	11
House of Jazz	2
McLean's Pub	16
Peel Pub	9
Le Vieux Dublin	19

would be offered to the public. Opposite stands the elegant **Cours Mont-Royal**, the largest hotel in the British Commonwealth when completed in 1922 and catalyst for the street's commercialization. Although no longer a hotel, it's worth taking a peek inside to gawk up at the fourteen-storey-high atria (surrounded by condos and offices), and to check out the lower four floors of shops, where a number of expensive designers jostle with stores geared to club kids.

Place Ville Marie

Heading back to rue Ste-Catherine and continuing east a block, you'll come across Downtown's most visible landmark, the silver, cross-shaped **Place Ville**

Marie, designed by I.M. Pei and Montréal's first truly defining skyscraper. Although a number of the city's other towers have reached similar lofty heights, the 46-storey skyscraper remains one of the city's defining features with its powerful searchlights strafing the night sky. Sadly, there is no public viewing deck – in fact, none of Montréal's skyscrapers has one – but for the price of a drink at *Altitude 737* (see p.147) you can check out the city from the top floor; the entrance is from the rue University side of the tower.

The base of the tower is integrated into the shopping mall that was the catalyst for the Underground City (see box, p.50). Set in the pavement in the centre of the mall's landscaped roof is a granite compass indicating true north. It's not particularly exciting in itself, but because the city's street grid is tilted 45 degrees, most Montrealers would argue that north actually lies in the direction of avenue McGill College (which is geographically to the northwest). Now you can prove them wrong. Ignoring the compass and looking "north" beyond Gerald Gladstone's abstract copper sculpture, *Female Landscape*, you'll see one of Downtown's best **views**. Framed by office towers are the gates leading to McGill University's main campus, with the cross atop the mountain visible in the distance beyond.

In the opposite direction, you can see the dully modernist *Queen Elizabeth Hotel* (see p.135), directly south of Place Ville Marie. Surprisingly enough, it was in room 1742 of this hotel where John Lennon and Yoko Ono held their Bed-in For Peace and recorded *Give Peace a Chance* on June 1, 1969.

Avenue McGill College and around

Redesigned in the early 1980s as a wide, tree-lined boulevard, **avenue McGill College** extends north from Place Ville Marie and bustles with cafés overflowing onto the wide sidewalks alongside occasional art displays, buskers and street vendors. One block north of rue Ste-Catherine, on the eastern side of the street, stands one of the city's most notable sculptures – Raymond Mason's larger-than-life *The Illuminated Crowd*. The numerous white fibreglass figures, facing an illumination (both in the literal and metaphorical sense of "seeing the light"), are meant to represent the fragility of man – only a short distance separates the healthy folk in front from the particularly gruesome figures furthest from the light. Ironically, the character at the front of the group is pointing across to the other side of the street, where Léa Vivot's charming bronze sculpture, *The Secret Bench*, depicts two youngsters cosying up to one another at the end of a park bench. Further along, the boulevard terminates at the gates to the expansive campus of McGill University (see p.59).

Back on rue Ste-Catherine and just east of avenue McGill College, you'll be confronted with another juxtaposition. Across the road from the families streaming out of Centre Eaton – a large shopping mall with a pretty run-of-the-mill selection of shops and restaurants – is a two-storey-high neon sign fronting "Club Super-Sexe", featuring scantily clad "superwomen" (see p.173). Adjacent to the Centre Eaton is an Italianate building with shop windows set within ornamental columns and arches – this was where the venerable Eaton's department store stood for seven decades until the chain went into receivership in 1999. The building's new tenant, the Complexe Les Ailes shopping mall, has carved up the interior with a striking elliptical atrium. The mall's real must-see, however, will be the ninth-floor restaurant, *Le 9e*, an Art Deco marvel originally designed in 1931 by Jacques Carlu, when it finally reopens.

Christ Church Cathedral

The seat of Montréal's Anglican diocese, **Christ Church Cathedral**, one block east of the Centre Eaton at 635 rue Ste-Catherine O (daily 8am–6pm; ⓣ514/843-6577, ⓦwww.montreal.anglican.org/cathedral; Métro McGill), is best remembered by many Montrealers as the "floating church". For most of 1987, the cathedral was supported on concrete struts while, underneath, developers tunnelled out the glitzy **Promenades de la Cathédrale**, a boutique-lined part of the Underground City. This curious development came about when the cathedral authorities, facing a shortage of funds, leased the land beneath the church. They also leased the land behind the church, where La Place de la Cathédrale, a mirrored Postmodern office tower, now reflects the symmetry of the 1859 church's tripartite Neo-Gothic facade.

The cathedral's other architectural oddity is its steeple – the original stone spire threatened to crash through the roof and was replaced by a replica of aluminum plates moulded to look like stone. Inside the cathedral, soaring Gothic arches are decorated with representations of angels and the evangelists, while the carved foliage is typical of what grew on Mount Royal. The copy of *The Last Supper* that hangs in the chancel was only saved from the fire that destroyed the earlier church on rue Notre-Dame by the derring-do of a soldier who cut it from its frame with his sword. The cathedral's most poignant feature, though, is mounted to the left of the pulpit: the small Coventry Cross, made from nails salvaged from the bombed Coventry Cathedral in Britain. The cathedral makes for a good spot to escape Downtown's bustle, especially during the concerts on Saturdays (occasionally other days as well) throughout the year; they're usually free but a small donation is expected.

One of the best features of the church is actually outside it – around back, you'll find benches set about a small and well-manicured public **garden**, centred around a trickling fountain that helps shut out the sounds of the city. The stone building separating the garden from rue University was the church's **rectory**, but has since been converted into the airy *Le Parchemin* restaurant (see p.148).

Square Phillips and around

Spreading back from rue Ste-Catherine another block east from Christ Church, **Square Phillips** has little in the way of greenery. Instead, the square offers a line of market stalls towered over from the centre by a bronze statue of **Edward VII** sculpted by Louis-Philippe Hébert, who also sculpted the pulpit at the Basilique Notre-Dame and had a lock on most public art commissions at the turn of the century. Thomas Phillips, a prominent merchant who bought the land in 1840, decreed that the buildings around the square should be the most beautiful in Montréal, and although they fall short of fulfilling his wish – the east side is a forgettable mishmash of cheap modern styles – a couple of the buildings fit the bill. The 1894 **Henry Birks and Sons building**, a jewellery store on the square's west side, has, behind the smooth-cut sand-coloured stone of its facade, a lovely interior full of marble columns supporting a frothy cream ceiling. On the square's north side, the distinctive dark red-sandstone building with the arched windows that dates from 1890 now houses **La Baie** (The Bay), a department store descended from the Hudson's Bay Company, which operated the trading forts throughout the Canadian wilderness from the seventeenth to nineteenth centuries. To the south, the **Canada Cement Company Building**, defined by its Ionic columns and a scallop-motif parapet, is (somewhat) notable for being the first reinforced-concrete office building in Canada.

Immediately east of Square Phillips, **St James United Church** is tucked behind a row of shopfronts, leaving only a pair of large steeples – one unusually suspended atop flying buttresses – and a neon sign advertising its presence at 463 rue Ste-Catherine O. The authorities of the city's largest Protestant church sold the land in front of the facade in the 1920s to stave off bankruptcy, but its impressive sandstone bulk is still visible from the grotty churchyard around the west side of the block on rue City Councillors. The church's hours are sporadic, but it's worth ducking in, if possible, to see the bright and airy interior – especially during one of the summer organ recitals (Tues 12.30pm; free).

Scattered about the upper floors of the mercantile building across the street at 460 rue Ste-Catherine O are eight contemporary art galleries, showcasing the work of mainly younger artists working in a variety of styles and media – check out Occurrence on the third floor for large-scale social commentary pieces. You can find more of the same at **Édifice Belgo**, a bit further east at no. 372, whose fifth floor also houses the Association des Galeries d'Art Contemporain (AGAC) (ⓣ514/861-2345, ⓦwww.agac.qc.ca), who have information on the various gallery shows around town. Note that most of these galleries are only open towards the end of the week (generally Wed–Sat noon–5pm).

St Patrick's Basilica

Of Montréal's four basilicas, **St Patrick's**, a block south and east from Square Phillips at 460 boul René-Lévesque O (daily 8.30am–6pm; ⓣ514/866-7379, ⓦwww.stpatricksmtl.ca; Métro Square-Victoria or McGill), receives the least attention. However, when the first Mass was celebrated, appropriately enough on March 17, 1847, the church must have been an imposing sight on the hill overlooking Vieux-Montréal, where its Irish parishioners lived. Enter from the main south entrance, where the rather drab Gothic exterior gives way to a dramatic interior full of warm hues. Although at first glance the dozen pillars supporting the vault appear to be a red, veined marble, they are in fact each crafted from pine trees 30m tall. The combination of the pillars' polished glow, the cream and peach colour of the ceiling and walls decorated with shamrocks and fleurs-de-lys contrasts with the cool and distant tones of the **sanctuary**. It's hard to miss the elaborate sanctuary lamps over the main altar – the larger of the two weighs almost a tonne and is surrounded by two-metre-tall angels.

Place des Arts and around

A couple of blocks east of Square Phillips, rue Ste-Catherine slopes down towards **Place des Arts**, Montréal's leading performing-arts centre, opened in 1963 and home to events like the famous Festival International de Jazz de Montréal (see p.214). Place des Arts comprises five performance halls and the **Musée d'Art Contemporain de Montréal** in an ensemble of buildings set around a large plaza, with a series of gardens and fountains and a wide set of steps creating a seating area for tired tourists and for spectators during outdoor concerts. Note that the entrances to all the performance halls are via an underground concourse, best entered directly from the Métro Place-des-Arts or at 175 rue Ste-Catherine O, where information on cultural events is available in the lobby. For details of Place des Arts' resident symphony, ballet, theatre and opera companies, see Chapter Fourteen, "Performing arts and film".

Plans are afoot to expand the cultural attractions in this area, with an additional outdoor **Parc des Festivals** on the southwest corner of rues Ste-Catherine and Jeanne-Mance, adjacent to the concert hall and jazz club that will form the hub of the new **Complexe Spectrum** (see p.176). With the change of government in spring 2003 – and requisite spending review – plans for a new symphony hall on the northwestern corner of the intersection are on hold. Many locals consider this to be a blessing, though – the proposed glass cube is an uninspired design that looks more like a government office building.

Musée d'Art Contemporain de Montréal

Occupying the west side of Place des Arts, the **Musée d'Art Contemporain de Montréal** (Tues–Sun 11am–6pm, Wed till 9pm; $6, free Wed evenings; ⓣ514/847-6226, ⓦwww.macm.org; Métro Place-des-Arts) was Canada's first museum devoted entirely to contemporary art. The city's foremost showcase for work produced by Québécois painters and sculptors since 1939, the museum also has a number of pieces by other Canadian and international artists. The collection overlaps with that of the Musée des Beaux-Arts and the Musée National des Beaux-Arts du Québec (see p.257) a fair bit, so don't be surprised when you see the same names (and occasionally very similar paintings, like those by Borduas and Riopelle – see box, p.56) cropping up again from one museum to the next. If you're not really into contemporary works – or don't fancy the temporary exhibition on show – head to the Musée des Beaux-Arts instead.

The building design is fairly low-key, although a photograph of a pair of lips smiling down from the rooftop adds a light-hearted touch. Inside, a two-storey rotunda links all of the museum's main components, including the *La Rotonde* restaurant (see p.148), whose terrace is often filled with diners enjoying live music. The exhibit space is divided into two wings, one of which hosts temporary exhibitions of major artists, while the other displays recent acquisitions of contemporary works alongside highlights of contemporary Québécois art culled from the 6000-item permanent collection.

Besides paintings, the museum's collection is also impressively stocked with sculpture, photography, video and installation art, as well as featuring the occasional multimedia performance. There is also a small, hard-to-find **sculpture garden**, entered through a partially hidden doorway in the last room of the temporary-works wing in the museum's northeast corner. Although there's only a handful of pieces here, it's worth seeking out for the totem-pole-like Henry Moore bronze of an abstract human form, *Upright Motive no. 5*, standing amidst the greenery.

The long-term exhibition of works from the Forties to the Sixties – known as the **Place à la Magie** – occupies a couple of small rooms in the museum's southeast corner, to your left as you reach the top of the stairs. Among the most significant pieces in the museum's collection are those of **Paul-Émile Borduas**, founder of the influential group, Les Automatistes (see box below). Scoot through the first gallery to the side room devoted to his output – you can follow his progression clockwise as his realistic early works give way to increasingly gestural pieces like the *Surrealist Artist's Palette, or 3.45 (State of Mind, Composition with Eggs)*, awash in broad stokes of glistening colour. By the early 1950s, his palette becomes more muted, with ever-increasing volumes of slathered whites, culminating in his best-known paintings – abstracts reduced to black blobs on a field of thick white paint.

Fellow Automatistes represented in the main gallery include **Jean-Paul Riopelle**, most notably his untitled 1949 piece filled with thick dabs of colour overlaid with drizzles of black and white. His later paintings, like *Landing*, burst with vibrant energy and colour, laid on sharply with a palette knife to produce a mosaic-like effect. Automatiste compatriot **Fernand Leduc** has a number of

Les Automatistes

Along with the formation of the Contemporary Art Society in 1939, the initial impetus of contemporary art in Montréal came with **Alfred Pellan**'s return from Paris after World War II broke out, bringing with him the main strands of the **avant-garde** – Cubism, Fauvism, Primitivism and Surrealism. Although parallel to the evolution of Abstract Expressionism in New York around this time, the art scene in Montréal developed along a divergent path thanks to one artist in particular.

A rival of Pellan, **Paul-Émile Borduas** drew upon the theory of automatism (automatic writing) espoused by surrealist poet André Breton and applied it to his painting, repudiating figurative art for a visual expression drawn from the subconscious mind. He and his group of followers, dubbed **Les Automatistes** in a review of their second Montréal show in 1947, published a landmark manifesto *Refus global* (total refusal) the following year, sparking outrage among the establishment. The manifesto's challenging of the conformist, Church-dominated society and demand for freedom of artistic expression and "resplendent anarchy" influenced a generation of Québécois and kindled the spirit that led to the Quiet Revolution and secularization of Québec in the following decades. For a mimeographed text that saw only 400 copies printed, it had a profound impact on cultural thinking in Québec that extended well beyond art.

Many of Québec's best-known artists were among the signatories, including Françoise Sullivan, Pierre Gauvreau, Marcelle Ferron and Jean-Paul Mousseau, who instigated the incorporation of non-representative art in the Métro's stations. **Jean-Paul Riopelle** left the group in 1950, developing his Pollock-like lyrical abstraction, slathering his canvases with thick blobs of colour overlaid with paint drizzles, before adopting a palette knife to produce the large-scale mosaic-like works that are among the most collectible in Québec. Other Automatistes such as **Fernand Leduc** later joined the Mondrian-influenced **Les Plasticiens** (Neo-Plasticists), producing works further abstracted to a unity of form, colour and line.

You can catch these artists' works at the province's big three art museums – in addition, the Musée des Beaux-Arts National du Québec devotes a room solely to Riopelle (see p.257), the Musée d'Art Contemporain sets aside space for Borduas (see p.55) and the Musée des Beaux-Arts showcases both painters (see p.63).

geometric abstracts dotted around the exhibition, though none are particularly exciting – more interesting are the rigorous abstract pieces, typified by hard-edged bands of vertical colour, produced in the 1960s by fellow member **Guido Molinari**.

In the second room of the exhibition, there's a small sample of the colourful stained-glass works of **Marcelle Ferron**, another Automatiste, but it pales next to her large-scale panels that adorn the Champ-de-Mars Métro station (see p.74). Likewise, the monochromatic landscape of **Jean-Paul Lemieux**'s *Winter Moon* – just the moon, dark sky and a flat grey plain – though evocative, doesn't convey the radical style changes throughout his career that are better displayed at the Musée National des Beaux-Arts du Québec (see p.257). Sculpture of the period is represented by a pair of vertical abstract sculptures by two Montrealers – both **Yves Trudeau**'s *La Cité*, made of welded segments of iron tubes, and the cut and welded metal planes of **Ivanhoé Fortier**'s *Sublunar Tower*, cast shadows that are almost as interesting as the sculptures themselves.

East of Place des Arts

As you follow rue Ste-Catherine east from Place des Arts, the blocks get increasingly seedy and there's not much of note along this stretch as far as sightseeing goes. The present-day **Théâtre du Nouveau Monde**, at the corner of rue St-Urbain, was once the notorious Gayety Burlesque Theatre, where Lili St-Cyr performed (see p.188). Though the building was given a sleek style update by Dan Hanganu (architect of the Musée d'Archéolgie) and is fronted by a trendy café, the plays are mainly from the classical French canon (see p.188). Further along rue Ste-Catherine, its intersection with **boulevard St-Laurent** has been a long-time hangout for prostitutes and is surrounded by some of the city's larger concert venues. Things don't get much more wholesome between here and the Quartier Latin, what with places like the nightclub **Les Foufones Électroniques** (literally, The Electric Buttocks – see p.175), although the area is gradually cleaning up as the Université de Québec à Montréal encroaches from the west. Plans to clean the area up are nothing new, however – citizens were complaining about its seedy, red-light district character as long ago as the 1840s. The area is safe to enough to walk though in the daytime, and even at night with a modicum of common sense, but if you're footsore you can skip it by taking the Métro two stops from Place-des-Arts station to Berri-UQAM in the Quartier Latin (see p.85).

Complexe Desjardins and south

Place des Arts marks the northern point on one of the Underground City's main axes, with a tunnel connecting it to **Complexe Desjardins**, a collection of office towers and the *Wyndham* (see p.135) surrounding a shopping mall just across rue Ste-Catherine. The complex's enormous central atrium hosts exhibitions on subjects of mainly local interest. You can surface at the south side of the complex to explore Chinatown or continue to the hulking **Palais des Congrès** (Ⓦwww.congresmtl.com), the city's main conference centre built over the Autoroute Ville-Marie (Hwy-720) opposite the northern edge of Vieux-Montréal. If you're passing through, be sure to check out the centre's surreal *Lipstick Forest*, comprising electric-pink concrete casts of actual trees. The new square fronting the centre's multicoloured western facade, **Place Jean-Paul-Riopelle**, was designed around the artist's *La Joute*, a group of sculptures surrounded by water and licked by flames.

Chinatown

A block south of rue Ste-Catherine and just north ofVieux-Montréal, a large Chinese gate rises above boulevard St-Laurent, replete with temple-like roofs and Chinese characters and flanked by a pair of white marble lions, one of several gates that mark the entrances to Montréal's small **Chinatown**. Although the Chinese immigrants who constructed the nation's railway lines settled here in the mid- to late nineteenth century, their descendants later dispersed throughout the city, leaving Chinatown to evolve into a primarily commercial and cultural centre. The traffic-choked blocks on boulevard St-Laurent contain a chaotic mix of produce shops and cheap but good restaurants, with crowds picking through the vegetables amid delivery vans double-parked along the sidewalks.

Extending westward as far as the plaza in front of the Palais des Congrès, the car-free portion of rue de la Gauchetière is quieter, though no less busy as crowds of pedestrians search out a place for dim sum or an evening meal (for reviews, see p.150). Many of the city's Chinese residents also venture here from the suburbs, outnumbering the tourists as they stock up at grocery shops selling dry goods and herbal remedies. If you're coming here by train, Métro Place-des-Armes is the nearest stop.

Although it's not a patch on the far more impressive Chinese Garden at the Jardin Botanique (see p.114), **Place Sun-Yat-Sen**, a granite-paced square at the corner of rues Clark and de la Gauchetière, offers a respite from the commercial bustle with cultural shows and impromptu street performers. Performances take place on the raised stage area, guarded by a dragon and with polished stone panels engraved with Chinese landscapes as a backdrop, while the east side of the square is bordered by a small pavilion inspired by palatial Imperial architecture.

The Golden Square Mile and around

The **Golden Square Mile**, a dignified neighbourhood of limestone mansions that cascades down the slopes of Mont Royal and is encroached upon by Downtown's western core, was Montréal's epicentre of English privilege at the beginning of the twentieth century. Its name derives from the area it covers, roughly one square mile – from rue University west to rue Guy, and avenue des Pins south to boulevard René-Lévesque – and from the riches of its residents who, at the neighbourhood's zenith in 1900, possessed 75 percent of Canada's wealth.

Things are slower-paced and more genteel in the area just north and west of Downtown, which has retained much of its character and where you can easily spend an afternoon visiting **rue Sherbrooke**'s heavyweight cultural institutions, such as the **Musée McCord d'Histoire Canadienne** opposite **McGill University**. The university spreads up Mont Royal's slopes, where it occupies a number of stately mansions in the core of the Golden Square Mile. This enclave's gentrified airs extend west through a district of chic boutiques and pricey art galleries towards the venerable **Musée des Beaux-Arts**.

South of here, there's no coherent identity to the area where the western edge of Downtown and the Victorian townhouses of the Golden Square Mile overlap, and the nightlife of rues Bishop and Crescent gives way to **Concordia University**'s urban campus and studenty residential area. It's worth the trek, though, to the impressive **Centre Canadien d'Architecture**, in the Shaughnessy Village neighbourhood to the southwest.

Some history

Originally settled by fur merchants like James McGill – who maintained a summer home here and an "everyday house" in Vieux-Montréal – shipping, railroad and banking magnates began colonizing the Mile for year-round living in the 1860s. Upon arrival, they built ostentatious mansions, embellishing them with an array of cornices, ornamental cherubs and bas-relief-detailing that loudly announced their economic standing. But after the 1929 stock market crash, many of these residents were forced to flee west to smaller – but still relatively lavish – homes in nearby Westmount (see p.122). The neighbourhood's character changed drastically as the Downtown core spread, and skyscrapers sprouted up where mansions once had been. Thankfully, much of the area north of rue Sherbrooke has remained relatively untouched, and most of the mansions there maintain their sumptuous facades – even though they've nearly all been turned into university faculties, hospital wings and apartments. You can take a virtual tour of McGill's holdings in the district at Ⓦhttp://cac.mcgill.ca/campus.

Musée McCord d'Histoire Canadienne

Near Downtown's centre, close to the corner of rue University at 690 rue Sherbrooke O, sits the **Musée McCord d'Histoire Canadienne** (Tues–Fri 10am–6pm, Sat & Sun 10am–5pm, Mon 10am–5pm, closed Mon in winter except holidays; guided tours Sat 2pm; $9.50, free Sat before noon; Ⓣ514/398-7100, Ⓦwww.mccord-museum.qc.ca; Métro McGill), a handsome early-twentieth-century limestone building that faces its one-time administrator, McGill University. The three-storey museum, dedicated to Canadian history, was inaugurated in 1921 following the donation of wealthy magistrate David Ross McCord's collection of 15,000 artefacts, and moved to its present location in the 1960s. The current collection numbers nearly a million objects, photos and documents, although the majority of these only come out during high-calibre temporary exhibitions. However, you can also view much of the collection on the museum's website – the slide show of famous Montrealers in fancy dress ball costumes is a hoot.

A cedar *gayang* (totem pole) greets you on the way to the second floor, where more than 800 pieces are displayed in **Simply Montreal**, a permanent exhibition addressing the city's social and commercial development. Though lacking cohesiveness – it seems as if nearly every aspect of Montréal life is touched on in only a few rooms – the exhibit does have its strong points. Photos confirming the worst you've heard about the city's punishing winters accompany displays of furry mitts, an image of a tram converted into a snowplough and mid-nineteenth-century ice-skates – all of which reveal how Montrealers adapted to, and even enjoyed, the climate. The real stunners, though, are the gritty floor-to-ceiling black-and-white **photographs** of the city taken by William Notman at the turn of the nineteenth century. These anchor the displays in galleries 3 and 4 and provide the exhibit's most visceral contrasts: an image of rue St-Jacques bustling with streetcars and *calèches* is around the corner from a forlorn shot of workers' houses, with sagging wood frames and crooked stone chimneys. Equally sterling are the **aboriginal items**, such as a collection of wampum beads once used as trading currency and a delicately carved and painted Iroquois baby carrier. The delightful array of memorabilia from elite Montréal families shows off things like an intricately detailed mourning necklace, with its onyx and pearl pendant, worn to honour the dearly departed. The gift shop is worth a look-in as well for its books on Canadiana and native and folk-art items.

McGill University

While the expansive campus of Québec's first English-language university, **McGill University** (Ⓣ514/398-6555, Ⓦwww.mcgill.ca; Métro McGill or Peel), spreads from rue Sherbrooke up to Mont Royal, and west from rue University to rue Peel, the main thrust of the university lies behind the semicircular **Roddick Gates** that enclose the top of avenue McGill College. The gates' colonnades open onto the campus's main road lined with grassy quads on either side, and on the right a **statue** of founder James McGill surveys the land. The main road leads directly to the Neoclassical **Arts Building**, the campus's first (1843), situated on a slight promontory at the northern end of the campus. It's distinguished from the rest by McGill's red-and-white flag atop its cupola – stand on the front steps for a fine view of Downtown and the surrounding campus.

McGill was the greatest beneficiary of the Golden Square Mile's decline, inheriting a number of mansions vacated by the neighbourhood's wealthy merchants. Along with the stone facades of the main university buildings, these give the grounds a dignified air, and the picturesque setting on the slopes and foreground of Mont Royal produces a quietude that's unexpected so close to the bustle of Downtown.

Musée Redpath

Before reaching the Arts Building, the main road splits, with the western fork cresting in front of the **Musée Redpath** (Mon–Fri 9am–5pm, Sun 1–5pm; late June to Aug closed Fri; free; ⓣ514/398-4086, ⓦwww.mcgill.ca/redpath; Métro McGill), an unusual museum devoted to zoological and ethnological pursuits. The 1882 Greek Revival structure in which it is housed lays claim to being the province's first custom-built museum. Upstairs there's an impressive two-storey-high oval atrium with a wrapround mezzanine. An ongoing facelift to brighten up the once fusty exhibits will continue until late 2005 but the majority of the displays remain accessible.

Architecture aside, though, this is an odd place all in all, featuring a hodgepodge collection of stuffed and fossilized creatures, geology specimens and ethnological tidbits, with a few interesting relics tucked here and there. There's the briefest of glimpses of marine life as you enter, including a massive "fragment" of a bowhead whale skull, but the main collection is upstairs, where a seven-metre-long menacing *Albertosaurus* dinosaur skeleton known as "Zeller" strides over the atrium's centre. The surrounding panels detailing the evolution of various species throughout the eras lend an educational aspect to the array of fossils and minerals but the only recently departed animals at the far end are more diverting (and are as close as you're likely to get to some of Canada's wildlife). Here, stuffed birds of prey perch between the windows looking out to the mountain, foregrounded by a wooly musk-ox, snarling wolverine and a whooping crane whose eyes seem to follow you – as well as the requisite beaver. Peer into the top floor landing's shelves of cultural artefacts and you'll see some spooky Kongo sculptures from Africa and ancient Egyptian sarcophagi behind the glass; a computer screen shows a CT scan of the mummy's insides. Extending out from the landing, the mezzanine's rounded walls provide a round-the-world trip through other ancient cultures.

Rue Sherbrooke

For decades, the stretch of **rue Sherbrooke** between rue University and rue Guy that forms the core of the Golden Square Mile was known as Canada's Fifth Avenue, as it was home to the country's choicest boutiques. Although the strip lost its five-star rating when much of the city's money shifted to Toronto years ago, it retains elements of its former shopping glory nonetheless: Ralph Lauren hobnobs with Escada and Giorgio Armani, as well as Holt Renfrew, Canada's answer to Neiman Marcus. Those allergic to high-priced clothiers will still enjoy a stroll down this length of rue Sherbrooke, as impressive ornamental details like demonic gargoyles, wrought-iron entrance grilles and

A house-hunting detour

The Golden Square Mile's most noteworthy mansions are on the slopes of Mont Royal north of rue Sherbrooke, cradled by lush foliage and Mont Royal's rugged rock face. The roads around here are quite steep – although the superb views of Downtown along the way offer plenty of excuses for a breather. Begin by heading to the north end of rue McTavish, McGill campus's western artery, to avenue des Pins ouest. On the north side of the street, at no. 1025, looms **Ravenscrag**, a magnificent Tuscan-style villa, now home to a psychiatric institute, but originally built for shipping magnate Sir Hugh Allan in 1864. Hemmed in by a weighty stone and wrought-iron gateway, the mansion's two sprawling wings connect to a central watchtower that rises high above the roofline. Allan himself often stood in the windowed tower to observe his ships docking at the port far below, and for decades its rough-cast stone facade welcomed Montréal's finest, along with royalty like Japan's Prince Fushimi, to waltzes in the grand Second Empire ballroom.

The most attractive of the fine mansions absorbed by McGill on the south side of avenue des Pins was built for Sir Hugh's brother, Andrew. The red brick **Maison Lady Meredith** at no. 1110 has a Romanesque Revival influence, and leading architects of the day Edward and William Maxwell took a more light-hearted approach than with their mannered Musée des Beaux-Arts, with conical turrets and a looping arch pattern in the brickwork. Ten minutes further west, at no. 1418, stands the **Maison Cormier**, its handsome Art Deco facade decorated with a sleek female statue above the door. Former Prime Minister Pierre Elliott Trudeau died here in 2000, and it is still occupied by his family. Across the street at no. 1415 is the former **Cuban Consulate**'s digs, recently converted into condos. The location hints at the longstanding friendship between Trudeau and Fidel Castro – a bond so strong that Castro was a pallbearer at Trudeau's funeral.

Four residences back east along avenue des Pins, a long set of stairs on the south side of the street leads down to avenue du Musée. The three eclectic mansions closest to the base of the stairs on the left form the **Russian Consulate**, and it's thought the United States was closely monitored from here during the Cold War. Whatever the Soviets were up to, they clearly didn't want anyone knowing about it: when fire broke out in 1987, they kept the firemen outside for fifteen minutes while they loaded document-filled boxes into waiting cars. From here, it's a five-minute walk to the bottom of avenue du Musée and the Musée des Beaux-Arts.

detailed bas-relief carvings add to the street's architectural panache. Beginning as far east as the Musée McCord, a series of plaques highlights the most notable buildings still in existence with photos and a historical overview.

Of the many structures in this area converted to commercial purposes, **Maison Alcan**, the aluminium giant's headquarters just west of rue Peel at no. 1188, is the most impressive, integrating a pair of nineteenth-century townhouses and an old, 1920s-era, red-brick hotel into an office building clad, naturally enough, in aluminum. Inuit and other sculptures are scattered about the atrium connecting the buildings, and there's a sunny garden and café in back that's good for a rest.

One of the finest examples of the street's heyday is the Beaux-Arts expanse of the **Ritz Carlton** hotel (see p.135), built in 1911 and announcing its grandeur with a sinuous frieze of acanthus leaves and twinkling lights from the entranceway's chandeliers. The accommodations for the street's permanent residents in bygone times were almost as grand – a number of colossal apartment buildings were erected for those who couldn't afford to maintain a Golden Square Mile mansion – notably across the street at no. 1321, where the aptly named **Appartements Le Château** rises like a fortress, topped by battlements, turrets and copper roofs.

Musée des Beaux-Arts

Canada's oldest art museum - it was inaugurated in Square Phillips in 1879 – the **Musée des Beaux-Arts** (Sept–June Tues–Sun 11am–5pm, special exhibits Wed till 9pm, Mon 11am–5pm (July & Aug); free, except special exhibits $10–15, half-price Wed after 5pm; ⓣ514/285-1600, ⓦwww.mbam.qc.ca; Métro Guy-Concordia) moved to its rue Sherbrooke location in 1912. It's renowned for the excellent quality of its visiting exhibits and the sheer size of its collection, which now spans two buildings (1379 and 1380 rue Sherbrooke O, connected by an underground passageway) and 65 rooms. Seeing everything on display could easily take a full day, but doing so need not be a priority as the permanent collection is actually rather spotty. Certain aspects, like the post-1945 contemporary-art collection, are of high calibre, as are many of the pieces by the likes of Picasso, Rodin, El Greco and Dalí. Unfortunately, these are surrounded by many lesser-known and inferior works often grouped in a seemingly haphazard fashion. If you're looking for a particular piece, ask at the reception counters located on the buildings' main floors, where you can also pick up a museum map.

Although the original building appears more inviting, at press time visitors were required to purchase tickets and check coats and bags in the modern building on the south side of the street.

Pavillon Jean-Nöel Desmarais

The blockbuster temporary exhibits and the best of the permanent collection are housed in the modern **Pavillon Jean-Nöel Desmarais** on the south side of rue Sherbrooke ouest. Designed by Moshe Safdie, the pavilion merges the red-brick facade of a pre-existing apartment building alongside a new Postmodern wing built of Vermont marble and incised with a sloping glass roof supported by a lattice of tubular aluminum.

Begin on the fourth floor, where pieces from the museum's **European decorative arts** and **Old Masters** from the twelfth- to nineteenth-century collections are on display; visit the rooms clockwise to get the clearest sense of chronological order. The oldest works are **religious paintings and sculptures**, beginning in the foyer with an almost marionette-like Christ on the cross sculpted in twelfth-century Italy, and continuing in the first gallery, which has a Jan de Beer triptych with pastoral overtones as the centrepiece. Straight ahead and in a small room to the left, the collection of late-sixteenth-century works matches El Greco's ethereal *Ecstasy of St Francis* with Hendrick de Clerk's orgiastic aftermath of *Moses Striking the Rock*.

The adjoining rooms, furthest from the entrance, feature a good selection of sixteenth- and seventeenth-century **Dutch and Flemish art**. Amongst the still-lifes and high-key portraits, scenes capture the varied lives of commoners; the visceral imagery of Lucas van Valckenborch's *A Meat and Fish Market (Winter)* contrasts with the almost cartoon-like drunkards of *Return from the Inn* by Bruegel the Younger. Next door, Rembrandt's *Portrait of a Young Woman*, her face brilliantly illuminated against an almost black background, gets pride of place, although Emmanuel de Witte's *Interior with a Woman Playing Virginals* is more artfully situated – seeing it through a doorway adds an extra layer to the sequence of rooms and delightful play of light in the painting itself.

Back towards the entrance and adjacent to the first room, the portraits, pastoral views and allegorical scenes seem to be linked only by time period, spanning from the mid-seventeenth to late eighteenth century. The best of the lot are English painter Thomas Gainsborough's immense *Portrait of Mrs George Drummond* and *Interior of San Marco, Venice* by Canaletto. The progression continues via a passageway to the museum's east side, filled mainly with French works; pause for the hurried brushstrokes speaking of the urgency of the flight of Honoré Daumier's *Women Pursued by Satyrs*. The final gallery culminates with a couple of the collection's stand-outs: James Tissot's splendid oil painting *October*, featuring an elegant young lady tucked amongst golden autumn foliage, and the hypnotic stare of the little girl in William Bouguereau's *Crown of Flowers*.

The temporary exhibition halls that mount the museum's high-calibre shows are down a floor. On the opposite side of the elevators from these are two small galleries, the first of which displays a fine collection of **Impressionist** pieces by Monet, Cézanne, Sisley, and a gloomy Degas alongside three Renoirs, whose *Vase of Flowers* overflows with vibrant colours. Rodin's bronze, *The Call to Arms*, grabs attention in the centre of the room away from the cool forms of his white marble sculpture of *The Sirens*. The second gallery here hosts **twentieth-century European Art**, with stand-outs by Giacometti, Matisse, Otto Dix and Dalí, whose pre-Surrealist *Portrait of Maria Carbona* turns her face from Picasso's sexually charged *Embrace*, a Cubist take on entwined lovers.

In the basement, the superb post-1945 **contemporary art** collection has a strong accent on works by Canadian artists. Abstract painter Jack Bush, and hyperrealists Alex Colville and Christopher Pratt are all represented, but the best of the pieces belong to **Québécois artists**. Look for Claude Tousignant's acrylic *Gong 96*, depicting a pastel-hued bull's-eye – stare at it too long and you may go cross-eyed. Jean-Paul Riopelle has an entire room devoted to him: the drizzled lines and daubs of primary colour that stand out against the blacks of his *Crosswind* mark the beginnings of his trademark style, best exhibited in his magnificent oil painting *Austria*, its hundreds of geometric daubs of colour surrounding a starkly white centre. Riopelle's art is given as much emphasis as that of fellow **Automatiste** Paul-Émile Borduas (see box, p.56), who gets an entire gallery in the back. Examine Borduas' pieces counterclockwise to follow his artistic progression – early works are much more fluid and bright than later pieces, which are sparsely coloured but highly textured. Bourduas' work culminates with *The Black Star*, its putty-coloured background heavily sculpted and layered with his painting knife.

Gallery of Ancient Cultures

Slightly jarring after the vivid colours of the contemporary works are the much older products of ancient civilizations, worth at least a cursory look as you pass through the tunnel between the museum's two buildings. Grouped by region, the **Gallery of Ancient Cultures**' displays begin on your left with masks, shields, carved figures and other ritual objects from Oceania and Africa, followed by a number of Asian and Islamic pieces, notably the glazed Persian ceramics and tableware, which include a handsome thirteenth-century ewer with a lapis lazuli glaze. On the right side of the passageway, pre-Columbian treasures range from a *zapotec* (funerary urn) to stone carved objects used for ball games.

Pavillon Michal et Renata Hornstein and Pavillon Liliane et David M. Stewart

Designed by architects Edward and William Maxwell, the elegant Beaux-Arts temple of art on the north side of rue Sherbrooke ouest comprises two joined pavilions. Its wide steps lead past a colonnaded portico to the original half of the building, the **Pavillon Michal et Renata Hornstein,** whose main hall's majestic grand staircase leads to the upstairs *salles* hosting temporary exhibitions.

In back, the Hornstein fuses with a more modern annex, the **Pavillon Liliane et David M. Stewart,** which contains the thrust of the museum's Canadian collection on its upper floor and a wide-ranging survey of decorative arts below.

Straight ahead after you've ascended the Hornstein's grand staircase, the **Canadian collection** occupies the second-floor galleries of the Pavillon Stewart annex. The furthest gallery to the left is crammed with decorative arts, the showstopper being an outrageously extravagant white-oak Renaissance revival sidebar; dogs' heads protrude on both sides of a central mirror while their catch – fish and fowl – hang by their feet and tails on the lower side panels. The middle gallery is busy with Inuit soapstone carvings; *Finger Pulling Game*, a palm-sized Iqaluit soapstone showing two hunched men with bony forefingers cocked for action, is particularly delightful.

The main gallery's collection of pre-1945 **Canadian paintings** is less than spectacular and confusing to boot, as numerous dividing walls break up the flow. The most worthy collection here is the series of landscapes by the **Group of Seven**, a group of Canadian artists that set the standard for landscape paintings throughout much of the twentieth century. Tom Thompson, the instigator of the group's creation, has several works here, including his magnificent *In the Northland*, which resonates with the orange hues typical of northern Canadian autumns. Also of note are Lawren Harris's moody landscapes of simple, rounded rock forms in the far north typified in *Baffin Island*.

Don't miss the side gallery devoted to **Alfred Laliberté**, whose discovery of Rodin while at the École des Beaux-Arts in Paris is evident in his angry-looking *Dollard des Ormeaux*. The successor to Louis-Phillipe Hébert as the main sculptor of public art in the first half of the twentieth century, Laliberté captures numerous aspects of Québécois life in the works on display here, as well as in the 200 bronzes commissioned for the Musée du Québec (see p.255).

The entire floor below the Canadian collection spans more than five centuries of **furniture and domestic objects** – to get here from the Hornstein's main hall, pass to either side of the grand staircase. Some of its most impressive and oldest pieces are the intricately inlaid wooden panels, depicting prominent Romans, that date from 1420s Siena. The rest of the first gallery's eclectic contents include an elaborate seventeenth-century English writing desk, with an ornate Rococo dragon-headed sleigh from France and delicate Sèvres and Meissen porcelain. The Neo-Classical and Victorian furniture in the next two galleries are not as memorable as the Art Deco stained-glass peacock-motif window and snake-wrapped floor lamp towards the end. If frou-frou isn't so much to your taste, you'll better appreciate the large collection of **twentieth-century design** that rounds out the exhibition. Gerrit Rietveld's classic *Red-Blue Chair* gives way to fabulously shaped creations like Marcel Breuer's sinuous wood-laminate lounge chair and Eero Saarinen's cow-patterned *Womb* armchair. Other twentieth-century luminaries who also get a look in for their furniture and household objects include Alvar Aalto, Charles and Ray Eames, Isamu Noguchi, Arne Jacobsen and Ron Arad. After you leave the museum, be sure to check out the colourful sculptures by Keith Haring – 3-D versions of his signature humanoid figures – that enliven the Hornstein's eastern side on avenue du Musée.

Quartier du Musée and Concordia University

The southern verge of the Golden Square Mile may be a mish-mash of architectural styles and purposes where it interweaves with Downtown but there are a few distractions en route to the excellent architecture centre located here (see below). The area immediately around the Musée des Beaux-Arts, dubbed the **Quartier du Musée** by the tourist authorities, contains some fine remnants of the Square Mile's golden age, elaborated on in the free two-hour tour of the district that departs from the museum's main lobby (mid-June to mid-Aug 11am & 2pm; ⓣ514/288-6176, ⓦwww.quartierdumusee.com). Included in the itinerary is **rue Crescent**, where the row of nineteenth-century town houses below rue Sherbrooke host some of the city's most upscale boutiques. Closer to rue Ste-Catherine, bars and dance clubs catering to a mix of Anglophone office workers, students and tourists proliferate – see pp.164 & 171.

A block to the west are the profoundly ugly structures that make up the nucleus of **Concordia University**'s urban campus: the 1960s-vintage Henry F. Hall Building appears to be clad in urinals – perhaps the inspiration for the use of what appear to be bathroom tiles for the exterior of the Postmodern J.W. McConnell Building, opposite. The latter's saving grace is the preserved **Royal George Apartments**, a 1912 Renaissance Revival building on rue Bishop adorned with white-glazed terra cotta floral detailing. Behind its facade but entered through the main building at 1400 boul de Maisonneuve O is the **Leonard and Bina Ellen Art Gallery** (Tues–Sat noon–6pm; free; ⓣ514/848-2424, ext 4750, ⓦwww.ellengallery.com; Métro Guy-Concordia), whose collection of contemporary art alternates with student shows. Hurrying along to rue Ste-Catherine and west past rue Guy will bring you to the **Faubourg Ste-Catherine**, one of the city's more interesting malls with its collection of craft stands and the city's best food court, comprising a lot of small operations rather than the usual mega-chain outlets (see p.197).

Centre Canadien d'Architecture (CCA)

Situated in the neighbourhood of limestone houses and low-slung red-brick apartment blocks known as Shaughnessy Village, on the outskirts of the Golden Square Mile a couple of blocks southwest from the Faubourg, stands the **Centre Canadien d'Architecture (CCA)**. Its significant collection of architectural prints, drawings and scale models is housed in an immensely formal building set back from landscaped grounds at 1920 rue Baile (June–Sept Tues–Sun 11am–6pm, Thurs to 9pm; Oct–May Wed & Fri 11am–6pm, Thurs 11am–8pm, Sat & Sun 11am–5pm; $6, free Thurs after 5.30pm; ⓣ514/939-7026, ⓦwww.cca.qc.ca; Métro Guy-Concordia). The severe, grey-limestone facade is broken up by an aluminum allusion to a parapet and very few windows, a minimalist approach echoed in the angular metal-and-glass portico over the entrance to the grounds themselves. But what the CCA lacks in detail on its side facing rue Baile it more than makes up for on the side that fronts boulevard René-Lévesque. Here, two Golden Square Mile-era houses collectively known as the **Shaughnessy House** have been ingeniously incorporated into the building, and their refurbished interiors offer the most luxurious places in the city to sit and rest. Outfitted with marble fireplace mantles and archways supported by grooved columns, the setting may make you linger long enough to forget about seeing the exhibits. One-hour guided tours of the building and the Shaughnessy House are offered on weekends (Sat & Sun 3.30pm) with the price of admission.

The CCA mounts anywhere from three to eight exhibitions a year using pieces from its archives and elsewhere – past shows have focused on the works of Frank Lloyd Wright, Frederick Law Olmsted and Carlos Scarpa, with whimsical displays on Disney theme parks and garden implements also receiving critical acclaim. If you're in town between exhibits, there is no permanent collection to tour as such, and though museum staff insist the architecture of the Shaughnessy House fills that function, it alone isn't worth the entry price. If you are into design and architecture books, the museum's bookstore will feel like heaven. The CCA's **gardens**, on the south side of boulevard René-Lévesque, are also open to the public (daily 6am–midnight; free), and are scattered about with an incongruous collection of fragments of buildings, miniature temples and other architectural allusions designed by local artist/architect Melvin Charney.

2

Vieux-Montréal

The clichés that abound about **Vieux-Montréal** (Old Montreal) in reality apply only in parts. Yes, there are stretches of cobblestone streets and eighteenth-century residences which feel like an old French village – and an extremely well-kept one at that – but the bulk of the original city is actually characterized by tall, dark canyons of nineteenth- and early-twentieth-century commercial buildings. Likewise, the sight of Victorian lampposts and the sound of horse-drawn *calèches* echoing off the stone structures can produce a Dickensian reverie – until it's broken by the occasional car rumbling down the area's narrow lanes. The neighbourhood's delights lie more in turning down its small, secretive streets and in ogling the Industrial Revolution-era embellishments – deeply rusticated stone walls, fanciful carved garlands or serious-looking busts – adorning many of the facades in Canada's one-time financial powerhouse. Even the buzz and cheesiness of the more touristy bits have an infectious appeal, especially the sense of anticipation that builds on Wednesday and Saturday summer evenings when the whole circus shuffles down to the Vieux-Port to ooh and ah the fireworks.

Roughly coinciding with the limits of the old town walls, Vieux-Montréal is braced by rue St-Antoine to the north, rue Berri to the east, rue McGill to the west and the St Lawrence to the south. Relatively compact, it is best visited on foot, and you could easily spend a day just strolling the streets and squares, starting with **Place d'Armes**, the old heart of the city, framed by buildings from the main epochs of Montréal's history. Much of that history was determined by the forces of commerce and the Church, represented here by lavish banks and the soaring **Basilique Notre-Dame**, while the edifices of government, including the ornate **Hôtel de Ville**, lie east along **rue Notre-Dame**. It passes the jostling tourist centre of Vieux-Montréal, **Place Jacques-Cartier**, adjacent to one of the neighbourhood's best museums: the **Musée du Château Ramezay**, which showcases hundreds of fascinating artefacts dating from the city's fur-trading days through to its financial zenith.

The old city's other, and more attractive, main thoroughfare, **rue St-Paul**, runs parallel to and south of rue Notre-Dame, extending from the intimate **Chapelle Notre-Dame-de-Bon-Secours** and silver-domed **Marché Bonsecours** (both of which also face onto the Vieux-Port and the St Lawrence) in the east to the Old Customs House in the west. The latter is part of the excellent **Musée d'Archéologie**, whose main building is located on the precise spot of Montréal's founding in 1642 and full of centuries-old artefacts excavated from the soil beneath.

Vieux-Montréal was not only the birthplace of the city's institution as a Catholic mission (see box, p.72) but was also Canada's financial and commercial hub up until the early twentieth century. Afterwards, it was largely left to decay when businesses moved to the present Downtown area in the first half of the twentieth century.

Vieux-Montréal practicalities

The best way to get to Vieux-Montréal is by the **Métro**'s orange line – Place-d'Armes is the most central station, due north of the eponymous square; to the east, Champ-de-Mars is the closest to Place Jacques-Cartier, while Square-Victoria serves the western end of the district. A **bicycle path** runs south to the end of rue Berri but you'll have to dodge pedestrians after it then turns west to run the length of the Vieux-Port. If you bring your **car**, there are parking lots on Quai King-Edward and Quai de l'Horloge ($2 per half-hour up to $12 for 12 hours), but traffic can be a nightmare, especially during the fireworks displays (see p.212) and other big events. A better bet is the parking garage under the Chaussegros de Léry building just east of the Hôtel de Ville or under the Centre de Commerce Mondial off rue St-Antoine.

The city-run **tourist office** is located on the northwest corner of Place Jacques-Cartier; see p.73 for details. Vieux-Montréal's official website is ⓦwww.vieux.montreal.qc.ca. For information on activities in the Vieux-Port, there's a counter in the front of the large pavilion on Quai Jacques-Cartier (May–Sept) and on the port area's website: ⓦwww.vieuxportdemontreal.com.

Horse-drawn *calèches* can be hired at Place d'Armes, on rue Notre-Dame est near the Hôtel de Ville and at the bottom of Place Jacques-Cartier along rue de la Commune for $35/30min and $60/1hr. If you'd prefer to hoof it, there are also regular **walking tours** of the district (see p.29) and the city publishes a self-guided tour booklet, *Discover Old Montreal*, available at the tourist office and Vieux-Montréal museums for $5.99.

The decision to hold Expo '67 on the islands facing Vieux-Montréal (see p.117) helped bring people back into the neighbourhood, kick-starting the long process of refurbishment that continues to this day with a recent explosion of boutique hotels and condo-conversions.

After the heady history of Vieux-Montréal, the **Vieux-Port** (Old Port), wedged between rue de la Commune and the St Lawrence, makes a great place to chill out, its car-free parkland providing plenty of places to sit and watch the crowds pass by. Its quays offer terrific views and, with the **Centre des Sciences de Montréal** and its **IMAX Theatre**, a good escape if the weather turns bad, especially if you've got kids in tow.

Place d'Armes and around

Start exploring at **Place d'Armes**, the square braced by rues St-Jacques and Notre-Dame that was once the financial centre of the city but which now banks mostly on tourism, thanks to its location directly in front of the Basilique Notre-Dame. In the colony's early days, the square served as both a cemetery and a common battlefield – the most legendary confrontation saw a supposedly unarmed Paul de Chomedey, Sieur de Maisonneuve, take on an armed Iroquois chief in 1644 and emerge victorious. A century later, French regiments surrendered their arms here in 1760, after the British captured the city.

The square's centrepiece is a century-old **fountain** commemorating the founding of Montréal, capped by a strident flag-bearing statue of de Maisonneuve. Among the key figures of the early colony represented on the base of the fountain, designed by sculptor Louis-Philippe Hébert, is Pilote, the dog whose barking allegedly warned de Maisonneuve and his troops of the impending 1644 Iroquois attack. You can see the Montréal flag fluttering nearby, its four emblems – French fleur-de-lys, English rose, Scottish thistle and Irish shamrock – recalling the nations that built the city.

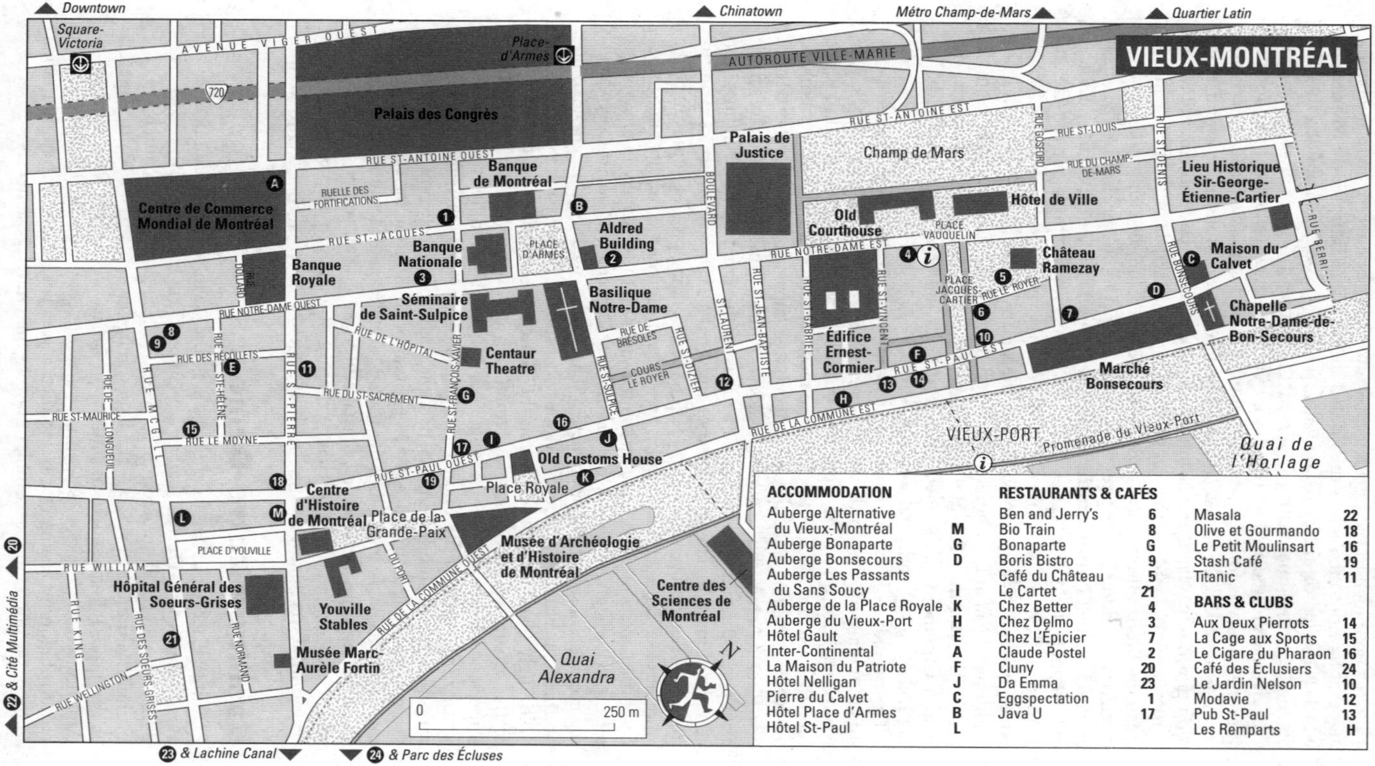

VIEUX-MONTRÉAL

ACCOMMODATION

- Auberge Alternative du Vieux-Montréal **M**
- Auberge Bonaparte **G**
- Auberge Bonsecours **D**
- Auberge Les Passants du Sans Soucy **I**
- Auberge de la Place Royale **K**
- Auberge du Vieux-Port **H**
- Hôtel Gault **E**
- Inter-Continental **A**
- La Maison du Patriote **F**
- Hôtel Nelligan **J**
- Pierre du Calvet **C**
- Hôtel Place d'Armes **B**
- Hôtel St-Paul **L**

RESTAURANTS & CAFÉS

- Ben and Jerry's **6**
- Bio Train **8**
- Bonaparte **G**
- Boris Bistro **9**
- Café du Château **5**
- Le Cartet **21**
- Chez Better **4**
- Chez Delmo **3**
- Chez L'Épicier **7**
- Claude Postel **2**
- Cluny **20**
- Da Emma **23**
- Eggspectation **1**
- Java U **17**
- Masala **22**
- Olive et Gourmando **18**
- Le Petit Moulinsart **16**
- Stash Café **19**
- Titanic **11**

BARS & CLUBS

- Aux Deux Pierrots **14**
- La Cage aux Sports **15**
- Le Cigare du Pharaon **16**
- Café des Éclusiers **24**
- Le Jardin Nelson **10**
- Modavie **12**
- Pub St-Paul **13**
- Les Remparts **H**

Downtown
Chinatown
Métro Champ-de-Mars
Quartier Latin
Square-Victoria
Place-d'Armes
Avenue Viger Ouest
Autoroute Ville-Marie
720
Palais des Congrès
Rue St-Antoine Ouest
Rue St-Antoine Est
Palais de Justice
Champ de Mars
Rue Gosford
Rue St-Louis
Rue du Champ-de-Mars
Rue St-Denis
Lieu Historique Sir-George-Étienne-Cartier
Rue Berri
Banque de Montréal
Centre de Commerce Mondial de Montréal
Ruelle des Fortifications
Rue St-Jacques
Banque Nationale
Place d'Armes
Aldred Building
Boulevard St-Laurent
Hôtel de Ville
Old Courthouse
Place Vauquelin
Rue Notre-Dame Est
Rue Notre-Dame Ouest
Château Ramezay
Maison du Calvet
Rue Bonsecours
Chapelle Notre-Dame-de-Bon-Secours
Banque Royale
Rue Dollard
Séminaire de Saint-Sulpice
Basilique Notre-Dame
Rue de Brésoles
Cours Le Royer
Rue St-Dizier
Rue St-Sulpice
Rue St-Jean-Baptiste
Rue St-Gabriel
Rue St-Vincent
Place Jacques-Cartier
Rue Le Royer
Édifice Ernest-Cormier
Rue St-Paul Est
Marché Bonsecours
Rue des Récollets
Rue Ste-Hélène
Rue de l'Hôpital
Centaur Theatre
Rue du St-Sacrement
Rue St-François-Xavier
Rue St-Pierre
Rue McGill
Rue St-Maurice
Rue de Longueuil
Rue Le Moyne
Rue de la Commune Est
Vieux-Port
Promenade du Vieux-Port
Quai de l'Horlage
Old Customs House
Rue St-Paul Ouest
Place Royale
Centre d'Histoire de Montréal
Place de la Grande-Paix
Place d'Youville
Musée d'Archéologie et d'Histoire de Montréal
Rue de la Commune Ouest
Du Port
Rue William
Hôpital Général des Soeurs-Grises
Rue King
Rue des Soeurs-Grises
Rue Normand
Rue Wellington
Youville Stables
Musée Marc-Aurèle Fortin
Centre des Sciences de Montréal
Quai Alexandra
N
0 250 m
22 & Cité Multimédia
20
23 & Lachine Canal
24 & Parc des Écluses

There's not much to the square itself – most items of interest are in the buildings that face onto it, such as the domed shrine of the **Banque de Montréal**, which is located on the north side at 119 rue St-Jacques O. Founded in 1817 by local Scottish merchants, it served the entire nation until the Bank of Canada was created in the 1930s. The current structure, built three decades after the bank was founded, is credited with initiating rue St-Jacques' development as the "Wall Street of Canada". The Banque de Montréal was by far the most glorious bank in the area; outwardly modelled on the Pantheon in Rome, it has interior chambers that reek of opulence with deluxe marble counters, gleaming bronze fittings and dark green syenite columns with gilt Corinthian capitals supporting an ornate coffered ceiling. Off to the left of the main entrance, a small **Numismatic Museum** (Mon–Fri 10am–4pm; free) displays old account books, banknotes and coins – be sure to check out the cheque written on sealskin. Several of the other banks that comprised Canada's Wall Street presided over the blocks west of the square, their ornate facades adorned with carved garlands, elaborate lintels and detailed cornices – a style exemplified by the **Banque Royale** at 360 rue St-Jacques, the tallest building in the British Commonwealth when erected in 1928 and possessing a central banking hall of almost cathedral-like grandeur.

The east side of Place d'Armes is equally imposing, starting with the red-sandstone building on the northeast corner built in 1888 for the **New York Life Insurance Company**. At eight storeys high, it was the city's first skyscraper, though you won't be able to check the view – access is limited to the dimly lit lobby, whose ceiling is stamped with handsome copper mouldings. Next door, at 507 Place d'Armes, the 23-storey Art Deco **Aldred Building** is the city's finest example of the ziggurat style made famous by the Empire State Building, both completed in 1931. The set-back roof answered a 1929 city ordinance mandating that structures over ten storeys design their building profiles to maximize the amount of sunlight let onto nearby streets. Its streamlined verticality and simplified ornamentation marked the first shift away from the classically inspired architecture that still gives Vieux-Montréal much of its character. The Art Deco detailing continues inside the lobby, where a stained-glass window casts a golden hue on the copper and brass friezes of swallows sitting atop telegraph poles.

The ugly black monolith housing the **Banque Nationale** on the west side of the square would be nothing more than an eyesore but for its symbolic importance. Towering over its neighbours, the 1967 building is seen as representing the power of the Francophone business class over their former oppressors, the Church and the English. Its vault, the black granite box jutting out on the opposite side from Place d'Armes, is suspended in the air to make it near impossible to break into. Until the tower's installation, little thought was given to conserving the architectural heritage here, so at least one positive aspect is that it provided a catalyst to change the planning laws to emphasize the conservation of the neighbourhood's historic character.

Basilique Notre-Dame

Framing Place d'Armes to the south is the twin-towered, Gothic-Revival **Basilique Notre-Dame** (daily 7am–5pm; $3, light show $10; ⓣ514/842-2925, ⓦwww.basiliquenddm.org; Métro Place-d'Armes), church of the Catholic faithful since 1829 – the largest religious building in North America at the time. It made such an impression on its architect, a Protestant Irish-American named James O'Donnell, that he converted to Catholicism six months before its inauguration. He died a year later and is buried in a rather unprepossessing (and inaccessible) grave in the church basement.

The basilica is for some reason often compared to Notre-Dame-de-Paris, but more closely resembles Westminster Abbey, thanks to its severe towers, named La Persévérance and La Tempérance (neither is open to the public). Persévérance, the westernmost of the two, holds the twelve-ton Jean-Baptiste bell affectionately called *le Gros Bourdon* (the big bumblebee), which required twelve bell-ringers to get it moving before electricity was installed. Though rarely rung nowadays – the former Prime Minister Trudeau's state funeral in 2000 was a notable exception – its low rumbling peals could be heard as far as 25km away in the days before urban development blocked the sound.

The lushness of the vast interior comes as a surprise after the stern exterior. For its first four decades or so it was equally austere until Victor Bourgeau drew inspiration from the Ste-Chapelle in Paris to embellish it in a lush French Catholic manner. The basilica positively explodes with colour, the wooden mouldings above the 3500-seat vault painted in dense blues, reds, golds and greens. The vibrant blue ribs adorned with hundreds of gold-leaf stars give the impression of sitting under a midnight sky, while light from three rose windows located, unusually, in the ceiling combine with flickering votive candle flames to create a sense of intense warmth and intimacy. The rich hues of the stained-glass windows portray the colony's early days – to the right of the altar, de Maisonneuve carries the cross to the top of the mountain.

About halfway toward the altar, you'll find an ornately decorated staircase leading up to the pulpit; the base is guarded by Louis-Philippe Hébert's exceptional woodcarvings of the prophets. Backlit in brilliant cobalt blue light, the soaring altar itself is a masterpiece of detailing by Frenchman Henri Bouriché, whose exquisite sculptures of biblical figures themed on the Eucharist have Christ's crucifixion as the focal point.

Behind the altar lies the surprisingly bright and modern **Chapelle Sacré-Coeur**, fondly referred to as the Wedding Chapel – up to five weddings a day are held here on summer weekends. Destroyed by an arsonist in 1978, the ground floor's delicately carved walls and richly embellished capitals supporting the mezzanine were reconstructed to the original design, while the upper layers – including a pine-panelled vault that fairly glows – are decidedly modern. Against the back wall, an enormous 16-metre-high bronze altarpiece by Charles Daudelin depicts man's progression from birth to heaven, the gates of which are represented by the sweeping wings of a dove over Christ's head.

Time your first visit so that you can catch the "And then there was light" *son et lumière* spectacle, which details the early history of the church and colony on giant screens before they are drawn back to reveal the interior architecture in all its glory, with artful lighting emphasizing its architectural features. The basilica provides an equally resplendent setting for concerts by the Orchestre Symphonique de Montréal and other classical ensembles (see p.185). Otherwise, to get the most out of your visit, take one of the free twenty-minute guided tours that start every half-hour or so from the reception desk near the entrance.

Séminaire de St-Sulpice

Adjoining the presbytery on the western side of the basilica is Vieux-Montréal's oldest building, the mock-medieval **Séminaire de St-Sulpice**, whose main doorway is topped by North America's oldest public clock, installed in 1701. The central part of the building dates from 1685 and was built as the headquarters of the Paris-based order of Sulpician priests that instigated Montréal's establishment as a religious colony and held title to the island for two centuries (see box, overleaf). There is no public access to the building: 25 Sulpicians still live there today and maintain the basilica.

Messieurs de Montréal

Montréal was originally conceived and run as a French religious colony, a plan that entailed the conversion of the many Natives – particularly Iroquois and Algonquin – to Catholicism. This momentous task fell to a group of missionaries, the **Messieurs de St-Sulpice**, an order of Sulpician priests trained in a seminary outside Paris.

It was a question of finances and determination more than anything else that led the Sulpicians to win spiritual dominion of Montréal. Their supporters had deep pockets and, crucially, eagerly emptied them when informed of the personal spiritual rewards to be gained from the practice. The first four priests to arrive came ashore in 1657 with a tidy sum of 75,000 *livres* and went on to found the parish of Notre-Dame. Their influence stretched beyond the sacred when they were given title to the island as its *seigneurs* in 1663, allowing them to rent it out to tenants. This system hampered efforts by industrial and mercantile barons to develop the land and, in tandem with other reforms, the Sulpician's right of seigneury was rescinded in 1859. Headquartered at the **Séminaire de St-Sulpice**, the society's seemingly endless funds had a lasting impact on the city's public face. On a civic note, they contributed to the city's urban planning – one needed roads, after all, to get the faithful to church, school and hospital – and the creation of many Montréal streets, like **rue St-Paul** (see p.77), can be credited to Sulpician leader François Dollier de Casson. Domestically, the Sulpicians funded the creation of the **Maison St-Gabriel** (see p.124), the eventual home and school of the *filles du roi* – women sent from the motherland to help populate the colony (see p.126). The priests would also assure their longevity by training newcomers at a facility built for the purpose in 1840, the **Grand Séminaire**, located northwest of Downtown; over 6000 priests have studied in its hallowed halls since its inception.

Not surprisingly, the most obvious remnants of Sulpician rule are the churches the order's alms helped erect. The most significant of these can still be visited in Vieux-Montréal: the **Chapelle Notre-Dame-de-Bon-Secours**, which received construction subsidies from the priests, and the 1829 **Basilique Notre-Dame**, arguably the Sulpicians' most lasting contribution to Montréal architecture and religious history. The basilica is certainly their only sanctified domain today – managed by what few Sulpician priests remain in Montréal.

Rue St-Sulpice, rue le Royer and the Palais de Justice

From the basilica, head south along **rue St-Sulpice**, a street rife with history. Many of the continent's first explorers lived here, and while some of the houses are today still private residences – those that aren't have been converted into shops – they are embellished with a variety of sometimes hard-to-spot historical plaques. Daniel Greysolon, Sieur du Lhut – the man for whom Duluth, Minnesota was named – lodged in the corner building at 88 rue Notre-Dame in 1675. Also, the Le Moyne brothers, who founded the American cities of Biloxi, Mobile and New Orleans, as well as the colony of Louisiana, were born and raised at no. 404.

About halfway down the street on the east side is **rue le Royer**, an austere courtyard lined with late-nineteenth-century warehouses that recall Montréal's past as a major shipping port. The site of Montréal's first hospital, it was run by nuns who later made a fortune building the warehouses and then renting them out. They were converted into offices and apartments about three decades ago, the first such development in the revival of Vieux-Montréal.

Walking to the courtyard's far end will bring you to boulevard St-Laurent, from which it's a short block north to the intersection with rue Notre-Dame. Running the length of Vieux-Montréal and along the south side of Place d'Armes, rue Notre-Dame is home to the city's main administrative bodies. The region east of boulevard St-Laurent is presided over by the mammoth **Palais de Justice**, the courthouse that handles most legal cases today. Two different courthouses in its shadow once did legal duty, the first being the **Old Courthouse**, at 155 rue Notre-Dame E, which was built by the British in 1856, and designed to look like a Greek temple. The third storey and incongruous grey dome were added 35 years later. Across the street at no. 100 is the other courthouse, the colonnaded **Édifice Ernest-Cormier**, which held criminal trials after the courts were separated in 1926. Massive bronze doors embossed with the symbols of justice guard the entrance to what had been converted into a music conservatory and was only recently renovated for the appellate court. Further along, at no. 160, the **Maison de la Sauvegarde**, built in 1800 with a rough-hewn limestone facade, high chimneys and steeply pitched roof and dormers, is one of the last houses built in the local French style, which persisted for four decades after the English conquest. Typical of the period, shops occupied the ground floor and the merchant and his family resided above.

Place Jacques-Cartier

The main activity on rue Notre-Dame est is found east of the courthouses, around the cobblestoned **Place Jacques-Cartier**, which served as the city's public market from 1804 to 1960 and stretches down to the Vieux-Port (see p.81). The only echo of its former use are the few small stalls selling flowers and prints at the square's north end daily throughout the summer. Most of the action now is in the form of buskers and artists hustling for change from the crowds that swarm to the square's bustling restaurants and terrace-fronted cafés. The city-run tourist office (early June to early Sept 9am–7pm; early Sept to early June 9am–5pm) occupies the stone building at the square's northwest corner, while off its lower reaches is tiny **rue St-Amable**, infested with watercolour-hawkers but providing access to a shady courtyard where jewellery stalls offer some decent artisan-crafted pieces.

The **Nelson Monument** at the north end of the square features a likeness of Admiral Nelson atop a drab column one-third the height of its better-known London counterpart. The statue is interesting less because of its composition than the controversy that continues to dog it. Funded by a group of Montréal Anglophones delighted at Nelson's defeat of the French at Trafalgar in 1805, it later became a source of sovereignist ire, reminding some of British colonialism. A faction plotted to blow the statue up as early as 1890, and grumbling about it continued well into the 1970s, when the surrounding taverns were hotbeds of sovereignist activity. Debate renewed as recently as 1997, when the city proposed moving it to a faraway Anglophone neighbourhood. Public opposition allowed Nelson to keep his spot, although he still came down from his perch for two years for cleaning. The statue there now is actually a reproduction of the original; it turned out Nelson was so weather-ravaged he had to be replaced.

Place Vauquelin and Champ de Mars

Facing Place Jacques-Cartier on the north side of rue Notre-Dame, the intimate **Place Vauquelin** features the Francophone answer to the Nelson Monument: a statue of French naval commander Jean Vauquelin, who harried

A fortified city

Even though Vieux-Montréal was a walled fortress for over a century, all that remains of the **fortifications** that once surrounded it are stretches in the Champ de Mars and an extensive chunk inside the Musée d'Archéologie et d'Histoire (its former course is also marked in the paving elsewhere). The first wall, a 2800-metre-long row of cedar posts, was erected in 1687 to protect against Iroquois attack. The structure ended up being more useful as firewood, and by 1713 it was deemed an insufficient barrier against the city's new enemy: the British. Construction on new walls began soon after, and by 1744 the city was wrapped in a stone cocoon that measured about 4m high in places. Those thirty-odd years of labour proved unnecessary, though – the war they were built to defend against was fought in Québec City in 1759 (see p.242). When the British took over the colony, they dropped Montréal as the military centre and focused on fortifying the capital. In 1796, a public petition requested that the walls, by then unkempt and blocking the town's expansion, be demolished. The public's will was approved in 1801, and the walls came down after an act was passed to advance the city's "Salubrity, Convenience and Embellishment" – official-speak for urban development.

the British during the Seven Years' War. Once the site of the city jail, Place Vauquelin has been a public space since 1858 and is outfitted with a pretty fountain surrounded by stone and wood benches.

At the square's north end, a set of stairs leads down to the **Champ de Mars**, a grassy expanse named for the god of war, though the only action it ever experienced consisted of military drills. By the 1820s, the park became a public promenade that Montrealers took to in their finest Sunday dress and was also, ironically, the city's favoured spot for public hangings. Though converted into a car park in the early twentieth century, it was transformed back into parkland in honour of the city's 350th anniversary, when remains of the **stone fortifications** that once surrounded the city were excavated (see box above) – you can see the parallel scarp and counterscarp cutting through the grass.

Hôtel de Ville

East of Place Vauquelin hulks the immense **Hôtel de Ville** at 275 rue Notre-Dame E (Mon–Fri 8am–5pm; free; Métro Champ-de-Mars). The building itself is quite opulent for a city hall, with its mansard roof and turreted entranceway, and the interior is just as impressive after renovations following a serious fire in 1922 were undertaken in the Beaux-Arts style. These produced the grand two-storey-high Hall of Honour adorned with bronze railings and marble pilasters, and overhung with an immense (and hideous) bronze chandelier. The bronze statues of a man sowing seed and a woman carting a wooden bucket flanking the entrance foyer were done by Alfred Laliberté and intended as a reminder of Québec's agrarian past. If the municipal government isn't in session, take a peek into the council chambers, where five stained-glass windows depict Montréal at the beginning of the twentieth century in mauve-tinted hues.

The Hôtel de Ville's second-floor balcony was chosen by French **President de Gaulle** as the launchpad for his incendiary rallying cry, "Vive le Québec libre!" during his state visit to Expo '67. His words left the city's Anglophones reeling at the thought that Québec was on its way to independent status and rekindled Francophones with a political fervour that peaked with the 1970 October Crisis (see p.271). French presidents have since then stayed notably mum – publicly anyway – as to their views on Québec's independence.

Musée du Château Ramezay and around

The history of the **Château Ramezay** (June–Aug daily 10am–6pm; Sept–May Tues–Sun 10am–4.30pm; $7; ⓣ514/861-3708, ⓦwww.chateauramezay.qc.ca; Métro Champ-de-Mars), the low, fieldstone manor house opposite the Hôtel de Ville at 280 rue Notre-Dame E is as interesting as the articles now on display in its many chambers. When built in 1705 for the eleventh governor of Montréal, Claude de Ramezay, it was the finest of the colony's 200 homes. It then served as the North American headquarters of the Compagnie des Indes Occidentales, a fur-trading company, before passing into the hands of the British after the conquest in 1760. Fifteen year later, Benjamin Franklin and his cohorts set up shop here during the fleeting American invasion and attempted to persuade the young colony to join the United States.

Since 1895, the Ramezay has served as a historical **museum**, and its lack of pretension is tremendously appealing. Many of the displayed artefacts from the eighteenth and nineteenth centuries have a genuinely used feel about them – an eighteenth-century missionary's prayerbook is weather-stained and leather firemen's hats are creased from wear. These items contrast with the glistening beaver-pelt top hat and other well-preserved relics of the upper classes. Their portraits hang alongside old maps like Lord Dorchester's 1795 vision of Québec with very un-Québécois county names like Kent and Buckinghamshire. Nearby is a Dion-Bouton, a turn-of-the-century luxury car that apparently so confused city authorities that they refused to provide a carriage permit for it, instead granting the owner a bicycle licence – a state of affairs rectified a few years later when it received the province's first licence plate, "Q1". In the whitewashed vaults downstairs, the exhibits take on more of an educational slant, recreating domestic scenes that include a kitchen with a dog-powered roasting spit.

But even if these don't interest you, the Ramezay's reconstruction of the **Salle de Nantes** of the Compagnie des Indes Occidentales is alone worth the entrance fee. The two-room salon has walls of rich mahogany imported from their headquarters in Nantes, France, lavishly textured with rose trellises, cherubs and musical instruments. It's the work of Germain Boffrand (principal architect for Louis XIV and Louis XV), and the Ramezay honours the salon's musical theme by putting on concerts here the last Sunday of the month (free with museum admission; call ⓣ514/861-3708 for information). Fieldstone walls surround the small gardens in back, recently laid out in the traditional manner; in summer, you can observe the gardens while sitting at the terrace café (see p.151).

Lieu Historique Sir-George-Étienne-Cartier

A five-minute walk east from Château Ramezay brings you to the edge of Vieux-Montréal. At 458 rue Notre-Dame E, the **Lieu Historique Sir-George-Étienne-Cartier** (late May to Aug daily 10am–6pm; Sept to late Dec & April to late May Wed–Sun 10am–noon & 1–5pm; $4; ⓣ514/283-2282, ⓦwww.parkscanada.gc.ca/cartier; Métro Champ-de-Mars) comprises two adjoining houses that were inhabited by the Cartier family between 1848 and 1871. Sir George-Étienne Cartier was one of the fathers of Confederation, persuading the French-Canadians to join the Dominion of Canada. Today, leaders of Québec nationalism decry Cartier as a collaborator, and the displays in the east house diplomatically skirt over the issue of whether he was right or wrong and instead emphasize his role in the construction of Canada's railways. Such conservatism is carried out in a decidedly bizarre fashion, however:

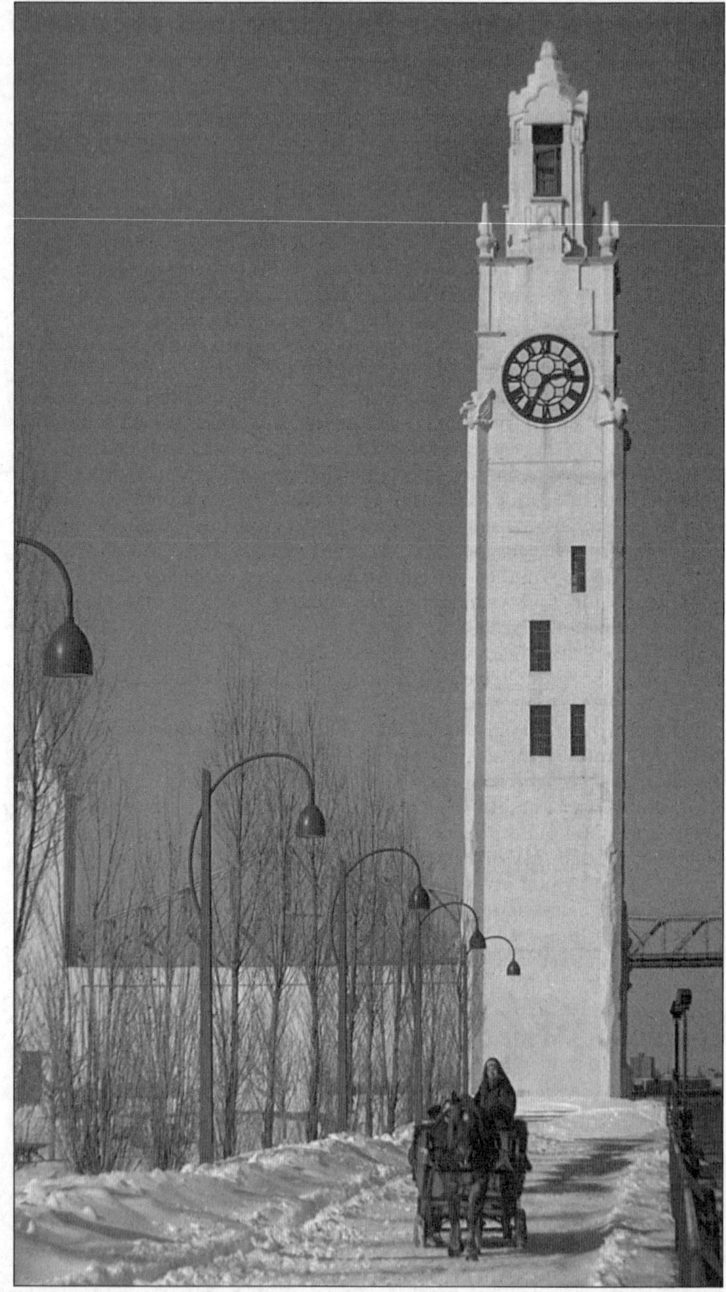

△ Tour de l'Horloge

Muppet-like figures represent the founding fathers on the main floor, while eight white-painted papier-mâché models of Cartier himself sit around in different poses at a glass-domed, round table upstairs. The stuffily decorated rooms in the west house re-create the period when Sir George lived here, though in no less hokey a manner: original domestic objects are tied around a dinner theme and recordings of monologues by fictitious house staff start playing once you walk into the rooms. They do, however, dish out the odd bit of salacious gossip, like Cartier's penchant for staying at the nearby Rasco Hotel rather than at home.

Rue St-Paul and around

One block south of the Cartier museum is one of the city's oldest and most attractive thoroughfares, **rue St-Paul**, which runs parallel to rue Notre-Dame the length of Vieux-Montréal. The nineteenth-century commercial buildings and Victorian lampposts that line rue St-Paul look much the same today as they did back when Charles Dickens stayed at the **Rasco Hotel** (now an office building) at nos. 281–295 in 1842. Many of the street's storefront windows house upscale art galleries, antique stores and clothing boutiques, with some tacky souvenir shops thrown in. But if you walk around to the back of these buildings on rue de la Commune – which parallels rue St-Paul just to the south and faces the Vieux-Port – you'll note that several of them resemble warehouses from the rear. It's an architectural trompe l'oeil that reflects the habits of the time, when goods were delivered to the back and sold in the front.

The street's most attractive building is the three-storey **Maison du Calvet**, at 409 rue St-Paul E, built in 1725 for the American Revolution supporter Pierre du Calvet. The house, now part of the inn that bears his name (see p.137), is the city's finest example of French domestic architecture, retaining two of the style's most distinctive characteristics: exterior stone walls that extend past the rooftop and "S"-shaped irons inset into the walls. The walls were built higher to prevent blazes from spreading between houses, and the irons are anchors – they connect to rods that hold the opposing fieldstone walls in place.

Kitty-corner to the Maison du Calvet, the splendid silver-domed **Marché Bonsecours** at 350 rue St-Paul E (Ⓦwww.marchebonsecours.qc.ca), is Vieux-Montréal's quintessential marketplace. Erected in 1846 as an interior counterpart to Place Jacques-Cartier's outdoor market, its upper floor served a very brief stint as United Canada's House of Parliament and was Montréal's City Hall for a few decades in the 1800s. Produce stalls bustled on the ground floor until 1964. After being taken over entirely by municipal offices, the building was restored to its former duty as a marketplace in 1992 and now houses very high-priced designer boutiques and commercial art galleries. If you're looking for more affordable shopping, try the blocks west of boulevard St-Laurent, where galleries offer anything from incredibly cheesy landscapes to vibrant contemporary works and even oriental art.

Chapelle Notre-Dame-de-Bon-Secours

Facing Maison du Calvet at 400 rue St-Paul E is the delicate and profusely steepled **Chapelle Notre-Dame-de-Bon-Secours**, its fieldstone walls supporting six copper-and-stone spires of various heights. The location near the St Lawrence earned it the nickname of the Sailors' Church, and mariners would endow it with model ships as thanks for having safely reached the shore – many of these are still on display as votive lamps hanging in the nave. The chapel, which served as Montréal's first church, was initiated by **Sœur Marguerite Bourgeoys** (see below) in 1655. The structure you see today, though, postdates her by some seventy years as it was rebuilt in 1771 following a serious fire. Inside the chapel, white marble panels and pilasters lend it an airy feel while overhead the vault's light grey and sepia tones make it hard to discern what are structural arches or merely painted decoration. To the left of the marble altar, a wax statue of Bourgeoys reposes in a glass-sided coffin – the tiny wooden statue of the Virgin and Child above was given to her in 1672.

Musée Marguerite-Bourgeoys

Adjacent to the chapel, a **museum** (May–Oct Tues–Sun 10am–5pm; Nov to mid-Jan & mid-March to April 11am–3.30pm; $6; ⓣ514/282-8670, ⓦwww.marguerite-bourgeoys.com; Métro Champ-de-Mars) devoted to Bourgeoys adds a touching note; one small room is filled with 58 handcrafted miniature doll scenes that tell her life's story, from birth to death. She arrived in Montréal in 1653 and quickly set to work as a teacher, founder of the colony's first school (in a stable donated by de Maisonneuve) and driving force behind the chapel's construction. She also established the farm and vocational school in Pointe St-Charles that helped women (including the King's Wards – see p.126) to establish homes and adopt to the harsh life of the colony. For all this, she was known as the "Mother of the Colony" and her piety eventually led her to become Canada's first saint, in 1982.

The museum itself isn't all that exciting, but it's the only way to gain access to the narrow staircase leading up 69 steps to the small **aerial chapel**, which gives excellent views over the port and the crammed network of streets around the church. A further flight leads to an open-air belvedere with glorious views.

Pointe-à-Callière and Place Royale

Montréal is one of those rare cities that can pinpoint the exact location on which it was founded: **Pointe-à-Callière** a triangular spit of land that juts out into rue de la Commune (the shoreline of the St Lawrence in the mid-1600s) at the western edge of Vieux-Montréal, a 10–15-minute walk from the Marché Bonsecours. But while the founding's location is clear, the precise date of the event is slightly murky – the only thing for sure is that it happened mid-May, 1642. It proved an ill-fated spot, prone to flooding, so the colony was moved a little to the north across the Petite Rivière St-Pierre (now channelled below Place d'Youville), near present-day **Place Royale**. From its earliest days, Place Royale was a meeting space, serving first as an Indian campground, then the site for annual fur-trading fairs in the colony's early days, and later as a marketplace and a public square replete with fountain and gardens fronting the Neoclassical Customs House. It may appear fairly drab today but beneath the raised expanse of granite paving stones lies one of the Musée d'Archéologie's highlights.

Musée d'Archéologie et d'Histoire de Montréal

Visible the length of the Vieux-Port, the splendid main building of the **Musée d'Archéologie et d'Histoire de Montréal**, 350 Place Royale (late June to early Sept Mon–Fri 10am–6pm, Sat and Sun 11am–6pm; early Sept to late June Tues–Fri 10am–5pm, Sat & Sun 11am–5pm; $10, $16.50 for two at the gift shop only; ⓣ514/872-9150, ⓦwww.pacmuseum.qc.ca; Métro Square-Victoria) rises up from the point of de Maisonneuve's landing, looking much like a ship that's run ashore. Inside the contemporary limestone structure, the boat motif carries on with finishing touches like portholes that are inset in the entrance floor, and industrial stairwells connecting the building's four levels. The name of the edifice equally captures its shipping theme – it's known as the **Éperon** (cutwater).

The museum has three main components: the Éperon, the underground archeological crypt and the **Old Customs House**, a Neoclassical building from the 1830s that backs on to rue St-Paul. Temporary exhibits are hosted on the first floors of the Éperon and the Customs House, and the café on the top floor of the former offers great views of the port. The crypt is a series of underground passageways and rooms – all of which connects the basements of the Éperon and Customs House buildings, passing below Place Royale en route – and is where you'll find the museum's stellar collection of archeological finds excavated from the soil surrounding the buildings between 1983 and 1992.

Before heading to the subterranean exhibits, start your visit with the fifteen-minute-long multimedia history presentation in the Éperon's main-floor theatre. By far the best way to experience the rest of the museum is on one of the free hour-long guided tours that begin at the ground-floor ticket desk (Sat 1.30pm, but call ahead as this may change). Otherwise, the interactive map downstairs can help you get your bearings.

Once downstairs, the most riveting find is a Catholic **cemetery** dating from 1643 – the oldest vestiges of the original settlement – discovered during the construction of the present-day Éperon building in 1989. Some 38 bodies were buried on this site, although only seven of the gravesites have been unearthed thus far. You can see the impressions left in the clay by the coffins but not the remains – the one skeleton not washed away by centuries of floods has been removed. Traces of three generations of buildings dating back as far as 1796 can be found layered on top of one another within the labyrinth of foundations, interspersed with exhibits of beads, eighteenth-century wine bottles and other artefacts left behind by the site's occupants. Keep an eye out for the subterranean windows – evidence that the street level today is three metres higher than it was centuries ago.

Further along (as you pass below Place d'Youville), a walkway takes you over an eighteenth-century water main and sewage system lined with cobblestones, the tamed **Petite Rivière St-Pierre** that threatened the first inhabitants with inundation – during the spring thaw, the sewer still gets filled. Beyond that, an exhibition chamber contains five intricate scale models of the surrounding area from different time periods. Set under glass below the floor, they illustrate the area's history from when only Natives roamed the grassy shores up to the late 1800s, and provide some guidance to the jumble of stone remains nearby, below Place Royale itself. Beside the privy pipe of an inn built in 1800 on the ruins of the fortifications, steps lead to a catwalk passing over and through earlier foundations, where spotlights highlight traces of seventeenth-century stockade posts and a stretch of eighteenth-century cobblestone street. From here, you can take the stairs up to the Old Customs House, home of the museum's gift shop and a couple of dull exhibitions on trade and the Customs House's own history.

Place d'Youville and around

Directly west of the archeology museum stands **Place d'Youville**, a narrow public square constructed atop the former watercourse of the little river (and later sewer) that is still visible from inside the museum. The square's eastern end was renamed **Place de la Grande-Paix** in 2001, to mark the tricentennial of

Renting wheels in the Vieux-Port

A bicycle or a pair of rollerblades not only makes scouting out the Vieux-Port's kilometre and a half of parkland less tiring, they also provide an ideal excuse to head out west through the former industrial heartland along the Lachine Canal's bike path (see p.128) or to wend your way over to the islands (see Chapter Seven, "Parc Jean-Drapeau"). Although there are also sillier (four-wheel buggies) and more expensive (motorized scooters) options, you're best to stick to bikes or blades, available from Vélo Aventure on the Quai des Convoyeurs, 100m west of Quai King-Edward (☎514/847-0666, Ⓦwww.veloaventure.com) and Ça Roule, 27 rue de la Commune E, facing Quai King-Edward (☎514/866-0633, Ⓦwww.caroulemontreal.com). Both charge $8–9/hr for blades, though Ça Roule is cheaper for longer periods ($20/24hrs versus $25–30/24hrs). For bike rental, Vélo Aventure has the better deal in the short term ($7–7.50/hr versus $8–9/hr), though they even out for an 8-hour day's rental at around $20–25. Note that the higher prices are for weekend rentals. Both also offer lessons and guided tours. Montréal En-Ligne Sport, 55 rue de la Commune O (☎514/849-5211) also rents bikes and in-line skates but its rates are a bit higher.

the Great Peace of Montréal, a treaty signed here to end the conflict between the Natives and French settlers. Passing the century-old "Founder's Obelisk", keep an eye out for the entrance to the **Youville Stables** on your left. The name is a misnomer – the 1825 complex of gardens, shady courtyard and stone buildings, which today houses yuppified restaurants and offices, was in fact a warehouse – the stables were next door. It's a nice enough place to stop in at if you're walking by, but not worth going out of your way for.

Further along and dividing the square in two is a converted red-brick fire station housing the **Centre d'Histoire de Montréal** (May–Aug Tues–Sun 10am–5pm, Sept–April Wed–Sun 10am–5pm; $4.50; Ⓦwww.ville.montreal.qc.ca/chm; Métro Square-Victoria), which focuses on the city's social history. Inside, displays depict Montréal from the first European settlement to its present expansions – fine for a sketchy overview but not terribly engaging. The competing soundtracks of films shown in the warren of rooms upstairs (includ-

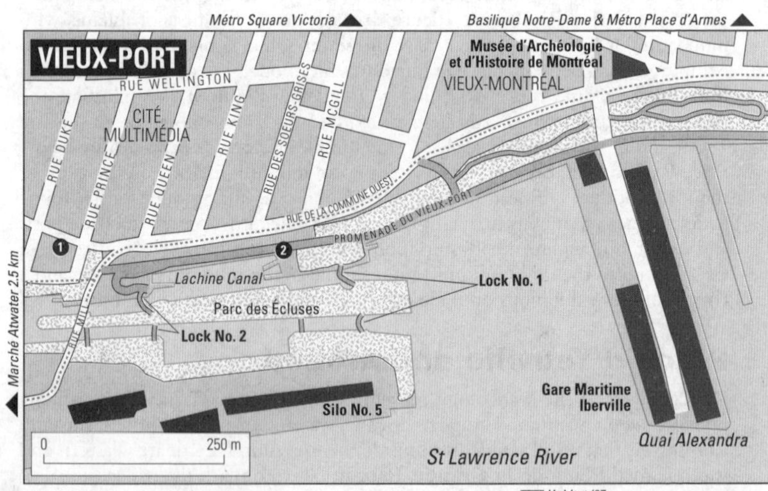

ing a locker room and a kitchen circa 1950) attempt to capture daily life in Montréal – the most amusing of these displays is the mock tram with images scrolling past the windows as a bus driver's voice calls out the stops.

The barren car park covering the western half of Place d'Youville gives no indication that this was once a marketplace, which also served as the Parliament of United Canada from 1844 until it was torched by Tory rioters in 1849. To the south, between rues St-Pierre and Normand, the **Hôpital Général des Soeurs-Grises** cared for the colony's sick, old and orphaned children, though all that remains of the original H-shaped structure is the west wing and half of the late-seventeenth-century chapel's stone walls – its original footprint is marked out in paving stones on rue St-Pierre. Next door, the **Musée Marc-Aurèle Fortin**, at no. 118 (Tues–Sun 11am–5pm; $5), is a small gallery dedicated to the prolific Québécois landscape painter of the early to mid-twentieth century who considered himself the first to found a "Canadian school" that wasn't influenced by Europeans. Judging by the mundane works inside, he probably could have used the help.

The Vieux-Port

Running the full length of Vieux-Montréal, between rue de la Commune and the St Lawrence, the **Vieux-Port** (Old Port) was once the most important harbour in Canada, its strategic location at the head of the Lachine Canal that connected ships with the Great Lakes assuring its maritime dominance for centuries. The construction of the St Lawrence Seaway in 1959 – allowing ships to bypass the canal altogether – ended the Vieux-Port's glory days, leaving it to deteriorate for three decades. Refurbishment came about in the early 1990s, as part of the city's 350th birthday celebration, and the parkland that was created turned this stretch of waterfront into one of Montréal's most idyllic playgrounds. The area is graced with superb biking, cross-country skiing and rollerblading paths (see box opposite for where to rent wheels) that offer spectacular vistas onto the waterfront to the south and the former warehouses lining rue de la Commune to the north.

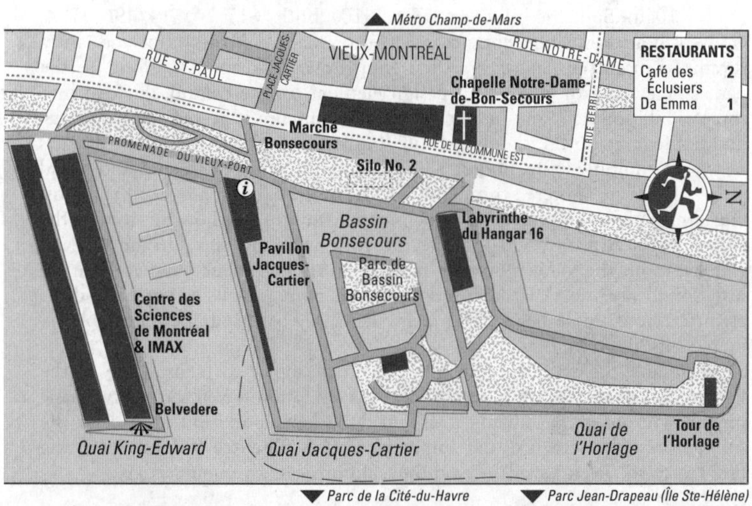

Traces still remain of the port's former shipping duties in the ghostly junkyard remnants of grain elevator **Silo no. 2**, at the port's eastern end, and the **Tour de l'Horloge**, a watchtower completed in 1922. But these sights are largely overlooked by those in search of summertime activities, like pedal-boating the calm waters of the **Bassin Bonsecours**, a protected reservoir that cascades into the St Lawrence. Fronting the massive Silo no. 5, the narrow **Parc des Écluses** marks the start of the Lachine Canal – recently reopened to pleasure boats – and its **bike path**, which embarks from the port's westernmost end. Overlooking the first set of locks, a striking wedge-shaped pavilion is home to a waterside terrace café and viewing balcony. The activity all but dies out come winter, or at least moves indoors to the cavernous halls on the **Quai King-Edward**, where a portside hangar incorporates the interactive science exhibits of the **Centre de Sciences de Montréal** and its **IMAX theatre**.

Quai King-Edward and the Centre des Sciences de Montréal

The lively **Quai King-Edward** at the southernmost end of boulevard St-Laurent is the hub of the Vieux-Port and a good place to start your waterfront explorations. The area immediately west of the quay is lined with a row of bright stalls whose stock of antique books and etchings occasionally yields a find. The real estate to the east of the quay is equally colourful, with caricaturists and musicians on hand to amuse passers-by. If you want to get away from the hubbub, walk to the southernmost end of the quay and take the stairs over the car park to reach a quiet **lookout** point.

Here, you can get a rare panoramic view of the city stretching north to the mountain and south to the islands of the St Lawrence. To your right and across from the Vieux-Port, on a long spit jutting into the St Lawrence, are the staggered Cubist blocks that comprise **Habitat**, a unique apartment complex built for Expo '67 by Moshe Safdie, who later designed the new pavilion at the Musée des Beaux-Arts (see p.62). Next to Habitat is the **Parc de la Cité-de-Havre**, a little-known getaway accessible by car or bicycle via industrial rue Mill at the port's western end; the bridge you see links the Habitat and park to Île Ste-Hélène and Île Notre-Dame (see Chapter Seven, "Parc Jean-Drapeau"), across the St Lawrence.

The port's main indoor attraction is the **Centre des Sciences de Montréal** (daily 10am–5pm; exhibit or film $10, both $17; ⓣ514/496-4724, ⓦwww.montrealsciencecentre.com; Métro Place-d'Armes), located in a revamped industrial hangar on Quai King-Edward (keep an eye out for the panels describing the high-tech design elements of the centre). Divided into three exhibition halls, the interactive science museum is geared towards families and focuses on the themes of Life, Information and Matter, with displays heavy on multimedia technology – interactive touch screens, and audio and video players are scattered throughout. Most of the exhibits are dull – the most engaging activities in the upstairs Technocité exhibit show how to produce the perfect paper airplane and let you record your own radio show. In the adjacent Eureka! room, the focus is on pure rather than applied science, and you can see how soundwaves work by talking to someone 50m away using parabolic dishes or test how a pole helps tightrope-walkers stay balanced (a comfortable six inches off the ground).

Downstairs, the interactive movie game will appeal to teens while in the Dynamo's Lair interactive playground, kids aged four to seven learn about basic physics without even realizing it. If you don't have kids, head instead for the seven-storey film screen of the complex's **IMAX Theatre** (English screening times vary, so check ahead) – even the 2D films can give you vertigo.

Quai Jacques-Cartier and Quai de l'Horloge

Heading eastwards, the next pier along is the **Quai Jacques-Cartier**. There are no attractions per se here but you'll find an information booth, grounds that host summertime concerts and the departure points for ferries to Parc Jean-Drapeau (see box, p.117) and various river cruises (see p.30). This is also where **Cirque du Soleil** pitches their big top when they're in town (see p.187). A walkway at the end of the pier gives a great view of Alexander Calder's colossal grey planar sculpture, *Man*, and the tracery of the Biosphère on Île Ste-Hélène, and connects to the more tranquil **Parc du Bassin Bonsecours** with its bridges arching over pedal-boaters in summer ($5.40 per half-hour per person) and ice-skaters in winter.

The easternmost, L-shaped pier, **Quai de l'Horloge**, serves as the departure point for wild and wet excursions to the Lachine Rapids (see p.127) and is presided over by the simple **Tour de l'Horloge**, a sandstone clock tower that rises 65m above sea level. The views of Vieux-Montréal, the islands and Mont Royal from its highest platform are superb, but it's a workout to get there – there are nearly 200 steps and the last fifty or so are quite narrow and steep. The lookout point on the grounds immediately east of the tower is an excellent spot to watch the annual fireworks competition (see p.212).

3

The Quartier Latin and the Village

Before rue Ste-Catherine plunges from Downtown into the eastern suburbs, it passes through the **Quartier Latin**, the haunt of Francophone university students, and the **Village**, home to the city's gay and lesbian community. Both are exciting, vibrant districts filled with cafés, restaurants and boutiques and thronged with revellers passing from bar to bar in the evenings. And while both have also undergone a number of changes through the years, they seem to have gone in opposite directions – whereas the Quartier Latin has changed from a district of the intellectual bourgeoisie in the nineteenth century to having a more downmarket, studenty vibe, the formerly working-class, industrial Centre-Sud district from which the Village evolved is on the upswing as gentrification sets in.

Quartier Latin

Like its Parisian counterpart, Montréal's bohemian **Quartier Latin**, on the eastern edge of Downtown, bounded roughly by boulevards St-Laurent and René-Lévesque and rues Sherbrooke and St-Hubert, derives its name from the fact that in the late nineteenth century the area's large student population studied in Latin. The Université de Montréal was based here before it moved north of the mountain, and the scholastic tradition continued with the foundation of the **Université du Québec à Montréal** (UQAM) in 1969, now attended by 40,000 students. For most visitors, though, the Quartier Latin's main appeal lies in just wandering through the boutiques or grabbing a drink at one of the many street-side terraces clustered on the stretch of **rue St-Denis** between rue Sherbrooke and rue Ste-Catherine to the south.

Rue St-Denis and around

Rue St-Denis has long been the main street for the city's Francophone residents. Above rue Sherbrooke is the preserve of the well-heeled, while the lower stretches have a rawer edge thanks to the youngsters who study and party here. You can begin your tour in the thick of things from Métro Berri-UQAM, but for a better introduction proceed south from Métro Sherbrooke for an

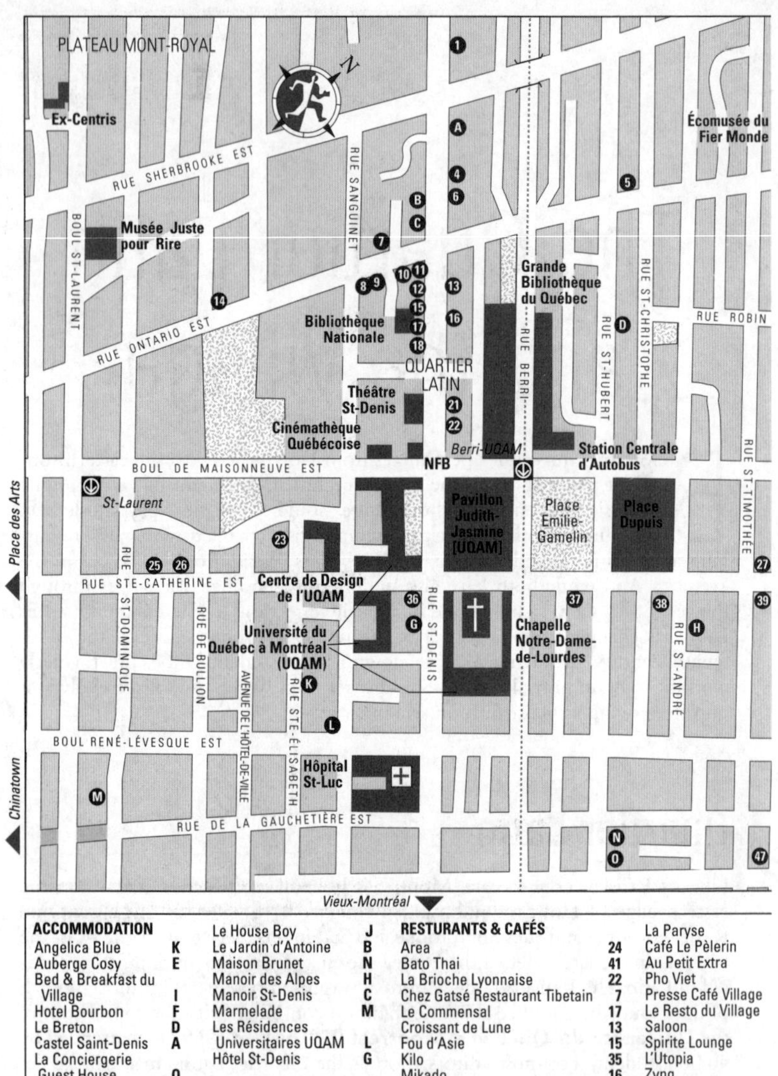

overview of the street scene as rue St-Denis descends from the ridge that marks the edge of the Plateau. The district's Victorian greystone houses, topped with turrets and fanciful parapets, visible above the shopfronts, have seen much better days since they were constructed in the 1860s. The focus here is now much more at street level, where terraces spill out from the numerous cafés and bars in order to accommodate the throngs of customers.

Otherwise, the area's principal attractions are its cultural institutions lodged between boulevard de Maisonneuve and rue Ste-Catherine, including the sym-

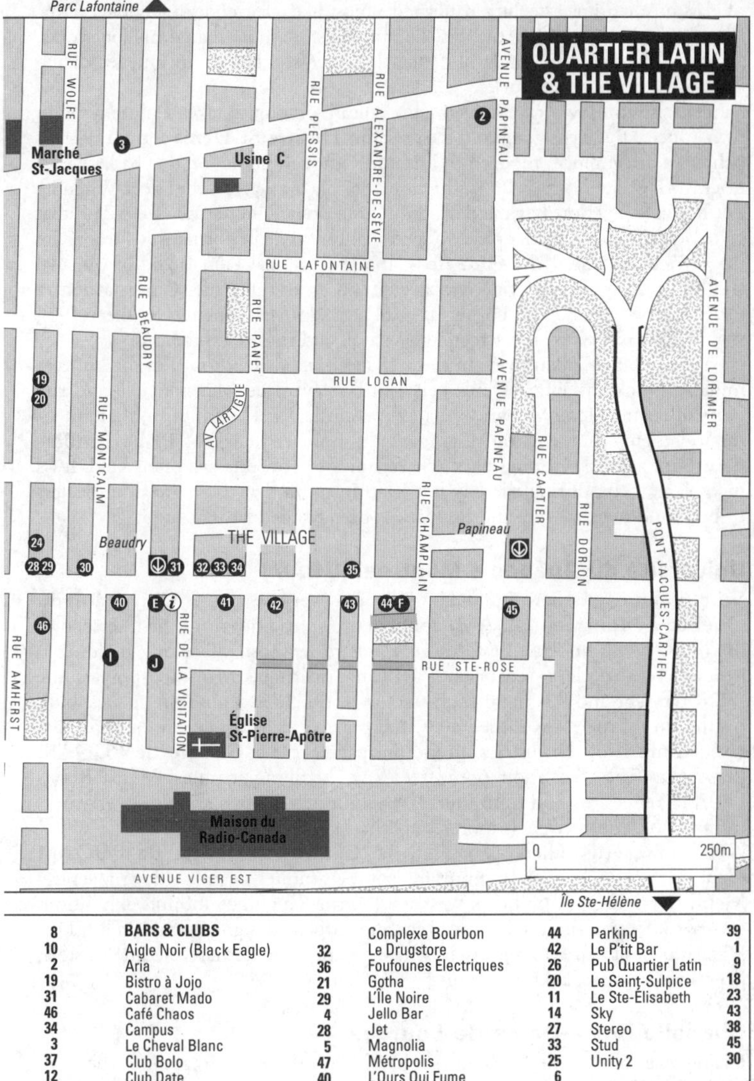

metrical Beaux-Arts **Bibliothèque Nationale** at 1700 rue St-Denis (Tues–Sat 9am–5pm; ⓣ514/873-1100, ⓦwww.bnquebec.ca). The library has housed a satellite of Québec's national library since its founding in 1967 and hosts occasional free art exhibitions. Built half a century earlier as a library for the Sulpicians, it will close when the **Grande Bibliothèque** (ⓦwww.grandebibliotheque.qc.ca) opens a block east (opposite the bus terminal on boulevard de Maisonneuve) in 2005. Its nearly $100-million price-tag wasn't without controversy, nor was the overlooking of more daring designs in favour of one where louvers and long strips of glass give it a linear feeling, patterned almost like a bar code. Bringing a number of collections together, the new library will store more than 4 million works, and you'll be able to consult all of the documents published in Québec dating back more than two centuries.

Further south down rue St-Denis, the culture on display takes a more populist turn. One of the city's grand old theatres, the **Théâtre St-Denis** at no. 1594, lies behind a streamlined modern-style facade, though some of the basketweave brickwork of the original 1900 structure is visible from across the street. When it's not hosting the comedy galas during the Juste pour Rire festival (see p.214) that takes over the street, it's the place to see Broadway-style performances. Nearby are the **Office National du Film du Canada** (National Film Board of Canada) and its unique robotic video jockey at no. 1564 and the **Cinémathèque Québécoise** around the corner at 335 boul de Maisonneuve E (see p.190), which hosts repertory film screenings, festivals and related exhibitions.

The only bit of green space in the area lies immediately south of the bus terminal, a block east of St-Denis between boulevard de Maisonneuve and rue Ste-Catherine. Here, Melvin Charney's whimsical steel sculptures of architectural elements mounted on stilts mark the northern edge of **Place Émilie-Gamelin**, a gently sloping park where summer concerts are often held. It's a nice place to be during the day but keep in mind that there are drug dealers to be found here as well, and the park is best avoided later at night.

Université du Québec à Montréal (UQAM)

With seemingly a new building going up every year, the **Université du Québec à Montréal (UQAM)** continues to spread out from the intersection of rue St-Denis and rue St-Catherine, where its most interesting building is located. The modern red-brick **Pavillon Judith-Jasmin** incorporates the south transept and 90-metre-high steeple of the 1858 Église St-Jacques, built on the site of the city's cathedral, which burned in the great fire of 1852 that ravaged much of the district. Inside the pavilion, **La Galerie de l'UQAM** (Sept–May Tues–Sat noon–6pm; free; Ⓦwww.galerie.uqam.ca; Métro Berri-UQAM), easiest to find from the 1400 rue Berri entrance, showcases artworks from its students as well as more established contemporary artists.

The university's other main sight, the **Centre de Design de l'UQAM** (Sept–May Wed–Sun noon–6pm; free; Ⓦwww.unites.uqam.ca/design/centre; Métro Berri-UQAM), a block west at 1440 rue Sanguinet, mounts exhibitions on architectural, industrial, graphic and urban design themes. The Dan Hanganu-designed building itself, with its stark, deconstructed facade of steel, glass and concrete, fits this premise quite well.

Chapelle Notre-Dame-de-Lourdes

Facing the old Église St-Jacques church's south transept at 430 rue Ste-Catherine E, the stocky Romanesque **Chapelle Notre-Dame-de-Lourdes** (Mon–Sat 7am–8.30pm, Sun 7.30am–6.15pm; Ⓣ514/842-4704, Ⓦwww.pages.infinit.net/lourdes/; Métro Berri-UQAM), ornamented with white marble detailing on its smooth grey stone facade, goes unnoticed by most of the people hurrying past. But when *La Vierge dorée*, the Virgin statue with a crown of stars to be lit at night, returns after a lengthy restoration to her perch atop the roof gable on her 2004 centenary, the church will be quite hard to miss. The interior of the Sulpicians' 1881 church is worth pausing for, its vault heavily embellished in soft hues leading to a large cupola that seems to be supported by the angels painted on the pendentives where the arches intersect. Beyond the ornate altar, the side-lit statue of a young Mary was the first major work by the prolific sculptor of public monuments, Louis-Philippe Hébert.

The Village

The **Village**, the heart of the city's gay and lesbian community, begins around **rue Amherst**, a few blocks east of the Quartier Latin, and extends along **rue Ste-Catherine** as far as rue Papineau, just shy of the massive green girders of the Pont Jacques-Cartier. Montréal's gay district was once centred on rue Stanley Downtown, but the city pressured bar owners out of the area in the run-up to the 1976 Olympics. The bars relocated to this run-down part of rue Ste-Catherine, and appearances have gradually improved, as has the city's attitude to the gay community – the local Métro stop, Beaudry, even incorporates the colours of the rainbow flag into its design. The **information centre** across the street on the second floor of 1260 rue Ste-Catherine E (Mon–Fri 10am–6pm, weekends during major events; ⓣ514/522-1885, ⓦwww.infogayvillage.com) is similarly targeted towards gay visitors. The Village occupies part of the Centre-Sud district – a working-class neighbourhood built up during the Industrial Revolution. With the exception of the Molson brewery, whose neon sign glows to the southeast near the St Lawrence, though, much of the Centre-Sud's industrial heritage has disappeared, been repurposed (as in the case of the Usine C theatre space, which occupies a one-time jam factory) or taken over by new industries such as media – Radio-Canada, TVA and Télé-Québec all have broadcast studios in the area.

Rue Amherst

Over the past few years, **rue Amherst** has become something of a twentieth-century design mecca, with a cluster of shops selling 1930s to 1970s furniture and decorative arts, notably along the east side of the street north of boulevard de Maisonneuve. Before heading north, duck into the more current **Centre de Diffusion en Arts Subversifs** half a block east at no. 1126, with its graffiti-culture-inspired street art and DJ events. Rue Amherst's retro shops have an architectural counterpart in the pair of Art Deco buildings located where the strip peters out at rue Ontario. On the northeast corner, the blooming flowers and pyramids of fruits and vegetables add colour to the stalls fronting the first of these, the streamlined orange-brick **Marché St-Jacques**, a former market building since given over to municipal offices.

Cross to the west side of rue Amherst, to see the other Art Deco structure **Écomusée du Fier Monde** at no. 2050 (Wed 11am–8pm, Thurs & Fri 9.30am–4pm, Sat & Sun 10.30am–5pm; $6; ⓣ514/528-8444, ⓦwww.ecomusee.qc.ca; Métro Beaudry). It occupies a former public bath, whose more fanciful facade is patterned in cream-coloured brick. Graceful arches soar over the light-filled space, where rotating art exhibitions are held in the former pool, the depth markings still visible in the tiles. The permanent exhibition, which runs along the mezzanine and covers the social and industrial history of the formerly working-class neighbourhood, doesn't warrant the admission fee on its own – if there's no temporary show on, you can still get a good peek at the interior from the reception desk.

Rue Ste-Catherine and around

The blocks of **rue Ste-Catherine** between rues Amherst and Papineau form the heart of Montréal's gay and lesbian community, and it's here that you'll find the majority of the city's **gay bars and clubs**. Scattered throughout are numerous restaurants that are equally popular with the media types working for the big French-language broadcasters in the vicinity. Listings of bars and clubs, as well as community resources and gay-friendly accommodation, can be found in Chapter Thirteen, "Gay Montréal" (see p.177). Just by wandering along rue Ste-Catherine, you can't miss the activity – most bars open their windows wide to the streets in the warmer months and couples wander blithely hand-in-hand past rainbow-flag-decked shopfronts while an unending stream of cars cruise by.

Largely commercial- and nightlife-oriented, there's not much in the way of sights on this stretch of rue Ste-Catherine itself – the main exception being **Station C** at the corner of rue Plessis, a colonnaded stone building that began as a post office in 1912, was the one-time home to the legendary *K.O.X.* nightclub in the 1990s and is now being developed as a performance and exhibition space. It's worth exploring the side streets, which in this neighbourhood are lined with attractive townhouses and well-tended gardens. The most interesting of these streets is **avenue Lartigue**, northeast of the Métro via rue de la Visitation and boulevard de Maisonneuve. Its winding path, reminiscent of an English mews, derives from the route the workers took to the early factories, whose owners weren't too concerned whether the streets lined up or not.

A block south of rue Ste-Catherine, at 1201 rue de la Visitation, the **Église St-Pierre-Apôtre** is a delicate 1851 Neo-Gothic church supported by buttresses and topped by a slender tin-plated steeple. Within its finely embellished interior lies the "Chapel of Hope", dedicated to those who have died of AIDS. A less successful AIDS memorial marks the corner of rue Ste-Catherine and rue Panet – many locals think the **Parc de l'Espoir**, with its concrete expanse ranged with black granite blocks and plain metal poles sporting now-ratty ribbons of remembrance, was better left as green space. A couple of blocks to the east, the gaudy extravagance of the Complexe Bourbon's hotel, bars and cafés at the corner of rue Alexandre-Desève goes some way to recalling "Gay Paree" – if it were to be re-created by a theme-park developer or Vegas casino designer, that is.

4

Plateau Mont-Royal and north

No neighbourhood is as emblematic of Montréal as **Plateau Mont-Royal**, a dense urban area that manages to capture the city's duelling English and French traditions, as well as its immigrant legacy. Plateau Mont-Royal, called just the Plateau by most, occupies **Mont Royal**'s east flank; the edge of the plateau where the land drops down towards the St Lawrence is clearly visible along the district's southern border, rue Sherbrooke. It extends east as far as rue d'Iberville and north to the Canadian Pacific Railway tracks, with the exception of the area's northwest corner, which is taken up by the **Mile End** neighbourhood. Mile End runs alongside the former town of **Outremont**, its bagel bakeries and Greek tavernas a stone's throw from the latter's trendy cafés and fine food shops. Further to the north, **Little Italy**, as its name suggests, is the heart of Montréal's Italian community, and has a terrific public market as well.

Plateau Mont-Royal and around

The Plateau's tight grid of streets was laid out in 1860, shortly after the first horse-drawn trams began trundling through what had been a mostly rural landscape. The district's main arteries developed along the tram routes, prompting the building boom of the Plateau's characteristic townhouses. While the eastern half of the Plateau has remained steadfastly Francophone, the western part has been home to a rotating cast of immigrants (see box, p.97) since the late 1800s – although, as of late, yuppies have been the largest group of arrivals.

While pretty much devoid of standard tourist attractions, the neighbourhood is nonetheless a fabulous place to wander about. The main drags – **avenue du Mont-Royal**, **rue St-Denis** and especially **boulevard St-Laurent**, or "The Main" – hum with a constant energy, and the area is home to many of the city's finest restaurants, bars and clubs. Add to that a wide selection of trendy boutiques and charming green spaces, **Square St-Louis** and larger **Parc Lafontaine** in particular, and you've got yourself a great day out.

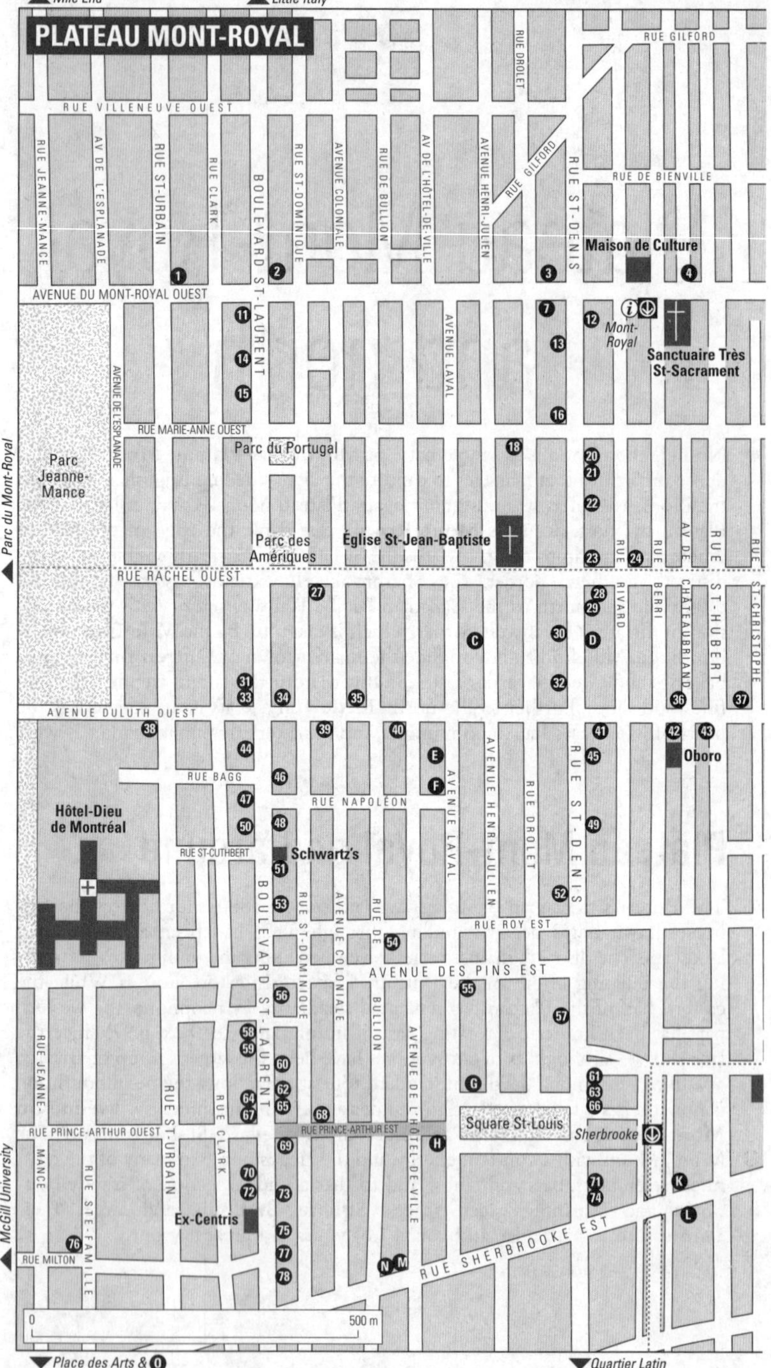
PLATEAU MONT-ROYAL
Mile End
Little Italy
Parc du Mont-Royal
McGill University
Place des Arts & O
Quartier Latin
RUE GILFORD
RUE VILLENEUVE OUEST
RUE DE BIENVILLE
AVENUE DU MONT-ROYAL OUEST
RUE MARIE-ANNE OUEST
RUE RACHEL OUEST
AVENUE DULUTH OUEST
RUE BAGG
RUE NAPOLÉON
RUE ST-CUTHBERT
RUE ROY EST
AVENUE DES PINS EST
RUE PRINCE-ARTHUR OUEST
RUE PRINCE-ARTHUR EST
RUE MILTON
RUE SHERBROOKE EST
RUE JEANNE-MANCE
AV DE L'ESPLANADE
AVENUE DE L'ESPLANADE
RUE ST-URBAIN
RUE CLARK
BOULEVARD ST-LAURENT
RUE ST-DOMINIQUE
AVENUE COLONIALE
RUE DE BULLION
AV DE L'HÔTEL-DE-VILLE
AVENUE DE L'HÔTEL-DE-VILLE
AVENUE HENRI-JULIEN
RUE DROLET
AVENUE LAVAL
RUE ST-DENIS
RUE RIVARD
RUE BERRI
AV DE CHÂTEAUBRIAND
RUE ST-HUBERT
RUE ST-CHRISTOPHE
RUE STE-FAMILLE
Maison de Culture
Mont-Royal
Sanctuaire Très St-Sacrament
Parc du Portugal
Parc des Amériques
Église St-Jean-Baptiste
Parc Jeanne-Mance
Hôtel-Dieu de Montréal
Schwartz's
Oboro
Square St-Louis
Sherbrooke
Ex-Centris
0
500 m

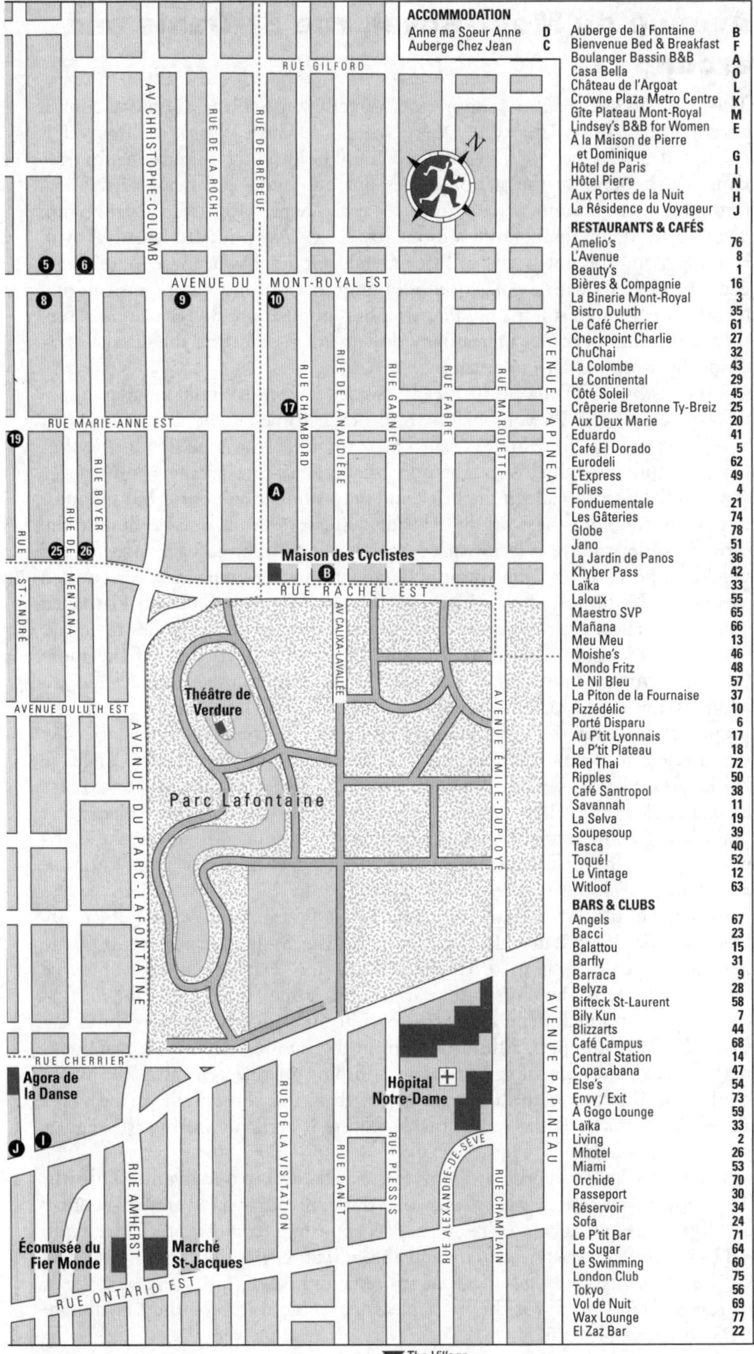
ACCOMMODATION
Anne ma Soeur Anne D
Auberge Chez Jean C
Auberge de la Fontaine B
Bienvenue Bed & Breakfast F
Boulanger Bassin B&B A
Casa Bella O
Château de l'Argoat L
Crowne Plaza Metro Centre K
Gîte Plateau Mont-Royal M
Lindsey's B&B for Women E
À la Maison de Pierre et Dominique G
Hôtel de Paris I
Hôtel Pierre N
Aux Portes de la Nuit H
La Résidence du Voyageur J
RESTAURANTS & CAFÉS
Amelio's 76
L'Avenue 8
Beauty's 1
Bières & Compagnie 16
La Binerie Mont-Royal 3
Bistro Duluth 35
Le Café Cherrier 61
Checkpoint Charlie 27
ChuChai 32
La Colombe 43
Le Continental 29
Côté Soleil 45
Crêperie Bretonne Ty-Breiz 25
Aux Deux Marie 20
Eduardo 41
Café El Dorado 5
Eurodeli 62
L'Express 49
Folies 4
Fonduementale 21
Les Gâteries 74
Globe 78
Jano 51
La Jardin de Panos 36
Khyber Pass 42
Laïka 33
Laloux 55
Maestro SVP 65
Mañana 66
Meu Meu 13
Moishe's 46
Mondo Fritz 48
Le Nil Bleu 57
La Piton de la Fournaise 37
Pizzédélic 10
Porté Disparu 6
Au P'tit Lyonnais 17
Le P'tit Plateau 18
Red Thai 72
Ripples 50
Café Santropol 38
Savannah 11
La Selva 19
Soupesoup 39
Tasca 40
Toqué! 52
Le Vintage 12
Witloof 63
BARS & CLUBS
Angels 67
Bacci 23
Balattou 15
Barfly 31
Barraca 9
Belyza 28
Bifteck St-Laurent 58
Bily Kun 7
Blizzarts 44
Café Campus 68
Central Station 14
Copacabana 47
Else's 54
Envy / Exit 73
À Gogo Lounge 59
Laïka 33
Living 2
Mhotel 26
Miami 53
Orchide 70
Passeport 30
Réservoir 34
Sofa 24
Le P'tit Bar 71
Le Sugar 64
Le Swimming 60
London Club 75
Tokyo 56
Vol de Nuit 69
Wax Lounge 77
El Zaz Bar 22
RUE GILFORD
AV CHRISTOPHE-COLOMB
RUE DE LA ROCHE
RUE DE BREBEUF
AVENUE DU MONT-ROYAL EST
RUE CHAMBORD
RUE DE LANAUDIÈRE
RUE GARNIER
RUE FABRE
RUE MARQUETTE
AVENUE PAPINEAU
RUE MARIE-ANNE EST
RUE BOYER
RUE DE MENTANA
RUE ST-ANDRÉ
Maison des Cyclistes
RUE RACHEL EST
AV CALIXA-LAVALLÉE
Théâtre de Verdure
AVENUE DULUTH EST
AVENUE DU PARC-LAFONTAINE
AVENUE ÉMILE-DUPLOYÉ
Parc Lafontaine
RUE CHERRIER
Agora de la Danse
Hôpital Notre-Dame
RUE DE LA VISITATION
RUE PANET
RUE PLESSIS
RUE ALEXANDRE-DE-SÈVE
RUE CHAMPLAIN
RUE AMHERST
Écomusée du Fier Monde
Marché St-Jacques
RUE ONTARIO EST
The Village

Avenue du Mont-Royal, rue St-Denis and around

The Mont-Royal Métro station exits directly onto Place Gérald-Godin, a paved plaza named after the Québécois poet whose *Tango de Montréal* is excerpted on the wall of a nearby building. The brightly coloured **information kiosk** opposite the station dishes out brochures and maps of the area throughout the summer (late June to early Sept Mon–Wed 10am–7pm, Thurs–Sun 10am–9pm; Ⓦwww.mont-royal.net). **Avenue du Mont-Royal**, running along the north side of Place Gérald-Godin, has become increasingly gentrified of late, with a collection of boutiques, cafés and restaurants catering to a diverse, though still mainly Francophone, population. But as you head further east, things becomes increasingly downmarket, reflecting the district's traditionally working-class population.

To get a flavour of the distinct, early-twentieth-century residential architecture typical of the Plateau, take a stroll down some of the side streets that branch off avenue du Mont-Royal to the east, notably avenue de Christophe-Colomb and rue Fabre. Wrought-iron balconies, ornate parapets and *tourelles* (turret-like dormers) adorn the brick and grey-stone townhouses, but the most notable features are the rows of exterior staircases – built outside despite the snow, in order to save interior space. Search out as well the back lanes of this neighbourhood where the dynamic landscape of washing lines, tin-covered sheds, circular fire-escape staircases and balconies wrapped around U-shaped courtyards reflect a more intimate side of life – dubbed "Balconville" by locals.

Many of the same architectural details appear on the facades of the more bourgeois townhouses lining **rue St-Denis**, which intersects avenue du Mont-Royal two blocks west of the Mont-Royal Métro station. Long *the* shopping street for the city's Francophones, rue St-Denis continues to draw well-heeled shoppers with its array of fashion boutiques, French-language bookstores, interior-design shops and a multitude of cafés, bars and bistros. It's a great spot for a stroll as the chic stores are mostly one-of-a-kind places that put a lot of effort into their window displays – they need to, given the competing distraction of the terraces where Montrealers linger over bowls of *café au lait* and check out the people passing by.

A couple of blocks south of avenue du Mont-Royal, and just west of rue St-Denis, is the 1912 Italian Baroque-style **Église St-Jean-Baptiste**, 309 rue Rachel E (daily 1–8pm; Ⓣ514/842-9811), the Plateau's most impressive church and one of the city's largest. Its smooth stone facade, fronted by classical columns and pediment, leads to a spacious interior that can accommodate up to 3000 worshippers, a third of them in the unusual circular mezzanine. A magnificent baldachin of gilded wood and pink marble rests atop the white marble altar, although the Casavant organ that runs the length of the choir above the entrance is the most notable feature – certainly during the regular concerts held here.

A block further south, rue St-Denis crosses red-brick-paved **avenue Duluth**. To the west spreads a funky mix of ethnic restaurants, twentieth-century antique shops and corner stores, and spots appealing to more alternative types – a folk café, vegetarian restaurant and a store that sells drums for tam-tam percussionists. Lined with *apportez votre vin* restaurants (see p.146) the blocks east of rue St-Denis make for the most pleasant, scenic route for the ten-minute walk to Parc Lafontaine.

Parc Lafontaine

The Plateau's central park, **Parc Lafontaine** (daily 6am–midnight; Métro Mont-Royal or Sherbrooke), offers a green respite from the crowded streets nearby. Its western half features a promenade that makes for a lovely stroll around two large man-made ponds, while to the east a network of lamp-lit pathways are shaded by tall trees. Locals swarm to the park in warmer times to bask in the sun, take a lazy turn on a pedal-boat or cruise around on rollerblades. The outdoor **Théâtre de Verdure**, on the western side of the ponds, regularly stages free summertime performances that range from classical concerts to Shakespeare (see p.184). In winter the frozen-over ponds create a perfectly romantic scene for **ice skating** (see p.203).

Square St-Louis and rue Prince-Arthur

Back on rue St-Denis and heading south, you'll pass an enormous silver-domed edifice built as the Institut des Sourdes-Muettes (a home for deaf-mutes) and typical of the city's late-nineteenth-century architecture; it now houses government offices. Just before rue St-Denis crosses rue Sherbrooke into the Quartier Latin (see p.85), it adjoins **Square St-Louis**, Montréal's most attractive square. The elegant ensemble of grey-stone Victorian residences with fanciful *tourelles* – some painted in vivid red or purple – that border it were originally occupied by the city's Francophone elite. Accordingly, the square itself has a formal layout, centred around a large fountain with pathways radiating outward beneath the overarching trees. Some of those hanging out here are a bit scruffy – but they tend towards the hippyish rather than thuggish, and you shouldn't encounter any problems other than offers to buy sub-standard pot (and an increased police presence has diminished that likelihood).

On the opposite side of avenue Laval from the square begin the five pedestrianized brick-paved blocks of **rue Prince-Arthur**, lined with restaurants and bars with plenty of outdoor seating. Tourists crowding around the street performers and artists' stalls set up here can make it a bit difficult to navigate, but even Montrealers occasionally get caught up in the hubbub and park themselves on a terrace shaded by umbrellas with a pitcher of sangria to watch the busy parade. Though the relentless hawking for customers and the small souvenir shops dotted about reflect the street's surrender to tourism, a bit of the old 1960s anarchic spirit shows up on the frequent occasions when the fountain with sculpted lily pads halfway along gets spiked with washing powder.

The Main

The pedestrianized part of rue Prince-Arthur ends at the equally crowded **boulevard St-Laurent** (Ⓦwww.boulevardsaintlaurent.com; Métro Sherbrooke or Saint-Laurent; bus #55), usually jammed with revellers passing to and from the many bars and restaurants on the city's most famous strip. Appropriately known as "**The Main**", boulevard St-Laurent, the traditional divide between the Catholic, French-speaking east of the city and the Protestant, English-speaking west (designated in 1792 as the official divide from which streets are numbered), captures much of the city in microcosm, reflecting its ethnic diversity and attracting citizens of all stripes with its pulsing vibe. The nonstop stream of automobile traffic moving northward echoes the movement of the immigrants who walked up the Main from the port, stopping, as legend has it, when they heard their own language being spoken.

Eastern Europeans, Jews, Greeks, Hungarians, Portuguese and Latin Americans have all passed through, leaving behind a trail of wonderful shops and restaurants. The "discovery" of the area's cheap rents and ethnic flavour by artists and students in the 1970s and 80s gave it a hip reputation that has led to rapid gentrification on the stretch above rue Sherbrooke, though the continuing tug-of-war between the various communities further along has kept the area dynamic and interesting.

There's not really anything specific to see here – the street's charm is appreciated by just wandering along – though you might want to check out trendy **ex-Centris**, the multimedia cinema at no. 3536 on the Main's flashiest block of clubs and *m'as-tu vu?* ("did you see me?") restaurants between rues Sherbrooke and Prince-Arthur. Behind the cinema's colonnaded facade are bizarre ticket booths where you're face-to-face with a video image of the ticket-seller (eerily, real human hands pass you your ticket).

Northwards from rue Prince-Arthur, you'll find more of the Main's former life – bakeries, butchers, kitchenware and fabric shops in early commercial buildings like the 1892 Baxter Block on the west side – struggling in vain against the tide of new bars and cafés advancing from the south. One classic storefront that won't be going anywhere soon, though, is **Schwartz's**, a tiny deli further up the Main at no. 3895. No visit to the city would be complete without a classic Montréal smoked-meat sandwich, and this unassuming spot, open since 1930, is the best place to tuck into one (see p.155). Further north, a couple of small parks interrupt the commerce – a bit of faux Central American temple serves as a backdrop to occasional concerts in the **Parc des Amériques** at the corner of Rachel, while the **Parc du Portugal** at the corner of rue Marie-Anne more successfully reflects the local Portuguese community with its glazed tiles and central gazebo. The Main's mutability shows up again on the blocks between the parks, where the garment trade's former digs have given way to some of the city's trendiest furniture showrooms.

North of the Plateau

To the northeast of the mountain, the Francophone elite have long inhabited the tony enclave of **Outremont**, which reluctantly merged with Montréal as part of the creation of the "Mega-City" (see p.273). The former town abuts the **Mile End** neighbourhood, settled by Greek immigrants in the 1950s and considered an increasingly desirable place by a crowd of students and arty types looking for the atmosphere that once characterized the Main, prior to its gentrification. Further north, a different ethnic flavour infuses **Little Italy**, home to some of Montréal's best espresso, and a major foodie destination as well, thanks to the bustling **Marché Jean-Talon**.

Outremont and Mile End

The neighbourhoods to the northwest of the Plateau are a bit of an odd couple. **Outremont** has long been the abode of the island's wealthy Francophones, the houses increasing in grandeur as they scale the northeast slopes of the hill for which it is named, and more modest as you head to the northern boundary at the rail tracks just beyond avenue Van-Horne. The main shopping and promenading street for Outremont's stylish set is lively

The Main's ethnic flavour

While much of boulevard St-Laurent, aka The Main, gets its traffic nowadays from boutique-shoppers and café-dwellers, strolling various pockets still affords a taste – quite literally – of the city's various immigrant waves. Food, as is to be expected, played an important role in Montréal's ethnic communities, and, unsurprisingly, some of their most lasting contributions to the city's social fabric are the grocery stores and restaurants that still line the street. Come hungry to get the best samples. The best place to get a flavour for the neighbourhood is to head to the central part of the Main, an area bounded to the south by avenue des Pins and the north by avenue du Mont-Royal. It's here, in the heart of the Plateau neighbourhood, that you'll find Montréal's greatest concentration of ethnicities. The Main's original inhabitants were newcomers from **Eastern Europe** – including a large Jewish population fleeing the pogroms of late-nineteenth-century Russia – while more recent arrivals hail from Latin America, Africa and Portugal; all of these groups are huddled together in a few short and easily walkable blocks.

Heading north from avenue des Pins, you'll hit upon La Vieille Europe, at no. 3855, a fantastic cheese and meats shop that caters to the Old World community, across the street from Berson and Sons, a Jewish tombstone-maker that's been in business for four generations. The overlapping communities on the Main are something of a palimpsest, with traces of the older Jewish community – left behind when later generations moved to the suburbs – intermingling with the rotisseries of the **Portuguese**, who settled throughout the area in the 1950s. In addition to the rotisseries, you'll find cafés on avenue Duluth full of old Portuguese men watching football, and the Santa Cruz church on the corner of rues St-Urbain and Rachel, the site of riotous festivals on saints' feast days.

avenue Laurier, full of chic cafés, restaurants and upscale boutiques. The main north–south commercial street, avenue du Parc, is actually in adjacent Mile End (see below), but for a fix of Outremont's stately old homes you can walk north from avenue Laurier along **avenue Bloomfield**. The Gothic-revival Église St-Viateur at the intersection of the two marks the start of one of the area's most attractive residential streets, passing leafy Parc Outremont and striking Beaux-Arts Académie Querbes, now a primary school, before reaching avenue Bernard (see below).

The pavement terraces and expensive but delectable fine-food emporia of avenue Laurier continue past rue Hutchison, the western border of **Mile End**. Extending north to the rail lines and blending with the Plateau towards avenue du Mont-Royal, the neighbourhood's more pronounced ethnic character and cheaper rents are drawing businesses that were once lower down on the Main, earning it the "new Plateau" label. Oddly enough, avenue Laurier's flair doesn't spill over onto the main drag, **avenue du Parc** – as soon as you turn the corner, the shops and restaurants to the north and south are cheap rather than chic.

For the next couple of blocks north, the places of interest lie on the side streets – Jewish bagel bakeries are the main draw on **avenue Fairmount** and **rue St-Viateur**, not far from the city's largest community of Hasidic Jews. Don't expect to see much in the way of an architectural presence – the Hasidic synagogues tend to be in modest dwellings and the synagogues of the other Jewish sects were demolished or converted to schools or other uses in the decades since the community moved to western suburbs such as Côte-des-Neiges, Hampstead and Côte-St-Luc. On rue St-Viateur, the black-clad men with curls peeking out of their hats provide a striking contrast to the laid-back

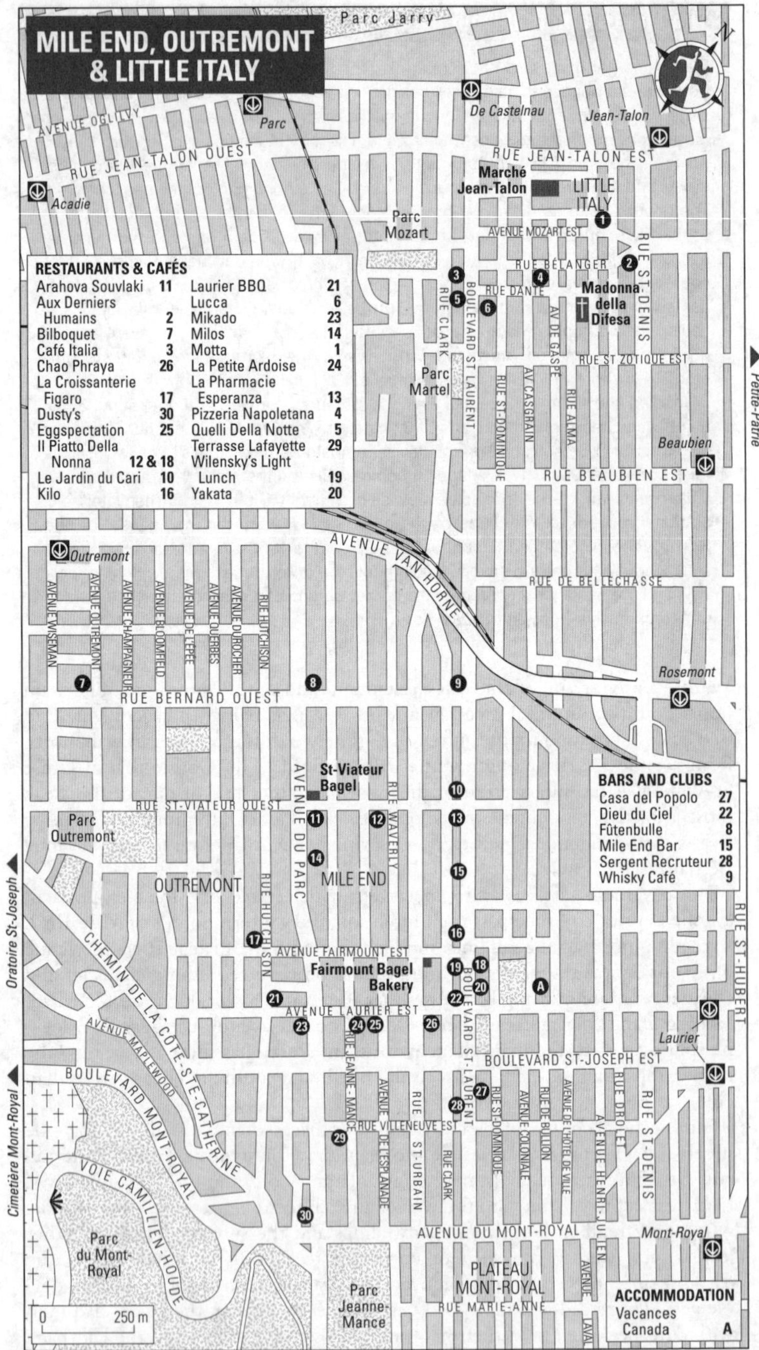
MILE END, OUTREMONT & LITTLE ITALY

RESTAURANTS & CAFÉS
Arahova Souvlaki 11
Aux Derniers Humains 2
Bilboquet 7
Café Italia 3
Chao Phraya 26
La Croissanterie Figaro 17
Dusty's 30
Eggspectation 25
Il Piatto Della Nonna 12 & 18
Le Jardin du Cari 10
Kilo 16
Laurier BBQ 21
Lucca 6
Mikado 23
Milos 14
Motta 1
La Petite Ardoise 24
La Pharmacie Esperanza 13
Pizzeria Napoletana 4
Quelli Della Notte 5
Terrasse Lafayette 29
Wilensky's Light Lunch 19
Yakata 20

BARS AND CLUBS
Casa del Popolo 27
Dieu du Ciel 22
Fûtenbulle 8
Mile End Bar 15
Sergent Recruteur 28
Whisky Café 9

ACCOMMODATION
Vacances Canada A

Parc Jarry
Parc
De Castelnau
Jean-Talon
Acadie
Avenue Ogilvy
Rue Jean-Talon Ouest
Rue Jean-Talon Est
Marché Jean-Talon
Little Italy
Parc Mozart
Avenue Mozart Est
Rue Bélanger
Rue Dante
Madonna della Difesa
Rue St-Denis
Rue Clark
Boulevard St-Laurent
Av de Gaspé
Rue St Zotique Est
Parc Martel
Rue St-Dominique
Av Casgrain
Rue Alma
Petite-Patrie
Beaubien
Rue Beaubien Est
Avenue Van Horne
Rue de Bellechasse
Outremont
Avenue Wiseman
Avenue Outremont
Avenue Champagneur
Avenue Bloomfield
Avenue de l'Épée
Avenue Querbes
Avenue Durocher
Rue Hutchison
Rosemont
Rue Bernard Ouest
Avenue du Parc
St-Viateur Bagel
Rue Waverly
Rue St-Viateur Ouest
Parc Outremont
Outremont
Mile End
Oratoire St-Joseph
Chemin de la Côte-Ste-Catherine
Avenue Fairmount Est
Fairmount Bagel Bakery
Avenue Laurier Est
Avenue Maplewood
Rue St-Hubert
Laurier
Boulevard St-Joseph Est
Boulevard Mont-Royal
Rue Jeanne-Mance
Avenue de l'Esplanade
Rue St-Urbain
Avenue Coloniale
Rue de Bullion
Avenue de l'Hôtel de Ville
Rue Drolet
Avenue Henri-Julien
Rue Villeneuve Est
Cimetière Mont-Royal
Voie Camillien-Houde
Parc du Mont-Royal
Avenue du Mont-Royal
Mont-Royal
Plateau Mont-Royal
Avenue Laval
Parc Jeanne-Mance
Rue Marie-Anne
0 250 m
Downtown

students and artists who frequent the quirky shops, family-run restaurants and no-nonsense Italian cafés that are turning this into one of the city's funkier streets. The district's commercial flavour is concentrated north of here along avenue du Parc, a bustling stretch with excellent Greek restaurants leading to **avenue Bernard**. As with avenue Laurier, fashionably attired bourgeois Francophones promenade past artsy cafés and swish boutiques and restaurants on the western, Outremont portion of the street.

Little Italy

The vibrant neighbourhood of **Little Italy** is a marvellous place to poke about, especially if you've got food on the brain. The city's largest **outdoor market** is here (see p.198) and the whole area around boulevard St-Laurent between rues St-Zotique and Jean-Talon is dotted with **cafés** and **restaurants** dishing out authentic Italian cuisine and some of the city's strongest coffee (some of the best is provided by the atmospheric *Café Italia*, at 6840 rue Jean-Talon, see p.161). While it's a short ride from Downtown to Métro Jean-Talon, and just a half-hour walk from the Plateau, most people bus it here on the #55 that runs up boulevard St-Laurent. You'll know you've arrived when you see Italian flags waving everywhere. Although the neighbourhood had a palpable Italian presence for a long time beforehand, it really took on its character in the years following the World War II when economic migrants left Italy in search of a better future in Canada. And although Montréal's largest Italian districts are now in northeastern suburbs like St-Léonard, Little Italy has retained its authentic feel and is still, aside from the areas described below, a largely residential district.

Hop off the bus at **Parc Martel**, where locals cluster on benches near the large gazebo and which faces the former Église St-Jean-de-la-Croix (converted into condos), notable for its twin bell towers whose cupolas are supported by appropriately Roman-style arches. Stylish restaurants and cafés line the stretch of boulevard St-Laurent north of here, though the family-run trattorias on eastward-running **rue Dante** hold more appeal. The fourteenth-century Italian poet also lends his name to the charming local park that runs alongside the blocky red-brick **Madonna della Difesa church**. The impressive frescoes on the vault and apse are the work of Florence-born Guido Nincheri, whose inclusion of a horse-back Mussolini among the figures to the right of the altar led to his detainment in 1940 as a Fascist sympathizer.

The area's main attraction, **Marché Jean-Talon** (shops: Mon–Wed & Sat 8am–6pm, Thurs–Fri 8am–9pm, Sun 9am–5pm; stalls: times vary; Ⓦwww.marchespublics-mtl.com), lies two blocks to the north. Bakers, *fromageries* and fishmongers surround a large square centred on an open-air, covered marketplace brimming with colourful fruits, vegetables and flowers picked over by the jostling crowds. From here, it's a five-minute walk northeast to Métro Jean-Talon, next to the Casa d'Italia community centre at the intersection of rues Jean-Talon and St-Denis.

5

Mont Royal and northwest

The large, rounded hill rising up north of Downtown dominates the city's skyline and its inhabitants' perceptions to the extent that, although it is only 233m high and actually comprises three separate summits – Mont Royal, Westmount and Outremont – everyone simply calls it **the mountain**. Confusingly, locals refer to "the mountain" or "Mont Royal" when talking about the whole mass, just the summit of Mont Royal or even **Parc du Mont-Royal**.

The park is the area's chief attraction, covering the summit of Mont Royal and its southern and eastern slopes. Wound about with heavily used trails, the park draws active Montrealers from all over the city, many of whom stop to ogle the spectacular views of Downtown from the various lookout points.

The largest green space on the mountain, though, is not the park itself, but the two vast **cemeteries** on the northern slopes offering a tranquil escape from the city: the woodsy Cimetière Mont-Royal wound about with meandering paths, and the more precisely ordered Cimetière Notre-Dame-des-Neiges. Overlooking the latter is the mammoth dome of the **Oratoire St-Joseph**, an unmissable presence on the mountain's northwest side that's visible from miles away due to its enormous dome. It's an important pilgrimage site that's equally worth a visit for non-believers. The **Côte-des-Neiges** neighbourhood to the northwest is mostly residential but features an attraction that is less physically monumental but more emotionally compelling than the oratory: the **Centre Commémoratif de l'Holocauste à Montréal**, its haunting exhibits documenting the horrific experiences faced by Europe's Jews in the concentration camps.

Parc du Mont-Royal

The mountain itself is crowned by **Parc du Mont-Royal** (daily 6am–midnight; Ⓦ www.lemontroyal.com; bus #11 and numerous buses on the periphery), which was opened in 1876 as the result of demands for the mountain's preservation after a number of its trees were cut for firewood after a particularly harsh winter. Occupying some 544 acres – a fifth of the mountain's total area – it was designed by the American landscape architect Frederick Law Olmsted, whose works include New York City's Central Park and Golden Gate Park in San Francisco. Although the Ice Storm of January 1998 damaged trees to the extent that 4000 had to be felled, it wasn't as catastrophic as Mayor Jean

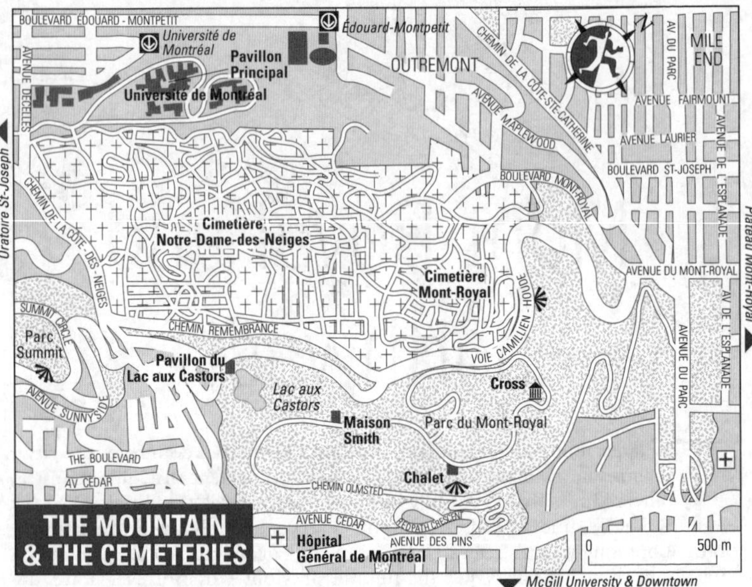

Drapeau's 1950s "morality cuts" of the underbrush on the summit, which were intended to thwart amorous pursuits, causing Mont Royal to be dubbed "Bald Mountain". Autumn is the best time to visit, when the leaves are a palette of reds, oranges and yellows, while in winter you can wander through a beautiful monochromatic landscape with black tree trunks silhouetted against the snow.

Ascending the mountain

From the intersection of boulevard St-Laurent and rue Rachel, head west to **Parc Jeanne-Mance**, where a path continues on past soccer fields, tennis courts and a paddling pool to Parc du Mont-Royal's main access point – easy to spot by the **Sir George-Étienne Cartier monument**, topped by a winged angel and guarded by four reclining lions. The surrounding plaza draws large crowds on summer Sundays from noon until dusk for the **Tam Tam** (Ⓦ www.montrealtamtam.com), a large drumming jam session and improvized market with hippyish overtones that's a great place to chill out. Begun by a group of musicians who came to practise here in the late 1970s, the Tam Tam soon became an almost pagan celebration with people dancing uninhibitedly to the incessant rhythms of the drums while hundreds of Montrealers of all stripes picnic on the surrounding grassy slopes.

North of the monument, **chemin Olmsted**, the gravel path designed by Olmsted for horse-drawn carriages, ascends the 4.5km up to the Chalet and cross in a series of gentle looping slopes. The lazy hour-long stroll up the main path offers several memorable vistas of the city below, but there's a shortcut halfway along if time is limited. Just after the two-kilometre mark, look for the 200-odd steps that lead up to the Chalet (see opposite) – a treacherous climb when covered in snow and ice, and exhausting at any time.

Atop the mountain

If you stick to chemin Olmsted, the trees open out into a large grassy expanse surrounding the man-made **Lac aux Castors** (Beaver Lake) twenty minutes further along. Pedal-boats ($8 per half-hour) rather than beavers glide across the surface of the former swamp, and the immediate area is popular for winter activities like inner-tube sledding ($7, $3.50 for children under 13), and skating on the lit trails running amongst the nearby trees. You can rent snowshoes, cross-country skis and ice skates from the pavilion next to Lac aux Castors (Ⓣ514/843-8240).

On the slope above the lake the mostly stone abstract sculptures dotted about are a relic of the 1964 sculpture symposium, when a dozen international artists created the works from scratch. The sculptors stayed in the **Maison Smith** (daily 9am–5pm; free; Ⓣ514/843-8240, Ⓦwww.lemontroyal.com), a squat stone structure further east that now houses an information centre and exhibition on Mont Royal. Ask for the brochures detailing various themed walking tours of the mountain or join one of the Sunday guided walks (times and prices vary) that depart from here.

Five to ten more minutes of walking up chemin Olmsted brings you to the rustic mountaintop **Chalet** (daily 10am–8pm), part of Olmsted's original plan but not built until the early 1930s, and the nearby 30-metre-high **cross**, one of the city's most recognizable landmarks and visible from miles around. The Chalet's long, low, stone building is a good spot to warm up on colder days, with a passable canteen (10am–4pm), toilets and a gift shop. Keep an eye out for the squirrels nestled in the rafters high up in the large main hall – they're more interesting than the paintings of Montréal history hung high on the walls (although a couple are by Paul-Émile Borduas, you'd be hard-pressed to see anything of the renowned abstract artist's style in them). The chief attraction, though, is the large semicircular plaza in front of the Chalet that offers outstanding **views** of Downtown's skyscrapers and beyond.

Although it's possible to walk east along chemin Olmsted to the base of the cross, it's not nearly as impressive up close. The illuminated metallic structure, erected in 1924 by the St-Jean-Baptiste Society, recalls the wooden one that de Maisonneuve, the founder of Montréal, carried up the mountaintop and planted here in 1643 in honour of the fledgling colony being spared from a flood. Further along, gaps in the trees frame views of the city's northern sprawl and a set of stairs leads to the lookout on voie Camillien-Houde for a panorama that takes in the Stade Olympique and eastern Montréal.

The cemeteries

The winding paths amidst large pockets of trees and shrubs make the 165-acre Protestant **Cimetière Mont-Royal** (June–Sept Mon–Fri 8.30am–7pm, Oct–May until 5pm, Sat & Sun 9am–5pm; south gate closes at 4pm every day; Ⓣ514/279-7358, Ⓦwww.mountroyalcem.com), founded in 1847, another wonderful place to wander around. Easily accessed from the car park behind the Maison Smith in Parc du Mont-Royal, the cemetery draws relatively few people, and the surrounding ridges help cut out most of the city's noise, making it feel like taking a stroll through a tranquil patch of countryside. The reception centre, located at the bottom of the slope next to the north entrance on chemin de la Forêt, off boulevard Mont-Royal, has a guide for birdwatchers (145 species of birds have been spotted here, from tiny sparrows and warblers on up to owls and kestrels) in addition to a map listing the burial sites of prominent citizens – the Molson brewing family's mausoleum is particularly impressive. Among the other memorials, the fireman-topped column that marks the resting place of fire-fighters killed on duty is especially poignant, while the simple grave of Anna Leonowens of *The King and I* fame is perhaps the most unexpected.

The adjacent (but not directly connected) **Cimetière Notre-Dame-des-Neiges** (daily April–Oct 8am–7pm, Nov–March to 5pm; ⓣ514/735-1361, ⓦwww.cimetierenddn.org) has been the favoured resting place for the city's Catholics since 1855. It is mainly notable, though, for its vastness – with nearly one million resting souls, it is one of the largest cemeteries in North America. There's a gate on chemin Remembrance opposite Lac aux Castors, but for information about the gravesites you'll need to visit the main reception, a fifteen-minute walk away. To get there, head west along chemin Remembrance and turn right on chemin de la Côte-des-Neiges; you can also walk from Métro Côte-des-Neiges or take bus #165, #166 or #535 directly to the cemetery from Métro Guy-Concordia Downtown. Among the who's who of Québécois artists and politicians interred here are poet Émile Nelligan and Fathers of Confederation Sir George-Étienne Cartier and Thomas D'Arcy McGee. The most attractive memorial centres on a full-size marble reproduction of Michelangelo's *La Pietà*, located towards the Cimetière Notre-Dame-des-Neiges' northwest corner. Nearby, a gate opens onto avenue Decelles from where it's a five-minute walk to the Oratoire St-Joseph.

Oratoire St-Joseph

Towering over the northwestern slopes of Mont Royal is the immense granite **Oratoire St-Joseph** (daily late June to late Aug 6.30am–9.30pm, late Aug to late June 7am–9pm; ⓣ514/733-8211, ⓦwww.saint-joseph.org; Métro Côte-des-Neiges or bus #51, #165, #166 or #535), a monumental domed shrine set on a promontory far back from chemin Queen-Mary. Upon approaching the main entrance at no. 3800, you may pass pilgrims – in search of physical cures – heading up the structure's hundred-odd steps on their knees. Such displays of devotion are the norm from visitors who often feel divinely inspired by the life of its late founder, Frère André Bessette (see box, p.106). For those unable to scale the steps, the church provides a free minibus service.

The sheer size of the structure almost lives up to its mythical aura as a pilgrimage destination. Topped by a remarkable 45-metre-high copper dome, which is surpassed in size only by that of St Peter's basilica in Rome, the interior chambers are so widely dispersed that escalators link the complex's main sights, including the hypnotic **Votive Chapel**, majestic **basilica** and an **exhibition** on Frère André that features one of Montréal's most bizarre spectacles (see p.106). The Oratory also provides a suitably grand space for regular organ and carillon **recitals**. Enter through the doors to the left of the main portico, where detailed guidebooks are available free of charge; guided tours are also available (times vary).

The ground-floor **Votive Chapel** is the Oratory's eeriest room – the flames of 10,000 votive candles illuminate a colossal collection of wooden canes, crutches and braces left behind by pilgrims (their sheer numbers seeming to be directed against visiting sceptics). A central statue of St Joseph with his arms outstretched stands between two doorways leading to a simple room containing Frère André's **tomb**, where parishioners can often be found touching the black-marble slab in an attempt to establish a connection with the man.

The landing at the top of the first set of escalators leads to an outdoor terrace with terrific **views** across the northern swathes of the city, and to the

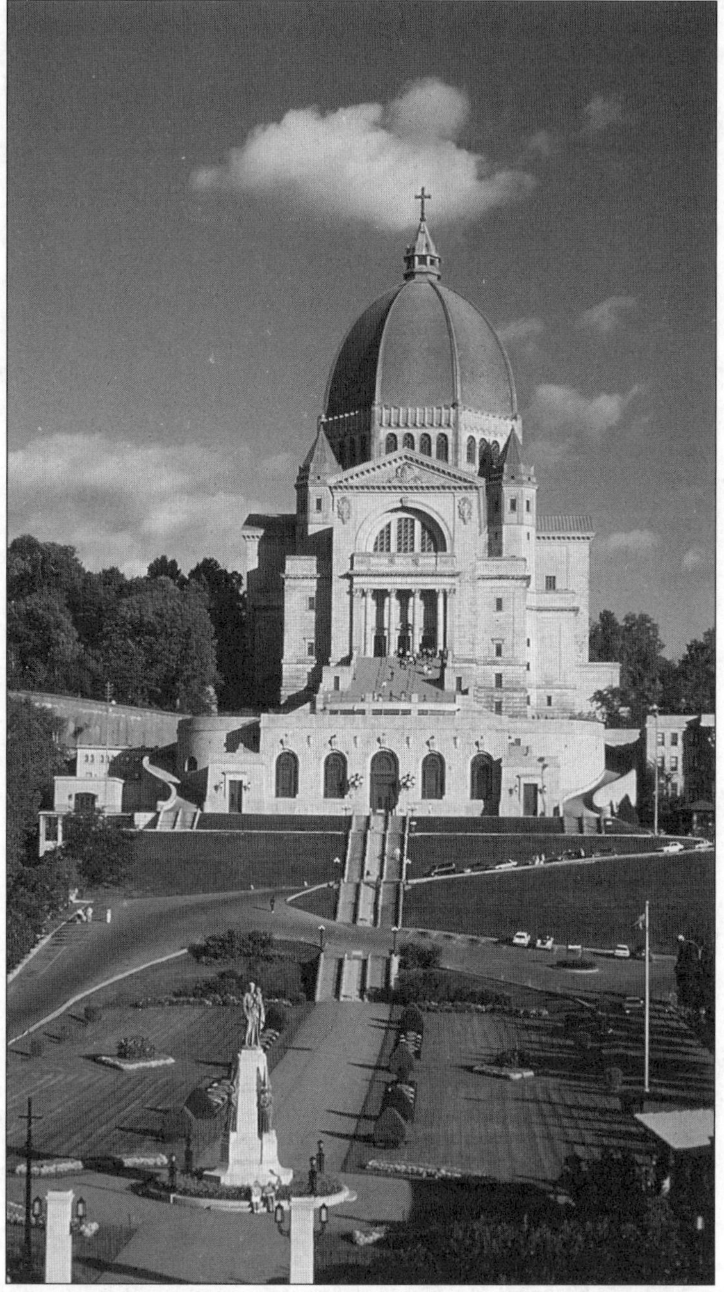

△ Oratoire St-Joseph

Montréal's miracle man

The founder of the Oratoire St-Joseph, the **Blessed Brother André** (1845–1937), is one miracle away from sainthood. Pope John Paul II recognized the first of his necessary two posthumous miracles in 1982, after a cancer-stricken New Yorker returned home from the Oratory disease-free. Still, André Bessette's early years didn't portend such greatness. At the age of 25, he was asked to leave the religious order of the Holy Cross because he was too sickly to perform the manual labour asked of him. After the bishop of Montréal intervened, André was allowed to stay on as a lay brother and was given the lowest job on the order's totem pole: porter of Collège Notre-Dame, a boys' school facing where the Oratory stands today.

It was here that André's extraordinary curative powers began to show, as after he tended to ailing parishioners many of them soon healed completely. He attributed his abilities to the oil he applied to their afflictions – an unguent that came from a lamp below a small statue of St Joseph in the college chapel. As knowledge of André's abilities spread, thousands of sick pilgrims began visiting the school. To make room, he built a primitive chapel in St Joseph's name at the top of the future oratory's grounds in 1904, using $200 saved, in part, from tips received for cutting the boys' hair. More than four hundred cures were recorded here in 1916 alone.

Brother André never took credit for the cures pilgrims received, but always deferred to St Joseph's divine generosity. Indeed, André's devotion to St Joseph was so intense that he deemed the chapel an insufficient monument to his patron saint, and began canvassing for donations to build the massive shrine that stands today. André never saw it finished – he died in 1937, 18 years before the basilica was inaugurated. Impressively, one million mourners came to see his body laid out in the Votive Chapel.

Oratory's **gardens** of the Way of the Cross, landscaped by Frederick G. Todd, the man behind Île Ste-Hélène (see p.118) and Québec City's Plains of Abraham (see p.254).

Tucked away on a mezzanine two floors up from the chapel is the Frère André **exhibition**. Here, three rooms central to his life have been re-created with their original furnishings. His bedroom, with its tiny bench-like bed and small roll-top desk, illustrates his ascetic ways. The main draw on this floor is on the other side of the exhibition where, amazingly, a gold box atop a marble column holds Frère André's **heart**. It has been preserved as a sign of admiration, and some pilgrims have claimed it has twitched in their presence.

Further up is the **basilica**, an enormous space with a soaring domed ceiling. After the heavy iconography found in the lower levels, the basilica's lack of frills is quite refreshing. Its cruciform layout is simply ornamented by six wooden carvings of the apostles mounted at the end of each transept and a few stone representations of Christ's procession with the cross, inset in the connecting corridors. A corridor behind the altar accesses the most richly decorated part of the basilica, the **Chapel of the Blessed Sacrament**, painted from floor to ceiling in gold leaf and anchored by chunky green-marble columns. The doors to the right lead outside to Frère André's original rustic **chapel** to St Joseph, with decor common to Québec's hinterlands, particularly the cross over the small altar – it's festooned with vanity-mirror lightbulbs. As you leave the chapel, the driveway exits onto Summit Crescent, leading to Summit Circle and the Westmount lookout (see p.124).

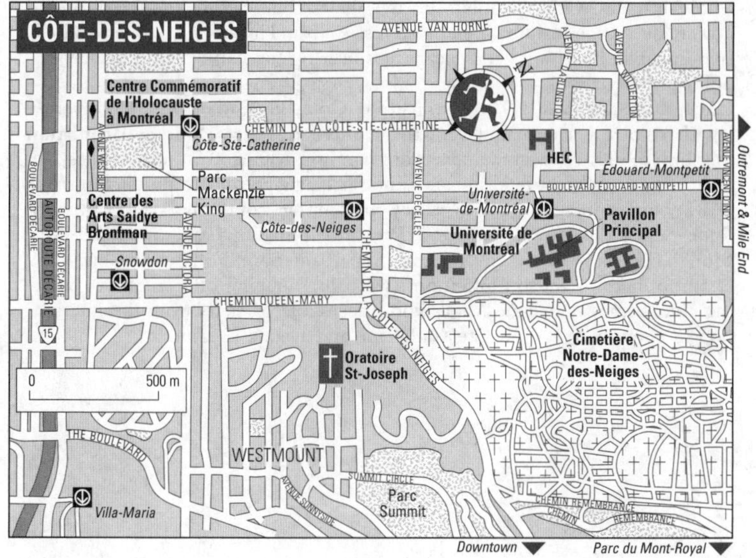

Côte-des-Neiges

The neighbourhood overlooked by the Oratory, **Côte-des-Neiges**, is largely residential, populated with families and some of the 50,000-plus students who attend the **Université de Montréal**. You can get a glimpse of the area from the #51 bus, which passes in front of the Oratory and along the length of the university campus which spreads along the mountain's northern slopes. Its most notable feature is Ernest Cormier's **Pavillon Principal**, a massive yellow-brick Art Deco structure whose tripartite wings frame a central block dominated by the university's signature tower (unfortunately, although the tower promises some incredible views, it is inaccessible). Other than providing visual appeal, however, the campus offers little of interest to visitors, and you're just as well to continue eastward on the bus past the handsome Outremont homes to avenue Laurier (see p.97).

Centre Commémoratif de l'Holocauste à Montréal and the Centre des Arts Saidye Bronfman

About 25 minutes' walk northwest of the Oratory via avenue Victoria is the recently expanded **Centre Commémoratif de l'Holocauste à Montréal** (Montréal Holocaust Memorial Centre). Located in the same building as the Jewish Public Library at 5151 chemin de la Côte-Ste-Catherine (Mon–Fri 10am–4pm; suggested donation of $5; ⓣ514/345-2605, ⓦwww.mhmc.ca; Métro Côte-des-Neiges), the centre is a repository not just of artefacts relating to the Holocaust but also of videotaped testimonies from survivors, many of whom, along with their descendants, live in the area and the suburbs to the west. The museum's exhibits are as poignant as you'd expect but rather than portraying the Jews sent to the concentration camps merely as victims, it also highlights the many small acts of defiance, through keepsakes like a heart-shaped autograph book crafted as a birthday present for a young woman by her fellow inmates. Other exhibits portray Jewish life before the Nazi rise to power, illustrating just how much was lost – a panel listing 5000 towns and villages inhabited by Jews stands near walls bearing the names of the concentration camps that took their place.

Across the street at 5170 chemin de la Côte-Ste-Catherine, contemporary Jewish culture is the mainstay of the **Centre des Arts Saidye Bronfman** (Ⓣ514/739-2301, Ⓦwww.saidyebronfman.org; Métro Côte-des-Neiges), an arts centre that hosts Yiddish- and English-language theatre productions (see p.187) and contains an art gallery presenting contemporary exhibitions (June–Sept Mon–Thurs 9am–7pm, Fri 9am–4pm, Sun 10am–5pm; Oct–May Mon–Thurs 9am–9pm, Fri 9am–2pm, Sun 10am–5pm). You can take bus #129 east from here to get to Outremont (see p.96), hopping off as it curves below the chic homes of avenue Maplewood, accessible by stairs from the intersection of chemin de la Côte-Ste-Catherine and avenue Laurier.

6

Parc Olympique and Jardin Botanique

On a clear day, the **Parc Olympique**'s striking architectural forms act like a magnet, enticing visitors from Montréal's Downtown to the Hochelaga-Maisonneuve neighbourhood, six kilometres to the east. Rising on the slope above the district's residential and industrial tracts, the flying-saucer-shaped **Stade Olympique** anchors the site of the 1976 Olympic Games. Climbing up the stadium's eastern side is the **Tour de Montréal**, an inclined tower with terrific views from its observation deck. The nearby Vélodrome, another relic of the Games, was transformed in 1992 into the **Biodôme**, an engrossing sort of indoor zoo that re-creates four distinct ecosystems.

While the sheer scale of the stadium may draw your attention at first, the real reward for venturing this far from the urban core is the colourful **Jardin Botanique**, one of the largest botanical gardens in the world. Among its gardens and greenhouses are a Ming Dynasty replica **Chinese Garden**, a traditional **Japanese Garden** and the unique **Insectarium**, crawling with all manner of six- and eight-legged creatures.

Leave time as well for a tour of the elegant **Château Dufresne**, a restored Beaux-Arts residence built in the early twentieth century for two brothers who were prominent players in the development of the short-lived, visionary city of **Maisonneuve** to the south.

Park practicalities

The easiest way to reach this area from Downtown is the fifteen-minute Métro ride on the green line to the Viau or Pie-IX (pronounced "pee neuf") stations, though you can also get out there by cycling along the rue Rachel bike path – it's about twenty to thirty minutes from rue St-Denis. The gardens and the park cover a huge area but fortunately a half-hourly shuttle bus (11am–5pm; free) links each attraction with the Métro Viau stop.

The "Nature Package" lets you visit the Biodôme, Jardin Botanique and Insectarium for $17, while the "Get an Eyeful" pass also includes the Tour de Montréal for $25. These are available only at the attractions themselves. **Places to eat** are a bit thin on the ground; there are cafeterias in the Biodôme and the Jardin Botanique (in the warmer months) but your best bet is to pack a lunch beforehand for a picnic in the grassy areas east of the stadium or in Parc Maisonneuve, adjacent to the Jardin Botanique (be sure to get your hand stamped for re-entry).

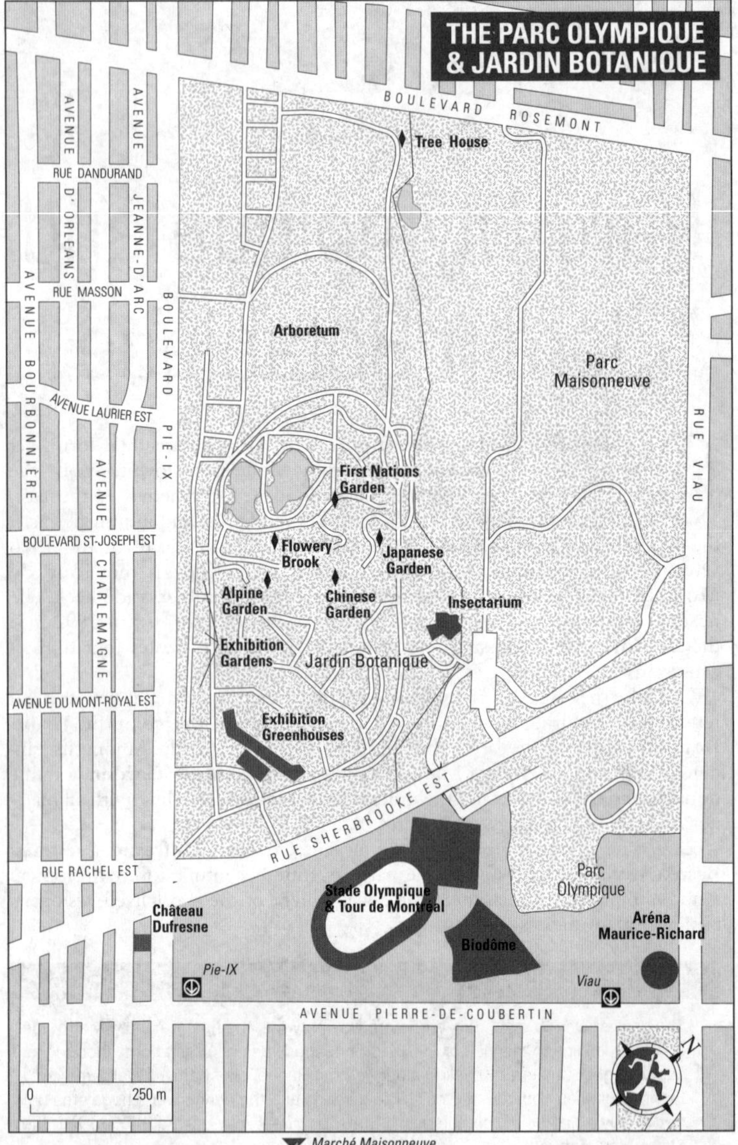

The Parc Olympique

The 1976 Olympics resulted in one of the city's most recognizable landmarks – and also one of its biggest follies. French architect Roger Taillibert, who also designed the Stade du Parc des Princes in Paris, was enlisted to create the **Parc Olympique**, the Games' massive arena and housing complex, and was told money was no object. Indeed, then-mayor Jean Drapeau even declared: "It is as unlikely that Montréal will incur a debt as for a man to bear a child." Biology has yet to catch up, but the complex ended up costing $1.4 billion (over $2 billion with subsequent maintenance and interest) – a large chunk of which is still outstanding. In addition to travails with the Kevlar roof and a falling concrete beam in 1991, the stadium's bad luck extended to Canada's Olympic hopefuls – it was the only country not to win a gold medal while hosting the Games.

The Stade Olympique and the Tour de Montréal

At the centre of the Parc Olympique complex looms the **Stade Olympique** (daily mid-Feb to late June & early Sept to Dec 9am–5pm; late June to early Sept 9am–7pm; tower: $10, tour: $5.50, both: $12.50; ⓦwww.rio.gouv.qc.ca; Métro Viau or Pie-IX), home to a varied line-up of rock concerts, monster truck races, trade shows and baseball games. It's an impressive sight, with huge concrete ribs rising out of an asphalt expanse to enclose the stadium's shell. Locals refer to the stadium as the "Big O" – ostensibly because of its shape or for the "O" in Olympic, but more often for the fact that the city still owes so much money for its construction. Adding insult to injury, the **Expos**, the Major League Baseball team who play here are perennially threatening to move. There are half-hour **guided tours** (ⓣ514/252-4737 or 1-877/997-0919 for schedule), but for the time being at least, the best way to see the stadium is from the (invariably) cheap seats during an Expos baseball game (see p.202).

Adjoining the stadium and rising above it in a graceful arc is the 175-metre-high **Tour de Montréal**, the world's tallest inclined tower. Although it was designed to hold the steel cables that (in theory) would raise the stadium's 65-tonne roof, at the time of the Games it was still just a concrete stump – the upper section was not completed until 1987, and the movable roof was installed soon after (it never really worked properly, though, and was replaced by a fixed roof in 1998). The Tourist Hall in the base of the tower sells tickets for tours and rides on the funicular, which rumbles up along the tower's spine, rewarding riders with a panoramic view across the city from the top – on a clear day you can see as far as the Laurentians 60km to the northwest. It's worth noting, though, that you can get an equally striking view for free from atop Mont Royal. The tower's lower floor houses an interesting **exhibition** of photographs on Montréal's development throughout the twentieth century that makes the tower's ticket price somewhat more worthwhile.

Biodôme de Montréal

The Parc Olympique's old Vélodrome, the scalloped-roof structure south of the tower, is now the **Biodôme** (daily 9am–5pm, summers until 7pm; $10.50; ⓣ514/868-3000, ⓦwww.biodome.qc.ca; Métro Viau), an environmental museum comprising four distinct ecosystems. Taillibert's design has proven as well suited for its current role as it was for Olympic cycling events, as the large, column-free roof span allows visitors to wander freely through the flora- and fauna-filled zones.

While touring the hot and humid **tropical rainforest** section keep an eye out for the sloths; they move so slowly that their fur grows algae, quite unlike the lively tamarins and tiny black callimico monkeys that swing through the trees above. It's hard to miss the screeching scarlet macaws, but you may need to ask the keen-eyed guides to point out the shyer creatures. It's noticeably cooler in the **Laurentian forest** portion, where you can look at an actual beaver dam and take a televised peek inside its lodge. Beyond that, in the

The City of Maisonneuve (1883–1918)

The neighbourhood directly south of the Parc Olympique was, for 35 years, the independent city of **Maisonneuve**. It was founded by wealthy Francophones who decided they would be better off on their own rather than being amalgamated by Montréal. Influenced by the **City Beautiful** reform movement, prominent citizens such as the Dufresne brothers hoped that Maisonneuve would be a model industrial city. Buoyed by its proximity to both the St Lawrence River and railways, Maisonneuve did indeed become a major independent (albeit short-lived) manufacturing centre.

Followers of the City Beautiful movement believed in part that a beautiful city would encourage moral and civic virtue in its citizens. Maisonneuve's elite thus began construction on wide boulevards and elegant Beaux Arts public buildings. Architect Marius Dufresne was instrumental in designing many of these, including the **Bain Morgan**, an ornate public bath fronted by classical Ionic columns, and **Marché Maisonneuve**, a large public market topped by a copper-covered cupola and chateau-style corner towers (fruit and veg are now sold at stalls in a modern building just to the east). Both are fronted by statues sculpted by Alfred Laliberté and face onto the plaza at the intersection of rue Ontario est and avenue Morgan, a kilometre south of the Stade Olympique. Further south, and seemingly parachuted in from nowhere, the 1915 **fire station** bears an uncanny resemblance to Frank Lloyd Wright's Unity Temple in Chicago. Despite the wealth generated by local industry, such grand projects ultimately led to the municipality's bankruptcy in 1918, and the city of Maisonneuve was soon after annexed by Montréal.

Further information is available from Tourisme Hochelaga-Maisonneuve (Ⓣ514/256-4636, Ⓦwww.tourismemaisonneuve.qc.ca), who operate an info kiosk on the plaza in the summer months and occasionally offer guided tours of the district's churches and historical buildings.

St Lawrence marine ecosystem, petrels, terns and kittiwakes fly overhead, occasionally touching down on an impressive tidal rock pool complete with foaming waves and a multicoloured population of anemones, crabs, lobsters and starfish. In the final **Polar zone** there are both Arctic and Antarctic ecosystems – puffins bob and dive along a replica Labrador coast, while close by four different species of penguins waddle amusingly on snow-covered slopes.

Jardin Botanique de Montréal

With its harsh winters, Montréal seems an unlikely locale for one of the world's largest botanical gardens, but the **Jardin Botanique de Montréal** (daily: 9am–4pm, late June to early Sept until 6pm, mid-Sept to early Nov until 9pm; $10.50 May–Oct, $7.75 Nov–April; Ⓣ514/872-1400, Ⓦwww.ville.montreal.qc.ca/jardin; Métro Pie-IX), immediately north of the Parc Olympique, is just that, second in size only to London's Kew Gardens. Begun in 1931, the 185-acre site, which comprises some thirty thematic gardens and ten greenhouses, can easily take a full day to explore. The **main gate** at the corner of boulevard Pie-IX and rue Sherbrooke provides the most dramatic approach, passing by a procession of colourful flowerbeds and a statue of founder Frère Marie-Victorin on the way to the Art Deco administration building. Behind the latter is the **reception centre**, where you can find out when the various guided tours of the site (and of specific gardens) take place. Between May and October, a free mini-train travels from the reception centre to the Insectarium and Tree House every fifteen minutes.

The exhibition greenhouses

The reception centre leads to the **Molson Hospitality Greenhouse**, where fan palms, bamboo and other sub-tropical plants provide a backdrop to introductory displays on plant biology. From here, the rest of the greenhouses branch off in two narrow rows. The hot and humid **east wing** begins with a simulated **tropical rainforest** canopy, the fake tree limbs hosting several types of bromeliads, rootless plants which collect water in their funnel of leaves to survive. The next conservatory may look similar, but the **tropical economic plants** flourishing here – which provide everything from coffee to medicines – help illustrate society's dependency on the rapidly disappearing rainforests. Next door in the most striking greenhouse, scores of multicoloured **orchids** and **aroids**, such as the elegant calla lily, appear to have colonized an ancient ruin, the walls of which were actually built from salvaged Vieux-Montréal cobblestones.

The pathways in the east wing are narrow, and, when crowded, you may prefer the more varied, and less busy, **west wing**. First up is the **begonias and gesneriads** conservatory, whose bright flowers contrast greatly with the **arid regions** room next door, where a desert landscape supports spiky aloe, prickly pears and giant cacti straight out of a Road Runner cartoon. Further on, the footbridge and ponds of the aptly named **Garden of Weedlessness** create a memorable stage for the impressive Chinese *penjings* (dwarfed trees), tended and pruned with exacting care, while the two-tiered **Main Exhibition Greenhouse**, at the end of the west wing, showcases everything from springtime perennials to a carved pumpkin competition.

The outdoor gardens and Arboretum

The first part of the Jardin Botanique to be developed, the **Exhibition Gardens**, bordering boulevard Pie-IX, are laid out in a formal French manner with a central axis interrupted by vine-covered pergolas and decorative fountains. Nearest to the reception centre are the **Perennial Garden** and **Economic Plant Garden**, installed to educate visitors on the practical uses of plants such as indigo and camomile. The axis terminates with a cluster of smaller gardens, including a collection of **poisonous plants** – fortunately fenced off.

The path opposite the Garden of Innovations – a showcase of landscaping trends located midway along the axis – leads to the **Alpine Garden**, where hardy dwarf conifers poke out of the scree and delicate alpine poppies cling to a pseudomountainous landscape. A small waterfall flows into a stream, along whose banks lies the English-style **Flowery Brook** garden of lilies, irises and peonies. The brook itself feeds the ponds at the centre of the Jardin Botanique, one of which borders on the **First Nations Garden**, celebrating native-peoples' relationship with the land and also serving as the site of related activities and performances.

Beyond the ponds, and covering more than half of the botanical garden's area, is the sprawling **Arboretum**, a popular spot for local birdwatchers (a leaflet on captive species is available at the reception centre) and, in winter, cross-country skiers. It's at its loveliest in autumn when many of the 200-odd species of trees and shrubs turn fiery shades of yellow and orange. In the far northeast corner here, the **Tree House** interpretation centre holds a unique collection of dwarf North American trees, cultivated in the same manner as Japanese bonsai.

The Chinese and Japanese gardens

The true highlights of the Jardin Botanique are the two gardens based on traditional landscaping principles of China and Japan. To get to them, head east from the reception centre, where you'll first come across the **Rose Garden** and then the **Marsh and Bog Garden**, whose lotuses and water lilies are laid out in a grid of ponds with sunken pathways so you can see the plants up close.

From here, a pathway to the left leads through a grand pagoda-like arch guarded by stone lions to the **Chinese Garden**'s entrance courtyard, where a full-moon gate provides a perfect frame for the ensemble of seven pavilions interconnected by pathways and bridges – all often filled with human traffic. The design is a replica of a Ming Dynasty garden, and its most arresting feature is the **Tower of the Condensing Clouds**, a delicate 14-metre-high pagoda perched on the rock face above a small lake. The tree peony blooms – described by Marco Polo as "roses the size of cabbages" – are another startling sight, though you'll only see these bursts of soft pink if you visit in June. Throughout the year, Scotch pine and some twenty species of bamboo provide a green backdrop to numerous *penjings* (dwarfed trees), magnolias, azaleas and artfully placed stones, many of which were imported from China. The best time to visit is on an autumn evening, when hundreds of Chinese lanterns illuminate the garden.

Far more serene, the **Japanese Garden** is a short walk to the northeast. The simple compositional elements of water, rock, plants, bridges and lanterns reward you with carefully planned views along the perimeter of its pond – save perhaps from the north side, with the Olympic Stadium in the distance breaking the harmony. The garden might be best appreciated from the **Japanese Garden Pavilion**, especially during the occasional tea ceremonies ($2–6; ⓣ514/872-1400 for schedule), which also allow access to the *roji* (tea garden); free guided tours are also available. Designed in the style of a traditional family home, the pavilion also has within its precincts a Zen garden and a collection of bonsai, the oldest of which are around 350 years old – almost the age of Montréal itself.

Insectarium

Much shorter-lived than the ancient bonsai are the inhabitants of the nearby **Insectarium** (ⓦwww.ville.montreal.qc.ca/insectarium), a building to the southeast shaped like a stylized housefly and devoted solely to insects and arthropods. The upper level is the more educationally oriented, with interactive displays on insect physiognomy standing alongside a collection of mounted butterflies – though in summer, it's more fun to see them in action in the adjacent **butterfly house** where local species flit about. There's also a transparent beehive that lets you see the busy inhabitants go about their work.

The bulk of the collection is downstairs, where some of the mounted beetles look like beautifully wrought jewellery, though the horned rhinoceros beetles might put you off ever wanting to visit the tropics. The live scorpions, tarantulas and giant centipedes are hardly more comforting, even behind glass. If you can overcome your fears, consider dropping by in November for the insect-tasting sessions when local chefs sauté scorpions and wrap other critters in pastry or chocolate (see box, opposite).

Le Château Dufresne

In contrast to the modernistic, fluid forms of the Stade Olympique across boulevard Pie-IX, the Beaux-Arts **Château Dufresne** at 2929 av Jeanne-

Crunchy snacks

When people speak of Montréal's many culinary delights, they're not typically referring to concocting mealworm-filled biscotti. And yet, a dish just like this one has graced the menu at the Insectarium for ten years running.

Inaugurated in 1993, and held annually over several weekends between early November and early December, the Insectarium's novel **Croque-insectes** (Insect Tastings) event has since attracted over 250,000 brave souls to nibble on critters ranging from ants to scorpions. Sautéed, baked and marinated by chefs from the highly regarded Institut de Tourisme et d'Hôtellerie du Québec, the wide-ranging menus have introduced exotic delicacies such as Madagascar morsels (spicy grilled scorpion or stick insects), cricket basbousa (couscous and honey cake garnished with crickets), and ant macaroons (infused with coconut). More than 100,000 mealworms, upwards of 60,000 crickets and approximately 5000 silkworm pupae are used to create the innovative snacks. Somewhat alarmingly, you'll find numerous very-much-alive and squirming examples of the very critters you're eating inhabiting the display cases located near the food-laden buffet tables.

Friday-night visitors have also been invited to sit at the so-called **Bug Bar** for the *5 à 7*, noshing on creepy-crawly tidbits and imbibing a non-alcoholic drink that invariably features a multi-legged creature or two. One year, the elixir of the moment was ant nectar – a "refreshing" number combining orange juice, bananas, honey and ants.

Officially intended to raise awareness of insects as a high-protein food group common to several African, Latin American and Asian diets, the event's unofficial drawing power is the test of will it exacts over its attendees. Even if you can't muster the courage to taste some insects yourself, it's still every bit worth attending just to watch others attempt to do so. It's not very often you see people eating with their eyes scrunched tightly shut – in trepidation.

d'Arc (Thurs–Sun 10am–5pm; $6; ⓣ514/259-9201, ⓦwww.chateaudufresne.qc.ca; Métro Pie-IX) presents a mannered and dignified sight. Inspired by the Petit Trianon palace at Versailles, the symmetrical facade gives no indication that there are actually two separate residences within, built between 1915 and 1918 for two brothers influential in the development of Maisonneuve (see box, p.112). The west wing housed the mansion's architect Marius Dufresne, while the east was home to his elder brother Oscar, an industrialist who headed the family's shoe-manufacturing company. After a mid-century stint as a religious boys' school, the building was abandoned. Although the chateau was restored as a museum in the late 1970s, restorers are still trying to uncover murals painted over by the Holy Cross Fathers – apparently the images were too provocative for their young charges.

The entrance is in back, where a small exhibit on the history of the building and the Dufresnes gives a bit of context, although the free guided tours in the afternoon (Thurs & Fri 3pm; Sat & Sun 2pm & 3.30pm) best bring the period to life. The tour begins by ascending a staircase to the main foyer of **Oscar Dufresne's residence**, where his visitors must have been impressed by the gold-damask walls and opulent marble staircase. A hallway leads past Oscar's study to a large drawing room designed with business rather than socializing in mind, its decorative restraint limited to a few features like the elaborate candelabra set against the mahogany-panelled walls. Before heading down the hall, check out the small salon to your left – the decidedly secular decoration is the work of Guido Nincheri, the Italian artist whose works feature in more than a dozen Montréal churches (see p.100). Keep an eye out for the "modern" touches in what initially appear to be classical scenes on the pastel-shaded walls

– the painted nude in one is framed by electricity poles, still a novelty back in the early 1900s.

A winter garden occupies the rear of Oscar's apartment, and through the breach made in the partition wall you can see its mirror image in **Marius Dufresne's residence**. Once inside the second brother's home, you'll notice almost immediately that it's less austere, and the eclectic mix of styles and comfortable design indicate a more intimate and domestic lifestyle. There's also more scope for whimsy, as the "Turkish lounge", with its bacchanalian frieze, plush cushions and hookah, attests. Recent renovations have uncovered another of Nincheri's works here – an eye-catching ceiling fresco of an angel and an elegant woman among the clouds.

Parc Jean-Drapeau

The roars and rumbles that spill out from the city's amusement park and annual auto races do much to obscure the more simple outdoor pleasures found at **Parc Jean-Drapeau**, the collective name of the two islands across from the Vieux-Port. With a combined 660 acres of greenspace – dotted with canals, parks and public art – the park is a popular urban escape, especially during the summer months as the breeze from the St Lawrence provides a welcome respite from the heat. Breaking up all the greenery are various buildings left over from the **1967 World's Fair** (the Universal Exposition whose theme was "Man and His World" and which is best known as simply Expo '67) that drew some fifty million visitors to **Île Ste-Hélène** and **Île Notre-Dame**. The National Archives of Canada has a detailed website (Ⓦwww.archives.ca/05/0533_e) about the event – don't skip the intro or you'll miss the hilarious Expo '67 theme song.

Note that you're unlikely to hear Montrealers refer to the islands as Parc Jean-Drapeau, a name given to commemorate former Mayor Jean Drapeau, the man responsible for Expo '67, who died in 1999. Instead, you're more likely to hear them identified by their individual names or as Parc des Îles.

Island practicalities

Parc Jean-Drapeau is easily reached from Downtown. The most efficient way is on the **Métro's** yellow line to the Jean-Drapeau station on Île Ste-Hélène. Île Notre-Dame is accessible from here by walking over one of the two **bridges** that connect the islands, or by taking bus #167 that stops to the left of the Métro station's exit and makes a tour of both islands. From mid-May to early October, a ten-minute **ferry** ride connects Île Ste-Hélène with the Quai Jacques-Cartier in the Vieux-Port (call Ⓣ514/281-8000 for schedules; $3.75). The **bike path** from the Vieux-Port will get you here in about thirty minutes; head west and take the turn-off to Cité du Havre that passes under Hwy-10 and over the Pont de la Concorde; access is not available during the week surrounding the major motorsports events. If you're heading back after dusk, you may want to pop your bike on the Métro instead (see p.27). You can also **drive** over either of the two bridges – though on-island parking is scarce and costs $10.

A seasonal **information** booth (late June to late Aug daily 9am–6pm; Ⓣ514/872-6120 or 7708, Ⓦwww.parcjeandrapeau.com) near the Métro gives out maps of the islands. While it's possible to walk around the islands, riding a bike or rollerblading are the best ways of getting around; a kiosk near the Métro station used to rent both of these and plans are afoot to find another concession – expect to pay around $8 per hour.

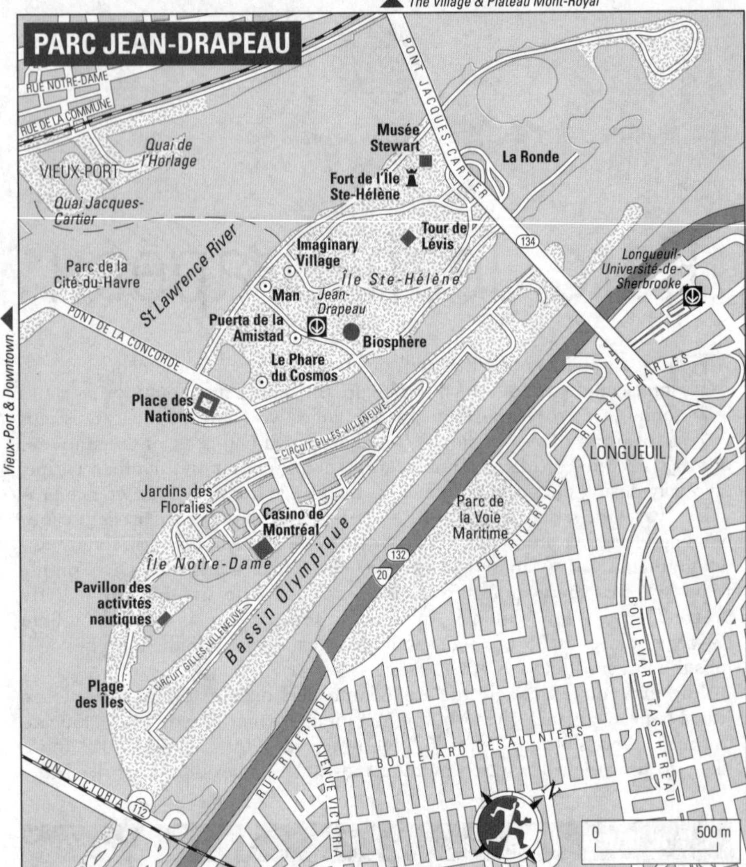

Île Ste-Hélène

Île Ste-Hélène, named after the wife of explorer Samuel de Champlain, who stumbled onto its shores in 1611, is the larger and more historic of the park's two islands. The island was the last French possession in North America to be surrendered to the British in 1760; 60 years later, they built a military garrison along its shores, but eventually ceded the island to Canada. Montréal purchased it in 1908, promising to turn the land around the old military camp into a public park.

The city made good on its vow, and the island now provides visitors with ample spots to lounge about and picnic. Designed by Frederick G. Todd, who also landscaped the gardens at the Oratoire St-Joseph (p.106) and Québec City's Plains of Abraham (p.254s), the park spreads out around a 45-metre-high grassy hillock, and is circled by one main road, the chemin du Tour de l'Île. The biggest draw, **La Ronde** (the city's **amusement park**), lords over its easternmost point, while the remains of the **military fort** are nearby along the northern shore. On the southern side looms the aluminium sphere that encloses the **Biosphère**, an engaging ecological museum that should not be confused with the Biodôme (see p.111).

La Biosphère

As you loop around to the left after exiting the Métro, you can't miss Buckminister Fuller's twenty-storey-high geodesic dome – built to house the United States pavilion during Expo '67 – rising ominously out of the greenery. Composed of thousands of interlocking aluminium triangles, the sphere was left to decay following the World's Fair, and lost its protective acrylic cover to fire in 1976. It was spruced up in 1992, and the **Biosphère** (June–Sept daily 10am–6pm; Oct–May Mon & Wed–Fri noon–5pm, Sat & Sun 10am–5pm; $8.50, $15 with Musée Stewart; ⓣ514/283-5000, ⓦwww.biosphere.ec.gc.ca; Métro Jean-Drapeau), an interactive centre with a focus on water ecosystems – the St Lawrence and Great Lakes in particular – moved in.

Using the raised platforms that remained inside the dome, the Biosphère created a structure resembling an oil rig with four large interior halls dedicated to watery pursuits. Several of the permanent installations employ a playful tone that aims to amuse as much as educate: there's a scale that measures your weight in water and a soothing Water Delights hall where you can bang on tonal water drums or soak your feet in a tiled Roman bath (towels are thoughtfully provided). Still, the best reason to visit the Biosphère may just be the **view** of the city and islands through the dome's metallic trusses from the fourth-floor observation deck.

Fort de l'Île Ste-Hélène and Musée Stewart

A twenty-minute walk from the Biosphère around the winding chemin du Tour de l'Île will get you to the grounds of Montréal's only **fort**, its U-shaped layout situated close to the river's edge. Built by the British between 1820 and 1824 as a defence against the threat of American invasion, its four low-lying buildings are made of stone culled from the island's core and surrounded by fortifications indented with loopholes and parapets. On the parade grounds between the walls is a heavy bronze **cannon** bearing George II's royal coat of arms; lost during a storm in 1760, it was recovered in 1957, during the creation of the St Lawrence Seaway.

The complex never saw battle and got heavy use as an ammunitions storehouse instead. The British withdrew in 1870, and Canadian soldiers patrolled the fort until the end of World War II, when the barracks served as a prison camp for some 250 Nazis and Canadian deserters. Opened as the **Musée Stewart** (mid-May to mid-Oct daily 10am–6pm; mid-Oct to mid-May Wed–Mon 10am–5pm; $8, $15 with Biosphère; ⓣ514/861-6701, ⓦwww.stewart-museum.org; Métro Jean-Drapeau) in 1955, the fort is staffed in the summer by costumed guides that lead informative, 45- to 60-minute tours and run loads of activities for kids. To get the most out of a summer visit, arrive in the early afternoon, when actors dressed as a ceremonial military corps perform drills on the parade grounds. The only building open to the public is the museum itself, in the former storehouse. Inside, there's an extensive collection of military memorabilia, full of uniforms and their accoutrements – French *justeaucorps* and pointy tricorn hats included – and all manner of threatening pistols, revolvers, rapiers and bayonets, some of which are etched with their original owner's insignias.

Public art on the islands

Among the more unique attractions in Parc Jean-Drapeau are several mammoth pieces of **public art**, their soaring steel and stone forms providing a striking contrast to the surrounding verdant landscape. While dotted about both islands, the most exceptional examples are clustered on the western tip of Île Ste-Hélène, including Mexican sculptor **Sebastián**'s fiery-red *Puerta de la Amistad*, on the chemin du Tour de l'Île west of the Métro (straight ahead as you exit). The openings between its three columns play tricks on the eyes – depending on where you stand, one shrinks and the other expands. Around 100m northwest, the grey-steel stabile *Man*, by **Alexander Calder**, stands at 20m high and 29m wide, the largest work ever produced by the American sculptor, and its lumbering mass of sweeping wings and curved angles is poised over a belvedere with terrific views across to the city. Over by the ferry wharf, five white-granite pillars rising high up from the ground comprise Portuguese sculptor **João Charters de Almeida**'s *Imaginary Village*, which looks strangely like a modern version of Roman ruins. A path leads south from Calder's piece to **Yves Trudeau**'s *Phare du Cosmos*, a 9.5-metre-high sculpted robot whose chunky torso sits atop a tripod base. His head and body used to move, but nowadays his mini-telescopic eyes are permanently transfixed on the Pont de la Concorde.

La Ronde

The shrieking sounds that can be heard all over the island's eastern point emanate from **La Ronde** (mid- to late May Sat & Sun 10am–8pm; early to mid-June daily 10am–8pm; mid-June to late Aug daily 10am–10.30pm; Sept Sat & Sun 10am–7pm; Oct Fri 5–9pm, Sat noon–9pm, Sun noon–8pm; rides: $29.55 plus tax, grounds only $22.60 plus tax; Ⓣ514/397-2000, Ⓦwww.laronde.com; Métro Jean-Drapeau and bus #167). Sold by the city to Six Flags in 2001, this amusement park is shedding its run-down image but at the price of increased corporatization – picnic hampers were banned in 2003, causing a local outcry. The line-ups for the forty-plus rides are usually short and the diversions good fun – the best is *Le Monstre*, the world's highest wooden double-track roller coaster. Close behind in thrills is *Orbite*, a rocket-launch simulator that shoots passengers 45m in the air before dropping them with a stomach-lurching plummet. With synchronized concert performances, La Ronde is also a good spot to watch the spectacular fireworks competition held every June through July (see p.212).

Île Notre-Dame

The man-made island **Île Notre-Dame** rose from the St Lawrence in the mid-1960s, its elongated teardrop shape consisting solely of silt and rock dredged from the riverbed and the construction of Île Ste-Hélène's Métro line. Today, its major draws are the massive **casino** complex along the shores of its lake and, for a couple of long summer weekends, the **Grand Prix** and **Molson Indy** (see p.202 for details) – which turn the island into a giant pit stop of fumes, screeching tires and concession stands, and make much of the island inaccessible to visitors. Île Notre-Dame is in fact completely encircled by the 4.42km **Circuit Gilles-Villeneuve** racetrack, which when not in use by race-car drivers is open to the public for rollerblading, cycling and cross-country skiing. More worthwhile, though, are Île Notre-Dame's **parklands** – its 300 acres are ideal for strolling as they're delightfully laced with canals overarched with wooden footbridges.

Casino de Montréal

The diamond-shaped building that held Expo '67's French pavilion presides over Île Notre-Dame like the centrepiece of a giant engagement ring. Shielded from the sun by aluminium shards, the five-storey building is a marvel of concrete, steel and glass, and served a stint as the Palais de Civilisations, a museum showcasing treasures from ancient cultures, before being reconfigured as a **casino** (Ⓣ514/392-2746, Ⓦwww.casinos-quebec.com; Métro Jean-Drapeau and bus #167) in 1993. It quickly proved too small to serve its growing clientele, and was expanded in 1996 to include the sawed-off pyramid (formerly home to Expo '67's Québec pavilion) to the east. The casino is now host to a whopping 3000 slot machines and 120 gaming tables, and the place teems with players around the clock. A free hourly shuttle bus runs directly to the casino from the Centre Infotouriste (see p.44) in summer (May–Oct noon–7pm, July & Aug until 9pm).

The beach and gardens

Most of Île Notre-Dame's outdoor activities are clustered around the casino, and clearly signposted along the island's footpaths. The chunk of land immediately north of the casino envelops the perennially blooming **Jardins des Floralies**, a garden laced with willow-shrouded canals and treed parklands whose benches and calming fountain invite lingering stays. Southwest of the casino, you'll find the city's only beach, the **Plage des Îles** (late June to late Aug 10am–7pm; $7.50, $4.50 after 4pm; Ⓣ514/872-6120), forming a sandy crescent moon along the southern edge of the man-made lake in the island's centre. You can rent pedal-boats and other watercraft to cruise the canals and lake at the **Pavillon des activités nautiques** (Ⓣ514/872-0199) at the beach's north entrance for $12/hour.

8

The western neighbourhoods

To experience a small-town atmosphere not easily found in central Montréal, head out to the city's western neighbourhoods. **Westmount**, which borders Downtown's western fringes and was until 2002 an independent city, has a picturesque English feel, complete with Victorian houses and tree-lined streets. The mansions belonging to the city's Anglo-Saxon elite look down – literally – from here over the city's poorer neighbourhoods flanking the banks of the **Lachine Canal**. Both **Pointe St-Charles** and **St-Henri** are throwbacks to the industrial era, their landscapes crossed by railroad tracks and dominated by tenement housing. Aside from the former's seventeenth-century Maison St-Gabriel, and the teeming Marché Atwater and "antique alley" of the latter, the area's main draw is the **Lachine Canal bike path** that starts from the Parc des Écluses in the Vieux-Port. At the western end of the 14km bike path lies the town of **Lachine**, a once booming fur-trade burg whose skyline is a miniature version of Vieux-Montréal's, silver dome and church spires included.

Westmount

The wealthy residential neighbourhood of **Westmount**, which tumbles down from the slopes of the mountain's western peak, became the new epicentre of Anglo-Saxon wealth after the stock market crash of 1929 forced Golden Square Milers to settle permanently into their one-time summer cottages. The choicest of these grand "cottages" remain perched high up on the mountain slopes, and while it's a hike to see them, the views from up top make the effort well worth it.

Westmount's few notable sights are clustered within a seven-block radius of avenue Greene, which is lined with upscale boutiques and presided over by a triad of impersonal black-steel and tinted-glass towers designed by Mies van der Rohe and collectively known as **Westmount Square**. The Atwater Métro station's underground passageway connects to the Square's shopping concourse, from where you can exit onto avenue Greene. Once outside, turn right and then left onto boulevard de Maisonneuve to reach Westmount's architectural standout at the corner of rue Clarke, the chunky Romanesque **Église St-Léon** anchored by a gabled bell tower. The church's interior is a visual feast of Italian marble floors, columns embellished with Florentine mosaics and superbly coloured frescoes, painted by the prolific Guido Nincheri (whose sec-

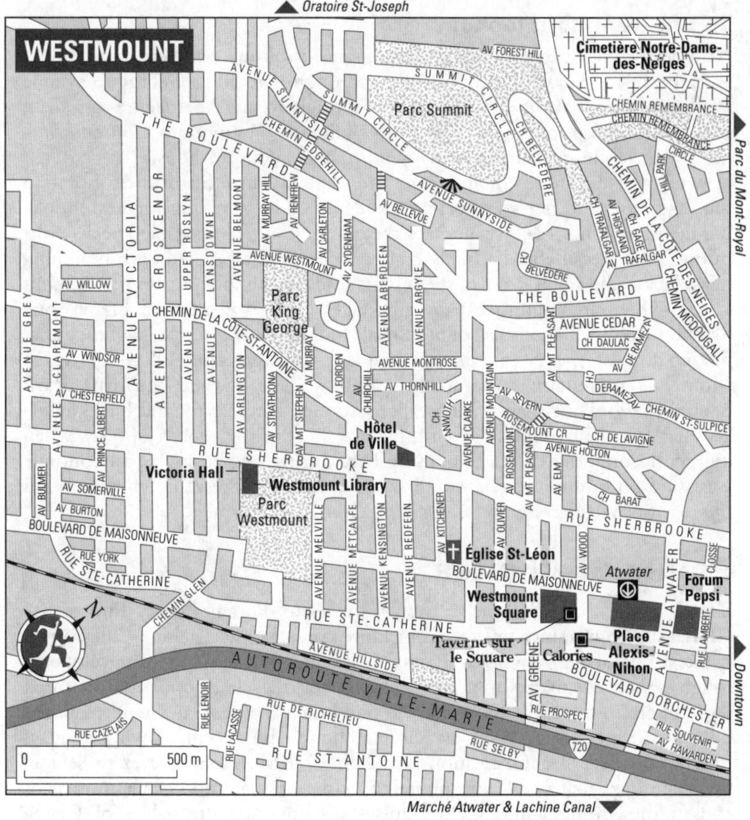

ular, allegorical paintings adorn the Château Dufresne; see p.115), on every inch of the domed ceiling. Nincheri's altar painting is the most intriguing work on display here, as it shows the church's namesake standing with Attila the Hun; he's hardly the personage you'd expect in a religious portrait, but it turns out that St Leo (the fifth-century Pope Leo I) was instrumental in convincing Attila to leave Italy.

One block north of the church, and another block west on rue Sherbrooke ouest, is the Neo-Tudor **Hôtel de Ville** (City Hall), at no. 4333. There's not much to see inside; more action is found at the rear, where locals, doffed in sporty whites, frequently play croquet or lawn bowls on the village green in the summer. West of here is one of the oldest public libraries in the province, the 1899 **Westmount Library**, 4574 rue Sherbrooke O (Mon–Fri 10am–9pm; Sat & Sun 10am–5pm), its leaded windows engraved with the names of influential writers and philosophers. There's a cheerful domed **greenhouse** inside the library with goldfish-filled pools and park benches; the door at its western end leads to the ground-floor atrium of **Victoria Hall**, where local artists' works are showcased. More upscale boutiques are found west of the library on rue Sherbrooke ouest; for a list of Westmount's best shops, see p.191.

To the Westmont lookout

No one road leads directly up to Westmount's **lookout**, a fifteen-minute walk away. From the library, head northward through Parc King-George to avenue Westmount, and take it eastward until you reach avenue Aberdeen. From here, strike north again to the curvy **avenue Bellevue**, Westmount's most enchanting street. Its heady hairpin turns wind past gingerbread houses, ivy-covered brownstones and stone cottages before reaching **avenue Sunnyside**, home to the neighbourhood's ritziest private residences. The rambling medieval-looking mansion at no. 12–14 is perhaps the grandest of all – its gabled peaks poke through the trees behind a finely crafted gridiron gate etched with blooming lilies. Across the street, a set of steep stairs leads to the lookout on rue Summit Circle, where an impressive panorama takes in the gabled roofs of the tony neighbourhood, the expanse of industrial lands bordering the St Lawrence and, poking out of the river valley, the distant Monteregian Hills – of which Montréal's mountain is the westerly outpost. The 45-acre **Summit Park** behind the lookout is an unlandscaped, wooded nature park and bird sanctuary that's particularly popular with birdwatchers in the month of May, when high concentrations of passerines stop here during migration. If you continue westward on Summit Circle, you'll arrive at Summit Crescent, which accesses the rear of the Oratoire St-Joseph (see p.104).

Pointe St-Charles

Slightly more than a kilometre west of the Vieux-Port lies gritty **Pointe St-Charles**, a community severed from Downtown by the Lachine Canal and a string of major highways. The Pointe, as it's affectionately called, developed a rough reputation thanks to a largely Irish, working-class population that first settled here in the early 1800s to help build the canal and later worked in the now-defunct factories along its shores. Though pretty run-down nowadays (despite pockets of gentrification), the Pointe's Irish legacy is ever-present in the shamrocks that emblazon the neighbourhood's bar and corner-store signs and in the wrought-iron Celtic crosses ornamenting the gables of **Grace Church** at 2083 rue Wellington.

Maison St-Gabriel

In the Pointe's south end at 2146 Place Dublin stands the neighborhood's main attraction, the **Maison St-Gabriel** (late June to early Sept Tues–Sun 11am–5pm, early April to late June & early Sept to mid-Dec Tues–Sun 1–4pm on the hour; $7, $3 site only, Sat 11am–3pm free; ⓣ514/935-8136, ⓦwww.maisonsaint-gabriel.qc.ca; Métro Charlevoix and bus #57), a picturesque duo of seventeenth-century fieldstone buildings tucked behind a monstrous 1960s apartment complex. The lovely manor house, trimmed by two stone chimneys and capped by a petite bell tower, once served as the school and residence of the King's Wards (see box, p.126); livestock was sheltered in the rustic barn nearby. The estate's location is unexpected, given the Pointe's industrial tenor, but there was little else around when Sœur Marguerite Bourgeoys purchased the land in 1668 and founded the school, a decade after initiating the Chapelle Notre-Dame-de-Bon-Secours (see p.77). Besides housing her order of nuns, the house also served as a neighbourhood school and farm.

The current house dates from 1698 – the original burned five years earlier – and opened as a **museum** in 1966. Members of the congregation founded by

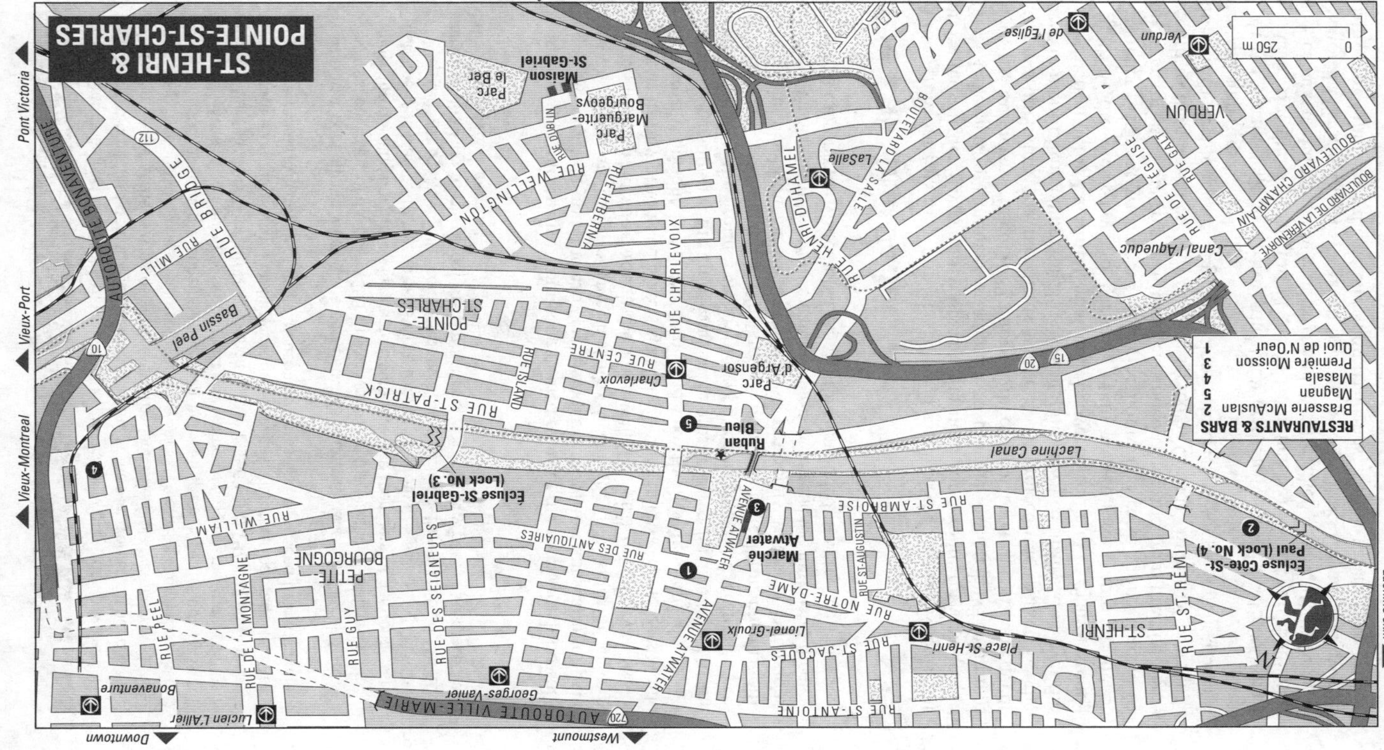
ST-HENRI &
POINTE-ST-CHARLES
Vieux-Montreal
Vieux-Port
Pont Victoria
Downtown
Westmount
Lachine 8km
Pont Champlain & Île des Soeurs
AUTOROUTE BONAVENTURE
AUTOROUTE VILLE-MARIE
RUE PEEL
RUE DE LA MONTAGNE
RUE WILLIAM
RUE GUY
PETITE-BOURGOGNE
RUE DES SEIGNEURS
RUE DES ANTIQUAIRES
AVENUE ATWATER
RUE ST-ANTOINE
RUE ST-JACQUES
RUE NOTRE-DAME
RUE ST-AUGUSTIN
RUE ST-AMBROISE
RUE ST-RÉMI
ST-HENRI
Lachine Canal
Écluse St-Gabriel (Lock No. 3)
Écluse Côte-St-Paul (Lock No. 4)
Marché Atwater
Ruban Bleu
Parc d'Argensor
RUE ST-PATRICK
RUE ISLAND
RUE CENTRE
RUE CHARLEVOIX
POINTE-ST-CHARLES
RUE WELLINGTON
RUE HIBERNIA
RUE DUBLIN
Parc Marguerite-Bourgeoys
Parc le Ber
Maison St-Gabriel
Bassin Peel
RUE MILL
RUE BRIDGE
RUE HENRI-DUHAMEL
BOULEVARD LA SALLE
RUE DE L'ÉGLISE
RUE GALT
VERDUN
Canal l'Aqueduc
BOULEVARD CHAMPLAIN
BOULEVARD DE LA VERENDRYE
Bonaventure
Lucien L'Allier
Georges-Vanier
Lionel-Groulx
Place St-Henri
Charlevoix
LaSalle
de l'Église
Verdun
0 250 m
RESTAURANTS & BARS
Brasserie McAuslan 2
Magnan 5
Masala 4
Première Moisson 3
Quoi de N'Oeuf 1

The King's Wards

When France settled Québec in the mid-1600s, the majority of residents were male bachelors recruited to defend against Iroquois attack; the few women on hand were either married or in the service of the church. The lack of eligible women vexed the men, who responded by carousing with native women. This behaviour was quickly deemed unsuitable, and a scheme was soon hatched to provide the colony with "honest" wives. King Louis XIV sent almost 800 women, who became known as the **King's Wards** (*filles du roi*), to New France between 1663 and 1673. Most of these women were orphans who, in return for their services, had their passage paid for and received a royal dowry of useful household items that enhanced their marriage value.

The first contingents were dispersed between Montréal, Québec City and Trois Rivières, but many of the post-1668 arrivals resided at the Maison St-Gabriel. There, under the guidance of Sœur Marguerite Bourgeoys and members of her congregation, the girls learned domestic skills while awaiting betrothal.

The plan was a success: the colony's population doubled between 1666 and 1672, enabling the king to phase out the programme which, in any case, had proved a drain on the royal treasury.

Bourgeoys give informative, hour-long guided tours of the rooms, each boasting unique pieces dating from the early eighteenth century. Most unusual among the items on display are the two large shelf-like sinks made of black stone, cleverly designed to drain outside through the stone wall. The girls' dormitory is also of interest as its tiny canopy beds are stacked high with pillows so the girls would sleep virtually upright lest death come and take them while lying down – a common superstition at the time – and, more prosaically, to aid digestion. During summer Sundays, the grounds are given over to concerts (11am), costumed performances and weaving and lace-making demonstrations (call for information). Next to the neighbouring barn, which hosts temporary historical exhibitions, the New France-style farmhouse garden's plots of vegetables, herbs and medicinal plants can only be visited on a guided tour (included in entry fee).

The Lachine Canal

Although Montréal's early importance owed much to the Lachine Rapids that prevented further navigation westward, the need for a route through to the Great Lakes led to a number of attempts to provide a water link, beginning with the Sulpicians' failed 1689 effort. Others went bankrupt in subsequent attempts, including the merchants whose 1819 project was sparked by the development of the competing Erie Canal. The province finally took over the construction of the **Lachine Canal**, built between 1821 and 1825 and extending from the Vieux-Port to Lachine, 14km west on the shore of the St Lawrence where it widens out as Lac St-Louis. The canal soon attracted so many factories to the area that it was expanded twice, and from the mid-eighteenth to the mid-nineteenth century served as Canada's industrial heartland, lined with steel foundries, sugar and flour refineries, factories, warehouses and rail and shipyards.

At the canal's peak, just before the 1929 crash, it was used by 15,000 ships annually. But the construction of the St Lawrence Seaway all but obliterated the canal's usefulness; it was closed and mostly filled in by 1970. Now a National Historic Site, it was taken over in 1978 by Parks Canada and cycling paths were built along the derelict industrial landscape but the area's real turnabout came in the late 1990s as various government bodies pumped $100 million into the area, re-opening the canal to pleasure boat traffic in 2002. Alongside this, private developments have converted the former factories and warehouses into offices for high-tech firms and expensive condos, and further projects such as marinas and waterside cafés are in the works. For now, it's still refreshingly untouristy, the impressive hulks of factories and warehouses providing a backdrop to a great spot to exercise, though guided tours allow the more cerebral to delve into the canal's industrial heritage.

St-Henri

The neighbourhood of **St-Henri**, northwest of the Pointe between the Lachine Canal and Westmount, is perfect for a pit stop if travelling along the canal's bike path (see box, p.128). Visible across the canal from the trail is the Art Deco **Marché Atwater** (shops: Mon–Wed & Sat 8am–6pm, Thurs–Fri 8am–9pm, Sun 9am–5pm; market stalls: times vary; Ⓦ www.marchespublics-mtl.com), which is highlighted by a large clock tower and holds a public market brimming with stalls selling mouthwatering foodstuffs. One of the finest is the Première Moisson, a delectable gourmet shop at the market's southern end selling heavenly patés – among other sundry treats like dainty pastries and prepared salads – that are perfect for lunching along the canal. Also worth a peek is the section of rue Notre-Dame ouest just north of the market, between rue Atwater and rue Guy, known as "rue des antiquaires" due to the numerous **antique shops** (see p.192) that line the street; frustratingly, most are closed on Sundays.

While browsing is the main trade in St-Henri nowadays, the neighbourhood's blue-collar history has its origins in leather tanneries. Though there's little left of the bygone era, its working-class roots are still evident a few blocks west of the market, on **rue St-Augustin**, a narrow residential street lined with quaint clapboard houses dating from the 1870s and the inspiration for Gabrielle Roy's *The Tin Flute*. Some have recently been covered with unattractive aluminium siding, but the restored private residences at nos. 110 and 118 exude a rustic charm with their small front porches, tiny dormer windows and brightly painted exteriors.

Lachine

The canal (and its bike path) ends in its namesake, the scenic town of **Lachine**, which sits on land granted to Robert Cavelier de La Salle in 1667 by the Messieurs de St-Sulpice, the priests that held title to Montréal for nearly two centuries (see box, p.72). La Salle was so obsessed with finding a passage to China that Montrealers of the time mockingly referred to his territory as "La Chine" (China) – the name stuck even though he never found the route. He somehow managed to chart Louisiana instead.

Lachine grew up to be an important fur-trading post due to its location near the **Lachine Rapids**, which hindered ships from travelling to Montréal prior to the canal days; shipments were unloaded here for transportation to Montréal by land. Those days are remembered in Lachine's major attraction, the **Commerce-de-la-Fourrure-à-Lachine**, an interactive historical museum lodged in a former fur storehouse, while the once unnavigable rapids are now plied by rafts and jet boats (see p.205). While the resulting wealth contributed to the steeples and domes that make the skyline so attractive, the rest of the former town (merged with Montréal on January 1st, 2002) is an uninteresting suburban sprawl.

Exploring the Lachine Canal

For years, the Lachine Canal was mainly the preserve of active Montrealers who came to bike or blade its length. But thanks to the re-opening of the locks and the area's increasing popularity, you can now cruise its waters or take a walking tour of the industrial legacy that most people obliviously whiz past. In tandem with the Pôle des Rapides (ⓣ514/364-4490, ⓦwww.poledesrapides.com), the tourist body for the whole region surrounding the canal, Parks Canada operates a number of **info kiosks** (mid-May to mid-Oct) and runs free **guided tours** in the National Historic Site (mid-May to early Sept; ⓣ514/283-6054 or 637-7433, ⓦwww.parkscanada.gc.ca/lachinecanal) centred on the canal itself. In addition to info on area attractions, the kiosks provide a free map (a more useful one is available for $2).

From east to west, there's an information kiosk at the south side of the Peel basin and a more substantial one at Écluse St-Gabriel (lock no. 3), whose daily tours cover the area's industrial heritage. Further along, the kiosk at the foot of the pedestrian bridge leading to Marché Atwater is the departure point for tours detailing the canal's history and urbanization (Wed–Sun). Two kilometres further west, the Écluse Côte-St-Paul (lock no. 4) gives tours of the area on weekends only. If you've worked up a thirst by now, you might consider a pint at the *Terrasse St-Ambroise* (Wed–Fri from 4pm, Sat & Sun from 11am), opposite at 5080 rue St-Ambroise; it's run by the Brasserie McAuslan, a local brewery that also offers tours of their facilities (ⓣ514/939-3060 for schedule; ⓦwww.mcauslan.com). Finally, you can also find out more about the canal at its terminus, Écluse de Lachine (lock no. 5), where, in addition to tours, the Lachine Visitors Services Centre (mid-May to mid-Oct daily 10am–6pm) has an exhibition of historic photos and a snack bar to boot. En route, keep an eye out for panels that are illustrated with historic photos and give more in-depth accounts of the canal's former life.

The nearest Métro stations to the sector of the canal in front of the Marché Atwater are Charlevoix and Lionel-Groulx, while the handiest station for the Vieux-Port end is Métro Square-Victoria. Numerous bus routes also traverse the area.

Cycling the canal

The cycle paths that run along the canal are popular with Montrealers and visitors alike, to the extent that it can be slow going on sunny summer weekends – if you're

Lieu historique national du Commerce-de-la-Fourrure-à-Lachine

The **Commerce-de-la-Fourrure-à-Lachine** (Fur Trade at Lachine) occupies an attractive low-lying fieldstone building near the Lachine waterfront at 1255 boul St-Joseph (April to mid-Oct, Mon 1–5.30pm, Tues–Sun 10am–12.30pm & 1–5.30pm; mid-Oct to Nov, Wed–Sun 9.30am–12.30pm & 1–5pm; $3.50; ⓣ514/637-7433, ⓦwww.parkscanada.gc.ca/fur; Métro Angrignon and bus #195). Built in 1803 as a storehouse for the country's leading fur-trading company, the North West Company, today the museum is jam-packed with hands-on exhibits dealing with the fur trade. The costumed mannequins guarding some of the displays are pretty cheesy, but you do get to handle some exquisite furs, the softest of which are beaver – a nearby price list notes a keg of rum bought three. There's also a weigh-station that determines your qualifications as a *voyageur*; their measurements were capped at 178cm and 63kg (5'7"/139lbs) so as not to upset the canoe in which they spent up to 18 hours a day. A fine example of their water transport, a 12-metre-long birchbark canoe, is also on display.

main goal is exercise, go early in the morning. The path begins at the Vieux-Port, where you can hire **bicycles** and **rollerblades** (see box, p.80) and extends westward for 14km to the canal's terminus in Lachine, passing locks, swooping under bridges (the steep grades may be a problem for first-time bladers) and crossing back and forth between the north and south banks. Plan on a minimum of two hours for the full circuit if you're in good shape and cycling outside the busiest times. The grassy Parc René-Lévesque, a peninsula that juts out from the end of the bike path, and adds about 3km to a round trip, has a fantastical collection of contemporary sculptures and offers prime views onto Lachine's attractive skyline. For a change of scene on the way back, follow the des Berges cycle path along the banks of the St Lawrence and past the Lachine Rapids. Pick up a cycling map beforehand at one of the info kiosks (see above) for a list of repair shops and amenities – as well as how to navigate your way back to the canal if you make a detour.

On the water

Don't even think about swimming in the canal (it's prohibited anyway), its sediment is legendarily polluted after a century of use as the backbone of "Canada's Pittsburgh". There are plenty of options to **cruise** along its surface, though. The most sedate way to experience it is the glass-topped boat *L'Éclusier*, which departs from in front of the Marché Atwater (see p.127) and travels eastward through the St-Gabriel locks to Peel basin and back with a Parks Canada guide providing an Industrial Revolution history lesson on the two-hour cruise (mid-May to mid-Oct Sat & Sun 1pm & 3.30pm (late June to early Sept daily); $17.50; Ⓣ514/846-0428, Ⓦwww.croisierecanaldelachine.ca).

If you'd rather chart your own course (and forgot to bring your own boat with you), you can hire **kayaks** and **pedal-boats** (from $10/hr) as well as electric **motorboats** (from $33/hr) from Ruban Bleu (Ⓣ514/938-4448, Ⓦwww.rubanbleu.ca) on the south side of the canal just east of the footbridge from the Marché Atwater. Further west, near Hwy-15, you can hire kayaks starting at $15/hr from H_2O Adventures, whose dock is on the south side of the canal just before the Pont Monk bridge (200m west of the Côte-St-Paul lock), at 5527 rue St-Patrick (Ⓣ514/842-1306, Ⓦwww.h2oadventures.com; Métro Vendôme and bus #37). For $39, they offer a two-hour lesson and tour and, if you're with a group, they'll even pick you up in town.

Listings

Listings

9

Accommodation

Montréal definitely does not lack for **accommodation**, as it has thousands of available rooms, and more options show up each year. However, even as the number of rooms has increased, so has the number of visitors to the city, which has effectively put an end to the days of being able to score cheap rooms in upmarket **hotels** year-round. During the **high season**, which runs from mid-May to early-September, and briefly again around Christmas, you should reserve well in advance – especially if you're coming on Grand Prix weekend (mid-June) or during the Jazz Festival (late June to early July). Throughout the rest of the year, though, when vacancies are higher, good weekend specials can sometimes be found and many small hotels offer weekly rates. The main exception is accommodation aimed at **gay travellers** (see p.179), which fills up quickly on the big party weekends throughout the year.

In many of the **smaller hotels**, there is often a fair amount of variety – room size, view, brightness, bath or shower – in rooms available for around the same price. In any event, don't hesitate to ask to see a couple of a hotel's rooms in order to find one that best suits you.

Despite Montréal's reputation as a smoker's heaven – which is due to a combination of less restrictive smoking laws and the city's French roots – hotels are required to have at least 60 percent non-smoking rooms and many smaller hotels won't allow you to light up at all. One other thing to check when booking a room is what type of **breakfast** will be served – a continental breakfast can be as skimpy as a croissant and coffee, while a "continental buffet", "deluxe continental" or "continental plus" might include yogurt, cheese, cold-cuts and fruit. A full (or American) breakfast should include eggs and other hot dishes, but may be served as a buffet.

Due in large part to rising hotel rates, **bed and breakfasts** are becoming increasingly popular and many of them are tucked into handsome greystones in ideal locations like the Plateau and Quartier Latin. Budget-conscious travellers also have a good selection of options, as Montréal's universities open the doors to their residence halls in summer, and there are also several decent **hostels** to choose from.

You can also check the Tourisme Montréal website (Ⓦwww.tourisme-montreal.org) for packages and last-minute details; they don't handle online bookings but Tourisme Québec (Ⓣ1-877/266-5687, Ⓦwww.bonjourquebec.com) does; you can also book upon arrival at the Centre Infotouriste (see p.22).

Accommodation maps

In the Guide chapters you'll find maps listing hotel locations in many different areas of Montréal. These can be found on the following pages:

Downtown	p.46–47
Vieux-Montréal	p.69
Quartier Latin and the Village	p.86–87
Plateau Mont-Royal	p.92–93
Mile End, Outremont and Little Italy	p.98

Hotels

The major weakness of Montréal's hotel scene is a shortage of quality **mid-range** rooms – we've listed the best of a small supply below. If you're willing to spend at least $150 a night, there are plenty of quality **upmarket hotels** to choose from. And if you're on a tight budget, somewhat shabby **bargain hotels** abound, many of them fortunately concentrated in energetic neighbourhoods like the **Quartier Latin** and on the edge of the **Plateau**. Hotels around the bus station in the Quartier Latin are especially cheap, but keep in mind the immediate area is a popular drug-dealing spot that attracts unsavoury types day and night. **Downtown** finds an assortment of **chains** geared towards corporate travellers, with a few winning independent hotels thrown into the mix. In contrast, **Vieux-Montréal's inns** and its many new **boutique hotels** are intimate and wonderfully atmospheric, but at a price – you're paying for the history of your surroundings as well as exclusive amenities.

Downtown

L'Appartement Hôtel **Ⓣ514/284-3634 or 1-800/363-3010, Ⓦwww.appartementhotel.com; Métro McGill or Place-des-Arts.** Studios, 1-bedroom and 2-bedroom apartments with kitchenettes, a/c, phones and TVs, on the border of Downtown and the Plateau. Daily, weekly and monthly rates include access to outdoor pool and sauna, though parking is extra. ❹

Château Versailles **1659 rue Sherbrooke O Ⓣ514/933-3611 or 1-888/933-8111, Ⓦwww.versailleshotels.com; Métro Guy-Concordia.** Spacious, individually decorated rooms in this complex of four greystones built in the 1800s. The deluxe suites have classy touches like chandeliers and gas fireplaces, while the sleek standard rooms have perks like CD players, modem hook-up, bathrobes and fancy toiletries. Book early, as this place is extremely popular, and ask about the various specials when doing so. Continental buffet breakfast included. ❻

Le Germain **2050 rue Mansfield Ⓣ514/849-2050 or 1-877/333-2050, Ⓦwww.hotelgermain.com; Métro Peel or McGill.** Every last detail in this boutique hotel has a designer touch to it – the airy rooms feature dark woods, down duvets and a sheer glass wall that divides the bedroom from the shower (there is a wrap-around shower curtain for privacy-seekers). In-room extras like CD player, bathrobes and fresh fruit just add to the overall package. Continental buffet breakfast included. ❼

Hôtel de la Montagne **1430 rue de la Montagne Ⓣ514/288-5656 or 1-800/361-6262, Ⓦwww.hoteldelamontagne.com; Métro Peel.** The lobby is something out of an *Arabian Nights* fantasy: two large sculpted elephants guard the front desk while a nearby flowing fountain, complete with rotating golden water nymph, shines under a massive crystal chandelier; tacky and yet somehow classy. After this spectacle, though, the guestrooms are four-star standard. The lively singles' bar, *Thursdays*, is on the ground floor (the main entrance faces onto the rue Crescent strip) but the choicest spot for a drink is next to the pool on the twentieth-floor terrace. Breakfast included on weekends. ❺

Manoir Ambrose 3422 rue Stanley ⓣ514/288-6922, ⓦwww.manoirambrose.com; Métro Peel. Two adjoining nineteenth-century Victorian houses on a quiet street, offering budget accommodation with character, albeit in slightly tatty condition. Some of the high-ceilinged rooms have a/c and private bathroom, for a bit extra. Continental breakfast included. ❸

Marriott Château Champlain 1050 rue de la Gauchetière 0 ⓣ514/878-9000 or 1-800/200-5909, ⓦwww.marriotthotels.com; Métro Bonaventure. Popular with executive travellers as it's huge, well-appointed and connected to the Underground City (see p.50), this chain's most distinctive features are the rooms' unusual half-moon windows. Ask for quarters facing Place du Canada – the views are excellent. ❻

Quality Inn Downtown 1214 rue Crescent ⓣ514/878-2711 or 1-800/221-2222, ⓦwww.choicehotels.ca; Métro Guy-Concordia. This reliable chain hotel gets packed during the June Grand-Prix weekend as its rue Crescent location puts guests right in the thick of the three-day F1 street party (see p.212). All the rooms are junior suites with two double beds or a king and pull-out sofa, and can sleep four. Street-facing rooms have private balconies with a bird's-eye view of the festivities. Continental breakfast included. ❺

Queen Elizabeth 900 boul René-Lévesque 0 ⓣ514/861-3511 or 1-800/441-1414, ⓦwww.fairmont.com; Métro Bonaventure. The grande dame of Montréal's big hotels, the *Queen Elizabeth* doesn't quite command the same kind of clientele as it did in 1969 when John Lennon and Yoko Ono staged their "Give peace a chance" bed-in here. Nowadays, its thousand-plus rooms play host to convention-goers, and the place can seem quite desolate when nothing corporate is going on. ❻

Ritz-Carlton 1228 rue Sherbrooke 0 ⓣ514/842-4212 or 1-800/363-0366, ⓦwww.ritzcarlton.com; Métro Peel. Standard luxury chain accommodation. Still, the lobby is spectacular, the charming garden-side restaurant is a lovely oasis in summer, and the hotel is conveniently located near the city's finest shopping. ❽

Le Square Phillips 1193 Place Phillips ⓣ514/393-1193 or 1-866/393-1193, ⓦwww.squarephillips.com; Métro McGill. More stylish than your average apartment-hotel, the high-ceilinged studios and suites are done up in creams, taupes and dark wood accents and have full kitchens, dining tables and high-speed Internet access. Ask for a room overlooking the square. Cheaper weekly and monthly rates available. ❺

Le St-Malo 1455 rue du Fort ⓣ514/931-7366, ⓦwww.hotel-saint-malo.com; Métro Guy-Concordia or Atwater. A reasonably priced option on the western edge of Downtown. The building lacks charm, but its thirteen rooms are bright, comfortable and come with cable TV. Some rooms have a/c; the cheapest are on the small side. ❷

Travelodge Montréal-Centre 50 boul René-Lévesque 0 ⓣ514/874-9090 or 1-800/578-7878, ⓦwww.travelodge.com; Métro Place-d'Armes or St-Laurent. There's not a lot of character here, but it's modern, clean and well located on the outskirts of Chinatown, close to Vieux-Montréal. Cable TV and in-room coffeemaker included. ❹

Wyndham 1255 rue Jeanne-Mance ⓣ514/285-1450 or 1-800/361-8234, ⓦwww.wyndham.com; Métro Place-des-Arts. A glass elevator silently whisks you up the

Accommodation price codes

Accommodation prices vary throughout the year, with the highest rates from mid-May to early-September, and again around Christmas. The price codes given below for **hotels** and **B&Bs** reflect the average price for the least expensive double-occupancy room in high season, excluding special offers and price-gouging during the Grand Prix weekend and Jazz Festival.

The prices do not include **tax**, which comes to about 15 percent (some of which may be refundable – see p.32), plus there's an additional $2-per-night occupancy tax.

❶ up to $50	❷ $50–75	❸ $75–100	❹ $100–150
❺ $150–200	❻ $200–250	❼ $250–300	❽ $300+

outside of the building to the elegant third-floor lobby with granite floors so polished they squeak. The 600 expansive rooms lack personality but come with modem hook-ups and free newspapers. When the Jazz Festival is on (see p.214), you won't find a better location – the third-floor terrace overlooks the main stage, though check to see that it won't be closed for private functions during your stay. ❺–❻

Vieux-Montréal

Auberge Bonaparte **447 rue St-François-Xavier ⓣ514/844-1448, ⓦwww.bonaparte.com; Métro Place-d'Armes.** A handsome upscale inn, steps from the Basilique Notre-Dame, built in 1886 and shaded by smart burgundy awnings. Inside, the quarters are decked out with wrought-iron headboards, hardwood floors, high ceilings and French dormer windows. The more expensive rooms overlook the private gardens of the Séminaire de Saint-Sulpice and have jacuzzis. The ground-floor restaurant serves up rich French fare (see p.151). Breakfast included. ❺

Auberge Bonsecours **353 rue St-Paul E ⓣ514/396-2662; Métro Champ-de-Mars.** Set back in a courtyard behind *Le Beau Soleil* B&B (see p.139), this seven-room inn occupies the former stables buildings and has a lovely breakfast room with exposed stone walls. The quarters are decorated with colourful bedspreads and eclectic furnishings like wrought-iron tables and painted Indian wardrobes, all of which help to compensate for some of the hotel's more questionable modern renovations. Some rooms have shared bath. ❺

Auberge de la Place Royale **115 rue de la Commune O ⓣ514/287-0522, ⓦwww.aubergeplaceroyale.com; Métro Square-Victoria or Place-d'Armes.** The standard rooms have exposed stone walls and queen beds, but look onto a back lane. Pay a bit more and you can get a view of the Vieux-Port, along with four-poster beds and whirlpool tubs. All the rooms, though, are a bit dowdy. A full breakfast, served on a sidewalk terrace in summer, is included. ❺

Auberge du Vieux-Port **97 rue de la Commune E ⓣ514/876-0081 or 1-888/660-7678, ⓦwww.aubergeduvieuxport.com; Métro Place-d'Armes.** This waterfront hotel dates from 1882 and is dotted with 27 loft-style rooms offering spectacular views onto the Vieux-Port or rue St-Paul from large casement windows. Original stone walls, hardwood floors and brass headboards add to the rooms' overall appeal. The roof terrace, open to the public, is a fantastic spot to survey the Vieux-Port with a drink or light meal. Eleven large lofts that can sleep up to four are available in the building behind, with full kitchen and washer/dryer. Full breakfast and wine-and-cheese cocktail hour included. ❻–❽

Auberge Les Passants du Sans Soucy **171 rue St-Paul O ⓣ514/842-2634, ⓦwww.lesanssoucy.com; Métro Place-d'Armes.** This charming inn is full of nice touches like flowerpots on the windowsills and lace curtains throughout. Brass beds and hardwood floors contribute to the romantic atmosphere, and some rooms have wooden beams and stone walls. Breakfast, served in a skylit nook, is included. ❹

Hôtel Gault **449 rue Ste-Hélène ⓣ514/904-1616 or 1-866/904-1616, ⓦwww.hotelgault.com; Métro Square-Victoria.** Most glamorous of the recent crop of boutique hotels, the *Gault* is the place to stay – if you can afford it. The 30 individually designed loft-style rooms are a design-junkie's dream, from the Arne Jacobsen fixtures and Artemide lamps to the white-oak panelling and custom-made linens. The sleek lobby's colourful furniture contrasts nicely with the cast-iron columns that are vestiges of the 1871 former warehouse that now houses the hotel. ❽

Hôtel Nelligan **106 rue St-Paul O ⓣ514/788-2040 or 1-877/788-2040, ⓦwww.hotelnelligan.com; Métro Place-d'Armes.** Another of the recent spate of boutique hotels, the *Nelligan* has a cozy lobby with exposed brick wall, fireplace and leather sofas that give a hint of the similarly comfortable rooms. Down duvets keep you warm in winter while in summer windows open onto Vieux-Montréal's charming streets. The included breakfast and *5 à 7* cocktails are served in an atrium overlooked by wrought-iron balconies, adjacent to the hotel restaurant *Verses*, serving high-quality regional cuisine. ❻

Hôtel Place d'Armes 701 Côte de la Place d'Armes ⓣ514/842-1887 or 1-888/450-1887, ⓦwww.hotelplacedarmes.com; Métro Place-d'Armes. The location of this eight-storey boutique hotel can't be beat – it's right on Place d'Armes, facing the Basilique Notre-Dame. The spacious rooms are sleekly tailored in neutral tones, and extras like in-room CD player, high-speed Internet access and cocktail hour by the lobby fireplace complete the package. Deluxe continental breakfast included. ❺

Hôtel St-Paul 355 rue McGill ⓣ514/380-2222 or 1-866/380-2202, ⓦwww.hotelstpaul.com; Métro Square-Victoria. This most minimalist of Vieux-Montréal's new boutique hotels is located on the district's western edge in a century-old building that was originally a bank. Its ground floor has a striking, free-standing, white marble fireplace and a very trendy restaurant, *Cube*. Upstairs, white walls and linens contrast with the dark wood floors and elegantly simple furnishings of the rooms and suites. ❻

Inter-Continental 360 rue St-Antoine O ⓣ514/987-9900 or 1-800/361-3600, ⓦwww.montreal.intercontinental.com; Métro Square-Victoria. It's plush and expensive, but well worth the price. The rooms have huge floor-to-ceiling windows overlooking either Vieux-Montréal or Downtown, and each comes equipped with marble bathrooms and modem hook-ups. Impeccable service is guaranteed, and you have a choice of either free breakfast or parking. ❺–❻

Pierre du Calvet 405 rue Bonsecours ⓣ514/282-1725 or 1-866/544-1725, ⓦwww.pierreducalvet.ca; Métro Champ-de-Mars. The *Pierre du Calvet* is housed in one of Vieux-Montréal's finest buildings (see p.77), and the accommodation is as fine as the grand exterior – guestrooms include oriental rugs, gas fireplaces and original masonry walls. The ground floor has a superb wood-panelled library and sunken dining room – trio of mounted deer heads included – and hot breakfast is served in a plant-filled greenhouse that's home to several squawking parrots. ❼

Quartier Latin

Le Breton 1609 rue St-Hubert ⓣ514/524-7273 or 1-888/231-3113, ⓦwww.lebreton.ca; Métro Berri-UQAM. A clean and friendly European-style hotel with well-priced though smallish rooms in a late-nineteenth-century building near the bus station and the Village. Half the rooms have a/c, most feature a private bathroom, and all have cable TV and free continental breakfast. Good family rates are available. ❶–❷

Castel Saint-Denis 2099 rue St-Denis ⓣ514/842-9719, ⓦwww.castelsaintdenis.qc.ca; Métro Berri-UQAM or Sherbrooke. A good budget hotel right on trendy rue St-Denis in, the heart of the Quartier Latin. Though the rooms lack flair, they're clean and include a/c and cable TV; most have private baths. ❷

Hôtel St-Denis 1254 rue St-Denis ⓣ514/849-4526 or 1-800/363-3364, ⓦwww.hotel-st-denis.com; Métro Berri-UQAM. One of the city's better mid-range hotels has an excellent location on busy rue St-Denis, immaculate and nicely furnished rooms, friendly service and a downstairs café-bistro that serves a reasonably priced breakfast. ❸

Le Jardin d'Antoine 2024 rue St-Denis ⓣ514/843-4506 or 1-800/361-4506, ⓦwww.hotel-jardin-antoine.qc.ca; Métro Berri-UQAM. One of the nicest Quartier Latin inns, though the decor in the 25 rooms may be a bit too frou-frou for some, with floral bedspreads and wallpaper. Amenities include a/c, cable TV, telephone and workspace, and you can eat your hot buffet breakfast (included) on the vine-covered patio. ❹

Maison Brunet 1035 rue St-Hubert ⓣ514/845-6351, ⓦwww.maisonbrunet.ca; Métro Berri-UQAM or Champ-de-Mars. Don't let the ratty reception area put you off – the main part of this budget hotel occupies a 125-year-old house with a leafy terrace out back. The furniture's old rather than antique, but the rooms are clean (if a bit cramped) and come with a/c, TVs and continental buffet breakfast; the cheaper ones have shared bath. They also rent loft studios (❹) with kitchen and space for six; longer-term rates are available. ❷–❸

Manoir des Alpes 1245 rue St-André ⓣ514/845-9803 or 1-800/465-2929, ⓦwww.hotelmanoirdesalpes.qc.ca; Métro Berri-UQAM. A friendly, good-value hotel in a Victorian-era building with adequate rooms that have cable TV; parking and buffet breakfast included. A couple of them feature exposed brick and whirlpool tubs as well. ❸

Manoir St-Denis 2006 rue St-Denis ⓣ514/843-3670 or 1-888/567-7654,

ⓦ www.manoirstdenis.com; Métro Berri-UQAM. Bargain-basement lodging at the Quartier Latin's busiest intersection – the sagging front terrace overlooks the action on the street. Many of the rooms are dark due to the rustic pine-clad walls and ceilings, but they're reasonably clean and include private bathroom, cable TV and minifridge. Continental breakfast included. ❷

Plateau Mont-Royal

Anne ma Soeur Anne 4119 rue St-Denis ⓣ 514/281-3187, ⓦ www.annemasoeuranne.com; Métro Mont-Royal. Situated on a prime stretch of rue St-Denis, this stylish seventeen-room hotel is a great find. The sunny, yellow rooms are clean and fresh and feature kitchenettes, large bathrooms and high-speed Internet access – some have "Eurobeds" that tuck up into a wall unit for more space during the day. Suites have their own private terraces out back. ❹

Auberge de la Fontaine 1301 rue Rachel E ⓣ 514/597-0166 or 1-800/597-0597, ⓦ www.aubergedelafontaine.com; Métro Mont-Royal. This hotel scores high on charm and location, right across from Parc Lafontaine and close to the restaurants and shops of av du Mont-Royal. Its modern rooms are brightly painted, have queen or twin beds, and private bathrooms. Extras like private balcony and jacuzzi are also available. Breakfast, snacks from the kitchen and parking included. ❺

Casa Bella 264 rue Sherbrooke O ⓣ 514/849-2777 or 1-888/453-2777, ⓦ www.hotel-casabella.com; Métro Place-des-Arts. A surprisingly good and affordable option in a three-storey limestone townhouse a few short blocks west of boul St-Laurent. The rooms are basic but most have private bathrooms and the price includes continental breakfast and parking. Ask for a room at the back as they're quieter. ❸

Château de l'Argoat 524 rue Sherbrooke E ⓣ 514/842-2046, ⓦ www.hotel-chateau-argoat.qc.ca; Métro Sherbrooke. A fanciful cream-coloured fortress offering 25 spacious and attractive rooms with high ceilings, quaint chandeliers and large windows. All have private bath – in the cheaper rooms they're quite cramped, while the more expensive have whirlpool baths. Breakfast and parking included. ❸

Crowne Plaza Metro Centre 505 rue Sherbrooke E ⓣ 514/842-8581 or 1-800/561-4644, ⓦ www.cpmontreal.com; Métro Sherbrooke. Despite the name, this 23-storey hotel tower is actually perched on the edge of the Plateau, overlooking the Quartier Latin. The rooms are as tastefully inoffensive as you'd expect from a four-star hotel, which is fine as you'll be goggling at the views – ask for a west-facing room for Downtown or south for the river, unless you manage to nab a larger, corner room. ❺

Hôtel de Paris 901 Sherbrooke E ⓣ 514/522-6861 or 1-800/567-7217, ⓦ www.hotel-montreal.com; Métro Sherbrooke. Spread across three separate properties on rue Sherbrooke near rue St-Denis, the *Hôtel de Paris*'s reception occupies a mansion with a lively ambience but tiny beds in the cheaply furnished rooms. There's a balcony café to hang out in, and the rooms have cable TV, telephone and private bathroom; most have a/c. Several apartments (❹) with kitchenettes are available and there are youth hostel dorms in the basement (see p.141). ❸

Hôtel Pierre 169 rue Sherbrooke E ⓣ 514/288-8519; Métro Sherbrooke. A darkly lit bargain hotel with few amenities near rue St-Denis whose twelve rooms are individually decorated in quirky styles that can't quite hide the shabbiness – ask to see them first if you're picky about lodging in the "princess room", for instance. All the rooms have a/c and TVs, most have a kitchenette, and laundry service is available. ❸

La Résidence du Voyageur 847 rue Sherbrooke E ⓣ 514/527-9515; ⓦ www.hotelresidencevoyager.com; Métro Sherbrooke. A good-value hotel just east of rue St-Denis on busy rue Sherbrooke. The 28 air-conditioned rooms are clean and modern if dull, and all have private bathrooms, telephones and cable TV. Rates include continental breakfast. ❷–❸

B&B listings and rental agencies

Use one of these agencies below to book a B&B for you.

BBCanada.com Ⓦ www.bbcanada.com. The oldest and possibly best-known Canadian B&B website covers the whole country. It takes some work, however, as even though over a hundred B&Bs turn up under its Montréal listings, many are in fact hotels and there's no narrower geographical search – accommodation in distant suburbs is indistinguishable from that on the Plateau, for example.

Bed & Breakfast à Montréal Ⓣ 514/738-9410 or 1-800/738-4338, Ⓦ www.bbmontreal.com. Montréal's original B&B agency lists good-quality houses Downtown, in the Quartier Latin, and Québec City, starting at $85 for shared bath, $115 for private, for two people in high season.

Downtown B&B Network in Montréal Ⓣ 514/289-9749 or 1-800/267-5180, Ⓦ www.bbmontreal.qc.ca. Dependable agency that nearly always has a vacancy either Downtown or in the Quartier Latin, starting at $85 for shared bath, $115 for private.

Fédération des Agricotours Ⓦ www.agricotours.qc.ca. An excellent service listing quality-inspected B&Bs throughout Montréal and the province, should you be moving on afterwards – you must book directly with the B&Bs, however. The service's information is also published in the annual *Inns and Bed & Breakfasts in Québec* guide ($17.95), which can be ordered online or by calling Ⓣ 514/252-3138. Rates for B&Bs start at $65.

Bed and breakfasts

Quebecers have been slow to take to **bed-and-breakfast** accommodation, for a long time preferring to stay in similarly priced though characterless motels. In recent years, however, B&Bs have multiplied, having proven they can provide superior accommodation for less – many of them charge under $100 a night. In addition to highly personalized service, B&Bs are also most often found on quiet, leafy side streets rather than the main drags and usually in interesting neighbourhoods where hotel rooms are scarce. If you have an aversion to family pets (or want to bring one or more with you), be sure to ask before booking, as many B&Bs are animal-friendly.

Angelica Blue 1213 rue Ste-Elisabeth Ⓣ 514/844-5048 or 1-800/878-5048, Ⓦ www.angelicablue.com; Métro Berri-UQAM. An attractive B&B in a Victorian townhouse on a pretty side street near the Quartier Latin. The five rooms have lots of character – exposed brick walls, high ceilings and original antiques – and all the rooms are en suite. Guests can use the kitchen to prepare meals and eat in the "bistro" (actually just a breakfast room decorated like a bistro), where the full breakfast is served. An additional two-bedroom apartment (❼) with full kitchen and private entrance can sleep a family of five. ❸

Le Beau Soleil Ⓣ 514/871-0299; Métro Champ-de-Mars. A friendly owner, central Vieux-Montréal location opposite the Marché Bonsecours and pretty, high-ceilinged rooms filled with antique Canadiana are the high points of this B&B on the top floor of an 1830s building. The drawback is that there are 52 outdoor steps to climb to reach the rooms. All have shared bath. ❸

Bienvenue Bed & Breakfast 3950 av Laval Ⓣ 514/844-5897 or 1-800/227-5897, Ⓦ www.bienvenuebb.com; Métro Sherbrooke. Montréal's original B&B (started in 1983) is in a handsome Victorian house on a picturesque Plateau street. The twelve rooms don't live up to the exterior, though, as they're quite plain and the whole place has the feel of a small hotel rather than a B&B – instead of a hot breakfast, they serve a "continental-plus" buffet. Half the rooms have private bathrooms; the others have in-room sinks. They have a second property (same name and contact information) just above rue Sherbrooke that does fit the B&B mould, with four high-ceilinged bedrooms and full breakfasts. ❸

Boulanger Bassin B&B 4293 rue Brébeuf ⓣ514/525-0854, ⓦwww.bbassin.com; Métro Mont-Royal. The chatty owner of this B&B on the cycle path just north of Parc Lafontaine knows the Plateau neighbourhood well and will offer plenty of advice over extravagant breakfasts like eggs Benedict with a smoothie starter, served next to the goldfish pond in the garden. The three bright and colourful rooms are simple but nicely furnished with a few quirky touches and all have private bath. Kids under twelve stay free. ❹

À la Maison de Pierre et Dominique 271 Square St-Louis ⓣ514/286-0307, ⓦwww.pierdom.qc.ca; Métro Sherbrooke. A charming navy-blue-trimmed house facing Square St-Louis with three tastefully decorated ground-floor rooms and a cheerful breakfast area. None of the rooms have private bathrooms, and there's a small sitting area with a mini-fridge. ❸

La Maison du Patriote 169 rue St-Paul E ⓣ514/397-0855, www.bbcanada.com/patriote; Métro Champ-de-Mars. Surprisingly cheap given that it's around the corner from the action on Place Jacques-Cartier, though the rooms here are a bit thrown-together. Despite the exposed beams and sloping ceilings it feels like a student flat, a notion reinforced by the youth of the friendly owner and the fact that you can rent the entire top floor and squeeze in up to twelve people for $240. ❷

Marmelade 1074 rue St-Dominique ⓣ514/876-3960, ⓦwww.total.net/marmelad; Métro Place-d'Armes or St-Laurent. An inviting five-room B&B on the outskirts of Chinatown with bonuses like sloped ceilings, a flower-filled terrace that's wonderful in the summer, and two indoor lounges – one with a cozy fireplace – for the rest of the year. Shared bathrooms. $100 deposit required. ❹

Petite Auberge les Bons Matins 1393 av Argyle ⓣ514/931-9167 or 1-800/588-5280, ⓦwww.bonsmatins.com; Métro Lucien-l'Allier. Located in adjoining townhouses on a tree-lined street near the Centre Bell, this well-appointed B&B-style inn has six spacious apartments and fifteen large, en-suite rooms. Each has picture windows and additional details like arched ceilings and polished hardwood floors. Several have a fireplace. Rooms: ❹ apartments: ❻

Aux Portes de la Nuit 3496 av Laval ⓣ514/848-0833, ⓦwww.bbcanada.com/767.html; Métro Sherbrooke. Well-situated on one of the Plateau's most attractive streets, this Victorian house has five comfortable rooms; all with private bath, though two of these are in the corridor. One of the least expensive has a balcony overlooking Carré St-Louis; the priciest has a rooftop terrace. ❸

University residences and hostels

Montréal has several large **universities** scattered about the city, and from about mid-May to mid-August they open their residences to visitors. These provide excellent value if you're not picky about frills, though you will get a linen service, access to a kitchenette and a common room with cable TV. The city also has a number of youth **hostels** offering primarily dormitory-style accommodation, most of which should be booked far in advance come summer.

Auberge Alternative du Vieux-Montréal 358 rue St-Pierre ⓣ514/282-8069, ⓦwww.auberge-alternative.qc.ca; Métro Square-Victoria. Montréal's finest hostel is located in a refurbished 1875 Vieux-Montréal warehouse. The common room, with its exposed masonry wall and modern cooking facilities, is a great place to lounge, and the dormitories, with arched windows and wood floors, sleep from six to twenty on bunkbeds. Singles and doubles also available, which include a free help-yourself breakfast (costs $3.50 extra if staying in a dorm). Rates include Internet access, and coin-laundry facilities are available. $18/dorm, $45/single.

Auberge Chez Jean 4136 av Henri-Julien ⓣ514/843-8279, ⓦwww.aubergechezjean.com; Métro Mont-Royal. You'll either love or hate this very unofficial (and concurrently not terribly rules-oriented) youth hostel located dead-central in the Plateau. Guests bunk down all over the common rooms on its three floors, making it a great place to make new friends quickly, but forget about privacy unless you take one of the closed rooms or sleep in the van out back. Each floor has its own kitchen and there are plenty of bathrooms. The friendly, knowledgeable staff will give suggestions on where to go out and offer advice about onward travel. $20 per person.

Auberge de Jeunesse Internationale de Montréal 1030 rue Mackay ⓣ514/843-3317 or 1-866/843-3317, ⓦwww.hostellingmontreal.com; Métro Lucien-l'Allier. A well-equipped Downtown hostel with over 200 beds. Dorms sleep a maximum of ten, and single, double and family quarters are also available. The lounge has a pool table and cable TV, and reservations are advised between June and September. Foreign guests must be members of Hostelling International – if not, a day membership costs $4.60. $22/dorm, $58/single (with membership card); $26/dorm, $68/single (Canadian non-members).

Auberge de Paris 901 Sherbrooke E ⓣ514/522-6861 or 1-800/567-7217, ⓦwww.hotel-montreal.com; Métro Sherbrooke. The grim basements of the *Hôtel de Paris*' three properties (see p.138) on the edge of the Plateau district have dark and tiny bunk rooms with wobbly locks and sleep four to fourteen. Guests have access to cooking facilities, café, garden and TV room. $20/dorm, $3/sheets (if needed).

Gîte Plateau Mont-Royal 185 rue Sherbrooke E ⓣ514/284-1276 or 1-877/350-4483, ⓦwww.hostelmontreal.com; Métro Sherbrooke. Bright six- to eight-bed dorms and private rooms (with shared bath), an extremely chill common room to hang out in and proximity to Plateau and Quartier Latin nightlife make this one of the city's best backpacker options. Price includes sheets and a self-serve breakfast; Internet and laundry are extra. The main drawback is that the kitchen is only open 5–8pm. In summer, they have an extra fourteen beds in a second house opposite Parc Lafontaine at 1250 rue Sherbrooke E. $23/dorms, $50–75/rooms.

Hôtel Y des Femmes (YWCA) 1355 boul René-Lévesque O ⓣ514/866-9942, ⓦwww.ydesfemmesmtl.org; Métro Lucien-l'Allier or Guy-Concordia. Single, double and triple rooms are available for men and women in this rather pricey Downtown YWCA, but only women have access to the pool and gym facilities. Other extras include kitchen and laundry facilities and Internet access. Shared bath: $60/single, $75 double, $95 triple; private bath: $75/single, $85 double.

La Maison du Prêt d'Honneur 1 boul René-Lévesque E ⓣ514/982-3420 ext 5501 or 5502, ⓕ514/982-3424; Métro Place-d'Armes or St-Laurent. Located on the edge of Chinatown, this residence of the Cégep du Vieux-Montréal junior college offers studios with one or two single beds as well as a few two-bedroom apartments. All have kitchenette, private bath, telephone and Internet access, plus there's a café, laundry room and fifth-floor terrace. Mid-May to mid-Aug; $57.50/single, $62.50/double, $100/apartment; an extra cot costs $10.

McGill University Residences 3935 rue University ⓣ514/398-6367, ⓦwww.residences.mcgill.ca/summer.html; Métro McGill. Up to 900 single rooms with shared kitchenettes, bathrooms and lounge areas are split between Royal Victoria College, near Downtown at 3425 rue University, and the four residence buildings on the mountain's slope. Sheets and towels are provided, as is free Internet access. Very popular among visiting Anglophones and, consequently, often full. Mid-may to mid-Aug only; $39–45.

Les Résidences Universitaires UQAM 303 boul René-Lévesque E ⓣ514/987-6669, ⓦwww.residences-uqam.qc.ca; Métro Berri-UQAM. Over a hundred clean and simply furnished studios with double bed, kitchenette and private bath, as well as apartments with two, three or eight bedrooms in this Quartier Latin student residence. Price includes linen service; there's also a café and laundry facilities. Mid-May to mid-Aug; $55/studio, $38.25-$51.25/apartment (per person).

Vacances Canada 5155 av de Gaspé ⓣ514/270-4459, ⓦwww.vacances-canadamd.montrealplus.ca; Métro Laurier. Up to 200 beds are available all year – double that in July and August – at this residence (used during the school year by the Collège Français) with two to six beds per room. The northern Plateau location makes it very popular, and it's frequently booked-up by Francophone school groups. $14.50/dorm, $21.50/double, $39.50 single. They also offer basic studio apartments in the Plateau area for $325/month.

10

Eating

One of the greatest pleasures of any visit to Montréal is **eating** out; the city is easily the number three foodie destination in North America, after New York and San Francisco. On top of the expected authentic **French cuisine**, there's a huge selection of **international foods** in which to indulge. Where the city truly excels is between the extremes of speedy lunchtime diners and formal dining extravaganzas – the bewildering array of moderately priced restaurants in Montréal serve up meals of a quality you'd be hard-pressed to find elsewhere at these prices. Another bonus is that they're often clustered close together, making it easy to just walk along and see what takes your fancy.

Montréal's European flavour is nowhere more evident than in its small **cafés**, where you can usually sit and read or talk undisturbed for hours while sipping on a drink. The majority of the cafés listed below also dish out delicious **snacks** such as *croque monsieur* and panini, and some go as far as serving light bistro fare. Montrealers tend to grab a quick fry-up **breakfast** or a croissant or muffin with their coffee on weekday mornings, but weekend **brunch** is an altogether different affair (see box, p.150).

In addition to cafés, you can seek out one of the city's many **diners** for deli-style meals, or try healthier food like soups, salads and sandwiches in smaller spots spread around the city. **Lunches** also offer the chance to try cheaper two- or three-course *spécial du midi* (lunch special) menus at the city's pricier restaurants, and a number of bars serve up grub at lunch or in the early evening (see Chapter 11, "Drinking"). If quick and cheap matters more than atmosphere, there are plenty of **food courts** in the basements of Downtown's malls and loads of noodle bars towards the west end. On hot and humid days, nothing beats **ice cream** – see box, p.154, for our roundup of Montréal's best.

Montréal **restaurants** start filling up for **dinner** between 7 and 8pm and serving until around 10 or 11pm. Most offer a three-course *table d'hôte*, which works out cheaper than ordering an individual starter, entrée and dessert à la carte. While it's easy to splurge on an expensive French restaurant in Montréal, the multitude of less formal ethnic spots can be just as satisfying and far more memorable, not to mention a good deal cheaper. Note that in French, an appetizer is called an *entrée*, while the main course is a *plat principal*. See the glossary (p.282) for more words likely to be on the menu.

If you want to grab a **late-night** bite, there are numerous places scattered along rue Ste-Catherine and in the Plateau (see box, p.156). Less conveniently, many smaller restaurants close Sunday and/or Monday, and places that cater to the business lunch crowd may not be open until dinnertime on the weekend; call ahead to avoid disappointment. It's a good idea to reserve in advance, but there are enough choices on rue St-Denis, rue Prince-Arthur, avenue Duluth,

Restaurants by cuisine

boulevard St-Laurent and avenue Laurier to stroll around and see what grabs you. Below, we've divided our listings up by neighbourhood (see box, p.146, for an overview), separated into spots that are best for a lighter meal during the day and those where you can settle down for a drawn-out evening dinner. You'll also find a complete list of restaurants cross-referenced by cuisine – see box, above.

Downtown

Cafés and light meals

Basha 930 rue Ste-Catherine O ⓣ514/866-4272; Métro Peel. Mosaic floors and subdued lighting help dispel the cafeteria feel of this cheap but good second-floor Lebanese spot overlooking rue Ste-Catherine. Fill up on falafel, spit-roasted *shish taouk* (chicken) or lamb *shawarma* for around $3 wrapped in a pita, or $5–6 with rice, salad and houmus. Sun–Thurs until midnight, Fri & Sat to 1am.

Ben's Delicatessen 990 boul de Maisonneuve O ⓣ514/844-1000; Métro Peel. Lithuanian Ben Kravitz opened his deli in 1908 and it's still run by his sons and grandsons. Their tasty smoked-meat sandwiches continue to draw people into the wee hours, and the gaudy 1930s interior and yellowing celebrity photos on the wall of this Montréal institution attest to an earlier, more prosperous time. Sun–Wed 7.30am–2am, Thurs

7.30am–3am, Fri & Sat 7.30am–4am.

Brûlerie St-Denis Maison Alcan, 1188 rue Sherbroooke ⓣ514/985-9159, ⓦwww.brulerie.com; Métro Peel. If it's sunny out, forgo the large, red-trimmed café interior and nab a seat on the glorious terrace along the garden path linking rues Drummond and Stanley. This is the nicest location of a local chain known for its terrific coffee and a good spot for a sandwich (most are under $7) and a pastry if you've got room. Mon–Fri 7am–7pm.

Café République 93 rue Ste-Catherine O ⓣ514/840-0000; Métro Place-des-Arts. Popular with media types, this relaxed café is close to Place des Arts and serves up a fine cup of coffee. Good for breakfast (until 3pm), light lunches – burgers, filled pitas and salads – and decadent cakes at decent prices. The branch at 1429 rue Crescent (ⓣ514/845-5999) has more of a lounge feel and a terrace overlooking the action, while the one facing Square Dorchester at 1200 rue Peel (ⓣ514/875-1200) has a classy atmosphere with velvety red banquettes, swag lampshades and a pricier evening menu.

Café Tramezzini 2125 rue de la Montagne ⓣ514/842-5522; Métro Peel. This cool and quiet basement café feels bigger than it is thanks to a wall of mirrors reflecting the stone walls. Try the namesake *tramezzini* – small sandwiches on white bread with the crusts cut off for $4 – or panini filled with prosciutto, shaved parmesan and arugula. Closed Sun.

Ciné-Express 1926 rue Ste-Catherine O ⓣ514/939-2463; Métro Guy-Concordia. A mix

Dining by district

Many of the city's priciest dining places are **Downtown**, where gastronomic French restaurants and higher-end ethnic eateries are tucked away on the side streets around rue Ste-Catherine. Here, you'll also find plenty of cheaper lunch spots and a smattering of fast-food joints. Over in **Chinatown**, rue de la Gauchetière is thronged with people seeking out not only Cantonese and Szechuan dishes, but also cheap and filling Vietnamese food. There are a few good options in **Vieux-Montréal**, as well, but many of the establishments here are overpriced tourist joints that don't offer much in the way of imaginative cuisine. The **Quartier Latin**'s main appeal lies in its terrace-fronted cafés – the restaurants tend to be more hit-or-miss. In the neighbouring **Village**, the gay contingent filling up before heading to the bars contributes a lively buzz to many establishments, but media types who work in the area also stick around for the casual but quality restaurants serving up a variety of international cuisines.

The best place to eat out is on the **Plateau**, where stylish restaurants serve up innovative cuisine on rue St-Denis and boulevard St-Laurent just above Sherbrooke. Greek-style tavernas serving *brochettes* (souvlaki) and a mix of other ethnic eateries vie for the tourist trade on **rue Prince-Arthur**. Better though, to head north a few blocks to **avenue Duluth**, where more authentic cuisine from Portugal, Italy, Afghanistan and even the tiny Indian Ocean island of Réunion can be found. The majority of restaurants on both these streets aren't licensed to sell liquor – instead they invite you to *apportez votre vin* (bring your own wine), a practice quite common in Montréal; see p.198 for recommendations on where to pick up a bottle. For Greek food that's more authentic than that served at many of the tavernas mentioned above, head up to **Mile End**, where you'll also find the best bagel bakeries. Adjacent **Outremont** is full of cafés, bistros and slightly pricier but still good-value ethnic joints on and around avenue Laurier, while to the north, **Little Italy** is the place for pizzerias, trattorias and fancier Italian cuisine.

Restaurant maps

In the Guide chapters you'll find maps listing the cafés, restaurants, clubs and bars of Montréal's liveliest areas. These can be found on the following pages:

of students and downtowners come for the cheap all-day breakfasts (served 8am–11pm) and $7 specials (a dollar more after 5pm) like the moussaka, Philly steak and primavera sandwich (veggies on a ciabatta). It's a long, casual space broken up by old sofas and tables for playing chess. The small terrace out front is a good spot to share a $9 pitcher of beer. 24hr.

Marché Mövenpick 1 Place Ville Marie ⓣ514/861-8181; Métro McGill. Labyrinthine "marketplace" that combines some of the tackiest motifs of the countries whose cuisine is on offer here, including serviceable Italian pastas, Japanese sushi and Swiss *rösti* potatoes. Take a ticket (and map), pick and choose from the different food stands (order hot dishes last), then pay as you leave. Daily 7.30am–2am.

Montréal Pool Room 1200 boul St-Laurent; Métro St-Laurent. A Montréal institution: nothing much but a steel counter facing the grill where steamies (hot dogs) topped with coleslaw have been the order of the day since 1912. Two dogs, fries and a Coke will set you back $3.99.

Reuben's Deli 1116 rue Ste-Catherine O ⓣ514/866-1029; Métro McGill or Peel. An old-school deli glammed up in black and mahogany tones that, despite management's efforts to the contrary, continues to draw diners for the wealth of smoked meats served up in a frantic atmosphere with friendly service. A favourite with local business types, and thus packed at lunchtime. If you're on a budget, head to the second location a few blocks east at no. 888 (☎514/861-1255); as it's in a basement (warmed by stained-glass panels), the food's a buck or two cheaper. Main location open daily 6.30am–1am.

Sushi Shop 915 boul de Maisonneuve O ☎514/847-1188, Ⓦwww.sushishop.com; Métro Peel. Part of a sleek new chain with large backlit images of the sushi, maki and sashimi that you can take away for a picnic on the nearby McGill campus or munch on a park bench. Boxed up and ready to go starting at $5 but it's worth the wait for them to roll you up something fresh.

Restaurants

Altitude 737 1 Place Ville Marie (rue University entrance) ☎514/397-0737; Métro McGill or Bonaventure. Very expensive. The prices may be sky-high, but so is the 360-degree view from this restaurant perched over 700 feet above sea level with the whole of the city spread out below. There are European touches on the menu, but French predominates – try the pan-fried fillet of beef or the grilled salmon. There's also a club and lounge with an outdoor terrace downstairs. Dress up. Closed Sun.

Bar-B-Barn 1201 rue Guy ☎514/931-3811, Ⓦwww.barbbarn.ca; Métro Guy-Concordia. Moderate. A fun, lively and loud restaurant on two floors serving tasty ribs and chicken in a faux Western setting. The hundreds of business cards stuck in the log rafters attest to its popularity with the local business world, and it's always packed to the hilt.

Bâton Rouge 180 rue Ste-Catherine O ☎514/282-7444, Ⓦwww.batonrougerestaurants.com; Métro Place-des-Arts. Moderate–expensive. The main draw here is the size (as opposed to the unspectacular preparation) of their portions of ribs, fries and other American, Cajun-tinged standards. Best enjoyed on the terrace facing Place des Arts, as inside is a bit claustrophobic, with low, dark wood ceilings over the booths and large tables for groups.

Boccacinos 1251 av McGill College ☎514/861-5742, Ⓦwww.boccacinos.com; Métro McGill. Moderate. A decent spot for a bite Downtown, with loads of tables on two floors and a good, crowded buzz – the place is heaving at lunchtime. The range of breakfasts starts at $4 and is served until 3pm or thereabouts; otherwise choose from burgers, pasta and salads or heftier dishes like steaks and Atlantic salmon.

Le Café des Beaux-Arts 1384 rue Sherbrooke O ☎514/843-3233; Métro Peel or Guy-Concordia. Moderate. Second-floor lunch spot in the Musée des Beaux-Arts where the food – French bistro with a regional Québécois touch – and table service are equally good. There's a wide range of wines by the glass and stand-out meals include the lamb shank and the portobello mushroom risotto. Dinner is only available Wednesday evenings.

Le Café du Nouveau-Monde 84 rue Ste-Catherine O ☎514/866-8669; Métro Place-des-Arts. Moderate–expensive. Located in the Théâtre du Nouveau-Monde's lobby, this is a place to see and be seen, as much as to sample the high-quality bistro fare and simpler sandwiches. The food is a bit richer in the upstairs half, where you can dine on the likes of duck *confit*, salmon tartare and *bavette* (flank steak). There's always a good buzz before showtime in the theatre (see p.188) and if it's sunny out the terrace is always packed. Closed Sun; open until midnight other nights.

Les Chenêts 2075 rue Bishop ☎514/844-1842, Ⓦwww.leschenets.com; Métro Peel or Guy-Concordia. Expensive. Superior French cuisine served up in a warm candle-lit room adorned with copper cookware. Highlights include wine-soaked escargots and good game dishes, such as pheasant breast smothered in wild mushrooms. With an extensive

Restaurant prices

The restaurant listings are price-coded into four categories: inexpensive (under $15), moderate ($15–25), expensive ($25–40) and very expensive (over $40). This assumes a three-course *table d'hôte* for one person, not including drinks, tax or tip. Taxes come to just over 15 percent, and a 15 percent tip is standard (but don't be hasty, the tip is occasionally included on the bill as a service charge).

wine list, referred to by staff as "the bible", selecting a vintage to accompany your meal won't be easy; there are also some 800 varieties of cognac.

Ferreira Café Trattoria **1446 rue Peel ⓣ514/848-0988, ⓦwww.ferreiracafe.com; Métro Peel.** Very expensive. Portuguese *azulejos* (glazed tiles) lining the walls hint at the authenticity of the delicious cooking here, notably fish dishes like the grilled sardines coated in sea salt. If you're on a budget, drop by for the two-course weekday lunchtime special ($22–28) served up in a lively atmosphere. Comprehensive port and wine selection. Closed Sun; no lunch Sat.

Le Grand Café **1181 av Union ⓣ514/866-1303; Métro McGill.** Expensive. The rattan chairs yell bistro, and the lunch menu delivers here, though with a few Asian-fusion twists like dumplings and sashimi thrown in. Evening selections are more classically French – think duck *confit* and rack of lamb – and the prices jump accordingly, though the wine list remains reasonable. Closed Sun.

Il Cortile **Passage du Musée, 1442 rue Sherbrooke O ⓣ514/843-8230; Métro Guy-Concordia.** Expensive. The name translates as "courtyard", and that's one of this classic Italian restaurant's most winning features – it spreads into a red-brick mews decked with blooming hanging baskets. The elegant interior is also appealing, and in either you can get carried away with the *crespella al ripieno* (crepes stuffed with ricotta and spinach) followed by scampi risotto, tagliolini with porcini mushrooms or the rich veal scalopine.

Katsura **2170 rue de la Montagne ⓣ514/849-1172; Métro Peel.** Expensive. Large and popular Downtown Japanese restaurant where kimono-clad waitresses bring sushi, sashimi and chicken or salmon teriyaki to your table. Traditional Japanese paintings add a subtle touch to the already-understated decor. For weekday lunches (11.30am–3pm), head upstairs to the *Katsura Delicatessen* for similar, though cheaper, dishes as well as Bento boxes (sushi, maki and tempura) for $13. No lunch on the weekend.

Le Parchemin **1333 rue University ⓣ514/844-1619; Métro McGill.** Moderate–expensive. Classic French dishes with *nouvelle* touches like seared tuna or tender chicken in a honey-almond sauce are served in this light-filled former presbytery built in 1876. It's the same menu and price for the *table d'hôte* at lunch but those on a budget can pick a dish from the bistro menu and a glass of wine from $11.95. No lunch Sat; closed Sun.

Queue de Cheval **1221 boul René-Lévesque O ⓣ514/390-0090, ⓦwww.queuedecheval.com; Métro Lucien-l'Allier or Peel.** Very expensive. Just north of the Centre Bell, this high-end steakhouse is one of the best in the city. Specials such as the arctic char – flown in fresh – cost a small fortune, but the main draw is the beef, like the juicy porterhouse steak, which they dry-age in house. With two waiters to a table, service is attentive to say the least.

La Rotonde **185 rue Ste-Catherine O ⓣ514/847-6900; Métro Place-des-Arts.** Expensive. It can be a bit noisy here – wrapped as it is around the atrium of the Musée d'Art Contemporain – but the food is well worth it. Provençal and southern French dishes like the roasted duck breast in a pear and honey sauce draw a busy evening crowd. Cheaper at lunch ($15–19) when there's a similar though toned-down menu (*magret de canard* rather than *confit de canard* and *bavette* instead of filet mignon, for instance). Open evenings when there's a performance on at Place des Arts for pre-show sittings only.

Takara **Cours Mont-Royal, 1455 rue Peel ⓣ514/849-9796; Métro Peel.** Moderate–expensive. Tucked away on the fourth level of the Cours Mont-Royal mall (there's a direct escalator from the rue Metcalfe entrance), this somewhat formal Japanese restaurant serves reasonably priced and nicely presented sushi and maki. If fish doesn't appeal, go for the *sukiyaki* – fat noodles and slices of beef simmering in a black cauldron. Kick your shoes off and sit around one of the lowered tables to make the most of the evening.

Zen ***Hôtel Omni*****, 1050 rue Sherbrooke O ⓣ514/499-0801; Métro Peel.** Expensive. Spicy Szechuan dishes are the order of the day in this elegantly minimalist basement restaurant, with specialties like crispy duck, beef with ginger and green onion and a particularly good General Tao chicken. Your best bet, though, is the "Zen experience" – for $29 you choose as many dishes as you want but the more you order, the smaller each portion served. There's a $15 lunch special, as well.

Montréal specialities

If you've come looking for local **Québécois cuisine**, you may have to look long and hard. Apart from a few traditional standbys such as *tourtière* (meat pie) and *fèves au lard* (baked beans with fatty bacon), such cuisine is nearly nonexistent, with *La Binerie Mont-Royal* (see p.157) one of the few holdouts. What you will find, though, is a number of gourmet restaurants that serve **cuisine du terroir** – literally "cuisine of the soil" – the focus of which is on regional produce wherever possible in the menu. Expect to see game from around the province, shrimp from Matane and ducks from Lac Brome (the fine-feathered friends are guests of honour at an annual festival – see p.234).

Cuisine du marché (market cuisine) places a similar emphasis on market-fresh ingredients, reflected in menus that vary with the season – and often daily, depending on what the chef was able to source that morning. Both are typically based on French cuisine, but usually with a lighter *nouvelle cuisine* approach and often a fusion with Mediterranean or Asian cooking styles. Many of the restaurants listed here will have some dishes that fit the bill, but the ones that have it as part of their defining ethos include:

Le Café des Beaux-Arts	p.147
Chez L'Épicier	p.152
La Colombe	p.158
Globe	p.155
Toqué!	p.159

The provincial and regional tourist boards do a fair job of setting out various gourmet routes and the Fédération des Agricotours has a searchable database of producers and places serving regional cuisine on their website (Ⓦ www.agricotours.qc.ca).

Local favourites

At the cheaper end of the scale, Québec has developed a number of variations on comfort food found throughout North America. Often the differences are minor (like *steamés* – steamed hot dogs in a steamed bun, served with grated cabbage), but when it comes to something as simple as barbecued chicken, you'll find that in Québec, they spit-roast the bird *rôtisserie*-style and serve it in quarters. For a taster, try *Laurier BBQ* (see p.160) or one of the many branches of the *Rôtisseries St-Hubert* (Ⓦ www.st-hubert.com) chain. The fast-food *poutine* (fries smothered in gravy and topped with cheese curd) is another stand-by, available at *casse-croûtes* (snack bars) around the province, and often in variations such as Italian *poutine* (with a tomato and meat sauce); try *Mondo Fritz* (p.155) for a sampler.

What many locals consider quintessentially **Montréal delicacies** were adopted from the European Jews who settled here in the early twentieth century. Top of the list is **smoked meat**, beef brisket cured in brine and then smoked (similar to pastrami or corned beef), which is sliced thick and piled high on rye bread. *Schwartz's* (p.155) is the undisputed king, but *Ben's* (p.144) and *Reuben's* (p.146) are reasonable Downtown alternatives.

Another Montréal classic is its variation on the rather prosaic **bagel** – denser and chewier than those found elsewhere – which are boiled first in honey water before being baked in a traditional wood-burning oven and sprinkled with sesame seeds. You can join the greedy crowds lining up to take home a bag-full at the bakeries themselves (see p.197) or have one as the base for eggs Benedict or topped with cream cheese and lox at most brunch spots (see p.150 for a list).

Brunch

In Montréal, **brunch** is a long and drawn-out affair, the meal generally used as an antidote to the previous night's partying, and most places serve until mid-afternoon – go early (before 11am) to avoid the queues. The Plateau – avenue Laurier in particular – has great spots to linger lazily over crepes, *pain doré* (French toast) or more lunch-like dishes. For a completely different brunch experience, head to Chinatown and get stuffed on dim sum.

Best brunch spots

L'Avenue	p.157	*Beauty's*	p.154
Le Café Cherrier	p.157	*Café Le Pèlerin*	p.152
Côté Soleil	p.158	*Dusty's*	p.159
Eggspectation	p.151	*L'Express*	p.158
Folies	p.157	*Laïka*	p.155
Lotté-Furama	p.150	*La Petite Ardoise*	p.159
Ruby Rouge	p.150	*Quoi de N'Oeuf*	p.161
Savannah	p.156		

Chinatown

Cafés and light meals

Idée Magique 30 rue de la Gauchetière O ☎514/868-0657; Métro Place-d'Armes. Although they serve cheap Chinese food, the main draw at this café is the "bubble tea". You start with cream tea, choose one of a dozen zippy flavours (such as mango, sesame or even egg yolk) and then jellies to put on top – it's the tapioca beads that give the tea its nickname, but you can try coconut berries or green tea crystals, too.

Pho Bac 97 1016 boul St-Laurent ☎514/393-8116; Métro Place-d'Armes. This small canteen-style Vietamese restaurant is typically crowded as they don't cheat on the Tonkinoise fixings, so expect plenty of coriander, basil and mint with your noodles and beef, chicken or veg. The iced coffee, laced with condensed milk, is serious rocket fuel. If this place is full, head down the block to the similar *Pho Bang New York* at no. 970 (☎514/954-2032). Neither accepts credit cards.

Restaurants

Hong Kong 1023 boul St-Laurent ☎514/861-0251; Métro Place-d'Armes. Moderate. Despite the army of roasting ducks in the window, this place is best known for its seafood – try the Cantonese-style lobster, flavoured with ginger, garlic and soy sauce. The vast menu at this Chinese restaurant is one reason it's packed with Chinese-Canadians.

Jardin de Jade 67 rue de la Gauchetière O ☎514/866-3127; Métro Place-d'Armes. Inexpensive. It's a bit of a factory, but the all-you-can-eat buffet is a bargain at $7.75 for lunch, $11 for dinner ($12.25 Fri–Sun) and $8.95 for a "late dinner" (9–11pm). The wide selection gives you a chance to try a variety of Cantonese and Szechuan dishes, from dumplings to spicy stir-fried beef.

Lotté-Furama 1115 rue Clark ☎514/393-3838; Métro Place-d'Armes. Moderate. Two large banquet halls are crowded with Chinese-Canadian families choosing dim sum dishes from the passing trolleys – the dumplings, like shrimp and coriander in a translucent rice wrapper, are wonderful. In the evenings, wedding parties take over the upper floor but you can still tuck into Peking duck and seafood at the large round tables on the chandelier-lit main floor.

Ruby Rouge 1008 rue Clark ☎514/390-8828; Métro Place-d'Armes. Moderate. Montréal's vast temple to dim sum is right in the heart of Chinatown. The menu is very well priced and you'll have to fight back the urge to grab spring rolls and fried seafood dumplings every time they wheel the trolley by. There are often long queues for dim sum (trolley service 11am–3pm) so get there early. If you go in the evening, opt for the Peking duck, Chinese fondue (winter only) or fresh lobster and crab, served Cantonese or Szechuan style.

Vieux-Montréal

Cafés and light meals

Bio Train 410 rue St-Jacques O ⓣ514/842-9184; Métro Square-Victoria. A self-serve health-food restaurant with tasty soups and hearty sandwiches. The muffins here – especially the tangy cranberry ones – make great snacks.

Café du Château Château Ramezay, 280 rue Notre-Dame E ⓣ514/861-3708; Métro Champ-de-Mars. Enjoy a warm-weather lunch on this stone-walled château's terrace overlooking the New France-style gardens. The short menu of carpaccio, panini, salads and the like are from *Claude Postel* (see below), though the prices are higher here ($8–12) than at *Postel*. You'll need to reserve at peak lunch hours. Daily 10am–6pm, summer only.

Le Cartet 106 rue McGill ⓣ514/871-8887; Métro Square-Victoria. If the weather's decent, head here for healthy sandwiches and complete boxed lunches to go – it's not far from the Vieux-Port's many green spaces. Otherwise, there's plenty of space to eat in, with a number of large, family-sized tables.

Claude Postel 75 rue Notre-Dame O ⓣ514/844-8750; Métro Place-d'Armes. A real find, this classy high-ceilinged café with honey-coloured walls sells panini and sandwiches, with fillings that include terrine de campagne and mousse de foie, at decent prices. For afters, there are decadent chocolates, elegant little cakes for $3 and mini crème brûlées for $2, as well as home-made ice cream.

Cluny 257 rue Prince ⓣ514/866-1213; Métro Square-Victoria. A trendy spot that shares digs with an art gallery in the Cité Multimédia just west of Vieux-Montréal. Best for lunch, when you can take your artfully crafted baguette sandwich or salad to one of the long wooden tables and listen in on your neighbours discussing the latest high-tech fads.

Eggspectation 201 rue St-Jacques O ⓣ514/282-0119, ⓦwww.eggspectation.ca; Métro Place-d'Armes. 198 av Laurier O ⓣ514/278-6411; Métro Laurier or bus #80. 1313 boul de Maisonneuve O ⓣ514/842-3447; Métro Peel or Guy-Concordia. A variety of antique objects are scattered about the Vieux-Montréal, Downtown and Mile End branches of this great local chain that's packed at weekends. Look for the cheaper "Classics" buried in the menu between the scrumptious crepes, french toast, eggs Florentine and the like. Mon–Fri 6am–3pm (until 4pm or 5pm weekends, depending on demand; de Maisonneuve branch daily until 4.45pm).

Java U 191 rue St-Paul O ⓣ514/849-8881; Métro Place-d'Armes. The name of this cheap chic café is misleading – it's part of an otherwise unremarkable chain that started up for the student crowd Downtown. At this particular location, however, the pressed-tin ceiling and ornate columns contrast with a hip design of soft modular seating set to a soundtrack of funky acid jazz. The tapas-style menu offers some unusual choices – profiteroles with blue cheese mousse, tandoori calamari and a "skinny" dip platter – and cheaper panini at lunchtime.

Olive et Gourmando 351 rue St-Paul O ⓣ514/350-1083, ⓦwww.oliveetgourmando.com; Métro Square-Victoria. Delectable bakery that serves up salads and hot and cold sandwiches throughout the day. The menu changes regularly, but it often features items like smoked trout or toasted focaccia with goat's cheese. Open Tues–Sat 8am–6pm.

Titanic 445 rue St-Pierre ⓣ514/849-0894; Métro Square-Victoria. Businesspeople and tourists alike fill the large communal tables crammed into this small Italian-style deli serving antipasti, sandwiches and healthy-sized salads from 8am to 3pm.

Restaurants

Bonaparte 443 rue St-François-Xavier ⓣ514/844-4368, ⓦwww.bonaparte.ca; Métro Place-d'Armes. Moderate. Located on a picturesque cobblestone street, this French restaurant's rich-red carpeting and dark-panelled wainscotting provides a perfect backdrop to dishes like rack of lamb in port wine or lobster stew with a vanilla sauce; if you're feeling indulgent try the seven-course tasting menu ($57). No lunch on weekends.

Boris Bistro 495 rue McGill ⓣ514/848-9575, ⓦwww.borisbistro.com; Métro Square-Victoria. Moderate–expensive. Although it serves good bistro fare like duck *confit*, salmon and beef tartares and braised rabbit, the main draw here is the phenomenal tree-shaded terrace, separated from the street by the free-standing facade of an old limestone building.

Chez Better **160 rue Notre-Dame E ⓣ514/861-2617; Métro Champ-de-Mars.** Inexpensive. An early-nineteenth-century house provides a suitable setting for this restaurant's warming platters of Old World sausages like spicy *debrecziner*, Bavarian *weisswurst* and mild *schublig* served with fries or sauerkraut.

Chez Delmo **211 rue Notre-Dame O ⓣ514/849-4061; Métro Place-d'Armes.** Very expensive. Seafood is the forte here, as evidenced by two long oyster bars up in front. In the back dining room, typically brimming with local stock-exchange workers, the fish and seafood dishes come perfectly cooked – the chowder is also a treat. No lunch Sat, closed Sun, no dinner Mon.

Chez L'Épicier **311 rue St-Paul E ⓣ514/878-2232, ⓦwww.chezlepicier.com; Métro Champ-de-Mars.** Expensive–very expensive. Updated French classics and comfort food – the shepherd's pie is made with snails, the quail is glazed with mole sauce – in a bright eighteenth-century building. There's a tasting menu if you want to explore a range of flavours and posh groceries are also on sale in the attached boutique. Lunch is a more reasonable $13–16 for two courses and there's a good selection of wines by the glass. No lunch at weekends.

Da Emma **777 rue de la Commune O ⓣ514/392-1568; Métro Square-Victoria.** Very expensive. Fantastic Italian cooking served up in a stylishly renovated basement in one of Montréal's oldest buildings. Standout mains include fettucine *al funghi porcini* and succulent *abbachio* or *maialino al forno* (huge chunks of lamb or suckling pig). Save room, if you can, for the homemade sorbets and addictive tiramisu.

Masala **995 rue Wellington O ⓣ514/287-7455; bus #61 or Métro Square-Victoria or Bonaventure.** Moderate. Punjabi and Kashmiri dishes are prepared with style and skill in this stripped-back warehouse space – about a ten-minute-walk west of rue McGill, through the Cité Multimédia district – warmed with orange and maroon walls and Indian fabrics. Start with the rich and creamy dahl before filling up on the tasty butter chicken, but leave room for the lime tart or cardamom cake. The chef-owner also offers cooking lessons for $50, including the dishes you prepare. Open for lunch (Mon–Fri 11am–3pm) and evenings later in the week – call ahead. *Apportez votre vin.*

Le Petit Moulinsart **139 rue St-Paul O ⓣ514/843-4779, ⓦwww.lepetitmoulinsart.com; Métro Place-d'Armes.** Moderate–expensive. If you didn't recognize the Belgian flag outside, the Tintin paraphernalia scattered about should give you an idea of the cuisine here. Top of the list is mussels, the dozen variations ranging from *marinières* to a sake, Chinese basil, pepper leaf and mushroom sauce. For adventurous carnivores, there's beef or horsemeat tartare; otherwise try the *bavette* with shallots and butter or *lapin à la moutarde* (rabbit in mustard sauce). In fine weather, sit in the courtyard terrace out back.

Stash Café **200 rue St-Paul O ⓣ514/846-6611; Métro Place-d'Armes.** Moderate. Sit on an old church pew and nosh on Polish comfort food like borscht, pierogies and meatier dishes in an equally warm atmosphere of stone walls and low lighting with a request-taking piano player.

Quartier Latin and the Village

Cafés and light meals

La Brioche Lyonnaise **1593 rue St-Denis ⓣ514/842-7017; Métro Berri-UQAM.** The smell of freshly baked French pastries like flaky *mille-feuille* and chocolate eclairs should lure you in to this café-patisserie. Try, too, the savoury crepes filled with egg, ham and cheese. Daily morning to midnight (11pm on slower nights).

Café Le Pèlerin **330 rue Ontario E ⓣ514/845-0909; Métro Berri-UQAM.** Some of the best coffee in the city, but if that's all you're after, drop by in the late afternoon as it's packed at lunch for the sandwiches, *croques* and other light bistro dishes. Brunch served until 2pm on the weekend.

Croissant de Lune **1765 rue St-Denis ⓣ514/843-8146; Métro Berri-UQAM.** A cozy, stone-walled Quartier Latin café set a few feet below street level. There's a range of savoury and dessert crepes available, as well as omelettes, salads and sandwiches, all in the $5 range.

Kilo **1495 rue Ste-Catherine E ⓣ514/596-3933; Métro Beaudry.** The healthy salads and sandwiches served here are merely teasers for the wild array of killer desserts on offer – the cheesecake is particularly deadly. Open until midnight, 1am weekends. They've got another diet-buster location in Mile End at 5205 boul St-Laurent (ⓣ514/277-5039).

La Paryse 302 rue Ontario E ⓣ514/842-2040; **Métro Berri-UQAM.** Delicious hamburgers loaded with goodies – try *Le Spécial*, which is topped with cream cheese and bacon – served up in a cheery, 1950s-style diner. Vegetarians have three types of burgers to choose from – tofu, pinto bean and veggie paté – with toppings to complement each.

Presse Café Village 1263 rue Ste-Catherine E ⓣ514/528-9530; **Métro Beaudry.** One of the best spots in the Village for people-watching, especially when its front window is open, this busy 24hr café serves up fine basic salads and sandwiches along with Internet access for $5 per hour.

Le Resto du Village 1310 rue Wolfe ⓣ514/524-5404; **Métro Beaudry.** Down a side street from rue Ste-Catherine, this small *apportez votre vin* diner serves filling comfort food such as *pâté chinois* (shepherd's pie) and *poutine* to a largely gay crowd. It's open 24 hours and packs up quickly once the nearby clubs close.

L'Utopia 552 rue Ste-Catherine E ⓣ514/844-1139; **Métro Berri-UQAM.** An unassuming door facing Place Émilie-Gamelin leads upstairs to this ramshackle studenty hangout with mismatched chairs and sofas strewn about a warren of rooms and skylit nooks. A non-profit outfit, it serves organic vegetarian meals for $7–8, hosts an eclectic range of nightly musical performances and has Internet terminals for $4 an hour.

Zyng 1748 rue St-Denis ⓣ514/284-2016, ⓦwww.zyng.com; **Métro Berri-UQAM.** Create your own meal by choosing a meat, shrimp or tofu base and one of eight seasonings, then fill your bowl from an assortment of veggies and hand it to a nearby chef who whips it all up. Definitely not haute cuisine, but it's cheap and decent and the tight-packed tables ensure a good conversational buzz.

Restaurants

Area 1429 rue Amherst ⓣ514/890-6691, ⓦwww.rest-area.qc.ca; **Métro Beaudry.** Very expensive. Well-designed restaurant with a stylish and airy atmosphere – ornamented by creamy-grey banquettes and chairs and minimalist floral arrangements against the white and exposed-brick walls – reflected in the presentation of the yellow fin tuna and salmon tartare, tempura shrimp in Madras curry and other French and Asian fusion dishes. Dinner only; closed Sun & Mon.

Bato Thai 1310 rue Ste-Catherine E ⓣ514/524-6705; **Métro Beaudry.** Inexpensive–moderate. Thai restaurant in the Village with horrendously slow service, but the food's worth the wait – especially the satay chicken served with deep-fried spinach. Lunchtime specials start at $6.50, but it's closed for lunch on the weekend.

Chez Gatsé Restaurant Tibetain 317 rue Ontario E ⓣ514/985-2494; **Métro Berri-UQAM.** Inexpensive. Tibetan restaurant serving *mômos* (dumplings stuffed with cheese, beef or veg), egg-noodle *thukpas* with beef and veg, and curry-spiced beef and chicken *shaptas*. If you like the decor, you can buy colourful Tibetan fabrics and handicrafts in the store upstairs. There's also a big tree-shaded courtyard out back. No lunch weekends.

Le Commensal 1720 rue St-Denis ⓣ514/845-2627; **Métro Berri-UQAM.** Inexpensive. Choose from dozens of vegetarian dishes, including salads, couscous, stir-fried tofu and lasagne from the buffet, then pay by weight ($1.69 per 100g) and enjoy your meal in the large, glazed front room looking onto the street. A warning – it's easy to over-fill your plate and end up paying for more than you can eat. There's a Downtown branch at 1204 av McGill College (ⓣ514/871-1480).

Fou d'Asie 1732 rue St-Denis ⓣ514/281-0077; **Métro Berri-UQAM.** Inexpensive–moderate. More stylish than many of its Quartier Latin neighbours, this Asian fusion restaurant applies Thai and Vietnamese flavours to beef, chicken and seafood, served up with noodles. The sushi bar is also a popular draw.

Au Petit Extra 1690 rue Ontario E ⓣ514/527-5552, ⓦwww.aupetitextra.com; **Métro Papineau.** Moderate. Large, lively and affordable bistro with amazing food and an authentic French feel, reflected in the selection of sweetbreads and kidneys, in addition to the tasty duck breast and fish dishes on the weekly-changing menu. There's also a good range of wines at affordable prices. Closed for lunch on the weekend.

Pho Viet 1663 rue Amherst ⓣ514/522-4116; **Métro Beaudry.** Inexpensive. Almost literally a hole-in-the-wall, this tiny, barely furnished Vietnamese restaurant is nonetheless popular with those in-the-know, especially for its beef or chicken Tonkinoise soup. Lunch during the week only and closed Sunday. Reservations recommended for dinner. No cards. *Apportez votre vin*.

Crème de la crème glacée

During Montréal's icy winters, the last thing you'd want is something cold to lick, but on warmer days people flock to the city's **ice cream parlours**. At great personal hardship, we've sampled some of the city's best:

Ben and Jerry's 1316 boul de Maisonneuve O ⓣ514/286-6073; Métro Peel or Guy-Concordia. The former Vermont independent still dishes up favourites like Cherry Garcia and Chunky Monkey as the Jersey cows painted on the walls look patiently on. Daily 11am–10pm, except summer Sun–Wed 10am–1am, Thurs–Sat 10am–3am. There's a second outlet on Place Jacques-Cartier in Vieux-Montréal.

Bilboquet 1311 av Bernard O ⓣ514/276-0414; Métro Outremont. Delectable homemade ice cream is the reason to visit this popular spot, where people line up until midnight on summer nights. The banana ice cream is loaded with real chunks, and the seasonal specialities, like the Maple Taffy flavour, are brilliantly original. Numerous Downtown cafés also stock *Bilboquet*'s products. Closed late December to mid-March.

Meu Meu 4458 rue St-Denis; Métro Mont-Royal. They pack a lot of flavours into this tiny Plateau parlour, applied to tasty and well-crafted sorbets, frozen yogurt and ice cream (including a number of soya varieties) – even the ice cream sandwiches are homemade.

Ripples 3880 boul St-Laurent ⓣ514/842-1697; bus #55. Nowhere's cooler on the Main come summertime – they do an ace job on vanilla and chocolate standards, as well as zestier sensations like the ginger ice cream.

Roberto 2221 rue Bélanger ⓣ514/374-9844; Métro D'Iberville. Miles from anywhere but they serve the best gelatto in town. The *nocciola* has a heavenly creamy hazelnut flavour but the *baci* takes it a step further by mixing it with chocolate.

Saloon 1333 rue Ste-Catherine E ⓣ514/522-1333; Métro Beaudry. Moderate. A reliable menu of pizzas, burgers, salads and brunch draws a mixed crowd of young and old, gay and straight to this two-level Village hangout, but it's the Thai-style grilled chicken that stands out. The steak frites isn't bad, either.

Spirite Lounge 1205 rue Ontario E ⓣ514/522-5353; Métro Beaudry or Berri-UQAM. Moderate. High-concept vegetarian dining that you'll either love or hate. The deal is that you must completely finish one course to be allowed to eat the next, and a fine (given to charity) is levied if you don't finish your meal. The largely organic menu is different every day and can be a bit hit-or-miss.

Plateau Mont-Royal: the Main and around

Cafés and light meals

Beauty's 93 av du Mont-Royal O ⓣ514/849-8883, ⓦwww.beautys.ca; Métro Mont-Royal or bus #55. A brunch institution that's been serving meals to customers snuggled up in their booths for over sixty years. The "Beauty's Special" – bagel, lox, tomato, red onion and cream cheese – is the best such combo in the city. Be prepared to get up extra early on the weekend to avoid the line-up. Daily from 7am (Sun 8am) until around 5pm.

Café Santropol 3990 rue St-Urbain ⓣ514/842-3110, ⓦwww.santropol.com; bus #55 or Métro Sherbrooke or Mont-Royal. This outstanding and mostly vegetarian café on the corner of av Duluth has a lovely "secret garden" back terrace, and retains its charm in winter thanks to a cozy atrium. Massive, inventive sandwiches (the "Midnight Spread" contains honey, peanut butter, cream and cottage cheeses, nuts, raisins and bananas) on chewy dark bread are accompanied by loads of fresh fruit. Vegetarian pies, salads and soups also available. Save space for the thick, to-die-for milkshakes. No credit cards.

Eurodeli 3619 boul St-Laurent ⓣ514/843-7853; Métro Sherbrooke or bus #55. Long a popular favourite with Plateau students, this is a great spot for a quick espresso or cheap pasta or calzone while people-watching on the Main. You can also take away a variety of deli fixings. Daily until 3.30am.

Laïka 4040 boul St-Laurent ⓣ514/842-8088; bus #55 or Métro Sherbrooke or Mont-Royal. The sleek interior draws urbane hipsters from the Plateau for daily specials and excellent *cafés au lait*. Floor-to-ceiling windows open onto the street in summer, and a small brunch selection, including eggs Florentine, frittatas and crepes, is available on the weekends. Daily 8.30am–3am (food until 2am).

Mondo Fritz 3899 boul St-Laurent ⓣ514/281-6521; bus #55 or Métro Sherbrooke. Great laid-back place for fries and a beer, as there's a wide array of dips for the former and a large, international selection of the latter. Good spot for vegetarians: both the *poutine*, served with a meat-free gravy, and the garden burgers are worth a try. Daily until 1am (3am Fri & Sat).

Schwartz's 3895 boul St-Laurent ⓣ514/842-4813; bus #55 or Métro Sherbrooke. A small, narrow, ten-table deli that's been serving colossal sandwiches since 1930, *Schwartz's* consistently (and deservedly) tops the *Mirror's* annual "best smoked meat" list – choose the *gras* style for the full-fat experience. There's usually a line-up out the door and surly service, but it's well worth it. Daily 9am–12.30am (until 1.30am Fri, 2.30am Sat).

Soupesoup 80 av Duluth E ⓣ514380-0880; bus #55 or Métro Sherbrooke or Mont-Royal. Does what it says on the tin – a daily changing menu of classic soups such as ratatouille and concoctions like the lemony squash, mussels and fennel combo are served in a small space with colourful ceramic tile tabletops and walls panelled with old doors. Closed Mon; no dinner weekends.

Restaurants

Amelio's 201 rue Milton ⓣ514/845-8396; Métro Place-des-Arts or bus #24. Inexpensive. Hearty pastas and pizzas – including their unusual five-cheese "white pizza" – are served in this tiny restaurant tucked away in the heart of the McGill University student ghetto. The service is friendly and the raspberry cheesecake heavenly. Daily 11am–8.45pm (Mon & Sat from 4pm); closed Sun. *Apportez votre vin*.

Bistro Duluth 121 av Duluth E ⓣ514/287-9096; Métro Sherbrooke or Mont-Royal. Inexpensive. This casual and friendly spot is as good a spot for a drink on the terrace as for the cheap but good meals served until 3am. It's picked up more of a Portuguese flavour from its neighbours in recent years, adding grilled fish to the standby sausage plates and bowls of mussels (all-you-can-eat Sun–Wed).

Checkpoint Charlie 50 rue Rachel E ⓣ514/842-0191; bus #55 or Métro Mont-Royal. Moderate. Third location of this long-time favourite, where the beer steins hanging over the open kitchen more than hint at the German menu of sausages and wienerschnitzel, though there are a few surprises such as Peking duck and rabbit prepared *à la française*. Have a schnapps or Jägermeister for a great finish. Wed–Sat, dinner only.

Globe 3455 boul St-Laurent ⓣ514/284-3823, ⓦwww.restaurantglobe.com; Métro Sherbrooke or St-Laurent or bus #55. Very expensive. Best of the flashy restaurants on this block of the Main, *Globe* scores high for food as well as for its sleek, simple decor. The seasonal produce – fiddleheads in late spring, kale in winter, for instance – are locally sourced and simply but expertly combined with a variety of fish, seafood and meats like roasted chicken and braised rabbit.

Jano 3883 boul St-Laurent ⓣ514/849-0646; bus #55 or Métro Sherbrooke. Moderate. The gaily decorated rooster out front seems blissfully unaware of its cousins – along with sardines, sole, rabbit and lamb chops – visible grilling away through the front window of this long-time Plateau restaurant. Other Portuguese dishes like *chourico* and squid are available but the focus is very much on the grilled meats. Open until midnight.

Laloux 250 av des Pins E ⓣ514/287-9127, ⓦwww.laloux.com; Métro Sherbrooke. Expensive. Creamy yellow walls lined with gilt mirrors add an elegant touch to this Parisian-style bistro serving exquisite *nouvelle cuisine*. The chef likes to contrast flavours, serving, for instance, foie gras with grapes. Follow it up with the marvellous sweetbreads with white port and morels, but make sure to try the chocolate cake with tarragon and Pernod ice cream, a memorably sweet/zesty/bitter medley.

Maestro SVP 3615 boul St-Laurent ⓣ514/842-6447, ⓦwww.maestrosvp.com; Métro Sherbrooke or bus #55. Expensive–very expensive. If you're in the mood for oysters, this is the place – some fifteen species are served up in a myriad of ways. Try them

Rockefeller (pesto, cheese and white sauce), raw with lemon one-by-one ($2–8) or in a shooter with vodka and horseradish sauce. The $65 "Maestro Platter" for two is another sure bet, loaded with clams, mussels, calamari, shrimp, king crab and lobster.

Moishe's 3961 boul St-Laurent ⓣ514/845-3509, ⓦwww.moishes.ca; bus #55 or Métro Sherbrooke. Very expensive. This steakhouse with dark, panelled walls has been a favourite haunt of Montréal's business community since 1938. Excellent (and huge) charcoal-broiled steaks, but very expensive, with notoriously bad-tempered service. No lunch at weekends; reservations recommended.

Red Thai 3550 boul St-Laurent ⓣ514/289-0998; Métro Sherbrooke or Saint-Laurent. Expensive. This restaurant serves up delightful Thai in a decor straight out of *Anna and the King*. They've got a sizzling seafood plate, Mekong scampi and chicken satay, and you can sample cheaper "Bangkok lunch" specials ($9–18) until 3pm (Tues–Fri only).

Savannah 4488 boul St-Laurent ⓣ514/904-0277, ⓦwww.savannahrestaurant.com; Métro Mont-Royal or bus #55. Expensive. The American chef-owner here tempers Southern fusion cuisine with a Montréal sensibility. Before jumping into Creole and Cajun standards like jumbalaya or blackened catfish, try the foie gras wrapped in wild boar bacon and doused with maple syrup – a complex and memorable melange of flavours. The large terrace is surrounded by hedges, which screen it from the street. Live jazz Friday and Saturday nights and for Sunday brunch.

Tasca 172 av Duluth E ⓣ514/987-1530, ⓦwww.bistrotasca.com; Métro Sherbrooke or Mont-Royal. Moderate. Authentic tapas restaurant filled with Portuguese families, especially at weekends when an accordionist plays. Pick a few dishes from the wide range of charcoal-grilled fish and seafood to share – try the octopus, either grilled or marinated in a herb and onion sauce.

Late-night eats

Whether it's for a late bite after a show or for something to soak up the alcohol after a night on the tiles, there are plenty of places in Montréal that close around midnight (a bit later on weekends) or even well after.

'Round midnight

Basha see p.144
La Brioche Lyonnaise see p.152
Le Café du Nouveau-Monde see p.147
Le Continental see p.158
Kilo see p.152
La Petite Ardoise see p.159
Schwartz's see p.155

Into the wee hours

Arahova Souvlaki see p.160
Ben's see p.144
Bistro Duluth see p.155
Ciné-Express see p.145
La Croissanterie Figaro see p.159
Eurodeli see p.154
L'Express see p.158
Folies see p.157
Laïka see p.155
Marché Mövenpick see p.146
Mondo Fritz see p.155
Presse Café Village see p.153
Le Resto du Village see p.153
Reuben's see p.146

Plateau Mont-Royal: rue St-Denis and east

Cafés and light meals

Aux Deux Marie 4329 rue St-Denis ⓣ514/844-7246; Métro Mont-Royal. One of the better of the many rue St-Denis cafés, *Aux Deux Marie* roast their own coffee beans (stacked in burlap sacks by the entrance) and serve cheap cakes to go with the finished brew. You can also have sandwiches, quiches, *croques* or salads on the terrace or at one of the wooden tables alongside the exposed brick walls.

La Binerie Mont-Royal 367 av du Mont-Royal E ⓣ514/285-9078; Métro Mont-Royal. Just four tables in this hole-in-the-wall diner, which prides itself on traditional Québécois cuisine served here since 1938. The house specialty is *fèves au lard* (baked beans doused with ketchup, vinegar or maple syrup), and other worthwhile dishes include a mean *tourtière* and the *pouding au chômeur* ("unemployed pudding") – a variation on bread pudding. Cheap, filling breakfasts served all day. Mon–Fri 6am–8pm, Sat & Sun 7.30am–3pm.

Le Café Cherrier 3635 rue St-Denis ⓣ514/843-4308; Métro Sherbrooke. An older Francophone crowd congregates here for guilt-free weekend brunches – the buttery eggs Benedict oozes calories – often making it hard to find a table. *Croques* and quiches fill the afternoon gap before the fuller bistro menu is available in the evening.

Café El Dorado 921 av du Mont-Royal E ⓣ514/598-8282; Métro Mont-Royal. A sleek café with friendly service that's warmed by exposed-brick walls and red-wood tables and floors. They serve a mean cup of coffee to go along with their large breakfasts. Grab a seat at the large front window to watch the passing streetlife or the folks queuing at *L'Avenue* (see below).

Folies 701 rue Mont-Royal E ⓣ514/528-4343, ⓦwww.folies.tv; Métro Mont-Royal. A hip café-lounge perfect for an excellent breakfast (and wider-ranging brunches on the weekends) on the umbrella-shaded terrace or in the retro-space-age interior full of sleek curves. Later on, choose from pastas, burgers and bistro dishes or nibble away at tapas while the DJ spins electronic beats. No credit cards. Mon–Fri 11am–1am, Sat & Sun 10am–2am.

Les Gâteries 3443 rue St-Denis ⓣ514/843-6235; Métro Sherbrooke. Opposite Square St-Louis, the warm ochre-and-cream interior of this café makes for a great spot to indulge in one of the excellent cakes on offer – a big slice of dark chocolate *mousse royale* goes for $6. If you want something less sweet, the typical standbys – sandwiches, quiches and inventive *croques* – are also available.

Porté Disparu 957 av du Mont-Royal E ⓣ514/524-0271; Métro Mont-Royal. Folksy café with dark wood furnishings and exposed brick walls that's a good place to read or hang out. Cheap and generous three-course lunch specials for around $7.50, occasionally accompanied by impromptu piano playing by customers. Schedule of evening gigs – from flamenco to jazz – is posted at the door.

Restaurants

L'Avenue 922 av du Mont-Royal E ⓣ514/523-8780; Métro Mont-Royal. Moderate. Extremely popular among the hip Plateau set and full of stylish decor, from the giant silver starfish scaling the facade to a wall of water in the bathroom. Sit at one of the sparkly gold booths and tuck into huge portions of thoughtfully prepared updates on classic diner food – like goat's cheese and wild-mushroom topped hamburgers – which share the menu with salads, pastas and really good *bavette*. Long queues for weekend brunch – *Café El Dorado* (see above), opposite, is a reasonable alternative if you're too hungry to wait. No credit cards but they have an ATM.

Bières & Compagnie 4350 rue St-Denis ⓣ514/844-0394, ⓦwww.bieresetcompagnie.ca; Métro Mont-Royal. Moderate. A stylish restaurant/bar with large booths and dim lighting, serving up $16 all-you-can-eat platters of mussels (Mon–Wed), beer-soaked sausages and a range of burgers made with exotic meats – try the rich buffalo burger served with homemade mayonnaise for dipping the great fries into. It should also rank high on any beer fanatic's list as there are around a hundred types of brews to choose from, including a wide Belgian selection.

ChuChai 4088 rue St-Denis ⓣ514/843-4194, ⓦwww.chuchai.com; Métro Mont-Royal or Sherbrooke. Moderate. Terrific and fresh vegetarian Thai food featuring a wide array of tasty mock meats, including a delicious crispy "duck". Get the divine deep-fried seaweed as an accompaniment. The adjoining *Chuch Express* is more casual and lively and serves the same food as well as cheaper ready-prepared dishes to eat in or take away; the $6 lunch special includes soup, two dishes and rice.

La Colombe 554 av Duluth E ⓣ514/849-8844; Métro Sherbrooke or Mont-Royal. Expensive. Open for dinner only, this small, stylish bistro attracts a well-heeled Francophone crowd and serves a higher level of cuisine than the average *apportez votre vin* restaurant. Fresh seasonal ingredients accompany mains like venison or *jarret d'agneau* (lamb shank) served *au jus*. Non-smoking. Closed Mon.

Le Continental 4169 rue St-Denis ⓣ514/845-6842; Métro Mont-Royal. Expensive. An always packed French bistro that has a few Italian dishes thrown into the à-la-carte-only menu – the carpaccio, fish bisque, lamb medallions and steak frites are tops. The Art Deco-influenced retro decor attracts an artsy crowd, and those eating at the bar add to the talkative buzz. Finish off with the decadent chocolate-mousse cake. Open for dinner only until midnight Sun & Mon, until 1am other nights. Reservations advised.

Côté Soleil 3979 rue St-Denis ⓣ514/282-8037; Métro Sherbrooke or Mont-Royal. Moderate. Light, Mediterranean-influenced bistro fare, including a delicious roasted goat's cheese salad, served in a welcoming space with exposed-brick walls. Great terrace for surveying the St-Denis scene, especially when lingering over one of the gorgeous brunches – try the "Ibiza" eggs accompanied by a zesty tomato salsa.

Crêperie Bretonne Ty-Breiz 933 rue Rachel E ⓣ514/521-1444; Métro Mont-Royal. Moderate. Despite the incredibly tacky decor with pictures of Brittany and traditional costumes, this family-style creperie has drawn a local following for over four decades. Their large crepes are the real thing, filled with ingredients like sausage, apples or asparagus in béchamel sauce. Daily from 11.30am.

Eduardo 404 av Duluth E ⓣ514/843-3330; Métro Sherbrooke or Mont-Royal. Inexpensive–moderate. Cheap, crowded Italian restaurant featuring huge portions of veal, trout in lemon sauce and *tuto mare* (linguini with shrimp, clams and scallops in a rosé sauce) served in a dark and cozy space with back-lit stained-glass windows. No lunch on the weekend. *Apportez votre vin*.

L'Express 3927 rue St-Denis ⓣ514/845-5333; Métro Sherbrooke. Expensive. Fashionable Parisian-style bistro whose hectic but attentive service adds to the atmosphere. Try the steak tartare if you're feeling adventurous; otherwise opt for the safer steak frites or *canard confit* (slow-roasted duck). Table reservations are essential – though you might be able to squeeze in at the bar unannounced. Mon–Fri from 8.30am (Sat & Sun from 10am) until 2am (1am Sun).

Fonduementale 4325 rue St-Denis ⓣ514/499-1446, ⓦwww.fonduementale.com; Métro Mont-Royal. Expensive. Set in a red-brick Victorian two-storey house, *Fonduementale*'s main living room is fitted with late-nineteenth-century lights and mouldings and warmed by a fireplace in winter, and there's a blooming outdoor terrace in summer. The fondue here is exquisite – especially *Le Mental*, which features chunks of venison and caribou. Be sure to leave room for the chocolate fondues for dessert.

Le Jardin de Panos 521 av Duluth E ⓣ514/521-4206, ⓦwww.lejardindepanos.com; Métro Sherbrooke or Mont-Royal. Moderate. Bring-your-own-wine *brochetterie* serving heavy meals – the standard is chicken or beef shish kebabs with fried potatoes accompanied by Greek salad, though the grilled salmon filet is a lighter option – in a warren of rooms. The food's better than similar spots on rue Prince-Arthur and it has a garden terrace to boot.

Khyber Pass 506 av Duluth E ⓣ514/844-7131; Métro Sherbrooke or Mont-Royal. Moderate. The cozy furnishings and music here feel as authentic as the menu of Afghan specialties, including kebabs, koftas and kormas. The *sabzi khalaw* – lamb shank with spinach and three kinds of basmati rice – is the standout. Dinner only. *Apportez votre vin*.

Mañana 3605 rue St-Denis ⓣ514/847-1050; Métro Sherbrooke. Moderate. Tuck into tasty beef fajitas and vegetarian quesadillas in this small stone-walled spot opposite Square St-Louis, surrounded by Mexican masks, sombreros and colourful woven tablecloths.

Le Nil Bleu 3706 rue St-Denis ⓣ514/285-4628; Métro Sherbrooke. Moderate. Walls of water, grass wreath sculptures and candlelight give this Ethiopian restaurant a dark and close feel. It's a perfect atmosphere for the spicy *doro wat* stew with beef, chicken, lamb or just vegetables that's served on top of spongy *injera* bread. Dinner only.

La Piton de la Fournaise 835 av Duluth E ⓣ514/526-3936; Métro Mont-Royal or Sherbrooke. Moderate. This cute little restaurant features the cuisine of Réunion – the French island colony in the Indian Ocean –

and the mix of the three cuisines is flavoured with turmeric, ginger, garlic and Thai pepper, applied to dishes like the shark or octopus stew. Evenings only; two seatings Fri & Sat (5.30/6pm & 8.30/9pm); closed Monday. *Apportez votre vin*.

Pizzédélic 1250 av du Mont-Royal E ⓣ514/522-2286; Métro Mont-Royal. Inexpensive–moderate. The signature square pizzas at this great local chain come with adventurous toppings like goat's cheese, walnuts and black olives, or smoked salmon, capers, cream cheese, red onion and ginger. The curvy ceiling painted in primary colours adds to the fun atmosphere while the garage-door front opens up to the street on balmier days. The decor is more sober in the branch at 3467 boul St-Laurent (ⓣ514/845-0404) but the pizza's equally good.

Au P'tit Lyonnais 1279 rue Marie-Anne E ⓣ514/523-2424, ⓦwww.auptitlyonnais.com; Métro Mont-Royal. Expensive. A number of Lyonnais specialities like frog's legs, *andouillette* (tripe sausage) and *quenelles de brochet* (pike dumplings) feature on the menu at this small French bistro decked out with sunny yellow walls and glazed tile floor. A three-course lunch runs $13–15 (Wed–Fri only), and there's no mark-up on the wines. Closed Mon.

Le P'tit Plateau 330 rue Marie-Anne E ⓣ514/282-6342; Métro Mont-Royal. Expensive–very expensive. A French bistro whose warm interior bubbles with conversation in between courses of foie gras, smoked pork terrine or cassoulet, and mains of duck, lamb, pork or salmon but hushes when the golden crème brûlée arrives. Evening only – two services at 5.30/6.30pm and 8.30pm; closed Sun & Mon. *Apportez votre vin*.

La Selva 862 rue Marie-Anne E ⓣ514/525-1798; Métro Mont-Royal. Inexpensive. Simple, hearty Peruvian dishes fill you up for a pittance at this family-run place that draws a steady local clientele to this quiet corner of the Plateau. Go for the popular grilled fresh fish of the day or try the chicken in a rich and mild peanut sauce. Non-smoking. No credit cards. Dinner only; closed Sun & Mon. *Apportez votre vin*.

Toqué! 3842 rue St-Denis ⓣ514/499-2084, ⓦwww.restaurant-toque.com; Métro Sherbrooke. Very expensive. World-renowned Chef Normand Laprise holds court here, and the results are a mouth-watering fusion of styles prepared with fresh market ingredients. Definitely try the seared foie gras and perhaps the local venison with sautéed craterelle mushrooms, roasted scallops or guinea fowl, depending on the season. Ultrachic, high-end and unforgettable – if you can get a seat. Dinner only; reserve at least a few weeks ahead. Closed Sun & Mon.

Le Vintage 4475 rue St-Denis ⓣ514/849-4264; Métro Mont-Royal. Expensive. Set in an intimate, stone-walled half-basement, this Portuguese restaurant serves up tapas in addition to a long list of fish and seafood dishes, notably the cod grilled with fried onions and olive oil, and succulent calamari, grilled or stuffed with chorizo sausage. Closed Sun; no lunch Sat.

Witloof 3619 rue St-Denis ⓣ514/281-0100; Métro Sherbrooke. Moderate–expensive. Belgian bistro tailor-made for carnivores – the menu features many forms of game, steak tartare, mussels, horse flank and even blood pudding *à la Bruxelloise*. Wash it all down with a Belgian beer on a terrace facing Square St-Louis. No lunch on weekends; closed Sun in winter.

Mile End and Outremont

Cafés and light meals

La Croissanterie Figaro 5200 rue Hutchison ⓣ514/278-6567; bus #80. Delightful café that everyone just calls *La Croissanterie*. Marble-topped tables and dark wood fixtures lend it an Old World feel perfect for coffee and pastries – the almond croissants alone make the trip here worthwhile. You can also settle in for light meals and rich cakes on the wrap-around terrace. Daily 7am–1am.

Dusty's 4510 av du Parc ⓣ514/276-8525; bus #80. A good spot to fill up before tackling the mountain, this old-school diner with its vinyl booths and counter stools has been around since 1949. The basic fry-up – eggs, bacon, fried potatos, toast and coffee – will only set you back $3.95. Daily 7am–7pm.

La Petite Ardoise 222 av Laurier O ⓣ514/495-4961; Métro Laurier or bus #80. The *ardoise* (blackboard) in question is reflected in the intellectual make-up of the Francophone Outremont regulars, who come for rich breakfasts, salads, quiches and the like in this cheery yellow and blue café. The secluded garden terrace is an idyllic spot to sip your *café au lait*. Daily 8am–midnight.

La Pharmacie Esperanza 5490 boul St-Laurent ☎514/948-3303; bus #55. A laid-back, funky café with mismatched charity shop furniture and changing art installations that draws local artists and musicians, who hang around for drinks in the evening. During the day, there's a basic selection of soups, salads and sandwiches to accompany the organic coffee. Daily 8am–10pm.

Wilensky's Light Lunch 34 av Fairmount O ☎514/271-0247; Métro Laurier or bus #55. A lunch counter whose decor hasn't changed since 1932, and that includes the till, the grill and the drinks machine – you can still get an old-fashioned cherry coke. The $2.75 Wilensky Special includes bologna and three types of salami on a kaiser roll. Mon–Fri 9am–4pm.

Restaurants

Arahova Souvlaki 256 rue St-Viateur O ☎514/274-7828; bus #80. Inexpensive–moderate. Superb choice for authentic Greek cuisine. The basic dishes are the best, such as the souvlaki and fried calamari, all of which are served up in a taverna-style restaurant with pictures of the old country hung about. Open until 5am Fri & Sat, 2am other nights. Also at 1425 rue Crescent (☎514/499-0262); same hours.

Chao Phraya 50 av Laurier O ☎514/272-5339, ⓦwww.chao-phraya.com; bus #55 or Métro Laurier. Moderate–expensive. One of the city's top Thai restaurants, with an elegant but unfussy decor. Start with the *tom yum gai* (hot and sour chicken soup) to loosen your tastebuds for the fish and seafood highlights – choose either the *pad ped ta-lay* (a spicy combo of crab claws, scallops, shrimp, squid and fish) or the buttered shrimp in spicy sauce. Dinner only.

Le Jardin du Cari 21 rue St-Viateur O ☎514/495-0565; bus #55. Inexpensive. A simply furnished and friendly spot to sample Caribbean specialities like goat curry and curried chicken or shrimp wrapped in a roti, as well as Guyanese-style chow mein and fried rice dishes.

Laurier BBQ 381 av Laurier O ☎514/273-3671; bus #80. Inexpensive–moderate. Great hunks of typical Québec-style rôtisserie chicken (see p.149), served drizzled with the delicious house barbecue sauce, have made this comfortable family-run restaurant a favourite for over half a century. If you're after comfort food, the homemade macaroni and cheese with meat sauce is hard to beat.

Mikado 368 av Laurier O ☎514/279-4809; bus #80. Expensive. Excellent sushi, sashimi and maki served in a smashing modern Japanese setting that draws a fun but dressy crowd. The grilled salmon and chicken teriyaki are tasty alternatives if you prefer your food cooked. Three-course lunch (Thurs & Fri only) costs $11–14. They have a second restaurant at 1731 rue St-Denis (☎514/844-5705) in the Quartier Latin.

Milos 5357 av du Parc ☎514/272-3522; bus #80. Very expensive. *Milos* is the finest Greek restaurant in the city. The seafood is exceptionally fresh and dishes are prepared simply and skilfully – try the grilled Mediterranean sea bass or delicately sea-soned grilled lobster. A cheaper but more limited four-course menu served 5.30–6.30pm and on Sundays costs $35. Reservations are essential.

Il Piatto Della Nonna 176 rue St-Viateur O ☎514/278-6066; bus #55 or 80; and 5171 boul St-Laurent ☎514/843-6069; Métro Laurier. Inexpensive. A pair of tiny family-run restaurants serving well-prepared Italian specialities from Calabria like roast rabbit and lamb. The St-Laurent location, with its pressed-copper ceilings and wide-plank pine floors, is a great spot for char-coal-grilled veal sausage or to wolf down a pasta fagiola for lunch on the weekend. Otherwise head to the more rustic St-Viateur branch where grandma cooks up a storm in the open kitchen.

Terrasse Lafayette 250 rue Villeneuve O ☎514/288-3915; bus #80. Moderate. A great little neighbourhood restaurant, popular for its wraparound terrace, where you can tuck into *pikilia* (Greek hors d'oeuvre platter), fried calamari and tender pita bread stuffed with chicken or souvlaki. The Greek specialities are best, though the spinach, shallot and feta pizza is really good as well. *Apportez votre vin*.

Yakata 5115 boul St-Laurent ☎514/272-8667; Métro Laurier or bus #55. Expensive. The fish swimming in the aquarium here aren't the ones that the chefs roll up at the bar, but you might wonder given how fresh the sushi is – try it at lunch for $9.95. The tempura prawns and scallops are other tasty choices, while for a satisfying finish try the green-tea ice cream. No lunch at weekends; reservations recommended for dinner.

Little Italy

Cafés and light meals

Aux Derniers Humains 6950 rue St-Denis ⓣ514/272-8521; Métro Jean-Talon or Beaubien. At the southeastern edge of Little Italy, this artsy café (works of a different artist are displayed each month) serves up great breakfasts and a cheap but good array of international dishes like pizzas, risottos, crepes and *confit canard*. Closed Mon.

Café Italia 6840 boul St-Laurent ⓣ514/495-0059; bus #55. Inexpensive. Boisterous Italian debates and mismatched tables await at this atmospheric café that froths up cappuccino with a potency nearing jet-fuel. They've got biscotti and panettone to go with it, as well as grilled panini if you need something a bit more substantial. Daily from 6am (7am Sun) to 11pm.

Motta 303 rue Mozart E ⓣ514/270-5952; Métro Jean-Talon. A speciality Italian food emporium selling gourmet goodies, coldcuts and pastries that's also a great spot to sit down for a quick bite. Order one of the really good spinach or seafood pies from the deli counter, or try one of the authentic one-person pizzas or more substantial pasta meals.

Restaurants

Lucca 12 rue Dante ⓣ514/278-6502; bus #55. Expensive–very expensive. A rustic trattoria where the constantly changing daily menu emphasizes refreshing antipasto combinations, delicious grilled meats and light seafood. The deep-fried calamari on a bed of red pepper *aïoli* and the grilled veal chop on creamy polenta with wilted spinach and roasted red peppers make frequent appearances. The three-course lunch is more affordable (pasta $15–25, meat and fish $18–25). No lunch Sat; closed Sun. Reservations recommended.

Pizzeria Napoletana 189 rue Dante ⓣ514/276-8226, ⓦwww.napoletana.com; bus #55. Moderate. A casual restaurant with a lively outdoor terrace in the summer and hearty pizzas – try the sausage and mushrooms *tutta bella* – and pastas like canelloni, penne *arabiata* and tortellini in rosé sauce on the menu. Save space for the decadent tiramisu or tartufo. *Apportez votre vin*.

Quelli Della Notte 6834 boul St-Laurent ⓣ514/271-3929, ⓦwww.quelli.com; bus #55. Expensive. Stylish restaurant complete with grand staircase spiralling down to a cigar lounge. Standouts on the dinner menu include grilled striped bass and homemade ravioli stuffed with veal and porcini mushrooms. Cheaper at lunch – two courses for $15–23. No lunch Sat; closed Sun.

Westmount and the Lachine Canal

Cafés and light meals

Calories 4114 rue Ste-Catherine O ⓣ514/933-8186; Métro Atwater. In contrast to the imposing Square Westmount opposite, the dark wood wainscoting and ochre walls give this café a hidden-away feel. The food is dead cheap – panini, salad and homemade iced tea for a fiver – and the cakes are divine. Choose one of the imaginative cheesecakes (mango or Baileys) or go whole hog on the goopy chocolate fudge Mudfight.

Quoi de N'Oeuf 2745 rue Notre-Dame O ⓣ514/931-3999; Métro Lionel-Groulx. Lively breakfast joint whose exposed brick walls and wood floors invite lingering over crepes, omelettes and eggs Benedict (with the option of bacon or sausage) before you head to the nearby shops on "antiques row". They also serve light lunches during the week. Open daily 7am–3pm (Sun from 8am).

Restaurants

Magnan 2602 rue St-Patrick ⓣ514/935-9647, ⓦwww.magnanresto.com; Métro Charlevoix. Moderate. Mention the name "Magnan", and most Montrealers go dreamy-eyed thinking about the excellent steaks that have been served at this restaurant-tavern since the Thirties. From around mid-May to mid-June – about the time the terrace opens – it becomes a pilgrimage destination for the "festival du homard" (lobster festival). Fortunately, the Lachine Canal is nearby so you can work off those extra pounds.

Taverne sur le Square 1 Westmount Square ⓣ514/989-9779 or 9967; Métro Atwater. Expensive. Hardly a tavern, this restaurant at the corner of rues Ste-Catherine and Wood has a clean, modern look, done up in creams and earth tones, with art for sale on the walls. The food is equally posh, with a menu featuring barbecued salmon belly, as well as lamb shank on a bed of lentils and shrimp risotto. It's all accompanied by a long wine list writ large in the freestanding wine cellar.

△ rue Prince-Arthur

11

Drinking

With its 3am closing time and minimum drinking age of 18, Montréal's vibrant **bar scene** has earned it a reputation as the party capital of Canada. Starting with a bustling *5 à 7* happy hour (see box, p.165), many bars remain packed well into the early hours, especially on the weekend – which for many here begins on Thursdays. Quite a few bars, however, only tend to get going around 11pm.

Several of the places listed below are part café or restaurant (but best for drinking), and may have a small dance floor or host bands on some nights. Similarly, many clubs and live-music venues keep things well lubricated with cocktails and pitchers of beer (see Chapter 12, "Nightlife"). And anywhere with a decent terrace will be packed with drinkers for the *5 à 7*. For quieter spots to quaff a few, see our café and restaurant reviews in Chapter 10, "Eating". Without a doubt, the best spot to bar hop is the **Plateau**, where on weekends it feels like the whole city has come there to party. There's a great mixing of Francophones and Anglophones, although the smaller bars on and around **rue St-Denis** tend to have a more Gallic flair. **Boulevard St-Laurent** has everything from flashy resto-bars to grungy student watering holes, with some fabulously hip lounges sprinkled in between.

The **Downtown** scene is also reliable, if (not surprisingly), less exciting, with bars catering to businesspeople and McGill and Concordia students dotted about. The action here centres on **rue Crescent**, where the block north of rue Ste-Catherine is choked with bars and pick-up joints, but there's less testosterone and a more neighbourly feel in a couple of the watering holes on parallel **rue Bishop**.

The **Quartier Latin**'s terrace-fronted bars on **rue St-Denis** draw a rollicking crowd, while nearby bars in the **Village** are covered in Chapter 13, "Gay Montréal". **Vieux-Montréal** is low on the drinking radar – except for the terraces lining **Place Jacques-Cartier**, which often have a festive vibe. In **Mile End** and **Outremont** you're better off having a glass of wine in a café or restaurant on **avenue Laurier**.

Note that you should tip the bar staff 15 percent (about a buck a beer, a little more for cocktails) – the perks constitute the main whack of their wages. Even so, don't ever expect to see your pint filled to the brim. And, if you're planning on a long night, leave the car behind; **drinking and driving** penalties are harsh and taxis are cheap and plentiful. Be forewarned that beer tends to be stronger here than in the US or the UK – 5 percent is standard, dry beers and the like are around 6 percent and some of the local brews (see box, overleaf) are even more lethal.

Les bières

For years, it was hard to find much in the way of well-crafted **beers** in Montréal – the market was dominated by the Labatt and Molson giants, with their same-tasting brands, enlivened every year or two by fads like dry beer and ice beer. Over the past decade or so, however, a number of **microbreweries** have started up, adding some much-needed flavour for the discerning beer-drinker. Although the majors still dominate in nightclubs, most bars serve many of the newer, local varieties. **Québec breweries** to look out for include Brasserie McAuslan, who craft beers under the St-Ambroise and Griffon labels at their Lachine Canal brewery, opened in 1989, Les Brasseurs du Nord (producers of Boréale), and Brasseurs RJ (Cheval Blanc and Belle Gueule). Unibroue, who ramp up the alcohol content for Belgian-style beers like Maudite and La Fin du Monde, also have regular-strength brands like Blanche de Chambly, a wheat beer. You'll often find that, rather than be classified as ales, lagers and the like, beer is differentiated by **colour**: blonde, *rousse* (red), *ambrée* (amber) and *noir* (dark).

For many of Montréal's local brews, you'll have to sample the product in-house – see below for a cross-referenced list of brewpubs we review. Finally, if you're in town in early June, be sure to visit the **Mondial de la Bière** beer festival (see p.212).

Brewpubs

Brutopia p.164
Le Cheval Blanc p.167
Dieu du Ciel p.169
Réservoir p.168
Sergent Recruteur p.169

Downtown

Alexandre et Fils 1454 rue Peel ⓣ514/288-5105; Métro Peel. A Parisian café, bistro and brasserie rolled into one, replete with marble-topped tables and rattan chairs facing the street. Pose with the rest of the *beau monde* while quaffing one of the dozen wines by the glass.

Brutopia 1219 rue Crescent ⓣ514/393-9277, ⓦwww.brutopia.net; Métro Peel or Guy-Concordia. A cozy yet occasionally boisterous pub with exposed-brick walls serving up a great selection of tasty ales, porters and stouts that are brewed in the vats next to where customers chat or play board games. Live music most nights, but no cover charge.

Café Sarajevo 2080 rue Clark ⓣ514/284-5629; Métro Saint-Laurent. Decorated like someone's comfortable rec-room, *Café Sarajevo* is a great place to hang out and listen to spoken word performances and occasional bands playing Balkan gypsy music, jazz or folk – Rufus Wainwright often played the piano here before hitting it big. There's a lovely garden out back, which they're still trying to get a permit to re-open, as of this writing. Closed Sun & Mon.

Cock 'n' Bull Pub 1944 rue Ste-Catherine O ⓣ514/933-4556; Métro Guy-Concordia. There's a good mix of old, crusty regulars and fresh-faced Concordia students at this unpretentious watering hole at the western end of Downtown. The cheap tap beers keep many of them rooted until closing.

Hurley's Irish Pub 1225 rue Crescent ⓣ514/861-4111, ⓦwww.hurleysirishpub.com; Métro Peel or Guy-Concordia. Located a little south of the rue Crescent carnival, *Hurley's* is one of the city's best Irish pubs, its warren of stone-walled rooms filled with friendly regulars downing pints of Guinness in the hope that it'll improve their dart-tossing skills. There's a nice selection of single malts and good pub food served from 11am until just after the live bands start up at 9.30pm.

Jimbo's Pub 1238 rue Bishop ⓣ514/398-9661; Métro Guy-Concordia. A dark and smoky local favourite with a friendly Anglophone crowd that surges before and after the comedy and improv shows at *Comedyworks* upstairs (see p.188). There's karaoke on the main floor whenever the owner is in the mood.

Luba Lounge 2109 rue de Bleury ⓣ514/288-5822; Métro Place-des-Arts. Chilled-out lounge near Place des Arts that attracts a trendy twenty- and thirty-something set. DJs and occasional live bands play against a backdrop of cushy old sofas and red-velvet curtains.

Madhatter Café 1230 boul de Maisonneuve O ☎514/987-9988; Métro Peel. Although popular with students from nearby Concordia, the main studies in this rumpled campus pub involve who can down a pint of *rousse* or other microbrew the fastest. Nightly drink specials.

Magnétic Terrasse *Hôtel de la Montagne*, 1430 rue de la Montagne ☎514/288-5656; Métro Peel. Like a little piece of Miami perched twenty floors up, this rooftop terrace lets you sip on a cocktail by the pool while gazing out over Downtown and the St Lawrence. Busiest for the *5 à 7*, but also popular with Downtown workers looking for a quick lunchtime dip in the pool and with strippers working on their tans. Open mid-May to early Sept (11.30am–3am), whenever the sun is shining.

McKibbin's Irish Pub 1426 rue Bishop ☎514/288-1580; Métro Guy-Concordia. Wood timbers, floors and tables give this relaxed pub a cozy feel conducive to conversations fuelled by pints of Guinness, Harp, Tartan, Hoegaarden and the like – but stick to the basement level if you don't want to be interrupted by the cover bands that play most nights from around 9.30pm. There's also a dance club upstairs and a terrace out back.

McLean's Pub 1210 rue Peel ☎514/392-7770, Ⓦwww.mcleanspub.com; Métro Peel. Centrally located near the Centre Infotouriste and facing Square Dorchester, this attitude-free tavern lacks a cohesive identity – TVs beaming sports matches contrast with the ornate beamed ceiling, and the crowd is equally varied with businessmen at lunch and for the *4 à 8*, and students in the evenings. Stick to local brews as the imports are pricey.

Peel Pub 1107 rue Ste-Catherine O ☎514/844-6769, Ⓦwww.peelpub.com; Métro Peel. A pilgrimage spot for first-year McGill students who come for the cheap pitchers of draft and largely forgettable food (try the cheap rib steak, if pressed) in a mess-hall atmosphere. You can come back to pay for your sins the next morning – $1.99 fry-ups are available from 8am.

5 à 7

Thanks in part to Montréal's continued economic health, there's still plenty of bars throughout the city offering **happy-hour specials**, like two-for-one beers, once the work day is done. Rather than referring to "happy hour", you're more likely to hear Montrealers say such-and-such bar has a great *5 à 7* (*cinq à sept*) – literally 5 to 7pm, the standard time for cheap booze – though many bars are stretching things to *4 à 8*. Unlike in many other North American cities, however, this deal rarely extends to food, though a few places may offer cheap nibbles. This keeps the focus on drinking, with the best spots (including almost anywhere with a terrace on a sunny day – see below) usually packed full of boisterous people.

Numerous Downtown bars entice the after-work crowd; elsewhere, you could start at *Pub Quartier Latin* (p.167), *Sky* (p.182) in the Village, *Réservoir* (p.168) on the Plateau or *Dieu du Ciel* (p.169) in Mile End.

Top terraces

After months of huddling indoors, Montrealers take full advantage of the warm weather by heading in droves to anywhere with a **terrasse** – pavement tables, patios or garden or courtyard seating. The few places that aren't lucky enough to catch the al fresco trade will usually at least have a few tables that are next to windows opened wide to the street. Some of the city's best terraces are:

Café des Éclusiers	p.166
Magnétic Terrasse	p.165
Les Remparts	p.166
Réservoir	p.168
Le Saint-Sulpice	p.167
Le Ste-Élisabeth	p.167
Sir Winston Churchill Pub	p.166
Le Sugar	p.168

Sharx **1606 rue Ste-Catherine O ☎514/934-3105; Métro Guy-Concordia.** Popular, stylish pool hall in the Faubourg Ste-Catherine (see p.197) that draws a mix of young Downtown workers to its 36 tables ($10/hr for two players, $12/hr for four; $20 deposit). You can chill out in the cigar lounge as well, or give one of the ten bowling lanes a try ($4.50 per person per game, except Fri & Sat $29/hr for two, $44/hr for three or more).

Sir Winston Churchill Pub **1459 rue Crescent ☎514/288-3814; Métro Peel or Guy-Concordia.** A prime pick-up joint, this English-style pub, also known as "Winnie's", attracts an older crowd of local and visiting Anglophone professionals. Though there are pool tables, a small dance floor, and a wine bar upstairs, the real action is on the front terrace, *the* place to be seen on the Crescent strip.

Stogies **2015 rue Crescent ☎514/848-0069; Métro Peel or Guy-Concordia.** Swanky cigar lounge, popular with businessmen, where you can puff away on a *cubano* from the humidor while sipping a martini ($8.50 and up), or get down on the dance floor where a DJ spins jazz and R&B. It's sandwiched between the small and friendly ground-floor *London Pub* and the chilled *Ice* bar-lounge (weekends only) up top.

Le Vieux Dublin Pub & Restaurant **1219A rue University ☎514/861-4448; Métro McGill.** Don't let the windowless facade put you off – the inside of the *Old Dublin* (as it's better known) has a warm glow furnished by back-lit stained-glass panels, polished wood and the best pint of Guinness in town. Irish bands create a rollicking mood by cramming onto the corner stage nightly.

Vieux-Montréal

Café des Éclusiers **rue de la Commune at rue McGill ☎514/496-0762, ⓦwww.cafedeseclusiers.com; Métro Square-Victoria.** The striking wedge-shaped pavilion housing the café provides a terrific backdrop for the canal-side terrace, which always fills up first. Nab one of the moulded seats on the raised promenade for views of the Vieux-Port. Clever salads and pastas appear on the lunch *table d'hôte*, while the *5 à 7* crowds nibble at tapas.

La Cage aux Sports **395 rue Le Moyne ☎514/288-1115, ⓦwww.cage.ca; Métro Square-Victoria.** If there's a big game on, then head to this branch of a province-wide sports bar chain for a pitcher of beer and some popcorn while watching one of the dozens of TVs surrounded by baseball pennants and portraits of hockey players. Don't come hungry, though – the food is mediocre at best.

Le Cigare du Pharaon **139 rue St-Paul O ☎514/843-4779; Métro Place-d'Armes.** The hints of Tintin at the adjacent *Le Petit Moulinsart* (see p.152) run riot in this fun bar, named after his *Cigars of the Pharaoh* adventures. You can rent one of the small coffins painted with mummified Tintin characters to store a bottle of your favourite tipple; otherwise, if the weather's warm, settle down in the loungey front bit or the courtyard terrace (given over to diners in the evening). Jazz acts and the like on Friday evenings cost $7 at the door.

Le Jardin Nelson **407 Place Jacques-Cartier ☎514/861-5731, ⓦwww.jardinnelson.com; Métro Champ-de-Mars.** Most come here to enjoy a glass of wine on one of the finest terraces on Place Jacques-Cartier, but there are decent crepes and light meals as well. A jazz band plays daily at noon (joined by a vocalist for evening sets) and there's a classical trio weekend mornings. Closed in winter.

Modavie **1 rue St-Paul O ☎514/287-9582, ⓦwww.modavie.com; Métro Place-d'Armes.** Although they serve pasta, steaks and grilled fish, the focal point of this bistro is the huge bar at its centre, popular with bureaucrats from nearby city hall who come to puff on a stogie while sipping scotch or port. Live jazz every evening.

Pub St-Paul **124 rue St-Paul E ☎514/874-0485, ⓦwww.pubstpaul.com; Métro Place-d'Armes.** A large and friendly pub with passable grub and a good range of suds on tap. Its atmospheric location amid the stone buildings of one of Vieux-Montréal's prettiest cobblestone streets and its portside views ensure that it's packed. Rock and alternative bands play Fri & Sat.

Les Remparts **93 rue de la Commune E ☎514/392-1649; Métro Place-d'Armes.** For the best view of the Vieux-Port you can get with a drink in hand, head to this unnamed rooftop terrace on the top of the *Auberge du Vieux-Port* (take the lift to the fifth floor, then the stairs). It's run by the ground-floor *Les Remparts* restaurant, who provide good but pricey light meals on the rooftop – stick to drinking unless you're feeling flush. Open in decent weather from mid-May to mid-September (noon–10pm).

Quartier Latin

Le Cheval Blanc **809 rue Ontario E ☎514/522-0211; Métro Berri-UQAM.** Old-style Montréal pub, with the same Art Deco decor as when it opened in the 1940s; popular with a fun Francophone crowd. They brew their own beer, which is quite good – try one of the seasonal varieties or from the regular cast of amber, *rousse*, dark, bitter and wheat varieties.

L'Île Noire **342 rue Ontario E ☎514/982-0866; Métro Berri-UQAM.** Named after the Tintin book in which he travels to Scotland (*The Black Island*, in English), this pub with cushy, dark-green booths attempts to help their clientele do the same. It certainly succeeds on the Scotch front, with an amazing selection of single-malt whiskeys, which you can chase with a pint of Tartan, bitter or stout.

L'Ours Qui Fume **2019 rue St-Denis ☎514/845-6998; Métro Berri-UQAM.** Drawing *habitués* of all ages with its faded charm, this small brasserie feels like it could be in Paris. Go when there's a blues band playing (Thurs–Sat 10.30pm) and you'll find a loud, boisterous crowd.

Pub Quartier Latin **318 rue Ontario E ☎514/845-3301; Métro Berri-UQAM.** Stylish pub that attracts thirtyish professionals for the *5 à 7* on the terrace, followed by students chilling out later in the evening. Occasional bands play anything from jazz and funk to R&B and electronica ($7 cover), with DJs spinning a mix of house, funk and electronic beats the rest of the time.

Le Saint-Sulpice **1680 rue St-Denis ☎514/844-9458, ⓦwww.lesaint-sulpice.com; Métro Berri-UQAM.** A bar complex comprising paired three-storey greystone houses that's as active outside as inside. The lively terrace in front is a good place to watch the human traffic on rue St-Denis, but it's even more fun out back in the massive, boisterous garden. Inside is a warren of often-crowded rooms, with atmospheres conducive to either chilling out or energetic dancing.

Le Ste-Élisabeth **1412 rue Ste-Élisabeth ☎514/286-4302; Métro Berri-UQAM.** Boxed in by high brick walls, the ivy-covered courtyard terrace is one of Montréal's finest – but if it's full (and it likely will be), a window seat on the upper floor is the next best thing. In winter, an open fire keeps things cozy for knocking back a scotch or imported beer along with the casual but boisterous crowd of UQAM students and slightly older regulars.

Plateau Mont-Royal

Bacci **4205 rue St-Denis ☎514/844-3929, ⓦwww.baccistdenis.com; Métro Mont-Royal.** You shouldn't have a problem scoring a table – there are 22 of them – in this large pool hall, plus there are table-football games for the cueless. If you're a fan of loud Top 40, R&B and the like, you'll feel right at home. $11.50/hr for two players.

Barraca **1134 av du Mont-Royal E ☎514/525-7741; Métro Mont-Royal.** The glam but somehow unpretentious crowd creates a great vibe in this long, narrow tapas bar that glows with light from parchment-shaded lamps. They may stop serving the $4–5 tapas dishes early on, but the bar still offers a dozen Spanish wines by the glass, rums from all over the Caribbean and also happens to make a mean mojito. A DJ spins funky, jazzy beats most nights.

Bifteck St-Laurent **3702 boul St-Laurent ☎514/844-6211; Métro Sherbrooke or Saint-Laurent.** A loyal crowd of students and ex-students frequent this tavern to drink cheap pitchers of Boréale Rousse ($9, $10.50 weekend evenings) between sets of pool. The stereo blasts anything from hip-hop to hard rock, and band members occasionally drop in (Melissa Auf der Maur, who played bass for both Hole and Smashing Pumpkins, once worked here).

Bily Kun **354 av du Mont-Royal E ☎514/845-5392, ⓦwww.bilykun.com; Métro Mont-Royal.** Tiled floors lend an Eastern European feel to this hopping Plateau bar, where stuffed ostrich heads look down on a mixed Anglo/Franco crowd. The music's too loud to really worry what language someone's speaking anyway, and the range of microbrews from mother bar *Le Cheval Blanc* (see above) provide more than adequate distraction. Occasional live bands play everything from Francophone folk-pop to jazz and electronica here as well as in the *O Patro Vys* hall upstairs.

Blizzarts **3956A boul St-Laurent ☎514/843-4860; bus #55 or Métro Sherbrooke or Mont-Royal.** Funked-out lounge with retro '60s chairs, semi-circular booths, exhibitions by local artists on the walls and a dozen varieties of beer on tap. The tiny dance floor gets packed every night – there's a $3 cover charge for the dub and reggae (Wed) and breakbeats (Thurs) nights. It's a buck more for the grooving afrofunk and hip-hop vibe on Fridays and the great electro set on Saturdays. Opens at 8pm.

Copacabana 3910 boul St-Laurent ⓣ514/982-0880; bus #55 or Métro Sherbrooke or Mont-Royal. Despite the truly awful decor – fake palm trees and surfboards – the *Copa* attracts a loyal following of Anglo hipsters for a game of pool and lots of cheap beer ($11.25 for a large pitcher of Boréale Rousse). If happy hour seems to go on all night, it does – prices are low all the time.

El Zaz Bar 4297 rue St-Denis ⓣ514/288-9798; Métro Mont-Royal. The garish piñata-coloured stairs and solarium of this second-floor bar create a festive feel perfect for knocking back margaritas and sangria. The rest of the bar is dark and close, with a dance floor beneath a low ceiling cluttered with giant vines. There's a nightly $2–5 cover charge after 9.30pm for DJ sets and live bands (Tues, Fri & Sun) playing anything from Québec pop to reggae or hip-hop.

Else's 156 rue Roy E ⓣ514/286-6689; Métro Sherbrooke. A great neighbourhood bar where you can hang out and play board games at the collage-covered tables while quaffing pints of local brews amid a good-natured buzz. There's also a choice selection of imported beers and scotches – the only downside is that to keep your table you need to order food (starting at only $2 for bar snacks, fortunately).

À Gogo Lounge 3682 boul St-Laurent ⓣ514/286-0882; Métro Sherbrooke or Saint-Laurent. A long and narrow bar with psychedelic paintings on the walls and a great vibe on the weekends. There are loungey areas at the front and back where you can listen to the funky Sixties to early-Eighties tunes playing on the stereo while sitting in the palm of a giant, red plastic hand.

Laïka 4040 boul St-Laurent ⓣ514/842-8088; bus #55 or Métro Sherbrooke or Mont-Royal. Hip café by day, trendy lounge by night, *Laïka*'s urbane decor looks like it was torn from the pages of *Wallpaper* magazine, with designer fibreglass chairs set against the large tiles on the wall. In summer, the windows slide open letting the sounds of the DJ sets spill onto the street. Open 8.30am–3am.

Mhotel 951 rue Rachel E ⓣ514/522-9773 Métro Mont-Royal. An unassuming exterior belies the hip touches inside this local lounge. Sit at the long bar to survey the quirky Seventies lamps, sofas on raised platforms, faux-fur on the ceiling and forest of (wallpaper) birch trees down at the end. The laidback mood is enhanced by the ambient tunes spun by the DJ. Open from 9pm Sat & Sun (4pm during the week).

Miami 3831 boul St-Laurent ⓣ514/845-2300; bus #55 or Métro Sherbrooke. A total dive, but this dingy watering hole for Plateau nihilists and eternal students has cheap beer and shots of tequila and Jameson's that allow for some serious drinking. The rooftop terrace in back makes for a great escape from the crowded Main.

Le P'tit Bar 3451 rue St-Denis ⓣ514/281-9124; Métro Sherbrooke. Though technically on the Plateau (it's just north of rue Sherbrooke), this small *boîte à chanson*, with its regular customers and Francophone appeal, has more in common with the Quartier Latin scene. French singers perform nightly; during the day, content yourself with checking out the cartoon-strewn walls. Shows are free but they pass a hat around for the musicians.

Réservoir 9 av Duluth E ⓣ514/849-7779; bus #55. One of the spots of the moment, *Réservoir* serves up fancy bar snacks like scallops and endive salad to accompany the ales and bitters brewed on the premises. If the stripped-back decor isn't to your liking, head upstairs and grab a seat on the terrace overlooking Duluth – if you can find a seat.

Sofa 451 rue Rachel E ⓣ514/285-1011, ⓦwww.sofa-bar.com; Métro Mont-Royal. A wonderful little port and cigar lounge filled with low-slung couches tucked into cozy nooks. The dark-blue and burgundy interior is a bit gloomy in the day but at night it feels just fine for listening to bands playing soul, funk or even swing (Thurs–Sun 10.30pm; $4–6).

Le Sugar 3616 boul St-Laurent ⓣ514/287-6555; Métro Sherbrooke or Saint-Laurent. Give the downstairs club of the same name a miss and head up the external stairs on the right to one of the city's coolest terraces – the roof's been removed from the second floor to allow for drinking under the stars. They fire up the heat lamps on cooler nights.

Le Swimming 3643 boul St-Laurent ⓣ514/282-7665, ⓦwww.leswimming.com; Métro Sherbrooke or Saint-Laurent. A bar that wears many hats: while live bands perform nightly, the dozen or so pool tables ($12.60/hr) in the back are *Le Swimming*'s mainstay the rest of the time. There's a great balcony overlooking the Main in the summertime, and regular drink specials year-long – from 4–8pm you can buy $9 pitchers and two-for-one bottles of beer.

Vol de Nuit **14 rue Prince-Arthur E ⓣ514/845-6243; Métro Sherbrooke or Saint-Laurent.** Forgo the unremarkable interior here and nab a table on the pavement. In the summer, *Vol de Nuit*'s location at one of the busiest spots on rue Prince-Arthur's pedestrian strip makes it a mighty fine spot to share a big pitcher of sangria on a nice evening.

Mile End and Outremont

Dieu du Ciel **29 av Laurier O ⓣ514/490-9555, ⓦwww.dieuduciel.com; Métro Laurier or bus #55.** Comfortable neighbourhood pub that fills up for the *5 à 7* when the tasty ales and lagers (brewed on the premises) go for $3.75 a pint. There's a constantly changing beer menu with some seven or eight brews (of the thirty or so house recipes, which include some potent abbey beers) – on tap at any given time.

Fûtenbulle **273 av Bernard O ⓣ514/276-0473; Métro Outremont or bus #80 or #535.** One of the largest selections of beers in Montréal – over eighty bottled varieties and another score on tap – draws a noisy crowd of well-off thirtyish Outremont regulars. Belgian favourites like mussels and sausages are available to soak up the suds.

Mile End Bar **5322 boul St-Laurent ⓣ514/279-0200, ⓦwww.mileendbar.com; bus #55.** A sleek bar with pale woods, zincs and linear lighting that won an award for its design – something that may or may not impress the stylish pretty-young-things who head straight upstairs for the techno-funk remixes on the dance floor ($5 cover Fri & Sat). Closed Sun & Mon.

Sergent Recruteur **4650 boul St-Laurent ⓣ514/287-1412, ⓦwww.sergent-recruteur.com; Métro Laurier or bus #55.** The British-style ales brewed here include a rich cream ale, as well as a stout and hand-pumped bitter. Live music on Saturday (and occasionally other) nights runs the range from rock to Celtic and folk (9.30pm; free); if you want to practice your French come on Sunday for storytelling night (Sept–May).

Whisky Café **5800 boul St-Laurent ⓣ514/278-2646, ⓦwww.whiskycafe.ca; Métro Outremont or bus #55.** Way up at the corner of avenue Bernard, this elegantly decorated bar draws a wealthy clientele of all ages – the prices aren't cheap, but then the liquor's purely top shelf. The design-conscious approach even extends to the toilets, with water cascading down a zinc wall in the boys', and the only girls' urinal in Montréal.

12

Nightlife

On weekend nights, Montréal's main drags are an endless parade of glamorous fashionistas ready to cruise the city's spectacular **nightlife** scene. The city has long been considered Canada's nightlife capital, and with good reason – dozens of **clubs** pulsate until the wee hours, pumping out music that ranges from Madonna remixes to thumping drum'n'bass, with a roster of home-grown and international DJs manning the turntables.

Filling out the city's nightlife possibilities is a wide range of **live music** venues. Montréal's strong **jazz** roots – Louis Armstrong, Ella Fitzgerald, Dizzy Gillespie and Billie Holliday all played to sold-out crowds here during the Roaring Forties, Charlie Parker recorded *Montréal 1953*, and the city produced its own jazz star in Oscar Peterson – are still very much in evidence in today's talented groups that play anything from bebop to fusion. But traditional **rock**, **punk** and **ska** bands also take their share of the limelight, and a small **folk** and **spoken-word** scene adds a pleasantly low-key vibe. When heading out to catch a show, keep in mind that bands usually get off-stage no later than 1am, and some end as early as 11pm. Accordingly, Montrealers treat seeing a band as an evening's primer – not its climax.

Though some live venues close once the show is over, Montréal's clubs serve alcohol until 3am, and even then the party goes on. Heavy-hitting DJs keep the dance floors packed well past dawn at the large (and legal) **after-hour clubs**, which serve up juice and caffeine-laced drinks rather than alcohol; it's not hard to figure out how the denizens stay up.

Clubs

Montréal's **clubs** are easy to find – just look for the jostling line-ups spilling out onto the sidewalks either Downtown or in the Plateau, along the stretch of the Main between rue Milton and avenue des Pins. **Dance clubs** in the latter neighbourhood tend to groove to house and techno, with some R&B and funk also clambering on deck, drawing young and up-for-it Francophones and Anglophones while Top 40 and retro pop generally rule Downtown, especially among the clubs catering to a slightly older and mainly Anglophone crowd on and around rue Crescent. Downtown's clubs also offer the most in the way of "Ladies' Nights" – decide for yourself whether the free entry and drinks outweigh the meat-market aura.

Most clubs open around 10pm but only really get busy at about 1am, and usually apply a cover charge ranging from $5–10, with entry fees towards the higher end at weekends, which for club kids begin on Thursdays (some clubs only open Thursday to Saturday or Sunday). The city's best **gay clubs**, often the most happening spots in town, are listed on p.181. The popular trend towards **DJ bars and cafés** continues unabated in Montréal, offering a more relaxed environment in which to still hear great music; we cover some of the best in Chapter 11, "Drinking".

If you're off to one of the larger clubs, it's a good idea to **dress up** – you likely won't be refused entrance, but if you don't you may feel a tad out of place. At most lounges, and the clubs in the Village, though, dress codes are virtually nonexistent. Note that some clubs have a 21-and-over policy on some nights. The evening doesn't have to end when the clubs call it a night at 3am, as number of excellent **after-hours spots** pick up the slack on weekends, getting started only when the others close shop. To suss out the latest club **flyers**, head to any of the Plateau's record shops or club-wear boutiques, where you can also pick up the current issue of *NightLife Magazine* (identified as just *nl* on its cover), a free club guide that's also available online at ⓦwww.nightlifemontreal.com. There are a host of other Montréal nightlife websites - ⓦwww.montreal-clubs.com is one of the more up-to-date English ones.

Another form of nightlife "entertainment" is the city's **strip clubs**, whose neon signs glow brightly throughout Downtown (see box, p.173).

Dance clubs

Angels 3604 boul St-Laurent ⓣ514/282-9944; Métro Sherbrooke or bus #55. A two-floor Plateau club frequented by McGill University students; the first floor has a pretty nondescript atmosphere with pool tables and Top 40 hits, while dark and smoky upstairs resonates with pounding house music, R&B and hip-hop all week.

Central Station 4432 boul St-Laurent ⓣ514/842-2836, ⓦwww.clubcentralstation.com; Métro Mont-Royal. This Plateau hotspot draws a big late-twenties crowd to its large main dance floor grooving to house. The a/c and sleek Miami-style decor keep things feeling and looking cool, though the hip-hop room in back gets packed to capacity fast. Fri–Sun only.

Club 6/49 1112 rue Ste-Catherine O ⓣ514/868-1649; Métro Peel. Long-running Latin dance club with plenty of tables to sit at if you don't have the spirit for salsa and merengue. If you do have the urge but don't know how, drop by for free salsa lessons on Monday and Thursday nights. Friendly crowd but can be a bit cruisey on the weekends, which also feature live bands.

Club Vatican 1432 rue Crescent ⓣ514/845-3922, ⓦwww.clubvatican.com; Métro Peel or Guy-Concordia. The pope certainly didn't sanctify this rue Crescent club, notable for its Gothic-lounge decor of white brick walls and stained-glass windows. The irreverent name doesn't seem to bother the hordes of Anglophone twentysomethings that strut their stuff to R&B, hip-hop and house on the dance floor. Thurs–Sun 10pm–3am.

Dôme 32 rue Ste-Catherine O ⓣ514/875-5757, ⓦwww.clubdome.com; Métro St-Laurent. A massive, decade-old club on Downtown's eastern fringe with dance floors on two levels and caged go-go dancers. The cast of DJs from Montréal radio stations as well as international guests play a mix of hip-hop, R&B and house to a preppy collegiate crowd. When not dancing, the clientele is usually lined up at one of the 16 bars for the frequent drink specials.

Envy 3553 boul St-Laurent ⓣ514/848-0200; Métro Sherbrooke or bus #55. A young, fun crowd lounges on white vinyl sofas and chairs at the front of this low club space before heading out under the grid of mini disco balls to groove to R&B, old school and house on the smallish dance floor. Gauzy white curtains mark out more chill-out spaces and all the while tiny TV screens embedded in the wall play psychedlic images.

Exit 3553 boul St-Laurent ⓣ514/285-2223, ⓦwww.exit3553.com; Métro Sherbrooke or bus #55. The decor in this long and narrow space above *Envy* (see above) is minimal, stripped back to the steel beams, leaving the focus firmly on dancing. The hip-hop sessions from Thursday to Saturday attract a mostly under-25 crowd; older clubbers head to the top floor (open Sat only) for Christian Pronovost's popular house set. Cover $10.

Jet 1003 rue Ste-Catherine E ⓣ514/842-2582, ⓦwww.jetnightclub.com; Métro Beaudry. One of the city's top spots for danceable R&B, with a dash of old school, house and club anthems. Make sure to dress up as the door turns away clubbers wearing baggy trousers, jeans, hats or running shoes. Fri & Sat 10pm–3am.

Living 4521 boul St-Laurent ⓣ514/286-9986, ⓦwww.livingnightclub.com; Métro Mont-Royal or bus #55. *Living* took an old Plateau bank building, kept its classical facade, and turned the interior into a three-floor club frequented by under-35 yuppies and musically ruled by urban beats ranging from R&B to deep house. The ground-floor bar, with its lofty ceiling and snug sitting areas, is the best spot to scope out the action. Wed–Sun; open bar for women Wed & Sun until midnight.

London Club 3523A boul St-Laurent ⓣ514/288-4994; Métro Sherbrooke or bus #55. A sleek, two-level club for a fashionable moneyed crowd (no jeans, no hats, no trainers). Old school and classic house (with a bit of R&B thrown in) fill both the cool blue first floor and the upper floor, dominated by red padded benches and lightboxes. There's an awesome terrace (with jacuzzi) overlooking the Main. Wed–Sat; $10–15; ages 21 and up.

Newtown 1476 rue Crescent ⓣ514/284-6555, ⓦwww.newtown.ca; Métro Peel or Guy-Concordia. The streamlined horizontal louvers on the facade hint at the sleek design inside F1-racer Jacques Villeneuve's nightlife complex. The bright and beautiful head for the rooftop terrace, stopping off at the club's own restaurant for pricey Mediterranean food or a drink in the lounge before bopping to disco, house and R&B grooves in the basement club.

Orchid 3556 boul St-Laurent ⓣ514/848-6398; Métro Sherbrooke or bus #55. A swanky second-floor nightclub whose large island bar separates the dance floor from tucked-away booths and the comfy lounge chairs overlooking the Main. Very popular with fashionable young things on the make who dance to a mix that ranges from commercial house to hip-hop or R&B, depending on the night of the week. Thurs–Sun from 10pm; Sun 25 and over; $10 cover.

Passeport 4156 rue St-Denis ⓣ514/842-6063; Métro Sherbrooke or Mont-Royal. An intimate bar-club that evokes the polished 1980s – spot lighting cuts through the black-painted decor, booze is served from a burnished wood-and-steel bar, and the smallish dance floor gleams with stainless steel. Not surprisingly, Eighties music is the norm. Dress stylishly in black and you'll fit right in.

Société des Arts Technologiques (SAT) 1195 boul St-Laurent ⓣ514/844-2033, ⓦwww.sat.qc.ca; Métro St-Laurent. A large, stripped-down warehousey space where you can catch some cutting-edge electronic sounds. It's part of an evolving digital culture centre that will feature a gallery and performance space and a funky café-bar in front with video and music sets for the weekday *5 à 7*.

Tokyo 3709 boul St-Laurent ⓣ514/842-6838, ⓦwww.tokyobar.com; Métro Sherbrooke or bus #55. A busy club in the thick of the Main that attracts a mixed ethnic crowd to its main room decked out with Japanese lanterns, plush and intimate booths, and R&B and Top 40 tunes. A smaller room off to the left, known as the Blue Room, spins house and techno to scenesters lounging on sunken oval sofas. There's a smashing rooftop deck in summer. Thurs–Sun 10pm–3am.

Urban Complex Forum Pepsi, 2313 rue Ste-Catherine O ⓣ514/933-6786 or 1-888/933-6786, ⓦwww.514productions.com; Métro Atwater. Carved out of the Canadiens' old arena, this complex will include four separate club spaces that can be combined – along with the former centre-ice in the ground-floor atrium – to host mega-parties of up to 17,000 ravers. At press time, only 750-capacity *Industry* had opened for the mainstream clubbing crowd, along with a re-invigorated *Sona* – an afterhours club along the lines of *Aria* and *Stereo* (see opposite). They'll be followed later in 2004 by *Republik* (part DJ shop, part café-bar) and *Megaplex*, with a capacity of up to 4000 for rock and other concerts and occasional club nights.

Wax Lounge 3481 boul St-Laurent ⓣ514/282-0919, ⓦwww.waxlounge.ca; Métro Sherbrooke or Saint-Laurent. Situated on the Main's flashiest block, this lounge is decorated with antique chandeliers and fringed lamps that give it an air of faded elegance. The chic crowd, mostly in their twenties and thirties, spend as much time dancing to the

Sin City

Though certainly not to everyone's tastes, strip clubs are – and have been since the early part of the twentieth century – an integral part of Montréal's entertainment scene, and can in fact be found right on the main Downtown commercial streets, rather than relegated to a destitute tenderloin district. Back in the old days, dancers like Lili St Cyr were even accorded a sort of legendary status. Even if much of the style (and talent) is absent from today's performances, having been replaced by dancers who peel their clothes off rather than putting on a show, and by more than a whiff of sleaze (especially in the clubs that allow "contact dances"), a few Downtown clubs still pack them in.

If you're interested in seeing a "show", expect to encounter typical businessman crowds, alongside some more down-at-the-heel types – entrance after all is free, with a one-drink minimum (the doorman also expects a $2 tip). The classiest of such establishments is the lounge-like Wanda's, 1458 rue de la Montagne (Ⓣ514/842-6927; Métro Peel), where from the plush chairs you might opt to admire the ornate frescoes on the walls as much as what's happening on stage. Only slightly more downmarket is Chez Paree, 1258 rue Stanley (Ⓣ514/866-0495; Métro Peel), full of gleaming brass fixtures and offering a lunch buffet. Most popular of all is probably Super Sexe, 696 rue Ste-Catherine O (Ⓣ514/ 861-1507; Métro McGill); you'll hardly fail to notice the massive neon sign, or, once inside, the "erotic bed" on stage.

Montréal's hedonistic reputation extends beyond merely looking, though – the past few years have seen a big rise in the swingers' scene, with members-only clubs like *L'Orage* on boulevard St-Laurent being quite open about things (after tussles with the police over the past five years, they secured a court victory in 2003 legalizing swingers clubs, subject to certain restrictions). If you're a "lifestyler", you can find out more from the Québec Swingers Association (Ⓣ514/990-5723, Ⓦwww.aeqsa.com). The city also has a co-ed sauna, but it's questionable whether it'll last long (too many men, not enough women, apparently) – Montréal's gay saunas (see p.180) see a lot more business. For more on the city's underbelly laid bare, pick up the free quarterly *Montréal Confidential* magazine.

loud funk and R&B beats as they do chilling on the clusters of sofas and stuffed chairs. Quieter Thursdays are free, otherwise it's $10 for the weekend, including Friday's live "soul sessions" of funk and R&B.

After hours clubs

Aria 1280 rue St-Denis Ⓣ514/987-6712, Ⓦwww.arianightclub.com; Métro Berri-UQAM. From 1.30am until 10am, Montréal's club kids dance the night and morning away in this former cinema to house music, with occasional detours into techno and trance, all of it pumping from a massive sound system. Big-name guest DJs keep the main room going while residents energize the urban room. Fri & Sat only; $20–25.

Stereo 858 rue Ste-Catherine E Ⓣ514/286-0325, Ⓦwww.stereo-nightclub.com; Métro Beaudry. Founded by local hotshot DJ Mark Anthony and New York's DJ David Morales, and outfitted with a stellar sound system, this Quartier Latin club blasts techno and house from 2am to 10am (there's also a bar to get primed in from 11pm to 3am). The guest DJ roster includes local talent and brilliant out-of-towners too; a host of UK and US DJs like Danny Tenaglia, as well as Dutch superstars Armin Van Buuren and Tiesto, have headlined here. Friday and Saturday only; $25, $30 for big-name guests.

Live music venues

Unlike dance clubs, the city's **live music** venues are pretty well dispersed throughout the city. **Jazz** spots have the highest profile and there's quite a bit of **worldbeat**, but **folk**, **rock**, **punk** and **ska** also have a good hold on the performance scene. Going to a gig in Montréal is nowhere near as much of a regular night out as it is in Toronto and similarly sized US cities, however. Many of the locales do double duty as watering holes or dance clubs, but when there is a performance on, it typically begins around 9pm, with headliners taking the stage around 11pm. Big-ticket bands play in the city's **large venues**, most of which are located in or around the Quartier Latin, though some marquee names headline open-air shows at Parc Jean-Drapeau. None of the major venues has a favourite genre, and instead book whoever can fill the place.

Covers range from $3 at smaller clubs on weekdays to upwards of $25 at the larger music halls on the weekends, with freebie shows occasionally thrown in during the week – you're best bet for free shows, though, are the city's Irish and brew pubs, reviewed in Chapter 11, "Drinking". For up-to-the-minute show listings, consult the *Mirror* (Ⓦwww.montrealmirror.com) and *Hour* (Ⓦwww.afterhour.com), two free English-language weeklies available in stores and on newspaper stands. *The Montreal Gazette* (Ⓦwww.montrealgazette.com), the English-language daily, also carries comprehensive listings; its Friday weekend guide is best. Tickets for big shows are available through the Admission network (Ⓣ514/790-1245 or 1-800/361-4595, Ⓦwww.admission.com), which adds a $4.10 service charge, and at each venue's box office. Note that larger concert halls are non-smoking except in the bar and lounge areas.

Jazz and blues

Bistro à Jojo 1627 rue St-Denis Ⓣ514/843-5015, Ⓦwww.bistroajojo.com; Métro Berri-UQAM. A step below sidewalk level, the low ceilings and stone walls give this blues cave an intimate feel, as do the wooden chairs and tables at close quarters. It's been an unpretentious spot for a pitcher of beer and an earful of blues since 1975. Shows nightly from 10 or 10.30pm.

House of Jazz 2060 rue Aylmer Ⓣ514/842-8656; Métro Peel. Known as *Biddles* until the eponymous Charlie Biddle passed away in 2003, this Downtown jazz joint offers up a sampling of jazz with a side order of ribs. For a paltry $3 cover charge, you can skip the meat and savour a pint at the bar while being serenaded by the in-house band from 8pm–midnight.

Jello Bar 151 rue Ontario E Ⓣ514/285-2621; Métro St-Laurent. Live acid jazz, blues and funk acts frequently take to the tiny stage at this Quartier Latin bar-cum-lounge furnished with 1960s and 1970s novelties like lava lamps and loveseats. They serve superb martinis, too.

Upstairs 1254 rue Mackay Ⓣ514/931-6808, Ⓦwww.upstairsjazz.com; Métro Guy-Concordia. *Upstairs* is actually downstairs in a half-basement ensconced between walls of exposed rock and wood. It's certainly the city's most easy-going jazz spot, with fresh jazz and blues on tap nightly (except Wed–Sun in summer, post-Jazz Festival) in a wonderfully attitude-free atmosphere. There's also a pleasant outdoor terrace come summertime. Admission charges on Friday to Sunday are between $10 and $20 unless it's an exceptional act.

Worldbeat and folk

Aux Deux Pierrots 104 rue St-Paul E Ⓣ514/861-1686 or 861-1270; Métro Champ-de-Mars. Québécois folk singers are the mainstay of this Vieux-Montréal club where everyone sings along. There's usually a good crowd, but don't expect to understand a word unless your French is excellent. There's an outside terrace in the summer.

Balattou 4372 boul St-Laurent Ⓣ514/845-5447; bus #55. The city's main nightclub for African music (with forays into Latin and worldbeat) has been around so long – since 1986 – that it's nearing institution status. The dark and smoky establishment attracts a mostly older crowd out to the Plateau for weekends of African, Caribbean and Latin American music – think salsa, souk and lambada. Tuesdays and Wednesdays usually showcase live worldbeat acts from just about anywhere.

Barfly 4062A boul St-Laurent ⓣ514/284-6665; bus #55. This Plateau hole-in-the-wall is the city's least pretentious showcase for local folksy and alternative bands. The beer is cheap, there's a pool table to while away the time and the odd time a cover applies, it's usually next to nothing.

Belyza 410 rue Rachel E ⓣ514/849-9363, ⓦwww.belyza.com; Métro Mont-Royal. Cabaret lounge done up in warm woods and curvy, sculptural elements that packs in an array of worldbeat sounds often fused with techno and house. Acts playing Latin rock, Afro-funk, reggae and even a bit of local Québécois music hit the stage at 8pm, before a DJ takes the tribal sounds further from 11.30pm until close. Tickets are normally in the $6–10 range.

Casa del Popolo 4873 boul St-Laurent ⓣ514/284-3804, ⓦwww.casadelpopolo.com; bus #55 or Métro Laurier. "The House of the People" is a sofa-strewn, low-key Plateau spot where high-calibre spoken-word evenings and folk and other bands perform for a marginal fee. A good spot to mingle with the locals anytime from noon until 3am. Some similar shows take place at *La Sala Rossa* down the block at no. 4848, which is owned by the same people as *Casa*.

Rock, punk and ska

Café Campus 57 rue Prince-Arthur E ⓣ514/844-1010; Métro St-Laurent. A low-frills venue with two stages showcasing local bands that run the gamut from rock to pop, and a DJ that keeps things humming when there's no band in the house.

Café Chaos 2031 rue St-Denis ⓣ514/844-0738, ⓦwww.cafechaos.qc.ca; Métro Berri-UQAM. Punk, metal and alt rock bands play upstairs at this Quartier Latin co-operative; DJs take over when the stage is quiet. The ground-floor bar, lined with bright blue walls and wood panelling, is a laid-back studenty hangout. Occasional art shows and theatre happenings as well.

Foufounes Électriques 87 rue Ste-Catherine E ⓣ514/844-5539, ⓦwww.foufounes.qc.ca; Métro St-Laurent. Don't let the bizarre name ("The Electric Buttocks") throw you; this graffiti-strewn complex on the Quartier Latin's western outskirts is the best place in Québec to catch punk and ska acts – and has been for two decades. In addition to punk outfits like Ripcordz, Ab Irato and Hands of Death, you might also catch groups from across the alt spectrum, from hardcore to stoner rock. There's a huge outside terrace that's perfect for summer evenings while downstairs there's usually one or two people involved in some form of body painting in the ground-floor bar, crowded with young Francophones knocking back cheap pitchers of beer. Admission to the bar is free; if you want to catch an act on one of the two stages upstairs, you're looking at $5–15 or more depending on how massive the band is. Club nights (in the second room or after the band has packed up) take a different theme each night (eg Wednesday is skater night) and vary from free early in the week to $8 on Saturday.

Large venues

Cabaret Music Hall 2111 boul St-Laurent ⓣ514/845-2014; Métro St-Laurent. *Cabaret* has hosted the likes of The The and Ninja Tune's Amon Tobin. For acoustic acts, it can be a cozy spot with high ceilings and a wrap around mezzanine lined with bistro tables, less so when they put the tables away to pack in up to 500 fans for rock bands and the like. Get there early if you want a seat, as the ground floor is usually standing room only. Entrance is through the front doors to the Musée Juste Pour Rire.

Centre Bell 1260 rue de la Gauchetière O ⓣ514/932-2582, ⓦwww.centrebell.ca; Métro Bonaventure. The Canadiens' ice rink is covered over for mainstream stadium rock and pop acts in Montréal's 21,000-seat main arena.

Club Soda 1225 boul St-Laurent ⓣ514/286-1010, ⓦwww.clubsoda.ca; Métro St-Laurent. Small enough to remain intimate, but still large enough to attract quality acts like French DJ Laurent Garnier and the Thievery Corporation. It's especially popular during the Jazz Festival.

Métropolis 59 rue Ste-Catherine E ⓣ514/844-3500 or 861-5851, ⓦwww.metropolismontreal.ca; Métro St-Laurent. Hosts bands with fairly large followings like Björk, The White Stripes and The Flaming Lips in a 2200-capacity venue that started off as a vaudeville theatre. With recent renovations, they've improved the sightlines throughout the large main floor space and from the balconies.

Spectrum 318 rue Ste-Catherine O ⓣ514/861-5851, ⓦwww.spectrumdemontreal.ca; Métro Place-des-Arts. Excellent acoustics, hundreds of candlelit tables, and an upstairs balcony with great views of the stage. You should get there early to get a seat. Drum'n'bass star Roni Size has played here as has Brazil's Bebel Gilberto. Plans for a new performance hall mean that the *Spectrum* will likely close soon – no completion date for the new *Spectrum* has been set yet.

13

Gay Montréal

Montréal is rightly considered to be one of the most open and tolerant cities in the world. The province of Québec was one of the first jurisdictions anywhere to begin recognizing the rights of same-sex couples (see box, p.179). Things haven't always been so welcoming, though. Until the mid-1970s, the city's gay district was located around rue Stanley, but in an effort to present a "cleaner" image of Montréal for the Olympic Games, city authorities harassed bar owners out of the area. They relocated to the then-run-down Centre-Sud neighbourhood, where the **Village** (see p.89) has since developed along the dozen or so blocks of rue Ste-Catherine between rues Amherst and Papineau, and you'll find the majority of the city's gay services, **accommodation** and **nightlife** here as well as an open, often cruisey, attitude. Matters steadily improved for the gay community, thanks in part to a joint police-community committee (despite police raids, which happened occasionally up until the mid-1990s). The Village continued to diversify, with the bars being joined by shops and restaurants that catered to both the gay community and workers in the nearby media institutions. And with prices rising in the Plateau, the streets surrounding rue Ste-Catherine are becoming an increasingly desirable place to live, regardless of one's sexual orientation.

The city tourist board now heavily promotes Montréal as a top gay destination, and with good reason. From the extravagant **circuit parties** and huge **pride celebrations** to the city's wealth of cafés, restaurants, shops, saunas, bars and nightclubs that are hopping throughout the year, there is a wealth of possibilities here for gay visitors, be they leather boys, drag queens and even sedate, long-term partners.

Information and resources

It's pretty hard to find English-language **information** about gay and lesbian life in Montréal – such publications tend to come and go, *to be* being the latest – although the English weeklies *Mirror* and *Hour* (see p.174), may also have some info to get you started. As long as you know just a smattering of French you should be able to decipher the **listings** in the free French-language magazines found in bars and cafés. Of these, the monthly *Fugues* (Ⓦwww.fugues.com) is best, with a comprehensive directory of gay resources and event listings – their bilingual *Rainbow Guide*, published in May and October, is especially useful. On the **radio**, catch the weekly *Queercorps* show of gay news and features on CKUT 90.3FM (Mon 6–7pm), immediately followed by *Dykes on Mykes* every other week. Still, your best bet is the **Internet**:

Big gay events

Montréal is a major stop on the gay party circuit, with a number of large events that tend to attract the gym-toned, clubbing crowd. More inclusive are the annual pride week celebration, Divers/Cité, and the gay and lesbian film festival, image+nation; for details on these, as well as the Black & Blue party, see Chapter 18, "Festivals". Info about the other circuit parties is available at Ⓦwww.bbcm.org, except for Ⓦwww.balenblanc.com. Major events include:

Events calendar

Mid-Feb Red Weekend (circuit party)
Easter Bal en Blanc (White Party)
Late May Hot & Dry / Fresh (circuit party)
Early July Festival des Arts du Village (gay and lesbian art festival)
Late July to early Aug Divers/Cité (gay and lesbian pride celebration), see p.215
Early Aug Twist Weekend (circuit party)
Late Sept image+nation (film festival), see p.215
Early to mid-Oct Black & Blue (circuit party and cultural week), see p.215
New Year's Eve Bal des Boys (party)

2006 Gay Games

You'll need to reserve way ahead if you are planning to visit Montréal when it hosts Gay Games VII from July 29 to August 5, 2006. In addition to the 20,000 or so athletes and artists – there's also a cultural aspect to the games – organizers expect as many as a quarter of a million visitors. Begun in San Francisco in 1982, the games have become a major international event – both the Amsterdam (1998) and Sydney (2002) games were hugely successful. Montréal looks likely to also do well, thanks to its already strong pull as a gay destination and sporting facilities that are a legacy of the 1976 Olympics. The Montréal 2006 website (Ⓦwww.montreal2006.org) is the best place to keep informed as the date draws near.

there is some content and links for lesbians on the mostly gay-oriented Ⓦwww.gaybek.com, while Tourisme Montréal has a number of pages on gay and lesbian Montréal at Ⓦwww.tourism-montreal.org/gay.

In the Village itself, the **tourist information centre** at 1260 rue Ste-Catherine E, Suite 209 (late June to early Sept Mon–Thurs 11am–6pm, Fri–Sun 10am–8pm; early Sept to late June Mon–Fri and weekends during major events 10am–6pm; Ⓣ514/522-1885 or 1-888/595-8110, Ⓦwww.info-gayvillage.com), can help with queries about accommodation, services and entertainment. The city's main queer **resource centre** is the Centre Communautaire des Gais et Lesbiennes de Montréal, 2075 rue Plessis, Suite 110 (Mon–Fri 10am–noon & 1–5pm; Ⓣ514/528-8424, Ⓦwww.ccglm.qc.ca), which has information on community groups and a well-stocked library (Wed & Fri 1–8pm). Bulletin boards and event information can be found at the store Priape (see p.200), which also sells event tickets. Montréal no longer has a gay and lesbian bookshop, following the closure of L'Androgyne in 2002 – after nearly three decades in business, it was unable to compete with the big chain bookshops (see p.193), most of which now carry a decent selection of gay and lesbian books.

General **information and help lines** for gay men and lesbians are Gay Line (daily 7–11pm; Ⓣ514/866-5090, Ⓦwww.gayline.qc.ca), the McGill student-run Queer Line (Mon–Sat 8–11pm; Ⓣ514/398-6822, Ⓦwww.ssmu.mcgill.ca/queer) and the French-language Gai Écoute (Ⓣ514/866-0103, Ⓦwww.gai-ecoute.qc.ca). Information on HIV and AIDS is available from Info-Sida (Ⓣ514/521-7432).

Accommodation

Although you shouldn't have a problem staying in any of the accommodations listed in Chapter 9, there is a decent range of options for visitors wanting to stay in a specifically gay **hotel**, **guesthouse** or **B&B.** Note that if you're arriving in the summer or for one of the major annual events, it's best to book way ahead. If the accommodation choices listed here are filled, try the resources listed above or a gay accommodation site like Ⓦwww.purpleroofs.com. Note that most Village establishments offer only a continental breakfast to get you started, rather than a large, cooked breakfast to fill you up.

Auberge Cozy 1274 rue Ste-Catherine E Ⓣ514/525-2151, Ⓦwww.aubergecozy.com; Métro Beaudry. A tastefully furnished hotel in the heart of the Village, whose fourteen simple rooms come with a/c and TV. There's a jacuzzi for relaxing in as well. Price includes continental breakfast. ❸

Aux Berges 1070 rue Mackay Ⓣ514/938-9393 or 1-800/668-6253, Ⓦwww.auxberges.ca; Métro Lucien-l'Allier or Guy-Concordia. Billing itself as "Canada's Finest All-Male Hotel", this recently spruced-up 42-room Downtown

Gay rights in Montréal

Montréal has become one of the most tolerant places in the world for gays and lesbians, thanks to a succession of provincial and federal laws. In 1967, Justice Minister (and subsequently Prime Minister) **Pierre Elliott Trudeau** declared "Take this thing on homosexuality. I think the view we take here is that there's no place for the state in the bedrooms of the nation", and the following year homosexuality was decriminalized.

The road to acceptance has had more than a few obstacles, though, what with the attitudes of police lagging behind that of the rest of society, and with landmarks **raids** on the *Truxx* bar in 1977 and the Sex Garage loft party in 1990, both resulting in large demonstrations. Things have since improved, with a liaison between the police and community activists and, of late, much of the police attention (and arrests) have shifted to heterosexual swingers' clubs (which have also scored partial victories).

On the political front, gay and lesbian Montrealers have fared better than these heavy-handed police raids suggest. A year after the Parti Québécois rolled into office, they introduced **Bill 88** in December 1977, which included "sexual orientation" in the province's charter of rights, a move in keeping with the spirit of openness fostered by the Quiet Revolution (see p.271). A series of court cases forced the Canadian government to follow suit, finally adding sexual orientation to the list of prohibited discrimination in the **Canada Human Rights Act in 1996**.

More recently, major victories came when Québec's Bill 32, which gave same-sex partners the same legal rights and responsibilities as common-law heterosexual couples, passed unanimously in the Assemblé National on June 10,1999, followed by a similar act at the federal level the following spring. These rights were expanded when Québec passed Bill 84 in June 2002, giving **same-sex civil unions** a legal status almost equal to that of marriage, including inheritance and adoption rights.

Montréal was trumped by Toronto on June 10, 2003, however, when the Ontario Court of Appeal declared that marriage should no longer be restricted to opposite-sex couples. This led to dozens of foreign gay and lesbian visitors travelling to Toronto to celebrate their nuptials while Montréal awaits the enactment of a federal law that would allow gay marriage coast-to-coast. While politicians and ordinary Canadians are evenly split on the issue of gay marriage, it looks likely that upcoming legislation (currently under review by the Supreme Court of Canada to determine whether it would withstand a constitutional challenge) will make Canada only the third country in the world to recognize gay marriages.

The sauna scene

Montréal's cruisey reputation is no doubt helped by the dozen or so **saunas** (bathhouses), about half in the Village and the rest scattered about town. Prices and clientele at each establishment tend to differ depending on the time of day but most are open 24hr and busiest for *cinq à sept* (5–7pm) and late at night when the clubs close. All offer rooms and lockers, and most include a steam room, jacuzzi and sauna, as well as secluded corners and somewhere to watch videos. The saunas with the best reputations are Oasis Spa, 1390 rue Ste-Catherine E (Ⓣ514/521-0785, Ⓦwww.thebestspa.com), for the young and fit; Le 456, 456 rue de la Gauchetière ouest (Ⓣ514/871-8341, Ⓦwww.le456.ca), which also has a gym; and Le 5018, 5018 boul St-Laurent (Ⓣ514/277-3555, Ⓦwww.le5018.com), which has a varied clientele, student specials and a roof deck. A complete list of the city's saunas is available in Fugues (Ⓦwww.fugues.com).

hotel (3km west of the Village) has been around since 1967. Most rooms have private bath, though the spa facilities – sauna, steam room and jacuzzi – are definitely shared. For outdoor relaxation, the small bar has an ivy-covered terrace or you can sun yourself on the clothing-optional roof deck. ❹

Bed & Breakfast du Village 1279 rue Montcalm Ⓣ514/522-4771 or 1-888/228-8455, Ⓦwww.bbv.qc.ca; Métro Beaudry. Clean and cozy B&B in the Village spread over two floors and equipped with a hot tub. Four of the eight rooms have shared bath. You can have the included continental breakfast on a secluded terrace. Indoor parking is $5 extra. ❷–❸

La Conciergerie Guest House 1019 rue St-Hubert Ⓣ514/289-9297, Ⓦwww.laconciergerie.ca; Métro Berri-UQAM. A Victorian town house with duvet-covered queen-sized beds in 17 comfortable air-conditioned rooms, around half of which have private bath. There's also a rooftop terrace, indoor jacuzzi and an exercise room. Continental breakfast included. ❸–❹

Hotel Bourbon 1578 rue Ste-Catherine E Ⓣ514/523-4679 or 1-800/268-4679, Ⓦwww.bourbonmontreal.com; Métro Beaudry. The ever-expanding *Complexe Bourbon* includes restaurants, bars and the *Backtrack* nightclub (see opposite), which is good if you want to be in the centre of things. The hotel itself has 30 rooms and 5 suites, the largest of which has two bed-rooms, a lounge and a jacuzzi. ❹

Le House Boy 1281 rue Beaudry Ⓣ514/525-1459 or 1-866/525-1459, Ⓦwww.lehouseboy.com; Métro Beaudry. A friendly B&B with a quiet garden and large cooked breakfasts. The six brightly painted rooms have contemporary IKEA-style fur-nishings, and the bathrooms are shared (as is the hot tub on the terrace). Non-smoking. Men only. ❸

Lindsey's B&B for Women 3974 av Laval Ⓣ514/843-4869 or 1-888/655-8655, Ⓦwww.lindseysmontreal.com; Métro Sherbrooke. A Plateau B&B in an 1887 Victorian house that caters to lesbians only. Two attractively furnished rooms share a bathroom with four-poster tub while the suite has private bath and fireplace. Decadent breakfasts are served in a light-filled conservatory. ❸

Nightlife

Montréal has an energetic and varied **bar** and **club** scene for gay men. But with nightspots forever renovating or closing down, it's best to ask around or check one of the listings magazines (see p.177) for the latest hotspot. The city is notoriously fickle when it comes to entertainment for **lesbians** – bars and clubs open every year just to close down again after a few months – and at press time, *Magnolia* was the only venue catering primarily for women, though *Le Drugstore* is a popular mixed hangout. The larger dance clubs usually have **cover charge** of around $6 at the weekend, but cost only a couple of dollars or are even free on quieter nights. There are plenty of cafés and restaurants in the Village, which draw a mix of straight and gay customers - see p.152. More bars and lounges outside the Village – many of them gay friendly – are covered in Chapter 11, "Drinking".

Agora 1160 rue Mackay ⓣ514/934-1428; Métro Guy-Concordia. Downtown bar frequented by businessmen complemented by a few students from nearby Concordia University. A horseshoe-shaped bar takes up most of the small space downstairs, the high stools giving a good vantage-point to watch the nightly karaoke singers (from 10pm). If you can't bear to watch, there are a couple of cushy sofas for chilling upstairs (but they're still within earshot).

Aigle Noir (Black Eagle) 1315 rue Ste-Catherine ⓣ514/529-0040, ⓦwww.aiglenoir.com; Métro Beaudry. A favourite haunt of leathermen, this dark and narrow bar is appropriately decked out in industrial decor and lots of chains. The "donjon" in back is an even darker cruisey space. 8am–3am. Men only.

Cabaret Mado 1115 rue Ste-Catherine E ⓣ514/525-7566, ⓦwww.mado.qc.ca; Métro Beaudry. Local drag celebrity Mado and her cohorts put on shows attracting a large number of straight people as well as a loud and appreciative gay contingent. There are also live cabaret-type or jazz-style bands on some nights.

Campus 1111 rue Ste-Catherine E ⓣ514/526-3616, ⓦwww.campusmtl.com; Métro Beaudry. One of the best known of the Village's handful of strip joints, it's as cheesy as you'd expect with mirrored walls and young men baring it on the stage or at your table. Women allowed on Sundays after 8pm.

Club Bolo 960 rue Amherst ⓣ514/849-4777, ⓦwww.clubbolo.com; Métro Beaudry. Don your cowboy hat and boots for two-step, line and country dancing at this friendly gay and lesbian western club. You can either take lessons ($10; first lesson free; call for schedules), come to dance on Friday or Saturday night (10pm–2am; $8 including drink) or try the Sunday T-dance (4–9pm; $10 including dinner).

Club Date 1218 rue Ste-Catherine E ⓣ514/521-1242; Métro Beaudry. Most younger gay men walk right past this piano bar, though the karaoke (every night from 11pm) can be a lot of fun if you're able to leave your attitude at the door. Open from 8am.

Complexe Bourbon 1560–1594 rue Ste-Catherine E ⓣ514/523-4679, ⓦwww.clubbacktrack.com; Métro Papineau or Beaudry. If a Las Vegas casino were designed for gay men, it might look something like this complex of bars, restaurants, nightclub and hotel decked out with hundreds of light bulbs. The street-corner pavement tables of the *Café Européen* are a good place to check out the passing traffic, while around back there's a parody of a pedestrianized European street – complete with water-wheel. The pastiche continues inside, with the café blending in to an Irish pub, an *Orient Express* restaurant-cum-railcar and the long-standing 1950s-style *Club Sandwich* diner. Tucked away in the basement, *Club Backtrack* draws a mainly male crowd for free sessions of retro tunes in an industrial decor.

Le Drugstore 1366 rue Ste-Catherine E ⓣ514/524-1960; Métro Beaudry. A central stairwell lit up like Times Square connects the many levels of this gay and lesbian entertainment complex. If you don't fancy drinking or dancing, you can grab a bite to eat or even get your hair cut here. In summer, the roof terrace overlooking the action on rue Ste-Catherine is the place to be.

Gotha 1641 rue Amherst ⓣ514/526-1270, ⓦwww.aubergell.com/gotha; Métro Beaudry. This lounge bar, slightly removed from the rue Ste-Catherine hubbub, both geographically and in spirit, is a good spot to chill in a retro Sixties chair and have an audible conversation. A piano and a fireplace add to the relaxed ambience.

Magnolia 1329 rue Ste-Catherine ⓣ514/526-6011, ⓦwww.magnolia.com; Métro Beaudry. The only spot in Montréal that's primarily for lesbians, the quieter pub atmosphere of early evening bumps up a few notches as the place becomes pretty much one big dance floor, with R&B on Thursdays and house on the weekend ($3–5). Men are allowed as guests, and tend to take over for "Church", the Sunday T-dance (2pm–midnight; $8).

Parking 1296 rue Amherst ⓣ514/282-1199, ⓦwww.parkingbar.com; Métro Beaudry. Two-floor club, with an alternative bent on the hot and sweaty dance floor upstairs, and a smaller, often packed space for grooving to

R&B and other urban sounds downstairs, where a side room lined with oil drums and other industrial decor from the old *K.O.X.* bar is the haunt of leathermen. Cover of $3–5 after 11pm.

Sky 1474 rue Ste-Catherine E ☎514/529-6969; Métro Beaudry. Before *Unity* opened (later *Unity II*, see below), this was *the* place to go, and almost annual facelifts over the past decade or so keep people coming back (though they tend to be fickle about which night is "good"). The ground-floor bar opens onto the street and attracts an after-work and pre-clubbing crowd, while upstairs has a loungey chill-out room and dance floor playing a mix of retro pop hits and chart dance music. Best for the Friday *5 à 7*, Sunday T-dance and on the rooftop terrace whenever the weather's fine.

Stud 1812 rue Ste-Catherine E ☎514/598-8243, Ⓦwww.studbar.com; Métro Papineau. As the name suggests, you're more likely to find beefy boys than precious young things here, but the atmosphere is more friendly than intimidating. You can dance to a mix ranging from Eighties tunes to techno on the large dance floor or just chat or cruise in the quieter side bar. A bonus – the pool tables are free 10am–3pm. Men only except Wednesday nights.

Unity II 1171 rue Ste-Catherine E ☎514/523-2777, Ⓦwww.club-unity2.com; Métro Beaudry. A young and outgoing crowd fill the large dance floor here, though the *Bamboo Bar* upstairs tends to get more packed and sweaty – head to the rooftop terrace to cool off (also a great spot to catch the fireworks). Music varies by the night – if there's hip-hop and R&B upstairs, it'll be pop or house downstairs (and vice versa). Wed–Sun 10pm–3am.

14

Performing arts and film

Drawing on both its French and English cultural heritages, Montréal's richly varied performing arts scene ranges from highbrow **classical music** – led by the world-renowned Orchestre Symphonique de Montréal (OSM) – to excellent avant-garde **dance** companies like the explosive La La La Human Steps. Still, the city's best-known cultural attraction is undoubtedly the **Cirque du Soleil**, who've wowed audiences with their kaleidoscopic performances in more than 100 cities around the world (see box, p.187).

The city is blessed with a major performing-arts complex right Downtown: **Place des Arts** is home to the OSM and Les Grands Ballets Canadiens as well as opera and theatre troupes and a host of chamber-music ensembles (see box, below). It's also centre stage for the city's big **festivals** – notably the Festival International de Jazz de Montréal and Les FrancoFolies festival of French music – with stages festooned about the large plaza and the closed-off streets nearby. For more on these and other major festivals, see Chapter 18.

Compared to Montréal's rich array of opera, classical and dance offerings, English **theatre** is a bit of a letdown, and it especially pales next to the rewarding variety of French theatre on offer, from Molière to contemporary works by Québécois playwrights. You won't have a problem finding decent English-language **film**, though – in addition to the many mainstream movie theatres there's a clutch of repertory cinemas showing fairly diverse programmes, and the city hosts more than a dozen film festivals year-round.

Information on cultural events is available from the main concourse of Place des Arts, as well as in the *Montreal Gazette* and the free alternative weekly papers, *Hour* and the *Mirror*. You can also pick up a quarterly booklet listing special events and festivals from the Infotouriste office. Most companies or venues sell **tickets** directly, as well as through the Admission Network (Ⓣ514/790-1245 or 1-800/361-4595, Ⓦwww.admission.com), which adds a service charge of around $4.

Classical music and opera

Montréal's main **symphony** and **chamber** groups perform in the various halls at Place des Arts throughout the autumn–spring season, spreading out to other venues like the outdoor Théâtre de Verdure and the Basilique Notre-Dame in

Multidisciplinary venues

A number of Montréal's larger performance spaces don't stick to a single genre – instead they provide a range of programming choices throughout the year. The major companies performing at these spots are detailed individually elsewhere in this chapter, but the multipurpose venues you're likely to catch them at are:

Place des Arts ⓣ514/285-4200, 514/842-2112 (tickets), ⓦwww.PdArts.com; Métro Place-des-Arts. Montréal's premier performing-arts showcase is home to the city's flagship orchestra, opera and ballet companies. The two largest halls are the **Salle Wilfrid-Pelletier**, which seats 3000, and the **Théâtre Maisonneuve**, about half that size. Tickets for events here can also be purchased from the main concourse box office (Mon–Sat noon–9pm; Sun one hour before showtime only). Plans for a new concert hall to house the OSM just to the west were scuttled (at least temporarily) when the Liberals imposed a spending freeze following their 2003 election.

Salles du Gesù 1200 rue de Bleury ⓣ514/861-4036, ⓦwww.gesu.net; Métro Place-des-Arts. Located below the Église du Gesù (Jesuit Church), the Salle du Gésu's 425 seats arc around the front of the main stage, which hosts theatre, comedy and classical music, as well as jazz acts during the festival. Events are also sometimes held in the centre's smaller spaces.

Le Théâtre de Verdure ⓣ514/872-2237. The open-air theatre in Parc Lafontaine has the most eclectic scheduling in the city, with Shakespeare, contemporary dance, world music and cinema interspersed with appearances by the city's major ballet, symphony and chamber companies. Best of all, the performances are free.

Théâtre St-Denis 1594 rue St-Denis ⓣ514/849-4211, ⓦwww.theatrestdenis.com; Métro Berri-UQAM. The biggest names in comedy play here during the Just For Laughs festival (see p.214), while concerts and touring Broadway-style productions fill it up the rest of the year.

the summer. Other ensembles play at a number of smaller concert halls, particularly at the universities. **Opera** productions are staged at Place des Arts.

During the summer, there are also frequent lunchtime concerts in Montréal's churches (often free, though a donation is appreciated), as well as in city parks. St James United Church, 463 rue Ste-Catherine O (ⓣ514/288-9245), and Christ Church Cathedral, 635 rue Ste-Catherine O (ⓣ514/843-6577), both offer weekly concerts, while the Oratoire St-Joseph, 3800 chemin Queen-Mary, provides a suitably grand setting for the annual **Organ Festival** held on Wednesdays throughout the summer (ⓣ514/733-8211). Check out *The Gazette*'s entertainment listings for a full list of concerts and recitals or *La Scena Musicale*, a free monthly magazine distributed around town and on the web at ⓦwww.scena.org.

Companies and venues

Chants Libres ⓣ**514/841-2642, ⓦwww.chantslibres.org.** Although they only perform one or two operas a year, this company is known for pushing the genre's boundaries, with the lyrical singers accompanied by anything from techno music to multimedia spectacles.

I Musici de Montréal ⓣ**514/982-6038, ⓦwww.imusici.com.** From September to April, this celebrated chamber orchestra performs from a varied repertoire – Baroque classics to present-day compositions – under the direction of cellist Yuli Turovsky for two decades. Although you can catch them at McGill's Pollack Concert Hall or the Théâtre Maisonneuve for $27, the morning and afternoon "rush-hour" concerts in the Tudor Hall on the fifth floor of the Ogilvy department store (see p.196) are much more intimate and will only set you back $19.

Orchestre Métropolitain du Grand Montréal Théâtre Maisonneuve, Place des Arts ⓣ**514/598-0870, ⓦwww.orchestremetropolitain.com; Métro Place-des-Arts.** Though overshadowed somewhat by the OSM, the Orchestre Métropolitain still turns out a decent range of concerts at, no surprise, the Place des Arts, along with other performance spaces across the city. Tickets for the PdA shows start at $18.70, and the best seats cost a mere $36.

L'Opéra de Montréal **Salle Wilfrid-Pelletier, Place des Arts ⓣ514/282-6737 or 985-2258, ⓦwww.operademontreal.com; Métro Place-des-Arts.** L'Opéra de Montréal stages an impressive number of performances each year, and of the half-dozen or so annual shows at least two are house premieres. The backbone of the schedule is chosen from the European lyrical repertory, but twentieth-century composers like Debussy and Janáček are often on the programme. English and French surtitles are projected above the stage. Tickets range from $40 to $114.

Orchestre Symphonique de Montréal (OSM) **Salle Wilfrid-Pelletier, Place des Arts ⓣ514/842-9951, ⓦwww.osm.ca; Métro Place-des-Arts.** Founded in 1934 and the granddaddy of the city's classical scene, the OSM was led by the energetic Charles Dutoit for a quarter of a century until 2002. At press time, his successor had still not been decided, but he or she will have their work cut out for them – Dutoit ran a gruelling schedule of concert series built around guest artists, composers and nations, as well as crossover and contemporary performances. The symphony also manages to squeeze in Sunday afternoon shows and Wednesday morning matinees, summer concerts in city parks and at the Festival de Lanaudière, and sell-out Christmas and Easter performances in the Basilique Notre-Dame. Tickets for most shows start at $17.50 and run to $82 for the best box seats. If not sold out, rush tickets are available 90 minutes before concerts begin.

Pollack Concert Hall **555 rue Sherbrooke O, McGill University ⓣ514/398-4547 or 398-5145, ⓦwww.mcgill.ca/music/events; Métro McGill.** Located in McGill's Faculty of Music building, this modern concert hall offers the up-and-coming generation of musicians a chance to perform. Everything from recitals and chamber groups to symphonies and opera companies are heard here, oftentimes for free.

Pro Musica **Place des Arts ⓣ514/845-0532 or 1-877/445-0532, ⓦwww.promusica.qc.ca; Métro Place-des-Arts.** Every year, the non-profit Pro Musica society lines up a strong international selection of small chamber groups to perform in either the Théâtre Maisonneuve or Cinquième Salle at Place des Arts during the October to March season. They also offer musical workshops that engage kids aged five to twelve while their parents attend a concert. Tickets are normally $25–30, half that for students.

Redpath Hall **861 rue Sherbrooke O, McGill University Main Campus ⓣ514/398-4547 or 398-5145, ⓦwww.mcgill.ca/music/events; Métro Peel.** The more traditional of McGill's two main classical-music venues, Redpath Hall likewise gives students a chance to shine. The warm wood of its interior adds to the ambience of the many chamber and early-music concerts performed here, several of which are taped for broadcast by CBC Radio.

Tudor Hall **Ogilvy, 1307 rue Ste-Catherine O ⓣ514/873-4031, Métro Peel.** Tucked away on the fifth floor of a swank department store, this intimate Old World space is well suited to regular daytime chamber recitals, including those organized by I Musici (see opposite).

Dance

Montréal has a justifiably strong reputation in the world of **dance**, based not just on its well-regarded **ballet** and **jazz dance** companies – Les Grands Ballets Canadiens de Montréal and Les Ballets Jazz de Montréal – but on the huge variety of **experimental and contemporary dance** companies and performers. Dancers and choreographers like Marie Chouinard, Margie Gillis, and Édouard Lock and (formerly) Louise Lecavalier of La La La Human Steps have blazed an international reputation for the city – though unfortunately this means they're often out of town. Other companies to look out for are Montréal Danse, O Vertigo and PPS Danse. In addition to the local talent, Montréal hosts North America's premier dance festival, the **Festival**

International de Nouvelle Danse, held at various city locations biennially from late September to early October (see p.215). Some of the city's globe-trotting companies also come home for the Montréal High Lights Festival in February (see p.211). Cheaper and often wackier are the dance performances at the Fringe Festival (see p.212). Besides newspaper listings of performances, the French-language *Dfdanse* magazine (Ⓦwww.dfdanse.com) covers the city's contemporary dance scene.

Dance troupes and venues

L'Agora de la Danse 840 rue Cherrier Ⓣ514/525-1500, Ⓦwww.agoradanse.com; Métro Sherbrooke. This four-storey building is ground-zero for contemporary dance in Montréal – it's not only the city's main dance centre but a number of companies have their studios here. Performances cost $23 in the 260-seat Studio.

Les Ballets Jazz de Montréal Ⓣ514/982-6771, Ⓦwww.balletsdemontreal.com. For more than three decades, this company has been touring the world and showing off a brilliant fusion of dance and jazz. You might be able to catch them at Espace GO in spring, or for free at the Théâtre de Verdure (see p.184) in summer, if you're lucky.

Compagnie Marie Chouinard Ⓣ514/843-9036, Ⓦwww.mariechouinard.com. Since Marie Chouinard founded her dance company in 1990, she has staged some brilliant works combining classical scores, like Stravinsky's *The Rite of Spring*, with outrageous costumes, though lately the focus has been more on solo works.

Danse Danse Ⓣ514/848-0623, Ⓦwww.dansedanse.net. Danse Danse produces half a dozen shows from November to May, inviting guest choreographers from Québec (such as dancer Margie Gillis in 2003) and abroad. Tickets for the shows, performed at various spaces around town, run about $40.

Les Grands Ballets Canadiens de Montréal Théâtre Maisonneuve and Salle Wilfrid-Pelletier, Place des Arts Ⓣ514/849-0269 (information and subscriptions) or 842-2112 (PdA box office), Ⓦwww.grandsballets.qc.ca; Métro Place-des-Arts. Under the tutelage of Gradimir Pankov, Les Grands Ballets presents a season of classical ballet combined with more contemporary works, collaborating with some of the biggest names in the dance world. Tickets are normally in the $50–80 range, but go for as cheap as $25 in the furthest balcony. From mid- to late December every year, not surprisingly, seats are snapped up quickly for seasonal favourite, *The Nutcracker*.

La La La Human Steps Ⓣ514/277-9090, Ⓦwww.lalalahumansteps.com. Since 1980, choreographer Édouard Lock's highly gestural and energetic works have been blazing a trail across Montréal's dance scene. Lock's latest production *Amelia* is on a two-year world tour; book well ahead if you want to catch the Montréal dates at Place des Arts.

O Vertigo Ⓣ514/251-9177, Ⓦwww.overtigo.com. Artistic director and choreographer Ginette Laurin's gymnast training is evident in O Vertigo's lively works. This is one more Montréal dance company that you're more likely to catch abroad, though you'll find them at the Monument National during their few Montréal dates.

Tangente 840 rue Cherrier Ⓣ514/525-5584, Ⓦwww.tangente.qc.ca; Métro Sherbrooke. In the same building as L'Agora de la Danse (see above), this dance organization supports and produces pieces by up-and-coming choreographers and dancers in a smaller performance space, Éspace Tangente ($10–15).

Theatre

Montréal may be largely bilingual on the streets, but that rarely carries over to **theatre** productions, as most troupes perform in either French or English only – although when *Les Misérables* came to town, the same actors performed in English one night and French the next. While on the whole the finest theatres perform in **French** (as might be expected in a predominantly Francophone city), there are a few noteworthy **English** options in the city; the rest are scattered about the Anglophone bastion of the Eastern Townships (see p.233).

Cirque du Soleil

Started by a group of young street performers in 1984, the **Cirque du Soleil** (☎514/722-2324 or 1-800/678-2119, Ⓦwww.cirquedusoleil.com) has grown into Montréal's most famous cultural export. With a mix of street-theatre whimsy and big-top drama – without the animals – this human circus relies on acrobatic performers, colourful costumes and atmospheric lighting and music to keep your attention. And they do, as evidenced by sell-out shows throughout the world, including permanent residencies in Las Vegas and Orlando.

Not only were each of the Cirque's fourteen different productions (so far) created and produced in Montréal, but each new touring show premieres in the city and often returns between tours. When in town, they usually perform under the bright blue and yellow tent erected on Quai Jacques-Cartier in the Vieux-Port (see p.83).

We've noted a few of the finest Francophone theatres below also, but note that they're only worthwhile if your language skills are up to the task. Expect to pay around $15–40 for a regular-price theatre ticket regardless of the language spoken.

In addition to the local theatre productions, bigger Broadway-style shows play at Place des Arts and Théâtre St-Denis (see box on p.184). Festivals also supplement the regular September to May theatre season – the biennial **Festival de Théâtre des Amériques** is the best of the lot.

English-language theatre

Centaur Theatre 453 rue St-François-Xavier ☎514/288-3161, Ⓦwww.centaurtheatre.com; Métro Place-d'Armes. The old Stock Exchange Building that houses the Centaur's two stages is a grand and fitting setting for Montréal's most established English-language theatre company. Both modern and contemporary plays make up the half-dozen productions in the season, which runs from late September to early June. Regular tickets cost $38 ($20 for students); matinees and previews go for $28.50. Rush tickets ($8) are available 90 minutes before the show (if it isn't sold out).

Monument National 1182 boul St-Laurent ☎514/871-2224 or Admission ☎514/790-1245, Ⓦwww.ent-nts.qc.ca; Métro St-Laurent. Renovated by the top-calibre National Theatre School, this venue has three stages and still features plays put on by the students, at least a couple of which are in English. The rest of the year, smaller theatre companies and individual performers rent out the space.

The Other Theatre 5115 rue St-Denis ☎514/279-4853, Ⓦwww.othertheatre.com; Métro Laurier. For the past decade or so, The Other Theatre has striven to develop alternative and experimental theatre in the city, in both English and French, with excellent results.

Players' Theatre 3480 rue McTavish ☎514/398-6813, Ⓦwww.ssmu.mcgill.ca/players; Métro Peel. Hidden up on the third floor of the William Shatner University Centre (named after the famous McGill alumnus following a student referendum), this small black-box theatre sees half a dozen low-budget productions a year, put on by the entirely student-run resident company, with an emphasis on contemporary Canadian plays. Tickets are a snip at $8.

Saidye Bronfman Centre for the Arts 5170 chemin de la Côte Ste-Catherine ☎514/739-2301 or box office: 739-7944, Ⓦwww.saidye-bronfman.org; Métro Côte-Ste-Catherine. This multimedia centre's Leanor and Alvin Segal Theatre is home to the Yiddish Theatre, the only one of its kind in North America (translation in English is available); plays (including translations of pieces like *Fiddler on the Roof*) and dramatizations of Yiddish texts reflect the Jewish experience internationally as well as life in Montréal. The centre's English Theatre also stages three productions a year, and guest companies occasionally appear.

Comedy clubs

Though Montréal's **comedy** club scene officially blooms during the Just for Laughs Festival (see p.214), a couple of Downtown institutions keep patrons entertained year-round.

Comedyworks 1238 rue Bishop ⓣ514/398-9661; Métro Guy-Concordia. Montréal's best comedy club is a dark, low-ceilinged den that stages stand-up every night but Sunday starting at 9pm, with late shows on Fridays and Saturdays at 11.15pm. Monday is open-mike night, Tuesdays and Wednesdays belong to the club's in-house improv troupe, and weekends showcase out-of-town talent. Sit further back to avoid becoming part of the act. Tickets range from $3 (Mondays) to $12 (Saturday).

Comedy Zone Le Nouvel Hôtel, 1740 boul René-Lévesque O ⓣ514/937-3888, ⓦwww.montrealcomedyzone.com; Métro Guy-Concordia. If you want to fill your belly before the laughs begin, you can treat yourself to *Comedy Zone*'s $30 dinner-and-show package. Otherwise, it's $10 ($5 for students or for the Wednesday night shows featuring French comedians). Showtimes are Wed & Thurs 8.30pm, Fri & Sat 9 & 11.15pm.

Ernie Butler's Comedy Nest Jillian's, Forum Pepsi, 2313 rue Ste-Catherine O ⓣ514/932-6378, ⓦwww.comedynest.com; Métro Atwater. A comedy club with acts Wednesday through Saturday starting at 8.30pm, with a 10.30pm late show on Saturday night. Wednesdays feature local comedians for free; out-of-town headliners take the stage starting Thursday for $10 ($12 on Saturday).

French-language theatre

Théâtre d'Aujourd'hui 3900 rue St-Denis ⓣ514/282-3900, ⓦwww.theatredaujourdhui.qc.ca; Métro Sherbrooke. As the name suggests, "today's theatre" is the focus, and this company has been *au courant* for three decades now. Théâtre d'Aujourd'hui specializes in the work of Québécois playwrights and often stage premieres of their plays.

Théâtre du Nouveau Monde 84 rue Ste-Catherine O ⓣ514/866-8668, ⓦwww.tnm.qc.ca; Métro St-Laurent. At the time this French theatre company was formed in 1951, the theatre it now occupies was the Gayety Burlesque Theatre (where the famous stripper Lili St Cyr performed – see p.173). Recent renovations have brought the building up to date, but the company itself focuses on large-scale mainstream fare, staging French repertory standards like Molière as well as translations of Shakespeare and European works.

Théâtre Espace GO 4890 boul St-Laurent ⓣ514/845-5455 or tickets: 845-4890, ⓦwww.espacego.com; bus #55 or Métro Laurier. Innovative and contemporary still, despite having been around long enough to be considered an established theatre, they cram in 9 shows (mostly modern French theatre, with some dance) between early September and the very start of June, though half are outside productions. Regular price for tickets is $28.

Usine C 1345 av Lalonde ⓣ514/521-4493, ⓦwww.usine-c.com; Métro Beaudry. This former factory was converted into a superb multi-disciplinary performance space by Carbone 14, a company known for pushing the bounds of theatre with their innovative, multimedia productions (their show *Le Dortoir* toured internationally and the filmed version of it won an Emmy Award). The space is also used by a number of emerging and experimental theatre and dance companies. There's a funky café open for weekday lunch and from 6pm on performance nights.

Film

Like any large North American city, Montréal has a glut of **multiplex cinemas** showing the latest Hollywood releases and the odd independent or foreign film. Although only three of these are Downtown, they share forty screens between them and so offer plenty of choices. The multiplexes are supplemented by several quality **repertory theatres** – in addition to those listed below, cultural centres such as the Goethe-Institut at 418 rue Sherbrooke E (Ⓣ514/499-0149) and the Centre Canadien d'Architecture at 1920 rue Baile (Ⓣ514/939-7026) screen special series of films and provide venues for festivals. For a bigger than big screen experience, you can lose yourself in one of two **IMAX** cinemas.

To find out what's playing, listings are readily available in daily newspapers as well as the free weekly papers *Hour* (Ⓦwww.afterhour.com) and the *Mirror* (Ⓦwww.montrealmirror.com), and on the Cinéma Montréal website (Ⓦwww.cinemamontreal.com). Cinemas show either French or English versions, rarely both; unless noted otherwise, the cinemas listed below screen English films (versions of French and foreign-language films tend to be subtitled, unlike French versions of Hollywood blockbusters, which are more likely to be dubbed). If in doubt, ask before you make your purchase. The average movie ticket is $10, though matinees and Tuesday-night screenings are cheaper.

Multiplexes and IMAX

AMC Forum 22 Forum Pepsi, 2313 rue Ste-Catherine O Ⓣ514/904-1250; Ⓦwww.amctheatres.com; Métro Atwater. Part of the entertainment complex carved out of the old Forum arena – there's a mock-up of "centre ice" with a section of seating as a reminder – the 22 cinemas here tend to be on the small side but the seating's comfy. There's plenty of other money-draining activities for teenagers – arcade, bowling alley, climbing wall – and a clubbing complex for over-eighteens intending on making a late night out of it.

Cinéma IMAX du Centre des Sciences de Montréal Quai King-Edward (opposite boul St-Laurent) Ⓣ514/496-4629, Ⓦwww.montrealsciencecentre.com; Métro Place-d'Armes. The big screen on Quai King-Edward offers the usual eye-popping 2D and 3D IMAX fare, but its location provides a welcome escape if you are touring the Vieux-Port and the weather turns ugly. There are only a couple of English screenings throughout the day, so check schedules beforehand. The 45-minute films will set you back $10.

Famous Players Centre Eaton 705 rue Ste-Catherine O Ⓣ514/866-0111, Ⓦwww.famousplayers.com; Métro McGill. Tucked away on the top floor of the Centre Eaton, little about this six-screen cinema invites lingering – people just come for the mainstream first-run films shown in English here.

Famous Players Paramount Montréal 977 rue Ste-Catherine O Ⓣ514/842-5828, Ⓦwww.famousplayers.com; Métro Peel or McGill. Taking up a good chunk of the old Simpson department store, the Paramount was the first cinema in Montréal to offer stadium-style tiered seating. It's got the best "event" feel of the Downtown cinemas, with throngs of people in the lobbies – there's nearly four thousand seats shared among a dozen large floor-to-ceiling screens, along with an IMAX cinema.

Repertory and specialty cinemas

Centre Cinéma Impérial 1430 rue Bleury Ⓣ514/848-0300, Ⓦwww.ffm-montreal.org; Métro Place-des-Arts. The grandest of Montréal's film palaces began life as a vaudeville theatre, and after its most recent restoration the 780-seat cinema is again a great place to indulge in a movie, either in the balcony or the sweeping main floor.

Cinéma du Parc 3575 av du Parc Ⓣ514/281-1900, Ⓦwww.cinemaduparc,com; bus #80 or #129. This student standby, in the mall under the intersection of rue Prince-Arthur and avenue du Parc, stages week-long runs of worthy independents and a repertory programme of second-run and classic films on the other two screens. New releases are no longer a bargain here, but rep films cost $7 and it's only $6 for matinees and Tuesday screenings.

Cinémathèque Québécoise 335 boul de Maisonneuve E ⓣ514/842-9768, ⓦwww.cinematheque.qc.ca; Métro Berri-UQAM. Founded over forty years ago to preserve and promote film and television, the Cinémathèque now has a collection of over 50,000 predominantly French films and videos. Their programme features everything from retrospectives to a diverse series of festivals, by Québécois as well as international auteurs. Facilities include the "mediathèque" documentation centre (Tues–Fri 1–8pm), exhibition galleries (Tues–Fri noon–9pm, Sat & Sun 5–9pm; $5. Wed 6–8.30pm; free) and a boutique.

Ex-Centris 3536 boul St-Laurent ⓣ514/847-3536, ⓦwww.ex-centris.com; Métro St-Laurent or Sherbrooke or bus #55. This sleek art-house theatre has three screens and one very trendy café, *Café Méliès* (open until 2am). A mix of thoughtfully chosen independent films are shown in either English or French (but mostly the latter), supplemented by experimental works – the New Media Film Festival (see p.216) is held here annually. Purchasing the $10 tickets ($6 Mondays and weekday matinees) at the high-tech kiosks is an experience in itself.

NFB Cinema (Cinéma ONF) 1564 rue St-Denis ⓣ514/496-6895, ⓦwww.nfb.ca; Métro Berri-UQAM. The National Film Board of Canada showcases their own films here, as well as other Canadian productions in English and/or French. There are comfortable seats in the cinema and video-screening theatre, but for a novel experience try the individual "CinéScopes" ($3/hr; Tues–Sun noon–9pm), where viewers can select films and freeze the frame or fast-forward as the whim strikes. These gadgets are run by the unique "CinéRobothèque", a central robot that dishes out one of the 8000 available videodiscs like a twenty-first-century jukebox.

15

Shopping

While Montréal has its share of chain stores, the city's reputation as a stylish **shopping** centre stems from its trove of smart **boutiques**, most of which are clustered in neighbourhoods outside of Downtown. The city's real strength is its selection of designer and streetwear threads – and politically incorrect furs too. More recently, Montréal has also become a hotspot for record collectors and aficionados of twentieth-century design.

The best part of shopping in Montréal is the atmosphere on the streets themselves, as some of the best boutiques are wedged in beside terrace-fronted cafés perfect for a breather and to eye up the passing fashion parade for further inspiration. Nowhere blends shopping and drinking better than the Plateau's two main drags: **rue St-Denis**' forte is Québec-designer boutiques along with sleek home-decor shops and funky accessory outlets. In contrast, affordable-clubby chic is the mainstay of **boulevard St-Laurent**, or "The Main", which also has the city's most concentrated selection of techno-driven record shops, while further north designer furniture showrooms target the Plateau's yuppie residents.

On the Village's western border, **rue Amherst** is tops for retro twentieth-century furniture and collectibles (mostly from the Thirties to the Seventies), while more traditional antiques can be found along **rue Notre-Dame ouest** in St-Henri. Near the western end of this "antiques row", a different sort of feast awaits at the **Marché Atwater**, where farmers sell their wares outside and some of the city's best butchers and *fromageries* ply their trade along the interior arcade.

Otherwise, most of the action is concentrated Downtown along **rue Ste-Catherine**. Most **chains** have their Montréal flagship stores here, but the real standout is **Simons**, a Québec City original with highly affordable contemporary garb and upmarket designer threads to boot. There are also several shopping **malls**, the best being the **Cours Mont-Royal**, a former

Shopping categories

hotel that now hosts dozens of fashionable boutiques in a swanky setting. For art dealing, head to rue Sherbrooke near the Musée des Beaux-Arts, home to the city's finest commercial galleries.

Unless otherwise specified, the shops listed here keep standard opening hours: Mon–Wed 10am–6pm; Thurs–Fri 10am–9pm; Sat 11am–5pm; Sun noon–5pm.

Antiques and twentieth-century design

Montréal's greatest concentration of **antique dealers** ply their trade along rue Notre-Dame ouest between rue Guy and avenue Atwater, a stretch known as the **rue des antiquaires** (antiques row). Annoyingly, almost none are open for a Sunday browse, and during the rest of the week tend to keep shorter hours than most other shops (Mon–Fri 10 or 11am until 5pm, Sat 11am or noon until 4pm). The plenitude of **twentieth-century design** shops on rue Amherst likewise open later during the week and there are no late closings as the area gets a bit dodgy later on; typical hours are: Mon–Fri 11am–6pm, Sat 11am–5pm, Sun 1–4pm.

Cité Déco 1761 rue Amherst ⓣ514/528-0659; Métro Beaudry. The smart leather chairs in the front of this shop – which specializes in décor from the 1930s to the 1970s – are made in-house and sell for a tidy $2400 a pair. Cheaper, and cooler, are the Art Deco armchairs with sleek curved sides trimmed in aluminum. In back, look for Danish sofas from the 1960s and teak or rosewood sideboards and tables.

Couleurs Meubles & Objets du 20ème Siècle 3901 rue St-Denis ⓣ514/282-4141; Métro Sherbrooke. A twentieth-century design boutique tucked in a half-basement and full of pristine early-1960s Scandinavian teak tables and chairs, and exotic 1930s pottery pieces. Some knick-knacks cost as little as $7.

Grand Central 2448 rue Notre-Dame O ⓣ514/935-1467; Métro Lionel-Groulx. The classiest shop on the rue Notre-Dame strip, Grand Central stocks first-rate eighteenth-and nineteenth-century antiques. Superbly crafted chandeliers sway over a collection of dining tables, sculptures and gleaming gold-leaf candelabras.

Jack's 1036 rue Ontario E ⓣ514/596-0060; Métro Beaudry. Chrome retro Sputnik lamps and moulded plastic housewares in bright reds and yellows confront you as you walk through Jack's main entrance on rue Amherst. These flashy 1950s to 1970s design objects contrast with the clean and sober lines of the contemporaneous teak and rosewood Scandinavian furniture in the next room.

Milord 1870 rue Notre-Dame O ⓣ514/933-2433, ⓦwww.milordantiques.com; Métro Lionel-Groulx. The emphasis at this attractive shop is on European arts and furniture, and its showroom floor is laden with ornately carved writing desks, marble busts, and Rococo gilt mirrors. A second, more central shop is at 1434 rue Sherbrooke O (ⓣ514/286-2433).

Books

Despite the city's Francophone majority, the presence of so many Anglophone university students ensures there's a healthy trade in **English-language books**. Your best bet for mega-bookshops with hefty stocklists is Downtown around rue Ste-Catherine, while specialist and used booksellers are on Downtown's western fringes or the Plateau. **French bookstores** are all over, with the best selection of shelves on rue St-Denis. In sunny weather, the row of bookstalls in the Vieux-Port is the most pleasant spot to browse.

New books

Champigny **4380 rue St-Denis ☎514/844-2587; Métro Mont-Royal.** One of the finest French bookstores in town, located in a lofty, wood-toned space, Champigny stocks everything from CDs to cookbooks in addition to their large kids' and literature sections. Daily 9am–midnight.

Chapters **1171 rue Ste-Catherine O ☎514/849-8825, ⓦwww.chapters.ca; Métro Peel.** Montréal's biggest English-language bookstore (with a fair-sized French selection), where people tend to linger a while in the comfortable armchairs scattered amidst the four and a half floors. There's also a café, Internet stations ($2/20min) and regular readings and book-signings; 30 percent off bestsellers. Mon–Thurs 9am–10pm; Fri and Sat till 11pm; Sun 10am–9pm.

The Double Hook **1235A av Greene ☎514/932-5093, ⓦwww.doublehook.com; Métro Atwater.** A small but concentrated selection of Canadiana – most of the books and magazines are in English and all are by Canadian authors.

Indigo Books, Music and Café **Place Montréal Trust, 1500 av McGill College ☎514/281-5549, ⓦwww.indigo.ca; Métro McGill.** This bright and airy two-storey bookstore stocks titles on fashion, cooking, architecture, art, fiction, travel and music on the second floor, where the discount bins frequently turn up great finds for under $10. There's a pleasant café on the second floor, as well. New English and some French texts, as well as, surprisingly, housewares, are found on the main floor. Daily 9am–11pm.

Mojo and Bella **3968 boul St-Laurent ☎514/282-7730, ⓦwww.mojobella.com; bus #55.** While there's a very small section of carefully chosen fiction and kids' books on sale, the best reason for hitting up this shop is their eclectic collection of comics and 'zines. Their choices of new and used LPs are equally thoughtful and consist mainly of jazz, Afro and funk. Closed Mon.

Nicholas Hoare **1366 av Greene ☎514/933-4201; Métro Atwater.** A superb array of books – ranging from fiction to children's to travel, with a strong emphasis on British titles – adorn the shelves in an atmosphere reminiscent of an old boys' club, wood-panelled walls included. The top floor also stocks a selection of CDs, mostly classical and jazz. There's a second outlet in Ogilvy (see p.196).

Paragraphe **2220 av McGill-College ☎514/845-5811, ⓦwww.paragraphbooks.com; Métro McGill.** Though it was bought out a few years back by chain conglomerate Québecor, this bookshop has maintained an independent attitude and boasts well-chosen stock that's especially good for fiction, philosophy, and art. Frequent readings, too. Mon–Fri 7am–11pm, Sat & Sun 9am–11pm.

Secondhand bookstores

Footnotes **1454 rue Mackay ☎514/938-0859; Métro Guy-Concordia.** A hole-in-the-wall spot whose shelves are filled by nearby Concordia University students trading in their texts. The fiction is hit-and-miss, but there are plenty of good finds in philosophy and history.

Sam Welch **3878 boul St-Laurent ☎514/848-9358, ⓦwww.swwelch.com; bus #55.** On sunny days there's a bargain bin out in front, while inside there's always a good selection of modern fiction, sci-fi, and art books, guarded by the requisite bookstore cat.

The Word **469 rue Milton ☎514/845-5640; Métro McGill.** Aside from being the textbook dumping ground for nearby McGill University students, there's also a respectable collection of out-of-date publications bought from estate sales and a decent lit section.

Travel books and maps

Aux Quatre Points Cardinaux **551 rue Ontario E ☎514/843-8116 or 1-888/843-8116, ⓦwww.aqpc.com; Métro Berri-UQAM.** Although they carry travel guides and accessories, this store's real strength is globes and maps, including 1:50,000 topographic maps of Québec.

Librairie du Voyage Ulysse **4176 rue St-Denis ☎514/843-9447; Métro Sherbrooke or Mont-Royal.** The city's main shop devoted to selling travel guides and travel-related accessories also has a great selection of items like neck pillows, money belts and voltage converters, along with plenty of French and English guidebooks. Also at 560 av du Président-Kennedy (☎514/843-7222).

Clothing

Designer boutiques

Dubuc Mode de Vie 4451 rue St-Denis ⓣ514/282-1465, ⓦwww.dubucstyle.com; Métro Mont-Royal. Philippe Dubuc's flair for finely cut suits (from $800), ties and shirts produces sharp, sexy and *très* chic men's attire – a trend he's carried over to his women's line.

Marie St-Pierre 2081 av de la Montagne ⓣ514/281-5547, ⓦwww.mariesaintpierre.com; Métro Peel. Quebecers in the know can spot this designer's works from a mile away. The items on sale here are completely original, made out of exquisite hand-painted silks, crinkly chiffon and high-tech fabrics like polyamide, in innovative cuts that easily pass for *haute couture*. Expect to pay around $250–400 for a dress.

Nadya Toto 2057 av de la Montagne ⓣ514/350-9090; Métro Peel. Her clothing caters to women in their late twenties and early thirties, with comfortable, sporty threads and feminine skirts and dresses with a predilection for low necklines and clingy fabrics. Prices start around $150.

Revenge 3852 rue St-Denis ⓣ514/843-4379; Métro Sherbrooke. Revenge used to house only Québec designers but has since gone cross-Canada in scope, carrying Vancouver's Neto line in addition to locals like Nadya Toto (see above) and their own men's line. The selection caters mostly to an older, moneyed crowd, but the occasional trendy outfit for the younger set can be found.

Rugby North America 3526 boul St-Laurent ⓣ514/849-9759, ⓦwww.rugby-na.com; Métro Sherbrooke or St-Laurent or bus #55. Montrealers with a leather fetish tend to head for Rugby, where skirts, pants, and even halters made out of the material come in modern styles and fashionable colours. There's also a large selection of handbags, travel bags and jackets, as well as some stylish (and cow-free) clubbing clothes. There's another outlet in Complexe Les Ailes (see p.197).

Scandale 3639 boul St-Laurent ⓣ514/842-4707; bus #55. Designer Georges Lévesque's fashion sense matches fluid retro-styled knits and jersey fabrics with wild and bright colour combinations. Not the place to pick up the perfect little black dress, but an excellent stop for something no one else will have back home.

L'UOMO 1452 rue Peel ⓣ514/844-1008, ⓦwww.luomo-montreal.com; Métro Peel. The clothes here ooze quiet elegance – sedate grey and black tints abound – in labels like Kiton, Nino Cerruti, Giorgio Armani and Prada. The service is exceptional – no wonder Mick Jagger, Eric Clapton and Michael Jackson shop here when in town. Suits start around $1500, making the mid-July and late December sales – when stock is 30–50 percent off – very popular.

Chain stores

Club Monaco Cours Mont-Royal, 1455 rue Peel ⓣ514/499-0959, ⓦwww.clubmonaco.com; Métro Peel. Once designed by Toronto-born Alfred Sung, the clothes have lost some of their spark after this chain was bought out by Ralph Lauren several years ago. But while the line is decidedly more beige and conservative than it once was, it's still exemplary for its clean lines and modernist look – and you might find the odd funky piece.

Harry Rosen Cours Mont-Royal, 1455 rue Peel ⓣ514/284-3315, ⓦwww.harryrosen.com; Métro Peel. Making and tailoring fine clothes for the white-collar professional – read high-powered, high-salaried CEO – is Harry Rosen's mantra. His annual Boxing Day sale, where everything is marked down a minimum of 50 percent, has men lined up outside the front doors well before they open.

Parasuco Santana Jeans 1414 rue Crescent ⓣ514/284-2288, ⓦwww.parasuco.com; Métro Guy-Concordia. The jeans in this brand's name are some of the sexiest denim on the market, made to hug every curve and then some. The stock also includes slinky sweaters and halter-tops and some Italian imports. The men's collection is equally hot (if less curvy). Open until 9pm summer weekdays.

Roots 1035 rue Ste-Catherine O ⓣ514/845-7995, ⓦwww.roots.com; Métro Peel. Although founded by two Americans, Roots is treated by Canadians as a made-in-Canada phenomenon. The chain's hallmark leather jackets, bags and cotton sweat-shirts have a classically preppy sense about them that never goes out of style.

Furs and winter coats

Harricana 3000 rue St-Antoine O ⓣ514/287-6517, ⓦwww.harricana.qc.ca; Métro Lionel-

Groulx. Local designer Mariouche Gagné takes old fur coats and recycles them into new, fashion-forward threads and accessories – boot covers, sleeveless vests, handbags and pillow cases are among the standouts. Handbags start around $150, while pillow cases range from $200 to $600. She does coats, too – they'll set you back a grand. Closed Sun.

Kanuk 485 rue Rachel E ⓣ514/284-4494, ⓦwww.kanuk.com; Métro Mont-Royal. The massive ranks of winter jackets made and sold here are warm but pricey ($400–800) and you can even get the sleeve length adjusted – something that's well-nigh impossible at most places. There's also a stock of outdoorsy clothes, and a few sleeping bags and knapsacks.

Clubwear and street fashions

Fly 1970 rue Ste-Catherine O ⓣ514/846-6888; Métro Guy-Concordia. The coolest clubwear store in the city, with local independent labels Umsteigen, Castle Dream and Betty Blush displayed alongside imports from New York and Italy, trendy trainers and funky bags and jewellery. There's also a small selection of dance music on CD and vinyl – a DJ sets the pace on weekends.

Lola and Emily 3475 boul St Laurent ⓣ514/288-7598, ⓦwww.lolaandemily.com; Métro Sherbrooke or bus #55. It's hard to walk out of here empty-handed, especially since almost everything is for sale: it feels a bit like someone's loft, with antique Indian furniture and fun knick-knacks – though it's mainly about the clothes, with some unusal styles, fun labels like Juicy and Paul Frank and creations by Montréal designers.

Mosquito Cours Mont Royal, 1455 rue Peel ⓣ514/286-5244; Métro Peel. Most of the stock sports France's Kookaï label, the high-quality stuff, not the shoddy knock-offs they're known for back home. Expect clean lines, crisp colours and affordable, stylish items. Other locations at 1651 rue Ste-Catherine O (ⓣ514/939-6793) and 3521 boul St-Laurent (ⓣ514/288-6839).

Mousseline 1182 rue Ste-Catherine O ⓣ514/878-0661; Métro Peel. Seriously funky high-street clothes for both men and women, with lines like Rare, Imperial, Nolita and In Love imported from France and Italy. Some boots and shoes as well.

Zara Place Montréal Trust, 1500 av McGill-College ⓣ514/281-2001, ⓦwww.zara.com; Métro McGill. Decent quality knock-offs of Euro fashions arrive here before the original pieces they're modeled on even hit stores. The stock is hip and unbelievably cheap – and produced so quickly you'll be lucky if it lasts an entire season. But by then it will likely have gone out of style anyway.

Vintage, consignment and discount shops

Boutique Encore 2165 rue Crescent ⓣ514/849-0092; Métro Peel. Tucked away in this second-floor shop is a gold mine of designer names at cut-rate prices – you'll find Helmut Lang and Costume Nationale skirts for $200 and Christian Lacroix coats at $1200, some of which have never been worn. Tues–Fri 10am–6pm, Sat 10am–5pm, closed Sun & Mon.

Retro Raggz Friperie 171 av du Mont-Royal E ⓣ514/849-6181; Métro Mont-Royal. The mostly raver-style clothes here are in excellent condition, not to mention highly affordable; jeans retail for $20. But the best merchandise are the campy T-shirts emblazoned with Wonder Woman, Superman and Star Wars decals (also about $20). Mon–Wed noon–6pm, Thurs & Fri noon–9pm, Sat & Sun 11am–6pm.

J Schreter 4358 boul St-Laurent ⓣ514/845-4231 or 1-877/745-4231, ⓦwww.schreter.com; Métro Mont-Royal or bus #55. Schreter's (as it's better known) has been a fixture on the Main since 1928 (but only moved to its present location in the Fifties). Still family-run, it's a great spot for deep discounts on name-brand basics – especially jeans, socks and underwear – as well as sportswear and running shoes. There's a stronger selection for men than for women.

Twist Encore 3972 boul St-Laurent ⓣ514/842-1308; bus #55. Good retro shoes, original jewellery (including a spectacular array of chunky cufflinks) and a wicked used-coat selection are the hallmarks here, although there's also a fairly good in-house clothing line, Jong.

Village des Valeurs 2033 boul Pie-IX ⓣ514/528-8604, ⓦwww.villagedesvaleurs.com; Métro Pie-IX. When out by the Stade Olympique (see p.111), drop into this massive store to browse among dozens of racks rammed to the hilt with bargain-basement used threads. Of the five Value Villages in Montréal, this outlet is the best for decorative scarves, shoes and fur coats that often go for as low as $35.

Accessories

Agatha 1054 av Laurier O ⓣ514/272-9313, ⓦwww.agatha.fr; bus #80. Québec women's-fashion magazines favour this jewellery shop over all others when it comes to accessorizing their models. Hundreds of spectacular pieces of costume, silver and gold jewellery, mostly imported from home base in France, are crammed into a shoebox-sized space.

Henry Birks and Sons 1240 Square Phillips ⓣ514/397-2511, ⓦwww.birks.com; Métro McGill. Birks' turquoise blue boxes are as eagerly received as those from New York's Tiffany and Co – largely because they contain the same expensive types of goodies: Murano crystal, Breitling and Cartier watches, pearls and diamond rings. Birks also designs their own lines of watches and jewellery in platinum or white gold.

Kamikaze Curiosités 4156 rue St-Denis ⓣ514/848-0728; Métro Sherbrooke or Mont-Royal. By night, this eclectic shop transforms into the retro nightclub *Passeport* (see p.172). You'd never know it by day, though, when they somehow clear out the smoke before covering the walls and floor with hair accessories, hats, leggings, socks and nylons of all stripes and shades.

Voyeur 3844 rue St-Denis ⓣ514/288-6556; Métro Sherbrooke. An impressive collection of handcrafted silver jewellery for both men and women, as well as some imported pieces like Storm, Skagen and Boccia titanium watches. Closed Sun & Mon.

Department stores and malls

If the weather's too unpleasant to hit the generally more interesting street-front shops, Downtown Montréal has plenty of warm and dry malls and department stores for browsing. Except for Holts and Ogilvy, all of the following are integrated into the Underground City (see p.50).

Department stores

La Baie 585 rue Ste-Catherine O ⓣ514/281-4422, ⓦwww.hbc.com; Métro McGill or Place-des-Arts. With Eaton's downturn in fortunes, The Bay has regained its status as Canada's flagship department store. Though it's shortened its name from the Hudson's Bay Company, it still stocks the trademark striped blankets that began as bartering fodder in the fur-trading days and now go for $300–450 (though you can get a cozy throw for $125). The rest of the selection is quite contemporary – mid-priced name-brand clothing, electronics, housewares and so forth.

Holt Renfrew 1300 rue Sherbrooke O ⓣ514/842-5111, ⓦwww.holtrenfrew.com; Métro Guy-Concordia. Head here for your Chanel, Prada, Gucci and Calvin Klein fix. The in-house Studio line, found on the third floor, offers similarly chic styles at more affordable prices.

La Maison Simons 977 rue Ste-Catherine O ⓣ514/282-1840; Métro Peel. Simons' house-lines Twik and Trente-et-Un promise good-quality clothing for both men and women at very reasonable prices, and fashion snobs will be happy here as well; designer labels like Gaultier, Dolce & Gabbana, Calvin Klein and Tommy Hilfiger are on hand, occasionally at reduced prices.

Ogilvy 1307 rue Ste-Catherine O ⓣ514/842-7711, ⓦwww.ogilvycanada.com; Métro Peel. Stocks upscale fashions, including a Louis Vuitton boutique, in an atmosphere true to the original department-store concept. Chandeliers hang overhead as you browse along oak counters and a bagpiper serenades the place during the lunch hour.

Malls

Centre Eaton 705 rue Ste-Catherine O ⓣ514/288-3708, ⓦwww.centreeatondemontreal.com; Métro McGill. This large mall covers an area roughly the size of a city block, with close to 200 shops on four floors. It's the best place to shop if you're short on time since virtually every major chain store has an outlet here – in addition to The Gap and Levi's, you'll find local chains like Jacob, Pegabo, and Tristan and America. The high-end shops are on the second floor, mid-range gear is on the main floor, and cheapie togs and accessories dominate the lower levels. The basement has a food court; the top level has cinemas. Mon–Fri 10am-9pm, Sat 10am–5pm, Sun noon–5pm.

Complexe Les Ailes 677 rue Ste-Catherine O ⓣ514/285-1080, ⓦwww.complexelesailes.com; Métro McGill. Wrapped around a dramatic oval atrium carved out of the centre of the old Eaton's department store are sixty mid- to upper-end shops, including large Guess? and Tommy Hilfiger stores, Archambault (see p.199), the flagship SAQ outlet (see p.198) and some good lingerie and accessories boutiques. The main anchor, though, is Les Ailes de la Mode, a department store with four floors of high-end men's and women's fashions and housewares.

Cours Mont-Royal 1455 rue Peel ⓣ514/842-7777; Métro Peel. Three floors of high fashion – the dozen odd shops on the mall's second floor cater to the young, hip, clubby set, while the third floor goes way upmarket with Donna Karan and Giorgio Armani. The basement level is oriented towards budget shoppers.

Faubourg Ste-Catherine 1616 rue Ste-Catherine O ⓣ514/939-3663, ⓦwww.lefaubourg.com; Métro Guy-Concordia. Montréal's most distinctive mall almost feels like a marketplace, with its great selection of food shops and craftsy little boutiques. Unlike the other malls' more generic food courts, the bright, third-floor one here has a number of winning independents with a strong focus on Asian cuisines. Daily 9am–9pm.

Place Montréal Trust 1500 av McGill-College ⓣ514/843-8000, ⓦwww.placemontrealtrust.com; Métro McGill. Perhaps the most conservative mall in the city, Place Montréal Trust has gained some points by adding an excellent bookstore, Indigo (see p.193), and the high-street fashion vixen, Zara (see p.195), to its ground-floor offerings.

Food and drink

Gourmet food and wine shops

Au Festin de Babette 4118 rue St-Denis ⓣ514/849-0214; Métro Sherbrooke. A small gourmet shop selling rich delicacies like glazed duck gizzards, foie gras and truffles, along with sweets like dark chocolates, alcohol-preserved fruits and rich, creamy ice cream.

Pierre-Yves Chaput 1218 rue Bernard O ⓣ514/279-9376; Métro Outremont. Though off the beaten path in the northwest corner of Outremont, this shop is undoubtedly the best *fromagerie* in the entire province. More than sixty raw-milk cheeses are on offer here, with *chèvre* (goat's cheese) in the starring role. A handful of the cheeses are made by Pierre-Yves Chaput himself, a star in his own right as he's one of the only *maîtres affineurs* (loosely translated as master cheesemaker) in North America. As an extra bonus, you don't buy without tasting first.

Première Moisson 1490 rue Sherbrooke O ⓣ514/931-6540; Métro Guy-Concordia. A mouthwatering gourmet shop selling delectable patés, cheeses and pastries – to take away or eat in the cozy attached café. If you're on a diet, stay far away. Another of the numerous branches is in the Marché Atwater (see p.198).

Bakeries and sweets

Chocolats Geneviève Grandbois 162 rue St-Viateur O ⓣ514/394-1000, ⓦwww.chocolatsgg.com. They ought to put up warning signs at this stylish little boutique – the smells from the adjoining chocolate factory may drive you insane. The Chuao chocolates are outrageously expensive ($3.25 for a small cube) but the kind made with 25-year-old balsamic vinegar are especially exquisite and the taste lingers for a while after. Closed Sun & Mon; open until 10pm the rest of the week. They also have a stand in the Marché Atwater.

Fairmount Bagel Bakery 74 av Fairmount O ⓣ514/272-0667; Métro Laurier. The granddaddy of Montréal bagel shops, opened in 1951, produces nearly 2000 bagels an hour (the most popular are poppy and sesame seed, best when still warm). The lines on the weekend stretch outside the door, even in the middle of winter. 24hr.

Monsieur Félix & Mr Norton Faubourg Ste-Catherine, 1616 rue Ste-Catherine O ⓣ514/939-3207, ⓦwww.felixandnorton.com; Métro Guy-Concordia. This basic counter shop serves the most decadent cookies in town. The headliner, the *ménage à trois*, is a heady combination of dark, milk and white chocolates in one soft cookie.

Buying booze

As long as you're over 18, you'll have no problem picking up a bottle of your favourite tipple in Montréal. You can buy beer from the big chains and regional breweries (see box, p.164) as well as cheaper bottles of wine from supermarkets and just about any *dépanneur* (convenience store), including many that are handy for the Plateau's bring-your-own-wine restaurants. However, if you want to buy spirits or a quality vintage (ie, one that has a year on the label and doesn't come with a screw-top), you'll need to drop by one of the provincial liquor outlets, run by the Société des Alcools du Québec (SAQ). If neither of the following locations are handy, call ⓣ514/873-2020 or 1-866/873-2020, or visit ⓦwww.saq.com, to find the nearest branch.

SAQ Express 4053 rue St-Denis ⓣ514/845-5200; Métro Sherbrooke. Good for grabbing a bottle before heading to an *apportez votre vin* joint, this liquor outlet is conveniently located right at the corner of avenue Duluth and the busiest BYO restaurant strip in town; appropriately, they keep a wide range of whites and rosés perpetually chilled. Open until 9pm weeknights, 7pm weekends.

SAQ Signature Complexe Les Ailes, 677 rue Ste-Catherine O ⓣ514/282-9445 or 1-888/454-7007; Métro McGill. There's no cheap plonk at this liquor store – instead you'll find an exemplary port, spirit and rare-wine selection. Keep an eye out for local specialities like *pomme de glace*, a cider version of ice wine, and the incredibly smooth maple syrup whiskey.

Pâtisserie de Gascogne 237 av Laurier O ⓣ514/490-0235; Métro Laurier or bus #80. The French term for window-shopping is *lèche vitrine* (window licking), which is exactly what you'll want to do before the array of rich cakes and sweet tarts displayed behind the glass. For once, though, follow your parents' advice and sample the savoury cheeses, patés, quiches and fresh-baked breads before jumping right into the desserts.

St-Viateur Bagel 263 rue St-Viateur O ⓣ514/276-8044; bus #80. In business nearly as long as Fairmont Bagel (see above), this 24hr bakery produces a product with little discernible difference – except to Montrealers, who will invariably swear that one or the other is better.

Health-food stores

Optimum 630 rue Sherbrooke O ⓣ514/845-1015; Métro McGill. A one-stop Downtown health shop selling all the alternative health food and supplements you'd expect and some natural beauty products (soap and body washes) to boot.

Tau 4238 rue St-Denis ⓣ514/843-4420; Métro Mont-Royal or Sherbrooke. If you're looking for vitamin-enriched fruit juices, herbal medicines, soy milk and other organic foodstuffs, this small and helpful Plateau shop is bound to have it.

Markets

Marché Atwater 138 av Atwater ⓣ514/937-7754, ⓦwww.marchespublics-mtl.com; Métro Lionel-Groulx. A wonderfully atmospheric 1930s Art Deco market with an interior arcade that's home to forty-odd gourmet butchers, bakers and cheese-makers who often proffer bite-sized samples to passing customers year-round. It's a riot of colour and movement in summer with blooming flowers and tempting produce spilling out of the stalls.

Marché Jean-Talon 7075 rue Casgrain ⓣ514/277-1588, ⓦwww.marchespublics-mtl.com; Métro Jean-Talon. Little Italy's market buzzes with shoppers year-round as dozens of stalls display superb fresh produce, flowers and baked goods in a plaza lined with gourmet cheese and meat shops; worth checking out for the palette of colours alone, but great for loading up on snacks or picnic supplies, too.

Galleries

If money is no object when searching for that perfect *objet*, the galleries evoking the wealth of the Golden Square Mile era on rue Sherbrooke ouest should be your first stop. Otherwise, your best bet for contemporary works are the loft spaces on rue Ste-Catherine near rue St-Alexandre, with more than a dozen galleries to browse (see p.54). Diverse styles can be found in galleries scattered throughout the Plateau, as well as along rue St-Paul in Vieux-Montréal where the selection runs the gamut from cheesy landscapes to avant-garde pieces.

Galerie Claude Lafitte 1270 rue Sherbrooke O ⓣ514/842-1270; Métro Peel. The ritziest gallery in the city – indeed, it's located in the *Ritz Carlton* – dealing in European, Canadian and American masters. Works by Chagall, Picasso and Renoir have all made appearances. Mon–Sat 10.30am–5pm, Sun noon–5pm.

Guilde Canadienne des Métiers d'Art 1460 rue Sherbrooke O ⓣ514/849-6091, ⓦwww.canadianguild.com; Métro Peel. This nonprofit gallery sells a wide selection of native crafts, including sterling Inuit soapstone and West Coast Haida prints and carvings. The top floor has a free permanent exhibition of predominantly Inuit artworks supplemented by temporary displays. The shop is closed Sun & Mon; the exhibition is open Tues–Fri 10am–5pm only.

Oboro 4001 rue Berri ⓣ514/844-3250, ⓦwww.oboro.net; Métro Sherbrooke. This happening Plateau gallery has a penchant for multidisciplinary works from local artists. Installations commonly showcase video, radio and Internet projects. Tues–Sat noon–5pm.

Zeke's 3955 boul St-Laurent ⓣ514/288-2233; bus #55. A quirky upstairs Plateau gallery devoted exclusively to showcasing first-time artists' works, a bent that gets some innovative output like *Montreal Mirror* restaurant critic Spanky Horowitz's photographs of what he ate for six months. The concept extends to music – acoustic bands play a couple of times a week (you can buy CDs of the recorded sessions) – and other one-off cultural events like poetry readings. Sun–Thurs 3–8pm, but closed during baseball games (the owner's a big fan) and may be open at other times – either try the door or call ahead.

Music

Archambault 500 rue Ste-Catherine E ⓣ514/849-6201, ⓦwww.archambault.ca; Métro Berri-UQAM. This music superstore seemingly has every French artist who ever recorded. It also features one of the best electronica sections in town. As an extra bonus, you can listen to any of the CDs before buying. Other Downtown outlets are in Complexe Les Ailes and in the concourse of Place des Arts.

Cheap Thrills 2044 rue Metcalfe ⓣ514/844-8988, ⓦwww.cheapthrills.ca; Métro Peel. The stock is dictated by the musical tastes of local university students. You'll find an eclectic mix of used jazz, rock, world, soul, reggae and electronica on vinyl and CD here as well as a reasonable collection of used books.

Disquivel 2035 boul St-Laurent ⓣ514/842-1607; Métro Saint-Laurent. Electronica and lounge are the norm at this used music store, as well as some dance/club music and even rock and jazz, mostly on vinyl, though CDs are becoming more prevalent. They also carry some new stuff.

HMV 1020 rue Ste-Catherine O ⓣ514/875-0765, ⓦwww.hmv.com; Métro Peel. Sure it's mammoth and impersonal, but it's also practical. Listening booths abound, and with three floors packed with all musical styles, HMV is sure to have what you're looking for.

Inbeat Record Store 3814 boul St-Laurent ⓣ514/499-2063, ⓦwww.inbeatmusic.com; bus #55. Owned by DJ Christian Pronovost, a veteran of the electronica scene, the focus here is mainly on house. You can listen to the 12" singles that make up most of the stock (along with a few CD mixes and compilations) on one of the eight available decks.

Pop Shop 3656 boul St-Laurent ⓣ514/848-6300; Métro Saint-Laurent. World music, Francophone, club music and rock show up used on vinyl and CD alongside small jazz and techno sections that deal more in new imports.

Primitive 3830 rue St-Denis ⓣ514/845-6017; **Métro Sherbrooke.** A good stop for used rock, psychobilly, punk, garage and Francophone vinyl, as well as some disco, jazz and soul.

Specialty shops

Bella Pella 3933 rue St-Denis ⓣ514/845.7328, ⓦwww.bellapella.com; **Métro Sherbrooke.** You can find a gorgeous array of handcrafted beauty products here which are made from natural ingredients that smell good enough to eat: goat's milk soap, cranberry bubble bath and lavender shampoo bars are just the start.

Condom du Fun 2015 rue Crescent ⓣ514/847-9297; **Métro Guy-Concordia.** Looking for fruity or glow-in-the-dark condoms? Head to this tiny half-basement boutique where jars of tropical-flavoured rubbers are displayed like candy and sell for $1.50 a pop. There's an assortment of other sex toys too, including inflatable sheep – in case you left yours at home.

Curio Cité 3870 rue St-Denis ⓣ514/286-0737; **Métro Sherbrooke.** A great find, this little shop is tucked under a set of stairs and packed to the hilt with knick-knacks of a predominantly Asian-influence. The sushi plates, posters, cushions and handbags are all exquisite and, best of all, affordable.

Davidoff 1458 rue Sherbrooke O ⓣ514/289-9118; **Métro Guy-Concordia.** An unabashedly posh tobacco emporium selling swanky smoking accoutrements, fine cigarettes, and all manner of cigars – with the largest humidor in town, it's *the* place to get your Cubans (Americans will have to smoke them before they head home, though – it's illegal to import them). You can settle down in one of the clubby armchairs in the smoking room in back to test your purchase.

Essence du Papier 4160 rue St-Denis ⓣ514/288-9691; **Métro Sherbrooke.** A stationery store with everything related to the pleasures of writing – elegant gift cards, notepaper and pens are on offer, along with luxurious wrapping paper.

Priape 1311 rue Ste-Catherine E ⓣ514/521-8451, ⓦwww.priape.com; **Métro Beaudry.** This has been Montréal's unofficial gay department store since 1974, with all sorts of gifts, clothing, calendars, magazines, books and videos, and a more hard-core collection of leather gear and accessories downstairs. It's also a good spot to pick up event tickets and community info.

Sporting goods

Whether it's for heading out into the woods or onto the slopes, Montréal naturally has a wide selection of sporting goods shops. In addition to the all-rounders listed below, check out Kanuk for fine winter wear (see p.195) and Chapter 16, "Sports and activities" for cycle and in-line skate shops.

Altitude Sports Plein-Air 4140 rue St-Denis ⓣ514/847-1515 or 1-800/729-0322, ⓦwww.altitude-sports.com; **Métro Mont-Royal.** A small but friendly boutique to get geared up for the outdoors. They sell and also rent sleeping bags, tents, backpacks and stoves ($30/day altogether), along with shoes, boots, clothes and other camping gear.

Inukshuk 1472 rue Peel ⓣ514/288-8010 or 1-888/592-8010, ⓦwww.inukshukpleinair.com; **Métro Peel.** A friendly budget-traveller boutique with great rates on camping rentals; you can get all the necessary gear for around $35/day, including tent, sleeping bag, backpack, mattress and stove. Of course, you can buy the stuff too.

Mountain Equipment Co-op Marché Central, 8989 boul de l'Acadie, ⓣ514/788.5878, ⓦwww.mec.ca; **bus #100, 179 or 460.** Outdoorsy Canadians are often fanatical about MEC – and with good reason: most of the clothes and accessories are their own brand and, though they can be expensive, they're top-notch. The staff tend to be avid adventure-seekers who've road-tested much of what's on offer. MEC also has a wide range of gear to rent but charge more than the others listed here. As it's a co-op, you need to purchase a membership ($5 for life). The store is located out near the junction of highways 40 and 15, so you're best to drive there.

Sports Experts 930 rue Ste-Catherine O ⓣ514/866-1914; **Métro McGill.** A one-stop, all-season, sporting-goods superstore – if you can't find what you're looking for here, then it probably doesn't exist. Also does ski and snowboard tune-ups for around $20 and $30, respectively.

16

Sports and outdoor activities

Montrealers are among the continent's most fickle **sports** fans, and in recent years their attitudes towards their **major league teams** could best be described as dejected. There are constant rumours of baseball's **Expos** leaving town, and the onetime pride of this hockey-worshipping nation, the **Canadiens**, appear to have left their glory days well behind. Indeed, the only professional sport that gets a passionate response nowadays is Canadian football – the **Alouettes** are one of the league's best teams and their games consistently sell out. Tickets to sporting events can be purchased through the Admission network (Ⓣ514/790-1245 or 1-800/361-4595, Ⓦwww.admission.com), or at individual stadium box offices.

Though professional sports may be on a downturn, Montrealers continue to indulge in **recreational sporting activities**, especially during the winter months when **cross-country skiing**, **ice-skating** and even **snowshoeing** provide excellent antidotes to the winter blues. But the city is also blessed with warm summers and residents take full advantage of them by **bicycling** and **in-line skating** along the many bike paths at their disposal. The waterways also get full use come summer as **boating** and **whitewater rafting** outfits cast-off for wet and thrilling excursions. To find any public recreational facility and enquire about opening hours and fees, call **Accès Montréal**, the city's telephone information service (Mon–Fri 8.30am–5pm; Ⓣ514/872-1111 or the 24hr automated line Ⓣ514/872-2237, Ⓦwww.ville.montreal.qc.ca/loisirs).

Hockey

The **Montréal Canadiens** are the most fabled hockey team in the National Hockey League (NHL). Some of the league's greatest stars – Ken Dryden, Guy Lafleur and Maurice "Rocket" Richard – have donned the team's classic red and blue uniforms, helping them win an astounding total of 24 Stanley Cups, professional hockey's ultimate trophy. Still, even with their storied history, *Les Habitants* (or the Habs, as they're familiarly known), have lost some polish in recent years – the team hasn't won a Stanley Cup since 1993 and their losses pile up year after year. Some claim the move from the hallowed Forum – the Habs' former digs – into the Centre Bell in 1996 put a curse on the team's game.

A perhaps even more damaging blow to the team's aura came in January 2001 when American businessman George Gillett, Jr bought a controlling interest in the Canadiens. However, the resulting influx of cash has resulted in some solid acquisitions and may mean that the end of the team's current slump may not be far away. If Hart and Vezina trophy-winning goalie José Théodore plays to form and new GM (and veteran of the Habs' glory days) Bob Gainey brings the expected sparkle, things will be looking up, indeed.

The NHL's regular season runs from October to April, and the playoffs can carry on into June. Home-game schedules are posted on ⓦwww.canadiens.com; **tickets** vary between $22 and $160 and are pretty easy to get, even on a game day.

Baseball

The **Expos**, Montréal's major-league **baseball** team, have an uncertain future. Since the franchise was created in 1968 (and named after Expo '67), it's been dogged by two major handicaps: a poor stadium in which to play baseball (the Stade Olympique, see p.111), and insufficient funds to compete with major-market teams. And it's debatable whether the team will stay at all – after promises to give them a downtown stadium were dashed, the team was bought out by Major League Baseball itself in February 2002, which decided to stage some of the Expos' 2003 "home" games in San Juan, Puerto Rico. Pretty much the only reason Montréal hasn't yet lost the franchise is that no American city (that can afford the team) seems to want them.

The good news, though, is that **tickets** to a game are the cheapest in the league, starting at $8 – the most expensive cost a paltry $36 – and good seats abound since so few people actually attend the games. The season runs from April to October; check ⓦwww.expos.mlb.com for schedules.

Football

Canadian **football**, though lacking the panache of its American counterpart, is still good fun: it's played on a longer and wider field than its southern version, with twelve rather than eleven players on each team and three rather than four downs to advance the ball in ten-yard increments. The result is a faster-paced, arguably more dramatic game; and it's one that Montréal's team, the **Alouettes**, excel at. The Als won the league title – the Grey Cup – in 2002.

You'll need to buy tickets well in advance if you want to see the Alouettes play. The season runs from August to November, culminating with the Grey Cup playoffs, and the games are played at McGill University's recently renovated Molson Stadium, at 475 av des Pins O; catch bus #144 from either Sherbrooke or Atwater Métro stations or the shuttle from Bonaventure or McGill stations. **Tickets** cost $17.50 to $65 for regular games, but go up to $100 for playoffs. Home-game schedules are posted on ⓦwww.montrealalouettes.com.

Motorsports

Until recently, **motorsports** meant one thing in Montréal – the **Grand Prix** (ⓣ514/350-0000, ⓦwww.grandprix.ca). For 25 years, the Circuit Gilles-Villeneuve on Île Notre-Dame has been a spectacle of roaring engines and whizzing blurs of colours as the Formula 1 racecars sped around the track.

Downhill skiing

Although Montrealers may call it a mountain, Mont Royal is no place for downhill skiing. Instead, city-dwellers head out of town in droves for the ski hills in the Laurentides (Laurentian Mountains). The region begins with Mont St-Sauveur, which has good night skiing and a trendy après-ski scene, and heads as far north as all-inclusive Mont Tremblant, the biggest resort in the province. To the east, the spread-out hills in the Cantons-de-l'Est (Eastern Townships) have the most interesting terrain and gladed areas for expert skiers. The province's other main ski district is the Québec City area, with mountains close enough that you can base yourself in the country's most romantic city. For details, see the appropriate "Out of the City" chapters.

It's named after Gilles Villeneuve, who won his first Grand Prix race here during the track's 1978 debut, and died when his Ferrari flipped during qualifying at the Belgian Grand Prix four years later. His son, Jacques, carried on the family tradition, winning the Indianapolis 500 and CART championships in 1995 before moving to the F1 circuit, winning the 1997 world championship for Williams. His luck failed after joining the fledgling BAR (British American Racing) team in 1999 and at the end of 2003 his contract wasn't renewed. Things don't look much better for the Montréal Grand Prix itself: at press time it's uncertain whether the tradition will come to an end, due to the clash between government laws banning tobacco advertising and the cigarette logos emblazoned on many of the cars.

Fortunately for motorsports fans, Montréal was added to the CART circuit in 2002. While it doesn't have the same international cachet, the **Molson Indy** (Ⓣ514/394-9000, Ⓦwww.molsonindy.ca) is still a big deal, and will certainly absorb some of the hoopla surrounding the Grand Prix, should the city lose its biggest tourist draw. As with the Grand Prix, tickets go quickly – reserve well in advance.

Cross-country skiing

After a heavy snowfall, city residents often treat main streets as **cross-country ski** trails. During the rest of the winter, they tote their skis to the numerous **trails** located around town, though by far the most popular are the 20km of well-groomed paths winding around Mont Royal (the same paths that make great jogging trails in warmer months). Other hotspots for cross-country skiing are the Lachine Canal path and Île Ste-Hélène, which aren't groomed, but are far more serene than the heavily used mountain paths. Otherwise, the wintry flora and fauna of the Jardin Botanique can also be cruised on skis. Information on additional trails on the city's fringes and ski conditions is available through the **Parcs Nature** network (Ⓣ514/280-7272, Ⓦwww.ville.montreal.qc.ca/parcs-nature); your best option for ski **rentals** is Mont Royal's Pavillon du Lac aux Castors ($6/hr, $10/3hr; Ⓣ514/843-8240), which also rents **snowshoes** for stomping the trails ($5/hr, $8/3hr).

Ice-skating

A mind-boggling 166 public **skating rinks** are open from late December to late February in Montréal's parks, used for figure skating, "shinny" (informal

Snow fun

For a quick blast of winter fun, head to the slides at the top of Mont Royal, which are frozen over for **inner-tubing**, weather permitting (Wed–Fri 10am–5pm, Sat 10am–8pm, Sun 10am–6pm; $7 including inner tube at the Pavillon du Lac aux Castors).

If snow conditions are good, you can have as much fun simply sliding down the mountain's gentler slopes – locals often just bring carpets and sleds to the corner of the park near the intersection of avenues du Parc and du Mont-Royal.

To experience the full range of ways locals have made the cold climate more enjoyable, plan your visit to coincide with the Fête des Neiges (see p.211) and the more extravagant Carnaval de Québec (see p.259).

hockey matches) and just plain goofing off. The best of the lot are Mont Royal's Lac aux Castors (where rentals are available for $6/3hr) and Parc Lafontaine's ponds, though a much less crowded option is the Olympic Rowing Basin on Île Notre-Dame. The city-run sports and recreational service keeps daily tabs on rink conditions (Mon–Fri 9am–noon & 1–6pm; ⓣ514/872-2644), which vary greatly as nearly all are naturally frozen and exist at the whim of the temperature. Montréal's only artificial outdoor rink is the privately run one on Bassin Bonsecours down in the Vieux-Port (Mon–Wed 11am–9pm, Thurs & Fri 11am–10pm, Sat & Sun10am–10pm; $3; ⓣ514/496-7678) and it's always kept in smooth, polished shape by Zamboni machines. If you're looking to go **indoors**, head downtown to the year-round rink in the Atrium Le 1000, 1000 rue de la Gauchetière O (Sun & Tues–Fri 11.30am–6pm, Sat 11.30am–7pm; $5.50; ⓣ514/395-0555); there's also a DJ night for the over-sixteen crowd on Saturday nights from 7 to 10pm.

Cycling

Montréal gets high marks for its **bicycle**-friendly attitude, boasting 400km of trails throughout the city streets and parklands. You'll find bike stands on most major streets, and some thoroughfares also have two-way lanes and traffic lights specifically for cyclists – look for the sections marked off by waist-high metal posts. Still, the most popular routes are those totally immune to car traffic, the path alongside the Lachine Canal being among the most picturesque. The circuitous roads that traverse Île Notre-Dame and Île Ste-Hélène are also well travelled, while the nearby 2.4km Circuit Gilles-Villeneuve teems with cyclists when it's not in use by Formula One drivers. Further afield, the P'tit Train du Nord is an excellent 200km cycle trail on an old rail bed through spectacular Laurentian scenery (see Chapter 20, "The Laurentians"), part of the 4300km *La Route Verte* system of cycle paths that criss-cross the province (ⓦwww.routeverte.com).

The city's best **cycling resource** is the Maison des Cyclistes, 1251 rue Rachel E (ⓣ514/521-8356, ⓦwww.velo.qc.ca), an outfit that sells books, maps and gear and organizes the annual Féria du Vélo races (see p.212) and guided bike tours in the countryside. They also publish *Cycling in Montréal*, a detailed cycling guide with maps. Although they no longer do **rentals**, you can pick up wheels at nearby Cycle Pop, 1000 rue Rachel E (Mon–Wed 10am–7pm, Thurs & Fri 10am–8pm, Sat & Sun 9am–6pm; $15/4hr, $25/24hr; ⓣ514/526-2525, ⓦwww.cyclepop.ca); rollerblades are available for the same prices, as well as $7 for just one hour. In addtion, they offer a full-day 84km **tour** to the western tip of the island along the lakeshore and back for $60. Tours of other Montréal neighbourhoods are offered by Vélo-Tour Montréal, 3880 rue Rachel E (Ⓣ514/259-7272, Ⓦwww.velomontreal.com; Métro Pie-IX) on an ad hoc basis for $40 per person (minimum $200); they also rent bikes ($20/4hr, $30/24hr). For rentals and tours in Vieux-Montréal, see box, p.180.

Skateboarding and in-line skating

Most Montrealers show no regard whatsoever for the law banning **in-line skates** and **skateboards** from the streets of the city – though there are perfectly legal ways to partake of both activities. As with biking and cross-country skiing, the Lachine Canal and the Formula One racetrack get most of the action, but Parc Lafontaine draws its share of rollerbladers too.

Though the city's public squares get high traffic from boarders, especially after nightfall, neither the authorities nor the locals look favourably on the activity. There is a good outlet for skateboarders, however, in the **outdoor skate-park** of Parc Jarry. It's a bit out of the way, northwest of Little Italy, but it's equipped with brilliant ramps and half-pipes and, best of all, is free (daily 6am–midnight; Ⓣ514/872-1111). Otherwise, try the latest incarnation of Le TAZ Roulodôme, an indoor skate park and blading centre due to re-open in a former incinerator at 1310 rue des Carrières (Ⓣ514/284-0051, Ⓦwww.taz.ca; Métro Rosemont) – call ahead for schedule and prices. Several shops **rent** blades (along with wrist and kneepads) for around $7/hr or $30/24hr, including the Plateau's Cycle Pop (see opposite) and three outfits in the Vieux-Port area (see box, p.80).

Whitewater rafting, jet-boating and cruises

The Lachine Rapids that once prohibited ships from travelling between Montréal and Lachine get ample **boating** action nowadays in the form of inflatable zodiacs and jet-boats that **raft** the current. Two quality outfits (listed below) run trips down the choppy waters; you're guaranteed to get wet, so bring along a change of clothing.

Less demanding, but a nevertheless great way to see the city, are the meandering river **cruises** on glassed-in boats that depart from the Vieux-Port; more unusual is the amphibious **Amphi-bus** that sails on water and also drives along the streets of Vieux-Montréal. Both types of cruises are covered in "Land and water tours", p.30. For cruises and boat rentals on the **Lachine Canal**, see box, p.128. You can also rent watercraft on Île Notre-Dame (p.121) or take a turn on pedal-boats in the placid Bassin Bonsecours (p.83) and the ponds at Parc Lafontaine (p.95).

Bicycle practicalities

Note that in Montréal bicycles are subject to the same rules of the road as cars, though there's no equivalent to the seatbelt law (the city doesn't mandate that cyclists wear protective helmets). Bikes are also allowed in the Métro when it's not rush hour, but only in the first car (Mon–Fri 10am–3pm & 7pm–close; all-day Sat, Sun & holidays).

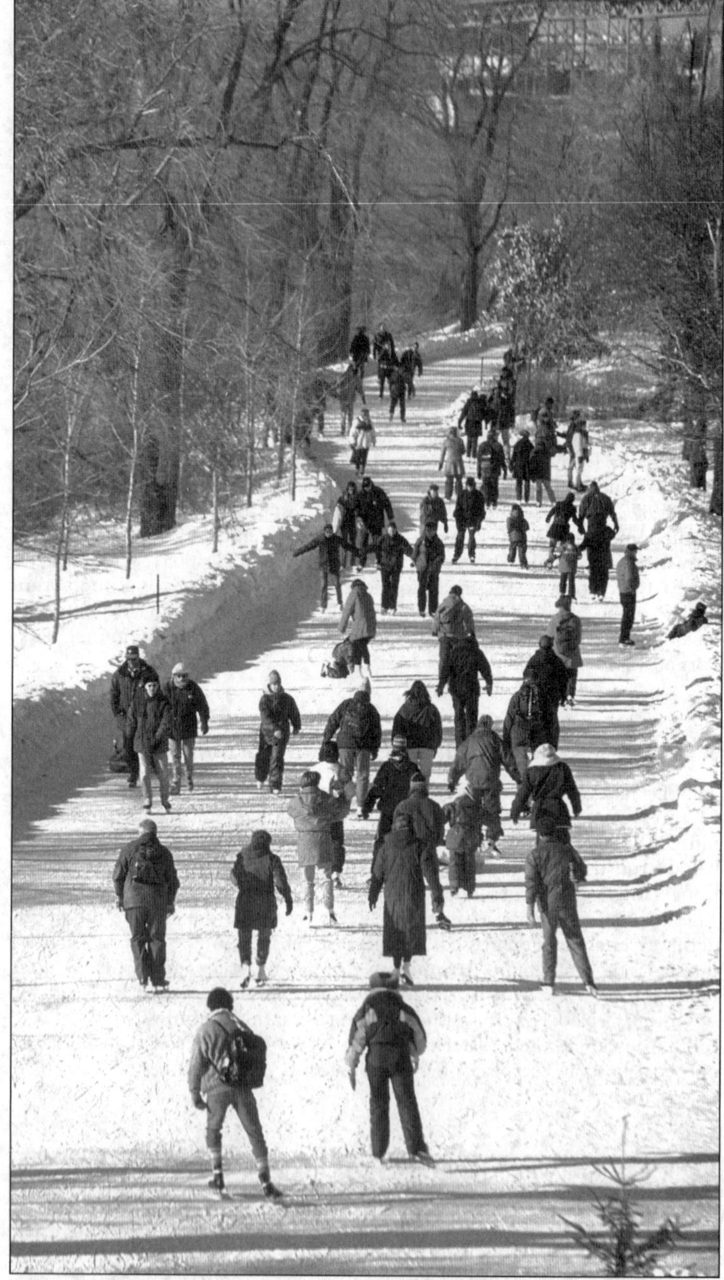

△ Skating at Parc Jean-Drapeau

Les Descentes sur le St-Laurent ⓣ **514/767-2230 or 1-800/324-7238,** ⓦ **www.raftingmontreal.com.** Located further afield than their competitor below, Les Descentes cast off from 8912 boul LaSalle (May–Sept daily 9am–6pm, times vary) and offer similar options of jet-boating (1 hour 15 minutes; $52) or rafting the frothy rapids (2 hours 15 minutes; $45). The best way to get there is via the shuttle bus service provided from the Centre Infotouriste at 1001 Square Dorchester. Reservations strongly recommended.

Saute-Moutons ⓣ **514/284-9607,** ⓦ **www.jetboatingmontreal.com.** Jet boats depart from the Vieux-Port's Quai de l'Horloge (May to mid-Oct every 2hr 10am–6pm; $55) for a wild and woolly 1hr ride through the Lachine Rapids (you can opt to raft down them as well). The company also runs 20-minute speedboat tours around the Vieux-Port ($22), which depart from the Quai Jacques-Cartier. Reservations recommended; arrive 45 minutes prior to departure.

17

Kids' Montréal

Montréal may not appear to be a child's city, with so much focus on the grown-up pursuits of shopping, dining and nightlife, but those with tots in tow can rest assured that there are plenty of activities tailor-made to keep kids engaged. The many **outdoor parks**, notably Mont Royal, Parc Lafontaine and Parc Jean-Drapeau – where you can picnic and ride pedal-boats along the waterways – are ideal for spending an afternoon simply playing and lounging about. **Boat trips** on the St Lawrence (see p.30) are another favourite pastime and a fun way to see the city – the same goes for the **funicular** ride up the leaning tower above the Stade Olympique (see p.111). There are also a number of exceptionally kid-friendly museums, listed and cross-referenced below. Be sure to ask about family rates before purchasing tickets for any of the attractions listed in this chapter.

Museums and sights

The **Biosphère**, where exciting exhibits on water ecology include squirt-guns and water drums (see p.119), stress the fun side of learning. The **Jardin Botanique de Montréal**'s lush gardens, especially the Chinese and Japanese pavilions, are equally captivating (see p.112). For animal spotting, head to the **Biodôme**, where monkeys frolic amidst the greenery (see p.111). The **Insectarium** (see p.114), with its creepy-crawly bugs, and the **Centre des Sciences de Montréal** (see p.82), filled with interactive science displays, are obvious places to let the kids loose; both appeal to the curious-minded, not to mention the always-important gross-out factor. For creative activities, the **Musée des Beaux-Arts** (see p.62), **Musée d'Art Contemporain** (see p.55) and **Musée McCord** (see p.59), have supervised art classes and activities, including summer day camps, for kids who might be too young to appreciate the main exhibitions.

Though further afield, both the **Centre-de-Commerce-de-la-Fourrure-à Lachine** (see p.128) and the **Maison St-Gabriel** (see p.124) historical sites provide good Sunday diversions with costumed performances, demonstrations and activities that bring the city's past to life.

Activities

For a less informative, but no less fun, kind of entertainment, you can visit one of the **arcades** along rue Ste-Catherine ouest, though your best bet for one-stop recreation is the big **movie complexes** (see p.189). In addition to video games and movie theatres decked out with comfy armchairs, the Paramount has an IMAX screen while the Forum has a bowling alley with UV-lighting, fluorescent pins, pounding music and video screens (and a bar nearby for over-stimulated parents). There's also plenty to do at the array of outdoor **festivals** (see Chapter 18) and more **active pursuits** to partake in (see Chapter 16, "Sports and outdoor activities"), notably along the Vieux-Port's promenade and on and along the Lachine Canal. Likewise, there's plenty of family-friendly activities a short drive from Montréal – both the Laurentians and Eastern Townships have beginners' ski runs in winter and water parks and a host of other activities come summer – see the "Out of the City" chapters of this book. Otherwise, any of the options listed below should prove to be worthwhile distractions. Your best resource for additional activities is the "Family" section in the *Montreal Gazette*'s daily "What's On" listings.

Finally, for sheer thrills, the city's **amusement park** (see p.120) can't be beat, though it will probably sap a great deal of energy (and dollars) on your part. For a more relaxed day, bring a picnic lunch and wander about the rest of the islands, perhaps taking a pedal-boat through the canals of the Jardins des Floralies.

Abracadabra! Musée Juste pour Rire, 2111 boul St-Laurent; $6. ⓣ514/845-5105 ⓦwww.hahaha.com; Métro St-Laurent. The not-so-funny Just For Laughs museum redeems itself with this exhibition for 4–12-year-olds. It comprises magic shows (including one where the tricks are revealed) and a room full of optical illusions that is itself an optical illusion. English-language shows are Sat 10am & 11.15am, but call to check if other times may be available.

Céramic Café Studio 4201-B rue St-Denis. Mon–Wed 10am–11pm, Thurs 10am–midnight, Fri & Sat 10am–1am, Sun 10am–10pm. ⓣ514/848-1119; Métro Sherbrooke or Mont-Royal. Children explore their creative sides by painting on ceramic mugs, bowls and plates. Just note that you'll need to go back and pick up the piece a week later ($5 for a three-day rush). Prices start at $8 for a mug, with $7 hourly fees added to the total to cover the paint and glazing. There's a second location near the Vieux-Port at 95 rue de la Commune E, ⓣ514/861-1611.

Labyrinthe du Hangar 16 Quai de l'Horloge, Vieux-Port. Mid-May to mid-June & Sept Sat & Sun 11.30am–5.30pm; mid-June to Aug daily 11am–9pm; Oct Fri 6.30–9pm, Sat 11.30am–9pm, Sun 11.30am–5.30pm; $11 adults, $10 teens, $9 children. ⓣ514/499-0099, ⓦwww.labyrintheduhangar16.com; Métro Champ-de-Mars. It might come as a shock to kids raised on computer games, but they will actually have to navigate corridors and overcome obstacles in person to solve the mystery of this maze.

Laser Quest 1226 rue Ste-Catherine O. Late June to early Sept Mon–Thurs 2–11pm, Fri & Sat noon–midnight, Sun noon–10pm; early Sept to late June Wed & Thurs 4–10pm, Fri 4pm–midnight, Sat noon–midnight, Sun noon–8pm. ⓣ514/393-3000; Métro Peel. A video game brought to life as players armed with lasers chase each other through a dark maze, along catwalks, and up various ramps while sound effects echo around them. Each game lasts 20 minutes and costs $7.50; twice the time is $10.

Planétarium de Montréal 1000 rue St-Jacques O. Late June to early Sept Sat–Mon 12.30–5pm, Tues–Fri 10am–5pm, also Fri–Sun 6.45–8.30pm; early Sept to late June Mon–Fri 9.30am–5pm, Sat & Sun 9.45am–5pm, also Fri–Sun 6.45–8.30pm; $6.50 adults, $3.25 under-17s. ⓣ514/872-4530, ⓦwww.planetarium.montreal.qc.ca; Métro Bonaventure. Documentaries about the solar system are projected onto the Planetarium's domed ceiling while you lie back in reclined chairs; the stars and planets swooshing above produce a fun out-of-body experience, and sneak in some education also. English and French showtimes are staggered – contact the Planetarium for schedules.

Shops

When the kids get tired of pushing buttons – both yours and the exhibits' – you can always get lost in one of Montréal's **malls** (see p.196). You won't find the best **children's stores** in the malls, though; they tend to be a bit more scattered about. We've listed a few of the best below.

Chez Farfelu 843 av du Mont-Royal E ⓣ514/528-6251; Métro Mont-Royal. The name means scatterbrained – and it's meant in the best way possible. The shop's shelves are chock full of amusing gimmicks and squishy toys. A second location across the street, at no. 838, brims with kid-friendly accessories like cartoon-decorated cups and saucers and colourful shower curtains.

Citrouille 206 rue Laurier O ⓣ514/948-0555; Métro Laurier or bus #80. This small Mile End boutique is the place to shop for unique, creative wooden toys like trains, building blocks and string puppets. Most are imported from Europe and are of excellent quality.

Franc Jeu 4152 rue St-Denis ⓣ514/849-9253; Métro Mont-Royal or Sherbrooke. Franc Jeu's shelves stock everything from board games to wooden toys and collectible stickers. Be sure to check the language of the game you buy though – they come in both French and English at this Plateau store.

Oink Oink 1343 av Greene ⓣ514/939-2634; Métro Atwater. The ground floor of this Westmount boutique is devoted to selling heaps of Hello Kitty gear alongside girly accessories like rhinestone headbands, fanciful make-up and feathery boas. Although the focus is much less on boys, they can have fun, too, with the model building sets, plastic figurines and board games upstairs. There's also a good selection of kids' clothing and some original novelty gifts, like old trading cards and squirting cameras, that'll appeal to nostalgic parents. Closed Sun.

Scarlett O'Hara Jr 256 av du Mont-Royal E ⓣ514/842-6336; Métro Mont-Royal. There aren't many used children's-clothing stores in Montréal to begin with, and there definitely isn't one to match Scarlett O'Hara Jr, where the focus is on quality brand names like Le Petit Bateau, OshKosh and Deux par Deux in sizes from 0–12 for both boys and girls.

Uni Foods 1029 boul St-Laurent ⓣ514/866-9889; Métro Place-d'Armes. Don't let the bland name put you off; Uni Foods is the most original candy store in town. Its Chinatown location gives it an exotic edge, and kids will go crazy over the Hello Kitty strawberry-flavoured pretzel sticks and candy boxes embossed with various Pokémon characters.

Le Valet d'Coeur 4408 rue St-denis ⓣ514/499-9970, ⓦwww.levalet.com; Métro Mont-Royal. A great spot for older kids (especially boys), as there's a wide selection of role-playing games and figurines here, in addition to board games, jigsaw puzzles, kites and a few toys like plastic dinosaurs.

Theatre and puppet shows

While there are several children's theatre troupes in Montréal, none of them have their own stages. Your best chance of seeing one perform is at the **Centaur**, 453 rue St-François-Xavier (ⓣ514/288-3161, ⓦwww.centaurtheatre.com), which hosts a Saturday Morning Children's Series (show time is 10.30am, tickets cost $5 adults, $3 children). Their children's classics performances are generally of high quality (they sell out fast), and a few educational pieces are thrown into the programme too. **La Maison Théâtre**, at 245 rue Ontario E (ⓣ514/288-7211, ⓦwww.maisontheatre.qc.ca) stages mostly Francophone plays, but occasionally puts on silent puppet shows. The curtain rises at 3pm Sat and Sun during the October to May season and tickets cost $17.25 adults, $13.25 children.

18

Festivals and events

Perhaps as a reaction to the long harsh winters, Montréal's social calendar is booked solid throughout the warmer months, with one or more big **festivals** happening nearly every week. Folks take to the blocked-off streets in the thousands for huge, wonderfully exuberant international events like the jazz and film festivals, where a wonderfully exuberant atmosphere pervades. In the cooler months the regular performing-arts season is supplemented by a host of smaller film festivals, and there's a variety of ethnic celebrations on offer all year long. Québec City's main festivals – including the famous Carnaval – are described on p.259.

While the selection of events below can give you a general idea of what's on, it's worth asking for the quarterly *What to do in Montreal* guide put out by **Tourisme Montréal** (see p.23).

January

La Fête des Neiges (late Jan to early Feb) Île Ste-Hélène is transformed into a winter playground for three straight weekends during the chilliest time of the year. There's a massive snow-castle to explore, ice-skating trails and toboggan-friendly hills to romp around on, as well as horse- and dog-sled rides. ⓣ514/872-4537, ⓦwww.fetedesneiges.com/en.

February

Festival Montréal en Lumière (late Feb) The Montreal High Lights Festival brightens up the city with video and pyrotechnic performances – with frequently spectacular results. DJ sets, gastronomic events, and theatre, music and dance performances by some of the city's top companies round out the ten-day festival. ⓣ514/288-9955 or 1-888/477-9955, ⓦwww.montrealhighlights.com.

March

Festival International du Film sur Art (mid-month) There are some fascinating subjects among the hundreds of documentaries shown at downtown cinemas during the ten-day International Festival of Films on Art. Profiles of architects, composers and writers run alongside screenings of creative output such as ballet performances. ⓣ514/874-1637, ⓦwww.artfifa.com.

St Patrick's Day Parade (mid-month) Regardless of their own ethnic heritage, most everyone in Montréal sports green for one of the largest and longest-running – the first parade was in 1824 – celebrations of all things Irish. The parade is always on the Sunday closest to March 17 and rolls down rue Ste-Catherine. ⓣ514/932-0512, ⓦwww.montrealirishparade.com.

April

Metropolis Bleu (early Apr) The five-day Blue Metropolis literary festival brings Québécois and international writers (such as Margaret Drabble and Norman Mailer) together for multilingual readings, signings, panel discussions and a "translation slam". ⓣ514/937-2538, ⓦwww.blue-met-bleu.com.

May

La Féria du Vélo de Montréal (late May to early June) The Tour de l'Île de Montréal is billed as the world's largest bicycle race – the 48km spin around the island attracts over 30,000 participants annually. It caps off a week of cycling events, including night-time and kids' rides, under the Montréal Bike Fest banner. Advance registration required. ⓣ514/521-8687 or 1-888/899-1111, ⓦwww.velo.qc.ca/feria.

Mutek (late May) A five-day festival of underground electronic music and digital culture, with acts like Señor Coconut and laptop techno-mixers Narod Niki. ⓦwww.mutek.ca.

Festival de Théâtre des Amériques (late May to early June) Half of the twenty or so plays staged at Montréal's largest theatre festival in English, performed by companies – often young and experimental – from throughout the Americas. The FTA runs in odd-numbered years; the related but much smaller Théâtres du Monde, with half a dozen plays, occurs in even years. ⓣ514/871-2224 or 1-866/844-2172, ⓦwww.fta.qc.ca.

June

Mondial de la Bière (early June) Once a year, for the better part of a week, Gare Windsor turns into a giant booze can, with more than 300 varieties of beer, scotch and whiskey on offer. There are various forms of entertainment, but testing one's limits of inebriation seems to be the main draw at this Wed–Sun bender. ⓣ514/722-9640, ⓦwww.festivalmondialbiere.qc.ca.

First People's Festival (mid-month) A celebration of Québec's First Nations takes over Place Émilie-Gamelin for a weekend of concerts, traditional dance and exhibitions of aboriginal sculpture and painting; a mini film festival runs concurrently at the NFB and the Cinémathèque Québécoise. ⓣ514/278-4040, ⓦwww.nativelynx.qc.ca.

Le Festival Fringe de Montréal (mid-month) With tickets priced at $9 or less, the Fringe Festival brings affordable theatre and dance to venues around the Main for ten days. The quality of productions varies wildly, so head first to the beer tent at Parc des Amériques to catch the buzz on what the must-see shows are (and listen to the free rock concerts). ⓣ514/849-3378, ⓦwww.montrealfringe.ca.

Grand Prix (mid-month) For one weekend every June, Formula One cars battle it out on the Circuit Gilles-Villeneuve on Île Notre-Dame. If you don't want to shell out the $50-and-up ticket price, at least check out the entertainment (including car and fashion shows) on rues Crescent and Peel, and boul St-Laurent. Note: at press time, the future of the Grand Prix in Montréal was in doubt, dependent on whether a way could be found to bypass legislation banning tobacco advertising. ⓣ514/350-0000, ⓦwww.grandprix.ca.

Montreal International Fireworks Competition (mid-June through July) Saturday evenings (as well as a couple of Wed nights) feature fantastic half-hour fireworks displays over the St Lawrence starting at 10pm. Although you can pay to hear an orchestra accompany the pyrotechnics at La Ronde ($35–45; includes ride pass), most Montrealers watch from the Pont Jacques-Cartier, the Vieux-Port or whatever rooftop terrace they can find. ⓣ514/397-2000, ⓦwww.lemondialsaq.com.

Fête Nationale du Québec (June 24) The provincial holiday – St-Jean-Baptiste Day – sees thousands parading down the street on June 24th, proudly waving the blue-and-white *fleur-de-lis* of the Québec flag. Many events take place the evening before, with fireworks, concerts and loads of neighbourhood block parties throughout the city. ⓣ514/849-2560, ⓦwww.cfn.org or www.fetenationale.qc.ca.

△ Festival International de Jazz de Montréal

Street sales

Just about anything can provide an excuse for outdoor festivities in Montréal, and street sales are no exception. While there are a number of sidewalk sales focused mainly on bargains – including one on rue Ste-Catherine in mid-July – two in particular, the Nuit Blanche sur Tableau Noir and Main Madness, are more like fairs than markets. In addition to racks of cheap clothing and piles of household goods, bars and restaurants stretch out terraces onto the street for al fresco drinking and dining, and there are stages set up here and there where you can catch free musical acts.

Things kick off in mid-June with the Nuit Blanche sur Tableau Noir on **avenue du Mont-Royal** (ⓦwww.mont-royal.net or www.tableaunoir.com), between rues St-Hubert and de Lorimier, where locals work into the wee hours painting murals on the road, setting a colourful stage for a weekend of shopping and entertainment. The following weekend, Main Madness sees **boulevard St-Laurent** (ⓣ514/286-0334, ⓦwww.boulevardsaintlaurent.com) become one massive four-day street party, with the blocks between rue Sherbrooke and avenue du Mont-Royal packed with people browsing and nibbling during the day, and carrying on for an amazing night out for drinking. Main Madness coincides with part of the Fringe Festival (see p.212), as well as the Magnifico series of outdoor film screenings opposite Ex-Centris, for some soberer evening fun. They shut down the Main again the second-last weekend in August for another splurge, while avenue du Mont-Royal's sidewalk sale the following weekend is more commercially oriented.

Festival Montréal Baroque (late June) Vieux-Montréal venues like the Chapelle Notre-Dame-de-Bon-Secours provide the appropriate ambience for the music of Bach and his contemporaries. There are also free concerts at Place-Royale and Baroque dance classes to get you in the mood. ⓣ514/845-7171, ⓦwww.montrealbaroque.com.

Festival International de Jazz de Montréal (late June to early July) During the world's best jazz festival, the streets around Place des Arts are shut down for hundreds of free concerts on a dozen or so stages; the major show, held the middle of the festival's second week, draws an audience of up to 200,000 good-humoured revellers. There's usually a range of other genres, from salsa to hip-hop, to check out if jazz isn't your bag, whereas there are jazz documentaries and concert films at the Cinémathèque and even an off-festival (ⓦwww.lofffestivaldejazz.com) for serious aficionados. ⓣ514/871-1881, or 1-888/515-0515, ⓦwww.montrealjazzfest.com.

July

Canada Day (July 1) While there's a parade along with fireworks, and festivities in the Vieux-Port promoted as Célafête, Canada Day is better known to most Montrealers as "moving day". A large percentage of leases end on July 1, and it's hilarious to watch the scramble as thousands try to move house on the same day. ⓣ514/866-9164, ⓦwww.celafete.ca.

Carifiesta (early July) It's too cold in February for a Caribbean-style Carnival, so the colourful parade along boul René-Lévesque takes place in summer instead. The calypso music and dancers of the *mas* bands move on to the big party at Champ de Mars afterwards, where you can, of course, tuck into some spicy Caribbean cooking. ⓣ514/735-2232, ⓦwww.carifiesta.ca.

Festival International Nuits d'Afrique (early to mid-July) Two-week African and Caribbean music festival best attended during the three days of outdoor concerts in Place Émilie-Gamelin. ⓣ514/499-3462, ⓦwww.festivalnuitsdafrique.com.

Juste pour Rire (mid-month) Over a thousand free shows (including street theatre and concerts) in the Quartier Latin and hundreds more at venues around the city comprise the Just for Laughs Festival, one of the world's largest comedy festivals. The best acts are always at the sell-out "Gala" shows at Théâtre St-Denis. ⓣ514/790-4242, ⓦwww.hahaha.com.

FanTasia (mid-July to early Aug) A great chance to see genre films, from Japanese animé fantasies to zombie gore-fests, that you won't otherwise catch on the big screen. ⓦwww.fantasiafestival.com.

Les FrancoFolies de Montréal (late July to early Aug) Hot on the heels of the jazz festival, rue Ste-Catherine is again closed for ten days for this celebration of French song and music from around the world. Indoor shows at various city venues supplement more than a hundred free outdoor shows ranging from traditional *chansons* to hip-hop. ⓣ514/876-8989 or 1-888/444-9114, ⓦwww.francofolies.com.

Divers/Cité (late July to early Aug) On the first Sunday in August, the biggest event of the year for Montréal's queer community takes place with a massive parade from Downtown to the Village, full of colourful and outrageous costumes, cheered on by more than half a million spectators. A week-long series of parties, concerts and events in celebration of gay and lesbian pride precedes the main event. ⓣ514/285-4011, ⓦwww.diverscite.org.

August

Rogers AT&T Canada Cup / Tennis Masters Series (early Aug) The brightest stars in the tennis universe descend on Parc Jarry (northwest of Little Italy) for an international tournament, with women playing even-numbered years and men the odd. The best seats are usually sold out half a year in advance. ⓣ514/273-1515, ⓦwww.tennis canada.com.

L'International de Montgolfières (mid-Aug) A great treat for the kids, the nine-day International Balloon Festival in St-Jean-sur-Richelieu (20min drive east of Montréal) features over a hundred colourful hot-air balloons in all sorts of wacky designs that are lit up at night like giant Chinese lanterns. Concerts and events help keep those on the ground (and unprepared to pay for a $150 flight) entertained. ⓣ450/347-9555, ⓦwww.montgolfieres.com.

Molson Indy (mid/late August) Montréal joined North America's premier motosports series in 2002. The turbo-charged Champ cars compete for the annual CART championships, roaring around the Circuit Gilles-Villeneuve at up to 240mph. ⓣ514/394-9000, ⓦwww.molsonindy.ca.

Festival des Films du Monde Montréal (late Aug to early Sept) Although Toronto's higher-profile festival tends to nab more premieres, you still might catch a few stars at the Montreal World Film Festival. Even if you don't, there's plenty happening, including films on the outdoor screen in front of Place des Arts. Screenings at the Cinéma Impérial and other downtown cinemas cost $10 – cheaper if you buy in bulk. ⓣ514/848-3883, ⓦwww.ffm-montreal.org.

September

Le Mois de la Photo (Sept–Oct) For over a month every odd-numbered year, Montréal becomes a giant photo gallery, with over a dozen simultaneous photography exhibitions scattered about town. ⓣ514/390-0383, ⓦwww.moisdelaphoto.com.

Image + Nation (late Sept to early Oct) The largest of its kind in Canada, Montreal's festival of gay, lesbian, bisexual and transgendered films offers thought-provoking and occasionally silly glimpses of the lives and fantasies of the queer community. ⓣ514/285-1562, ⓦwww.image-nation.org.

Festival International de Nouvelle Danse (FIND) (late Sept to mid-Oct) One of the world's best gatherings for energetic contemporary dance companies is centred at L'Agora de la Danse (see p.186). In addition to home-grown talent, the biennial festival (odd-numbered years) showcases top dance troupes from around the world. ⓣ514/287-1423, ⓦwww.find-lab.com.

October

Black & Blue Festival (early Oct) A festival of cultural events, sports and club nights fills the week leading up to the Canadian Thanksgiving weekend, when the Black &

Blue, a huge gay circuit party and AIDS fundraiser, fills the Olympic Stadium with some 18,000 all-night revellers. ⓣ514/875-7026, ⓦwww.bbcm.org.

Festival International Nouveau Cinéma Nouveau Médias (mid-month) Given the strength of the city's multimedia industry, it's fitting that the International Festival of New Cinema and New Media, showcasing cutting-edge works in cinema, video and digital media is held in the Plateau's suitably high-tech Ex-Centris cinema. ⓣ514/847-9272, ⓦwww.fcmm.com.

November

Cinemania (early to mid-Nov) Ten days of screenings of independent French-language films – all with English subtitles – at the Musée des Beaux-Arts. ⓣ514/878-0082, ⓦwww.cinemaniafilmfestival.com.

Santa Claus Parade (late Nov) The big guy in red draws over a quarter of a million spectators to rue Ste-Catherine, though for many Montrealers it's the unveiling of the Christmas display in the Ogilvy department-store window that truly marks the start of the holiday season.

December

Salon des métiers d'art du Québec (early to mid-Dec) Hundreds of mostly Québécois artisans display their creations for sale in the lead-up to Christmas at Place Bonaventure. ⓣ514/861-2787, ⓦwww.salondesmetiersdart.com.

New Year's Eve (Dec 31) In addition to the wide array of parties thrown in the city's clubs and bars, you can see in the new year under the stars at the Place Jacques-Cartier Formal Ball's heated outdoor dance area. ⓣ514/871-1873.

Directory

Airport Aéroport International Pierre-Elliott-Trudeau de Montréal ⓣ514/394-7377 or 1-800/465-1213, ⓦwww.admtl.com. Renamed at the beginning of 2004, it's better known as Aéroport de Montréal-Dorval, or simply Dorval airport. See p.25 for details.

Car rental Avis, 1225 rue Metcalfe ⓣ514/866-7906; Budget, 1240 rue Guy ⓣ514/938-1000; Discount, 607 boul de Maisonneuve O ⓣ514/286-1554; Hertz Canada, 1073 rue Drummond ⓣ514/938-1717; Thrifty, 845 rue Ste-Catherine E ⓣ514/845-5954; Via Route, 1255 rue Mackay ⓣ514/871-1166, which charges a bit less than the majors. See p.28 for toll-free reservation numbers and websites.

City information Accès Montréal (ⓣ514/872-2237, ⓦwww.ville.montreal.qc.ca) has recorded information on all manner of municipal services, from tennis courts to parking tickets.

Consulates France 1 Place Ville Marie ⓣ514/878-4385, ⓦwww.consulfrance-montreal.org; **Germany** 1250 boul René-Lévesque O ⓣ514/931-2277, ⓦwww.montreal.diplo.de; **Italy** 3489 rue Drummond ⓣ514/849-8351, ⓦwww.italconsul.montreal.qc.ca; **Japan** 600 rue de la Gauchetière O ⓣ514/866-3429, ⓦwww.montreal.ca.emb-japan.go.jp; **UK** 1000 rue de la Gauchetière O ⓣ514/866-5863, ⓦwww.britainincanada.org; **US** 1155 rue St-Alexandre ⓣ514/398-9695, www.usembassycanada.gov. For the following countries, contact the embassy in Ottawa: **Australia** ⓣ613/236-0841, ⓦwww.ahc-ottawa.org; **Ireland** ⓣ613/233-6281; **New Zealand** ⓣ613/238-5991, ⓦwww.nzhcottawa.org.

Currency exchange Most large downtown banks will change currency and travellers' cheques, or try the following: American Express, 1141 boul de Maisonneuve O ⓣ514/284-3300; Bureau de Change du Vieux-Montréal, 230 rue St-Jacques ⓣ514/284-8686; Calforex, 1250 rue Peel ⓣ514/ 392-9100; Thomas Cook, Centre Eaton, 705 rue Ste-Catherine O ⓣ514/284-7388.

Dentists Centre Dentaire, 3546 av Van-Horne (24hr dental clinic; ⓣ514/342-4444); Walk-in Clinic, 3rd floor, Montréal General Hospital, 1650 av Cedar (Mon–Fri 8am–noon & 1–4pm, but go as early as possible; ⓣ514/934-8397; after-hours call ⓣ514/934-8075).

Disability Kéroul (ⓣ514/252-3104, ⓦwww.keroul.qc.ca) provides information on, and publishes the *Accessible Québec* ($15) guide to, attractions around the province. See also, "Travellers with disabilities", p.39.

Electricity Voltage (110V) and plug types are the same as in the US.

Emergencies ⓣ911 for fire, police and ambulance.

Helplines Tel-Aide (ⓣ514/935-1101, ⓦwww.telaide.org) is a 24hr anonymous and confidential service for people who are feeling suicidal or just need to talk. For gay and lesbian concerns, see p.178. If you have been the victim of sexual assault, see "Rape crisis", below.

Hospitals Central English-language hospitals that are part of the McGill University Health Centre "superhospital" (ⓣ514/934-1934) are the Montréal General Hospital, 1650 av Cedar, on the mountain's slope northwest of downtown, and Royal Victoria Hospital, 687 av des Pins O, up the hill from McGill University.

Internet The cheapest access is often at photocopy shops, such as Allô Copie, 928 av du Mont-Royal E (10¢/min or $5/hr; ☎514/523-2488). Dedicated Internet cafés include *CyberGround*, 3672 boul St-Laurent ($7/hr; ☎514/842-1726), open until 11pm; *L'Inter-Café.net*, 1455 rue Amherst ($6/hr; ☎514/849-5477), open until 8pm (7pm weekends) and a number of places clustered around Concordia University, including *Net 24*, 2157 rue Mackay ($4/hr; ☎514/845-9634), which has free coffee to keep you going 24 hours a day. Larger Canada Post branches have free Internet access (15 minute limit).

Laundry Net-Net, 310 av Duluth E (☎514/844-8511), will wash, dry and fold your clothes in neat bags for you within 24 hours for 77¢/pound; doing it yourself works out to around $4–5. Buanderie du Village, 1499 rue Amherst (☎514/526-4084), will wash your clothes in a few hours for $6/load, around $4 if you do it yourself. Buanderie et Café Lab, 3565 av Lorne, serves drinks and snacks while you wait for the rinse cycle (9am–11pm). Most hotels have laundry service as well.

Left luggage There are $2 lockers at the main bus terminal (24hr only; $5/day charge thereafter) accessible until 11pm, as well as left-luggage storage ($4–6 with hefty late charges) open 7am to 7pm. The train station has left-luggage facilities for passengers only ($2.50/24hr, $5 oversized); open until 11pm.

Pharmacies Jean Coutu (Ⓦwww.jeancoutu.com) and Pharmaprix (Ⓦwww.pharmaprix.ca) are the major chains with branches all over the city. The Pharmaprix near the Oratoire St-Joseph at 5122 chemin de la Côte des Neiges (☎514/738-8464) is open 24hr. Closer to the centre and open until midnight are its branches at 901 rue Ste-Catherine E (☎514/842-4915) and 1500 rue Ste-Catherine O (☎514/933-4744). Jean Coutu outlets open until 11pm are at 501 av du Mont-Royal E (☎514/521-3481) and 1675 rue Ste-Catherine O (☎514/933-4221).

Police For emergencies, call ☎911. Dial ☎514/280-2222 for non-emergency situations.

Post offices The main downtown branch is at 1250 rue University (Mon–Fri 8am–5.45pm). Many smaller outlets can be found as counters in shops and pharmacies – contact Canada Post (☎1-800/267-1177, Ⓦwww.canadapost.ca) for your nearest branch.

Public toilets Your best bets are attractions such as museums, as well as shopping malls (usually near the food court). If pressed, you can always make a small purchase (eg a cup of coffee) in a bar or restaurant if they won't let you use the facilities otherwise.

Rape crisis Bilingual rape crisis line (☎514/934-4504).

Ridesharing Allô-Stop, 4317 rue St-Denis (☎514/985-3032, Ⓦwww.allo-stop.com), is a carpool service that matches drivers with passengers for destinations within Québec. Membership costs $6 per year, and you pay for your share of petrol. Québec City also has a branch, located at 467 rue St-Jean (☎418/522-0056).

Ski/snow reports Ⓦwww.quebecskisurf.com, as well as regular radio reports.

Tax Two taxes are applied to just about every purchase: the 7 percent GST (TPS in French) and the 7.5 percent QST (TVQ in French). For information on claiming a rebate, see box, p.32.

Taxis Taxi Diamond (☎514/273-6331) and Taxi Co-op (☎514/725-9885) are two reputable firms.

Telephones Local calls cost 25¢ at a payphone; more if you pay by credit card. Prepaid cards (see p.34) are available from Bell-Canada outlets, newsagents, the airport and the Centre Infotouriste. Dial ☎411 for information, 0 to reach the operator. Toll-free (freephone) numbers begin with 1-800, 1-866, 1-877 or 1-888.

Tickets The Admission network sells tickets for almost everything (☎514/790-1245 or 1-800/361-4595, Ⓦwww.admission.com).

Time Montréal is on Eastern Standard Time (EST), five hours behind GMT. Daylight Savings Time runs from the first Sunday in April to the last Sunday in October.

Tipping It's customary to tip 15 percent of the total before taxes to waiters and bar staff. Note that "TPS" or "GST" which appear on the bill are not abbreviations for "tips" or "Good Service Tip" – these are taxes. Taxi drivers and hairdressers also expect a 15 percent tip; for porters, doormen and bell hops, tip $1 per bag.

Travel agents Tourisme Jeunesse Boutique, 205 av du Mont-Royal (☎514/844-0287 or 1-866/461-8585, Ⓦwww.tourismejeunesse.org), and Club Voyages Tourbec St-Denis, 3419 rue St-Denis (☎514/288-

4455), are both excellent sources for budget travellers; the former has a branch in Québec City at 94 boul René-Lévesque O (ⓣ418/522-2552). Voyages Campus (Travel Cuts), 1455 boul de Maisonneuve O (ⓣ514/288-1130 or 1-866/246-9762, ⓦwww.travelcuts.com), 3480 rue McTavish (ⓣ514/398-0647), 225 av du Président-Kennedy (ⓣ514/281-6662) and 1613 rue St-Denis (ⓣ514/843-8511), books travel primarily for students with an International Student Identification Card (ISIC).

Weather and road conditions Environment Canada (ⓣ514/283-3010, ⓦwww.weatheroffice.ec.gc.ca) for info on weather and winter road conditions; Transports Québec (ⓣ514/284-2363, ⓦwww.mtq.gouv.qc.ca) for roadworks. Up-to-the-minute traffic reports are also on radio stations such as CJAD 800 AM.

Out of the City

Out of the City

20

Les Laurentides

Easily reached from Montréal, and a good choice if you want to stretch out a bit in the outdoors and perhaps do some skiing, the **Laurentides** (Laurentians) combines stretches of farmland dotted with relaxed, historic towns with a few splendid resorts in its mountainous upper reaches. Immediately north of Montréal and separated from it by the Lac des Deux-Montagnes and suburban island city of Laval, are the **Basses Laurentides** (Lower Laurentians). Once home to the region's main farmlands (some of which are still in operation), its flat and quiet landscapes are graced by centuries-old whitewashed cottages and manor houses. Here, two laid-back destinations make for pleasant afternoon detours: **St-Eustache**, along the Rivière des Milles-Îles, is notable for its battle-scarred historic centre, while on the shores of Lac des Deux-Montagnes lies **Oka**, home to one of North America's oldest monasteries, bordering on an attractive provincial park.

For more active pursuits, most visitors head straight for the Laurentian heartland beginning north of St-Jérôme – the area most Montrealers have in mind when they talk about the Laurentians. Here, the mountains begin to climb higher into the sky, affording great hiking in their forested glades and all manner of watersports in the lakes and rivers dotted about. Don't expect dramatic, jagged peaks, though – 500 million years of erosion have moulded one of the world's oldest ranges into a rippling landscape of rounded peaks and smooth valleys. The area boasts one of the largest concentrations of **ski** resorts in North America – come winter, skiers conquer dozens of hills, with those around the town of **St-Sauveur-des-Monts** being among the most accessible and popular. In contrast to the yuppified ski resorts found around here, artsy **Val-David** is better for cross-country skiing and snowshoeing – though it has its pistes too, along with a host of summertime pursuits. Continuing north, the mountains reach an altitude of nearly 1000m, with the famous **Mont-Tremblant** the biggest draw of all; as it is 130km north of Montréal, you pretty much need to make a weekend of it or longer – there are plenty of full-week ski packages available.

St-Eustache

After passing through the monotonous suburbs of Laval and crossing the Rivière des Milles-Îles to sprawling **St-Eustache** (forty minutes northwest of Montréal along Hwy-13 or 15 north to Hwy-640 west), the town's tiny historic core, **Vieux-St-Eustache**, comes as a bit of surprise. The riverside old town dates from the eighteenth century and its historic sites are clustered along two narrow streets: rues St-Louis and St-Eustache. The silver twin bell-towered **Église de St-Eustache** at 123 rue St-Louis looms over the whole district, and it was here that a faction of the Patriotes rebels protesting oppression of the

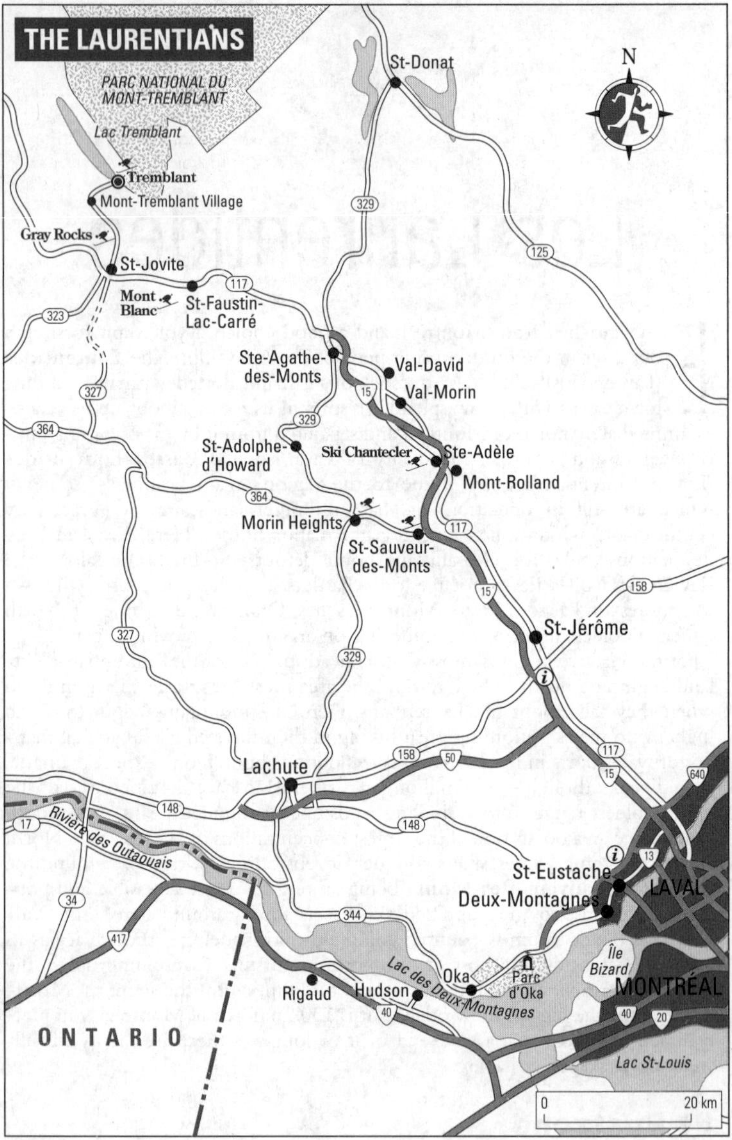

THE LAURENTIANS

Francophones under British rule was put down by military detachments in 1837. A third of the 150 men who took refuge in the church were killed after it was blasted by cannon fire, and the church still bears a few scars on its recently cleaned-up stone facade. The interior vault was rebuilt following the battle, with gold rosettes alternating with cream-coloured beams above an altar shimmering with gold leaf. British troops went on to raze much of the town, leaving

Practicalities

Access to the region by **bus** is provided by Limocar Laurentides (☎514/842-2281 or 1-866/700-8899, ⓦwww.limocar.ca), which stops at St-Sauveur (1 daily, 1hr 40min), Val-David (5 daily, 2 hr) and the St-Jovite sector of Mont-Tremblant (5 daily, 2hr 40min); there are additional runs on the weekend. The main regional **tourist information** office for the Basses Laurentides is located off exit 14 from Hwy-640, a short drive north of Vieux St-Eustache (daily: late June to late Aug 8.30am–6.30pm, late Aug to late June 9am–4pm; ☎450/491-4444, ⓦwww.basseslaurentides.com). For the rest of the Laurentides, there's an office at exit 39 off Hwy-15 (late June to Aug daily 8.30am–8.30pm, Sept to late June Mon–Thurs 8.30am–5pm, Fri 8.30am–7pm, Sat & Sun 9am–5pm; ☎450/436-8532 or 514/990-5625 or 1-800/561-6673, ⓦwww.laurentides.com) or you can stop by one of the smaller local offices described below.

ing a dozen-odd fieldstone buildings intact, most of which today are simply marked with heritage signs and form the core of Vieux-St-Eustache. The **Manoir Globensky** at 235 rue St-Eustache postdates the battle and is worth a quick visit if you're interested in the rebellion. Inside, the **Musée de St-Eustache et de ses Patriotes** (Tues–Sun 10am–5pm; $3) puts on a 15-minute film tied to temporary exhibitions on local history and has displays of various tools and weapons; most are reproductions, though the cannon ball and British rifle are legitimate articles. Also of historical interest is the **Moulin Légaré**, the oldest continually operating water-powered flour mill in North America, directly opposite; guided visits are available ($3; ☎819/974-5400 for schedules) and you can pick up fresh bread, as well. If you want to stop to **eat**, *Café Bistro Coincidence*, a block back towards the church at 198 rue St-Eustache (☎819/623-8094), is a good spot for cheap ciabatta sandwiches and salads in a house dating from 1812.

Oka

Some 20km southwest of St-Eustache on Hwy-344 lies the lakeside municipality of **Oka**, site of the controversial armed stand-off between the Mohawks and police in the summer of 1990 (see box, p.226). The tiny village itself is a sleepy spot – the areas of interest are located in the nearby countryside, which is dotted with apple orchards and dominated by the impressive **Abbaye Cistercienne d'Oka**, 1600 chemin d'Oka (daily 4am–8pm; ☎450/479-8361, ⓦwww.abbayeoka.com). Some thirty Trappist monks live in the abbey, built to house 200 monks and notable for its century-old bell tower rising amidst the enveloping hills. Given its diminishing numbers, the abbey has decided to move elsewhere, though that will likely not happen for a few years. The bright **church** inside has arched ceilings warmly offset by wood panelling on the lower walls, and the nearby monastery shop (closed Sun) sells organic Trappist products, including their trademark Oka cheese, a smooth and creamy semi-soft ripened cheese similar to Port Salut.

Pick up a wedge before heading to the splendid **Parc National d'Oka** (open year-round; $3.50 plus $5 parking; ☎450/479-8365 or 1-888/727-2652, ⓦwww.sepaq.com), which stretches south of the abbey to the shores of **Lac des Deux-Montagnes** (the main entrance is five-minutes' drive west of the abbey on Hwy-344). The park is laced with 45km of biking and hiking trails: the best of these is the scenic 5.5km **Calvaire d'Oka** trek that ascends to the top of a spectacular viewpoint, passing a grouping of seven deserted

Stand-off at Oka

In 1990, Oka was the stage for a confrontation between Mohawk warriors from Kanesatake and the provincial government when the town's council decided to expand its golf course onto the tribe's sacred burial ground (a territory for which they had been trying to settle a claim for decades). The Mohawks responded by arming themselves and staking out the territory, and Québec's public security minister sent in the provincial police to retake the land. A policeman was killed in the ensuing fracas – no one knows by whom – and the two sides became increasingly polarized. The federal government offered to buy the disputed land for the natives as long as they surrendered, but negotiations failed and the stand-off continued for 78 days, until the core group of 25 Mohawks was encircled by army soldiers and forced to give up.

The events drew national attention and the cause was taken up by other First Nations, including sympathetic Mohawks from the Kahnawake reserve south of Montréal, who set up barricades across the Mercier Bridge, one of Montréal's main commuter arteries. A particularly gruesome moment occurred when the Kahnawake natives tried to evacuate their women and children only to be pelted by stones thrown by white Québécois.

The clash at Oka ultimately led to some improvements for the Kanesatake residents, such as the introduction of democratic elections, a local police force and additions to the community infrastructure. But, like many other land claims across the country, the slow negotiation process to settle land claims continues.

stone chapels built around 1740 by the Sulpicians (see box, p.72). In winter, cross-country skiers and snowshoers take over the same trails – including the Pinède, a 4km trail lit up for evening skiing; rentals are available. One of the park's main draws is the long stretch of sandy **beach** along the shores of Lac des Deux-Montagnes (which faces across to the west end of the island of Montréal); bicycles and various watercraft can be rented at its western end (starting at around $10/hr). There are serviced **campsites** ($30.65) and more rustic spots to pitch a tent ($22); you can rent all the gear you need from $82 for a minimum of two nights (including pitch rental) – enquire at the entry kiosk.

St-Sauveur-des-Monts

Most visitors skip the Basses-Laurentides and head directly for the mountainous terrain of the Laurentian heartland. **St-Sauveur-des-Monts**, 60km north of Montréal, marks the beginning of the region and is its ritziest resort town. During the peak skiing season, the town's resident population of 7000 quadruples, and the main drag, rue Principale, boasts every type of restaurant, designer boutique and craft shop imaginable. Come nightfall, numerous flash clubs and discos fill quickly with tired skiers in trendy outfits. Rue Principale spreads out to either side of the **Église St-Sauveur**, a century-old greystone building typical of the province's massive parish churches with its tin-clad steeple and flanking cupolas; the vaulted interior is disappointingly plain. Even without snow, the town's still a pleasant spot to wander around, especially during the mid-July Festival des Arts de St-Sauveur (Ⓣ450/227-9935, Ⓦwww.arts-saintsauveur.com) – ten days of dance, chamber music and jazz concerts.

Information on shopping and skiing is available from the **tourist bureau**, near exit 60 from Hwy-15, at 605 chemin des Frênes (Mon–Fri 9am–5pm, late May to early Sept until 9pm; Ⓣ450/227-3417 or 1-800/898-2127,

Ⓦwww.saint-sauveur.net or www.tourismepdh.org); there's also a kiosk near the church on rue Principale in the warmer months.

Of the six separate nearby ski mountains, the best are **Mont St-Sauveur** and **Mont-Habitant**. The former features the most extensive night-skiing in the province and some decent expert runs and glades; it often has enough snow to keep the ski season going until June ($37–43/adults, $23–27/6–12 years; Ⓣ450/227-4671 or 514/871-0101, Ⓦwww.montsaintsauveur.com). The latter is a great spot for families with kids just starting out, with ten gentle slopes and a good ski school ($25–33/adults, $19–22/6–12 years; Ⓣ450/227-2637 or 1-866/887-2637, Ⓦwww.monthabitant.com). In summer, the area continues to be a good destination for families thanks to a number of **water parks** – the most popular is St-Sauveur's Parc Aquatique ($24, $19 for kids under 1.39m; Ⓦwww.parcaquatique.com), with a giant wave pool and slides you can race down in a raft, on a tube or on your butt.

Practicalities

If you need a **place to stay**, try *Les Bonheurs de Sophie*, 342 rue Principale (Ⓣ450/227-6116 or 1-877/227-6116, Ⓦwww.lesbonheursdesophie.com; ❸), a countrified B&B with three glossy wood-panelled rooms that have private bathrooms and cable TV; guests also have access to a garden and pool. Another quaint B&B is *Le Bonnet d'Or*, 405 rue Principale (Ⓣ450/227-9669 or 1-877/277-9669, Ⓦwww.bbcanada.com/bonnetdor; ❹), which has five handsome rooms, some with amenities like in-room fireplace that raise the price; all have private bathrooms and antique furnishings. For plusher digs, there's the massive complex of *Manoir St-Sauveur*, 246 chemin du Lac Millette (Ⓣ450/227-1811 or 1-800/361-0505, Ⓦwww.manoir-saint-sauveur.com; ❹), featuring 300 well-appointed rooms and suites, the best of which are on the top floor, nestled in the eaves.

The range of **dining** options runs the gamut from fast-food joints nearer the highway to expensive restaurants of both the posh and trendy varieties. For mid-range choices, there are local branches of a number of Montréal outfits such as *Pizzédélic*, 16 rue de la Gare. Or there are local favourites like *La Bohème*, 251 rue Principale (Ⓣ450/227-6644, Ⓦwww.restoboheme.com), serving French specialities like frog's legs *provençale* and *bœuf bourguignon* in a rustic ambience, and the lively Italian restaurant *Papa Luigi*, 155 rue Principale (Ⓣ450/227-5311, Ⓦwww.papa-luigi.com). For breakfast or a quick snack, along with excellent coffee, head to *Brûlerie des Monts*, 197 rue Principale (Ⓣ450/227-6157).

Val-David

Some 16km further north along Hwy-117 lies bohemian **Val-David**, the most laid-back of the Laurentians' towns, chosen by artists and artisans as a haven from the yuppie developments elsewhere. Its progressive credentials suffered a setback in 2003, however, when the municipal authorities bulldozed half a dozen low-rent homes to make way for a car park for the regional park; protesters, including one who shackled herself to the roof of her house, tried in vain to stop the move.

The main street, rue de l'Église, reflects the town's cultural bent with several galleries and craft shops that make for a pleasant afternoon of browsing, interspersed with the majority of the town's cafés, restaurants and bars. Also on rue de l'Église, at no. 2501, is the **tourist information** office (mid-April to mid-Oct Sun–Thurs 9am–5pm, Fri & Sat 9am–6pm; mid-Nov to mid-March daily

Hitting the slopes

The rounded and forested hills of the Laurentians that make up Montréal's winter playground are dotted with over a dozen **ski hills** served by **resort towns** that come alive at night with energized skiers. The ski resorts start under an hour's drive north of Montréal with the mountains surrounding the St-Sauveur valley. Tickets for **Mont St-Sauveur** (see p.227) are also valid at four associated resorts – of these, **Morin Heights** (Ⓦwww.skimorinheights.com) is mainly intermediate and has a number of night runs, while **Mont-Olympia** (Ⓦwww.montolympia.com) is geared more to beginners, as is independent **Mont-Habitant** (see p.227). Further north, near Ste-Adèle, the upscale resort of **Le Chantecler** (Ⓦwww.lechantecler.com) has 23 runs split between beginner and intermediate levels, many lit at night.

Surrounding **Val-David** (see p.227), a number of smaller hills depend on a good snowfall. In addition to the all-inclusive **Tremblant** operation further north (see p.231), nearby **Gray Rocks** (Ⓦwww.grayrocks.com) is a smaller, family-oriented resort with varied terrain. Its lift tickets are interchangeable with those at **Mont Blanc** (Ⓦwww.ski-mont-blanc.com), just off Hwy-117, 10km closer to Montréal than Tremblant; it has a 300m vertical, challenging intermediate tree run and the best-maintained half-pipe in the area.

As many of the region's towns are little more than bases for the ski hills, accommodation tends to be of the pricey resort variety, though a smattering of B&Bs, motels and a couple of hostels offer cheaper stays. Check with travel agents in Montréal (see p. 218) before heading out as weekend packages can be a bargain, or try the region's free accommodation service (Ⓣ450/436-8532, 514/990-5625 or 1-800/561-6673, Ⓦwww.laurentides.com). Keep in mind, though, that staying overnight need not be a priority if you're willing to leave early and come back late the same day. For up-to-date ski conditions visit Ⓦwww.quebecskisurf.com or listen out for regular updates on the radio.

For more comprehensive descriptions of runs, terrain, lift passes, facilities and the like, pick up a copy of *The Rough Guide to Skiing & Snowboarding in North America*.

9.30am–5pm; other times as per winter hours Wed–Sun; Ⓣ819/322-3104 or 1-888/322-7030 ext 235, Ⓦwww.valdavid.com).

Though surrounded by three small mountains – **Mont-Alta** has the most pistes at 22 (Ⓣ819/322-3206, $10/over-12, $6/under-13) – the town sets itself apart with non-ski-related attractions come summertime. In addition to the artistic sights, Val-David is a great base for exploring the Laurentian scenery as there are a number of **hiking** trails within a short distance and the relatively flat Le P'tit Train du Nord **bicycle trail** extends for miles to the north and south (see box, opposite). If you want to explore the trail, or just tool around the surrounding countryside, Pause Plein Air, 1381 chemin de la Sapinière (Ⓣ819/322-6880 or 1-877/422-6880, Ⓦwww.pause-plein-air.com), rents bikes for $6/hr or $18/day (including trail permit) and **canoes and kayaks** starting at $15; it also offers a number of packages including a downstream trip and return by bicycle. Phénix Sport et Aventure, 2444 rue de l'Église (Ⓣ819/322-1118 or 1-877/566-1118, Ⓦwww.phenixsport.com), offers similar deals.

The area is popular for **rock climbing** as well, with half a dozen well-developed sites: Passe Montagne (Ⓣ819/322-2123 or 1-800/465-2123, Ⓦwww.passemontagne.com) offers beginners' courses on summer Saturdays for $70. If you're an experienced climber, contact the Fédération Québécoise de la Montagne et de l'Escalade (FQME), the provincial mountain climbing association (Ⓣ514/252-3004 or 1-866/204-3763, Ⓦwww.fqme.qc.ca), for details of more challenging climbs.

In addition to its wealth of nature activities, Val-David happens to be home to the Laurentians' tackiest attraction, the **Village du Père Noel** at 987 rue Morin (early June to early Sept daily 10am–6pm, plus 3 weeks prior to Christmas, schedule varies; $8.50; ⓣ819/322-2146 or 1-800/287-6635, ⓦwww.noel.qc.ca), a Santa's village whose star attraction is the Wise Goat. This animal's wisdom apparently stems from an ability to climb an obstacle course and feed himself from pails suspended on pulleys – it's fun for kids anyway.

Practicalities

In contrast to some of the flashier resort towns, Val-David offers cheaper and generally laid-back **accommodation** in small inns and B&Bs, as well as a great, if sometimes noisy, youth hostel in a massive chalet with roaring fires in the winter and a pub with terrace in the summer. *Le Chalet Beaumont*, 1451 rue Beaumont (ⓣ819/322-1972, ⓦwww.chaletbeaumont.com) has dormitory beds for $20 and double rooms for $55 ($69 with private bath); there's a $4 discount for HI members and family rates are available; call from the bus station and they'll come pick you up. One of the nicer B&Bs, *La Maison de Bavière*, 1470 chemin de la Rivière (ⓣ819/322-3528, ⓦwww.maisondebaviere.com; ❸), backs onto river rapids, which you can see from the fireplace-warmed sitting room. All five rooms have private bath, and breakfasts include extravagances like cheese soufflés. Nearby, the woodsy *Auberge Le Relais de la Piste*, 1430 rue de l'Academie (ⓣ819/322-2280, ⓦwww.relaisdelapiste.com; ❸), has six comfortable rooms complete with slanted ceilings, cable TV and private bath. Price includes full breakfast; its restaurant has an evening *table d'hôte* for $22.50, with a range of gourmet dishes, including specialties from Seychelles and Martinique, on the menu. *La Sapinière*, 1244 chemin de la Sapinière (ⓣ819/322-2020 or 1-800/567-6635, ⓦwww.sapiniere.com; ❹), a relatively upscale ski lodge of log and stone offering 70 well-appointed rooms (some with fireplace), likewise offers dinner – they serve a five-course *table d'hôte* with a good range of meat,

Le P'tit Train du Nord

The bed of **Le P'tit Train du Nord**, a railway line that once ferried Montrealers to the Laurentians' resorts, now sees brisk business as a major **bicycle trail** as thousands of cyclists pedal their way among the mountains throughout the summer. The former stations have been renovated as well, now often housing tourist information centres, some with facilities such as showers and snack bars for cyclists taking a break. Access to the 200km trail, which runs north from St-Jérôme to Mont-Laurier, costs $5/day, $10 for the whole May to October season.

In winter, the snow-covered route is equally in demand by **cross-country skiers** ($7/day), who can explore numerous side-trails branching off into the hills between St-Jérôme and Val-David, and to **snowmobilers** – the Ste-Agathe to Mont-Laurier stretch is part of the network of thousands of kilometres of trails that criss-cross the province. **Information**, as well as a guide with maps and list of services (including cycle repair, baggage transport and accommodation) along the route, is available from the Association Touristique des Laurentides (see p.225).

For a combination of land and water fun, Les Excursions Rivière du Nord (ⓣ450/229-1889 or 1-866/342-2668, ⓦwww.riviere-du-nord.ca) gives you the chance to **canoe or raft** downriver for a couple of hours from Mont Rolland station (near Ste-Adèle) to Piedmont (just east of St-Sauveur) and then cycle the 7km back north, starting at $64 per couple. Similar trips are available for the 4-hour return trip from Val-David to Mont Rolland (see box, opposite).

fish (they smoke their own salmon) and vegetarian options on the menu - and has a host of outdoor activities on the property.

Other than the dining rooms in the hotels mentioned above, most of Val-Davis's **eating** spots are concentrated on rue de l'Église. On the corner at its north end, at 1337 chemin de la Sapinière, *L'Express* (℡819/322-3090) is a café-bistro that's great for breakfast or soup and sandwiches, as well as good daily specials like *tourtière* later on (open 8am–4pm, until 6pm weekends). Nearer the highway, earnest but fun staff at the ramshackle co-operative restaurant *Aux Vivres d'en Haut*, 2360 rue de l'Eglise (℡819/321-0766), serve fair-trade coffee and organic, vegan smoothies, sandwiches, sushi and daily stir-fry specials. Midway between the two at no. 2481, *Le Grand Pa* (℡819/322-3104) is a friendly restaurant serving simple and affordable French food that turns into a rollicking *boîte à chanson* on weekend evenings.

Mont-Tremblant

Situated some 50km north of Val-David, **Mont-Tremblant** is the Laurentians' oldest and most renowned ski area, focused on the range's highest peak (915m).

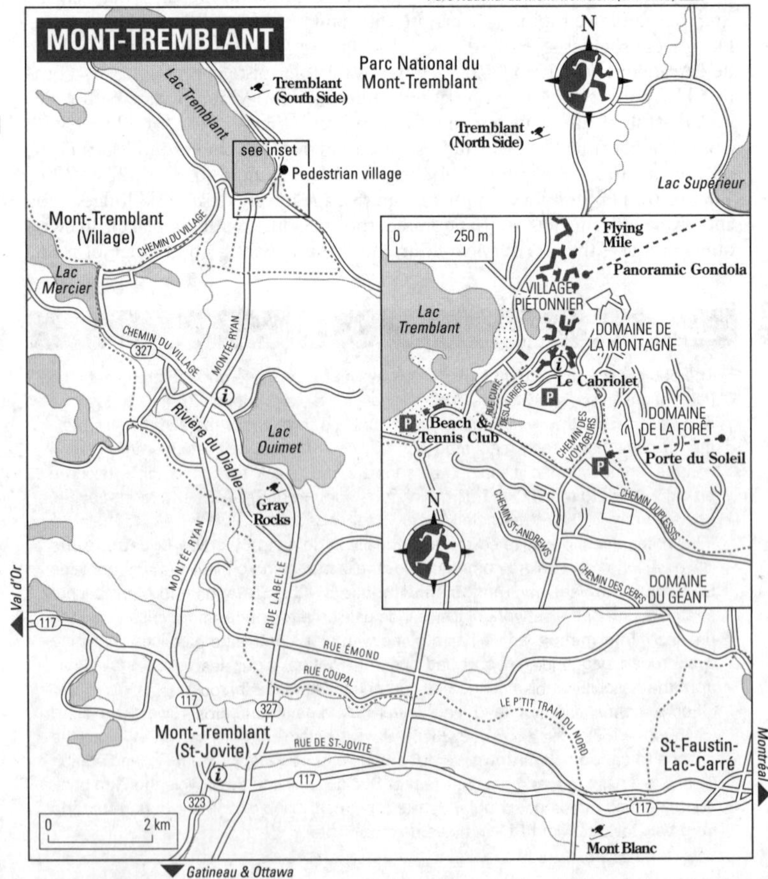

around its Disney-esque pedestrian village, is the liveliest spot in the whole area come winter (though there are plenty of hiking, cycling, boating and golfing activities in warmer months).

Practicalities

The main **tourist information** office is just off Hwy-117 as you enter Ste-Jovite, at 48 chemin de Brébeuf (June–Sept Sun–Thurs 9am–7pm, Fri & Sat 9am–8pm, Oct–May 9am–5pm; ⓣ819/425-3300 or 1-800/322-2932, ⓦwww.tourismemonttremblant.com); a second tourist office is located further north at 5080 montée Ryan (ⓣ819/425-2434). **Accommodation**, scattered throughout the area, includes more than a dozen B&Bs, as well as rustic chalets and ritzy resorts; the tourist office can provide more information, or phone ⓣ1-800/567-6760 for reservations.

Clustered on **St-Jovite**'s main drag, rue de St-Jovite, are a number of good **restaurants and bars**. *Le Bistro Brunch Café*, 814 rue de St-Jovite (ⓣ819/425-8233), serves breakfast until 4pm and has cheap pub food and a terrace to sit back with a pint; for a more expensive dinner, *Chez Roger*, around the corner at 444 rue St-Georges (ⓣ819/429-6991), offers rich French cuisine.

Although St-Jovite has some cheap motels, the second sector, **Mont-Tremblant Village**, 10km to the north, has better places to **sleep**, including a youth hostel, the *Auberge de Jeunesse International du Mont-Tremblant*, with dorms for $20 ($24 non-members), double rooms for $52/$64 and plenty of organized activities. Right where the P'tit Train du Nord bike path passes Lac Mercier, *Tremblant Onwego*, 112 chemin Plouffe (ⓣ819/429-5522 or 1-866/429-5522, ⓦwww.tremblantonwego.com; ❸), is a friendly B&B well-equipped for active visitors – it even has its own stretch of lakefront beach. Opposite, the *Hôtel Mont-Tremblant*, 1900 chemin du Village (ⓣ819/425-3232 or 1-888/887-1111, ⓦwww.hotelmonttremblant.com; ❸), offers more standard accommodation and has a wide terrace for chilling out.

The third sector is the aforementioned **Tremblant resort** itself, located another 3km east of the village between Lac Tremblant and the ski-slopes, with all manner of **après-ski** spots to eat and drink. **Hotels and chalets** are pricier here – the *Fairmont Tremblant* (ⓣ819/681-7653 or 1-877/441-1414, ⓦwww.fairmont.com; ❼) is the most glamorous of the lot – but in many cases you can ski right up to your front door, and with around 3500 beds, getting a place should be no problem. *La Place St-Bernard* (ⓣ819/861-2000 or 1-

Parc National du Mont-Tremblant

Mont-Tremblant ski resort is but a small part of the **Parc National du Mont-Tremblant** ($3.50; ⓣ819/688-2281 or 1-877/688-2289, ⓦwww.sepaq.com), a mammoth provincial park that sprawls out north of the mountain for almost 1500 square miles. Marked by undulating hills and hundreds of lakes, the park is a natural habitat for moose, white-tailed deer and beavers, and one of the best ways to spot them is by canoe, though determined landlubbers can head out on the plentiful hiking trails and bike paths that cut through the park. You can rent bicycles, canoes, rowboats, kayaks and pedal-boats in summer, and cross-country skis and snowshoes once the snow's arrived. **Camping** is available (mid-May to early Oct $16.52–40) and there are also huts and cabins if you'd rather have a solid roof over your head. The park has several entry points – the nearest accesses the Diable sector of the park, east of the Tremblant resort along chemin Duplessis; if you're heading there directly, exit Hwy-117 at St-Faustin-Lac-Carré.

800/461-8711; ❻) offers some of the best value lodging given its location next to the pedestrian village's slope-side plaza. If skiing is your main focus, check out the ski and accommodation **packages** offered by the resort itself – their website, Ⓦ www.tremblant.com, lists everything in the area and includes photos, rates and ski packages – as well as what's being promoted by the Laurentides tourist board (see p.225). You could also try one of the package tour operators listed in the "Getting there" section of "Basics" near the front of this book (see p.11).

21

Les Cantons-de-l'Est

Beginning 80km east of Montréal and extending south to the US border, the scenic **Cantons-de-l'Est** (Eastern Townships) was once Québec's best-kept secret, but its nineteenth-century villages are fast gaining popularity with shoppers seeking out antiques and discounted labels at outlet stores. A burgeoning service industry caters to summer cyclists and hikers, while the ski slopes and hiking trails of Mont-Orford and other resorts make it a great outdoorsy destination year-round. However, the region's charm still outweighs its ever-increasing commercialization, with plenty of picture-postcard villages, their white-clapboard or tin-steepled limestone churches and handsome Victorian manors clustered around glistening lakeshores.

The land, once home to scattered groups of aboriginal peoples, was later settled by Loyalists hounded out of the US after the American Revolution. Their loyalty to the crown resulted in freehold land grants from the British (as opposed to the tenanted *seigneuries* commonplace elsewhere), and settlements with very English names like Farnham and Bedford were soon founded. In the mid-nineteenth century the townships opened up to industry, which attracted an influx of French Canadians seeking work: today, nearly 95 percent of the Eastern Townships' 400,000 population are Francophone. For the most part, relations between the linguistic groups have been amicable, though pockets like the towns and villages around Knowlton and North Hatley remain staunchly tied to their Anglophone heritage, and the English-language cultural scene is much stronger than the size of the population would suggest.

The trek from Montréal to the Cantons-de-l'Est is worth it for the scenery alone, as the northern range of the Appalachian Mountains cuts through the region, especially majestic come autumn when the slopes explode with yellows, oranges and reds. The dull city of Granby, 85km east of Montréal, marks the beginning of the Townships region, which extends all the way east to the university town of Sherbrooke, but it's the picturesque villages nestled in the valleys between them that brim with character. Quaint **Knowlton** exudes Victoriana and boasts terrific antique shops, while **North Hatley**'s breathtaking collection of mansions lends the town a refined air. Between these two lies the paired towns of **Magog-Orford**, whose primary appeal is the wide selection of excellent year-round outdoor activities afforded by the impressive Lac Memphrémagog and the rugged **Mont Orford**, laced with hiking trails and ski runs.

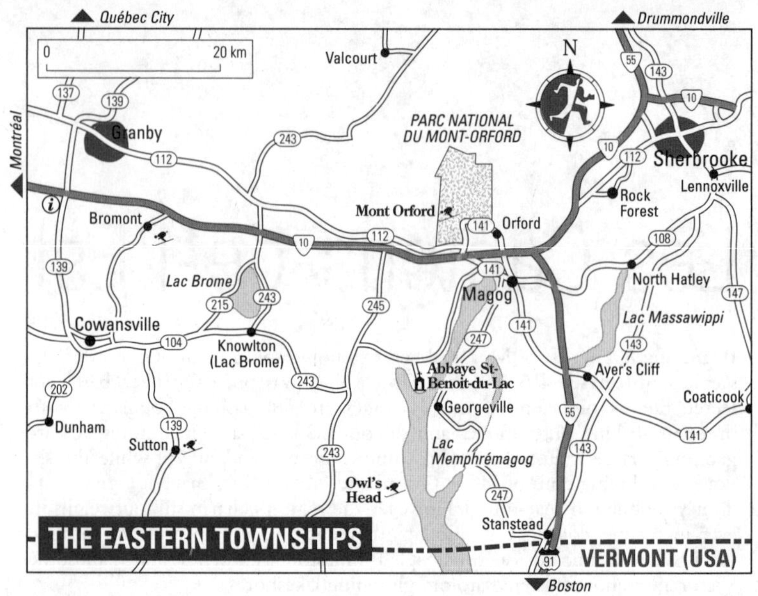

Knowlton

The peaceful township of **Lac Brome**, named for the twenty-kilometre-long shimmering lake at its centre, is home to seven sleepy communities, the most handsome of which is pocket-sized **Knowlton**. Settled at the lake's southern end, the town's Loyalist flavour is still strongly felt along its two main drags – chemin Lakeside and, perpendicular to that, chemin Knowlton – which boast an eye-catching combination of red-brick and clapboard houses. At the centre of town the small **Parc Coldbrook** sits at the edge of a quaint waterfall and stream. Lac Brome is renowned for the quality of its duck, celebrated during the annual **Duck Festival**, a jamboree of music and gastronomy held in October (Ⓣ514/281-6601, Ⓦwww.duckfest.com). At other times, you can pick up a duck meal, duck foie gras or a package of "hot ducks" (a pun on hot dogs) at Canards Lac Brome, 40 chemin Centre (Ⓣ450/242-3825, Ⓦwww.bromelakeducks.com).

The town's only museum, the cluttered **Musée Historique du Comté de Brome**, occupies a complex of buildings at 130 chemin Lakeside (mid-May to mid-Sept Mon–Sat 10am–4.30pm, Sun 11am–4.30pm; $5; Ⓣ450/243-6782), including an easy-to-spot white clapboard fire tower. A county history museum with a focus on local heritage, it's surprisingly strongest on military artefacts – the show-stopper is an original Fokker DVII airplane, the type flown by the Red Baron. Further down the street at Arts Knowlton, 9 chemin du Mont-Écho, the **Théâtre Lac Brome** (Ⓣ450/242-2270, Ⓦwww.cclacbrome.qc.ca/tlb) offers light-hearted fare during its late-June to mid-August season (other troupes stage short runs throughout the year); tickets are in the $22–25 range and there's a pub next door.

Most visitors overlook these cultural attractions in favour of shopping. **Antique shops** are clustered along chemin Knowlton, while designer **cloth-**

ing outlets selling discounted Polo Ralph Lauren and Vittadini labels, among others, are found on chemin Lakeside. The annual **antique show and sale** held at Raquettes Brome, 584 chemin Knowlton (mid-Oct; ⓣ450/243-6134), vies for popularity with the Duck Festival; the museum hosts a smaller antique sale on its grounds on a couple of summer Sundays.

Practicalities

Just off the *autoroute*, there's a seasonal **tourist office** near the intersection of highways 243 and 215 (May–Oct 9am–6pm, daily late June to August, otherwise weekends only). Knowlton is easily handled as an afternoon jaunt out of Montréal – it's just over an hour from the Pont Champlain – so there's no real need to stay the night. If the town's charm does grab you, however, there are plenty of country **inns and B&Bs** to choose from. The most centrally located B&B is *La Venise Verte*, a veranda-wrapped 1884 house with simple, country-style rooms and breakfasts made with local and/or organic products (ⓣ450/243-1844, ⓦwww.laveniseverte.com; ❸). Right at the town's main intersection, at 286 chemin Knowlton, the modernized *Auberge Knowlton* (ⓣ450/242-6886, ⓦwww.cclacbrome.qc.ca/ak; ❹) has been operating as an inn for a century and a half; the downstairs restaurant, *Le Relais*, is popular for its Brome Lake duckling ($15–20). Lighter **food** options include nearby *Frostys Bistro Pub*, 51 chemin Lakeside (ⓣ450/242-2929, ⓦwww.frostysbistro.ca), which serves pub grub on a terrace overlooking a stream, while *Le St-Raphaël*, 281 chemin Knowlton (ⓣ450/243-4168), offers scrumptious scones and rich duck pizza but closes at 5pm.

Magog and around

The resort town of **Magog**, about 30 minutes east of Knowlton along Hwy-10 or Hwy-112, combines some of the best swimming and cycling in the Eastern Townships. Magog fans out around one of the townships' largest lakes, **Lac Memphrémagog** – reputedly home to Memphré, a local variant of the Loch Ness Monster (see ⓦwww.memphre.com for a list of some of the 200-odd reported sightings since the mid-nineteenth century). Strangely enough, there's greater controversy at the moment over who owns the rights to the

Practicalties

Magog is the only town covered here that is accessible by **bus** from Montréal's Station Centrale d'Autobus (up to 8 trips daily; 1hr 30min on the express; call ⓣ514/842-2281 for schedules and fares). To stop at Knowlton or North Hatley, you'll have to rent a car (see p.28). From Montréal, the Autoroute des Cantons-de-l'Est (Hwy-10) flies across the top of the region, but the slower Hwy-112 is more picturesque as it unravels through the towns and villages at the heart of Loyalist country. If you've got time, detour onto the secondary roads nearer the US border that pass rustic barns, duck under covered bridges and wind through the province's fledgling vineyards. The region's main **information centre** is located off exit 68 on Hwy-10, southwest of Granby (daily: June–Sept 10am–6pm, Oct–May 9am–5pm; ⓣ819/820-2020 or 1-800/355-5755, ⓦwww.easterntownships.cc). For background info, historic photos and thematic itineraries, check out the *Townships Heritage WebMagazine* (ⓦwww.townshipsheritage.com).

Hitting the slopes

Although not as numerous as their Laurentian cousins, the Eastern Townships' four main **ski resorts** are generally larger and feature more interesting terrain, particularly on the expert runs and gladed areas. Independent **Bromont** (ⓦwww.skibromont.com) is the nearest to Montréal – making it possible to do some night skiing and still drive the 45 minutes back to the city well before the bars close – and offers well-groomed cruisers for intermediate skiers as well as a separate peak, Mont Soleil, for beginners. Due south, towards the Vermont border, **Sutton** (ⓦwww.montsutton.com) is suited to a range of abilities on its gladed runs. Further east, **Orford**'s three peaks (see p.238) also cater to all skill levels and the attractively forested slopes usually have the best snow conditions. South past Magog, **Owl's Head** (ⓦwww.owlshead.com) offers terrific vistas over Lac Memphrémagog from its varied beginner and intermediate trails. You can get an interchangeable lift ticket (four days or more) for the latter three resorts: contact the resorts themselves or visit ⓦwww.easterntownships.cc/ski for info.

Although it can make for a rather tiring excursion if you're heading to one of the further resorts, it's possible to get in a full skiing session as a day-trip from Montréal. Plenty of cozy B&Bs and charming (and sometimes pricey) inns supplement the resorts' slope-side accommodation but other than at Bromont, you'll need to head to one of the nearby towns for any après-ski nightlife. As when travelling to the Laurentians, check with Montréal travel agents before heading out as weekend packages can be a bargain, or try the tourist office's free accommodation service for the region (ⓣ1-800/355-5755). For up-to-date ski conditions visit ⓦwww.quebecskisurf.com or listen out for regular updates on the radio.

For more comprehensive descriptions of runs, terrain, lift passes, facilities and the like, pick up a copy of *The Rough Guide to Skiing & Snowboarding in North America*.

name – a Vermont woman is threatening to sue anyone who cashes in on "her" monster – than whether Memphré in fact exists.

Magog is a lively spot fairly teeming with bars and restaurants along its main street, rue Principale. Magog's north–south artery, rue Merry (Hwy-141) hosts much of the town's accommodation and also allows access to most of the area's outdoorsy activities since it both runs down the eastern shore of the lake and crests **Parc National du Mont-Orford**, passing through the uninteresting village of Orford's scattered houses and businesses along the highway. **Buses** from Montréal stop on rue Sherbrooke, near the intersection of rue Principale.

The **tourist office** is located at 55 rue Cabana, just off Hwy-112 on the way into Magog (June to mid-Oct daily 8.30am–8pm; mid-Oct to May daily 9am–5pm, Fri until 7pm; ⓣ1-800/267-2744, ⓦwww.tourisme-memphremagog.com).

Accommodation

Hotels tend to be expensive in Magog – your best bet is one of the two dozen or so **B&Bs** clustered around rues Merry Nord and Abbot if you want to stay in town. Mont-Orford is better for budget options, with a youth hostel and camping in the park (see below). For accommodation price codes see p.135.

Auberge du Centre d'Arts Orford 3165 chemin du Parc (Hwy-141) ⓣ819/843-8595 or 1-800/567-6155, ⓦwww.arts-orford.org/English/auberge/auberge.html; May–Oct. An excellent youth hostel right in the Parc du Mont-Orford with rustic chalets (July and Aug), and three large pavilions with a range of room options the rest of the summer. $18 dorm (with HI membership card); $23–25 per person in a room.

La Belle Échappée 145 rue Abbott ⓣ819/843-8061 or 1-877/843-8061,

Ⓦwww.bbcanada.com/echappee. A gabled 1880 house with three pretty rooms, wicker chairs on the veranda, and free use of bicycles – a good deal at this price. Shared or private bathroom. ❷–❹

La Belle Victorienne 142 rue Merry N Ⓣ819/847-0476 or 1-888/440-0476, Ⓦwww.bellevic.com. An attractive B&B in a Victorian home featuring beautiful gardens, an ivy-covered terrace, and five tastefully decorated rooms, all with private bathroom. ❸

Au Coeur du Magog 120 rue Merry Nord Ⓣ819/868-2511, Ⓦwww.aucoeurdemagog.com. A fine old house with individually themed rooms, some with private bath. There's a jacuzzi out back, near the deck where a hot breakfast is served on sunny days. ❷–❸

The Town

Much of Magog's activity centres on the **waterfront**, which is heaving on summer weekends and especially during **La Traversée Internationale du Lac Memphrémagog**, a 40km swim across the lake that provides the excuse for ten days of festivities and free concerts (late July to early Aug; Ⓣ819/847-3007, Ⓦwww.traversee-memphremagog.com). Strollers, bladers and cyclists roam the paths along the shore heading west from the centre of town, but swimmers skip the beach here for one further west (see below). Idyllic **boat cruises** ply Lac Memphrémagog daily during the summer and on weekends in September and October (1hr 45min tour; $15); unless you need a visa to visit the US, you can also opt for a day-long cruise south to Newport, VT ($55; Ⓣ819/843-8068 or 1-888/842-8068, Ⓦwww.croisiere-memphremagog.com); a tower marks the dock, located a third of the way along the promenade from rue Merry.

You'll want a bicycle or car to reach the sheltered Plage des Cantons, a sandy **beach** for swimming that fringes the lake further west. At a nearby kiosk, Voile Magog rents out water transport ranging from pedal-boats to sailboats (June to mid-Sept daily 9am–6pm; Ⓣ819/847-3181; $12–110); lessons are available. If you'd rather stay dry, there's a pricey **labyrinth** made up of chain-link fences that you can navigate on rollerblades or on foot (May to mid-Oct daily 10am–dusk; $7, $4 extra to rent in-line skates). You can also rent **in-line skates and bicycles** from Loca-Roule ($8/hr; Ⓣ819/847-4377), near the tourist office; in town, Ski-Vélo Vincent Renaud, set back from the main drag at 395 rue Principale O (Ⓣ819/843-4277, Ⓦwww.skivelo.com), rents bicycles ($15/half-day) and snowboards ($25/day) in season.

Eating

There are loads of **places to eat** along rue Principale in Magog and some fun drinking spots on rue Merry Sud. We've listed some of the best below.

Bistro Lady of the Lake 125 chemin de la Plage des Cantons Ⓣ819/868-2004, Ⓦwww.bistrolady.com. Expensive. Laid-back bar-bistro that feels like a Mediterranean beach house, complete with terrace overlooking the beach. The French and Italian fare is a bit pricey, but the two-course lunch is around $11 (from 2pm Mon–Wed, noon Thurs-Sun). They also brew their own beer on site.

Caffuccino 219 rue Principale O Ⓣ819/868-2225. Inexpensive. A trendy café serving up affordable breakfast fare, lunch (salads, panini, wraps and pizza bagels), sinfully sweet desserts and good coffee. Open 8am–11pm (until 10pm in winter).

Le Martimbeault 341 rue Principale O Ⓣ819/843-3182. Expensive. This upmarket French restaurant is heavy on rich meats like sweetbreads and steak, though there's also pasta and mussels on the menu. The five-course "fantaisie du chef" will set you back $40. Dinner only.

La Memphré 12 rue Merry S Ⓣ819/843-3405. Inexpensive. A pleasant bar in a charming house with views of the lake from the veranda; they serve quality pub food such as pasta, panini and burgers (lamb, bison and seitan – but no beef). The main draw, though, is the extremely tasty local beer named after the sea serpent that allegedly lives in the nearby lake.

La Petite Place 108 place du Commerce ☎819/847-3067. Inexpensive. A nondescript little place just off rue Principale that serves cheap vegetarian meals such as melted brie with pesto salad, veggie-paté or hummous tortillas and panini stuffed with feta. They have Internet access to boot ($2/15min or $6/hr). There's a second entrance at 280 rue St-Patrice O. No dinner Mon & Tues; breakfasts from 8.30am weekdays, 10am weekends.

Tonnerre de Brest 2197 chemin du Parc, Orford ☎819/847-1234, ⓦwww.tonnerredebrest.net. Moderate. Handy to Mont Orford, this Victorian house north of Magog on Hwy-141 has a large-windowed dining room where you can settle back to Belgian mussels or savoury Brittany-style crepes.

Parc National du Mont-Orford

A mature sugar maple forest blankets three-quarters of the 58 square-kilometre **Parc National du Mont-Orford** ($3.50 plus $5 beach parking; ☎819/843-9855 or reservations 1-877/843-9855, ⓦwww.sepaq.com), interspersed with stands of birch and conifers and laced with small lakes and rivers. The park's frontier lies ten minutes' drive north of Magog along rue Merry Nord (Hwy-141) via the blink-and-you've-missed-it village of Orford, and actually comprises three mountain peaks, of which Mont Orford is the tallest at 853m. In **summer**, the grassy slopes are a nature-lover's paradise with 80km of hiking trails, cycle paths, golfing, boating and supervised swimming. You can rent gear for most activities from park offices (see above for contact details). You can also **camp** at one of the sites dotted about or off in the woods (rustic $18, semi-serviced $22, serviced $24–32).

The park is equally lively in **winter**, when 52 downhill skiing runs, a snow park with half-pipe and challenging jumps, 70km of groomed cross-country skiing trails and 10km of snowshoeing trails all open. The chair lifts operate year-round. The ski hill and golf course are administered separately from the rest of the park (☎819/843-6548 or 1-866/673-6731, ⓦwww.orford.com).

If that all sounds too active, time your visit for one of the **classical music concerts** during the Orford Festival (late June to mid-Aug; $25–50; ☎819/843-9871 or 1-888/310-3665, ⓦwww.arts-orford.org) at the Centre d'Arts Orford, 3165 chemin du Parc (Hwy-141).

Abbaye St-Benoît-du-Lac

The Eastern Townships's most unique attraction, the **Abbaye St-Benoît-du-Lac** (☎819/843-4080, ⓦwww.st-benoit-du-lac.com), looms over Lac Memphrémagog 25km southwest of Magog, a fantastical, castle-like building colourfully trimmed with pinks, yellows and greens. To get here, take Hwy-245 south from the western edge of Magog and follow the signs to St-Benoît-du-Lac.

Sixty Benedictine monks, renowned for their **Gregorian chants**, reside in the abbey and perform three times daily in the barn-like church at its western end (daily: 7.30 & 11am, plus Fri–Wed 5pm and Thurs 7pm). They also make some of the region's best cheese – their light **Ermite blue cheese** started the abbey's tradition of making high-quality regional produce and is sold at the on-site shop (Mon–Sat 9am–4.30pm) along with cider and other goodies. In keeping with St Benedict's rule on hospitality, the monastery accepts men as guests (accommodation for women is available at the Villa Ste-Scholastique, ☎819/843-2340); a donation of $35 is all that you'll be asked for a night's stay and three meals but you'll need to reserve months in advance to secure a bed.

North Hatley

The region east of Magog is one of the few areas in Québec where you'll encounter vestiges of the snobbish Anglophone attitudes that once pervaded the whole province. No town epitomizes this more than picturesque **North Hatley**, 30-minutes' drive east from Magog along Hwy-108, where boutiques sell English teas and biscuits to a resident population that steadfastly refuses to change the town's name to "Hatley Nord". Grand manors, many of which house hotels and B&Bs, curve in a U-shape around the pleasant **Lac Massawippi** that extends south from the centre. Parking ($2/hr, $10/day) is tucked just behind the main strip, rue Principale, along with a small tourist information office (summer only; hours vary).

Just about the only organized activity here is theatre, as the province's longest-running English-language playhouse, **The Piggery**, stages several quality productions throughout the summer (mid-June to Sept; Ⓣ819/842-2431, Ⓦwww.piggery.com). Theatre aside, North Hatley is a quiet town with little to do but hang out with a good book and absorb the scenery. There's a public **beach** on the lake's western shores, and several small **art galleries** and **antique shops** clustered along rue Principale that make for a pleasant afternoon of shopping. If you fancy a spot of **fly-fishing** for trout and bass, contact the owner of the *Serendipity Bed & Breakfast* (see below) – a four-hour trip costs $100 per couple and lessons are available. One-hour motorboat **cruises** are also available from Roger Ross ($15; Ⓣ819/842-2279).

Practicalities

North Hatley's rarefied air extends to its **accommodation** – some of the best inns in the province are here, but you'll pay for the privilege of spending the night. Likewise, the B&Bs are pricier than those in Magog. One of the more elegant hotels is the *Auberge Hatley*, 325 rue Virgin (Ⓣ819/842-2451 or 1-800/336-2451, Ⓦwww.northhatley.com; ❼), which has lake views from its hillside location, sumptuous rooms, an outdoor swimming pool and a restaurant serving top-notch French cuisine. *Serendipity Bed & Breakfast*, 340 chemin de la Rivière (Ⓣ819/842-2970, Ⓦwww.bbcanada.com/1441.html; ❸), is a century-old house done up with country-style furnishings in the three rooms, one of which has private bath; the owner runs fly-fishing trips (see above). Further out is *Manoir Le Tricorne*, 50 chemin Gosselin (Ⓣ819/842-4522, Ⓦwww.manoirletricorne.com; ❹), well worth the 6km drive from town for the spectacular views over the lake and countryside from the 92-acre estate of this 145-year-old house. Converted to an inn, most of *Le Tricorne*'s twelve large and nicely furnished rooms have fireplaces; rates include breakfast and access to the swimming pool.

There isn't much of a drinking scene in this staid village – you'll most likely pass the evening lingering over a **meal**. *Café de Lafontaine*, 35 rue Principale (Ⓣ819/842-4242) serves standard salads, hamburgers, pastas and good desserts on the terrace when it's sunny out and has live musical acts in the colder months. The cozy *Café Massawippi*, 3050 chemin Capelton (Ⓣ819/842-4528), offers original remakes of international classics like smoked sturgeon carpaccio, venison tartare and seared scallops with tempura vegetables. Those with tighter budgets should try *Pilsen*, 55 rue Principale (Ⓣ819/842-2971, Ⓦwww.pilsen.ca), a gastronomic pub whose eclectic menu includes mussels, buffalo steak and terrific grilled salmon, best washed down with one of the local Massawippi ales while seated at the waterside terrace. The pricey *Manoir Hovey*, a posh inn at 575 chemin Hovey (Ⓣ819/842-2421, Ⓦwww.hoveymanor.com), has a game-heavy menu on which duck figures strongly, enhanced with delectable flavours like ginger and chokecherry – and an extensive wine list. Reserve a table overlooking the lake (or near the fireplace in winter).

22

Québec City

If Montréal is French-speaking Canada at its most dynamic, New France's religious and colonial legacy is more evocatively captured by **Québec City**, some 250km northeast. Spread over Cap Diamant and the banks of the St Lawrence, Québec City is Canada's most beautifully situated and historic city. At its centre stands **Vieux-Québec**, the only walled city in North America, a fact that prompted UNESCO to classify it as a World Heritage Site in 1985. In both parts of the old city – Haute- and Basse-Ville (Upper and Lower Town) – the winding and sometimes cobbled streets are flanked by seventeenth- and eighteenth-century stone houses and churches, graceful parks and squares, and countless monuments.

This is an authentically and profoundly French city: 95 percent of its 600,000 inhabitants are French-speaking. Though not as bilingual as Montrealers, the people of Québec City are generally friendlier and most speak some English. While Montréal feels international, Québec City is more than a shade provincial, often seeming too bound up with its religious and military past – a residue of the days when the city was not only the bastion of the Catholic Church in Canada, but also its strategic linchpin. The Church was responsible for the creation and preservation of the city's finest buildings, from the quaint Église Notre-Dame-des-Victoires to the opulent Basilique-Cathédrale Notre-Dame de Québec and the vast Séminaire. Austere and awe-inspiring defensive structures, like the massive Citadelle, reveal the military pedigree of a city dubbed by Churchill as the "Gibraltar of North America".

Some history

For centuries, the clifftop site on which Québec City sits was occupied by the Iroquois village of **Stadacona**. Permanent European settlement did not begin until 1608, when **Samuel de Champlain** established a fur-trading post in what is now Place Royale. To protect the rapidly developing inland trade gateway, the main settlement shifted to the clifftop in 1620 when Fort St-Louis (later Château St-Louis) was built. Québec's steady expansion was noted in London, and in 1629 Champlain was starved out of the fort by the British, an occupation that lasted just three years. Before the century was out, the long-brewing struggles between England and France spilled over into the colony again, prompting the Comte de Frontenac, known as the "fighting governor", to replace Champlain's Fort St-Louis with Château St-Louis, and begin work on the fortifications that ring Vieux-Québec.

During the Seven Years' War (1756–63), the most significant battle in Canada's history took place here, between the British under General James Wolfe and the French army, led by Louis Joseph, Marquis de Montcalm. The city had already been under siege from British forces on the opposite shore for

QUÉBEC CITY

0 — 500 m

Rivière St-Charles
Bassin Louise
Gare du Palais & Bus Terminal
Marché du Vieux-Port
ST-ROCH
AUTOROUTE DUFFERIN
Hôtel-Dieu
VIEUX-QUÉBEC (HAUTE VILLE)
Musée des Ursulines
Séminaire
VIEUX-PORT
Cruise ship terminal
Musée de la Civilisation
BASSE VILLE
Ursuline Convent
Château Frontenac
Citadelle
Parc de l'Esplanade
Hôtel du Parlement
Place George V
Discovery Pavilion
Parc Jeanne-d'Arc
Parc de Champs de Bataille (Plaines d'Abraham)
Martello Tower 1
Martello Tower 2
Martello Tower 4
Musée National des Beaux-Arts du Québec
Observatoire de la Capitole
Parc de l'Amérique-Française
Le Grand Théâtre de Québec
FAUBOURG ST-JEAN-BAPTISTE
Église St-Jean-Baptiste
MONTCALM
St Lawrence River
Lévis

BARS & CLUBS

L'Amour Sorcier	2
Dagobert	12
Le Drague	5
Maurice	14
Pub Java	9
Sacrilège	3

RESTAURANTS & CAFÉS

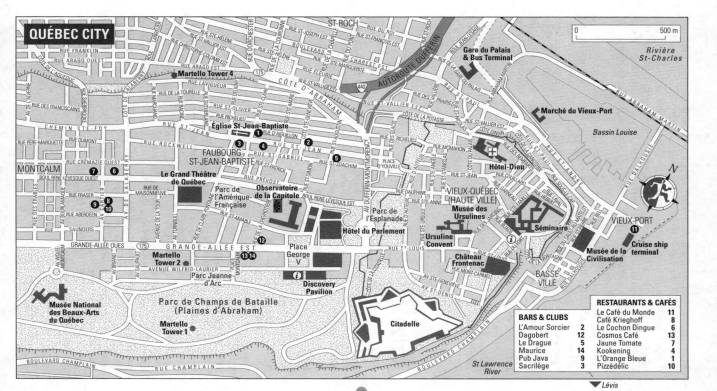

Le Café du Monde	11
Café Krieghoff	8
Le Cochon Dingue	6
Cosmos Café	13
Jaune Tomate	7
Kookening	4
L'Orange Bleue	1
Pizzédélic	10

three months, during which time Montcalm had carefully protected the city from any approach by water. Finally, in September 1759, Wolfe and his 4500 troops heard of an unguarded track, scaled the cliff of Cap Diamant and crept up on the unprepared French regiment. The twenty-minute **Battle of the Plaines d'Abraham** left both leaders mortally wounded and the city of Québec in the hands of the British, a state of affairs ultimately confirmed by the Treaty of Paris in 1763.

In 1775, the town was attacked again, this time by the Americans, who had already captured Montréal but were unable to take Québec City. For the next century the city quietly earned its livelihood as the centre of Canada's timber-trade and shipbuilding industry. By the time it was declared the provincial capital of Lower Canada in 1840, though, the accessible supplies of timber had run out. Ceasing to be a busy seaport, the city quietly declined, its way of life still largely determined by the Catholic Church until the Quiet Revolution in the 1960s and the rise of Québec nationalism (see p.271). Québec City has since grown with the upsurge in the economy, developing a suburban belt of shopping malls and convention centres as slick as any in the country. And with the waning influence of the once all-pervasive Church, many of the city's less historic religious structures are now being converted into condos.

Arrival

Québec City is easy enough to get to from Montréal, with excellent air, rail and road links. You won't save much time by flying once you've tacked transport and airport formalities onto the fifty-minute flight time; flights arrive at **Aéroport Jean-Lesage** (Ⓦwww.aeroportdequebec.com), 20km west of the city and the twenty-minute trip by taxi to the city centre is a fixed rate of $24.50.

VIA Rail **trains** from Montréal take three hours to reach the central Gare du Palais ($114; Ⓣ1-888/842-7245) in Basse-Ville. **Buses** are cheaper, and the regular express buses just as fast as the train, arriving at the main bus terminal, 320 rue Abraham-Martin (Ⓣ418/525-3000), adjoining the Gare du Palais. A slower but more scenic alternative is the **jet boat** (see p.15), arriving at the Vieux-Port. A **ridesharing** service between Montréal and Québec City is available through Allô-Stop – see p.29 for details.

If you come by **car**, there's a choice of two *autoroutes* for the two-and-a-half-hour journey from Montréal: Hwy-40 follows the north shore of the St Lawrence (if you have the time, switch over to the picturesque and much slower Hwy-138 – the old Chemin du Roy, or King's Highway – east of Trois-Rivières) and Hwy-20 the south, the latter being a marginally more interesting drive if you don't have time for the Chemin du Roy. On-street **parking** within the city walls can be a pain and, although there are car parks there (beneath the Hôtel de Ville, for instance), it's best to leave your vehicle outside the centre. Try the car park near the tourist office on avenue Wilfrid-Laurier outside Porte St-Louis or along the river in front of rue Dalhousie (but expect traffic jams during rush hour); the long-term car park is opposite the bus terminal. Note that motorcycles are not permitted in Vieux-Québec.

Information and city transport

Québec City's main **information centre**, which also offers an accommodation service, is located beside the Voltigeurs de Québec armoury at 835 av Wilfrid-Laurier (late June to early Sept daily 8.30am–7.30pm; early Sept to mid-Oct daily 8.30am–6.30pm; mid-Oct to late June Mon–Thurs & Sat 9am–5pm, Fri 9am–6pm, Sun 10am–4pm; ⓣ418/641-6290, ⓦwww.quebecregion.com). More information is available at the province-run **Centre Infotouriste** on the opposite side of Place d'Armes from the *Château Frontenac* at 12 rue Ste-Anne (daily: late June to early Sept 8.30am–7.30pm; early Sept to late June 9am–5pm; ⓣ1-877/266-5687, ⓦwww.bonjourquebec.com). It also has an accommodation service and counters for the various tour companies. Grab the free booklet *Greater Québec Area* from either for a detailed map.

Québec City's sights and hotels are packed into a small area, so **walking** is the most practical and pleasurable way to get around. A funicular and staircase near the *Château Frontenac* provide easy access down to Basse-Ville. For sights further out, like the Musée National des Beaux-Arts du Québec, RTC **local buses** (ⓣ418/627-2511, ⓦwww.rtcquebec.ca) are efficient and run from around 6am to 1am (certain routes run until 3am Fri & Sat). Fares are $1.95 per journey by prepaid ticket, available at newsstands and grocery stores across town, as are one-day passes ($5.25; valid for two people Sat & Sun); the cash fare per journey is $2.35, exact fare only. **Taxis** are available from Taxi Coop (ⓣ418/525-5191) and Taxi Québec (ⓣ418/525-8123).

Accommodation

There's a wealth of **accommodation** in Québec City, with dozens of **hotels** and **bed and breakfasts** in Vieux-Québec alone (see p.135 for price codes). Many of these are smaller, family-run affairs and generally do not offer parking (although they may be able to sell you a voucher for one of the car parks for around $10 a day). Because they are often in converted houses, the rooms may have various quirks – don't be afraid to ask to see a couple of rooms as they can vary greatly within a hotel (and may have one or two beds of various sizes). Generally, the cheaper rooms will be darker, smaller, and have one double bed and/or shared bath. There are also two **youth hostels** within the walls of the old city – the one on rue Ste-Ursule is surrounded by **budget hotels**. Always try to reserve rooms in advance, particularly during the summer months and the Carnaval in February.

Hotels

Auberge St-Antoine 10 rue St-Antoine ⓣ418/692-2211 or 1-888/692-2211, ⓦwww.saint-antoine.com. The stone walls and chunky wood posts and beams in the common areas of this swish hotel are as authentic as the artefacts on display at the Musée de la Civilisation, next door. The pricier of the sleekly modern rooms in the recently added wing have private terraces, while the older part has an elegant contemporary decor with French doors overlooking the courtyard or, in the more expensive rooms, river views. ❼–❽

Auberge St-Louis 48 rue St-Louis ⓣ418/692-2424 or 1-888/692-4105, ⓦwww.bonnesadressesvxqc.com. This simple inn along rue St-Louis is centrally located and comprises two three-storey houses dating from the

1830s whose muted olive-coloured rooms feature IKEA-style furnishings but are comfy nonetheless. Cheaper rooms have shared bath. ❸–❹

Le Château Frontenac 1 rue des Carrières ⓣ418/692-3861 or 1-800/441-1414, ⓦwww.fairmont.com. This opulent Victorian "castle" opened in 1893, and has accommodated such dignitaries as Churchill, Roosevelt, Madame Chiang Kai-shek and Queen Elizabeth II. It's the most expensive place in town and has magnificent views over the city and the St Lawrence, elegant dining halls, a tiled swimming pool and impeccably well-furnished rooms. If you can't afford to stay, you can still take a guided tour (see p.249). ❽

Hôtel Cap-Diamant 39 av Ste-Geneviève ⓣ418/694-0313, ⓦwww.hcapdiamant.qc.ca. Nine-bedroom guesthouse dating from 1826 with sumptuous Victorian furnishings located on a quiet street near the Jardin des Gouverneurs. All rooms are en-suite, and have a/c, minifridges and TVs. In summer, you can take your continental breakfast into the peaceful courtyard garden. ❹

Hôtel Clarendon 57 rue Ste-Anne ⓣ418/692-2480 or 1-888/554-6001, ⓦwww.hotelclarendon.com. The city's oldest hotel, dating from the 1870s, was given a number of Art Deco and Art Nouveau touches when renovated in the 1930s. The comfortable rooms feel a bit small but are nicely furnished in muted earth tones. ❹

Hôtel Dominion 1912 126 rue St-Pierre ⓣ418/692-2224 or 1-888/833-5253, ⓦwww.hoteldominion.com. Fabulous boutique hotel with all the touches – feather pillows and duvets, subdued lighting, stylish modern decor and cool frosted-glass sinks lit from below. Windows run the lengths of the rooms, offering terrific views of the St Lawrence or Vieux-Québec from the upper floors. ❻

Hôtel Le Clos St-Louis 69 rue St-Louis ⓣ418/694-1311 or 1-800/461-1311, ⓦwww.clossaintlouis.com. Elegant hotel in two interconnected 1840s houses with decor to match – Victorian stuffed chairs and settees, four-poster beds in some of the rooms, gilt mirrors and lots of antiques (including the armoires where the TVs are cached). Hot breakfast is served in the dining room. ❻

Hôtel Manoir d'Auteuil 49 rue d'Auteuil ⓣ418/694-1173, ⓦwww.quebecweb.com/dauteuil. Lavish 1835 townhouse by the city walls, refurbished a century later with 16 Art Deco rooms, now with a/c. Friendly service and a free continental breakfast is included. ❸

Hôtel Le Priori 15 rue de Sault-au-Matelot ⓣ418/692-3992 or 1-800/351-3992, ⓦwww.hotellepriori.com. The rooms in this renovated house have a bright, modern feel with deep purple carpets, cone-shaped stainless-steel wash basins and, in some of the rooms, clawfoot tubs. You can have your buffet breakfast in the hotel's tranquil courtyard. ❺

Hôtel Terrasse-Dufferin 6 place Terrasse-Dufferin ⓣ418/694-9472, ⓦwww.terrasse-dufferin.com. An 1830s mansion with some original details in the 19 rooms, all of which have private bath. The rooms at front have striking views over the St Lawrence, and thus need to be booked months in advance. ❹

Bed and breakfasts

B&B des Grisons 1 rue des Grisons ⓣ418/694-1461, ⓦwww.bbcanada.com/2608.html. A late-nineteenth-century home with high ceilings, wood-strip floors and antiques from various epochs. The larger of the five rooms have sofa-beds and all have shared bath. Hot breakfasts are served in the dining room, adjacent to the living room whose fireplace will also warm you up. ❸

Maison Historique James Thompson 47 rue Ste-Ursule ⓣ418/694-9042, ⓦwww.bedandbreakfastquebec.com. One of Vieux-Québec's original B&Bs, this historic 1793 house is surprisingly bright and strewn with antiques; there are sleigh beds in two of the three bedrooms. ❸

La Marquise de Bassano 15 rue des Grisons ⓣ418/692-0316 or 1-877/692-0316, ⓦwww.marquisedebassano.com. A tastefully decorated 1888 house with five tastefully decorated rooms – the more expensive have private bath and perks like four-poster beds or a roof terrace. The friendly young owner prepares fresh pastries to go with the continental-plus breakfast and occasionally plays the baby grand in the comfy living room. ❸–❺

Hostels

Auberge de la Paix 31 rue Couillard ☎418/694-0735, Ⓦwww.aubergedelapaix.com. Situated just off rue St-Jean, this is by far the better of Québec City's two youth hostels, with a friendly staff and a large courtyard to hang out in. Rates – $19.50 whether in dorms or one of the two private rooms – include a serve-yourself breakfast; bedding is an extra $2.50 per stay ($5 deposit). It fills up fast, so book ahead.

Centre International de Séjour de Québec 19 rue Ste-Ursule ☎418/694-0755 or 1-800/461-8585, Ⓦwww.cisq.org. The city's official youth hostel, in a former hospice run by nuns, can be impersonal and fills up quickly despite offering over 300 beds in large shared rooms and dormitories ($20 for members, $24 for non-members) and doubles ($46/$50 for the room, $65/$69 with private bath), triples, quads, etc. It's well kitted-out for budget travellers, though, with a cafeteria and bar, kitchen and laundry facilities, Internet access ($1 for 15min) and luggage lockers. No curfew, but you'll need to be buzzed in after 11pm. Discounts for children under 12.

The City

Québec City's historic highlights are mostly situated beside the St Lawrence, with the main attractions evenly distributed between the upper and lower portions of **Vieux-Québec** (Old Québec). Perched atop Cap Diamant and encircled by the city walls, **Haute-Ville** (Upper Town) forms the Québec City of tourist brochures, dominated appropriately enough by a hotel – the towering *Château Frontenac*. Its stupendous clifftop location accounts for part of its allure, and the wide boardwalk of the Terrasse Dufferin running along the front provides fantastic views over the St Lawrence River and **Basse-Ville** (Lower Town). Steep stairs and a funicular provide access to Basse-Ville, the site of some of the city's oldest and best-preserved buildings, as well as the worthwhile Musée de la Civilisation. Back away from the cliff edge, amid the jumble of streets in the middle of Haute-Ville are a number of museums and the city's most dramatic churches, while the fortifications are best seen at the western end ofVieux-Québec.You can follow them along to the star-shaped Citadelle, protecting the city from attack across the Plaines d'Abraham, although the only clashes there now are the bold colours of modernist paintings in the Musée National des Beaux-Arts du Québec at the far end of the former battlefield.

Haute-Ville

Most visitors begin their tour of **Vieux-Québec** in the walled upper town – **Haute-Ville** – drawn by the castle-like **Château Frontenac** and magnificent vistas over the St Lawrence from the **Terrasse Dufferin** running along in front. If you're only here for a short time, drop down into Basse-Ville (see p.258) before exploring the wealth of museums and sites on the narrow streets spreading out from **Place d'Armes** that convey the city's religious and military history. An imposing cathedral and seminary, along with a number of churches and convents, are reminders of the former, while the latter is most literally set in the stones that make up the encircling **fortifications** and massive **Citadelle** guarding the old town's southern flank.

Château Frontenac

Champlain established his first fort in 1620 on the site now occupied by the gigantic **Château Frontenac**, dominating the south side of Place d'Armes

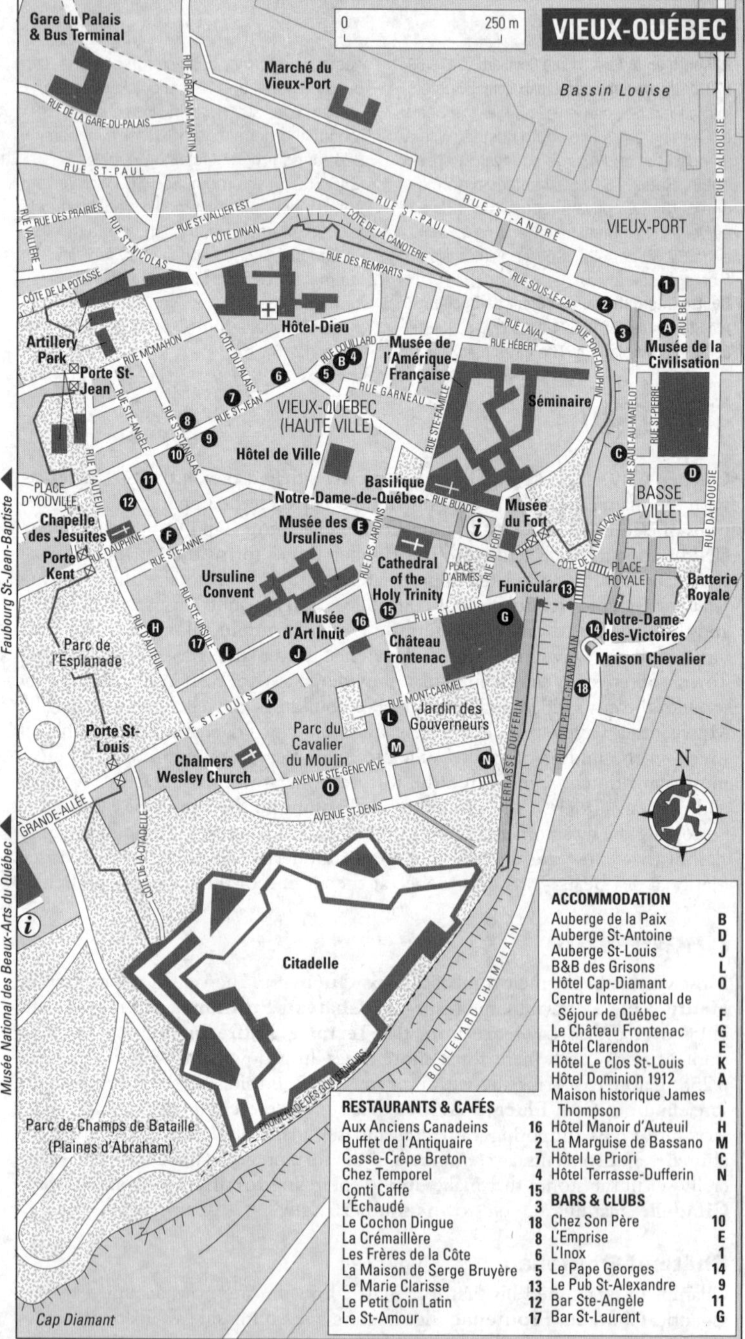
VIEUX-QUÉBEC
0 250 m
Gare du Palais & Bus Terminal
Marché du Vieux-Port
Bassin Louise
RUE DE LA GARE-DU-PALAIS
RUE ABRAHAM-MARTIN
RUE ST-PAUL
RUE ST-ANDRÉ
RUE DALHOUSIE
VIEUX-PORT
RUE VALLIÈRE
RUE DES PRAIRIES
RUE ST-VALLIER EST
CÔTE DINAN
CÔTE DE LA CANOTERIE
RUE ST-NICOLAS
RUE DES REMPARTS
RUE SOUS-LE-CAP
CÔTE DE LA POTASSE
Hôtel-Dieu
CÔTE DU PALAIS
RUE COUILLARD
Musée de l'Amérique-Française
RUE LAVAL
RUE HÉBERT
RUE PORT-DAUPHIN
RUE BELL
Musée de la Civilisation
Artillery Park
RUE McMAHON
Porte St-Jean
RUE GARNEAU
Séminaire
RUE ST-JEAN
VIEUX-QUÉBEC (HAUTE VILLE)
RUE STE-ANGÈLE
RUE ST-STANISLAS
RUE STE-FAMILLE
RUE SAULT-AU-MATELOT
RUE ST-PIERRE
Hôtel de Ville
Basilique Notre-Dame-de-Québec
RUE BUADE
Musée du Fort
BASSE VILLE
PLACE D'YOUVILLE
RUE D'AUTEUIL
Chapelle des Jesuites
Musée des Ursulines
RUE DES JARDINS
RUE DU FORT
CÔTE DE LA MONTAGNE
Porte Kent
RUE DAUPHINE
RUE STE-ANNE
Ursuline Convent
Cathedral of the Holy Trinity
PLACE D'ARMES
Funicular
PLACE ROYALE
Batterie Royale
RUE STE-URSULE
Musée d'Art Inuit
RUE ST-LOUIS
Notre-Dame-des-Victoires
Parc de l'Esplanade
Château Frontenac
Maison Chevalier
RUE DU PETIT-CHAMPLAIN
RUE MONT-CARMEL
Jardin des Gouverneurs
Porte St-Louis
Parc du Cavalier du Moulin
TERRASSE DUFFERIN
Lévis
Chalmers Wesley Church
AVENUE STE-GENEVIÈVE
N
GRANDE-ALLÉE
AVENUE ST-DENIS
CÔTE DE LA CITADELLE
Faubourg St-Jean-Baptiste
Musée National des Beaux-Arts du Québec
Citadelle
BOULEVARD CHAMPLAIN
PROMENADE DES GOUVERNEURS
Parc de Champs de Bataille (Plaines d'Abraham)
Cap Diamant
ACCOMMODATION
Auberge de la Paix B
Auberge St-Antoine D
Auberge St-Louis J
B&B des Grisons L
Hôtel Cap-Diamant O
Centre International de Séjour de Québec F
Le Château Frontenac G
Hôtel Clarendon E
Hôtel Le Clos St-Louis K
Hôtel Dominion 1912 A
Maison historique James Thompson I
Hôtel Manoir d'Auteuil H
La Marguise de Bassano M
Hôtel Le Priori C
Hôtel Terrasse-Dufferin N
BARS & CLUBS
Chez Son Père 10
L'Emprise E
L'Inox 1
Le Pape Georges 14
Le Pub St-Alexandre 9
Bar Ste-Angèle 11
Bar St-Laurent G
RESTAURANTS & CAFÉS
Aux Anciens Canadeins 16
Buffet de l'Antiquaire 2
Casse-Crêpe Breton 7
Chez Temporel 4
Conti Caffe 15
L'Échaudé 3
Le Cochon Dingue 18
La Crémaillère 8
Les Frères de la Côte 6
La Maison de Serge Bruyère 5
Le Marie Clarisse 13
Le Petit Coin Latin 12
Le St-Amour 17

and probably Canada's most photographed building. New York architect Bruce Price drew upon the local French-Canadian architectural style to produce a pseudo-medieval, red-brick pile crowned with a steep copper roof. Although the hotel he designed was inaugurated by the Canadian Pacific Railway in 1893, its distinctive main tower was only added in the early 1920s, resulting in an over-the-top design that makes the most of the extreme location atop Cap Diamant. Numerous celebrities and royalty, including Queen Elizabeth II, have stayed here, and the hotel has hosted at least one pair of newlyweds every night since it opened. If the steep prices are beyond your budget (see p.246), there are 50-minute guided tours departing on the hour from the lower level (May to mid-Oct daily 10am–6pm; mid-Oct to April Sat & Sun noon–5pm, call for weekday times; $7; reservations recommended ⓣ418/691-2166).

Terrasse Dufferin

Fronting the *Château Frontenac*, the wide clifftop boardwalk of the **Terrasse Dufferin** overlooks the *kebec* ("where the river narrows" in the Algonquin language), which is the source of the city's (and the province's) name. Underlying part of the boardwalk are the foundations of Frontenac's Château St-Louis, which served as the governor's residence for two centuries until a fire destroyed it in 1834. The leafy park running alongside the boardwalk was the château's garden – hence its name, the **Jardin des Gouverneurs**.

The boardwalk heads south from here, past the Charles Baillairgé-designed open-air pavilions and streetlamps, first electrified in 1885, and ends where the cliff rises to the Citadelle (see p.253). You can continue past it by taking a long flight of stairs up to the Promenade des Gouverneurs, a narrow boardwalk perched precariously on the cliff face below the Citadelle that leads to the Plaines d'Abraham. At the northern end of the walkway, near the *Château Frontenac*, you can access the funicular and staircase that lead down to Basse-Ville (see p.258). Nearby, the terrace broadens into a plaza lorded over by a romantic statue of **Champlain** and, beside it, a modern sculpture symbolizing Vieux-Québec's status as a UNESCO World Heritage Site

Place d'Armes

Terrasse Dufferin's northern end flows into Vieux-Québec's main square, **Place d'Armes**, which features a central fountain topped by a monument to the Récollet missionaries who arrived here in 1615, and is surrounded by a number of notable historic buildings. One of the finest, to the right of the *Château Frontenac* at 17 rue St-Louis, is the **Maison Maillou**, which houses the Québec Chamber of Commerce. This 1736 grey-limestone house, with metal shutters for insulation and a steeply slanting roof, displays the chief elements of the climate-adapted architecture brought over to Canada by the Norman settlers.

Among the hotels and restaurants on the square's north side is the entrance to the narrow alley of **rue du Trésor**, where French settlers once paid their taxes to the Royal Treasury; nowadays it's a touristy artists' market with vendors hawking saccharine cityscapes. You'll do better to visit the courtyard just west of Place d'Armes between rue Ste-Anne and the Cathedral of the Holy Trinity, where Québec-based artisans operate small crafts and clothes stalls in summer (daily 11am–10pm). To the east of the alley, the former Union Hotel, built in 1803, houses the **Infotouriste** office (see p.245).

History lessons

There is no escaping history in Québec City. In addition to panels illustrated with archival photos and text (mainly in French) scattered throughout the city, more than a dozen museums, interpretation centres and historic buildings each provide their own take on the past, based on a particular person, religious movement or district – we cover the best ones for a short visit. Most have loads of activities aimed at kids, including replica costumes to try on and use to re-enact the life of former days – an adult version is even on offer in the form of a mystery dinner in the **Martello Tower No. 2** ($31.75; ⓣ418/649-6157).

On top of all of this, there are at least half a dozen multimedia shows, though many of these are rather patchy or painfully hokey. The most whiz-bang is the 3D **Québec Experience**, 8 rue du Trésor, second floor (May–Oct daily 10am–10pm; $7.50; ⓣ418/694-4000, ⓦwww.quebecexperience.com), aimed at people with short attention spans. The grand setting of the basilica, though, makes the **Heavenly Lights** show, a multimedia presentation telling the church's history and spotlighting architectural features in the pitch-black basilica to wondrous effect, hard to beat (May to mid-Oct Mon–Fri 6 shows daily 3.30–8.30pm, Sat & Sun 3 shows daily 6.30–8.30pm; 30min; $7.50; ⓣ418/692-2533 or 694-4000, ⓦwww.patrimoine-religieux.com).

Although hardly cutting-edge (think LED lights), the 37-square-metre model of Québec City, circa 1750, that forms the sole exhibit of the **Musée du Fort** at 10 rue Ste-Anne (Apr–Oct daily 10am–5pm; call to reserve in winter; $7.50; ⓣ418/692-2175) gives the most detailed account of the six battles fought here (the gift shop also has a decent selection of history books in English).

Finally, there are a host of **tours**, ranging from the colourful banter of the *calèche* drivers ($60 for a 30–45 minute tour; departures from in front of the *Château Frontenac*, Porte St-Louis or Parc de l'Esplanade) to the informative go-at-your-own-pace **CD Tour** ($10; ⓣ418/990-8687), which covers exhibits in some of the museums as well as the sights, and is available at the Centre Infotouriste. As well as an array of bus and thematic (ghost, literary, historical) walking tours, there are also tours of specific areas, like the free guided visit of Place Royale available from the interpretation centre (see p.259). Parks Canada runs two 90-minute trips along the **fortifications** led by a costumed guide – the "Fortified City" tour leaves from the Frontenac kiosk on Terrasse Dufferin, while "Defensive City" focuses more on military history and leaves from the fortifications interpretation centre next to the Porte St-Louis ($10, under-16s free; ⓣ418/648-7016, ⓦwww.parkscanada.gc.ca/fortifications).

Basilique-Cathédrale Notre-Dame de Québec

From Place d'Armes, you can follow rue du Trésor directly towards the impressive bulk of the **Basilique-Cathédrale Notre-Dame de Québec** (Mon–Fri 9am–2pm, Sat & Sun 9am–5pm and between shows; free). Focal point for the oldest parish north of Mexico, the church was burnt to the ground in 1922 – one of many fires it has suffered – and was rebuilt to the original plans of the post-Conquest version (the original 1647 church on this site was much smaller and insulated with furs). Absolute silence within the basilica heightens the impressiveness of the creamy Rococo-inspired interior, which culminates in a painted ceiling of blue sky and billowy clouds. The altar, a gilded replica of St Peter's, is surmounted by an elaborate baldachin uncharacteristically supported by angelic caryatids rather than columns due to the narrow space, and is topped by a statue of Jesus standing on a gilded sphere. The pewter sanctuary lamp, to the right of the main altar, was a gift from Louis XIV and is one of the few treasures to survive the fire.

Underneath much of the area surrounding the cathedral and the Hôtel de Ville (City Hall) across the square are the largely forgotten cemeteries of the colony's early days. The basilica's crypt itself holds more than nine hundred bodies, including Frontenac, three other governors and most of Québec's bishops. (Champlain is also rumoured to be buried there, though archeologists are still trying to work out which body is his.) Unfortunately, the only part of the crypt you can see on the informative **guided tours** (8.30am–3.30pm, every half-hour) is a ho-hum modern corridor – skip it and the tour is free; otherwise it's a dollar. In the afternoons, access to the basilica is limited to half an hour at a time unless you pay for the worthwhile *Heavenly Lights* show (see opposite).

Opposite the basilica, Côte de la Fabrique leads down to Vieux-Québec's lively main commercial strip, rue St-Jean, which is filled with a plentiful selection of restaurants and bars (see "Eating, drinking and nightlife", p.261) interspersed with some decent boutiques.

Séminaire de Québec

The wrought-iron gates beside the basilica lead into a large courtyard flanked by austere white buildings with handsome mansard roofs, where the vast **Séminaire de Québec** – founded by the aggressive and autocratic Monseigneur François de Laval-Montmorency in 1663 – spreads out to the north. In the three decades he was in office, Laval secured more power than the governor and intendant put together, and any officer dispatched from France found himself on the next boat home if Laval did not care for him. With the founding of the Diocese of Québec in 1674, Laval became the first bishop of New France and undertook a pilgrimage to see his See – a long jaunt given that it spread as far as Louisiana in those days. Laval retired early due to ill health, brought on by a religious fervour that denied him blankets and proper food. He finally died in 1708 after his feet froze on the stone floor of the chapel during his morning prayer session.

The seminary was the finest collection of buildings the city had seen, causing Governor Frontenac to grouse that the bishop was now housed better than he. Primarily a college for priests, the seminary also educated young men pursuing other professions, and in 1852 it became Laval University, the country's first Francophone Catholic university. Today it still houses the faculty of architecture, while other buildings in the complex include the Petit Séminaire, now a school, and the Archbishop's Residence, neither of which is accessible to the public.

The Séminaire's main areas of interest – and the departure point for one-hour guided tours of the seminary – can be found in the ever-expanding **Musée de l'Amérique Française** (June–Sept daily 9.30am–5pm; Oct–May Tues–Sun 10am–5pm; $4, free on Tues Sept–June. Guided tours: weekends from mid-May to mid-Oct, daily in summer; included in entry fee; ⓣ418/692-2843; ⓦwww.mcq.org), whose main entrance is in the **Maison du Coin**, on your left as you face the main gate. The Maison du Coin contains a small upstairs exhibition on the early colonists. It also adjoins the high and narrow Roman-style **chapel**, whose Second Empire interior holds Canada's largest collection of religious relics, a few of which are on display. A side-chapel contains Laval's ornate marble tomb, but not his remains, which were moved to the basilica when the main chapel was deconsecrated in 1993. The whole interior is a bit of a sham, overall – fed up with rebuilding after the chapel burnt down yet again in 1888, the church authorities decided to construct the pillars and coffered ceilings out of tin and paint over them; the stained-glass windows have been painted on single panes of glass and even the "tapestries" are just the result of some deft brushwork.

From the chapel, an underground corridor runs to the **Pavillon Jérôme-Demers**, which displays mostly well-presented, historical exhibitions on the ground and first floors. Also on the Pavillon's first floor is a tiny sample of the eclectic items gathered by Québec's bishops and the academics at Laval: elaborate nineteenth-century scientific instruments, an Egyptian mummy, a small collection of European and Canadian paintings, as well as ecclesiastical silverware and some of Laval's personal belongings.

The museum's name derives from the exhibition on the second floor, **The Settling of French America**, which details the history of the settlement and emigration of the more than nineteen million North Americans of French stock. It may come as a bit of a surprise – given how thoroughly Franco-Americans have melted into the pot – that throughout the nineteenth century nearly 200 French newspapers were established in New England to serve the region's Francophone population. If yours is a French surname, you can search through the exhibition's genealogical panels to find your ancestors – the prolific Tremblays alone are responsible for some 85,000 households today.

Couvent des Ursulines

Heading south from the basilica along rue des Jardins brings you to narrow rue Donnacona, where a sculpted hand holding a quill – a monument to the women who, since 1639, have dedicated their lives to teaching Québec's young – rests on a pedestal. It points toward the **Couvent des Ursulines** on rue Donaconna, built by a tiny group of Ursuline nuns who arrived in Québec in 1639 calling themselves "the Amazons of God in Canada". Their task was to bring religion to the natives and later to the daughters of the settlers, a mission carried out in the classrooms of North America's first girls' school – the buildings still house a private school, run by the nuns.

The remains of the Ursulines' first mother superior, **Marie Guyart de l'Incarnation**, are entombed in the oratory adjoining the **chapel** (May–Oct Tues–Sat 10–11.30am & 1.30–4.30pm, Sun 1.30–4.30pm). Rebuilt in 1902, the chapel retains the sumptuous early-eighteenth-century altar and sculptures by Pierre-Noël Levasseur and a collection of seventeenth- and eighteenth-century paintings acquired from post-Revolution France in the 1820s. If you stand at the altar rail and look to the right, you can see the ornate, domed sisters' choir, positioned so that the nuns can remain cloistered while worshiping. A plaque nearby indicates General Montcalm's former resting place – he was buried in a hole created by a cannonball that punched through the roof of the chapel. However, during renovations some years later only his skull was to be found (it was recently moved to a military cemetery in the suburbs).

The lives of the early Ursulines, and Marie Guyart de l'Incarnation in particular, are the focus of the art and history **museum** (May–Sept 10am–noon & 1–5pm, Sun 1–5pm; Oct–April Tues–Sun 1–4.30pm; $5; ⓣ418/694-0694), opposite the chapel. Amongst the religious paraphernalia are gilded reliquaries containing partial skulls and bone fragments of a number of saints, while documents and household items stand as testament to the early colony's harsh living conditions. The collection of paintings includes a posthumous portrait of Marie, and Frère Luc's re-imagining of the Holy Family: Joseph presents a Huron girl to Mary as the St Lawrence flows past Cap Diamant in the background. What makes the entrance fee worthwhile, however, is the display of seventeenth- and eighteenth-century **liturgical ornaments** made by the nuns – wool and silk altar frontals shot through with gold and silver threads and equally richly embroidered vestments.

△ Quartier du Petit-Champlain from the Escalier Casee-Cou

Rue St-Louis and around

A short walk from the convent along rue des Jardins brings you to the intersection of **rue St-Louis** – Vieux-Québec's main tourist strip, teeming with overpriced and mostly uninteresting restaurants occupying dour greystone eighteenth- and nineteenth-century townhouses. On the corner at no. 34 stands **Maison Jacquet**, occupied by the restaurant *Aux Anciens Canadiens* (see p.262). The building's name comes from Québec's first novel, whose author, Philippe Aubert de Gaspé, lived here for a while in the middle of the nineteenth century. Dating from 1677, the house's thick stone walls, steeply sloping roof and dormer windows are typical features of seventeenth-century New France architecture, characteristics shared by the blue-and-white **Maison Kent**, at no. 25 on the other side of rue St-Louis, which was built in 1649. Once home to Queen Victoria's father, the Duke of Kent, it's best known as the place where the capitulation of Québec was signed in 1759 and now ironically houses the French consulate.

The delightful **Musée d'Art Inuit Brousseau**, 39 rue St-Louis (daily 9.30am–5pm; $6; ⓣ418/694-1828, ⓦwww.inuitart.ca), traces the development of Inuit art from the naive works of the mid-twentieth century to the highly narrative and intricately carved sculptures by contemporary artists. Inuit stone sculpture really only began in the 1940s, replacing the declining fur and hunting industries as a source of income – the Inuit artists used aspects of the everyday, like animals and hunting, for inspiration, but would also carve an ashtray if they thought they could sell it to a traveller passing through. The museum groups sculptures by region so that you can see the legends and daily rituals of the different Inuit cultures. The few ancient items on display are from the Dorset and Thulé cultures, nomadic peoples who worked in small, easy-to-carry pieces of ivory.

If you fancy a bit of greenery after all the grey stone of Vieux-Québec, take a detour up rue Haldimand (off rue St-Louis, just to the east of the museum) to the **Jardin des Gouverneurs**, overlooking the Terrasse Dufferin and formerly the preserve of the governors who inhabited the Château St-Louis. The monument to Wolfe and Montcalm, an obelisk erected in 1828, is rare in paying tribute to both the victor and the vanquished. A more intimate spot is the **Parc du Cavalier du Moulin**, a quiet little park two minutes west of the Jardin on rue Mont-Carmel and built on the remnant of the earlier French fortifications. The surrounding streets are home to some of the old town's most handsome residences – including those on rue de La Porte, on the Jardin's west side, and on parallel rue des Grisons. Both streets intersect with avenue Ste-Geneviève, from where you can ultimately work your way back to rue St-Louis near the city walls.

The fortifications and Artillery Park

Rue St-Louis leads directly from Place d'Armes to the **Porte St-Louis** (keep an eye out for the cannonball lodged in the tree roots at the corner of rue Corps-de-Garde along the way). The oldest (1878) of the four gates in the city wall, Porte St-Louis is surrounded by **Parc de l'Esplanade**, the main site for the Carnaval de Québec (see box, p.261) and departure point for the city's smart horse-drawn *calèches*, not to mention a good spot to begin the 4.5-kilometre stroll around the **fortifications** ringing the city (see box, p.250 for guided tours).

To the north lies the bulwark of the Citadelle (see opposite), while to the south, you can wander along the walls over the Porte Kent to Porte St-Jean, which separates the boutiques and restaurants of rue St-Jean from **Place**

d'Youville, scene of outdoor concerts. Further to the west, beyond Place d'Youville, rue St-Jean is the main street of the **Faubourg St-Jean-Baptiste** neighbourhood, whose studenty vibe, small gay district and down-to-earth restaurants and bars can be a welcome change from the history-steeped old town.

Immediately south of the Porte St-Jean lie the defensive structures of **Artillery Park**, raised in the early 1700s by the French in expectation of a British attack from the St Charles River, and subsequently a barracks for the Royal Artillery Regiment for more than a century. In 1882 it became a munitions factory, providing the Canadian army with ammunition in both world wars. The foundry, added in 1902, now houses an interpretation centre (April to early May Wed–Sun 10am–5pm; early May to mid-Oct daily 10am–5pm; $4; Ⓦwww.parkscanada.gc.ca/artillery), which has displays on the military pedigree of the city, including a vivid model of Québec City in 1808. It's also the starting point for one-hour guided tours ($4 extra) and visits of the site's four buildings, including the Officers' Quarters, furnished as it was in 1830, and the massive Dauphine Redoubt. The latter typifies the changes of fortune here: used by the French as the barracks for their garrison, it became the officers' mess under the British and then the residence of the superintendent of the Canadian Arsenal.

The Citadelle

Towering over the southern section of Vieux-Québec, the massive, star-shaped **Citadelle** can only be visited on one of the worthwhile guided tours (departing hourly: April 10am–4pm, May & June 9am–5pm, Sept 9am–4pm, Oct 10am–3pm; every half-hour: July & Aug 9am–6pm; once per day: Nov–March Mon–Fri 1pm; $8; Ⓣ418/694-2815, Ⓦwww.lacitadelle.qc.ca). The tour de force of Québec City's fortifications, the Citadelle occupies the highest point of Cap Diamant, 100m above the St Lawrence. This strategic site was first built on by the French, but most of the buildings still extant were constructed by the British under orders from the Duke of Wellington, who was anxious about American attack after the War of 1812.

The complex of 25 buildings covers 40 acres and is the largest North American fort still occupied by troops – it's home to the Royal 22nd Regiment, Canada's only French-speaking regiment. Around the parade ground are ranged various monuments to the campaigns of the "Van-Doos" (*vingt-deux*), as well as the summer residence of Canada's governor general and two buildings dating back to the French period: the Cap Diamant Redoubt, built in 1693 and thus one of the oldest parts of the Citadelle, and the 1750 powder magazine. The latter is now a mundane museum of weaponry from the eighteenth century to the present, military costumes and other artefacts – including a stuffed white goat, *Batisse IV* (an ancestor of the current regimental mascot). Other highlights of the tour are the views alongside the cannon atop the King's Bastion and the long, dank tunnel to the vaulted shooting gallery used to defend the external walls.

In addition to mandatory but entertaining hour-long guided tours (see above) around the Citadelle, other activities included in the admission price are the colourful **Changing of the Guard** (late June to early Sept daily 10am), which you can catch at the end of a 9am tour (otherwise arrive by 9.45am) and the **Beating of the Retreat** tattoo (July & Aug Fri–Sun 7pm), likewise at the end of the 6pm tour.

Outside the walls

Beyond the confines of Vieux-Québec's enveloping walls, most of the sights in the modern city lie directly to the west in what is technically also Haute-Ville as it's on the same escarpment. The area surrounding Grande-Allée, the westward continuation of rue St-Louis, is also known as Parliament Hill, much to the ire of English-speaking Canadians who feel the name should be reserved for the Canadian Parliament's setting in Ottawa. However, the provincial parliament is here, its **Hôtel du Parlement** meeting-place lying north of Grande-Allée's sweep of bars and cafés, while to the south unfurls the broad expanse of the **Plaines d'Abraham**, culminating with the city's premier art museum. The rest of the area makes for a good respite from the tourist hype, with the Faubourg St-Jean-Baptiste filling the gap between the parliament and the northern edge of the plateau, while to the west near the **Musée National des Beaux-Arts du Québec**, avenue Cartier brims with boutiques and mid-range restaurants popular with locals.

Hôtel du Parlement

Sweeping out from Porte St-Louis and flanked by grand Victorian mansions, the tree-lined boulevard of **Grande-Allée** bustles with restaurants, hotels and bars. At its eastern end stand the stately buildings of the **Hôtel du Parlement** (late June to early Sept Mon–Fri 9am–4.30pm, Sat & Sun 10am–4.30pm; early Sept to late June Mon–Fri 9am–4.30pm; ⓣ418/643-7239 or 1-866/DEPUTES, ⓦwww.assnat.qc.ca), designed by Eugène-Étienne Taché in 1877, using the Louvre for inspiration. Inside, finely carved and gilded walnut panels in the entrance hall depict important moments in Québec's history. From here the corridor of the Presidents' Gallery, lined with portraits of all the Legislative Assembly's speakers and presidents, leads to the Chamber of the National Assembly, where the 125 provincial representatives meet for debate. You can't see much, though, unless you take one of the free half-hour guided tours – call ahead as the schedule changes daily.

Among the government buildings clustered to the west of here, the Édifice Marie-Guyart, 1037 rue de la Chevrotière, is the tallest structure in the city. On its 31st floor, the **Observatoire de la Capitole** (late June to mid-Oct daily 10am–5pm; mid-Oct to late June Tues–Sun 10am–5pm; $4; ⓣ418/644-9841 or 1-888/497-4322, ⓦwww.observatoirecapitale.org) offers a 360-degree panoramic view over Vieux-Québec, the Citadelle and beyond, with panels providing useful background info on what you can see.

The Plaines d'Abraham

West of the Citadelle are the rolling grasslands of the **Parc des Champs-de-Bataille** (Battlefields Park), a sizeable chunk of land stretching along the cliffs above the St Lawrence. The park encompasses the historic **Plaines d'Abraham**, which were named after Abraham Martin, the first pilot of the St Lawrence River in 1620, and were the site on which Canada's history was rewritten (see p.268). The best place to start out is the park's **Discovery Pavilion**, below the tourist office at 835 av Wilfrid-Laurier E (daily 8.30am–5pm; mid-June to mid-Oct until 5.30pm; ⓣ418/648-4071, ⓦwww.ccbn-nbc.gc.ca), with maps, information panels and a short film on the site's history. It offers a multimedia history show (10am–4pm; $6.50), which, although featuring irksome 3D-enhanced "interviews" with Wolfe, Montcalm and other historical personages, nevertheless does a reasonable job of covering the after-effects of the Conquest, leading to the formation of Canada today.

Standing out amid the landscaped gardens, scenic drives, nature trails and jogging paths (cross-country ski trails in winter) of the wooded parklands designed by Frederick G. Todd in the 1930s is the **Martello Tower 1**, built in 1808 for protection against the Americans and today containing an unmemorable exhibition ($4). You can listen to free music performances at the Edwin-Bélanger bandstand, towards the park's western edge, on summer evenings (mid-June to mid-Aug Thurs–Sun 8pm; ⓣ418/648-4050).

Musée National des Beaux-Arts du Québec

Canadian art had its quiet beginnings in Québec City and the full panoply of this output can be found on the western edge of the Parc des Champs-de-Bataille in the **Musée National des Beaux-Arts du Québec** (daily 10am–6pm, Wed until 9pm; permanent collection free, special exhibitions $10; ⓣ418/643-2150 or 1-866/220-2150, ⓦwww.mnba.qc.ca; bus #11). The Grand Hall, with its cruciform skylight, connects the museum's two buildings (its original home, the Pavillon Gérard-Morisset, and a renovated Victorian prison renamed the Pavillon Charles-Baillairgé) and also serves as the main entrance.

For a chronological tour, start with Gallery 7 on the second floor of the **Pavillon Gérard-Morisset**, which provides a good survey of Québécois art from the early seventeenth through the late nineteenth centuries. As Québec churches were the primary art commissioners at the time, most of the earliest works are **religious art**, including the output of **Frère Luc**, represented here by *The Guardian Angel*, a painting depicting the story of Tobias and the archangel Raphael. The most notable contributions to the collection are by two dynasties: the works of brothers **Pierre-Noël** and **François-Noël Levasseur** from the mid-1700s and the three generations of **Baillairgés** who succeeded them, their copious output including the architecture of churches as well as their interior decoration. Under the British, the subject matter broadened to include portraiture, seen here in **Antoine Plamondon**'s poised *Madame Tourangeau*, and Canadian landscapes by Québec-born **Joseph Légaré** and, more famously, Amsterdam-born **Cornelius Krieghoff**, noted for his romanticized landscapes of landmarks in the region.

Gallery 8, opposite, covers the period spanning 1860 to 1945, from the late-nineteenth-century **salons** to the development of **modernist art**. In the first room, paintings fight for space on the walls; one that grabs your attention as you enter is **Horatio Walker**'s *Ploughing, the First Gleam at Dawn*, a romantic vision of the lives of the French-Canadian *habitants* who so engrossed him that he repudiated his Ontario roots. The tug-of-war of styles in Europe is played out in many of the subsequent works, including **Maurice Cullen**'s Impressionist-influenced view onto Basse-Ville, *Wolfe's Cove*, and the evocative scene of a horse-drawn carriage in a snowstorm, *Craig Street, Montréal*. Urban life is also admirably recorded by **Adrien Hébert**'s *Rue St-Denis*, which wonderfully captures the spirit of Montréal in the 1920s.

Downstairs, in Gallery 2, the impact of **Alfred Pellan**, who returned from Paris in 1940 to teach at Montréal's École des Beaux-Arts, plays out in the development of post-war **figurative and abstract art**. He introduced the modernism of Matisse and Picasso to Canada, and his comparative radicalism, evident in his Cubist-influenced still life, *Flowers and Dominoes*, was the catalyst for a generation of Québécois artists who flocked to Europe to pick up on the avant-garde movements of the time. The move to non-figurative representation can be seen in **Jean Dallaire**'s softly muted abstract figures in his 1957 *Julie*, which contrasts with his surreally colourful and strident *Coq Licorne* (Unicorn

Rooster) painted five years earlier. The process reaches its apogee with the Neo-Plasticism represented by **Fernand Leduc**'s boldly coloured geometric abstract *The Mountain Climber*.

At the same time, two of Québec's best-known artists were developing their signature styles. **Paul-Émile Borduas** applied the automatic writing technique of the surrealists to painting – his *Cabalistic Signs* is almost a doodle in oils. His progression to the increasingly spare canvases that have rooms devoted to them in Montréal's museums (see p.55 and p.62) can also be noted here. Gallery 3, across the hall, is devoted solely to the work of **Jean-Paul Riopelle**. The gallery's highlight is his *L'Hommage à Rosa Luxemburg* (1992), a 40-metre-long triptych in 30 segments, with ghostly spray-painted outlines of birds and man-made objects.

In the **Pavillon Charles-Baillairgé**, the red-brick interior walls of the former jail have been spruced up, creating a warm atmosphere surprisingly conducive to displaying art. Vaillancourt's *Tree on rue Durocher* sweeps up into the atrium, which then leads visitors into the galleries and a few of the old prison cells. These lie en route to Gallery 10, where "Je me souviens" portrays the personages and events in Québec's history through paintings and sculptures by some of the province's leading artists, and includes the studies for public works by sculptors Louis-Philippe Hébert and Alfred Laliberté. In the prison's tower, Montréal sculptor David Moore has created a unique two-storey sculpture of bodies scaling walls – just what you might expect in an old prison.

Gallery 12 on the third floor is devoted to Québec-born painter **Jean-Paul Lemieux**. His style varies wildly, from landscapes inspired by the Group of Seven such as the Charlevoix-set *Afternoon Sunlight*, through a phase of folk-art-style painting (including a fun look at the Corpus Christi parade winding down Côte de la Montagne), to end with a series of uncluttered Expressionist portraits.

Basse-Ville

The birthplace of Québec City, **Basse-Ville** (Lower Town), can be reached from Terrasse Dufferin by the **funicular** opposite the *Château Frontenac* and Place d'Armes, but it's best to save that for the weary journey back up. Instead, take the stairs at the north end of the terrace down to Porte Prescott (reconstructed in the 1980s – over a century after the original gate was demolished), where a path continues across the top of the gate to **Parc Montmorency**, the meeting place of Québec's first legislature in 1694. Descend the steps before crossing the gate, though, to reach the winding Côte de la Montagne from where the steep **Escalier Casse-cou** (Breakneck Stairs) leads to lively rue du Petit-Champlain (see p.259). Resist the temptation to descend it and carry another few metres along to where an unassuming staircase leads down to Place Royale, opening onto a lovely square of seventeenth-century stone buildings that offers perhaps the best introduction to Basse-Ville.

Place Royale and around

Champlain built New France's first permanent settlement at **Place Royale** in 1608, to begin trading fur with the native peoples. The square remained the focal point of Canadian commerce until 1759, and after the fall of Québec the British continued using the area as a lumber market, vital for shipbuilding during the Napoleonic Wars. After 1860, Place Royale was left to fall into scruffy disrepair until renovation began in the 1970s. Today, its pristine stone houses, most of which date from around 1685, are undeniably photogenic, with their

Hitting the slopes

Québec City makes a charming base for a ski holiday at one of the three surrounding resorts that are within an hour's drive. The largest, **Mont-Ste-Anne** (Ⓦwww.mont-sainte-anne.com), lies 40km to the east and offers a variety of good terrain at all skill levels, particularly intermediate runs and challenging expert terrain, and night skiing until 10pm. A further 33km east, **Le Massif** (Ⓦwww.lemassif.com) draws skiers as much for the spectacular vistas over the St Lawrence as for its intermediate-level carving slopes and some challenging expert runs. Beginners are best off at the locals' mountain, **Stoneham** (Ⓦwww.ski-stoneham.com), whose three interconnected peaks are just 6km north of Québec City's limits and also offer a good range of intermediate runs.

Mont-Ste-Anne has the most in the way of slopeside accommodation, but with Québec City and its array of dining and nightlife so close, you can easily make day-trips to any of the hills by car or with the Hiver-Express ski shuttle service (Ⓣ418/525-5191, Ⓦwww.taxicoop-quebec.com) to Stoneham or Mont-Ste-Anne (from where a free shuttle continues to Le Massif). The resorts along with the city tourist board offer ski packages and interchangeable lift tickets (Ⓣ418/827-5281 or 1-866/386-2754, Ⓦwww.fun2ski.com). For up-to-date ski conditions, visit Ⓦwww.quebecskisurf.com or listen out for regular updates on the radio.

For more comprehensive descriptions of runs, terrain, lift passes, facilities and the like, pick up a copy of *The Rough Guide to Skiing & Snowboarding in North America*.

steep metal roofs, numerous chimneys and pastel-coloured shutters, but it's a Legoland townscape, devoid of the scars of history. Fortunately the atmosphere is enlivened in summer by entertainment ranging from classical orchestras to juggling clowns, and by the Fêtes de la Nouvelle-France (see box, p.261), when everyone dresses in period costume and Place Royale briefly relives its past as a chaotic marketplace.

In Maison Hazeur, at 27 rue Notre-Dame, a merchant's house dating in part to 1684, the **interpretation centre** (late June to Aug daily 10am–5pm; Sept to late June Tues–Sun 10am–5pm; $3, free Nov–March and Tues except in summer; Ⓣ418/646-3167) outlines the history of Place Royale. Domestic objects and arrowheads are exhibited on the upper floors, while the original vaulted cellars have modern-looking stage sets of 1800s domestic scenes; kids will enjoy trying on the period costumes and acting out a role. The hokey multimedia show may also appeal to them, but the same ground is better covered in a tucked-away exhibit on level one illustrating the growth of the colony. The centre also runs free guided tours of the Place Royale area.

The **Église Notre-Dame-des-Victoires** (daily 9am–4.30pm), on the west side of the square where Champlain's residence once stood (the site of a former turret is outlined in paving stones in front of the church), was first built by Laval (see p.251) in 1688 but has been completely restored twice – after being destroyed by shellfire in 1759 and following a fire in 1969. Inside, the fortress-shaped altar alludes to the two French victories over the British navy that gave the church its name: the destruction of Admiral Phipp's fleet by Frontenac in 1690 and the sinking of Sir Hovenden Walker's fleet in 1711. Paintings depicting these events hang above the altar, while the aisles are lined with copies of religious paintings by Van Dyck, Van Loo and Rubens, gifts from early settlers to give thanks for a safe passage. The large model ship hanging over the nave is similarly an *ex voto*, donated by the Marquis de Tracy, the viceroy who commanded the Régiment de Carignan against the Iroquois in 1665–66.

Place Royale leads east past rue St-Pierre to **Place de Paris**, where a white cubic sculpture called *Dialogue with History* marks the disembarkation place of the first settlers from France. Further east beyond rue Dalhousie, you can see the promenade along the St Lawrence that passes the restaurants and attractions of the **Vieux-Port de Québec**, while to the south (past the Batterie Royale – see below) is the terminal for the **ferry** to Lévis (daily 6.30am–2am; $5 June–Sept; $4 Oct–May; Ⓣ418/644-3704, Ⓦwww.traversiers.gouv.qc.ca). A quick round trip affords great views of Québec City's impressive skyline.

Musée de la Civilisation

A walk north along rue Dalhousie from Place de Paris brings you to one of Québec City's most impressive museums, the **Musée de la Civilisation**, 85 rue Dalhousie (late June to early Sept daily 9.30am–6.30pm; otherwise Tues–Sun 10am–5pm; $7, free on Tues Sept–June; Ⓣ418/643-2158; Ⓦwww.mcq.org). Designed by prominent Canadian architect Moshe Safdie (who built Habitat '67 and the addition to the Musée des Beaux-Arts in Montréal), the museum references the steep-pitched roofs of the early settlers in a structure that incorporates a rooftop terrace with great views and three historic buildings. In the main foyer, a 1730s barque discovered on the site is displayed between a stone wall (the edge of the quay built a couple of decades later) and Astri Reusch's *La Débâcle*, a sculpture that symbolizes the break-up of the ice in the spring thaw.

Concentrating primarily on Canadian subjects but also diversifying into worldwide perspectives the museum presents worthwhile temporary exhibitions that have ranged from whimsical pop culture interests to serious looks at earlier historical periods. The first of the two permanent exhibitions upstairs, **Memories**, expertly displays life in Québec from the early days of the settlers to the present. Cross the atrium for the **Encounter with the First Nations** exhibition, set up in consultation with all eleven of the First Nations of Québec. It presents the history and culture of these earlier residents using artefacts and videotaped oral histories; the larger items – including a *rabaska*, an enormous birch-bark canoe – were crafted in recent years.

Be sure to check out the gift shop in the 1751 **Maison Estèbe**, which survived the British bombardment, adjacent to the museum's secondary entrance on rue St-Pierre. Even if you're not interested in reproductions of original tableware, the vaulted cellars are worth a peek (ask for the leaflet detailing the house's history).

Batterie Royale and Maison Chevalier

Depart the Musée de Civilisation by its secondary exit next to the Maison Estèbe onto rue St-Pierre. The heart of Québec City's turn-of-the-century financial district, rue St-Pierre leads south between Place Royale and Place de Paris to end at rue Sous-Le-Fort. Here, a gate provides the sole access to the **Batterie Royale**, a crenellated rampart that took a battering from the British during the siege of 1759 and was only restored (and a new array of cannons installed) in the 1970s.

Back on rue Sous-le-Fort, you can duck through the narrow stone vaulted passageway a few feet along, or turn left onto rue Notre-Dame, to reach narrow rue du Cul-de-Sac, which wraps around the 1752 **Maison Chevalier** (May to late June & early Sept to Oct Tues–Sun 10am–5pm; late June to early Sept daily 9.30am–5pm; Nov–April Sat & Sun 10am–5pm; free). An *hôtel particulier* (a somewhat grand townhouse) that served a stint as the London Coffee House, where merchants would meet up throughout the nineteenth century,

Québec City festivals

Québec City is renowned for its massive annual **festivals**. The **Carnaval de Québec** (☎418/626-3716 or 1-866/422-7628, Ⓦwww.carnaval.qc.ca) takes place over eleven freezing days in early February, when large quantities of the warming Caribou – a lethal mix of red wine, spirits and spices – are consumed amid parades and ice-sculpture competitions.

In early July, the ten-day **Festival d'Été** (☎418/529-5200 or 1-888/992-5200, Ⓦwww.infofestival.com) is an equally cheery affair. The largest festival of Francophone culture in North America attracts hundreds of performers for this musical celebration.

The **Fêtes de la Nouvelle-France** (☎418/694-3311 or 1-866/391-3383, Ⓦwww.nouvellefrance.qc.ca) returns Vieux-Québec's Basse-Ville to the seventeenth and eighteenth centuries in early August. It's great fun as thousands of Québécois from around the province dress up in period costume to crowd around the Place Royale's market stalls and engage in street theatre.

it's now an annex to the Musée de la Civilisation (see opposite). The entrance is through what was originally the rear of the house and leads to rooms displaying interior scenes that comprise period furniture, costumes and domestic objects. The plush drawing room and bedroom of a typical nineteenth-century bourgeois family contrast with the all-in-one common room that a tradesman and his family might have occupied a century earlier. Take a peek into the vaulted cellars, where local artisans today sell traditional works.

Quartier du Petit-Champlain

Maison Chevalier lies on the edge of the **Quartier du Petit-Champlain** (Ⓦwww.quartier-petit-champlain.qc.ca), the oldest shopping area in North America. Although there are a few dining and browsing distractions along boulevard Champlain leading south, you're better to take any of the stairways tucked between its buildings to the parallel and more atmospheric **rue du Petit-Champlain**. Dating back to 1685, this narrow, cobbled street is the city's oldest. The boutiques and art shops in the quaint seventeenth- and eighteenth-century houses are not as overpriced as you'd think, and they offer an array of excellent crafts, from weird and wonderful ceramics to Inuit carvings. The glass-blowing workshop and gallery, **Verrerie La Mailloche** (Ⓦwww.lamailloche.com), where the street meets the base of the *escalier casse-cou* is particularly interesting – you can watch the craftsmen blow glass straight out of the 1100°C furnace and purchase the gorgeous and unique result. Nearby is the Maison Louis-Jolliet, which was built in 1683 for its namesake, the retired discoverer of the Mississippi. It now houses the base station for the **funicular** (daily 7.30am–11pm, until midnight in summer; $1.50) – the least taxing way to scale the cliff back up to Terrasse Dufferin and Place d'Armes in Haute-Ville (see p.247).

Eating, drinking and nightlife

The French ancestry of the Québécois truly hits all the senses when it comes to **eating** in Québec City: the city's restaurants present a fine array of culinary delights adopted from the mother country, from lovingly presented gourmet dishes to humble baguettes. Quite a few places mix French and Italian on their menus, and there are increasing numbers of ethnic spots, from Indian to Moroccan, for a change of taste. **Nightlife** in Québec City is more relaxed than in Montréal: an evening spent in an intimate bar or a jazz or blues soiree is more popular than a big gig or disco – although many a young student would beg to differ.

Cafés and restaurants

Vieux-Québec is home to most of the gourmet **restaurants** and **cafés**, but other areas – notably along rue St-Jean (quirky and cheaper) and Grande-Allée (generally touristy and expensive), just outside the city walls – also have their fair share. Your best bet for moderately priced restaurants is to do as the locals do – head for avenue Cartier a kilometre west of the walls (buses #11, 800 or 801) near the Musée National des Beaux-Arts du Québec, and check out the menus of the numerous terrace-fronted restaurants. See p.147 for an explanation of restaurant price codes.

Haute-Ville

Aux Anciens Canadiens 34 rue St-Louis ⓣ418/692-1627, ⓦwww.auxancienscanadiens.qc.ca. Expensive. Touristy and overly expensive, it's nonetheless popular due to its charming location in the city's oldest house and the menu of Québécois specialities like *tourtière* (meat pie) and *pattes de cochon* (pigs' trotters) prepared much more finely than how the original *habitants* could have afforded.

Casse-Crêpe Breton 1136 rue St-Jean ⓣ418/692-0438. Inexpensive. Diner-style restaurant where $5 crepes are filled with items like cheese, ham and vegetables for a savoury snack, or fruit and chocolate for something sweeter. There's often a queue, but it moves quickly. Open from 7am to around 11pm.

Chez Temporel 25 rue Couillard ⓣ418/694-1813. Inexpensive. Bowls of steaming *café au lait*, croissants and *chocolatines* make this café, a few doors from the *Auberge de la Paix* hostel, a perfect place for breakfast or a late afternoon pit-stop. Soups and sandwiches are also available until 1.30am.

Conti Caffe 32 rue St-Louis ⓣ418/692-4191. Moderate–expensive. An offshoot (and sharing the kitchen) of the good but more expensive and formal *Le Continental* next door, this casual Italian eatery is the best choice on a street swamped with mediocre, touristy restaurants. Veal is a speciality – the medallions in porcini mushroom sauce are rich and succulent.

La Crémaillère 21 rue St-Stanislas ⓣ418/692-2216. Expensive. Superior French and Italian cuisine in a romantic, stone-walled 1829 residence that feels miles away from busy rue St-Jean just beyond the windows. You might start with marinated scallops, move on to the *suprême de poulet* (tender chicken with risotto and vegetables) or the Dover sole and then let the chocolate truffle cake finish you off. Reservations suggested.

Les Frères de la Côte 1190 rue St-Jean ⓣ418/692-5445. Moderate. A friendly and crowded bistro that draws locals as well as tourists for steaks, smoked salmon and great mussels and pizzas, as well as an excellent steak tartare. Make sure to check the daily specials on the blackboard.

La Maison de Serge Bruyère 1200 rue St-Jean ⓣ418/694-0618. Inexpensive–very expensive. Three restaurants under one roof: the *Restaurant la Grande Table* is one of the best in the city, serving fresh produce, beautifully prepared and presented. The eight-course *ménu découverte* ($85 per person, $145 with wine) is a French *nouvelle cuisine* extravaganza that changes with the season; reservations are required. The adjacent *Chez Livernois Bistro* is more affordable, serving the likes of fettucine with portobello mushrooms and roasted chicken. The café is cheaper still, but best for a simple *café au lait* on the terrace.

Le Petit Coin Latin 8.5 rue Ste-Ursule ⓣ418/692-2022. Moderate. Yellow-orange walls brighten up the exposed stone in this cozy café/bistro but, in nice weather, the secluded courtyard is the place to be. *Raclette* is a speciality, but they also serve steaks and a caribou *tourtière* (meat pie) for heartier appetites. Breakfast (7.30–11.30am, until 4pm weekends) ranges from straightforward fry-ups to eggs Benedict, while the two-course lunches are good value at around $10.

Le St-Amour 48 rue Ste-Ursule ⓣ418/694-0667, ⓦwww.saint-amour.com. Very expensive. As the name suggests, this is one of Québec City's most romantic restaurants, with a suitably elegant decor to match the finely wrought French recipes applied to local produce – the foie gras is exceptional. Ask for a table in the winter garden.

Outside the walls

Café Krieghoff 1089 av Cartier ⓣ418/522-3711, ⓦwww.cafekrieghoff.qc.ca. Moderate. This French café-bistro, just a ten-minute walk north of the Musée National des Beaux-Arts du Québec, serves up some of the city's best coffee, big breakfasts and light meals like chicken caesar salad, quiche lorraine and traditional *croûtons* (a baguette topped with garlic butter and melted cheese) for around $10 for two courses at lunch.

Cosmos Café 575 Grande-Allée E ⓣ418/640-0606, ⓦwww.lecosmos.com. Moderate. This café's cool decor and imaginative menu, with specials like trout with blueberries as well as a range of burgers, salads and pizzas, make it by far the best spot on the Grande-Allée. Crowded and lively at lunch and for the *5 à 7* cocktail hour.

Le Hobbit 700 rue St-Jean ⓣ418/692-0438. Moderate. A popular local spot where a mixed crowd of students and slightly older residents come for the great vegetarian options, as well as burgers, pasta and bistro dishes like steak and trout filet.

Jaune Tomate 120 boul René-Lévesque O ⓣ418/523-8777, ⓦwww.jaunetomate.com. Moderate. The sunny yellow walls and Italy-inspired decor in this terrace-fronted house set the mood for tasty and reasonably priced Italian dishes like *osso bucco*, *linguini del mare* and a range of pizzas. The two-course lunch is good and filling at around $10.

Kookening 565 rue St-Jean ⓣ418/521-2800. Inexpensive. Chilled-out restaurant-bar in the studenty part of rue St-Jean, ten-minutes' walk west of Vieux-Québec, with bright walls and board games that makes for a good hideout when the weather's rotten. The mainly Tex-Mex menu – tacos, fajitas and enchiladas – will also warm you up. Other eclectic choices are *Mole de canard confit* (duck with Aztec chocolate sauce) and kaiser rolls filled with tandoori chicken. Daily from 4pm.

L'Orange Bleue 526 rue St-Jean ⓣ418/524-5005. Inexpensive. A tiny vegetarian café co-op with changing art displays that uses mainly organic ingredients to make frittatas, pastas, pizzas, an *escalope de tofu* and a "faubourgeois" (a pun on *faubourg* and *faux hambourgeois*). Acoustic acts and pianists play here some nights. Closed Mon; no lunch weekends.

Pizzédélic 1145 av Cartier ⓣ418/525-5981. Inexpensive–moderate. A ten-minute walk north of the fine arts museum, this trendy spot dishes up creative pizzas (try the mascarpone and Black Forest ham or the salmon carpaccio) and pastas like linguini with red Thai curry and black tiger shrimp. The large, packed terrace is definitely the most fun of those lining the av Cartier strip.

Basse-Ville

Buffet de l'Antiquaire 95 rue St-Paul ⓣ418/692-2661. Inexpensive. An old-school diner popular with locals for breakfast (served from 6am) and home-cooked comfort food like *poutine*, *ragoût* (pork stew) and *pâté chinois* (shepherd's pie) as well as burgers and club sandwiches.

Le Café du Monde 84 rue Dalhousie ⓣ418/692-4455, ⓦwww.lecafedumonde.com. Expensive. This large and sleek Parisian-style bistro may be in the cruise ship terminal, but it's a hit with locals for its brash atmosphere and fantastic terrace overlooking the St Lawrence. And the food – mussels, veal sweetbreads, *confit de canard*, steak tartare and the like – is quite good, too.

Le Cochon Dingue 46 boul Champlain ⓣ418/692-2013, ⓦwww.cochondingue.com. Moderate. Casual restaurant with tiled floors and checkerboard tablecloths, where young and friendly staff serve the likes of brochettes, pasta, mussels, bavette and steak frites. There's a second branch at 46 boul René-Lévesque O (Ⓣ418/523-2013), near av Cartier.

L'Échaudé 72 rue du Sault-au-Matelot Ⓣ418/692-1299, Ⓦwww.echaude.com. Expensive. Upscale but unpretentious bistro with a terrace on the pedestrian portion of rue du Sault-au-Matelot. A good selection of wines accompanies classics like *confit canard*, steak tartare and stuffed quail, as well as daily fish specials.

Le Marie Clarisse 12 rue du Petit-Champlain Ⓣ418/692-0857. Very expensive. Named after an old schooner, the specialty in this late-seventeenth-century stone house with a terrace at the foot of the *escalier casse-cou* is market-fresh seafood. Try the large pan-seared bay scallops, served in a lobster and beet sauce with a touch of saffron or the house *marmite* – a fish stew similar to a bouillabaisse. The lunchtime *table d'hôte* is a good deal, under $20. With only twelve tables, you'll need to make a reservation.

Bars and clubs

Compared to Montréal, Québec City's **nightlife** feels quite laid-back, with plenty of quiet bars and the few louder ones – venues for folk, rock or jazz – being on the small side. That said, the clubs at either end of the Grand-Allée strip are a frenzy on summer weekends, drawing a young, dressed-up crowd who wouldn't be caught dead with one of the gimmicky drinks (like half-yards of ale) offered on the restaurant terraces along the way. The bars along rue St-Jean, especially beyond the walls, tend to be more down-to-earth.

Haute-Ville

Bar Ste-Angèle 26 rue Ste-Angèle Ⓣ418/692-2171. A dark and smoky neighbourhood bar with a beamed ceiling and cozy nook that doesn't seem to realize it's in the middle of tourist central. Cheap bottles of beer ($3.50) and single malts make it a popular student hangout as well. Open from 8pm.

Bar St-Laurent 1 rue des Carrières Ⓣ418/692-3861. The *Château Frontenac* address may be a bit stuffy, with glasses of wine and pints of beer costing $7.50 and a whopping $9.25, respectively, at the polished octagonal bar, but you don't need to dress to the nines and the view from the terrace is stupendous.

Chez Son Père 24 rue St-Stanislas Ⓣ418/692-5308, Ⓦwww.barchezsonpere.qc.ca. Québécois folk singers keep things humming in this lively bar just off rue St-Jean in Vieux-Québec. Nightly specials like $10 pitchers add to the buzz. Free admission.

L'Emprise 57 rue Ste-Anne Ⓣ418/692-2480. Located on the main floor of the *Hôtel Clarendon*, this bar's Art Deco surroundings attract a sophisticated touristy crowd to evenings of smooth jazz at 9.30pm (every night; weekends only in winter; free).

Le Pub St-Alexandre 1087 rue St-Jean Ⓣ418/694-0015, Ⓦwww.pubstalexandre.com. Yuppie English-style pub with a long mahogany bar set against the exposed-brick walls. With 40 single malts, 20 beers on tap – including Bass, Tartan and Newcastle Brown from $7.25 a pint – and ten times that many in bottles, it's a good spot to down a few.

Outside the walls

L'Amour Sorcier 789 Côte Ste-Geneviève Ⓣ418/523-3395. Popular, intimate lesbian bar with cheap beers and soft music (which gets louder and more danceable on weekend evenings) in a two-storey exposed-brick interior with a great roof terrace in summer. A ten-minute-walk west of the Porte St-Jean.

Dagobert 600 Grande-Allée E Ⓣ418/522-0393, Ⓦwww.dagobert.ca. This sprawling old house has been one of the city's most raucous nightspots for decades. Young dressed-up-for-it clubbers head upstairs for the large dancefloor, which feels trapped in the past decade with its smoke machine and flashing lights. Downstairs an only slightly older crowd sit at tiered tables to catch cover bands playing popular tunes from 10.30pm. There's rarely a cover charge.

Le Drague 815 rue St-Augustin ⓣ418/649-7212, ⓦwww.ledrague.com. Situated in Québec City's tiny gay district ten minutes west from the Porte St-Jean; beyond the front terrace there's a café, bar and basement nightclub with wraparound mezzanine – the Sunday night drag shows are great fun.

Maurice 575 Grande-Allée E ⓣ418/647-2000, ⓦwww.mauricenightclub.com. Happening club with a rotating crew of DJs that attracts a stylish twenties to mid-thirties crowd for R&B and house nights (Wed–Sun only in winter). Dress up to get by the selective door policy. The $3 cover ($4 on weekends) also gets you into the more laid-back *Charlotte* upstairs, with couches for chilling out or smoking a cigar, though on the funk and latino nights it can be just as hopping.

Pub Java 1112 av Cartier ⓣ418/522-5282. There's a good selection of imported and draught beers at this pub, that also draws locals for lunch (around $10) and breakfasts (8am–2pm, until 6pm weekends). For cozier surroundings, head upstairs to the *Salon Galway*, done up like an Irish pub with dark woods and large armchairs by the fireplace.

Sacrilège 447 rue St-Jean ⓣ418/649-1985. Friendly and often packed watering hole drawing students and locals, especially for the cheap beer ($4.25 a pint) and popular courtyard terrace in back. It's in the Faubourg St-Jean-Baptiste district, less than fifteen minutes west of Place D'Youville.

Basse-Ville

L'Inox 37 quai St-André ⓣ418/692-2877, ⓦwww.inox.qc.ca. Québec City's original brewpub's decor may be a bit cold, with greys and a metal central bar, but with artisanal cheeses and European sausages to accompany fine ales – such as the brown Scottiche (a winter warmer only) and Trouble-Fête, a refreshing Belgian blonde with coriander and lime – you won't complain for long.

Le Pape Georges 8 1/4 rue Cul-de-Sac ⓣ418/692-1320, ⓦwww.papegeorges.com. There's barely room for the guitarist squashed against the fireplace in this tiny cellar of a bar. If you're claustrophobic, you can have your wine or beer (along with a cheese plate) on the equally atmospheric terrace in front. Live music Wed–Sun; free.

Contexts

Contexts

A brief history of Montréal

The struggle between French and English has been a constant theme throughout most of Montréal's **history**, shaping it culturally, politically, socially and even physically. After seizing Québec City from the French in 1759, the British gained the upper hand, yet passage of the Québec Act in 1774 ensured the survival of the province's French culture. In the nineteenth century, British influence was most strongly felt in the increasing commercialization of Montréal, which made it Canada's largest and wealthiest city before it evolved into Canada's "sin capital" during Prohibition. The subsequent influx of immigrants has resulted in a great ethnic mix, a rich culture and an array of festivities that make this cosmopolitan city one of the continent's most fun and unique places to visit.

Beginnings

Little is known about the earliest peoples who roamed this part of Québec beyond that they were nomadic groups of **hunter-gatherers**, living off a plentiful supply of fish, fowl, moose, deer and caribou. What is known is that by around 1000 BC Iroquois-speaking peoples lived in the area, though it took another two millennia for these Iroquois nations to develop a sedentary lifestyle, cultivating crops – primarily corn, beans and squash – and making pottery in which to store food. These tribes surrounded their villages with wooden palisades, inside of which up to 1500 people would live in communal, bark-covered longhouses some twenty to thirty metres long.

It was such a settlement, named **Hochelaga** ("Place of the Beaver"), situated at the base of the mountain and occupied by the St Lawrence Iroquois, that **Jacques Cartier** stumbled across on his second trip to North America in 1535. The year before, he had claimed all of Canada for Francis I of France and had returned to look both for gold and a shorter trade route to Asia. While he found neither, he did manage to provide the source for Montréal's name, labelling the hill that towered over Hochelaga **Mont Royal** (although some argue he actually named it Monreale, for the bishop of that town who was one of his trip's sponsors).

The founding of Ville-Marie

It's uncertain whether warfare with other tribes or disease brought by the Europeans was at fault, but in the latter half of the sixteenth century the population of St Lawrence Iroquois plummeted. By the time French explorer **Samuel de Champlain** arrived in 1603, all traces of Hochelaga had vanished. Champlain briefly left the scene as well, travelling east to found Québec City in 1608, but he returned three years later to the Montréal area to begin the first European construction on the island at Pointe-à-Callière, naming the immediate area Place Royale. Champlain then turned his energies to the smaller island just offshore, naming it in honour of his twelve-year-old bride, Hélène – a decent thing to do given that he purchased it with her dowry.

The next few decades saw only intermittent European activity, the French settlement at Place Royale being little more than a small garrison. The Récollets (reformed Franciscans) and Jesuit missionaries – called the "Black Robes" by the natives who suspected them of sorcery – also maintained a small presence on the island, attempting to convert the Iroquois, more often than not being put to death for their pains. The priests' tasks were not made any easier by the fact that the French had aligned with the Algonquin and Huron nations to gain access to their **fur-trading networks**, while those groups' traditional enemies, the Iroquois Confederacy, had formed alliances with the Dutch and subsequently the British. Periodic bouts between the factions over control of the industry would continue over the next half-century.

Meanwhile, a group of French aristocrats and merchants soon obtained a title from Louis XIII to colonize Canada for commercial gain, and Paul de Chomedey, **Sieur de Maisonneuve**, was chosen to lead the mission. After wintering in Québec City, he established the colony of Ville-Marie on the site of Champlain's Place Royale along with some fifty settlers on either May 16 or 17 in 1642. That winter the settlement – which would before too long be known as Montréal – seemed destined to disappear as quickly as it came due to the impending threat of rising floodwaters. De Maisonneuve's fervent prayers were answered on Christmas Day when the waters receded, and in gratitude, he planted a **cross** near the mountain's summit, a gesture commemorated by the present-day landmark. Floods, though, were only the beginning of de Maisonneuve's problems, as native attacks plagued the colony; even after the Frenchman bested an Iroquois chief in single combat in 1644, settlers risked ambushes for the next two decades.

New France

Ville-Marie's survival remained tenuous until Louis XIV made Québec a royal province in 1663 (and granted the seigneury of the island of Montréal to the **Sulpicians**, an order of missionaries who would be the city's de facto landlords for roughly the next two hundred years; see box, p.72). The area's new status allowed for the dispatch of a thousand French troops, whose arrival further widened the existing gender gap. In order to rectify this imbalance, unmarried Frenchwomen, the so-called **filles du roi**, were shipped over by the boatload throughout the next decade (see p.126). Still, even with the much stronger (and now happier) military presence, periodic skirmishes between the French and British and their native allies continued to be a destabilizing factor, stunting the growth of the colony. Matters were resolved somewhat when 1200 colonists met with an even greater number of natives from across eastern North America at Pointe-à-Callière to sign **La Grande Paix**, the Great Peace treaty of 1701 between the French and 39 Indian nations. The signing of the Treaty of Utrecht with the British a decade later further allowed the fur trade to flourish, greatly increasing the town's fortunes.

It wasn't until mid-century that further serious conflict broke out, with the British and French again at odds in the **Seven Years' War** (also known as the French and Indian War). Although the early years of fighting were concentrated in the Atlantic colonies, the turning point took place in 1759 when, after a summer of punishing bombardment at Québec City, General James Wolfe defeated the French under the Marquis de Montcalm in the twenty-minute **Battle of the Plains of Abraham**. When Québec City fell, Montréal briefly served as the capital of New France, until the Marquis de Vaudreuil surrendered to the Brits a year later, without a shot being fired.

British control and the birth of a city

The transfer to **British rule** saw little change in the life of most Québécois, except for the fleeing of a few upper-class merchants. But when an attempt was made in 1763 to impose British administrative structures that threatened the status of the powerful Catholic clergy, grumbles rose from the largely Francophone and rural population. Worried that unrest similar to that occurring in the American colonies might be played out here, the British enacted the 1774 **Quebec Act**, a stopgap measure that allowed the French to maintain their language, civil code, seigneurial system and religion. This short-term solution was largely responsible for Québec's unique character, as well as the tensions that would continue to flare up throughout its future.

The British occupation suffered a brief hiccup in the mid-1770s when **American** soldiers, led by General Richard Montgomery, took over the city, and the likes of **Benjamin Franklin** tried to convince a skeptical populace to join the American struggle against the British. The Americans were soon defeated in Québec City, but after they won independence from Britain in their own land, a flood of British Loyalists fled across the Canadian border, settling primarily in the Eastern Townships and present-day Ontario. The new Anglophone residents, as well as the Francophone bourgeoisie, were chafing under the terms of the Quebec Act, and both wanted an elected assembly. The British response to these demands, was the 1791 **Constitutional Act**, which divided the territory into Lower and Upper Canada (present-day Québec and Ontario), giving both a legislative assembly. The act emphasized the inequalities between Anglophones and Francophones, however, as real power lay with the so-called **Château Clique** – an assembly composed mainly of members of the wealthy establishment and answerable to a British governor and council appointed in London.

Around this time, the city walls were becoming a serious impediment to growth, and their demolition was carried out between 1804 and 1809, with all traces of their existence wiped out by 1817. During this period, the first steamships began sailing between Montréal and Québec City, leading to further growth and, despite fears of an American invasion during the War of 1812, the city continued to prosper.

The town by now was well on its way to becoming Canada's commercial centre, a fact confirmed with the establishment of the **Banque de Montréal** in 1817. From around 1815, waves of British and Irish immigrants swelled the population enough that by the 1820s Montréal's total passed that of Québec City and in 1831 Anglophones formed the majority of Montréal's residents.

Resentment, however, was brewing just under the surface as the Château Clique vetoed bills passed in the Francophone-dominated assembly, occasionally resulting in riots. Francophone anger – exacerbated by a severe depression and punitive import taxes on British goods, as well as the favouritism shown Anglophones – boiled over in 1837, when the French **Patriotes** led by **Louis-Joseph Papineau** rose up against the British. Their insurgency failed, resulting in hangings, exiles and a particularly murderous punitive episode in St-Eustache (see p.223), and led to an investigation by the British-appointed governor general, **Lord Durham**, who concluded that English and French relations were akin to two nations warring within the bosom of a single state. His prescription for peace was immersing French-Canadians in the English culture of North America; the subsequent establishment of the **Province of Canada** with the 1840 Act of Union can be seen as a deliberate attempt to marginalize Francophone opinion within an English-speaking state. In 1844, Montréal became the capital of Canada, a role it held only until 1849 when a protesting mob of Anglophone Tories torched the parliament building (a former market on Place d'Youville) in anger at legislation compensating Francophones for damages caused by the British army in quelling the Patriotes' rebellion.

Industrialization and expansion

The mid-nineteenth century was a time for **industrialization** in Montréal – much as it was in urban areas across Canada and the US – spurred by the deepening of the channel between Montréal and Québec City and the construction of the Grand Trunk Railway, which reached from the ice-free port of Portland, Maine, to the island of Montréal itself when the Victoria Bridge was completed in 1859. Vast tracts of factories sprouted up along the **Lachine Canal** and in east-end towns like Hochelaga, refining grain and sugar, producing shoes and other leather goods, textiles, and heavy machinery for the rail and ship industries. Simultaneously, massive blocks of substandard row houses were built to accommodate, in part, the masses of rural Francophones who flooded into Montréal looking for work in the factories – by 1866 Montréal's language scale had tipped, leaving **Francophones in the majority** for good.

The city's hold on the national economy was further strengthened by the completion of the coast-to-coast **Canadian Pacific Railway** in the 1880s, and the city continued to jump its boundaries, absorbing 22 adjacent municipalities between 1883 and 1918. Meanwhile, the commercial centre of the city shifted to the present-day Downtown and an electric streetcar network began running in 1892, connecting the growing metropolis. Pogroms in Eastern Europe sent thousands of **Jews** fleeing to Montréal and with a continued exodus from the rural areas the city's population reached half a million in 1911, doubling in the next two decades with an influx of émigrés from war-torn Europe.

Morality and the early 1900s

For the first half of the twentieth century, Montréal's liberated mores stood out against the staid Puritanism of other Canadian cities, earning it a reputation as Canada's "**sin city**". US Prohibition in the 1920s allowed Québec to become the continent's main **alcohol supplier** – the Molsons (brewers), Bronfmans (owners of Seagram distillers) and their ilk made their fortunes here – while prostitution and gambling thrived under the protection of city and police officials.

Even the Great Depression couldn't dampen the carousing, in part because **Camillien Houde**, the off-and-on mayor of Montréal between 1928 and 1954, mitigated much of its effects with massive **public works projects** (like the construction of the Jardin Botanique). His magnanimity bankrupted the city, though, and it was forced into trusteeship by the province in 1940. Yet despite this, and the jail term he served for urging citizens to resist conscription for World War II, Houde's popularity did not cease, and he returned to power for another decade. With the war, the economy picked up again and by this time Montréal had forty nightclubs and lounge bars, whose lavish floor shows, big bands and visiting entertainers – including Harlem jazz acts at the famous Rockhead's Paradise – pulled in crowds until dawn.

The pace only let up when Pacifique "Pax" Plante became head of the **Morality Squad** in 1946. Whereas his predecessors had pretty much gone along with the times, organizing sham raids and scaring no one, Plante surprised everyone by shutting down the gambling joints and whorehouses virtually overnight. But rather than receive praise, he was ousted eighteen months later, and the city roared back to life. It wasn't until 1950 that citizens' outrage finally sparked a four-year-long judicial inquiry into corruption and other matters, and on the strength of its damning report, prosecuting lawyer **Jean Drapeau** won a landslide victory in the October 1954 mayoral race with his promise to clean up Canada's wide-open city.

The Drapeau years and the Quiet Revolution

Drapeau's reforming zeal did not sit well with the premier of Québec, **Maurice Duplessis**, who used his organizational might to fix the 1957 election against him. It was hardly a stretch for Duplessis, who had the support of both the Anglophone business elite and the clergy. Rural Québec at this time was almost a feudal state, held under the thrall of both the Church and the State, and despite their demographic strength Francophones continued to be ill-paid and badly housed in comparison to their Anglo counterparts. Frustrated by this disparity, a French-speaking middle class began articulating the workforce's grievances, leading to the so-called **Quiet Revolution** that began in 1960. The provincial government, led by **Jean Lesage** and his Liberal Party of Québec, took control of welfare, health and education away from the Church and, under the slogan "*Maîtres chez-nous*" (Masters of our own house), established state-owned industries that kick-started the development of a **Francophone business class**.

In 1960, Drapeau returned to power, and set about attending to his legacy: in large part, this meant changing Montréal's physical appearance during his next 26 years as mayor. He, like Camillien Houde before him, is remembered for the megaprojects bestowed on the city, such as Place Ville-Marie, the Underground City, Place des Arts and the **Métro system**. The first underground trains began running in 1966, just in time for the hugely successful 1967 Universal Exposition – better known as **Expo '67** – a world's fair that attracted 50 million guests and catapulted the city to international status.

One of those visitors was Charles de Gaulle, who made his famous "**Vive le Québec libre**!" speech from the balcony of the Hôtel de Ville, echoing the sentiments of nationalists who, woken by the social and cultural possibilities of the Quiet Revolution, were intent on making political results as well. Despite inroads into the corridors of real power, many still felt that it was Montréal's Anglophones who were benefiting from the prosperity of the boom that accompanied the Expo and the city's rapid expansion, and beneath the smooth surface Francophone frustrations were reaching dangerous levels.

The crisis peaked in October 1970, when the radical **Front de Libération du Québec** (FLQ) kidnapped the British trade commissioner, James Cross, and then a Québec cabinet minister, Pierre Laporte. As ransom, the FLQ demanded the publication of the FLQ manifesto, the transportation to Cuba of 25 FLQ prisoners awaiting trial for acts of violence, and $500,000 in gold bullion. Prime Minister **Pierre Trudeau** responded with the War Measures Act, suspending civil liberties and putting troops on the streets of Montréal. The following day, Laporte's body was found in the trunk of a car. By December, the so-called October Crisis was over: Cross had been released, and his captors and Laporte's murderers arrested. But the reverberations shook the nation, impacting politics not just in Québec, but Canada as a whole.

At last recognizing the need to redress the country's social imbalances, the federal government poured money into countrywide schemes to promote French-Canadian culture, while in Montréal, Drapeau funnelled money into the last of his grand projects – hosting the **1976 Summer Olympics**.

The ongoing threat of Separatism

Francophone discontent found a political voice in the Parti Québécois, founded by **René Lévesque** in 1968 with the chief goal of Québec sovereignty – still one of the party's main platforms today. Their message finally won the support of voters in the provincial election of 1976 and the consequent language law – the Charte de la langue française, better known as **Bill 101** – was enacted the following year. It established French as the province's official language, making it a compulsory part of the school curriculum and banning English-only signs on business premises (subsequently eased so that all signs had to at least be bilingual, with the French printed twice as large as the English). Tens of thousands of Anglophones promptly began an **exodus** from Montréal. Over a hundred companies, several head offices and a massive amount of capital moved west to Toronto, provoking a steep decline in housing prices, a halt on construction work and the withdrawal of investment.

For Québec to shape its own future, many nationalists felt the province needed control over laws and taxes, although they wanted to maintain an economic association with Canada. In 1980, a **referendum on sovereignty association** was held, but still reeling from the terrorist activities of the FLQ and scared that separatism would leave Québec economically adrift, the 6.5-million population voted 60/40 against. Prime Minister Trudeau then set about repatriating the country's **Constitution** in the autumn of 1981. Trudeau called a late-night meeting on the issue and did not invite Lévesque, literally denying Québec a seat at the table. "The night of the long knives", as the event became known, wound up imposing a Constitution on the province that placed its language rights in jeopardy and removed its veto power over constitutional amendments. Accordingly, the provincial government refused to sign it – and still hasn't to this day.

In October 1993, Québec's displeasure with federalism was evident in the election of Lucien Bouchard's Bloc Québécois to the vastly ironic status of Her Majesty's Loyal Opposition in Ottawa. The cause received added support in 1994 when the Parti Québécois was returned to provincial power after vowing to hold a **province-wide referendum** on separation from Canada. The referendum was held a year later and the vote was so close – the province opted to remain a part of Canada by a margin of less than one percent – that calls immediately arose for a third referendum (prompting pundits to refer to the process as the "neverendum").

Contemporary Montréal

Political uncertainty and continuing tensions, combined with a Canada-wide economic recession, had Montréal on shaky ground in the mid-1990s. After the 1995 referendum, however, a tacit truce was made on the issue of separation. The communal bonds between Québécois were further strengthened by the shared adversity of the **ice storm** of 1998, which plunged pockets of the province into darkness after torrents of icy rain downed power lines and left 1.4 million without electricity – some for weeks on end. The ice storm's impact on Montréal's green spaces was enormous, and most pronounced on the mountain, where some 80,000 trees were damaged.

The more stable political climate – the result of Francophones increasingly confident with their lot and Anglophones who have remained and adjusted to the turbulence and change – coincided with restored **economic confidence** that led to a good deal of rejuvenation on the city's commercial streets. Boarded-up shops that lined rue Ste-Catherine in the mid-1990s, for example, re-opened and continue to do bustling business. Derelict pockets on the edges of Downtown and Vieux-Montréal have been renovated to house the growing multimedia industry, just one element of the city's transition to a **new economy**. The industry was seemingly less affected by the burst of the dot-com bubble than many other cities thanks to specialization in animation and special-effects software, though the amount of new building in the Cité Multimédia and the towers of the Cité du Commerce Électronique (E-Commerce Place) has proven over-optimistic.

Even though most Quebecers – and certainly most Montrealers – have for now put the separatist dream on hold, Montréal still seems doomed to ongoing political squabbles. Not long after Lucien Bouchard stepped down as the leader of the Parti Québécois in January 2001, claiming that Quebecers weren't ready for sovereignty, and separatist firebrand Bernard Landry took his place, **Pierre Bourque**, the mayor since 1994, led the drive to create "One Island, One City". For years, Montréal had shared its island with a patchwork of 27 other municipalities, co-ordinating many services at the regional level as the Communauté Urbain de Montréal (CUM, or MUC in English). Proponents of a **Mega-City** that would amalgamate all of the island's towns and cities claimed everyone would benefit from economies of scale and that the tax burden for services in central Montréal used by everyone would be shared more equally. The idea did not sit well with many of the municipalities, especially the English-speaking ones in the West Island, who worried that they would not only pay more taxes for fewer services, but that the move was also an attempt to deprive many areas of bilingual status through re-districting. Mayor Bourque lost the November 2001 election, due largely to his support of the scheme, but the provincial government pushed the bill through anyway, creating the new island-wide city of Montréal on January 1, 2002.

Things don't look to be much easier for the new mayor, **Gérald Tremblay**, who now has to deal with the increased clout of Mega-City unions and calls from the former suburban mayors for a "**demerger**". Courting voters in these areas with the carrot of possible referendums to overturn the merger may have played a part in the election of **Jean Charest** and his Liberal party in April 2003. For most Quebecers, though, the reasons for casting out the Parti Québécois probably had more to do with meat-and-potato issues – fixing an ailing healthcare system, funnelling money into education and promising to reduce taxes in the highest-taxed province in the country – not to mention a well-earned rest from separatism, at least at the provincial level.

All of this will have little impact on visitors to Montréal, though, as the new *arrondissements* (boroughs) conform largely to the same boundaries that existed before the merger. More visible are the physical changes aimed at making the city a better place to walk around, like the redevelopment of the space between Downtown and Vieux-Montréal, where the scar left by the Autoroute Ville-Marie was covered over by new office buildings and new parks were created. Even within the confines of staid Vieux-Montréal, a crop of boutique hotels and river-view condos is making the neighbourhood more of a year-round place – and one convenient to the revitalized Lachine Canal, re-opened to pleasure boat traffic in 2002 and increasingly a popular recreation destination for visitors and Montrealers alike.

Books

The listings below represent a highly selective reading list on Montréal, with a couple of broader Québec-specific books thrown in. Wherever possible, they've been listed by their most recent edition and most accessible publisher; many should be readily available in Canada, the US and the UK. If they can't be found in bookstores, try to order through the publisher, or online from Montréal bookstores (see p.192). Highly recommended titles are signified by ★ . Out-of-print titles are indicated by o/p.

History, society and politics

Pierre Anctil *Saint-Laurent: Montréal's Main* (Les Éditions du Septentrion, Canada). Based on research for an exhibition at the Musée d'Archéologie, this history of Montréal's most vibrant street is in many ways a microcosm of the city's history itself – the Main always reflecting current trends if not actually instigating them.

Lucien Bouchard *On the Record* (Stoddart, Canada). A recording of the sovereignty movement's *raison d'être*, written by one of its most charismatic leaders; so persuasive you may wish to join up – that is, until you read Lawrence Martin's *The Antagonist* (see opposite).

Edgar Andrew Collard *Montreal Yesterdays* (o/p). Collard's light-hearted tomes often blend momentous stories with quirky anecdotes, and this volume, which combines a chapter on Mark Twain's visit to the *Windsor Hotel* with tales of haunted houses and reclusive hermits, is no exception.

John A. Dickinson and Brian Young *A Short History of Quebec* (McGill-Queen's University Press, Canada). Though not especially short, this book is nonetheless a readable trawl through the province's social, economic, governmental, cultural and religious histories with loads of suggestions for further reading.

John Gilmore *Who's Who of Jazz in Montreal* (Véhicule Press, Canada). A jazz aficionado handbook with hundreds of biographies of musicians that worked in the city from the dawn of the jazz era to 1970, including home-grown talents like Oscar Peterson and Americans like Louis Metcalfe and Slap Rags White.

Lawrence Martin *The Antagonist* (Viking, Canada). Martin's excellent biographies of influential Canadian politicians generally hinge on a controversial hypothesis; here he psychoanalyses former Separatist leader Lucien Bouchard as having "esthetic character disorder" – pyschobabble for highly unstable.

Jennifer Robinson (ed) *Montreal's Century* (Éditions du Trécarré, Canada). A good potted history of twentieth-century Montréal with essays on city life, politics and sports supplemented by scads of colour photographs from both the *Montreal Gazette* and *Journal de Montréal's* archives.

★ **William Weintraub** *City Unique* (McClelland and Stewart, Canada). This riveting narrative of the city in the 1940s and 1950s is full of salacious stories of corruption, sex and boozing, with an especially juicy section on the stripteaser Lili St-Cyr.

Architecture and photography

Pierre Phillipe Brunet and Jean O'Neil *Les Escaliers de Montréal* and *Les Couronnements de Montréal* (Hurtubise HMH, Canada). A pair of photo books focusing on some of the city's unique architectural details – the former captures the staircases that are such a prominent feature of

Montréal's residential streets, while the latter looks up at the city's rooflines and their fanciful parapets, dormers and *tourelles*. Text is in French only.

★ **Sandra Cohen-Rose** *Northern Deco – Art Deco Architecture in Montreal* (Corona, Canada). This glossy pictorial study beautifully captures the city's finest Art Deco buildings, including the interior of the private Maison Cormier (see p.61).

Bryan Demchinsky *Montréal Then and Now* (Éditions du Trécarré, Canada). A photo essay that captures the city's history in architectural terms – how spaces are used differently, what has passed away and what's surprisingly unchanged. Curiously, many of the century-old photos from *The Gazette*'s photographers look crisper than the modern-day ones. Bilingual text.

★ **Isabelle Gournay and France Vanlaethem** *Montréal Metropolis* (Stoddart, Canada). The definitive analysis of Montréal's architectural evolution from 1880 to 1930, complete with a studied collection of black-and-white photographs and layout plans (including projects never built).

Phyllis Lambert and Alan Stewart *Opening the Gates of Eighteenth-Century Montreal* (Canadian Centre for Architecture, Canada). A thorough, if academic, volume documenting the impact of Vieux-Montréal's fortifications on urban planning.

Andrzej Maciejewski *After Notman: Montreal Views – A Century Apart* (Firefly Books, Canada). Prolific late-nineteenth-century photographer William Notman documented a great deal of Montréal life and architecture. Here, his images from the Musée McCord's archives are placed side-by-side with Maciejewski's contemporary shots of the same scenes, giving a fascinating insight into how the city has changed.

Jean-Claude Marsan *Montreal in Evolution* (McGill-Queen's University Press, Canada). An analysis of Montréal's architectural trends and urban planning motifs that spans three centuries and culminates with an exhaustive look at the orchestration of Expo '67.

Jean–Eudes Schurr and Louise Larivière (eds) *Montréal Métropole* (Aux Yeux du Monde, Canada). A coffee-table book showcasing evocative photographs of the city taken by thirty photojournalists during a three-day blitz in the autumn of 1999.

Impressions, travel and specific guides

Nick Auf der Maur *Nick: A Life* (Véhicule Press, Canada). This regaling collection of works by the *Montreal Gazette*'s most illustrious columnist is as much about the late Auf der Maur's boisterous life as it is about Montréal.

Joe Fiorito *Tango on the Main* (Nuage Editions, Canada). Winner of the 1996 National Newspaper Award, Fiorito's compiled columns about the city's people, places and things make great, if sentimental, reading.

★ **Kristian Gravenor and John David Gravenor** *Montreal: The Unknown City* (Aresnal Pulp Press, Canada). A book full of fascinating trivia on all aspects of the city, including its scandals, quirkier personalities, hidden treasures and hare-brained ideas for projects that, if built, would have made the Big O look like a stroke of genius.

★ **Johnson and David Widgington** *Montréal Up Close* (Cumulus Press, Canada). Two great walking tours through the city that give the low-down on every gargoyle, frieze and bas-relief carving throughout Vieux-Montréal and Downtown; comes with a handy fold-out map.

Leif R. Montin *Get Outta Town* (No Fixed Address Publications, Canada). A terrific day-trip guide to

52 attractions within driving distance of Montréal.

Stuart Nulman *Beyond the Mountain: True Tales About Montreal*(Callawind Publications, Canada). Detailed explorations of quirky historical tidbits about the city's buildings, institutions and personages, though the question-and-answer format is annoying.

Sandra Phillips *Smart Shopping Montreal*. If you're serious about shopping in Montréal this guide (currently in its ninth edition) covers a myriad of ways to spend your money, with a focus on discount and specialist shops. Also available online (Ⓦ www.smartshopping.net).

John Symon *The Lobster Kids' Guide to Exploring Montréal* (Lobster Press, Canada). A comprehensive guide to kids' activities around and outside the city with listings of child-friendly restaurants, playlands, and the like.

Fiction and drama

Yves Beauchemin *The Alley Cat* (McClelland and Stewart, Canada). An engaging story centred on the *Binerie* restaurant (see p.157) and owner Florent Boissonneault's struggles to keep the place and his personal life afloat while one sinister Egon Ratablavasky strives to bring him down.

Andy Brown and Rob McLennan *You and Your Bright Ideas: New Montreal Writing* (Véhicule Press, Canada). Contemporary stories by mainly young local authors, many of whom are part of the city's energetic spoken word scene.

★ **Roch Carrier** *The Hockey Sweater* (Tundra Books, Canada). Every kid in Québec has read this story about a boy who longs for a Montréal Canadiens hockey jersey but gets a Toronto Maple Leafs one instead, much to the scorn of his fellow shinny players. A must if you have children in tow.

★ **Leonard Cohen** *The Favourite Game* (McClelland and Stewart, Canada). Songwriter Cohen's debut novel chronicles the escapades of the irresistible Lawrence Beavman through the streets, sheets and bars of Montréal and New York City, in punchy and lyrical prose. His follow-up, *Beautiful Losers* (McClelland and Stewart, Canada), a more uninhibited and experimental work, is a cult classic.

John Farrow *City of Ice* (HarperCollins, Canada). A tense thriller about the city's biker gangs with all the criminal activity you'd expect – CIA plants, crooked cops, dodgy lawyers and the like – set during a bone-chilling Montréal winter.

David Fennario *Balconville* (Talonbooks, Canada). This play adroitly captures the social interaction fostered by the facing balconies of Montréal's paired triplex apartment buildings. Set in Pointe-St-Charles, the Anglophone and Francophone neighbours talk of day-to-day things, separatism and the Expos.

Charles Foran *Butterfly Lovers* (HarperCollins, Canada). Ailing and embittered David LeClair's meandering narrative of self-discovery starts and ends in a Mile End bar called Remys, but spends a good chunk in China, where his relationship with a married woman prompts a profound metamorphosis.

★ **Hugh MacLennan** *Two Solitudes* (McClelland and Stewart, Canada). The story of Canada's French–English relations is mapped onto the equally epic but more poignant narrative of Paul Tallard's struggles as the son of a French-Canadian father and Irish mother; an even-handed and enlightening read. His wonderfully sentimental *The Watch that Ends the Night* is also worth picking up.

Kathy Reichs *Déjà Dead* (Pocket Books, US/Arrow Books, UK). A chilling forensic crime novel about one woman's attempts to track down a serial killer fond of dismembering women's bodies and stashing them about town; a serious page-turner that spawned a series of sequels.

★ **Mordecai Richler** *Barney's Version* (Alfred A. Knopf, Canada/Washington Square Press, US/Random House, UK). The late Richler's last novel, *Barney's Version*, is as much about himself as it is Barney Panofsky, his affable protagonist whose passions – hockey and Anglophone rights in Montréal – often get side-tracked by his fondness for women. Richler's debut, *The Apprenticeship of Duddy Kravitz* (McClelland and Stewart, Canada/Washington Square Press, US), introduced Canadian literature's greatest scoundrel, whose capers are told here in witty style.

Gabrielle Roy *The Tin Flute* (McClelland and Stewart, Canada). The houses crammed together on rue St-Augustin, with their backs to the railway tracks, inspired this touching novel about an impoverished family's struggles during World War II.

Michel Tremblay *The Fat Woman Next Door is Pregnant* (Talonbooks, Canada). A great title for a wonderful book chronicling the events of one day, May 2, 1942, in the life of a Plateau family; no one captures the ethos of working-class Francophone Montréal better.

Montréal on film

Low production costs, varied architecture and skilled locals have all made Montréal an increasingly in-demand locale for film shoots including recent major productions like *Gothika, Snake Eyes, The Aviator* and *The Art of War*. But other than fleeting glimpses – the Jacques-Cartier bridge in *Johnny Mnemonic*, the Big O in the Super Bowl scene of *The Sum of All Fears* and a post-apocalyptic McGill Arts Building in the atrocious *Battlefield Earth*, the city rarely appears as itself. There *are* some good films with Montréal in the starring role, though – a selective list appears below. Note that many of these were shot in French, but are available with either English subtitles or dubbed into English (alternate release titles indicated in parentheses followed by director and year of release).

The Apprenticeship of Duddy Kravitz (Ted Kotcheff 1974). Richard Dreyfuss plays Mordecai Richler's larger-than-life scamp as he schemes his way through Jewish Montréal and the Laurentians in the 1940s.

Le Confessional (*The Confessional*; Robert Lepage 1995). Top Québec playwright Lepage turns his hand to film with excellent results. The action flips back and forth between the present, as the main characters try to makes sense of their roots, and the secrets and events four decades earlier during the filming of Alfred Hitchcock's *I Confess* in Québec City in 1952.

Le Déclin de l'Empire Américain (*Decline of the American Empire*; Denys Arcand 1986). Grand themes of sex and society pervade this tale of a group of middle-class baby-boomers – the generation that transformed Québec with the Quiet Revolution.

Les Invasions Barbares (*The Barbarian Invasions*; Denys Arcand 2003). The characters (and cast) of *Déclin* reunite in Montréal nearly two decades later at the deathbed of the family patriarch. Older and wiser, they reflect on life and morality in twenty-first-century Montréal and wonder where their dreams went and how the next generation turned out so different.

Jésus de Montréal (*Jesus of Montreal*; Denys Arcand 1989). Lothaire Bluteau plays an actor hired to stage the passion play – but his updated re-telling, which re-examines Christ's story and principles in a contemporary context, infuriates church officials.

Léolo (Jean-Claude Lauzon 1992). Delightful and occasionally surreal film whose slightly mad child protagonist is convinced he's Italian – conceived when his mother fell into a bushel of tomatoes that an Italian farmer had masturbated on – despite being born into a large, poor Francophone family in 1950s Montréal. The traumas of growing up are comically and often brutally portrayed.

Mambo Italiano (Émile Gaudreault 2003). Warm-hearted comedy where Angelo falls in love with his childhood friend Nino, much to the dismay of their conservative Little Italy families. Based on the hit play by Steve Galluccio.

Montréal vu par (*Montreal Sextet*; various directors 1991). Six snippets of Montréal as seen by Québécois and Canadian directors like Denys Arcand and Atom Egoyan. The only common thread between the varied stories is Montréal itself.

Scanners (David Cronenberg 1981). Canadian horror-meister Cronenberg's thriller has telepaths using their psychic powers to battle it out with head-popping results, all beneath the ominous sweep of Place Ville-Marie's searchlights.

The Score (Frank Oz 2001) Vieux-Montréal features prominently as the setting for a jazz club owned by Robert De Niro, a safe-cracker who even speaks a bit of French in this one-last-heist flick co-starring Edward Norton.

Language

Language

French language and glossary

No amount of French training will prepare you for the vagaries of the Québécois dialect – even the European French have difficulty understanding the slurring drawl that's spoken here at lightning speed. Don't be embarrassed to ask people to repeat themselves more slowly (*s'il vous plaît, répétez plus lentement*), or just ask if they speak English (*parlez-vous anglais?*); most in Montréal do and they won't be offended at your asking. With **pronunciation** there's little point trying to mimic the local dialect – just stick to the classic French rules. Consonants at the ends of words are usually silent and at other times are much like English, except that **ch** is always sh, **ç** is s, **h** is silent, **th** is the same as t, **ll** is like the y in yes and **r** is growled. Vowel-wise, **é** resembles a long a, **è** is eh and **a** is ah. If you plan on spending much time in the province, consider the pocket-sized *Rough Guide to French* (Penguin, UK/US), in a handy A–Z format.

Words and phrases

Basics

Good morning/Hello	Bonjour
Good evening	Bonsoir
Good night	Bonne nuit
Goodbye	Au revoir
Yes	Oui
No	Non
Please	S'il vous/te plaît
Thank you	Merci
You're welcome	Bienvenue/De rien
OK	D'accord
How are you?	Comment allez-vous?/Ça va?
Fine, thanks	Très bien, merci
Do you speak English?	Parlez-vous anglais?
I don't speak French	Je ne parle pas français
I don't understand	Je ne comprends pas
Excuse me	Je m'excuse
Sorry	Pardon/Désolé(e)

Today	Aujourd'hui
Tomorrow	Demain
Yesterday	Hier
Morning	Matin
Afternoon	Après-midi
Evening	Soir
Night	Nuit
Monday	Lundi
Tuesday	Mardi
Wednesday	Mercredi
Thursday	Jeudi
Friday	Vendredi
Saturday	Samedi
Sunday	Dimanche
Except	Sauf
Here/there	Ici/là
With/without	Avec/sans
Near/far	Près (pas loin)/loin
More/less	Plus/moins

Questions

Where?	Où?
When?	Quand?

Why?	Pourquoi?
How much/many?	Combien?

How much does it cost?	Ça coûte combien?	**What is it?**	Qu'est-ce que c'est?
What?	Quoi?	**What time is it?**	Il est quelle heure?
		What time does it open?	À quelle heure ça ouvre?

Numbers

1	un/une	**14**	quatorze
2	deux	**15**	quinze
3	trois	**16**	seize
4	quatre	**17**	dix-sept
5	cinq	**18**	dix-huit
6	six	**19**	dix-neuf
7	sept	**20**	vingt
8	huit	**21**	vingt-et-un
9	neuf	**100**	cent
10	dix	**110**	cent-dix
11	onze	**500**	cinq cents
12	douze	**1000**	mille
13	treize	**2000**	deux milles

Accommodation

Hotel	Hôtel	**...for one/two weeks**	...pour une/deux semaine(s)
Inn	Auberge		
Youth hostel	Auberge de jeunesse	**How much is it?**	C'est combien?
B&B	Gîte (du Passant)	**Can I see it?**	Est-ce que je peux la voir?
room with a double bed	chambre avec un lit double	**Do you have anything cheaper?**	Avez-vous quelque chose de moins cher?
...with a shower /bath	...avec douche/salle de bain	**Is breakfast included?**	Est-ce que le déjeuner est compris?
...for one/two/three nights	...pour une/deux/trois nuit(s)		

Transport

Aeroplane	Avion	**Railway station**	Gare centrale
Bus	Autobus	**Ferry terminal**	Quai du traversier
Train	Train	**I'd like a ticket to...**	J'aimerais un billet pour...
Car	Voiture		
Taxi	Taxi	**One-way/return**	Aller simple/aller-retour
Bicycle	Vélo		
Ferry	Traversier	**Transfer**	Correspondance
Bus station	Terminus d'autobus/gare des autobuses	**Freeway (motorway)**	Autoroute

Eating and drinking

Do you have an English menu?	Avez-vous un menu en anglais?	**Set menu**	Table d'hôte
		Lunch special	Spécial du midi

Breakfast	Déjeuner	**Fish**	Poisson
Lunch	Dîner	**Chicken**	Poulet
Dinner	Souper	**Duck**	Canard
Appetiser	Entrée	**Pork**	Porc
Main course	Plat principal	**Ham**	Jambon
Dessert	Dessert	**Beef**	Bœuf
Sugar	Sucre	**Veal**	Veau
Milk	Lait	**Pasta**	Pâtes
Butter	Beurre	**Potato**	Patate
Salt	Sel	**Fries**	Frites
Pepper	Poivre	**Apple**	Pomme
Bread	Pain	**Lemon**	Citron
Coffee	Café	**Salad**	Salade
Tea	Thé	**Lettuce**	Laitue
Eggs	Oeufs	**Beer**	Bière
Sausages	Saucissons	**On tap**	En fût
Bacon	Bacon	**Glass**	Verre
Meat pie	Tourtière	**Pitcher**	Pichet
Baked beans	Fèves au lard	**White wine**	Vin blanc
Shrimp	Crevettes	**Red wine**	Vin rouge
Mussels	Moules	**Check, please**	L'addition s'il vous plaît
Lobster	Homard		

Glossary of Montrealisms

Because of the interweaving of Francophone and Anglophone cultures, it's not surprising that English-speaking Montrealers often throw the occasional French word or expression into a conversation. This glossary lists the most common of these occurrences, as well as local English slang and idioms you're likely to encounter.

2 & 20 Hwy-20; called that by older Montrealers as it used to link to Hwy-2 in Ontario.

450 (four-five-oh) Area code for off-island suburbs; derogatory term used for the people who live there (also "bridge and tunnel people").

5 à 7 (cinq à sept) Happy hour.

Allongé Long (or "stretched") espresso but still stronger than an Americano.

Allophone Montrealer whose ethnicity and/or native-tongue is neither English nor French.

Als Montréal Alouettes football team.

Anglophone English-speaker.

Angryphone Vocal Anglophone complaining about erosion of rights for English-speakers, especially on talk-radio phone-ins.

Apportez votre vin Bring your own wine; many smaller restaurants do not have a liquor license, but will uncork any bottle you bring.

Arrêt Stop (in theory – to Montréal drivers, it seems to mean slow down); unique to Québec – in France, signs say "Stop".

Arrondissement Borough.

Balconville Social space created by the proximity of balconies in many of the city's typical triplex houses.

Bavette Flank steak – the classic version is served with shallots.

Big O Stade Olympique.

Bill 101 Law promoting the use of French (and restricting the use of English).

Bio/biologique Organic.

Boîte à chanson Small folk-music bar.

Buanderie Laundromat.

Cabane à sucre Sugar shack; where maple syrup and its derivatives are produced in spring; usually open to the public to try out some samples.

Café au lait Espresso with steamed milk (similar, if not identical, to a caffè latte); often served in a bowl (*bol*).

Caisse pop Abbreviation of *caisse populaire*; credit union.

Calèche Horse-drawn carriage.

CÉGEP Acronym for Collège d'enseignement général et professionel, a junior college (in Québec, this replaces the final year of high school and first year of university, as compared to other provinces and states).

Centre-ville Downtown.

CLSC Acronym of Centres locaux de services communautaires; health clinic.

The Conquest English capture of Québec City in 1759 (and their take-over of the rest of New France the following year).

Courriel E-mail.

Demerger Calls to undo the merger that created the Mega-City.

Dep Abbreviation of *dépanneur*, convenience store or corner shop.

Équitable Fair-trade.

First Nations Generally preferred term for Native Canadian or Indian.

FLQ Front de Libération du Québec; 1960s separatist terrorist group – see p.271.

Francophone French-speaker.

Fripperie Second-hand clothes store.

GST/TPS Goods and Services Tax.

Guichet (automatique) ATM.

Habs Montréal Canadiens hockey team.

Hôtel de ville City hall.

Hydro Electricity (supplied by Hydro-Québec); some Anglo Montrealers also refer to natural gas as *gaz*, as the bills are from Gaz Métropolitain.

Je me souviens "I will remember"; motto on the Québec license plates and coat-of-arms. Although it is read as being a nationalistic slogan, the three-line poem from which it comes is open to interpretation: *Je me souviens / que né sous le lys, / je croîs sous la rose* (I remember / that born under the [French] lily / I grow under the [English] rose).

Joual Thick Québécois regional accent.

Language police Office de la Langue Français; they enforce the rules governing the size of English signs (they must be no larger than half the size of the French) and other vital matters.

Lavoir Laundromat.

Loonie Dollar coin; the two-dollar coin, released later, thus became known as a toonie.

Magasiner To go shopping.

The Main Boulevard St-Laurent.

Mega-City The amalgamation of all the island of Montréal municipalities into one.

The Met Short for the Metropolitan (Autoroute Métropolitaine); the portion of Hwy-40 on the eastern half of the island.

Monnaie French for coins or spare change.

The mountain In Montréal, apparently any land mass that's at least 233m high; Mont Royal; Parc du Mont-Royal; the combined summits of Mont Royal, Westmount and Outremont.

National What qualifies in other provinces as provincial (eg the Québec provincial parliament calls itself the Assemblée Nationale).

Patriotes Insurgents, mainly Francophone, in the early nineteenth century.

Pepsi Derogatory term for Francophones (due to their preference for Pepsi over Coke).

Péquiste A member or supporter of the PQ (Parti Québécois); sometimes used to refer to separatists in general.

Piastre French slang for dollar.

Poutine French fries topped with cheese curds and gravy; artery-busting and alcohol-absorbing.

Pur laine Pure wool; old-stock, hundred percent Francophone.

QST/TVQ Québec Sales Tax.

Quiet Revolution 1960s arising of an articulate, mainly Francophone, intellectual and political class against the domination of Church and State.

Refus global Artists' manifesto published in 1948 that had profound effects on Québec culture - see p.56.

Resto Restaurant.

Rez-de-chaussée Ground floor.

SAQ Société des Alcools du Québec; runs the provincial liquor outlets.

Seigneury Land granted by the crown to an individual or group; the seigneur then let parcels of the land to tenants (rural farmers of this sort were known as *habitants*).

Smoked meat Brine-cured and smoked beef brisket similar to pastrami; served on rye with a pickle on the side.

Sous French for cent(s).

South Shore Suburbs geographically east of the St Lawrence from Downtown.

Stationnement Parking; a "P" is used on traffic signs, however.

Steamée Hot dog – the classic Montréal version is steamed (rather than grilled or boiled) and served with mustard and shredded cabbage.

STM Société des Transports de Montréal (Montréal Transit Commission).

Tam-tams Tribal drum sessions (specifically the percussion jams on the mountain – see p.102).

Terrasse Terrace (patio/pavement seating); *terrasse en arrière* indicates there's a terrace in the back garden or courtyard.

Tisane Herbal tea; also *infusion*.

Tourelle Turret-like dormer window.

T-Can / Trans-Canada Autoroute Trans-Canadienne; the portion of Hwy-40 on the western half of the island.

Triplex Townhouse with three apartments, one above the other.

Vielle souche Old-stock Québécois, descended from the original French settlers.

West Island Mainly Anglophone suburbs on the western half of the island of Montréal.

Rough Guides

advertiser

Rough Guides travel...

UK & Ireland
Britain
Devon & Cornwall
Dublin
Edinburgh
England
Ireland
Lake District
London
London mini guide
London Restaurants
London & SE England, Walks in
Scotland
Scottish Highlands & Islands
Wales

Europe
Algarve
Amsterdam
Andalucía
Austria
Baltic States
Barcelona
Belgium & Luxembourg
Berlin
Brittany & Normandy
Bruges & Ghent
Brussels
Budapest
Bulgaria
Copenhagen
Corfu
Corsica
Costa Brava
Crete
Croatia
Cyprus
Czech & Slovak Republics
Dodecanese & East Aegean
Dordogne & The Lot
Europe
First-Time Europe
Florence
France
Germany
Greece
Greek Islands
Hungary
Ibiza & Formentera
Iceland
Ionian Islands
Italy
Languedoc & Roussillon
Lisbon
The Loire
Madeira
Madrid
Mallorca
Malta & Gozo
Menorca
Moscow
Netherlands
Norway
Paris
Paris Mini Guide
Poland
Portugal
Prague
Provence & the Côte d'Azur
Pyrenees
Romania
Rome
Sardinia
Scandinavia
Sicily
Slovenia
Spain
St Petersburg
Sweden
Switzerland
Tenerife & La Gomera
Turkey
Tuscany & Umbria
Venice & The Veneto
Vienna

Asia
Bali & Lombok
Bangkok
Beijing
Cambodia
China
First-Time Asia
Goa
Hong Kong & Macau
India
Indonesia
Japan
Laos
Malaysia, Singapore & Brunei
Nepal
Philippines
Singapore
South India
Southeast Asia
Thailand
Thailand Beaches & Islands
Tokyo
Vietnam

Australasia
Australia
Gay & Lesbian Australia
Melbourne
New Zealand
Sydney

North America
Alaska
Baltic States
Big Island of Hawaii
Boston
California
Canada
Chicago
Florida
Grand Canyon
Hawaii
Honolulu
Las Vegas
Los Angeles
Maui
Miami & the Florida Keys
Montréal
New England
New Orleans
New York City
New York City Mini Guide
New York Restaurants
Pacific Northwest
Rocky Mountains
San Francisco
San Francisco Restaurants
Seattle
Skiing & Snowboarding in North America
Southwest USA
Toronto
USA
Vancouver
Washington DC
Yosemite

Caribbean & Latin America
Antigua & Barbuda
Argentina
Bahamas
Barbados
Belize
Bolivia
Brazil
Caribbean
Central America
Chile
Costa Rica
Cuba
Dominican Republic
Ecuador
First-Time Latin America
Guatemala
Jamaica
Maya World
Mexico
Peru
St Lucia
South America
Trinidad & Tobago

Rough Guides are available from good bookstores worldwide. New titles are published every month. Check www.roughguides.com for the latest news.

...music & reference

Africa & Middle East
Cape Town
Egypt
The Gambia
Jerusalem
Jordan
Kenya
Morocco
South Africa, Lesotho & Swaziland
Syria
Tanzania
Tunisia
West Africa
Zanzibar
Zimbabwe

Travel Theme guides
First-Time Around the World
First-Time Asia
First-Time Europe
First-Time Latin America
Gay & Lesbian Australia
Skiing & Snowboarding in North America
Travel Online
Travel Health
Walks in London & SE England
Women Travel

Restaurant guides
French Hotels & Restaurants
London
New York
San Francisco

Maps
Algarve
Amsterdam
Andalucia & Costa del Sol
Argentina
Athens
Australia
Baja California
Barcelona
Boston
Brittany
Brussels
Chicago
Crete
Croatia
Cuba
Cyprus
Czech Republic
Dominican Republic
Dublin
Egypt
Florence & Siena
Frankfurt
Greece
Guatemala & Belize
Iceland
Ireland
Lisbon
London
Los Angeles
Mexico
Miami & Key West
Morocco
New York City
New Zealand
Northern Spain
Paris
Portugal
Prague
Rome
San Francisco
Sicily
South Africa
Sri Lanka
Tenerife
Thailand
Toronto
Trinidad & Tobago
Tuscany
Venice
Washington DC
Yucatán Peninsula

Dictionary Phrasebooks
Czech
Dutch
Egyptian Arabic
European
French
German
Greek
Hindi & Urdu
Hungarian
Indonesian
Italian
Japanese
Mandarin Chinese
Mexican Spanish
Polish
Portuguese
Russian
Spanish
Swahili
Thai
Turkish
Vietnamese

Music Guides
The Beatles
Cult Pop
Classical Music
Country Music
Cuban Music
Drum'n'bass
Elvis
House
Irish Music
Jazz
Music USA
Opera
Reggae
Rock
Techno
World Music (2 vols)

100 Essential CDs series
Country
Latin
Opera
Rock
Soul
World Music

History Guides
China
Egypt
England
France
Greece
India
Ireland
Islam
Italy
Spain
USA

Reference Guides
Books for Teenagers
Children's Books, 0–5
Children's Books, 5–11
Cult Football
Cult Movies
Cult TV
Digital Stuff
Formula 1
The Internet
Internet Radio
James Bond
Lord of the Rings
Man Utd
Personal Computers
Pregnancy & Birth
Shopping Online
Travel Health
Travel Online
Unexplained Phenomena
The Universe
Videogaming
Weather
Website Directory

Also! More than 120 Rough Guide music CDs are available from all good book and record stores. Listen in at www.worldmusic.net

Index

and small print

Index

Map entries are in colour

A

B

C

D

E

F

G

H

N

O

P

Q

INDEX

U

V

W

A Rough Guide to Rough Guides

In the summer of 1981, Mark Ellingham, a recent graduate from Bristol University, was travelling round Greece and couldn't find a guidebook that really met his needs. On the one hand there were the student guides, insistent on saving every last cent, and on the other the heavyweight cultural tomes whose authors seemed to have spent more time in a research library than lounging away the afternoon at a taverna or on the beach.

In a bid to avoid getting a job, Mark and a small group of writers set about creating their own guidebook. It was a guide to Greece that aimed to combine a journalistic approach to description with a thoroughly practical approach to travellers' needs – a guide that would incorporate culture, history and contemporary insights with a critical edge, together with up-to-date, value-for-money listings. Back in London, Mark and the team finished their Rough Guide, as they called it, and talked Routledge into publishing the book.

That first *Rough Guide to Greece*, published in 1982, was a student scheme that became a publishing phenomenon. The immediate success of the book – with numerous reprints and a Thomas Cook prize shortlisting – spawned a series that rapidly covered dozens of destinations. Rough Guides had a ready market among low-budget backpackers, but soon also acquired a much broader and older readership that relished Rough Guides' wit and inquisitiveness as much as their enthusiastic, critical approach. Everyone wants value for money, but not at any price.

Rough Guides soon began supplementing the "rougher" information about hostels and low-budget listings with the kind of detail on restaurants and quality hotels that independent-minded visitors on any budget might expect, whether on business in New York or trekking in Thailand.

These days the guides – distributed worldwide by the Penguin group – offer recommendations from shoestring to luxury and cover more than 200 destinations around the globe, including almost every country in the Americas and Europe, more than half of Africa and most of Asia and Australasia. Our ever-growing team of authors and photographers is spread all over the world, particularly in Europe, the USA and Australia.

In 1994, we published the *Rough Guide to World Music* and *Rough Guide to Classical Music*; and a year later the *Rough Guide to the Internet*. All three books have become benchmark titles in their fields – which encouraged us to expand into other areas of publishing, mainly around popular culture. Rough Guides now publish:

- Travel guides to more than 200 worldwide destinations
- Dictionary phrasebooks to 22 major languages
- History guides ranging from Ireland to Islam
- Maps printed on rip-proof and waterproof Polyart™ paper
- Music guides running the gamut from Opera to Elvis
- Restaurant guides to London, New York and San Francisco
- Reference books on topics as diverse as the Weather and Shakespeare
- Sports guides from Formula 1 to Man Utd
- Pop culture books from Lord of the Rings to Cult TV
- World Music CDs in association with World Music Network.

Visit **www.roughguides.com** to see our latest publications.

Rough Guide credits

Text editor: Chris Barsanti
Layout: Diana Jarvis
Cartography: Delhi team, Katie Lloyd-Jones, Ed Wright
Picture research: Jj Luck
Proofreader: Karen Parker

Editorial: **London** Martin Dunford, Kate Berens, Helena Smith, Claire Saunders, Geoff Howard, Ruth Blackmore, Gavin Thomas, Polly Thomas, Richard Lim, Lucy Ratcliffe, Clifton Wilkinson, Alison Murchie, Fran Sandham, Sally Schafer, Alexander Mark Rogers, Karoline Densley, Andy Turner, Ella O'Donnell, Andrew Lockett, Joe Staines, Duncan Clark, Peter Buckley, Matthew Milton; **New York** Andrew Rosenberg, Richard Koss, Yuki Takagaki, Hunter Slaton, Chris Barsanti, Thomas Kohnstamm, Steven Horak
Design & Layout: **London** Helen Prior, Dan May, Diana Jarvis; **Delhi** Madhulita Mohapatra, Umesh Aggarwal, Ajay Verma
Production: Julia Bovis, John McKay, Sophie Hewat
Cartography: London Maxine Repath, Ed Wright, Katie Lloyd-Jones; **Delhi** Manish Chandra, Rajesh Chhibber, Jai Prakesh Mishra, Ashutosh Bharti, Rajesh Mishra, Animesh Pathak
Cover art direction: Louise Boulton
Picture research: Sharon Martins, Mark Thomas, Jj Luck
Online: New York Jennifer Gold, Cree Lawson, Suzanne Welles; **Delhi** Manik Chauhan, Amarjyoti Dutta, Narender Kumar
Marketing & Publicity: **London** Richard Trillo, Niki Smith, David Wearn, Chloë Roberts, Demelza Dallow; **New York** Geoff Colquitt, David Wechsler, Megan Kennedy
Finance: Gary Singh
Manager India: Punita Singh
Series editor: Mark Ellingham
PA to Managing Director: Julie Sanderson
Managing Director: Kevin Fitzgerald

Publishing Information

This 2nd edition published February 2004 by
Rough Guides Ltd,
80 Strand, London WC2R 0RL.
345 Hudson St, 4th Floor,
New York, NY 10014, USA.
Distributed by the Penguin Group
Penguin Books Ltd,
80 Strand, London WC2R 0RL
Penguin Putnam, Inc.
375 Hudson Street, NY 10014, USA
Penguin Books Australia Ltd,
487 Maroondah Highway, PO Box 257,
Ringwood, Victoria 3134, Australia
Penguin Books Canada Ltd,
10 Alcorn Avenue, Toronto, Ontario,
Canada M4V 1E4
Penguin Books (NZ) Ltd,
182–190 Wairau Road, Auckland 10,
New Zealand
Typeset in Bembo and Helvetica to an original design by Henry Iles.

Printed in Italy by LegoPrint S.p.A

304pp includes index
A catalogue record for this book is available from the British Library

ISBN 1-84353-195-X

1 3 5 7 9 8 6 4 2

Help us update

We've gone to a lot of effort to ensure that the 2nd edition of **The Rough Guide to Montréal** is accurate and up-to-date. However, things change – places get "discovered", opening hours are notoriously fickle, restaurants and rooms raise prices or lower standards. If you feel we've got it wrong or left something out, we'd like to know, and if you can remember the address, the price, the time, the phone number, so much the better.

We'll credit all contributions, and send a copy of the next edition (or any other Rough Guide if you prefer) for the best letters. Everyone who writes to us and isn't already a subscriber will receive a copy of our full-colour thrice-yearly newsletter. Please mark letters: "**Rough Guide Montréal Update**" and send to: Rough Guides, 80 Strand, London WC2R 0RL, or Rough Guides, 4th Floor, 345 Hudson St, New York, NY 10014. Or send an email to **mail@roughguides.com**

Have your questions answered and tell others about your trip at **www.roughguides.atinfopop.com**

Acknowledgements

John Shandy Watson would like to give a big thank you to Gilles Bengle, Yves Pelletier and Jean-François Perrier at Tourisme Montréal, Richard Séguin and the staff at the Greater Québec Area Tourism and Convention Bureau, Roselyne Hébert and Bard Nordby at Tourisme Québec, and Ronald Poiré and Élyse Busque for informative city tours. Thanks also to Richard Burnett, Brett Shymanski, Pierre-Yves Legault, Charlie McKee, Robert Stewart, and especially Darren Henriet, Angela Songui and Stephanie Halley for specific advice and whole-hearted support in Montréal. Cheers to friends and flatmates in London for their support and patience – as you can see the book is finally done. Thanks also to the folks at VIA, Air Canada and Les Dauphins de St-Laurent for assistance in getting there and around and to Christian Williams for ski info. I couldn't have done it without the able assistance of the RG staff – thanks notably to Chris Barsanti and Andrew Rosenberg for fine-tuning the text and to Jj Luck for her patience in finding just the right pics. And finally, a big thanks to Arabella Bowen for writing a number of kick-ass context boxes when the crunch came, not to mention the better half of the first edition of this guide.

Arabella Bowen extends her thanks to John Shandy Watson, for spearheading the project; Chris Barsanti and Richard Koss, for fine-tuning her words; and Tyler Cole, for his camera and patience.

Readers' letters

Thanks to all the readers who took the trouble to write in with their comments and suggestions (and apologies to anyone whose name we've misspelt or omitted):

A big thank you to the readers who took the time to make suggestions for this guide: Juan Abad, Xavier Brebion, Gavin Hawe, Alicia Hunt, Eric Kronstadt, Janet McLean and the many folks who contacted us by email but preferred to remain anonymous.

Photo credits

Cover credits

Front main: Square St-Louis ©W.Bibikow/ jonarnold.com
Front small top: Marche Bonsecours & sculpture ©Getty
Front small lower: Montréal Cathedral © Getty
Back top: Ile St Helene ©Robert Harding
Back lower: ©Getty

Introduction

City skyline ©Old Port of Montreal Corporation Inc., A.P.E.S
Mount Royale ©Getty Images
Biosphère ©Biosphère Environment Canada
Lanterns Chinese Garden ©Montreal Botanical Garden, Michel Tremblay
St Place Jacques ©Tourisme Montréal, Stéphan Poulin
Caleche on de la Commune Street in Old Montreal ©Tourisme Montréal, Stéphan Poulin
McGill University, Royal Victoria Hospital and Mount Royal ©Tourisme Montréal, Stéphan Poulin
Santropol steak sandwich ©Garth Gilker
La fête des Neiges (Winter festival) ©Parc Jean-Drapeau, Éric St-Pierre

Things not to miss

1. Biosphere ©Tourisme Montréal, Stéphan Poulin
2. Notre-Dame Basilica ©Tourisme Montréal, Stéphan Poulin
3. The Plateau ©John Shandy Watson
4. The Village ©Tourisme Quebéc, Londa Turgeon
5. International Jazz festival ©Festival International de Jazz de Montréal, Jean-François Leblanc
6. Lineup at Schwartz's ©Chase-Wolfe
7. Mont Royal ©John Shandy Watson
8. Snowboarder (Mont-Tremblant) ©Tremblant
9. Marche bonsecours ©www.old .montreal.qc.ca, le photographe masqué
10. Lachine Canal (Seceur Pont des Seigneurs) ©Megapress/Philipchenko T.
11. Jean-Talon ©John Shandy Watson
12. St-Denis ©Tourisme Montréal, Stéphan Poulin
13. Insectarium ©Pierre Racine, Insectarium de Montreal
14. Montreal Canadiens ©Ladislas Kadyszewski/Montreal Canadiens Hockey Club
15. Molson Indy ©Dan R.Boyd/LAT Photographic
16. Canadian Centre for Architecture ©Canadian Centre for Architecture, Richard Bryant
17. Tamtams ©Pierre Desrosiers
18. St Joseph ©Canadian Tourism Commission, Pierre St-Jacques
19. Québec City ©John Shandy Watson
20. Fireworks/old port ©Earl & Nazima Kowall/CORBIS
21. Parc Fontaine ©John Shandy Watson

Black and white

Édifice Sun Life ©Tourisme Montréal, Stéphan Poulin (p.45)
Tour de l'Horloge ©A.P.E.S., Anton Fercher (p.76)
Oratoire St-Joseph ©Canadian Tourism Commission, Pierre St-Jacques (p.105)
Rue Prince Arthur ©Canadian Tourism Commission, Pierre St-Jacques (p.162)
Skating at Parc Jean-Drapeau ©Parc Jean-Drapeau, Sébastien Larose (p.206)
Festival ©Festival International de Jazz de Montréal, Jean-François Leblanc (p.213)
Quartier du Petit-Champlain from the Escalier Casee-Cou ©John Shandy Watson (p.251)

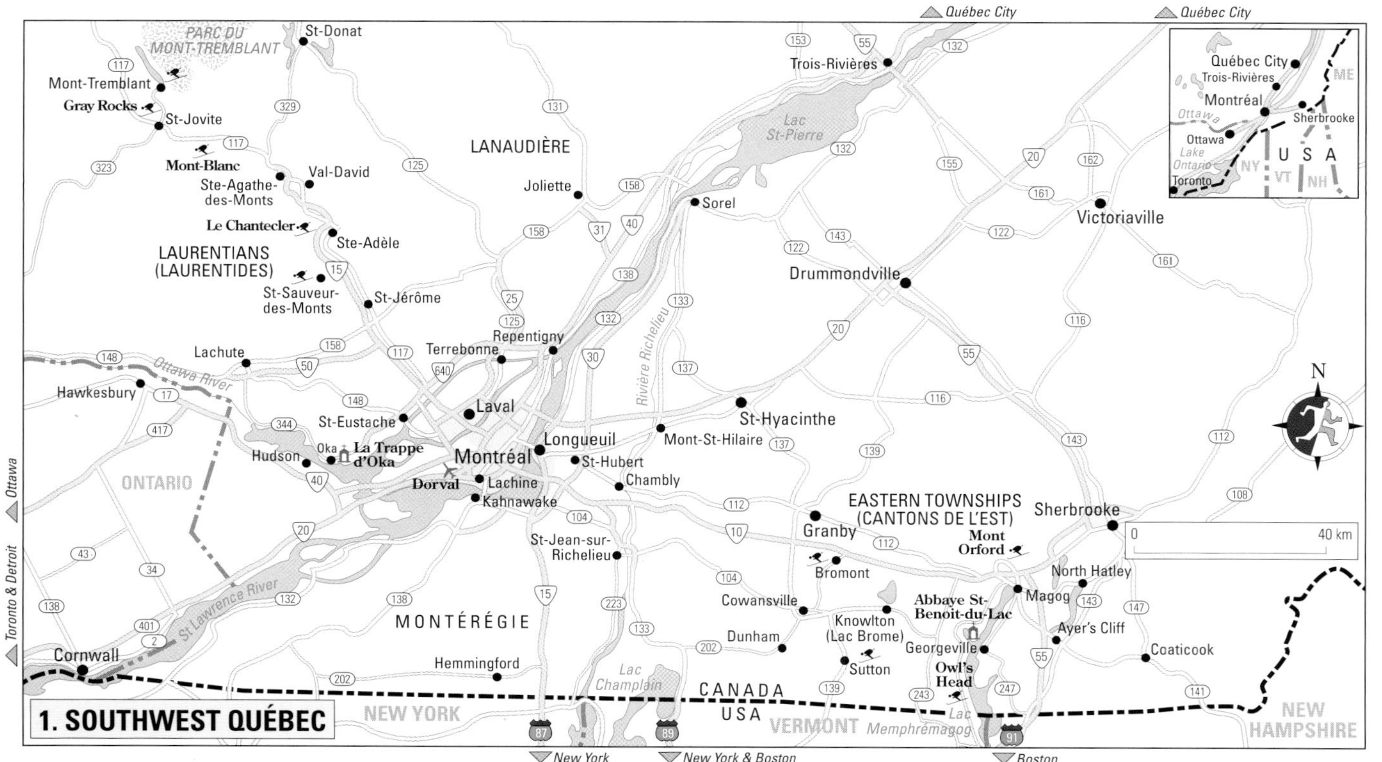
1. SOUTHWEST QUÉBEC
Québec City
Québec City
Ottawa
Toronto & Detroit
New York
New York & Boston
Boston
PARC DU MONT-TREMBLANT
St-Donat
Mont-Tremblant
Gray Rocks
St-Jovite
Mont-Blanc
Val-David
Ste-Agathe-des-Monts
Le Chantecler
Ste-Adèle
LAURENTIANS (LAURENTIDES)
St-Sauveur-des-Monts
St-Jérôme
LANAUDIÈRE
Joliette
Sorel
Lac St-Pierre
Trois-Rivières
Drummondville
Victoriaville
Lachute
Hawkesbury
Ottawa River
Terrebonne
Repentigny
Laval
St-Eustache
Oka
La Trappe d'Oka
Hudson
Montréal
Dorval
Lachine
Kahnawake
Longueuil
St-Hubert
Chambly
Mont-St-Hilaire
St-Hyacinthe
Rivière Richelieu
ONTARIO
Cornwall
St Lawrence River
MONTÉRÉGIE
Hemmingford
St-Jean-sur-Richelieu
Lac Champlain
EASTERN TOWNSHIPS (CANTONS DE L'EST)
Granby
Bromont
Cowansville
Dunham
Knowlton (Lac Brome)
Sutton
Mont Orford
Sherbrooke
North Hatley
Magog
Abbaye St-Benoit-du-Lac
Georgeville
Owl's Head
Ayer's Cliff
Coaticook
Lac Memphrémagog
CANADA
USA
NEW YORK
VERMONT
NEW HAMPSHIRE
N
0
40 km
Québec City
Trois-Rivières
Montréal
Ottawa
Sherbrooke
Toronto
Lake Ontario
U S A
ME
NY
VT
NH

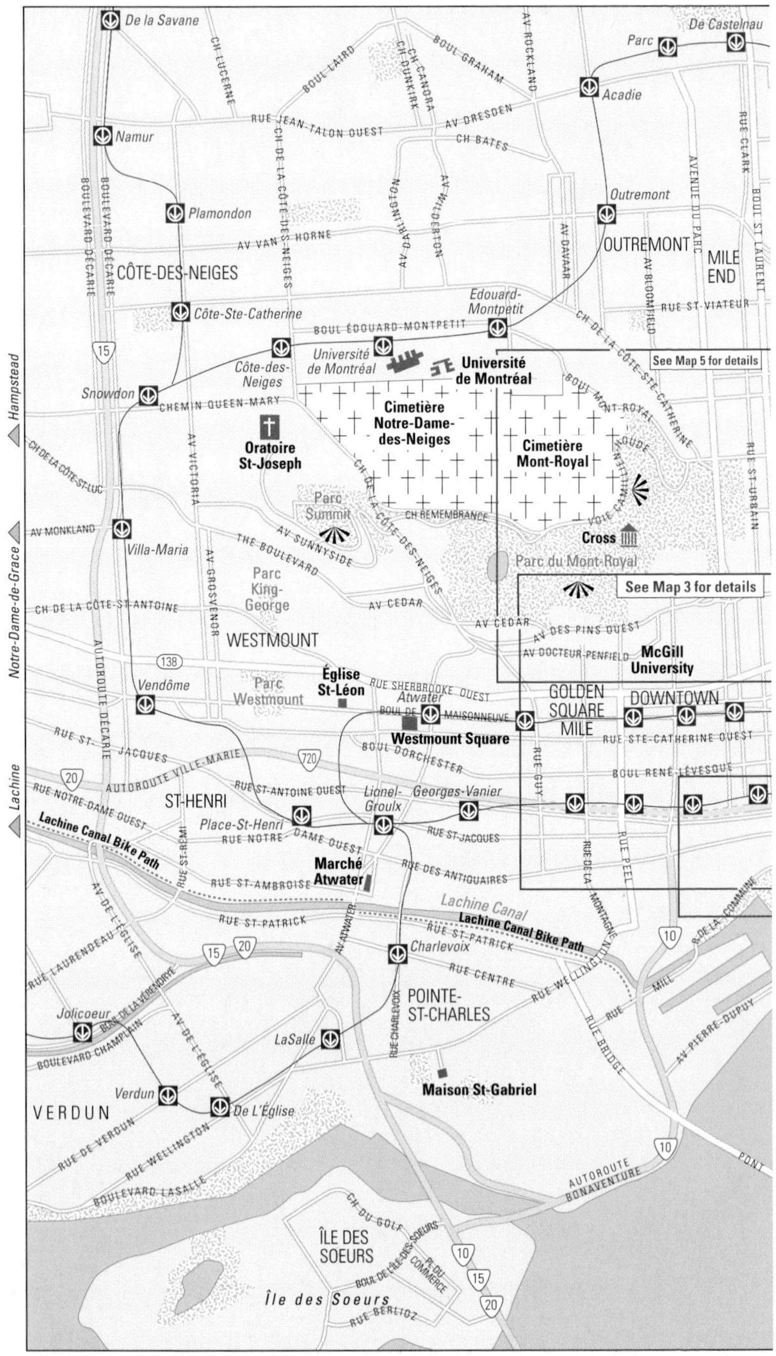

De la Savane
Namur
Plamondon
Côte-Ste-Catherine
Snowdon
Côte-des-Neiges
Université de Montréal
Edouard-Montpetit
Outremont
Acadie
Parc
De Castelnau
Villa-Maria
Vendôme
Atwater
Lionel-Groulx
Georges-Vanier
Place-St-Henri
Charlevoix
LaSalle
Jolicoeur
Verdun
De L'Église
CÔTE-DES-NEIGES
OUTREMONT
MILE END
WESTMOUNT
GOLDEN SQUARE MILE
DOWNTOWN
ST-HENRI
POINTE-ST-CHARLES
VERDUN
ÎLE DES SOEURS
Île des Soeurs
Université de Montréal
Cimetière Notre-Dame-des-Neiges
Cimetière Mont-Royal
Oratoire St-Joseph
Parc Summit
Cross
Parc du Mont-Royal
Parc King-George
Parc Westmount
Église St-Léon
Westmount Square
McGill University
Marché Atwater
Maison St-Gabriel
Lachine Canal
Lachine Canal Bike Path
See Map 5 for details
See Map 3 for details
Hampstead
Notre-Dame-de-Grace
Lachine
CH LUCERNE
BOUL LAIRD
CH DUNKIRK
CH CANORA
BOUL GRAHAM
AV ROCKLAND
RUE JEAN-TALON OUEST
AV DRESDEN
CH BATES
CH DE LA CÔTE-DES-NEIGES
AV VAN HORNE
AV DARLINGTON
AV WILDERTON
AV DAVAAR
AVENUE DU PARC
AV BLOOMFIELD
RUE CLARK
BOUL ST LAURENT
RUE ST-VIATEUR
BOUL ÉDOUARD-MONTPETIT
CH DE LA CÔTE-STE-CATHERINE
BOUL MONT-ROYAL
VOIE CAMILLIEN HOUDE
RUE ST-URBAIN
BOULEVARD DÉCARIE
CHEMIN QUEEN-MARY
CH DE LA CÔTE-ST-LUC
AV VICTORIA
CH REMEMBRANCE
AV MONKLAND
AV SUNNYSIDE
THE BOULEVARD
AV GROSVENOR
CH DE LA CÔTE-ST-ANTOINE
AV CEDAR
AV DES PINS OUEST
AV DOCTEUR-PENFIELD
AUTOROUTE DÉCARIE
RUE SHERBROOKE OUEST
BOUL DE MAISONNEUVE
RUE STE-CATHERINE OUEST
RUE ST-JACQUES
BOUL DORCHESTER
AUTOROUTE VILLE-MARIE
RUE GUY
BOUL RENÉ-LÉVESQUE
RUE ST-ANTOINE OUEST
RUE NOTRE-DAME OUEST
RUE ST-RÉMI
RUE DE LA MONTAGNE
RUE PEEL
RUE DES ANTIQUAIRES
RUE ST-AMBROISE
RUE ST-PATRICK
AV ATWATER
AV DE L'ÉGLISE
RUE LAURENDEAU
RUE CENTRE
RUE WELLINGTON
RUE DE LA COMMUNE
RUE MILL
RUE BRIDGE
AV PIERRE-DUPUY
BOUL DE LA VÉRENDRYE
BOULEVARD CHAMPLAIN
RUE CHARLEVOIX
RUE DE VERDUN
BOULEVARD LASALLE
AUTOROUTE BONAVENTURE
PONT
CH DU GOLF
BOUL DE L'ÎLE-DES-SOEURS
PL DU COMMERCE
RUE BERLIOZ
15
20
10
138
720

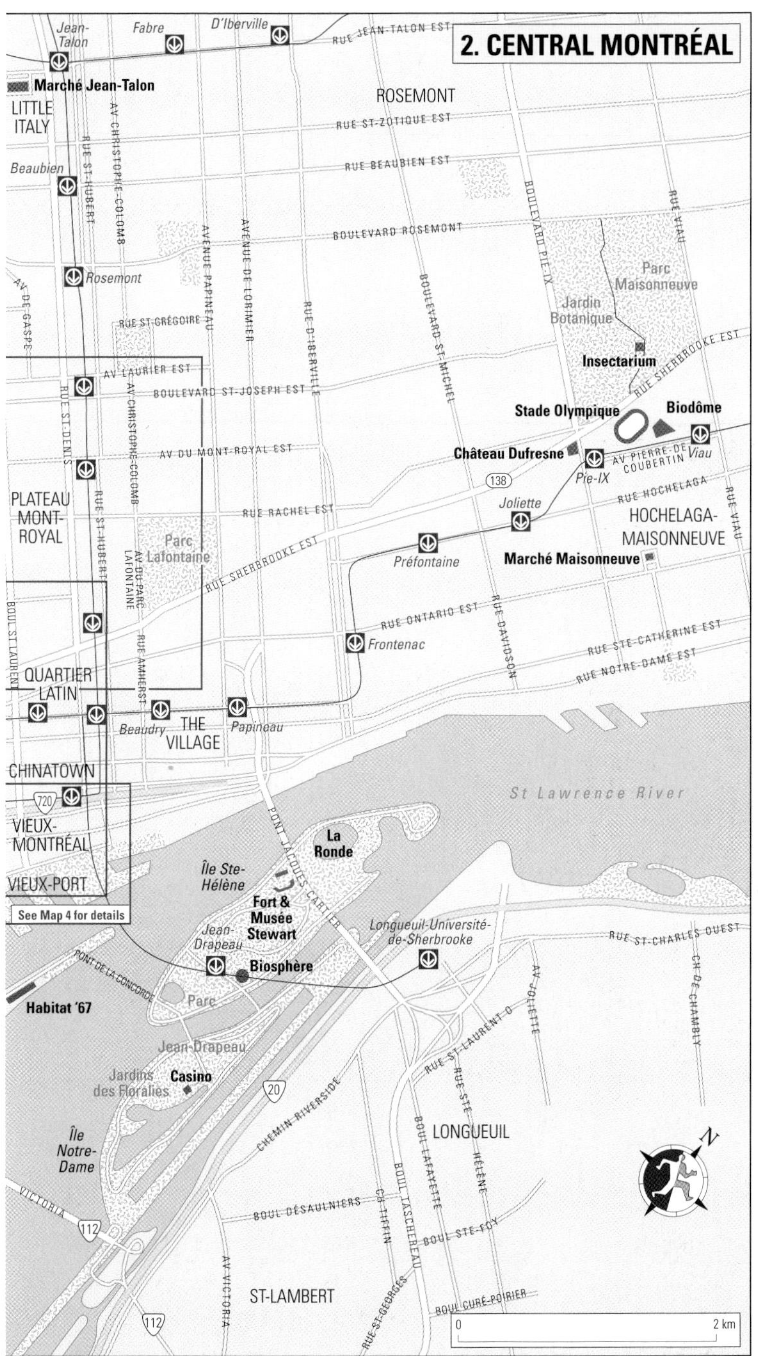
2. CENTRAL MONTRÉAL
Jean-Talon
Fabre
D'Iberville
RUE JEAN-TALON EST
Marché Jean-Talon
LITTLE ITALY
ROSEMONT
RUE ST-ZOTIQUE EST
RUE BEAUBIEN EST
Beaubien
AV CHRISTOPHE-COLOMB
RUE ST-HUBERT
BOULEVARD ROSEMONT
AVENUE PAPINEAU
AVENUE DE LORIMIER
BOULEVARD PIE-IX
RUE VIAU
Rosemont
AV DE GASPE
RUE ST-GRÉGOIRE
RUE D'IBERVILLE
BOULEVARD ST-MICHEL
Parc Maisonneuve
Jardin Botanique
Insectarium
RUE SHERBROOKE EST
AV LAURIER EST
BOULEVARD ST-JOSEPH EST
RUE ST-DENIS
Stade Olympique
Biodôme
AV DU MONT-ROYAL EST
Château Dufresne
AV PIERRE-DE COUBERTIN
Viau
Pie-IX
138
Joliette
RUE HOCHELAGA
PLATEAU MONT-ROYAL
RUE RACHEL EST
HOCHELAGA-MAISONNEUVE
Parc Lafontaine
AV DU PARC LAFONTAINE
Préfontaine
Marché Maisonneuve
RUE ONTARIO EST
RUE DAVIDSON
BOUL ST-LAURENT
RUE AMHERST
Frontenac
RUE STE-CATHERINE EST
RUE NOTRE-DAME EST
QUARTIER LATIN
Beaudry
THE VILLAGE
Papineau
CHINATOWN
720
St Lawrence River
VIEUX-MONTRÉAL
PONT JACQUES CARTIER
La Ronde
VIEUX-PORT
Île Ste-Hélène
Fort & Musée Stewart
See Map 4 for details
Jean-Drapeau
Longueuil-Université-de-Sherbrooke
RUE ST-CHARLES OUEST
PONT DE LA CONCORDE
Biosphère
AV JOLIETTE
CH DE CHAMBLY
Habitat '67
Parc Jean-Drapeau
RUE ST-LAURENT O
Jardins des Floralies
Casino
RUE STE-HÉLÈNE
20
CHEMIN RIVERSIDE
Île Notre-Dame
LONGUEUIL
BOUL LAFAYETTE
N
VICTORIA
BOUL DÉSAULNIERS
CH TIFFIN
BOUL TASCHEREAU
112
BOUL STE-FOY
AV VICTORIA
ST-LAMBERT
RUE ST-GEORGES
BOUL CURÉ-POIRIER
0
2 km

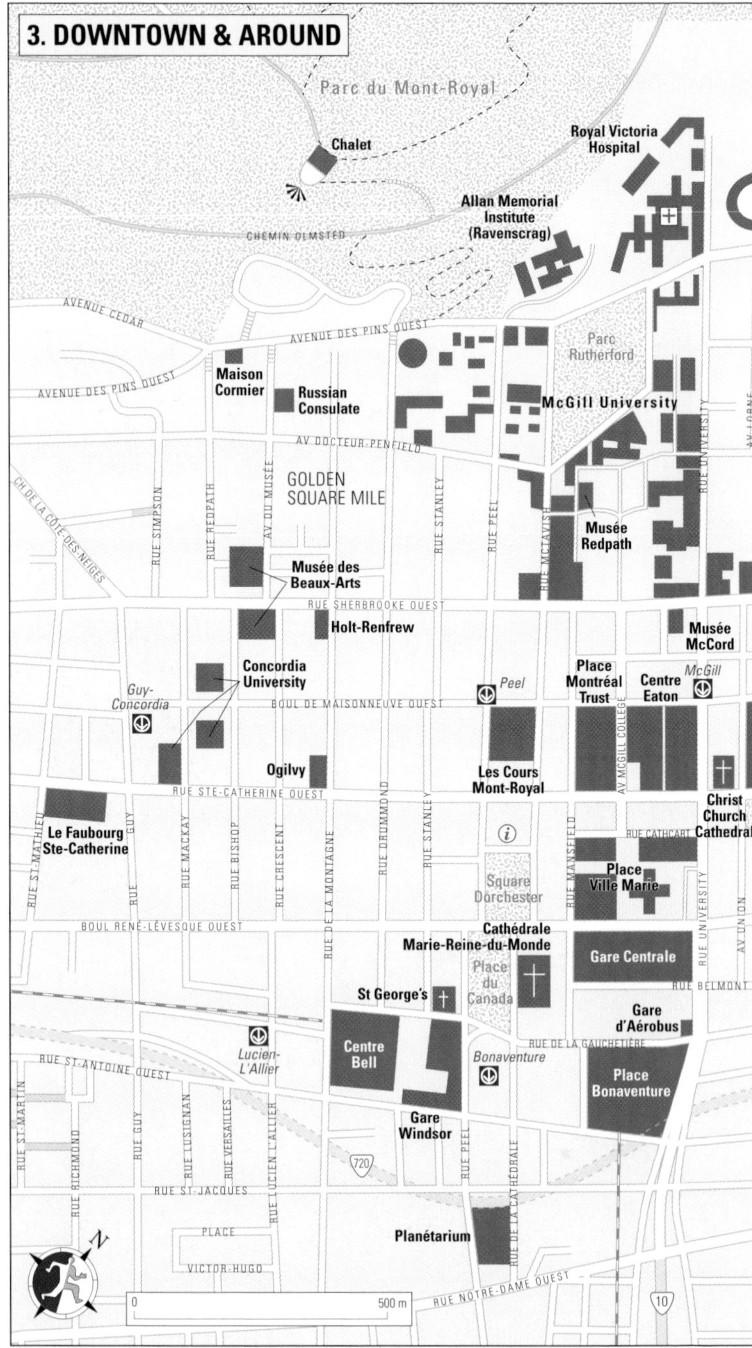

3. DOWNTOWN & AROUND
Parc du Mont-Royal
Chalet
Royal Victoria Hospital
Allan Memorial Institute (Ravenscrag)
CHEMIN OLMSTED
AVENUE CEDAR
AVENUE DES PINS OUEST
Parc Rutherford
Maison Cormier
Russian Consulate
McGill University
AV DOCTEUR-PENFIELD
GOLDEN SQUARE MILE
CH DE LA CÔTE-DES-NEIGES
RUE SIMPSON
RUE REDPATH
AV DU MUSÉE
RUE STANLEY
RUE PEEL
RUE MCTAVISH
RUE UNIVERSITY
AV LORNE
Musée Redpath
Musée des Beaux-Arts
RUE SHERBROOKE OUEST
Holt-Renfrew
Musée McCord
Concordia University
Guy-Concordia
Peel
Place Montréal Trust
Centre Eaton
McGill
BOUL DE MAISONNEUVE OUEST
AV MCGILL COLLEGE
Ogilvy
Les Cours Mont-Royal
RUE STE-CATHERINE OUEST
Christ Church Cathedral
Le Faubourg Ste-Catherine
RUE ST-MATHIEU
RUE GUY
RUE MACKAY
RUE BISHOP
RUE CRESCENT
RUE DE LA MONTAGNE
RUE DRUMMOND
RUE MANSFIELD
RUE CATHCART
Square Dorchester
Place Ville Marie
AV UNION
BOUL RENÉ-LÉVESQUE OUEST
Cathédrale Marie-Reine-du-Monde
Gare Centrale
Place du Canada
RUE BELMONT
St George's
Gare d'Aérobus
Centre Bell
Lucien-L'Allier
Bonaventure
RUE DE LA GAUCHETIÈRE
Place Bonaventure
RUE ST-ANTOINE OUEST
Gare Windsor
RUE ST-MARTIN
RUE RICHMOND
RUE LUSIGNAN
RUE VERSAILLES
RUE LUCIEN L'ALLIER
RUE DE LA CATHÉDRALE
720
RUE ST-JACQUES
PLACE VICTOR-HUGO
Planétarium
N
0
500 m
RUE NOTRE-DAME OUEST
10

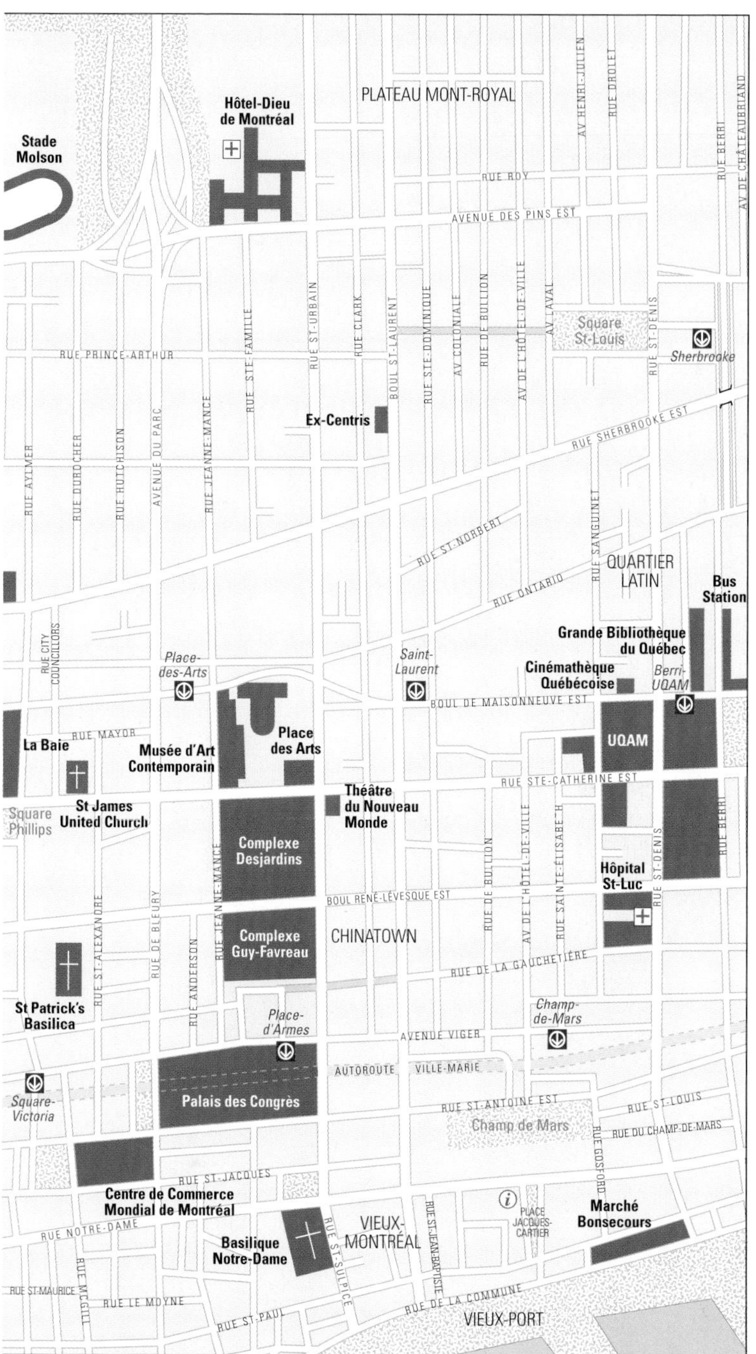
PLATEAU MONT-ROYAL
Hôtel-Dieu de Montréal
Stade Molson
AV HENRI-JULIEN
RUE DROLET
RUE BERRI
AV DE CHÂTEAUBRIAND
RUE ROY
AVENUE DES PINS EST
RUE ST-URBAIN
RUE CLARK
BOUL ST-LAURENT
RUE STE-DOMINIQUE
AV COLONIALE
RUE DE BULLION
AV DE L'HÔTEL-DE-VILLE
AV LAVAL
Square St-Louis
RUE ST-DENIS
Sherbrooke
RUE PRINCE-ARTHUR
RUE STE-FAMILLE
Ex-Centris
RUE SHERBROOKE EST
RUE AYLMER
RUE DURDCHER
RUE HUTCHISON
AVENUE DU PARC
RUE JEANNE-MANCE
RUE ST-NORBERT
RUE SANGUINET
QUARTIER LATIN
RUE ONTARIO
Bus Station
Grande Bibliothèque du Québec
RUE CITY COUNCILLORS
Place-des-Arts
Saint-Laurent
Cinémathèque Québécoise
Berri-UQAM
BOUL DE MAISONNEUVE EST
RUE MAYOR
La Baie
Musée d'Art Contemporain
Place des Arts
UQAM
RUE STE-CATHERINE EST
Théâtre du Nouveau Monde
St James United Church
Square Phillips
Complexe Desjardins
RUE SAINTE-ÉLISABETH
Hôpital St-Luc
BOUL RENÉ-LÉVESQUE EST
RUE ST-ALEXANDRE
RUE DE BLEURY
RUE ANDERSON
Complexe Guy-Favreau
CHINATOWN
RUE DE LA GAUCHETIÈRE
St Patrick's Basilica
Place-d'Armes
Champ-de-Mars
AVENUE VIGER
Square-Victoria
AUTOROUTE VILLE-MARIE
Palais des Congrès
RUE ST-ANTOINE EST
RUE ST-LOUIS
Champ de Mars
RUE DU CHAMP-DE-MARS
RUE GOSFORD
RUE ST-JACQUES
Centre de Commerce Mondial de Montréal
PLACE JACQUES-CARTIER
Marché Bonsecours
RUE NOTRE-DAME
VIEUX-MONTRÉAL
RUE ST-JEAN-BAPTISTE
Basilique Notre-Dame
RUE ST-SULPICE
RUE ST-MAURICE
RUE MCGILL
RUE LE MOYNE
RUE DE LA COMMUNE
RUE ST-PAUL
VIEUX-PORT

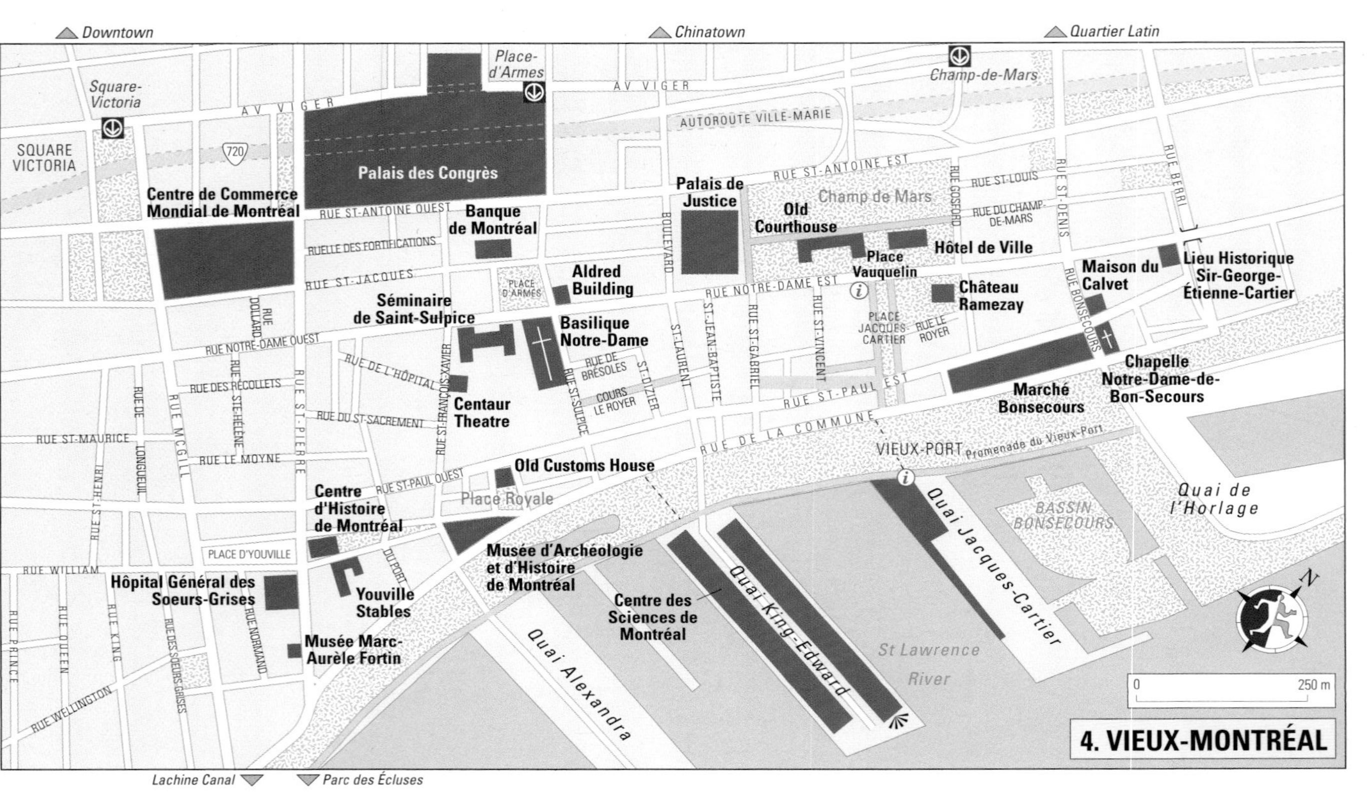
4. VIEUX-MONTRÉAL
Downtown
Chinatown
Quartier Latin
Lachine Canal
Parc des Écluses
Square-Victoria
SQUARE VICTORIA
Place-d'Armes
Champ-de-Mars
AV VIGER
AUTOROUTE VILLE-MARIE
720
Palais des Congrès
Centre de Commerce Mondial de Montréal
Banque de Montréal
Palais de Justice
Old Courthouse
Champ de Mars
Hôtel de Ville
Place Vauquelin
Château Ramezay
Maison du Calvet
Lieu Historique Sir-George-Étienne-Cartier
Aldred Building
Séminaire de Saint-Sulpice
Basilique Notre-Dame
Centaur Theatre
Chapelle Notre-Dame-de-Bon-Secours
Marché Bonsecours
Old Customs House
Place Royale
Centre d'Histoire de Montréal
Musée d'Archéologie et d'Histoire de Montréal
Hôpital Général des Soeurs-Grises
Youville Stables
Musée Marc-Aurèle Fortin
Centre des Sciences de Montréal
VIEUX-PORT
Promenade du Vieux-Port
Quai de l'Horlage
BASSIN BONSECOURS
Quai Jacques-Cartier
Quai King-Edward
Quai Alexandra
St Lawrence River
RUE ST-ANTOINE EST
RUE ST-ANTOINE OUEST
RUE ST-LOUIS
RUE DU CHAMP-DE-MARS
RUE GOSFORD
RUE ST-DENIS
RUE BERRI
RUELLE DES FORTIFICATIONS
RUE ST-JACQUES
PLACE D'ARMES
BOULEVARD
RUE NOTRE-DAME EST
RUE NOTRE-DAME OUEST
RUE DOLLARD
ST-LAURENT
ST-JEAN-BAPTISTE
RUE ST-GABRIEL
RUE ST-VINCENT
PLACE JACQUES CARTIER
RUE LE ROYER
RUE BONSECOURS
RUE DE L'HÔPITAL
RUE DE BRÉSOLES
ST-DIZIER
COURS LE ROYER
RUE ST-SULPICE
RUE ST-FRANÇOIS-XAVIER
RUE DU ST-SACREMENT
RUE ST-PAUL EST
RUE ST-PAUL OUEST
RUE DE LA COMMUNE
RUE DES RÉCOLLETS
RUE STE-HÉLÈNE
RUE LE MOYNE
RUE ST-PIERRE
RUE MCGILL
RUE DE LONGUEUIL
RUE ST-MAURICE
RUE ST-HENRI
PLACE D'YOUVILLE
DU PORT
RUE WILLIAM
RUE NORMAND
RUE DES SOEURS-GRISES
RUE KING
RUE QUEEN
RUE PRINCE
RUE WELLINGTON
N
0
250 m